65881

DATE DUE			

Canada's War
The Politics
of the
Mackenzie King
Government,
1939-1945

J.L. Granatstein

Toronto
Oxford University Press
1975

For Elaine, Carole, and Michael

F
1034
G68

Jacket design by
FRED HUFFMAN

ISBN-0-19-540228-6

Printed in Canada by
THE BRYANT PRESS LIMITED

65881

Contents

ILLUSTRATIONS

The illustrations between pages 212 and 213 are reproduced courtesy of the Public Archives of Canada.

The first troops leaving Halifax, December 1939.

Mackenzie King signing autographs, election day 1940.

Mackenzie King addressing troops, and beside his train on his western tour, summer 1941.

Mackenzie King on his western tour, summer 1941.

Lapointe's funeral, November 1941.

Mackenzie King and Churchill in Ottawa, December 1941; and Colonel Ralston, Minister of National Defence, 1940-44.

The conscription plebiscite in Toronto, 1942.

The Cabinet War Committee, 1943.

President Roosevelt in Ottawa, August 1943.

The Commonwealth Prime Ministers' meeting, May 1944.

Norman Robertson and Mackenzie King in London, May 1944.

Mackenzie King and his sister, and receiving a statuette of himself and his dog Pat, both on the twentieth anniversary of his leadership of the Liberal Party.

A cartoon on the conscription crisis of 1944.

Mackenzie King at the San Francisco Conference, 1945.

Victory celebrations in Ottawa, 1945.

A Liberal candidate's headquarters in Toronto during the election, 1945.

Preface

'I never travel without my diary', one of the characters in *The Importance of Being Earnest* says. 'One should always have something sensational to read in the train.' The diary of Mackenzie King may not contain much of that type of sensational material, and only a special kind of person would find it a good companion for a long journey, but to Mackenzie King his diary mattered, holding a place in his life that, for a married man, could only have been filled by a wife-confidante. In the diary King escaped from the prying eyes of the public, the press, and his political friends and foes. In the diary he revealed himself, set out his own personality, and indicated the spiritual nature of his yearnings and his soul. The diary was Mackenzie King's important safety valve in a world of high tensions and pressures.

The diary clearly reveals Mackenzie King as two men, almost completely separate entities. King, the political leader and Prime Minister, was a man of sagacity and cunning and, when necessary, ruthlessness. Mackenzie King, the secret self, was the spiritualist and sentimentalist and the mother-fixated boy. These natures co-existed well together; there was no schizoidal war between the two personalities. Each seemed complete on its own.

This study of Canada's War centres around the public Mackenzie King, the political leader who ran the war effort and shaped it. It is not a biography of King but a study of certain aspects of the national effort from 1939 to 1945 and an examination of the way King and his government grappled with a complex of issues, political, financial, economic, and racial. Much has been omitted here, in large part because others have dealt with certain specific areas, and very well. James Eayrs examined much of the war's foreign policy in his *In Defence of Canada*, Vols II and III, while Charles Stacey has dealt superbly with the entire sweep of military and policy questions in his *Arms, Men and Governments: The War Policies of Canada, 1939-1945*. Where I have gone over some of this well-tilled ground, it has usually been because of additional evidence, most notably from British sources, that added a new dimension. This study also ignores totally the events on the war fronts, dealing with them only as they affected affairs in Canada.

The theme of this book is nationalism and the way it developed during the Second World War in Canada. This country went to war in September 1939 in a state of half-hearted unity. The people's will was sapped by the depression, and public opinion was divided about the necessity for war. But Canada went to war because English Canadians still identified with Britain and Britons. Britain's war had to be Canada's war, and for the first nine months the war was a phoney one for Canada because it was a *sitzkrieg* for Britain. In this period the King government acted in what it defined as the national interest—although national self-interest might be a better term—bargaining (without much success) for economic benefits and playing a cautious, almost non-committal hand. In the 1939-40 war, there was nothing to inspire nationalism.

But the defeats in France and Flanders galvanized the country as never before, turning a half-hearted Dominion into Britain's ranking ally. Men and women enlisted in the hundreds of thousands, the factories boomed, and war production soared. The war truly became Canada's War, and the nation's pride and fate became identified with the battle in a fashion that all the propagandists of 1939 had been unable to make real. The story of Canadian financial aid to Britain from 1940 to 1945 is told here, for example, and even though the bargaining was tough on both sides, even though self-interest on both sides was a dominant factor, there was something more. Canada was no longer simply fighting Britain's war, but its own. Canadian foreign policy under Mackenzie King's direction too was always cautious and not very forceful, but the Department of External Affairs, full of able men and led by a Secretary of State for External Affairs who had his own conception of Canada's status and role, succeeded in carving out its own doctrine and a new stature as a middle power. In 1939 Canada had been a colony in everything but name. Six years later Canada's debt to its past had been paid and the nation, for a brief period, was as independent and powerful as it would ever be.

If it was Canada's War abroad, it was similarly Canada's War at home.

Canada and the People's War, a booklet issued by the Director of Public Information in September 1942, featured a quote from the movie 'Mrs. Miniver':

> This is not only a war of soldiers in uniform, it is a war of the people—of all the people—and it must be fought, not only on the battlefield, but in the cities and in the villages, in the factories and on the farms, in the home and in the heart of every man, woman and child who loves freedom! . . . This is the people's war! It is our war!

'Mrs. Miniver' was a British film, of course, but that quote reflected something true about Canada and Canadians too. People wanted and expected something better for themselves and their children. The casualties, the sacrifices, the rationing and shortages and hard work had to bring forth something more than a return to the *status quo ante.* A country that could double its Gross National Product and increase its national budget ten-fold in five years could also look after its citizens. It was the people's war, and the prosperity it brought in its train fed the conviction that victory had to be won at home too. This could best be discerned in the opinion polls, in the new electoral strength of the CCF, in the manoeuvrings of politicians poised unhappily on the crest of a wave. 'Bring Victory Home!' was one slogan the Liberals tested in 1944, and a popular one. In the end the government went to the people on the motto 'Build a New Social Order', a phrase that evoked the same spirit. In this sense the move to the left by the political parties, the adoption of social-welfare platforms by Liberals and Conservatives, the implementation of major steps towards the welfare state by the King government—all were reflections of the people's war.

The country shared a unity of spirit, a surprising consensus on goals, if not on means. This unity had to be preserved, and it was to this that Mackenzie King devoted himself. Canada's entry into the war and the conscription crises were the most crucial tests of French-English unity during the period, and there can be no doubt that King coped with them masterfully. There were divisions, demonstrations, and different attitudes in Quebec, but there was no breakdown in relations between the two cultures, no great cleavage as in 1917. Popular memories of the strife of the Great War years tended to forbid this, but Mackenzie King's policies and his skill at political management largely contributed to the eased relationship, as did a substantially greater war effort from French Canada. King's tack was to resist conscription as long as possible, to hold off, to delay, to move by half-steps. Not an exciting or satisfying policy, it was nonetheless effective and successful. And because King combined his conscription balancing act with a progressive policy on social-welfare questions, a policy that appealed to ordinary men and women in French and English Canada, he and his Liberal Party maintained a strong position in all regions of the nation in the 1945 election. King manoeuvred so that the Liberal government remained in the centre, so that the Conservative Party was destroyed on the shoals of conscription and social welfare, so that the CCF was crippled by the public's fears that it would alter too much too fast. King's task was to go no further than necessary towards conscription, as far as necessary towards social welfare, and to keep the party, the government, and the existing order together. The election results of 1945 and the renewed party he left his successors in 1948 demonstrate that King succeeded.

As the solitary political organization with substantial representation in all parts of the country, the Liberal Party was the leading agency of national unity during the war. As the manager of the war effort, King was very much in charge, and if he must assume the blame for his errors, he similarly must receive some of the credit for his and the nation's achievements. The accomplishments were impressive in every area, and although the war years were hard, Canadians emerged from them more united than could have been expected, confident of the worth of their war performance, and with their apprehensions about an uncertain future stilled somewhat by the creation of the social-welfare state. If, in September 1939, it had not been Canada's War, by V-E day it was.

This book is largely based on primary sources, most notably the papers of the key individuals concerned and of Canadian, British, and American government departments and offices.

The basic sources are the papers and diaries of W. L. Mackenzie King located in the Public Archives of Canada. King's correspondence, memoranda and notes, speeches, and diaries constitute a national treasure, for the Prime Minister kept everything and in his diary did his best to record it all. The *Mackenzie King Record*, published in four volumes by J. W. Pickersgill, is an ably edited version of the diary for 1939 to 1948, and I have cited the *Record* almost interchangeably with the manuscript diary.

The records left by Mackenzie King's colleagues are also crucial. The J. L. Ralston Papers in the Public Archives of Canada and the Angus L. Macdonald Papers in the Public Archives of Nova Scotia are good, large collections. The T. A. Crerar and Chubby Power collections at Queen's University have excellent material in them, particularly Power's on airforce matters and on Quebec politics, while Ian Mackenzie's Papers at the Public Archives of Canada are excellent on prewar defence policy and on the emergence of social-welfare legislation. Brooke Claxton's Papers at the Public Archives of Canada constitute one of the very best collections for the 1940s, and General McNaughton's Papers add some interesting matter on his brief tenure as Minister of National Defence. The J. G. Gardiner Papers at the Saskatchewan Provincial Archives are useful on Western politics, but unfortunately both the Ernest Lapointe and the C. D. Howe Papers at the Public Archives of Canada seem to have been thoroughly culled, unlike those of Senator Norman Lambert at Queen's, which constitute the best record of Liberal Party financing.

Other collections that I have found useful are those of the *Winnipeg Free Press* reporter, Grant Dexter (Queen's); of the U.S. Minister in Ottawa, Pierrepont Moffat (Harvard University); of *The Financial Post* editor, Floyd Chalmers (Toronto); and of President F. D. Roosevelt (Hyde Park, N.Y.). The Fondation Lionel-Groulx in Montreal holds the best collections relating to Quebec in the war years, most notably the Groulx Papers, the records of La Ligue pour la défense du Canada and the Bloc Populaire Canadien, and the papers of Georges Pelletier of *Le Devoir* and Maxime Raymond. The records of the National Liberal Federation, the Progressive Conservative Party, and the CCF are all held in the Public Archives of Canada. There are several collections left by Conservative politicians there as well, including those of R. J. Manion, Arthur Meighen, R. B. Hanson, Gordon Graydon, and John Bracken. The papers of H. A. Bruce and J. M. Macdonnell are at Queen's. M. J. Coldwell's Papers are at the Public Archives of Canada; Mitchell Hepburn's are in the Public Archives of Ontario; and those of F. Cyril James are held by McGill University.

W. Clifford Clark left filing cabinets full of material at the Department of Finance, the best source of data on war finance. The Department's massive records are held in the Public Archives of Canada, as are some of those of the Departments of External Affairs, National Defence, and Trade and Commerce. Other records are still held by the Departments concerned. The records of wartime agencies are also at the Public Archives of Canada, including the Wartime Prices and Trade Board and the Wartime Information Board. The Privy Council's records deposited there include the minutes and documents of the Cabinet War Committee and the Cabinet Conclusions for 1944 and 1945.

In Great Britain, the Public Record Office holds the very important collections of the Foreign and Dominion Offices, the Air Ministry and the Treasury, as well as the Cabinet and Prime Minister's Office records. In Washington, the United States National Archives have the clumsily indexed records of the State Department, the Office of Strategic Services, and the War and Navy Departments.

Additional manuscript collections, some of which have proven invaluable on specific points, are indicated in the references, as are secondary sources, monographs, theses, and articles.

Anyone who has written a book such as this will appreciate the innumerable debts that are incurred in the course of research and preparation. I have many.

I must acknowledge with gratitude the assistance and co-operation provided by the literary executors of Mackenzie King in permitting me to use the diaries and papers of Mr King for the war years. The Hon. J. W. Pickersgill, in particular, not only assisted greatly in this way but read the entire manuscript and submitted to a number of interviews. Without his co-operation and that of his colleagues this book would not have been possible.

I am grateful as well to Mrs Angus L. Macdonald for permitting me to use her husband's papers, stored at the Public Archives of Nova Scotia; to Mrs Grant Dexter for access to the splendid Dexter Papers at Queen's University; to Mr Floyd Chalmers and the late Hon. M. J. Coldwell for access to their papers; to the heirs of J. G. Gardiner, Ian Mackenzie, and Norman Lambert for access to their collections; to the Director of History, National Defence Headquarters, for permission to see the papers of General McNaughton; to the Department of Finance and Mr J. F. Parkinson for permission to use the very valuable collection of material left by W. Clifford Clark; to Mrs Stuart Ralston, the late Principal F. C. James, Mrs H. A. Bruce, and the Hon. T. A. Crerar for allowing me to see manuscript collections in their control.

A substantial number of very busy men let me harrass them with questions and query their recollections of thirty years back, and I am most grateful to them all. Archivists, too, assisted or interfered with my research. Ian Wilson at Queen's University runs the best small archives in Canada and was always of great help, as was the entire staff of the Public Archives of Canada. The same thing cannot be said of the Public Archives of Nova Scotia.

My colleagues and friends have helped in many ways. At York University, my colleagues Robert Cuff, H. V. Nelles, Christopher Armstrong, and many others in the History Department's Research Group have created a splendid atmosphere in which to work. Professor Cuff wrote with me an article on the Hyde Park Agreement of 1941, some of which is used herein. Professors Armstrong and Nelles criticized sections of the work at enormous expense to my liquor cabinet. Others outside York have helped, too. Mr Norman Hillmer guided me through the mysteries of British archives and saved me at least one month's work. Mr William Young allowed me to use his notes on several manuscript collections in British Columbia archives, gathered in the course of his own important research into public information during the war years. Professor Michael Cross was instrumental in getting copies of Mackenzie King's personal correspondence with his family for me. Messrs Hillmer and Young read substantial portions of the manuscript, as did Professors Charles Stacey, Robert Bothwell, William Kilbourn, and Peter Neary. Professor Bothwell and I together prepared an article on King's prewar foreign policy, some of which is used in Chapter 1. All these people assisted me greatly, but none of the blame for the result should be allowed to land on them. That is mine alone.

The research on which this work is based has been financed by the Canada Council and the C. D. Howe Foundation. Because of the Council's aid I was able to employ Mrs Linda Grayson, Miss Pat Oxley, and Mr Mark Moher as research assistants at various times. I am grateful to them all. Mrs Martha Dzioba at Oxford University Press worked mightily to achieve consistency of style in the text and in the notes. Ms Tilly Crawley, the senior Oxford editor for this work, a good friend and a constant goad, performed minor miracles on call and major ones on two days' notice. I could not have asked for better editing and assistance.

Finally, my wife Elaine and my children Carole and Michael have been very patient throughout. This book is theirs.

J.L.G.

1. The Coming of the War

'...I whistled as sharply as I could,' Mackenzie King wrote in his diary, 'and out of the mist came a voice, "I am here." It was J. [Mrs Joan Patteson] who had come over from Shady Hill, as she had promised last night to do, to give me the word which would come over the radio this morning...' Mrs Patteson, the Prime Minister's closest friend, lived during the summer with her husband in a cottage on Mackenzie King's Kingsmere estate. The word she brought was that Britain and France were at war with Germany.

It was September 3, 1939. Mackenzie King was calm, and early in the day he put his mind off the problems he now faced and contemplated his own role and that of those close to him. 'Little Pat,' he recorded of his dog, 'always seems to me a sort of symbol of my mother, as J. in her tender way makes me think very often of her. When she spoke it was as though my mother, through her, was giving me assurance of being at my side at this most critical of moments.' A little later King thought of his grandfather, William Lyon Mackenzie, and of how fitting it was that Mackenzie's grandson should have the responsibility 'of bringing the Canadian nation into war for freedom "at Britain's side". I feel it is all part of the same struggle—the struggle for the freedom of mankind.'[1]

These reflections were a stage in Mackenzie King's spiritual preparation for war. There was a gathering of forces at his side—his mother and her father, William Lyon Mackenzie; Joan Patteson; his dog. All were positive influences and on them King would have to rely for support and sustenance in the months and years that lay ahead. He would need all the strength he could muster.

I

From the very beginning of the crises that led to the outbreak of war there had never been any real doubt that Canada would go to war in support of Britain. Mackenzie King had been definitely determined on participation since the Munich crisis, and his every leaning had been in the same direction at least since the Imperial Conference in May and June 1937. At that time King had told Malcolm MacDonald, the Secretary of State for Dominion Affairs, that he would impress on Hitler 'that if Germany should ever turn her mind from constructive to destructive efforts against the United Kingdom all the Dominions would come to her aid and that there would be great numbers of Canadians anxious to swim the Atlantic!'[2] The Prime Minister was as good as his word in his interview with the Führer in Berlin,[3] and he repeated his commitment a few days later in a speech in Paris on July 2.[4] This kind of statement represented King's own views, but his political sense of the Canadian scene and the pressures exerted on him by O. D. Skelton and Loring Christie, his two chief advisers in the Department of External Affairs, often forced him to hedge and trim. After a speech in Parliament on January 16, 1939, for example, in which he had said that 'when Britain is at war Canada is at war,'[5] King wrote:

> ... I simply developed what had been most in my mind and particularly in regard to Canada's relations to Britain in time of war, made up my mind that I would not allow myself to take the one sided view that I was crowded into, speaking on External Affairs, last session which ignored the possibility of Canada being at war when Britain was at war.[6]

In his own mind at least, King's policy was crystal clear.

The British, however, had their difficulties in determining what Canada's position would be in the event of war. In part this was because their representatives in Canada were not of the first rank; in part, too, because King and Skelton took out their frustrations about British policy by haranguing the High Commissioner. Whatever the reason, after 1934[7] and even before King had returned to power, British officials and politicians worried about the senior Dominion. The Imperial Conference and King's more than satisfactory interview with Hitler did not still these worries. 'It would be clearly disastrous,' wrote Sir Maurice Hankey, the secretary of the Committee of Imperial Defence, 'if we laid our plans on the assumption that we could count upon Canada, and then when the day came we found that we had been building on false premises.' Britain would be willing to spend money in developing industrial war potential in Canada, he added, 'But we can't do that if there is the slightest risk of Canada's adopting a "neutrality set" or anything of the kind.'[8] Hankey obviously considered this a possibility. So too did Francis Floud, the High Commissioner in Ottawa until the fall of 1938. In a long letter to the Dominions Office in June 1938, he canvassed the possibilities. Mackenzie King, he reported, wanted to keep his eye 'on what he considers to be the main objective, viz. the preservation of Canada's unity'. As a result he was content 'again and again to insist on the supremacy of Parliament as the interpreter of the people's wishes if and when the time comes. He refuses resolutely to take any other line,' Floud said, 'and it is clear that however unsatisfactory this may be for those who are charged either here or at home with working out anything in the nature of Imperial defence plans, we cannot hope under the present regime, to get any further.' Floud then reviewed the legalities of the neutrality question and concluded that 'Canada seems well equipped at least to avoid getting herself entangled unofficially as it were in a war in which we were engaged,' a conclusion that few Canadian authorities accepted.[9] But in his summation Floud was more hopeful of Canadian co-operation:

Since it is inconceivable to you and to me that we shall embark on an aggressive war, and that any war in which we do ever get engaged will be other than a war of direct self-defence after an unprovoked attack, or a war which we are bound to wage in fulfillment of express undertakings shared by Canada or a war in which our undertakings are not actually shared by Canada but which is manifestly equivalent to a war of self-defence, it is surely inconceivable that Canada will not be with us in the end. All I myself really fear is a period of hesitancy, and I am afraid that we cannot necessarily count on Canada being in with us from the very beginning. There might be a delay of days, and those days might lengthen into perhaps two or three weeks. . . . After all what is the alternative? Personally I think that whatever Canada's own attitude might be, she would be brought in on our side in any case by the enemy's own action.[10]

Floud's successor as High Commissioner, Sir Gerald Campbell, was in general less sanguine. After Munich he found general support for British policy in Ottawa because, he reported, Mr Chamberlain's policy appealed to the Prime Minister who is 'temperamentally as well as politically attracted by a policy of settlement by negotiation'.[11] That was surely true, but when British policy began to stiffen, King became exceedingly uneasy. Chamberlain 'the appeaser' was more to the Prime Minister's liking, Lester Pearson wrote at the time from Canada's High Commission in London, than Chamberlain 'the avenger'.[12] The result was that on several occasions Campbell, the British Prime Minister's surrogate, was upbraided by King. On March 24, 1939, for example, Mackenzie King expressed the fear that Britain's conversations with the Soviet Union would cause difficulties among the anti-communist French Canadians and Roman Catholics. Campbell reported that King added, 'Generally the people of Canada would not be brought into any war which would appear to have been due solely to a Balkan dispute or a dispute between what he termed "African countries".' It was clear, Campbell concluded hopelessly, that 'he is if anything less disposed to co-operate with other countries in the defence of democracy than is the Government of the United States.'[13]

Considering that four days earlier King had told Parliament that if there was the prospect of an aggressor raining bombs on London, Canada would go to war,[14] Campbell's pessimism is difficult to comprehend. King believed in Chamberlain's policy of appeasement; he most emphatically did not agree with the new British policy of guarantees to Poland and Romania. And as Canada had received no advance notice of this policy and had not been consulted about it, the Prime Minister felt no particular compunction against registering his feelings towards it. British attitudes towards Canada and the other Dominions were not well calculated to win over the doubters or reassure the timorous. Far from it. London usually acted as if the Statute of Westminster had never been passed in 1931.

This particularly galled King, a man who wanted to support Britain and yet keep his country, his party, and his caucus together. He was prepared to go full distance, to walk that extra mile, in support of Chamberlain and appeasement. But a policy that in his view would lead Britain to war was a different story, particularly when Canada was virtually certain to become involved in that war. Not that the Prime Minister would try to keep Canada out of the war; not at all. King knew that if

Britain went to war, he would have to take Canada in and, indeed, he wanted to do so. But domestic politics demanded that at least the appearance of free choice be preserved, and King's speeches offered with one hand and took back with the other. On March 30, for example, just ten days after his remarks about Canada's response if bombs were falling on London, he spoke again to the House of Commons.

> The idea that every twenty years this country should automatically and as a matter of course take part in a war overseas for democracy or self-determination of other small nations, that a country which has all it can do to run itself should feel called upon to save, periodically, a continent that cannot run itself, and to these ends to risk the lives of its people, risk bankruptcy and political disunion, seems to many a nightmare and sheer madness.

The force of this neutralist oration was lessened, however, by King's pledge that should war come there would be no conscription for overseas service.[15] His anti-war sentiments never extended so far as to imply that Canada would stay out of a general war involving Britain.

In his discussions with Sir Gerald Campbell, however, Mackenzie King was never averse to appearing more cautious than he really was. For example on April 26, 1939 Campbell called and asked for a blanket guarantee of support for British policy, an appallingly foolish request. King reacted as if stung by a wasp and, as the High Commissioner reported, said that 'There were many people in Canada including some Ministers, and I gathered this included him, who disliked entanglements of this kind [being made in Eastern Europe by Britain]. . . . He could not forecast in advance of Parliament what line Canada would take if the United Kingdom went to the help of one of these countries and as a result were herself attacked.'[16] Pretty chilling stuff for the British policy-makers to ponder. Yet that same day King and O. D. Skelton agreed that 'Germany knew quite well that Canada would go into the fight if Germany were in any way an aggressor.'[17] King's complaints to the High Commissioner, therefore, were nothing more nor less than attempts to influence British policy, to steer Chamberlain back to the appeasement course that King considered most fruitful.

Once the Russo-German pact had been signed on August 23, however, King knew that war was inevitable. There was much bitterness about British policy, with Skelton calling the pact 'the greatest fiasco in British history' and King criticizing the 'blundering there has been in England's foreign policy all along the way'.[18] The Under Secretary summed it all up in a minute to a file on August 25:

> The first casualty of this war has been Canada's claim to control over her own destinies. If war comes to Poland and we take part, that war came as a consequence of commitments made by the Government of Great Britain, about which we are not in one iota consulted, and about which we were not given the slightest inkling of information in advance.[19]

Skelton still leaned towards neutrality, but he knew that the Prime Minister would—and could—consider no such course. The best the Prime Minister could offer his closest adviser was the assurance that 'If we get through this . . . there will be an Imperial Conference at which there will have to be some very plain speaking.'[20]

No one would get through this, and King well knew it. He did have faint hopes, however, that Hitler would come to his senses,[21] and he sought for ways to mobilize opinion to this end. Like several other world leaders, he telegraphed Chamberlain on August 26 to 'strongly urge' that George VI should personally appeal to Hitler to give time for further negotiations 'before resort is had to gamble. The appeal to be made by His Majesty in the interests of humanity as being above all nations, and whose interests are vastly more concerned than the special interests of individual nations.' That was a highly unusual view of the place of the monarchy, but Mackenzie King went on to suggest that the Queen should be associated with the gesture as well 'on behalf of women and children'. Such a move would have great effect in the Common-wealth, in the world, and not least in Germany. 'It would stir the hearts of the entire world and be immensely helpful later on, should war follow nevertheless.' Despite George VI's eagerness to take this step, Chamber-lain's reply implied that royal intervention would not be opportune.[22] The British clearly viewed Mackenzie King's suggestion as naive in the extreme, and they were certainly correct in deciding that such an appeal would have no effect on the Führer. Nonetheless King's proposal, with its guileful comment on its value even if unsuccessful, might have been worth an attempt. Similarly Mackenzie King's telegrams to Hitler, Mus-solini, and the Polish president on August 25 were worth the effort. The messages were couched in the same prose style as King's telegram to Chamberlain and hence seem to be the prattlings of an innocent.[23] In a sense King was an innocent, but his prolix, purple prose came close to meeting the desires of the people for some attempt by Canada to keep the peace.[24] It was futile and King realized this—at the same time that he despatched the telegrams he told the German and Italian representatives in Ottawa that Canada would fight—but the attempt had to be made.[25]

Meanwhile the Cabinet was turning to serious things. The question of Canada's going to war in the event of an attack on Poland was fully canvassed at its long meeting on August 24. Every member had his say, and everyone accepted the idea that, as C. D. Howe, the Minister of Transport, put it, 'Canada would have to participate.' There was no great enthusiasm for war, but King told his Cabinet that

> I was immensely relieved to find that on the all-important matter of Canada's participation in the event of Britain being drawn into war, we were of one mind and united. I said there appeared to be a difference of view as to the time at which we should state our policy. Some were for stating it immediately; others to await developments. I have been criticized for saying that Parliament would decide, impression having been gained that I meant by that that we would leave it to a sort of general discussion in Parliament, when Parliament was assembled, to see what the majority felt. That I had not meant anything of the kind, as they knew; that I thought the position to take lay between these two extremes and it was that we would not wait until Parliament assembled to announce our policy, but would, when summoning Parliament, let the country know what the policy was on the matter of participation leaving to Parliament to decide the details of nature, extent of, etc., etc. Our views on these would be given to Parliament immediately it assembled and the government would stand or fall by its policy as stated.

The Prime Minister recorded in his diary that 'I got general agreement and unanimity on this position. In the event of war we had now decided that Canada would participate ... that we would summon Parliament at the moment war was declared. ... At the same time we would announce our policy with respect to Canada's being at war; that Parliament could be brought together in at least a week ...'[26]

King told the High Commissioner of the Cabinet's decision and impressed upon him that it would be extremely harmful if anyone suggested that Canada should enter the war 'as though she were a Colonial possession'.[27] The procedure was extremely important to King and rightly so, for in the method of going to war Canada's national status would be tested. Mackenzie King had not really sought any role for Canada in the pre-war diplomacy, preferring to hang back because the fragile state of English-French relations in his view demanded such a policy. Now, with war about to begin, Canadian unity demanded that Canada go to war on its own, a concept that was very difficult for many British leaders to grasp. After the crucial Cabinet meeting on August 24, for example, King met with Lord Maugham, the British Lord Chancellor, who was in Ottawa for a visit. Maugham told the Prime Minister that he proposed to deliver a speech saying that he was pleased to learn that Canada would be at Britain's side in the event of war, a statement that appalled King who informed his nonplussed visitor that Canada had to avoid the impression 'that we might be in any way acting at the instance of Britain'. King added a characteristic aside: 'How desperately stupid some Englishmen are in appreciating any attitude other than their own.'[28]

So the decision had been made to fight. But where? And with what? This was much less clear. In the summer of 1939 Major-General A. G. L. McNaughton, the former Chief of the General Staff and the head of the National Research Council, had been very critical of Canada's defence preparations in a letter he had sent to Lord Gort, the Chief of the Imperial General Staff: 'The provision which has been made for the development of our defence is painfully inadequate but I think the situation is improving. . . . all one hopes is that sufficient time will remain available.'[29] An American military intelligence report was similar in tone. The permanent force, it said, was 'very efficient' and the militia was the 'best trained' in all the British Dominions, but the tiny size of both—the regulars numbered 4,261 on July 31, 1939 and the militia 51,418 on December 31, 1938[30]—greatly limited the combat value of the Canadian army. In any case, the report noted, the Canadians would fight along Great War lines.[31]

Even that conclusion was in doubt. No one in Ottawa truly knew what kind of force might be required for war or even if Canada would send an expeditionary force overseas. Everything and nothing was in the air. The Prime Minister's calculated refusal to permit consultation and liaison with London and the British forces, his persistent unwillingness to commit Canada in advance, had all but paralyzed co-operation. The political motives for this course more than justified it, in King's mind at least. But in a military sense the result was frantic scurrying in Ottawa at the end of August.

Skelton, the indispensable Skelton, raised points of this kind in a memorandum to Mackenzie King on August 24. There was, he argued, some real virtue in pointing publicly the direction the war effort would follow. Otherwise 'there will be agitation by individuals and newspapers for this or that course, based mainly on the conditions of 1914 rather than those of 1939.' Unstated, but clearly foremost in Skelton's mind and in his Prime Minister's, was the concern that public pressure would begin for a large army and for conscription to support it. Skelton assumed that there would be close consultation with London and Paris 'and equally important, discreet consultations with Washington'. But above all, in the Under Secretary's view, Canadian efforts should be devoted to the defence of Canada. 'Many statements have been made in the past year or two as to the impossibility in the event of war of Canada avoiding attack. If that is so,' he argued with impeccable logic, neatly nipping in the bud the contention that now that war was at hand the only danger was in Europe, 'our first business is to avert that attack.' Canada should consider extending assistance to Newfoundland and the West Indies, and any military action overseas in the first instance should be through the air force rather than the army. Finally, Skelton argued, 'it is in the economic field that we can give aid that will be most effective to our allies and most consistent with Canada's interests.'[32]

The Chiefs of Staff did not agree. In a memorandum prepared on August 29 and forwarded to the Cabinet the next day, the military leaders reviewed the situation and suggested a course of action. The government, they said, had already determined against neutrality and would act to defend Canada's coasts, harbours, trade and population centres. 'Active participation with other Empire forces has throughout been a secondary and incidental consideration,' the Chiefs conceded. 'But it may be confidently ... anticipated that the outbreak of a major war will produce in Canada an immediate and overwhelming demand for active intervention with armed forces in direct aid of Great Britain.' After a long justification of the necessity for planning for a major land war and an equally long disquisition on plans for orderly recruiting, the Chiefs got to the point: an Army corps of 60,000 men should be raised immediately and despatched 'abroad as soon as arrangements can be made, in co-operation with the British Government, to transport it and to make good such deficiencies in its war equipment as cannot be supplied from Canadian sources'.[33]

As might be expected, the Chiefs' blithe (if not incorrect) assumptions raised hackles. Loring Christie of the Department of External Affairs devastated their memorandum in notes to the Prime Minister: 'The paper may perhaps give some notion of why certain things have been left undone in the past years' by the Department of National Defence. 'They were spending most of their brains on this baby...' To Christie, the main reason advanced by the military for the despatch of 60,000 men overseas 'is the demand on Great Britain's man power for (a) air defence and (b) war industry. That is to say, British man power would work at home ... while at great expense Canadian man power would be transported across the ocean, across Great Britain and pitched into Europe.'[34] King needed no help with this. On September 4 he told J. L. Ilsley, the Minister of National Revenue and acting Minister of Finance, to refuse expenditures except for the defence of Canada, a move that was deliberately designed to prevent National Defence from ordering supplies for the fitting out of troops for overseas service.[35] The next day Ian Mackenzie, the Minister of National Defence, instructed his officials not to stimulate recruiting 'as it is probable that more men are now available than can be conveniently handled'.[36] In the Defence Committee of Cabinet* on September 5 and in a private conversation with the Chiefs of Staff, the Prime Minister objected to the assumptions in the military memorandum and reiterated that his government's policy was the defence of Canada. Taken aback, the military advisers said they had intended only to 'provide the organization of an expeditionary force if, in the light of developments, such were deemed advisable, and such were decided by the government.' The forces presently being mobilized, they assured King, were only for the defence of Canada.[37]

---

*The Cabinet organization for defence matters was not yet clearly or finally defined. The basic element was the Cabinet Sub-Committee on Defence that met infrequently. On September 5 this same body, its membership consisting of the Prime Minister, the Acting Minister of Finance, and the Ministers of National Defence, Justice, and Mines and Resources seems to have altered its name to the Defence Committee of Cabinet. By September 15 the title had altered again to the Emergency Council (Committee on General Policy) of Cabinet, and the Government Leader in the Senate joined its deliberations. The Emergency Council met several times until on December 5, 1939 the Cabinet War Committee, established by P.C. 4017½, replaced it. The Cabinet War Committee remained the key directing committee of the government until war's end, its membership initially consisting of the Prime Minister, the Ministers of Justice, Finance, National Defence, Mines and Resources, and the Senate Leader. On May 27, 1940 the Committee was enlarged to include the Ministers of Munitions and Supply and the Minister of National Defence (Air). Later the Minister of National Defence (Naval Services) was added. Other ministers participated as required.

King's position, in fact, was based in part on what he had learned from Britain's representative in Canada. On September 1 he had talked with the High Commissioner who reported to London that 'I told him that the United Kingdom Government were aware that Canada might be unwilling to consider the despatch of expeditionary force but I thought that there would be large number of volunteers eager to enlist for service in Great Britain and their assistance would be welcomed though the Government of the United Kingdom would not want to do anything to weaken defence forces of Canada.' Campbell then gave his superiors his 'personal impression . . . that while he wants a perfectly frank statement of your desires, he would prefer that no great account should be made at this juncture upon the despatch of an expeditionary force as he is eager to present the world with an almost unanimous vote when Parliament meets.'[38] King interpreted this conversation with Campbell to mean that 'Britain was not concerned in the matter of expeditionary force, if we did not wish to send an expeditionary force,' not an unfair version at all.[39] The next day the Cabinet discussed the question and, as King recorded, 'all were agreed we should not absolutely prohibit it, but should not seek to encourage anything of the kind.'[40]

Explicit support for this position came on September 6 when Chamberlain replied to a telegram from King asking for an assessment of the 'theatre and character' of British and Allied military operations. The British Prime Minister replied that 'We realize . . . the immediate task of the Canadian Government will be the defence of Canada,' thus accepting that no expeditionary force would be pledged in the first instance.[41] King was delighted—'to my great relief,' he recorded, '. . . the British had replied in a manner which will avoid the necessity of our thinking of an expeditionary force.'[42] The issue did not disappear so easily, and on September 7 King was surprised to discover that the Cabinet was more favourable to the expeditionary force in principle than 'I had imagined they would be, and growing feeling that it might become inevitable. I was also surprised to find considerable feeling for conscription or saying nothing against conscription.' That could not be tolerated and would have to be dealt with forcefully. 'It may conceivably come to conscription for our own defence,' King did note; 'nothing has been said against that.'[43]

For all this period, of course, Canada was still at peace. Britain and France had declared war on September 3, but while the position of the Dominion under international law might have been hazy, in practice the country was not at war. This had some importance, because in the United States the Neutrality Act had been put in force, effectively cutting off the sale of war supplies to the belligerents. The United States government was aware of Canada's position, for Fiorello LaGuardia, the Mayor of New York City, something of a gadfly and something of a friend of President Franklin D. Roosevelt, had written to the Secretary of State, Cordell Hull, with a copy to the President, in this vein. Canada not being at war, LaGuardia wrote, 'we would then be free to ship all sorts of material and supplies.... What happened to such shipments after that would not be our concern...'[44] Perhaps as a result of this letter, King was called on the telephone by Roosevelt and Hull on September 5, and he assured his two American friends that Canada was still neutral. War supplies as a result were shipped to Canada until the Canadian declaration of war took effect on September 10.[45]

The neutrality was only a formality. Col. Maurice Pope, the secretary to the Chiefs of Staff Committee, recalled that the Minister of National Defence instructed him on September 3 to convey to the Chiefs 'that they were to give effect to all the defence measures which would be required in a state of war and to fire on any blinking German who came within range of our guns—but that we were not at war.' 'You are certainly trying to have it both ways,' Pope replied, and the Minister, Ian Mackenzie, said, 'chuckling . . . "Of course we are."'[46] In his own fashion the Defence Minister was interpreting the decisions that had been reached in Cabinet that day. King had said that 'all our measures at present would be for the defence of Canada. That we were at war in the sense of being liable to be attacked. That Britain was at war and, if attacked, we should take means of defence and should not go beyond the defence of Canada at present, or do anything in the way of attacking ourselves. We would,' King added, 'have to take measures with respect to some aliens to protect against some internal difficulties and that all this should be done with caution and judgement.'[47]

Caution and judgement also demanded that the people be told of the government's intentions, and the Prime Minister spoke to the country on the radio. King made it clear that when Parliament met, Canada would go to war, but it would be up to Parliament to decide the form and scope of Canadian participation:

Parliament will meet Thursday next. Between now and then, all necessary measures will be taken for the defence of Canada. Consulta-

THE COMING OF THE WAR | 13

tion with the United Kingdom will be continued. In the light of all the information at its disposal, the Government will then recommend to Parliament the measures which it believes to be most effective for co-operation and defence. That Parliament will sanction all necessary measures, I have not the least doubt.[48]

The position of the government was now clear, but the next day King was upset by the press reaction to his speech. The Ottawa *Journal* had 'Not a line or a reference to our country's position and part,' he recorded, although it was full of the King's speech and Chamberlain's. 'It is this aspect of Toryism that fills me with grief, dismay and contempt. Anything if it is the King of England, but no mention whatever of Canada's own noble part or the words of her P.M. Is it any wonder that Liberal-minded men and women are driven to feel that the sooner they stand on their own the better . . .'[49] That type of press reaction to his speeches always infuriated King, as did the Anglocentrism of so many Canadians. King himself was susceptible to the appeal of Empire, but ordinarily he kept himself in check by noting the follies of British policy. The terrible news from Poland on September 6, for example, forced King to agree with Skelton 'that it is appalling that Britain should ever have allowed that nation, by promising its support in the way it did, to [be] where it ultimately would be completely destroyed.' Less understandably, King also added that 'I think the Poles themselves too are terribly to blame for not having hastened to meet Hitler's terms, though one can see . . . that he really has had conquest in view.' The whole picture was bleak, for King doubted that Britain and France would stop fighting even if Hitler wanted to, something that was equally unlikely. 'Heaven only knows whether socialist aims at world revolution, may not manifest themselves all over the world. What may the Japanese not do in the Orient! . . . I have no doubt that we shall have some bombing of our coast and possibly some inland bombing as well.'[50]

A few days later, when King learned that Britain and France were trying to win Italy's support by promising the former German colonies in southern Africa to her, he was again moved to think about the events that had led to war. In his view that news showed 'how criminally foolish those in authority in Britain and France have been in not getting down long before this, being prepared to give something in the way of concession to Germany which would have avoided this terrible war.' His own conscience was clear, however: 'I have right along impressed on the

British Government and persons with whom I have talked, the necessity of getting into conference, and seeking to adjust things by peaceful means.'[51] In King's mind appeasement had not failed; rather, it had not been pressed hard enough.

Canada's sham neutrality in an Empire at war could not last much longer. On September 7 the emergency session of Parliament met for the bleak speech from the throne: 'You have been summoned at the earliest moment in order that the government may seek authority for the measures necessary for the defence of Canada, and for co-operation in the determined effort which is being made to resist further aggression.'[52] The Prime Minister then tabled a long list of emergency orders in council covering expenditures for defence purposes, establishing pay rates for the armed forces, censorship regulations, a declaration of a state of apprehended war, and a host of other measures.

The most important business of the day, however, was Mackenzie King's announcement of the appointment of Colonel J. L. Ralston as Minister of Finance and of his acceptance of the resignation of Charles Dunning from the government and from this post. Dunning had been ill for some time and had sent his resignation to King in July. Ralston, who had been King's Minister of National Defence from 1926 to 1930, had been asked by the Prime Minister to enter the Cabinet in August as Minister of Finance. The Nova Scotian-turned-Montreal lawyer had refused, but he told King that he would do anything if war came. 'This,' King noted at the time, 'is what I had in mind in 'phoning, and I was glad he volunteered it before I had come to this second request.'[53] Now Ralston was in the government again.

The Colonel, in fact, had been offered his choice of Finance or National Defence[54] and had taken Finance. Ralston was a very strong man. A front-line battalion commander in the Great War, an able and successful corporation lawyer, he was a figure of recognized courage and power. Instantly upon entering the Cabinet he became, with King and Ernest Lapointe (the Minister of Justice and King's Quebec leader), one of the three most powerful men in the country. He would remain so for the next five years.

Mackenzie King delivered his first major address to Parliament the next day. 'Just a few minutes before I got up to speak, thoughts came to me quickly as to how best to introduce what I had to say,' he wrote later. 'I started in very quietly and, I thought, felicitously. I recognized at once that I was going to be in good form and that strength and power were being given to me.' More, King let himself go as he rarely did. 'The result was that I expressed my very soul. Did not keep back any thought or feeling which I had been cherishing in the last few days . . .'[55]

The Prime Minister began with a few graceful words of thanks to Dr R. J. Manion for the Leader of the Opposition's pledges of co-operation with the government, and he shortly turned to the war and to a definition of the administration's war policy:

> We stand for the defence of Canada; we stand for the cooperation of this country at the side of Great Britain; and if this house will not support us in that policy, it will have to find some other government to assume the responsibilities of the present.

That was clear enough, and so was King's almost proselytizing fervour as he addressed the neutral nations:

> I tell them if they remain neutral in this struggle, and Britain and France go down, there is not one of them that will bear for long the name it bears at the present time; not one of them. And if this conqueror by his methods of force, violence and terror . . . is able to crush the peoples of Europe, what is going to become of the doctrine of isolation of this North American continent? If Britain goes down, if France goes down, the whole business of isolation will prove to have been a mere myth. There will in time be no freedom on this continent; there will in time be no liberty. Life will not be worth living. It is for all of us on this continent to do our part to save its privileged position by helping others.

The Prime Minister was most effective when he explained the reasons for his often tortuous course since 1935:

> I have never doubted that when the fatal moment came, the free spirit of the Canadian people would assert itself in the preservation and defence of freedom, as it did a quarter of a century ago. I have, however, been anxious that when the inevitable hour came, our people should be as one from coast to coast in recognizing the magnitude of the issue which was presenting itself, and as one in their determination to meet it with all the strength and power at their command. I have made it, therefore, the supreme endeavour of my leadership of my party, and my leadership of the government of this country, to let no hasty or premature threat or pronouncement create mistrust and

divisions between the different elements that compose the population of our vast dominion, so that when the moment of decision came all should so see the issue itself that our national effort might be marked by unity of purpose, of heart and of endeavour.

In his discussion of the war measures the government would adopt, Mackenzie King laid greatest stress on economic steps and played down the prospect of an expeditionary force. He did, however, definitely pledge himself against conscription for overseas service:

> I wish now to repeat the undertaking I gave in parliament on behalf of the government on March 30 last. The present government believe that conscription of men for overseas service will not be a necessary or effective step. No such measure will be introduced by the present administration.[56]

This promise was flat and unequivocal. It was also supremely political, for with his references to the 'present' administration Mackenzie King was telling Quebec that while he could guarantee that there would be no conscription, if he should be defeated all such promises would be invalid. The pledge was also prescient, too, with its declaration against conscription for overseas service, not service in Canada.[57]

This long address, one of the most fateful of King's career, was in many respects entirely typical. It was too long, too boring by half, too much designed to conceal. It was, in fact, greatly exceeded in impact by Lapointe's masterly oration and plea for Quebec to support the war, delivered the next day.[58] But King's speech presented a full record of his government's actions, a complete guide to the public correspondence and telegrams. Everything was there, and everything was hedged or qualified as much as the Prime Minister deemed necessary. Except for the pledge on conscription; that was not hedged at all. It was a classic King speech, even to his concluding with a full fourteen stanzas of bad poetry.[59]

The rest of the brief emergency session of Parliament was anticlimactic except for the passing of a $100 million war appropriation bill[60] and for the courage of J. S. Woodsworth. In a great and noble speech, the CCF leader set out his unyielding opposition to war:

> I do not care whether you think me an impossible idealist or a dangerous crank, I am going to take my place beside the children and these young people, because it is only as we adopt new policies that this world will be at all a livable place for our children who follow us.

We laud the courage of those who go to the front; yes, I have boys of my own, and I hope they are not cowards, but if any one of those boys, not from cowardice but really through belief, is willing to take his stand on this matter and, if necessary, to face a concentration camp or a firing squad I shall be more proud of that boy than if he enlisted for the war.[61]

After another day of debate, it was all over on September 9. Ever the political manager, King privately talked to some of the Liberal isolationists from Quebec, and he discouraged P. J. A. Cardin, his Minister of Public Works, from making an effort to read them out of the party.[62] The result was that when Liguori Lacombe, the Liberal M.P. for Laval-Deux Montagnes, moved an amendment to the Address in Reply to the Speech from the Throne regretting that the government had not determined on neutrality, his efforts to mobilize Quebec Members failed and the amendment was easily turned down in a voice vote. The Address, in effect a vote on war or peace, was similarly carried despite a few nays. By the decision of her own Parliament, Canada had determined to enter the war.

Immediately after the close of proceedings on September 9, the Cabinet met to sign the order in council declaring a state of war so that word could be sent to the King. 'As I was about to sign,' Mackenzie King wrote, 'I suddenly lifted my eyes off the paper and was surprised to see my grandfather's bust immediately opposite, look directly at me—the eyes almost expressing a living light. He was the one person in my thoughts as I affixed my signature to the order-in-council.' Later, when he returned to Laurier House, King noted that he looked at his mother's picture in the library. 'All I could say was—and I could not help saying it—"The names Mackenzie and King will have an honoured place in the records of our country." That we had played our part . . .' Next to his mother and grandfather, King concluded, 'my thoughts were of Sir Wilfrid and Lady Laurier.'[63] George VI signed the proclamation of a state of war between Canada and Germany on September 10, and when Mackenzie King received word that Canada was now officially at war, 'I knelt and prayed for my country and for the cause of freedom, for strength and guidance in these times of need.' King added that he was relieved that the monarch's approval had come. 'I kept fearing that the jingo elements in the country would again be finding fault with me for not getting into the war as soon as we could. There will, I fear, be plenty of war before the end comes.'[64]

II

'My Prime Minister,' the Governor General, Lord Tweedsmuir, wrote in his slightly pompous way to a friend in England, 'has succeeded skilfully in aligning Canada alongside Britain with a minimum of disturbance. He, of course, is being criticized for not declaring himself roundly and clearly, but in my view his policy has been the right one.'*[65] The judgement was a good one. Mackenzie King's achievement was important, for with his policy of evasion and delay, of 'Parliament will decide', he had accomplished his end: he had brought Canada into the war by the virtually unanimous choice of her Parliament and with the minimum of disturbance and discontent in the country. A year earlier that had seemed almost an impossibility.

But in fact there was discontent barely beneath the surface. Neutralist sentiment in the country as a whole was weak, but it was powerful in the quality of its advocates and in the force of its arguments. In Quebec there was no enthusiasm at all for the war and much subdued muttering against it. On the Prairies, too, many European immigrants remembered 1917 and were unhappy. The simple fact was that to many Canadians it did not seem to be Canada's war. Why should we join in another European quarrel? Why should Canada be the only North American nation, the only independent state in the Western hemisphere, to enter the war? Wasn't this just another war of imperialisms?

Those were the important questions. Canadians perceived Hitler as a menace and as evil, yes; but in September 1939 few knew of concentration camps and genocide, and those who might have heard of such things

---

*The British High Commissioner, no admirer of the Prime Minister, said much the same thing. King 'is clearly justified now in claiming that his policy of not committing the Dominion in any way which might disrupt the union of Canada has proved to be right.' (Public Record Office, Foreign Office Records, FO 371/23966, Campbell to Harding, 13 Sept. 1939.) King George VI was said to agree. (Queen's University, John Buchan Papers, Sir A. Hardinge to Tweedsmuir, 30 Sept. 1939.) A more perceptive, albeit Liberal, response was Brooke Claxton's. The Montreal lawyer wrote a Tory friend that 'While King has been indefinite, I do think that he has done a magnificent job in getting the country started on its war effort in an intelligent way where greater definiteness on almost any point would have created endless difficulty and trouble.... King has taken the middle line, not only because it is in his nature to do so, but also because he thought it best for the country.' But Claxton was not fooled by the quiet in Quebec: 'no single French Canadian organization has passed a resolution favouring intervention, while literally hundreds have passed resolutions violently opposing it.' Canadian Institute of International Affairs, Edgar Tarr Papers, Claxton to J. M. Macdonnell, 16 Sept. 1939.

probably equated them with the phoney atrocity stories of 1914-18 when the Huns were alleged to have cut the breasts off Belgian nuns, to have spitted babies on their bayonets, and even to have crucified a Canadian officer. Credulity resisted similar horror stories in 1939. Hitler was aggressive, but few could work up any enthusiasm for Poland. Just a few months earlier, some Canadians remembered, the Poles had insisted on their pound of flesh from the corpse of Czechoslovakia, and the Polish leaders seemed as militaristic, if not as efficient, as Hitler. To talk of the defence of democracy was difficult in these circumstances. It was made harder still by the collapse of the world economy in the 1930s.

Canadians were no different from other North Americans in their perceptions of the emergent conflict in September 1939. But unlike the United States, Canada went to war. The reason why is clear: Canada went to war because Britain went to war. Not for democracy, not to stop Hitler, not to save Poland. Canada decided to fight in September 1939 only because Prime Minister Neville Chamberlain felt himself unable to escape the commitments Great Britain had made to Poland six months earlier.[66] If he had slipped free, Canada would have watched Germany devour Poland without in any way feeling compelled to fight.

The fundamental reason for this Canadian decision was sentiment. The ties of blood and culture that bound Canada to Britain proved strong enough to compel the government willingly to follow the course it did. In fact the government had little choice. To stay neutral would be difficult legally, given the old British rights to the naval bases at Halifax and Esquimault. To stay neutral involved an open challenge to the principle of the indivisibility of the Crown, a principle that seemed very real to many Canadians after the visit of the King and Queen to Canada in May.[67]

But in a sense the Canadian decision for war was almost *pro forma*. There was no enthusiasm, no desire for a battle to the death with godless Nazism and its ally in Stalinist Russia. This war was to be different from 1914; there would be no conscription crisis, no racial disunity, no hysteria, no vast expenditure of blood and treasure. Canadians were virtually obliged to participate, but we were not obliged to participate to the last man and the last dollar. This was to be a war in which Canada's primary assistance to England would be in the form of economic aid—a war of limited liability. In September 1939 this seemed both practical and possible; as important, it seemed to be what the public wanted.

What is striking about the first few days of the war is the coolness of the Canadian response. There were the usual fire-eaters, of course, but they stand out only because they were so firmly in a minority.* The war was not received with cheers and enthusiasm as it had been in 1914. There were no crowds around newspaper offices, no bands in the streets, no impassioned singing of *God Save the King* or *La Marseillaise*. The memories of 1914-18, the terrible casualties of that war, and the divisions it left in the fabric of the nation were still too deep for that. The disillusionment over the failures of the 1930s, over the collapse of the League of Nations, and over the weaknesses of British policy—all were too clear. Above all, the great depression had sapped the will of the people. For the first time many Canadians might even have wondered if the system were worth fighting for. From Winnipeg, Professor Arthur Lower wrote to a friend that 'people everywhere are apathetic or appalled; there is no enthusiasm. In the immortal words of General Griesbach [a Boer War and Great War veteran and a Conservative Senator], this war "will have to be sold to the young people".'[68]

So strong was this feeling that the Under Secretary of State for External Affairs could write in a memorandum that 'it is very doubtful if a majority of the people of Canada would in a free plebiscite have voted for war. There is little enthusiasm even among the war supporters. There is a widespread feeling that this is not our war, that the British government which blundered into it, should have been allowed to blunder out . . .' With his deep-set biases against the British, Skelton was not the most impartial judge of the situation, but he was undoubtedly correct when he observed that anti-war feeling 'has not found greater expression [because] it has not found leadership, [because] the organs of opinion are in control of the old and conservative, and not least [because of] the masterly strategy of the Prime Minister.'[69] Impartial observers such as the American Consuls-General in Vancouver and Winnipeg confirmed Skelton's assessment, although both American diplomats did note a determination to stick with the war until victory.[70]

But even this perception of events was different from popular sentiment in Quebec, where opinion probably favoured staying out of the war. Yet even in Quebec a realistic recognition of the fact that neutrality

---

*Addressing the Liberal caucus on September 12, Mackenzie King felt justified in telling the Senators and Members that his policy of no commitments had been the right one. 'I then said to them to look at the situation and they would see that this country had come into the war with a quietude and peace almost comparable to that of a vessel sailing over a smooth and sunlit lake; that we had kept down all passion and faction, and now were a united country.' King Diary, 12 Sept. 1939.

was simply impossible, given the blood ties of so many English-speaking Canadians to England, did exist. For the government the task was to keep this realism to the fore and not to permit the vocal isolationists to dominate the media. One of the key moulders of opinion, of course, was the Church, and Chubby Power, King's Minister of Pensions and Health, flew into Quebec City on September 1 expressly to see Cardinal Villeneuve. The ostensible purpose of his visit, Power wrote in a memorandum, was 'to seek the cooperation of the Authorities of the Province of Quebec' in air-raid precautions. The real purpose was to find out the Cardinal's views on the war, and to Power these were not entirely satisfactory. While the Cardinal was 'whole-heartedly against Germany . . . he believes he can help best by not appearing to become involved in any political discussions. He felt that it was his duty to assist and support the duly constituted Authorities in their undertakings, and he would do so.' This was qualified support at best, although Power had been impressed by the cordiality of his reception.[71]

Some of the Quebec press were less than cordial. The nationalist *Le Devoir* took the view that Canada should stay out of the war: 'Le Canada n'est pas Pays d'Europe,' it pronounced on September 2. *Le Droit* in Ottawa took essentially the same line, as did *L'Action Catholique* and *L'Evénement-Journal*. But the major newspapers in the province gave cautious support to the government, seeing the war as a righteous one and assigning full blame for it to Hitler. As for enthusiasm, however, there was none. *La Presse, Le Canada, Le Soleil*, good Liberal journals all, were very hesitant, and such reassurance for the future that they could find came from a belief that Mackenzie King would have due regard for the susceptibilities of French Canada.[72]

In English Canada some elements also favoured neutrality. The Communists followed the swerving party line, and with the Russo-German pact their fierce anti-fascism was transformed into a sudden desire for neutrality. More significantly, the legitimate socialist movement was badly split. The League for Social Reconstruction, the largely academic group that provided the Cooperative Commonwealth Federation with its ideas and intellectual credibility, stood basically against the war. Some of its members, most notably Professor Frank Scott—McGill law professor, constitutional expert, and CCF stalwart—had in fact been in the midst of conversations with Quebec nationalists with a view to the formulation of a joint statement on foreign policy.[73] But the coming of the war interrupted these talks and, faced with the certainty of Canadian participation, the LSR had to seek other means of action. The Toronto branch, for example, sent out letters on August 28 urging 'all possible steps to demand a plebiscite on the question of Canada's participation in the forthcoming war.'[74] These efforts were futile.

Within the Protestant churches, too, there was some substantial unease about the war. Too many clergymen remembered the hysteria of the 1914 war and in particular the role of the church in the 1917 election not to worry about being used once again. A number of clergy had been associated in the 1930s with the Fellowship for a Christian Social Order, a leftist and activist group that had been formed as a Christian response to the failure of the economic system. During the last years of the peace there had been debates on pacifism at the United Church's annual meetings, and there were even occasional cracks in the solid front of the Anglican Church. The result of this sentiment was the 'Witness Against War', a pacifist manifesto eventually signed by sixty-eight United Church ministers across the country. 'We find ourselves, not without pain and regret, unable to approve of this or any war,' the ministers' statement said. 'We take our stand upon the declaration of our own General Council in 1938, that "war is contrary to the mind of Christ". . .' It was magnificent, but it was war nonetheless, and the great majority of United Church ministers went out of their way to justify the struggle to their congregations.[75]

The CCF was equally torn. At its emergency National Council meeting from September 6-8, there was scant support for war. Two of those attending favoured full support, eight favoured qualified support, four were for neutrality in this war, and six were for neutrality in this or any war. The last group included J. S. Woodsworth, the party leader.[76] Much of the pacifist-neutralist sentiment sprang from deep conviction, but political calculation shaped some of it. Frank Scott, for one, believed that the war offered the CCF a chance to win support in Quebec. If it withheld its support for the war, the CCF would have its 'best opportunity for bridging the gap between Quebec and ourselves'.[77] In the end the party decided to offer its qualified support for the war but to oppose sending men overseas.[78] Woodsworth was left free to make an appeal for neutrality. Political realism—or at least a CCF version of it— had carried the day.

Not in British Columbia, where militant members of the CCF were crusading against the war. Harold Winch, M.L.A., the provincial leader, said in Kamloops in October that 'Not a man will leave Canada for overseas duty if we can prevent it,' and others made similar remarks. But the old and conservative were in charge there, too, and the B.C. Police began reporting on CCF meetings to the Attorney-General of British Columbia. The Deputy Attorney-General advised prosecution on the grounds that such speeches would prejudice recruiting, an offence against the Defence of Canada Regulations. Premier Duff Pattullo decided against prosecution, but he did issue a warning against any further breaches of the Regulations.[79] It was almost enough to justify *Life*'s comment that 'Democracy, including free speech and free press, went out the window as soon as Canada declared war.'[80]

The Conservative Party had fewer problems in shaping its response to war. Many Tories believed simply that once Britain was at war, Canada was at war. There could be no nonsense about separate declarations of war, no claptrap about 'Parliament will decide'. The Crown was indivisible, and Canada was at war.[81] The party leader, Dr Robert Manion, a Catholic married to a French Canadian and a man chosen party leader partly because he was believed to have popular appeal in Quebec, took essentially the same view, although he phrased it rather more moderately than some of his supporters might have hoped. 'There can be no neutrality for Canada while Britain is engaged in a war of life and death,' he said in a September 1 statement. 'Therefore, in my opinion the united voice of Canada will call for full co-operation with Britain and France . . .'[82] Manion's moderation was not at all surprising considering the efforts he had made through the summer of 1939 towards securing an alliance with the Union Nationale Party, led by Premier Maurice Duplessis of Quebec.[83] Nonetheless the coming of the war shattered Manion, who saw what it would do to disrupt his efforts to topple Mackenzie King. The Prime Minister, he told a friend, 'certainly has the luck of the very devil—just as he was on the verge of going out, this crisis comes along and allows people to forget his past sins.' To another Conservative, Manion wrote that 'I was convinced that we were going to sweep the country and I should not have been surprised at a real landslide. . . . However now with this affair on we can't even talk politics and I imagine he is in for a renewed lease of life . . .'[84]

The war had delayed any election, however. The Prime Minister had been contemplating an election in the fall of 1939, but by August he had started to worry what would happen if war came with Parliament dissolved. The prospect frightened him enough that, as he told his Cabinet on August 11, he had decided not to allow dissolution to occur as long as there was the prospect of war.[85] As a result when Manion came to see him on September 6 the Prime Minister indicated, as Manion recorded, that 'there would be no general election until after the next session—that is, the January session—but that he did not believe in the extension of the life of Parliament and said he thought that we would have a general election then, with which I wholly agreed.' King's pledge was also given in the House of Commons on September 12.[86]

III

With Canada in the war, the government's task now was to decide on the form that the Canadian contribution would take. Mackenzie King himself was lukewarm about sending troops overseas as late as September 12,[87] preferring to rely on the British assurances of September 1 and 6 that the defence of Canada remained the first and major charge of his government. But as a telegram from the Dominions Office to the British High Commissioner in Ottawa made evident, those assurances had just been British tact: 'In order not to embarrass the Prime Minister of Canada when he wished to bring Canada into the war with an almost unanimous vote in Parliament, we refrained from suggesting [an expeditionary force] too directly. The need for such a force does, however, exist and is increasing from day to day.'[88] Pressures within the country were increasing, too, and the Canadian Legion insistently demanded 'that the Government must make an immediate declaration of the nature and the measure of our effective cooperation with Great Britain.'[89]

A Cabinet sub-committee had been established on September 15 to prepare just such a program and to calculate its costs. The recommendations of the military chiefs amounted to $491,689,000 for the first year of the war,[90] a sum almost equal to the peacetime budget of the country. King and his advisers were staggered, and on September 18 the full Cabinet heard the Governor of the Bank of Canada, Graham Towers, and the Deputy Minister of Finance, W. Clifford Clark, declare that the country might be able to bear an expenditure of half that amount. King was delighted with the budget-paring presentation by the civil servants. It reminded him of his days at Harvard, he recorded, and 'It was an immense relief getting back to sound economics.'[91] Nonetheless King argued against any delay in reaching decisions. Politically it would be 'folly', he told the Cabinet, 'not to make known to the Canadian people at once that our war effort was going ahead.'[92]

Sound economics demanded a total force of two divisions of infantry, not three as suggested by the Chief of the General Staff. One division, King said, 'might be arranged for despatch overseas when required and trained in Canada meanwhile. A second in Canada to be kept available for despatch later if required.'[93] This view was accepted in the Cabinet the next day. 'It was apparent,' King wrote, 'that a third division could not be thought of at this time, if we were not to occasion protest across the country itself and even more to impair the credit of Canada so that ... we would not be able to get the money to carry on a long war.'[94] A few weeks later General McNaughton was named to command the First Canadian Division. Formerly one of Prime Minister R. B. Bennett's closest aides, the General was considered a Tory sympathizer. For that reason alone his appointment was useful in demonstrating that the government was not playing patronage games. In addition McNaughton, a 'scientific soldier', told the Prime Minister on October 6 that the major effort of the war should be along the lines of production and 'every effort should be made to arm and equip the troops to spare human lives.' Such sentiments were precisely those of Mackenzie King, for casualties meant heartbreak—and eventual conscription.[95]

The public was informed on September 19 that a division was to be prepared for service overseas. The press release announcing this was the last act of Ian Mackenzie as Minister of National Defence. Mackenzie was a bluff, likeable ladies' man and a popular figure in Parliament, in caucus, and with the Prime Minister. But he had got into trouble over letting munitions contracts and in controlling his Deputy Minister before the war, and his reputation had been tarnished by a Royal Commission investigation. More to the point, *The Financial Post* had been assailing him in each issue since the end of August,[96] complaining of patronage, incompetence, and inefficiency, and the Minister had clearly become a liability to the government at one of its most sensitive points.

King became convinced that Mackenzie had to be removed from National Defence within a few days of the declaration of war. On September 13 he began preparing his Cabinet for the switch when he spoke with Colonel Ralston, who agreed with his assessment and who recommended Norman Rogers, the Minister of Labour, as Mackenzie's replacement. 'I have all along been thinking of this myself,' King noted, adding that 'I am debating between finding an outside post for Mackenzie or keeping him in the government. Might possibly arrange an immediate exchange between him and Power,' the Minister of Pensions and Health. 'Have, of course, to watch Quebec portfolios.... Best at present to keep Cabinet intact and avoid by-elections.'[97] Much the same ideas were advanced to Ernest Lapointe, his closest colleague, the next day,[98] and to C. D. Howe, the Minister of Transport, on September 19. Howe demurred at the suggestion that Power should replace Mackenzie, arguing that Power's drinking problem made it too dangerous. 'We would never be forgiven if anything happened when the country was actually at war. I said I agreed,' King wrote. Howe also believed that Rogers would be best for National Defence, and after consulting Power, King finally decided on the switch.[99] Power became Postmaster-General, Mackenzie moved to Pensions and Health, and Norman McLarty left the Post Office to succeed Rogers at Labour.

The new Defence Minister was a former political science professor at Queen's University and probably King's favourite among his ministers. In addition to writing a glowing campaign biography of Mackenzie King for the 1935 election, Rogers had done well during the depression in his difficult Labour portfolio, some observers believing that he had initiated modern planning techniques in the government. A veteran of the Great War, Rogers was young, ambitious, and energetic. Above all King believed him trustworthy and unlikely to fall under the sway of the generals, unlikely to yield to demands for more men, more money, more of everything. He seemed the ideal choice, and King was delighted with Rogers' first performance as Minister of National Defence in Cabinet: 'We got the first intelligent and clear-cut statement from the Minister of the Department we have had in a year past.'[100]

But there was still criticism. The most reasoned attack on the war, on Canada's participation in it, and on the way the government was operating came from Professor Frank Scott. In a private letter to Mackenzie King that caused a good deal of uncomfortable squirming in his office and in Skelton's, Scott laid out the case against the government's course:

> ... the practice of your government during this war, if you will permit me to say so, has been quite at variance with its previously declared policy in one most important respect ... you have consistently maintained that it was for Parliament to decide the nature and extent, if any, of Canada's participation in war ...
>
> May I point out that your Cabinet, a 'group of individuals', took so many steps to place Canada in a state of active belligerency before Parliament [met] ... that you very greatly limited Canadian freedom of action to decide what course to follow. ... Thus our participation was only 'voluntary' if that adjective is used in a very special sense.
>
> Since Parliament was prorogued on September 13 this practice of executive commitment has continued. Your government allowed Parliament to disband on the distinct understanding that no expedition-

ary force had yet been decided upon. . . . Air pilots were the only men whom you hinted might be sent to Europe. The first thing the Canadian people learned officially about an expeditionary force was the announcement in the press that a division was going overseas. In like manner, I suppose, the people of India learned that their troops had been sent to Egypt.

That last shot stung, as did the implication throughout Scott's letter that the Prime Minister was sacrificing the future of the country by pushing the war effort too far and too fast. 'Our greatest enemy,' Scott said, 'is not Hitlerism, evil though that system is, but participation "to the last man and the last dollar". The only way Canada can lose this war is by fighting it too strenuously.' In a memo to the Prime Minister, Skelton commented that Scott's points 'are not easy to answer,' and although a careful reply was prepared, Mackenzie King decided that it should not be sent.[101]

Despite its force, Scott's letter was wrong in most of its arguments. The government had taken steps that virtually foreclosed any decision but war before Parliament was called, but it had not decided its position on an expeditionary force until after the emergency session ended. And no one except the most isolationist Canadian could claim that Mackenzie King's policy was even close to being that of 'the last man and the last dollar'.

Still, the initial decisions had been made. The money was allocated. The recruits were flocking to the colours. The war was on. But Mackenzie King's heart was not really in the war, not yet. As did many Allied leaders, he still believed that the war was all a mistake that somehow could be rectified. 'I keep feeling that if Italy appealed for an armistice,' he wrote on September 19 after a long walk at Kingsmere, 'it might even yet be worthwhile to see if European civilization could not be saved from destruction.' There was no doubt in King's mind that it was European civilization that was at stake. The Germans, with their society 'founded on force, and based on materialism', were out to destroy Britain and France, countries based 'on reason and . . . spiritual realities'.[102] If Germany won, it was 'the end of our civilization'. If Germany lost, it would be 'equally the same for it would mean the onrush of Communism —the control of Europe by the Communists'.[103] His profound pessimism verged on defeatism.

This fear of the future led King early in October to offer Prime Minister Chamberlain his plan for peace, part of which had been drafted while King was at church. The plan called for an investigation of the European situation by neutral countries and in particular by the President of the United States and the Kings of Italy and Belgium. The report of this committee of neutrals would be submitted to the belligerents who could do with it what they wished, but in the interim an unconditional truce would be in force. This suggestion, King wrote, 'is all in the lines of our Industrial Disputes Act and also of L[eague] of N[ations] procedure, the theory being that it is a form of compulsory consideration not arbitration, permitting opportunity for public opinion to be brought to bear.' The Prime Minister arranged for this suggestion to be conveyed unofficially. 'Gets advantages if any,' he observed of this procedure, 'without embarrassing British statesmen.' King expected nothing of this proposal,[104] and he was correct. But naive though it was, it was justified; anything that might bring peace was justified. 'I feel a sense of terror of what might be the most ghastly war ever witnessed,' he wrote.[105] Here too he was correct.

IV

The first real challenge to the war effort and to the slightly unnatural political peace it had brought to Canada came two weeks after Canada's declaration of war. Maurice Duplessis, the Union Nationale leader and the Premier of Quebec, dissolved his provincial legislature on September 25 and went to the people. The war seemed to offer Duplessis the opportunity to renew his mandate and to escape from the pressing financial problems and constraints that were making it all but impossible for him to borrow money and finance the operations of the province. He could, he obviously believed, capitalize on the very great unease in the province, turn his election campaign into a triumphant referendum against the war and, in the process, steal a march on his opponents. Nothing like this could be said openly, however, and in announcing his decision for an election, Duplessis spoke of Ottawa's long campaign to destroy provincial autonomy and of the way in which 'le prétexte de la guerre déclarée par le gouvernement féderale' had been used to foster 'une campagne d'assimilation et de centralisation'.[106]

Duplessis' contentions had an element of truth in them, for he had been engaged in a long and acrimonious series of battles with the federal government ever since he assumed power in 1936. There was never enough money for relief projects in the province, and the Liberals, with their strong base in Quebec, kept trying to encroach on the spheres the

Premier considered his. The result had been to force Duplessis into seeking an accommodation with the federal Conservatives, a process that speeded up after Dr Manion became leader. By August 1939 the alliance between the Union Nationale and the Tories had been sealed on the understanding that Duplessis would hold off his provincial election until it could coincide with the expected general election. Then the Union Nationale would attack Ottawa, and the federal and provincial campaigns would dovetail neatly together.[107] The war had altered all this, however, and Duplessis now was on his own, running against Ottawa.

The reaction in the national capital to the sudden election call came close to panic.[108] The Liberals had had high expectations that they could retain their dominance in the province federally,[109] but their position would be severely damaged if Duplessis won re-election in a campaign implicitly directed against the war effort. More to the point, both Mackenzie King's carefully constructed national unity and the war effort would be threatened. English Canada's reaction to a Duplessis victory, seemingly an anti-war victory, could easily be imagined. What would London, Paris, and most of all, Berlin, think? What harm would a Duplessis victory do to the status and position of Ernest Lapointe, the Minister of Justice, P. J. A. Cardin, the Minister of Public Works, and Chubby Power, the Postmaster-General, in Ottawa? The threats were very real, and Mackenzie King did no more than express the general opinion when he noted that 'It is a diabolical act on [Duplessis'] part to have made the issue Provincial Autonomy versus Dominion Government.'[110] The Quebec Premier was 'a little Hitler'.[111]

The Prime Minister, of course, was flooded with instant advice on how to meet the situation. A staff memorandum on September 26 cautiously suggested that the provincial Liberals should avoid the federal issue entirely and campaign against the Union Nationale's extravagant spending and waste. 'From the point of view of the federal government and from the point of view of the Liberal party in Quebec,' this memo argued, 'there is too little to gain and too much to lose to risk turning the contest into a Federal Election in Quebec. If the Liberals conduct a purely provincial campaign, they may not win, but at least they will not have compromised the future and driven a wedge between Quebec and the rest of the country.'[112]

Fear of this wedge quickly led the federal ministers from Quebec to the opposite conclusion. Chubby Power, the Liberals' leading election organizer, was the first to argue, as Senator Norman Lambert recorded it, that Duplessis' act 'challenges Quebec federal ministers & only thing to do is fight, arguing Quebec's invidious position and that Duplessis will bring conscription by his foolish act.'[113] Quickly convinced, Lapointe went to see Mackenzie King the day of the dissolution. The election was 'straight sabotage, the most unpatriotic thing he knew,' King recorded his Justice Minister as saying.

> He and Power both agreed that it would lead to a desperate fight for some of the constituencies. . . . They took the view that if Duplessis carried the province, it would be equivalent to a want of confidence both in themselves as Federal Ministers, and that they would feel it necessary to withdraw from the Cabinet as having lost all influence in Quebec. . . . They looked on the issue as the taking of Quebec out of Confederation at this time. They felt that they must go into the fight, with which I of course agree.

But where King broke away from his ministers' reasoning was at the suggestion that they should resign if Duplessis was returned.

> I do not agree that our Ministers should leave the Federal Cabinet if Duplessis wins, but as they see it, their strength lies in the fact that as long as they are in the Federal cabinet, there will not be conscription in Quebec; that if Quebec people think they are going to continue despite what Duplessis may say and do, they might give Duplessis their support. On the other hand, if they know Quebec Ministers were dropping out of the Federal arena, being fearful of having a conscription government come in Ottawa immediately after, they will probably stand by Lapointe and Cardin and Power. . . . It will be a great contest between the highest patriotism and the lowest forms of disloyalty.[114]

The logic of the argument was clear to King, but how could he govern without Lapointe, Cardin, and Power? On September 28 he argued with Lapointe and Power, beseeching them not to make any hard and fast promises about resigning. But the Quebec leaders remained adamant: 'They seemed very determined on that point claiming that it is the only way Duplessis can really be defeated.'[115]

King was wrong and Lapointe right, the risks notwithstanding. Quebec could not be permitted to opt out of the war by default, and Ottawa had to intervene. Certainly Brooke Claxton, a Montreal lawyer soon to be a Liberal candidate in St Lawrence-St George, took this view in a letter that circulated among Cabinet ministers and senior officials.

> . . . I don't see how anyone can minimize the importance of the Quebec

elections: they may mean the first shot in a Canadian civil war, or
the break-up of Confederation, or they may even mean the first serious
rebuff to the nationalist movement in fifty years. Truly judged, the
importance of the elections to Canada far outweighs for the moment
our war effort. In fact a resounding victory for Duplessis will mean
dissension and obstruction. As a first step in getting on with the war
we should get on with this election. As it happens Duplessis has raised
an issue which the Dominion Government cannot dodge. . . . Duplessis
has chosen to have an election now because he cannot go on borrowing
money in the States on outrageous terms. The reason why he needs
to borrow money and cannot is his own terrible record. He has put
himself and put the Province where they are now and he wants to
cover it up by blaming the Federal Government for having got into
a war to stop Hitler. His appeals to the Province go far further than
blaming the Federal Government. They challenge its right to represent the whole Canadian people. They isolate Quebec. Does Quebec
want to stand aside? . . .

In this election, I think the colours should be nailed to the mast
without compromise. If the P.M., Lapointe, Cardin, Ralston, and
every other minister join in to the extent of two or three speeches and
put Manion in default to do the same, they should get a majority of
the popular votes, provided Gouin remains in the field. . . . Even if the
Liberals only gain a seat from Duplessis, that can be represented as a
victory. If, however, the P.M., and the Federal Liberals do and say
little or nothing, then they will not only lose Quebec in this election
and in the Federal election, but they will also lose the other provinces in
the next election and the party will disappear with extreme rapidity.[116]

One important factor on the provincial scene, as noted by Claxton,
was Paul Gouin, the breakaway Liberal who had formed the Action
Libérale Nationale and then joined with Duplessis to create the Union
Nationale. The two men had fallen out just before the provincial election of 1936, and Gouin had been trying to reorganize his movement
since then. Now he refused all appeals to join a common effort against
Duplessis, and instead he organized his own slate of candidates, attacking
both the Liberals and the Union Nationale.[117] From Claxton's point of
view, this gave disgruntled nationalists a place to stand without forcing
a choice between Duplessis and the Liberals, an ideal state of affairs.
Less easily put into his niche, Dr Manion refused to follow the course
Claxton had predicted for him. The Conservative leader not only

refused to speak against Duplessis, but in fact came very close to supporting him publicly. In Manion's eyes it was not the war that motivated
Lapointe and his Cabinet colleagues, but 'politics'. 'Why they should
resign because of a provincial result no one knows', he wrote to his son,
'but, of course, their purpose was to try and frighten the French-
Canadians into voting against Duplessis and give Lapointe and his gang
a chance to get their filthy machine back in power down there.' There
was probably some truth in the complaint, and Manion was ready to
throw his support behind the Union Nationale until a Quebec Conservative Member of Parliament, Georges Héon, told him that he would
cost Duplessis votes if he did.[118] So much for Manion's hopes of gains
in Quebec.

Manion's sense of injustice was heightened by his awareness that the
provincial Liberals would have been unlikely to do well against Duplessis
on their own. The Liberal leader, Adelard Godbout, was an agronomist,
47 years old, and a moderate man in all respects. But Godbout suffered
in the eyes of some observers because he and many of his supporters
were survivors from the *ancien régime*, from the discredited Taschereau
administration of the 1920s and 1930s. His campaign was taken over by
the federal Liberals completely, and if at times it seemed that Chubby
Power acted as the campaign manager for Ernest Lapointe, the importance of the election justified this in Liberal thinking. In one speech the
Minister of Justice told his audience that 'La province de Québec ne
rendra pas un verdict qui serait acclamé à Berlin et à Moscou,' and
Liberal newspaper advertisements harked back to 1917 by reminding the
voters that 'Ce que Wilfrid Laurier, dans l'opposition, n'a pu faire, King
et Lapointe, au pouvoir, l'ont accompli. . . . 1917, Laurier combat la
conscription—1939, King, Lapointe, Cardin, Power, Dandurand nous
sauvent de la conscription.'[119] Upstaged by the Cabinet ministers, Godbout did his best:

> Je m'engage sur l'honneur, en pesant chacun de ses mots, à quitter
> mon parti et même le combattre, si un seul Canadien français, d'ici la
> fin des hostilités en Europe, est mobilisé contre son gré sous un régime
> libéral ou même un régime provisoire auquel participeraient nos
> ministres actuels dans le cabinet du très honorable M. King.[120]

This was a spendid pledge, and if in 1944 it would go unfulfilled along
with a host of others, no one in 1939 knew that.

Probably surprised by the vehemence of the federal response,[121]
Duplessis still tried to make 'autonomy' triumph over the fear of con-

scription. In Montreal on October 19, he defined provincial autonomy, hinting obliquely at what centralization could do to the province and to French Canada:

L'autonomie, c'est le droit, pour la population canadienne-française majoritaire et la population anglaise minoritaire de Québec, de faire ses propres lois sur tout ce qui a trait à la religion, à l'éducation, à l'agriculture, à la colonisation, à l'emploi de ses ressources naturelles. La perte de l'autonomie, cela signifie que les lois sur la religion, l'éducation, les ressources naturelles, au lieu d'être faites par la province de Québec, où la race canadienne-française est en majorité, seraient faites à Ottawa, où nous sommes en minorité.[122]

This was so mild that some observers were convinced that the Church had intervened with the Premier, telling him forcefully that he was endangering Catholics all across the country by his campaign.[123] Certainly Cardinal Villeneuve despatched emissaries to Toronto to see the press barons there and to assure them that he opposed Duplessis. King heard from Joseph Atkinson of the *Star* that Villeneuve 'was anxious that the Toronto papers should not do anything in the way of antagonizing Quebec by being ultra violent, etc. He did not want to see Duplessis succeed.'[124]

Yet few believed that Duplessis could lose. His party had won 77 of 90 seats in 1936, and even in the best of Liberal circumstances it seemed unlikely that he would lose more than 25 seats.[125] Although Mackenzie King had begun to receive optimistic reports about ten days before the October 25 election,[126] he feared the worst and had his office prepare a statement to be used in the event of another Duplessis victory: 'I feel that the vote has not clearly recorded the opinion of the Province with respect to the federal government's war policy. However, it would be useless for me to pretend that the result is not disappointing . . .'[127] This sombre statement proved unnecessary when the Liberals took 53 per cent of the popular vote and 69 seats in the Legislature.[128]

Jubilation personified, Mackenzie King praised the efforts of Lapointe, Cardin, and Power to the skies, giving Lapointe in particular a place on a par with Laurier and calling him a patriot second to none.[129] The press in English-speaking Canada reacted similarly. 'Quebec has answered,' the Toronto *Globe and Mail* said on October 26. The result 'confirms the confidence of the rest of the country in the soundness of the French-Canadian people' and, said the Toronto paper in an astonishing leap of faith, demonstrates that the 'great majority of the electors held fast to the substance of British citizenship.' The Montreal *Star* saw all the provinces now united in the war effort, and the Toronto *Star* claimed that the results registered Quebec's determination to do her utmost for the war effort.[130] The reaction of the French-language press was more varied and more realistic. *Le Devoir* argued that Duplessis had been mouse-trapped by the conscription issue and by an unexpectedly strong Liberal organization, while Sherbrooke's *La Tribune* flayed Duplessis' bungling strategy. Most papers saw the Union Nationale defeat resulting from mixed federal and provincial issues, and *Le Devoir*, lamely but probably correctly, suggested that the campaign for provincial autonomy had not been defeated.[131]

The gap between English Canada's perceptions of the results and reality was so great that Frank Scott felt compelled to try to set the record straight in an important article in the *Canadian Forum*. The eagerness to read approval for the war into the results, he argued, was 'highly dangerous to the national unity it pretends to understand'. The popular vote was relatively close with the Liberals securing only 30,000 more votes than the other parties. And insofar as it was possible to determine motivation, Quebec Liberals voted 'anti-conscription rather than pro-war. . . . That is why Mr Lapointe's intervention was so supremely important. Once he had announced . . . that in the event of a Duplessis victory he would resign with all his French colleagues in the Federal Cabinet, it became clear that a vote for Mr Duplessis would be more likely to bring on conscription than retard it.'[132] This was clearly so, as was Brooke Claxton's comment that the result was a 'great personal triumph for Ernest Lapointe who was magnificent'.[133]

The Liberal election victory also carried with it the additional benefit that the federal Conservative Party was left in ruins in Quebec. Manion was bitter at events, but he was out of sympathy with his own supporters in the province. One Montrealer wrote of his hard work to defeat Duplessis and told his leader that the Conservative vote against the Union Nationale was very large. But, he added, 'The Conservatives who opposed Duplessis are bitterly resentful toward those who supported him . . . it is impossible for us to ally ourselves in the future with [those] whose stand is so much at variance with our sincere beliefs.'[134] The Tory-Union Nationale alliance had been shattered along with the fragile links between English- and French-speaking Conservatives. In spite of his hesitations and doubts, Mackenzie King and his government had emerged from the election stronger than ever before. The opposition in Quebec was in ruins, the Tories were in disarray, and the Cabinet was solidly behind the Prime Minister. But Adelard Godbout's government would always be seen as subservient to Ottawa,[135] and Mackenzie King had made both his government and Godbout's hostage to his pledges against conscription. Still the country had been brought into the war, and the first overt challenge to Ottawa had been met and mastered.

---

1 Public Archives of Canada [PAC], W. L. Mackenzie King Papers, Diary, 3 Sept. 1939.

2 Public Record Office [PRO], London, Cabinet Records, Cab 23/88, Cabinet Conclusion 34(37)5, 16 June 1937. See also J. L. Granatstein and Robert Bothwell, ' "A Self-Evident National Duty": Canadian Foreign Policy 1935-1939', *Journal of Imperial and Commonwealth History*, III (Jan. 1975) for further details on King's policy before 1939.

3 James Eayrs, *In Defence of Canada*, Vol. II: *Appeasement and Rearmament* (Toronto, 1965), pp. 226ff.

4 Reported in Montreal *Gazette*, 3 July 1937. King claimed he had been misquoted. See King Diary, 3 July 1937.

5 House of Commons *Debates*, 16 Jan. 1939, p. 52.

6 King Diary, 16 Jan. 1939.

7 See J. L. Granatstein, 'The "Man of Secrets" in Canada, 1934', *Dalhousie Review*, LI (Winter, 1972), for Hankey's reports on Canada.

8 Cab 21/670, Hankey to Sir E. Harding, 9 May 1938.

9 E.g., R. A. MacKay and E. B. Rogers, *Canada Looks Abroad* (Toronto, 1938), chapter XV.

10 PRO, Dominions Office Records, DO 35/543, Floud to Harding, 21 June 1938. One could argue that the September 1939 war met none of these conditions.

11 PRO, Prime Minister's Office Records, Prem 1/242, Campbell to Dominions Office, 27 Oct. 1938.

12 Quoted in Eayrs, II, p. 74.

13 DO 114/98, Campbell to Dominions Office, 24 Mar. 1939.

14 House of Commons *Debates*, 20 Mar. 1939, esp. p. 2043.

15 *Ibid.*, 30 Mar. 1939, pp. 2605-13.

16 DO 114/98, Campbell to Dominions Office, 26 Apr. 1939.

17 King Diary, 24 Apr. 1939.

18 PAC, Department of External Affairs Records, Vol. 54, file 319-2, Memo, 22 Aug. 1939; King Diary, 22 Aug. 1939.

19 External Affairs Records, Vol. 54, file 319-2, 'Canada and the Polish War. A Personal Note', 25 Aug. 1939.

20 *Ibid.*, Memo by Skelton, 28 Aug. 1939.

21 King Diary, 21 Aug. 1939.

22 Cab 499/21, King to Chamberlain, 26 Aug. 1939 and reply, 26 Aug. 1939. J. W. Wheeler-Bennett, *King George VI* (London, 1959), pp. 402-3.

23 Cab 499/21, Campbell to Dominions Office, 25 Aug. 1939. For the Cabinet view of this, see King Diary, 25 Aug. 1939.

24 External Affairs Records, Vol. 109, 'French Canadian Press and the War', indicates substantial praise for King's efforts.

25 After the Canadian declaration of war on 10 Sept. 1939, King showed extraordinary personal courtesy to Dr Windels, the German representative in Ottawa, even calling on him and his wife. King Diary, 11-12 Sept. 1939.

26 King Diary, 24 Aug. 1939; cf. King Papers, Memo by Skelton, n.d., ff. C120071ff.

27 PRO, Foreign Office Records, FO 371/23966, Campbell to Dominions Office, 25 Aug. 1939.

28 King Diary, 24 Aug. 1939. In London, Maugham reported that King had told him that 'owing to the attitude of certain of his colleagues, it was not possible for him to make any further announcement of Canada's attitude until war had broken out, but that Canada would be in it with us.' Cab 23/100, Cabinet Meeting 47, 1 Sept. 1939.

29 PAC, A. G. L. McNaughton Papers, Series II, Vol. 128, 6 July 1939.

30 C. P. Stacey, *Six Years of War* (Ottawa, 1955), p. 34.

31 U.S. National Archives, State Department Records, 842.20 MID Reports/5/6, Canada Combat Estimates, 1 July 1939.

32 King Papers, Memorandum, 'Canadian War Policy', 24 Aug. 1939, ff. C155073ff.

33 PAC, Ian Mackenzie Papers, file x-71, Canada's National Effort (Armed Forces) in the Early Stages of a Major War', 29 Aug. 1939. Mackenzie, the Minister of National Defence, asked for this paper back on 4 Sept. 1939 but C. G. Power, at least, had a copy made. Queen's University, C. G. Power Papers, Mackenzie to Power, 4 Sept. 1939 and notation.

34 King Papers, Memos, 5, 6 Sept. 1939, ff. C155047ff.

35 King Diary, 4 Sept. 1939.

36 Mackenzie Papers, file 187-3, Senior to Deputy Minister, 5 Sept. 1939.

37 PAC, Privy Council Office Records, Cabinet War Committee Records, Memorandum re Defence Committee of Cabinet, 5 Sept. 1939; King Diary, 5 Sept. 1939.

38 Cab 66/1, W.P. (39) 4, Campbell to Dominions Office, 1 Sept. 1939. The British Chiefs of Staff to whom this telegram was sent noted that 'We should hope that Canada will exert her full national effort as in the last war including the despatch of an expeditionary force. But what was needed beyond a fighting unit "for sentimental grounds and for reasons of Canadian prestige" were technical and specialist units.' *Ibid.* See also Campbell's disingenuous account. Sir Gerald Campbell, *Of True Experience* (New York, 1947), esp. p. 98. The U.K. requests of Canada are in External Affairs Records, Vol. 67, file 388, High Commissioner to Under Secretary of State for External Affairs, 6 Sept. 1939.

39 King Diary, 1 Sept. 1939.

40 *Ibid.*, 2 Sept. 1939.

41 External Affairs Records, Vol. 67, Tel. King to Chamberlain, 3 Sept. 1939, and reply 6 Sept. 1939.

42 King Diary, 6 Sept. 1939.

43 *Ibid.*, 7 Sept. 1939.

44 F. D. Roosevelt Library, Hyde Park, N.Y., F. D. Roosevelt Papers, PPF1376, LaGuardia to Hull, 5 Sept. 1939.

45 J. W. Pickersgill, *The Mackenzie King Record*, Vol. 1: *1939-1944* (Toronto, 1960), pp. 30-1; Queen's University, Grant Dexter Papers, Memo, 8 Sept. 1939.

46 Maurice Pope, *Soldiers and Politicians* (Toronto, 1962), p. 140.

47 King Diary, 3 Sept. 1939.

48 Quoted in Pickersgill, I, pp. 16-17. A page was missing from the French translation of the speech, due to be read by Lapointe, and this upset King. King Diary, 3 Sept. 1939.

49 *Ibid.*, 4 Sept. 1939.

50 *Ibid.*, 6 Sept. 1939.

51 *Ibid.*, 10 Sept. 1939.

52 House of Commons *Debates*, 7 Sept. 1939, p. 1.

53 King Diary, 12 Aug. 1939.

54 *Ibid.*, 5 Sept. 1939.

55 *Ibid.*, 8 Sept. 1939. The British High Commissioner believed that 'The Prime Minister talked too long and wandered too far from the main issue . . .' FO 371/23966, Campbell to Harding, 13 Sept. 1939.

56 House of Commons *Debates*, 8 Sept. 1939, pp. 8-41.

57 Grant Dexter, very close to several Ministers at this time, noted (Dexter Papers, Memo, 8 Sept. 1939) that 'there is no objection in Quebec to Canada sending as many airmen, technicians, equipment, supplies, etc., as possible. The scare points in Quebec are conscription and union government and, to a much lesser extent, the expeditionary force.'

58 House of Commons *Debates*, 9 Sept. 1939, pp. 64-9.

59 King's poetry reading 'came near to bathos'. FO 371/23966, Campbell to Secretary of State for Dominion Affairs [SSDA], 20 Sept. 1939.

60 There were complications with the appropriations bill. It had been so hastily put together that no one was even sure if Cabinet had accepted it. King had to get Ralston and Ilsley to spend all day Sunday, September 10, preparing the bill. 'Ralston's work has been magnificent,' King noted. 'What we would have done without him I don't know.' King Diary, 9 Sept. 1939.

61 House of Commons *Debates*, 8 Sept. 1939, p. 47.

62 King Diary, 9 Sept. 1939.

63 *Ibid.*

64 *Ibid.*, 10 Sept. 1939.

65 Janet Adam Smith, *John Buchan, A Biography* (Boston, 1965), p. 458. King found the 'my Prime Minister' usage somewhat distasteful. See King Diary, 30 Mar. 1940.

66 See the latest study of the U.K. decision to go to war. Sidney Aster, *1939—The Making of the Second World War* (London, 1973), chapter XIV.

67 E.g., Wheeler-Bennett, p. 379: neutrality sentiment disappeared after the royal visit 'like thin clouds before a Biscay gale'.

68 University of British Columbia, Alan Plaunt Papers, Box 2, file 21, Lower to Plaunt, 21 Sept. 1939. I am indebted to Mr William Young for bringing this letter to

my attention. A novel that is evocative in dealing with Quebec opinion is Gabrielle Roy, *The Tin Flute* (New York, 1947), pp. 30ff. Cf. Barry Broadfoot, *Ten Lost Years* (Toronto, 1973), pp. 372-5.

69 External Affairs Records, Vol. 13, folio 74 (Vol. 6), Memo, 10 Sept. 1939. For the view of the old and conservative, see FO 371/23967, 'The Empire at War', a confidential set of letters emanating from the Empire Parliamentary Association, and containing long extracts from letters by anonymous Canadian public figures.

70 State Department Records, 711.42/184, G. D. Hopper to Secretary of State, 14 Dec. 1939; *ibid.*, 842.00/568, P. R. Josselyn to Secretary of State, 17 Nov. 1939.

71 Power Papers, Memorandum concerning visit to ... Villeneuve, 1 Sept. 1939.

72 Florent Lefebvre, *The French-Canadian Press and the War* (Toronto, 1940), *passim*; External Affairs Records, Vol. 109, 'French-Canadian Press and the War'; Power Papers, 'Memo for Mr Thompson', 21 Sept. 1939. For a good example of *nationaliste* neutrality sentiment, see Fondation Lionel-Groulx, Maxime Raymond Papers, Guy Vanier to Raymond, 20 Sept. 1939. For critical comment on one journal, see Pierre Godin, *L'information-opium: Une histoire politique de La Presse* (Montréal, 1973), pp. 104-5.

73 Michiel Horn, 'The League for Social Reconstruction: Socialism and Nationalism in Canada, 1931-1945', Ph.D. thesis, University of Toronto, 1969, 214.

74 *Ibid.*, 108.

75 This paragraph is based on an excellent paper by David Rothwell, 'The Crisis of United Church Pacifism, October 1939', York University, 1971; David Clifford, 'Charles Clayton Morrison and the United Church of Canada', *Canadian Journal of Theology*, xv (1969), 80ff.; *The Financial Post*, 16 Dec. 1939.

76 A. J. Groome, 'M. J. Coldwell and CCF Foreign Policy, 1932-50', M.A. thesis, University of Saskatchewan, 1967, 84.

77 Horn, 476.

78 The leading supporter for the war was G. H. Williams, the Saskatchewan party head. See PAC, M. J. Coldwell Papers, Williams file.

79 Public Archives of British Columbia, Dufferin Pattullo Papers, Deputy Attorney-General to Pattullo, 20 Oct. 1939 and att. police reports. I am indebted to William Young for bringing this material to my attention.

80 *Life*, 18 Dec. 1939, 69. Others, more important than Mr Luce's magazine, were concerned with the clamp on civil liberties. Chubby Power, for example, threatened to resign and even drafted a letter of resignation because of his belief that the Canadian regulations were more strict than those in force in the United Kingdom. Power Papers, Power to King, 4 Jan. 1940, not sent.

81 E.g., Sen. Meighen in Senate *Debates*, 9 Sept. 1939, p. 8; T. L. Church in House of Commons *Debates*, 9 Sept. 1939, p. 73; Toronto *Globe and Mail*, 4 Sept. 1939.

82 Progressive Conservative Party, Ottawa, Progressive Conservative Party Records, Manion File, press release, 1 Sept. 1939.

83 See J. L. Granatstein, *The Politics of Survival* (Toronto, 1967), chapter I; Marc La Terreur, *Les Tribulations des conservateurs au Québec de Bennett à Diefenbaker* (Québec, 1973), chapter IV.

84 PAC, R. J. Manion Papers, Vol. 12, Manion to R. H. Webb, 4 Sept. 1939; *ibid.*, Vol. 13, Manion to M. MacPherson, 8 Sept. 1939.

85 King Diary, 11 Aug. 1939.

86 Manion Papers, Vol. 45, Memorandum, 6 Sept. 1939; House of Commons *Debates*, 12 Sept. 1939, p. 157. Apparently the subject of national government was not seriously discussed at this meeting with Manion, although the U.S. chargé assumed that it would follow the outbreak of war as a matter of course. State Department Records, 842.00/557, Simmons to Secretary of State, 31 Aug. 1939. King also raised the idea of shortening the period between dissolution and the vote to three weeks, but Manion felt this too brief. King Diary, 3, 6 Sept. 1939.

87 DO 35/1003/WG3/13, High Commissioner to Dominions Office, 12 Sept. 1939.

88 *Ibid.*, Dominions Office to High Commissioner, 20 Sept. 1939.

89 King Papers, Black Binders, Vol. 14, file 52, Ian Mackenzie to King, 17 Sept. 1939, and *ibid.*, 'Memo of Submission . . . 19 Sept. 1939' from Canadian Legion.

90 *Ibid.*, Secret Memo for Council, 18 Sept. 1939.

91 King Diary, 18 Sept. 1939. But cf. PAC, L. W. Murray Papers, Vol. 4, Taped interview, May 1970 which indicates that Adm. Murray felt the RCN had all the money it wanted in September 1939.

92 King Diary, 18 Sept. 1939.

93 *Ibid.* Massey reported London rumours of a 'token' force of one division. King Papers, Tel. Massey to Secretary of State for External Affairs [SSEA], 18 Sept. 1939, f. C279012.

94 King Diary, 19 Sept. 1939.

95 Pickersgill, I, p. 38. There were substantial difficulties in settling arrangements with McNaughton. See King Diary, 5-6 Oct. 1939; McNaughton Papers, Vol. 241, Memos, 5 Oct. 1939.

96 *The Financial Post*, 26 Aug. 1939-2 Dec. 1939; Floyd Chalmers interview, 27 Sept. 1973.

97 King Diary, 13 Sept. 1939.

98 *Ibid.*, 14 Sept. 1939.

99 *Ibid.*, 19 Sept. 1939 and Power Papers, 'Excursions and Alarums Incident to Reorganization of Cabinet, September 19, 1939', a very revealing document.

100 Pickersgill, I, p. 26.

101 King Papers, Scott to King, 5 Jan. 1940, and atts, ff. 249688ff.

102 King Diary, 19 Sept. 1939.

103 *Ibid.*, 12 Oct. 1939.

104 *Ibid.*, 8 Oct. 1939.

105 *Ibid.*, 15 Oct. 1939.

106 Michel Brunet, *Histoire du Canada par les textes*, Tome II: *1855-1960* (Montréal, 1963), pp. 128-9; State Department Records, 842.00/561, Simmons to Hickerson, 5 Oct. 1939, and att.; cf. Robert Rumilly, *Maurice Duplessis et son temps*, Tome I: *1890-1944* (Montréal, 1973), pp. 529-33.

107 Manion Papers, Vol. 4, Hon. T. J. Coonan to Manion, 1 May 1939; Granatstein, *Politics of Survival*, p. 26.

108 State Department Records, 842.00/560, Simmons to Secretary of State, 26 Sept. 1939.

109 Dexter Papers, Memo, 28 June 1939.

110 Pickersgill, I, p. 35.

111 FO 371/23966, High Commissioner to SSDA, 3 Oct. 1939.

112 King Papers, Memo, n.d., ff. C116821ff.

113 Queen's University, Norman Lambert Papers, Diary, 25 Sept. 1939.

114 King Diary, 25 Sept. 1939. The matter was discussed in Cabinet two days later. See *ibid.*, 27 Sept. 1939.

115 *Ibid.*, 28 Sept. 1939. Long after the election Lapointe was still bitter about King's opposition to his tactics. 'Of course,' he told Grant Dexter, 'after these events which have taken my strength, those who opposed me have quite happily shared in any credit that was going.' Dexter Papers, Memo, 25 Oct. 1940. Others who believed that the ministers should not have threatened to resign, however, included Brooke Claxton (PAC, Claxton Papers, Vol. 137, Claxton to T. W. L. MacDermot, 5 Oct. 1939), Edgar Tarr, president of the Canadian Institute of International Affairs (Canadian Institute of International Affairs, Toronto, Edgar Tarr Papers, Tarr to Claxton, 7 Oct. 1939), and Senator Norman Lambert (State Department Records, 842.00/562, Simmons to Secretary of State, 14 Oct. 1939).

116 Claxton Papers, Vol. 44, Claxton to A. D. P. Heeney, 27 Sept. 1939. As Principal Secretary to the Prime Minister, Heeney was in a good position to circulate this letter, and he did so.

117 Robert Rumilly, *Histoire de la province de Québec*, Tome XXXVIII: *Ernest Lapointe* (Montréal, 1968), p. 47. Many *nationalistes* had already chosen Lapointe over Duplessis. Anyone was better than Duplessis, 'l'assassin du mouvement national'. Fondation Lionel-Groulx, Lionel Groulx Papers, P. Hamel to Groulx, 14 Oct. 1939; *ibid.*, R. Chaloult to Groulx, 7 Nov. 1939. According to Lionel Bertrand the reorganization of the ALN was one reason Duplessis called the snap election. *Mémoires* (Montréal, 1972), pp. 66-7. The best study of the ALN is Patricia G. Reid, 'Action Libérale Nationale, 1934-39', M.A. thesis, Queen's University, 1966.

118 Cited in Granatstein, *Politics of Survival*, pp. 33-4.

119 Cited in Rumilly, *Duplessis*, I, pp. 545-6. For some detail on Power's difficulties with money, see J. L. Granatstein, 'Financing the Liberal Party, 1935-45', in M. S. Cross and R. Bothwell, eds, *Policy by Other Means* (Toronto, 1972), pp. 188-9.

120 Brunet, II, p. 130; Antonio Barrette, *Mémoires* (Montréal, 1966), p. 53.

121 State Department Records, 842.00/561, Simmons to Hickerson, 5 Oct. 1939.

122 *Ibid.*, 842.00/562, Simmons to Secretary of State, 14 Oct. 1939; Rumilly, *Duplessis*, I, p. 548.

123 State Department Records, 842.00/562, Simmons to Secretary of State, 5 Oct. 1939.

124 King Diary, 7 Oct. 1939. Cf. Rumilly, *Duplessis*, I, pp. 553-4.

125 State Department Records, 842.00/563, Simmons to Secretary of State, 21 Oct. 1939, reporting views of Consuls in Montreal and Quebec. Manion seemed to share the optimism. Manion Papers, Vol. 5, Manion to Duplessis, 24 Oct. 1939. Rumilly, XXXVIII, p. 58 reports 'une confiance joyeuse' around Duplessis.

126 E.g., King Diary, 14 Oct. 1939. 'I have seldom seen men more certain of victory.'

127 King Papers, Draft Press Release for 25 Oct. 1939, ff. C116834-5.

128 For an analysis of the vote, see K. H. McRoberts, 'Contrasts in French-Canadian

Nationalism: The Impact of Industrialization upon the Electoral Role of French-Canadian Nationalism, 1934-44', M.A. thesis, University of Chicago, 1966, 131-3. The ALN received only 4.6 per cent of the vote.

129 Pickersgill, I, p. 35. To Duplessis, the defeat was a product of 'federal Liberal blackmail'. Barrette, p. 53.

130 King Papers, 'Press Comment on Quebec Election Results', ff. C116835ff.

131 *Ibid.*, 'French Canadian Press on Quebec Election Results', ff. C116851ff.

132 'The Real Vote in Quebec', *Canadian Forum*, XIX (December, 1939), 270-1. Motivation did vary, of course. The ladies of La Ligue des droits de la Femme campaigned for the Liberals because they promised female suffrage. Thérèse Casgrain, *Une Femme Chez les Hommes* (Montréal, 1971), p. 137.

133 Claxton Papers, Vol. 137, Claxton to G. Spry, 30 Oct. 1939. See also Buchan Papers, Hardinge to Tweedsmuir, 12 Nov. 1939, conveying the King's congratulations. The Foreign Office view in London was that Quebec was 'prepared to sacrifice a large measure of the autonomy of which they have hitherto been so jealous for the purpose of winning the war. For this phenomenon we may thank Hitler's new friend Stalin.' FO 371/23966, Minute by V. Cavendish-Bentinck, 26 Oct. 1939.

134 Manion Papers, Vol. 11, J. A. Ross to Manion, 27 Oct. 1939.

135 René Chaloult, *Mémoires Politiques* (Montréal, 1969), pp. 110-11.

2. Dealing with London

The concern for national unity that had been demonstrated by Canada's separate declaration of war on September 10, 1939 would continue to dominate Canadian policy. Nowhere was it more prominent than in the first few months of the war when Canada engaged in a series of difficult negotiations with London on military and economic matters.

To Mackenzie King and the Canadian government, national unity meant the relations between French and English Canadians above all. To keep harmony at home the war effort would have to be moderate in all things, particularly in contributions of manpower, or casualties overseas might lead to demands for conscription. But national unity was more than simply the relations between English and French. The economic war effort was important too, and the interests of the farmer and the manufacturer had to be protected and enhanced. Prairie wheat had to be sold at good prices, and orders for war materiel were necessary if the Canadian economy was going to recover at last from the lingering effects of the Great Depression. National unity meant getting a good price abroad for Nova Scotia apples just as much as it meant securing British orders for aircraft parts for Toronto heavy industry.

This sounded like self-interest, and it was. Canada was in the war out of a sense of duty, not because her own national interests were directly threatened. This being so, why shouldn't the war produce some benefits for Canadians, a people still suffering from heavy unemployment and depressed national productivity? This was selfish, but this Canadian attitude was matched, and more than matched, by the British attitude to Canada. Few orders would find their way to the Dominion until the fall of France relaxed the British government's insistence on steering contracts to British firms, and the financial and military relations between the two countries would be characterized by tough, difficult bargaining. Canadian national unity and Canadian self-interest demanded no less.

I

While the Quebec election was progressing towards its conclusion, the King government was beginning negotiations with the United Kingdom on a proposed Empire air-training scheme. The scheme, eventually to be known as the British Commonwealth Air Training Plan (BCATP), would become the major Canadian military contribution to the Allied war effort, training tens of thousands of air crew from Canada, Australia, New Zealand, and Britain and her colonies. But as with other war programs involving money, prestige, and concepts of Imperial relations, the genesis of the BCATP was troubled.

The BCATP's origins probably go back at least to 1926 when, at the Imperial Conference of that year, Mackenzie King himself had suggested in general terms the possibility that Canada and the United Kingdom might co-operate on bases, on the provision of helium for dirigibles, and on the creation of a reserve of airmen.[1] Nothing appears to have come of this suggestion, and nothing further was heard on the subject of air training until 1936 when the German threat was already looming. The Baldwin government began pressing the King government in that year to facilitate the recruiting of men in Canada for service in the Royal Air Force, but these suggestions foundered on the rock of autonomist objections from within the Department of External Affairs.[2] The British continued their interest despite the unenthusiastic response to their initial suggestion, changing their aim to securing a training school in Canada. The Cabinet was cool to this idea too.[3]

Pressure then subsided for two years, but in May 1938 the Chamberlain government returned to the charge with a new proposal that the Royal Canadian Air Force should conduct training for RAF candidates at one or more Flying Training Schools in Canada.[4] Unfortunately the High Commissioner and the Prime Minister became involved in a dispute over who had said what to whom during these negotiations, the result being substantial acrimony between London and Ottawa and yet another cool Canadian response.[5] Mackenzie King's primary objection, as he told the House of Commons, was to having 'a military station to be put down in Canada, owned, maintained and operated by the Imperial Government for Imperial purposes'.[6] This was very different in King's view from having British pilots train in Canada in Canadian establishments that were under Canadian control.

London clearly believed that King's House of Commons statement marked a change of position from opposition to any air-training scheme whatsoever, and the Air Ministry quickly sent a mission to Canada to explore the new state of affairs.[7] The British visitors, however, still found Canadian-made difficulties in their way, and after months of negotiations the British discouragingly noted that it seemed 'extremely dubious whether there is any possibility of persuading the Canadian Government to operate any scheme which involves financial contribution on their part'.[8] Further negotiations led to an agreement in April 1939; under its terms, fifty RAF pilots a year would receive medium and advanced flying training in Canada. The new scheme, an expensive one by the standards of the Air Ministry, cost £1,500 per pilot more than training in Britain, but presumably the involvement of Canada in Empire air training was considered worth the money.[9] No pilots had arrived in Canada for training by September 1939.

The initial British plans had foundered on London's persistence in ignoring Mackenzie King's clearly expressed views that only British pilots could be trained for the RAF in Canada and only in training stations under Canadian control. Given King's long insistence on autonomy, the British were beating their heads against a stone wall on this issue, as on others. An onlooker could admire their persistence, not their tactics. The same mistakes would be repeated again and again in the course of the air-training negotiations in the fall of 1939.

Understandably, on the outbreak of war the Air Ministry had no major plans for air training in Canada. The first suggestions were for the training of 2,000 pilots a year and as many air crew as possible.[10] Within a few days, however, RAF studies raised the number of pilots desired to 8,000 per year. The RAF view was that the RCAF should control this training scheme and make it the major role for the Canadian air force in the war. Naturally other Dominions were making proposals to London as well, and the need for a rationalized scheme was becoming clear. According to Vincent Massey, the Canadian High Commissioner in London, the idea for a giant British Commonwealth Air Training Plan originated with him, was discussed with his Australian counterpart in London, and then presented to Anthony Eden, the Secretary of State for Dominion Affairs on September 16.*[11] At no time apparently did Massey tell Ottawa of his part in this affair, a curious but understandable lapse of responsibility on the part of the Canadian government's representative in Britain. Massey's reputation with Mackenzie King and with the Department of External Affairs was not very high at this point;[12] had his superiors known of his role in the birth of the Air Training Plan their anger might have been very great.

The Air Training Plan idea won ready acceptance in London and by September 26 official telegrams were sent off by Prime Minister Chamberlain to the Dominion Prime Ministers. The message to Mackenzie King, partly drafted by Massey who knew his master well,[13] was carefully phrased:

> I am sure that you will agree that the scheme outlined is of first importance. For this reason, and because it invites co-operation with Canada to a very special degree, I want to make a special personal appeal to you about it. I feel that so far-reaching a project will strike your imagination particularly as it concerns an all important field of war activity in which Canada has already made so striking and gallant an individual contribution. May I therefore ask that the matter should receive very urgent attention?[14]

The British scheme was based on the need for 'not less than 20,000 pilots and 30,000 personnel of air crews annually for maintenance of [an] enlarged force. To provide for these, it is estimated that about ninety elementary and advanced flying training schools . . . would be necessary.' The British expected that elementary training would be carried out largely by each individual Dominion, but that since 'Canada has special advantages of nearness to the United Kingdom, greater potentialities for manufacture of service type of aircraft and proximity to the vast re-

*Massey's paternity is vigorously denied by the then Australian High Commissioner, Stanley Bruce, and by the Under Secretary of State for Air, Harold Balfour. In his memoirs Balfour goes to some length to award sole credit to the Australian: 'The Empire Air Training Scheme . . . was born with Stanley Bruce . . . as father.' Harold Balfour, *Wings Over Westminster* (London, 1973), pp. 112-13.

sources of the United States of America . . . advanced training for trainees from elementary training schools should be centred in Canada.' London also suggested a meeting of experts to discuss the plan and indicated that this should take place in Canada. The telegram noted the 'immense influence' such a scheme could have on the course of the war—'it might even prove decisive.'[15]

The careful wording of Chamberlain's telegram made its mark on Mackenzie King: 'It is felt that we might in this way render as great a service in bringing the war to a close as was rendered in the late war by the U.S. coming in at the end. This is the most important despatch so far.'[16] But the next day when he told Cabinet of the British proposal, he was somewhat less enthusiastic. 'It shows how quite unprepared the British . . . were in their plans that until now they have not been able to tell us definitely what really is the best of all plans, and which would have saved us having anything to do with an expeditionary force at the start.'[17] That was the key in King's view. The delay in suggesting the giant scheme had forced Canada to plan an expeditionary force, something that might otherwise have been avoided. Still, the reaction in Cabinet was extremely favourable to the suggestion. Cost was the major worry, along with the possibility that Canadian planning in other areas, already based on the maximum financial contribution of which Canada was believed capable, might have to be altered.[18] The Cabinet agreed that a telegram should be despatched to London accepting the scheme in principle, but raising certain questions: where would the aircraft come from? where would instructors be found? how would costs be shared? Those were the Cabinet's main questions, but Mackenzie King also had to redraft personally the telegram prepared by Dr Skelton. 'The truth is he, at heart, is against much in the way of co-operation,' King wrote. 'Quite rightly feels the British are very selfish but fails to see the larger significance of the fight for freedom that is being waged.'[20] The pot was calling the kettle black.

Before the public announcement of the air-training plan could be made, there was a small but not insignificant *contretemps* between London and Ottawa over its wording. Skelton and the Prime Minister wanted London's announcement to make clear that this was the most important Canadian contribution to the war, an effort that was clearly doomed to failure. King was disappointed but not surprised by the British attitude for he had 'felt they would stick at that in a public pronouncement. They were prepared, however, to use it to get us into the scheme.'*[21] The announcement, unsatisfactory as it may have been to Canada, was made on October 10.

The British Air Training Mission, headed by Lord Riverdale, a bluff and undiplomatic Sheffield industrialist, was already at sea and hard at work preparing the British plans. Riverdale aimed at an equitable sharing of the burden and its distribution in a manner that would cause the least difficulties with foreign exchange, already becoming critical in England. In the Air Ministry's view equity could best be achieved by dividing the costs on the basis of the numbers of trained personnel allocated to each of the several forces. That prospect, however, might lead the Dominions to reduce their share to keep costs down and that would weaken the British foreign-exchange position. The smaller the size of the RCAF, the Air Ministry noted, 'the smaller will be, not only the share of the total cost which Canada would bear, but also the amount of Canadian dollars which we would receive in respect of aeroplanes, bombs, stores, etc., manufactured in this country, and issued to the Canadian squadrons which come to Europe.' If possible Riverdale should attempt to have the Canadians 'fix the number of squadrons at which they propose ultimately to aim for despatch overseas, before the Mission becomes involved in discussing the division of costs...'[22] Money was clearly going to be a vital component of Riverdale's talks, and it seems clear that Riverdale approached the question as a cost-conscious industrialist, not as a negotiator skilled in dealing with sometimes balky Canadians. At the first meeting of the Mission staff he told his colleagues of the serious British dollar position, 'and it was not possible as yet to indicate what solution could be found. We had not yet promised to buy Canadian wheat,' he said, 'and it might well be that we could eventually make such a promise in order to facilitate the acceptance of the proposed training scheme by Canada.'[23] Riverdale was no fool, however, and he worried whether Canada had the financial resources necessary to support such a costly plan.[24]

---

*Skelton on Oct. 1, 1939 also drafted a mock paragraph for inclusion in the public announcement by King of the Plan: 'I could not let this occasion pass without reciprocating the courtesy of our London cousins by paying a tribute, in our turn, to the British statesmen whose sublime and effortless assurance, coupled with a gentlemanly vagueness on the sordid question of finance and a unique eminence in diplomacy, which if in some slight measure not so completely successful as usual in the European field, has retained its full potency among the native tribes, has done so much to lead us to concur in this great undertaking.' King Papers, Skelton draft, 1 Oct. 1939, f. C267906.

The result of the Mission's work during the sea voyage to Canada was passed to Canadian officials in the form of a memorandum on October 14. The British envisaged an intake of 2,910 aircrew trainees every four weeks, not including the British contribution. Canada was to raise 1,396 aircrew each four weeks, the remainder being found in Australia and New Zealand. Thirty-seven flying schools would be necessary in Canada plus thirty-five aircrew schools and an array of supply and record depots. No cost estimates were indicated.[25]

Mackenzie King received the British delegation on October 17. Riverdale began the interview badly both by referring to the plan as 'your scheme' and by creating in King's mind the impression that London was dictating to Canada. It was never hard to do this, of course, and King felt compelled to respond. It was very kind of Riverdale 'to speak of the scheme as ours,' he began, 'but it was really theirs, and how far we could go in developing it would depend very largely on what Britain herself would do.' King added in his diary that he 'was rather amused at the sort of railroading, taking for granted style which Riverdale adopted.' It was 'amazing how these people . . . from the Old Country . . . seem to think that all they have to do is tell us what is to be done. No wonder they get the backs of people up on this side.'[26] A Canadian officer who was present at this meeting remarked that he was impressed that King 'did not show any sign of surprise or give any indication that what was happening was anything out of the ordinary' although the Riverdale proposal was 'so far ahead of anything that we had thought of that everyone . . . was quite taken aback at its magnitude . . .'[27]

So, in his own way, was Riverdale. In conversation with W. D. Euler, King's Minister of Trade and Commerce, he learned that Canada contemplated an eventual expenditure of $300 million per year on defence. If there was added to this even $250 million for the air-training scheme, that would be more 'than the Canadian Government could face'.[28] As Riverdale wrote to Kingsley Wood, the Secretary of State for Air, in a letter on October 19, 'It is doubtful whether even if they doubled their taxation the Canadian Government would be able to find the money for our training scheme as well as the help which they are giving to the Navy and the Army . . .'[29]

It is strikingly clear from all this that the British had come to Canada with only a rough draft of a scheme, with little idea of the numbers of aircraft required or their source, and with only the scantiest idea of Canadian financial resources. All the financial calculations on the cost of the scheme were carried out in Canada by the RCAF, rushed and harried to produce the data that should have come from London.[30] In essence the British had found an idea and they brought it to Ottawa looking for someone else to put up the cash.

By October 31, when senior Canadian Cabinet ministers met formally with the British Mission, some of the cost data were ready. Capital expenditure was put at $400 million and maintenance for a three and one-half year period was set at $508.5 million. After a deduction for a cost differential, the cost of the Air Training Plan was fixed at $888.5 million.[31] In the British view this scheme was a good one for the Canadians, for 'a large part of the capital expenditure incurred . . . will go to provide employment in Canada and also that a large amount of employment in Canada is being provided by the orders which the British Government has placed and contemplates placing . . .'[32] The Canadians, having met earlier to consider the estimates,[33] were not impressed. Riverdale read his statement and then announced Britain's decision to make a contribution—a 'free contribution'—of $140 million in kind to the cost of the scheme. Of the remaining $748.5 million, he hoped that Canada would bear half the cost. Colonel Ralston, the Minister of Finance (called by one of the British negotiators 'a lawyer who was maddeningly pernickety'),[34] interjected at this point that this was the first time that any proportionate sharing had been suggested, a clear implication that the minister felt the Canadian proportion was out of line.

After Riverdale had concluded and after Captain Balfour, the British Parliamentary Under Secretary for Air, had added a few words, the Prime Minister took the floor.

The Prime Minister in reply [the British note of the meeting records] said that when the war broke out Canada lost no time in ranging herself on the side of Great Britain and France and declaring war on Germany, but it was not Canada's war in the same sense as it was Great Britain's, and it would do more harm than good if they were pressed to do more than they felt they were able to do; he was afraid there could be no question of taking on responsibility for the scheme in the proportion which Lord Riverdale had suggested today. . . . he . . . was afraid that the Canadian Government could not take the line that money would be found somewhere. They must only undertake what they were sure that they would be in a financial position to do. . . . He felt he must speak plainly on this question right at the beginning so that there should be no misunderstanding. He and his Ministers appreciated Great Britain's difficulties and they wished to co-operate in overcoming them, but they did not want to have the spirit of cooperation which animated them crushed at the outset by excessive demands. Lord Riverdale had talked about Great Britain making a contribution under the scheme as if it were a contribution to Canada but [it was] only a contribution to the cost of a scheme suggested by the British Government, and for which the British Government must be mainly responsible.

Mackenzie King concluded by observing that this 'was the kind of scheme in which they were happy to join and he wished that they had more money to put into it.'[35]

Ralston then spoke and expressed the view that while Canada hoped to do her utmost, it would simply not be possible to come within 'shooting distance' of the Riverdale estimates. The British, he argued, 'had made a point of the fact that the pilots and crews trained in these Canadian Schools would be maintained in the field by the United Kingdom; in his view it was quite right that they should be so maintained; these were schools for training crews for the British Air Force. They were being located in Canada simply because Canada was situated in a convenient position geographically. . . . the United Kingdom should pay for these men.' He did not want to put a damper on the scheme, Ralston said, effectively doing just that, but he 'had to look at it as a businessman.'[36]

The only agreement to emerge from this meeting was that the British would meet with Ralston and with C. D. Howe, the Minister of Transport, and continue the talks. Before these meetings could begin on November 3, however, Sir Gerald Campbell felt compelled to register his disapproval of Mackenzie King's remarks at the October 31 meeting. He had been shocked, he told Dr Skelton, to hear King say 'this is not our war.' That phrase had been conveyed to London and he didn't know what they would make of it there. One member of the Mission had wondered if the Prime Minister would dare to make such a comment in Parliament. Skelton's diplomatic reply gave nothing away: 'It certainly was not Canada's war in the sense that the war did not originate in any German threat against Canada or in any Canadian pledge in Eastern Europe. This of course did not mean that Canada had not made Great Britain's and France's cause her own.' As for any statement in Parliament, Skelton indicated, that might safely be left to Mackenzie King.[37]

When he learned of this, Mackenzie King was furious. Riverdale, he wrote, wanted to load the whole scheme onto the Dominions and he had given his hand away when he talked about free gifts from Britain to Canada. To King the British tack was 'to extricate themselves from the wrong position they were in by giving a wholly false interpretation to my remark that this was not our war, which was made in reply to Riverdale's statement "we are making this contribution to you." I had said in reply that so far as there were contributions, it was the other way, and that what we were doing was for the common cause.' King was disturbed enough about this imputation of near-disloyalty to see the Governor General and to urge him to call in Sir Gerald Campbell. Tweedsmuir agreed to do this.[38]

More important to the Prime Minister, however, was the very great cost of the British air-training scheme, and on November 3, the day detailed negotiations were to begin with the British Mission, King telegraphed to Chamberlain. The scope of the plan was staggering, King said, and for reasons that were well known in Britain Canada could not afford as great a proportion of her national income for war as could Britain. Moreover it was clear that Canada had not been successful in conveying a full understanding to the United Kingdom 'and particularly to its various agencies concerned with the purchase of Canadian products or with making arrangements in regard to the various aspects of our military contribution. I may instance the fact,' King stated baldly, 'that while the British Air Mission are pressing us in regard to their air training proposals which would involve a substantial increase in Canada's direct military expenditures, we on our part have for many weeks been pressing without satisfactory result for a decision in regard to wheat purchases which is the biggest single item in our whole economic programme and the most far-reaching in its public consequences. In our opinion,' the Prime Minister added, 'the questions of military and economic participation in the war effort are inextricably intertwined and cannot be dealt with separately.'[39] The Canadian Prime Minister was clearly interested in bargaining, but he was also right. Canada could not pump millions more into guns unless and until some of its butter—and wheat—were sold abroad.

King's ministers bargained equally hard. The Mission met with Ralston, Howe, Ian Mackenzie, now the Minister of Pensions and Health, and Norman Rogers, the Minister of National Defence, on November 3.

The Canadians hammered away at the outset at the British contribution of $140 million in kind. 'It was explained,' the British notes of the meeting record, 'that this sum represented the cost of all material to be manufactured in the United Kingdom which would be required as the first equipment of each school. The Canadian ministers felt that there was no logic in a proposal of that nature and that it would be necessary to devise a more rational method of dividing the costs.' The amount Canada was expected to shoulder in any case was too much. Ralston presented data showing that Canada was spending $190 million for defence in 1939-40 and planning to spend $352 million, $330 million, and $300 million in each successive fiscal year. The Finance Minister indicated that the national income was $3,575 million and an increase of 15 per cent in that figure might be expected as a result of war orders. Nonetheless government expenditures amounted to $1,490 million or 36.3 per cent of National Income. If this was raised to 42 per cent, adding a further $237 million to defence spending, Canada could not possibly carry the costs of the training scheme to anything like the extent envisaged by the British. C. D. Howe, in suggesting that the plan was too grandiose, added that Canada had made proposals early in September 'as to the form which the Canadian war effort was to take, and they had understood that these proposals had been welcomed by the United Kingdom Government. The United Kingdom Air Mission then arrived with proposals for the financing of an Air Training Scheme which apparently took no account of the defence commitments into which the Canadian Government had already entered.'[40]

Meanwhile the Australians and New Zealanders had arrived in Ottawa for discussions on their role in the Air Training Plan. They were friendly, but the Antipodean Dominions hoped to do as much air training as possible on their own territory, an attitude that forced new cost estimates to be made.[41] These figures were presented to the Canadian ministers on November 9. The capital and maintenance costs now were put at $686 million, a figure that was shortly lowered again to $650 million. Towards that cost Britain now offered $175 million. That left $475 million to be divided among the three Dominions, and the shares were expected to be Canada—$335 million, Australia—$115 million, and New Zealand—$25 million.

In the Canadian view this was better, but still too much. If this estimate were accepted, the Canadians argued, they would be unable to afford to send a second division overseas; Britain would have to pay more. The ministers insisted that Britain should pay for $23 million in air frames and engines already ordered as well as the freight charges on the additional aircraft she was providing, a further $20 million. This would bring the British share up to $218 million, leaving $432 million to be split among the Dominions. On November 13 it seemed that agreement was reached on this arrangement, with Canada bearing 72.5 per cent of the cost ($313 million), Australia 22.5 per cent ($97.4 million), and New Zealand 5 per cent ($21.6 million).[42]

The Cabinet War Committee considered this scheme and accepted it on the following day. King believed that the government was 'going much further than we intended' but that it was right 'so that the British Government might feel that we had acted generously'. Graham Towers of the Bank of Canada took this view, telling the ministers that British government purchasing officials 'would likely go much further with us if we were not niggardly with them.' King reassured himself by noting that the heavy costs did not fall at the beginning of the Plan and 'If war lasts two years or more, people . . . will be ready to stand the higher outlays.'[43] But there were two conditions laid down by the War Committee. The British would have to agree that the Plan took priority over all other forms that a Canadian contribution to the war effort could take, and there would have to be a satisfactory result to the economic discussions then underway in London.[44]

The British War Cabinet jibbed at everything. Kingsley Wood wrote to Riverdale that 'Just as the Canadian Government feel unable to give the all-clear pending the outcome of the discussions here on economic relations generally, so we for our part cannot commit ourselves in regard to the scheme until we know where we stand in the same respect.'[45] There were also some severe doubts about granting the Canadians the assurance on priority they sought. 'It is troublesome of Mr Mackenzie King . . . ,' Kingsley Wood's memorandum to the War Cabinet on November 18 said, but he did urge that approval be granted.[46] But when the matter was discussed a week later the Secretary of State for Dominion Affairs, Anthony Eden, balked and said 'we should probably have to take a firm line. The matter was a purely domestic one . . .'[47]

Of course it was, and that was why King was so adamant about it. He told the British High Commissioner that Canada would not sign the agreement unless Britain conceded these points, and both Sir Gerald Campbell and Lord Riverdale felt obliged to urge that the conditions be accepted.[48] On one point, at least, all parties agreed when on November 25 the British signified a willingness to meet the costs discussed on November 13.[49]

Regrettably those figures were already out of date. The Australians had decided to reduce the amount of time their trainees would spend in Canada and the Canadians insisted that the British raise their contribution to meet any increased costs. The new cost of the scheme was set at $607 million, of which Britain was to contribute $185 million, Australia $39.9 million, and New Zealand $28.6 million. The Canadian contribution was now $68 million for schools that would be used only for the training of Canadians plus $285.4 million to the joint scheme or a total of $353.4 million, an increase of more than $40 million over the November 13 figures and an amount that substantially exceeded the estimates the Canadians had rejected as too much a few weeks earlier. But this new estimate had been cleared comma by comma with the Canadian negotiators and the British hoped for quick acceptance.

They were to be disappointed. On King's recommendation the Cabinet War Committee delayed, deciding that a 'dissembling' telegram from Chamberlain was not satisfactory in its assurances on the two Canadian conditions.[50] Chamberlain had said only that 'I have no hesitation in giving this assurance as I entirely agree that it is for Canada to decide on the priority of her effort and therefore I should not think of interfering in it whatever our own opinions might be. I should explain that we ourselves have attached the highest priority to this Training Scheme .... which we believe may be a decisive factor in the war. If the Canadian Government decided to contribute to the scheme on the scale contemplated, their policy will be in the closest correspondence with our own. But,' Chamberlain said at the sticking point, 'we should not have liked to emphasise the priority of the Air Training Scheme lest it should have embarrassing effects on our relations with the French who are pressing us strongly to increase our effort on land.'[51] This reply did dissemble, for as King wrote on the telegram what he wanted was an assurance 'That in Br. Govt. view—the scheme will be considered as having priority to anything that may *subsequently* be put forward by Br. Govt.'[52] In these circumstances King would go no further than permitting a press release on November 27 stating that 'a basis of agreement' had been reached and referred to the various governments for decision.[53]

By this date Canada was insisting on five conditions before it would accept the Air Training Plan. The RCAF would have to administer the scheme. This was accepted. The British would have to help Australia and New Zealand raise the Canadian dollars needed to pay their costs. This was agreed. The financial discussions in London would have to be resolved satisfactorily. This eventually took place. The desired statement on the priority of the Training Plan would have to be issued. This was ultimately offered on December 7.[54] Surprisingly the final, crucial difficulty hinged on the Canadian insistence that aircrew be identified with Canada to the maximum extent possible once their training was completed.

From the first proposal on September 26 it had always been assumed that separate Canadian squadrons would be formed in the field. But not until December 7 were steps begun to arrange for this, and almost immediately there were problems.[55] On December 8 Norman Rogers wrote to Riverdale, setting out his understanding of a discussion between the two men that day: 'Canadian personnel from the training plan will, on request from the Canadian Government, be organized in Royal Canadian Air Force units and formations in the field.'[56] Riverdale's reply—Canadian requests would be met 'in all circumstances in which it is feasible'[57]—infuriated the Canadians who found it totally unacceptable. In King's view the British government was trying to 'keep Canadian squadrons at its disposal, merged into British forces, creating all the trouble in the air field that was created on land with the army in the last war. This,' he said, 'must be avoided at all costs and will be by my standing firm on this matter.' The next day he added that it was 'really shameful the way in which the British government in these matters seek to evade and undo and to change the meaning of the most definitely understood obligations.'[58]

The British viewed this problem very seriously. In the first place the Canadian position that the United Kingdom should pay for RCAF units in Europe understandably bothered the War Cabinet in London, all its members believing firmly in the principle 'that a Dominion unit must be paid for by the Dominion concerned.' Secondly, if an agreement was made with Canada to segregate Canadians into RCAF units, the other Dominions might demand equal treatment. Up to half the fighting personnel of the RAF could be made up of Dominion squadrons, but since the RAF would have to provide the supporting ground crew, far more than half the total personnel would be British.[59] The complaints about money were rather more soundly based.

The British offered a new proposal on December 14. If Canada provided the ground crews, the British suggested, then its squadrons could be identified as RCAF and placed under Canadian command. The RCAF favoured this, but Mackenzie King quickly pointed out that the financial provisions for the Training Plan were based on the RAF providing ground support.[60] For the next three days haggling was intense on this question. At one point on December 15 the parties reached agreement, but Riverdale quickly reneged. New British proposals, financially unacceptable to Mackenzie King, were then produced.[61] Riverdale's note referred to a new condition that 'the factor governing the numbers of such pupils to be so incorporated at any one time should be the financial contribution which the Canadian Government have already declared themselves ready to make towards the cost of the Training Scheme.' Previous discussion, King noted in his diary, had always been based on questions of feasibility and practicality. 'Now the message implied what we have all along thought, that the Air Ministry was trying to exact more in the way of money out of the Government of Canada, or make the position such as to render impossible command by Canadians where service crews were British.'[62] King also overheard one RAF officer with the Air Mission say that 'if Canadian squadrons were being serviced by British crews, it would mean that there would be a larger number of "Englishmen" under the command of Canadians. I said nothing at the time, but made a very careful note of the remark ... which really ... let the cat out of the bag.'[63]

The next day, December 16, King continued to press Riverdale to sign the agreement on terms satisfactory to the Canadian government. The reason for haste was in large part King's intention to make a national broadcast on December 17 in order to announce both the successful conclusion of the agreement and the arrival of the First Canadian Division overseas. The 17th was King's birthday, and for this reason the number 17 was one to which he attached near-mystical properties. Under this pressure the agreement was finally signed and sealed in the early morning hours of December 17, an added fillip for Mackenzie King who could now both announce his agreement and sign it on his birthday. The question of Canadian squadrons—later called 'Canadianization'—was left essentially unresolved.[64]

If Mackenzie King was jubilant, the British were not. The Secretary of State for Air felt that everything had turned out well, but the Chancellor of the Exchequer was gloomy, pointing out to the War Cabinet that he had sent no congratulatory telegrams after the signing of the agreement. 'He had not agreed that Canada could insist on unlimited units of the R.C.A.F. being provided at the expense of the United Kingdom taxpayer.'[65] The High Commissioner in Ottawa shared the gloom. His report on the negotiations, sent on December 19, is probably one of the more blistering despatches sent about one Commonwealth government by the representative of another:

> I can best begin by saying bluntly that the United Kingdom delegation . . . approached the common problems to be solved from an entirely different angle from that of the Canadian Government. . . . [We] never forgot that [we] were here to forge a weapon for use against the common enemy. The Canadian Government saw everything in terms of the advantage which might be secured for Canada and for themselves.
>
> . . . When the Empire training scheme was first proposed to them, the Canadian Government considered it and saw that it was good: good, that is, because if they played their cards right, they could employ the essential features of the scheme for the greater honour and glory of Canada. It would, incidentally, be an effective weapon against the enemy, and this fact had its own value, since the Canadian people were pressing for effective measures on the part of their Government. But first things come first, and here was a plan which promised a far better return in the way of political capital than the despatch of a mere division or two to the Western Front.
>
> Having thus decided, the Canadian Government, it must be conceded, played their hand remarkably well.

This extraordinary despatch then proceeded to list the concessions squeezed out by the Canadians: control of the administration of the plan; the British statement of the priority of the plan over other forms of contribution to the war; and the assurance that Canadian pupils would be placed into RCAF squadrons. Why such concessions were so difficult for Sir Gerald Campbell to swallow is difficult to conceive, but the blame for it all rested on one man:

> . . . the Prime Minister is the Government, and . . . a very complex character. On the one hand he goes far beyond the average Canadian in his mystical and idealistic talk of a crusade or holy war against the enemies of civilization and democracy. On the other hand he is the narrowest of narrow Canadian nationalists. It is this twofold outlook which makes him at one moment believe that he is serving humanity by dedicating Canada to the common cause, and at the next moment consider what the common cause can be made to do to help Canada.

It is thus that he is able simultaneously to compose his own exalted platitudes and to encourage the pettifogging niceties of the Minister of Finance.*[66]

A fairer comment on this difficult negotiation can be found in a memorandum made by Floyd Chalmers of *The Financial Post* after a discussion with Sir Christopher Courtney, a member of the British Air Mission:

> ... he had got the impression, when he was over on the BCATP in 1939 that Canada was inclined to bargain pretty hard. I suggested to him that *neither* Britain nor Canada were in the war with all they had in 1939 and if Canada's financial authorities—then feeling their way— were cautious in their estimate of Canada's financial limitations, the British were pursuing a policy of virtually ignoring Canada as a war workshop.[67]

In these two assessments combined there is probably something close to a reasonable judgement. Excised of its vindictiveness and spleen, Sir Gerald Campbell's despatch was quite shrewd. Mackenzie King was difficult to deal with when he was fighting to protect what he and his colleagues perceived as the Canadian national interest, a commendable objective even in wartime. The British, after all, were demonstrably acting in their own interests in trying to pass as much as possible of the costs of the BCATP onto the Dominions. King was fighting to protect national unity, too, for a successful BCATP seemed to him likely to be the best guarantor against heavy infantry casualties and a consequent demand for conscription. The agreement seemed likely to produce a successful air-training plan, and the alterations that the Canadian negotiators had won went some distance in protecting Canadian sovereignty, although the financial costs were very heavy.

The Prime Minister stressed these costs in his radio address on December 17, and he also put special emphasis on the British statement about the priority status of the British Commonwealth Air Training Plan:

*Harold Balfour, present throughout the negotiations as a British Ministerial representative, also offered his opinion of Mr King: 'I knew his Cabinet collectively and individually had no affection for him and distrusted him. I knew that he on his side felt the same about them. He ruled without question, playing off one section of Ministerial opinion against another, thus cunningly holding the balance of power in his own hands. . . . He was a bachelor and gave one the feeling that he was an entirely sexless creature.' Harold Balfour, *Wings Over Westminster* (London, 1973), p. 117.

The United Kingdom Government has ... informed us that, considering present and future requirements, it feels that participation in the
Air Training Scheme would provide for more effective assistance
towards victory than any other form of military co-operation which
Canada can give.[68]

The BCATP was a ten-strike for the Liberal Government. On the one
hand it was possible to feature it as Canada's greatest effort to help
Britain, a true and reasonable claim. On the other hand it was a form of
military effort that likely would not lead to enormous casualties, a positive inducement for French Canada to admire the government's wise
management of affairs. The BCATP, therefore, would receive a prominent place in Liberal propaganda in the coming election campaign. And
well it might, for the Plan was a great undertaking that would unquestionably rank as Canada's major contribution to the Allied war effort.
Still, there can be no doubt that Mackenzie King and his Cabinet fought
against the preconceived notions of the British government in the first
months of the war with more vigour than either Canada or Britain
mustered against Hitler.

II

Money. This was the major basis of the disagreements between British
and Canadian negotiators during the course of the BCATP discussions.
Who would pay how much and for what was bound to be of great importance in the opening phase of a war of limited liabilities. To the
British the important thing was to produce as much as possible of the
necessary war materiel in Birmingham, Manchester, and Sheffield, and to
import as little as possible at as cheap a price as could be obtained. To
the Canadians the goal was to secure orders for manufactured goods and
raw materials at as high a price as could be negotiated. There was bound
to be conflict, and it was certain to be exacerbated by what Mackenzie
King saw as exorbitant demands for Canadian aid on the one hand and
an absolute refusal to negotiate seriously on the other.

Clearly Britain began the war expecting very little in a material sense
from Canada. 'At first,' the historian of British war supply says with
characteristic understatement, Canada 'may not have figured very
largely' in British calculations. The country's industrial resources were

small, 'and in the nature of things Canadian munitions production could never reach sufficient volume, least of all in the crucial categories of tanks and aircraft, to alter the basic assumptions of British war production planning.' In addition there were serious 'doubts about the ability of Canadian industry to deliver the goods quickly' and a very real 'shortage of dollars'.[69]

Those assumptions were not entirely incorrect. Mackenzie King had been more than a little dubious throughout the last years of peace about turning Canada into a manufacturer of munitions. To do such a thing would effectively foreclose the Canadian option of choosing neutrality in a British war, and for domestic political reasons that option was one that Mackenzie King never chose to foreclose entirely. Only in mid-1939 did the King government begin to show some interest in seeking arms contracts. The Canadian Manufacturers Association began to demand assistance from Ottawa in negotiating with the British government and its agencies;* this was given;[70] and a CMA delegation visited England in August 1939 in an effort to get munitions orders. The reception the delegation received was heartening but by the time it returned to Canada war had broken out[71] and the situation had altered decisively.

From the British point of view the best financial aid Canada could give in the early stages of the war was to help Britain purchase goods in Canada. Chamberlain's telegram to Mackenzie King on September 6 made this very obvious: 'As regards supplies, there will undoubtedly be large requirements of Canadian dollars.' Canada had a trade surplus in normal years, the telegram went on, and war demands would likely increase it. 'For instance, if dollars are available for food defence department would like to increase our normal food imports from Canada by a very large amount, perhaps 100 million dollars.'[72] When Mackenzie King read this telegram to Cabinet, he noted that he thought his ministers were 'a little stunned at the amounts asked for by way of credits—some-

---

*Canadian business looked on the war as providing a golden opportunity. John C. Kirkwood, a Canadian business consultant, wrote in the fall of 1939 that 'It is not always wrong to turn other persons' misfortunes to one's personal advantage. . . . And by the same token, it is not wrong for Canadian enterprises to turn to profitable account their advantageous position and opportunity in respect of the current war. . . . our enterprises would be blameworthy if they failed to use their present opportunity to sell, to the maximum of possibility, all that they can . . . and to sell at prices established by the law of supply and demand.' J. C. Kirkwood, 'The War and Business', *The Quarterly Review of Commerce*, VII (Autumn, 1939), 5-6; cited in S. Purdy, 'Another Look at Order-in-Council P.C. 1003', York Univ. graduate paper, 1973, p. 20.

thing like $300,000,000 . . .'[73] The key words in Chamberlain's telegram, of course, were 'if dollars are available' and the shortage of dollars was soon to cause problems.

As Chamberlain noted, even in peacetime Britain had a large trade deficit with Canada. In 1938, for example, Canada exported $341,424,000 to Britain but imported only $119,292,000 from her, a surplus of $222 million.[74] Of course Canada needed this surplus to balance her large deficit with the United States. The problem for both Canada and the United Kingdom was certain to be compounded by the war and the consequent end of the free convertibility of sterling to dollars. Thus while Canadian purchases in the United States would eventually increase as a result of war needs, so too would United Kingdom purchases in Canada. The certain result was that both Commonwealth countries would be in difficulty.

The British saw the problem first, and their almost instinctive response was to cut non-essential imports from Canada and the United States to the bone. A Cabinet paper from the President of the Board of Trade on September 19 argued for restrictions 'for the purpose of enabling us to concentrate all available resources in dollar exchange on the purchase of commodities which are essential for the prosecution of the war.' Already, the minister stated, luxury imports and imports of goods that could be produced in Britain had been stopped. This amounted to about £5.25 million from Canada. Now controls had to be imposed on tobacco and fresh and canned fruit, the value of these Canadian imports being about £2.7 million per year.[75]

However necessary and reasonable these controls, the response from Canada was predictable. The Cabinet considered the question on September 20, and Mackenzie King noted that the restrictions had been made at the same time that Britain 'has undertaken to take all of Australia's wool supply and all her surplus agricultural products, and also after she had made equally generous arrangements with New Zealand. Our Government,' King fumed, 'has been the first to arrange to send an expeditionary force and yet we are the first to be cut off.'[76] Dr Skelton told the High Commissioner that when Canada was trying to make as many dollars as possible available to Britain 'it was hardly encouraging to find that two commodities in which Canada was specially interested and of which she is a large supplier should be restricted.' Sir Gerald Campbell noted that Skelton 'thought it was highly unsatisfactory that the whole question of handling dollar resources should be dealt with in a piecemeal manner.' The High Commissioner added that 'I confess I do not find this argument easy to meet . . .'[77] The official Canadian reply made the same points and urged a delay in any such decision. The breathing space was accorded, aided by a memorandum from the Dominions Secretary, Anthony Eden, to the Cabinet, which coolly noted that 'The Canadians will obviously feel that it is wrong that we should be pressing them to supply and even finance purchases in Canada essential to *our* interests while we are taking unilateral action which must damage *their* essential interests.'[78] These arguments succeeded in converting a ban on apples into restrictions,[79] a minor victory, perhaps, but one of importance in Nova Scotia and to its representative in the Cabinet, the Minister of National Revenue, J. L. Ilsley.

The apple incident, not of profound significance, did illustrate a certain British insensitivity to Canadian concerns. The High Commissioner, a constant critic of Mackenzie King and his policies, had been favourably impressed in early September by what he reported as 'several gratifying instances of a readiness to co-operate.'[80] But that willingness was being frittered away, as a memorandum prepared in the Department of Finance showed in October. The British already had indicated that they expected a trade deficit with Canada of about $445 million in the first year of the war,[81] and it was their expectation and hope that Canada would agree to finance all or a large part of this. But what had Canada got from Britain so far? At best, about thirty orders for $10 million;[82] an offer to purchase cheese at a price that was too low; a refusal to buy bacon at the Canadian price; an offer to purchase copper under the going rate. This was no way to win Canadian co-operation.[83]

But what did Ottawa want? Another Finance Department memorandum set out the Canadian position. Canada would supply food, supplies, some equipment and munitions, plus a small expeditionary force for which Canada would pay the costs. Britain and France would be charged for supplies they used, and Britain would ship them overseas. Canada, however, would assist Britain (and possibly France)[84] in financing purchases in Canada and in return the British would repatriate Canadian securities held in the United Kingdom.[85] The Canadian policy on negotiations with London also was stated simply. The program had to be considered as a whole, not piecemeal as had happened with apple imports. Financial assistance would be offered in a package, not with regard to specific commodities, and fair treatment would have to be shown to Canadian producers. In addition, under no circumstances would Canada tie the dollar to the pound sterling,[86] and Ottawa wished to use Canadian credit balances in London to reduce both public and private indebtedness to Britain.[87]

Clearly the Canadian policy was not one of *guerre à l'outrance*.[88] But as Graham Towers of the Bank of Canada told J. A. C. Osborne (the British Treasury representative in Ottawa and a former Deputy Governor of the Bank of Canada), 'the United Kingdom should realize how enthusiastically Canada has come into the war and that they are determined to put forward their maximum effort. . . . Of course,' Osborne observed, 'the term "maximum effort" is elastic and likely to mean different things to different countries according to their needs and the degree of immediate danger they experience, a thing we will not allow the Canadians to forget.'[89]

This was the heart of the Canadian argument. R. B. Bryce, the young but exceedingly able student of the great British economist, John Maynard Keynes, and a key aide to W. Clifford Clark, the Deputy Minister of Finance, laid out the Canadian position in a memorandum that argued persuasively that Canadians could not be expected to devote as large a proportion of their national income to the war as the British. 'The War is a European War in which the vital interests of the U.K. are at stake. . . . Not so with Canadians, who are 3,000 miles from the scene of war, who whether rightly or wrongly appreciate the protection they enjoy from their great southern neighbour, and who enter the war more from a sense of loyalty to the Mother country and in a spirit of a crusade for the protection of our ideals of freedom and democracy.' Moreover, Bryce argued, Canada was a sprawling country with 'a lesser degree of real national unity behind the prosecution of the war' and much less accustomed than Britain to the controls and regimentation that might make possible a large diversion of the national income to war. Furthermore the Canadian governmental structure was less efficient than the U.K.'s and Canada was 'relatively and absolutely . . . the greatest *debtor* country in the world.'[90] The Prime Minister had said exactly the same thing to the British Air Mission.

The Canadian position on financial questions was taken to London at the beginning of November by T. A. Crerar, the Minister of Mines and Resources. As a Manitoban, Crerar was particularly concerned about wheat sales, and he argued as vigorously as he could that Britain had an obligation to buy wheat from Canada at a price that would give a reasonable return to the Prairie farmer. At Treasury insistence, British policy thus far had been to buy on the world market at the going rate, a price well below the Canadian one.[91] But by November, when Crerar was beginning his negotiations, the British had decided to buy in Canada if the price was right.[92] It wasn't. The British maintained that 70¢ a bushel was fair while the minister said that such a sum 'could not be considered'.[93] Crerar suggested a Canadian guarantee to supply wheat for twelve months at 93½¢ or until July 1, 1941 at $1.[94] The British were unhappy, and Graham Towers, in London with Crerar, 'pointed out that Britain had obtained cheap food for nine years, except for brief periods, and Canadian farmers had had poor prices. It would be impossible to convince the Canadian farmer that he was unreasonable in asking for a better price now.' This speech prompted the British Minister of Food, W. S. Morrison, to argue that an increase of 30¢ per bushel would raise the price of bread in Britain by a penny and a half a loaf. 'Such an increase in the cost of living would have a very serious effect, not only on the spirit of the workers of this country, but on the whole capacity of the country to exert its maximum war effort.' This emotional blackmail failed to move Crerar, and the question remained unresolved, the British evidently preferring to continue to buy and sell on the open market.[95] London obviously hoped prices would stay low, while in Ottawa Mackenzie King and the Cabinet expected 'wheat will rise considerably from now on.'[96] In May 1940, finally, Britain contracted to take fifty million bushels at 82½¢, a price then still above the market price.[97] Further orders followed in August after the change in the war situation.

Crerar's discussions on the extent of Canadian aid were equally important. The British beyond doubt believed that Canada was acting in a niggardly fashion, and much of the discussion centred on how much of its national income each country was spending on the common cause.[98] Crerar presented the Canadian position in a paper, 'The War Finance of Canada'. The Dominion effort would take two forms, he said, military assistance and the provision and financing of supplies. The most that Canada could do during the next year was to spend $320 million for military purposes and about $200 million to finance British purchases in Canada. 'It was hoped,' Crerar said, holding out the carrot, 'that this last sum might possibly be increased if orders from the United Kingdom and other allied countries were placed in Canada promptly enough and on a large enough scale to give an immediate and substantial stimulus to the expansion of Canadian production and Canadian national income.' According to Crerar, Canada was already spending 47.3 per cent of national income on government operations and the war, and even if the war pushed the national income up 15 per cent this would still mean that governmental expenditures would be 41.1 per cent of national income. By contrast Britain, a principal power, was spending only 51.1 per cent of her national income on such uses.[99]

The British reaction to this kind of reasoning was amused contempt. 'Broadly speaking,' a Treasury note argued, 'the Canadian Treasury appears to be making elaborate calculations as to the cost of Canada's war effort in the first year and from this there emerges at the finish a figure which they say represents the maximum financial assistance which they could give by loan to the United Kingdom. The whole thing seems to us mildly preposterous.' Canada was underestimating its national income, and the calculations were based on 'theoretical reasonings and rough estimatings which make it a ridiculous method to choose.'[100]

Perhaps, but the Canadians held firm in the negotiations. Sir Frederick Phillips of the Treasury met with Graham Towers on December 1, and heard the Bank of Canada governor confirm that the total amount Canada could lend was $237 million less the cost to Canada for financing the first year of the BCATP, some $46 million. This was unfortunate, Phillips said. 'Mr Towers said that however unfortunate it might be they could not offer us a sum which they did not honestly believe they could find inside the economic structure of Canada.' Towers did add that if the estimates proved too low, Canada would do more. 'This,' Phillips sighed, 'seems to me reasonably satisfactory and I do not think we shall get more out of them.'[101] Towers had been at some pains to point out that the Canadian offer was not one that the country could bear with ease, but rather one that would entail considerable sacrifice by the Canadian people.[102]

Canadian generosity had been pushed as hard as it could be in the fall of 1939. More might have been forthcoming had the British demonstrated a willingness to place some orders in Canada, but even the British negotiators' own estimates showed only £7 million in orders as of November 21.[103] This failure, for so it was seen in Canada, provoked Mackenzie King enormously, and in an Ottawa press conference at the end of November he let fly. Grant Dexter of the *Winnipeg Free Press* recorded the Prime Minister's off-the-record remarks in a private memorandum:

This matter of war orders was admittedly difficult to explain to the public. But in fact the explanation was simple. The British were not in a position to place orders. And when they did decide to place orders it was usually discovered that one of two reasons existed which made action impossible: 1. some essential blueprint or pattern would be missing and would have to be brought out from England, entailing a very long delay; 2. the approval of the British treasury had to be obtained. He had never been able to understand why the British purchasing authorities at home did not get the approval of the treasury before instructing the war mission in Canada to make the purchase. Indeed, he said, there seemed to be very little co-operation between the British treasury and the purchasing authorities and, in consequence, orders in every direction were being held up. He said that no doubt the British treasury was very busy and greatly in arrears. Meantime everybody would have to be patient.[104]

Some people in Canada seemed to believe that the Treasury was determined to stop all orders to the Dominion.[105] That was probably too strong, but there was no doubt that, as Lester Pearson wrote to a friend from London some months later, British officials had been 'criminally short-sighted' in ignoring Canada as a base of supplies. The Canadians were not blameless, Pearson added with his usual willingness to see both sides of any problem, but Britain's very existence was at stake and there could be no excuse for not placing orders in Canada 'even if it might mean the loss of a few orders by their own manufacturers'.[106] The British, thinking of their own unemployment and profits, unfortunately did not see it this way, and they would not until the fall of France altered their views of the war. Ottawa's fiscal perceptions would change at the same time.

---

1 Public Archives of Canada [PAC], W. L. Mackenzie King Papers, Black Binders, Vol. 14, file 51, exhibit 1; C. P. Stacey, *Arms, Men and Governments: The War Policies of Canada 1939-1945* (Ottawa, 1970), p. 81.

2 PAC, Department of External Affairs Records, Vol. 42, folio 243, Vol. 1, 'Recruitment of Canadians for Service in Royal Air Force', 3 Mar. 1936; *ibid.*, Christie to Skelton, 5 May 1936.

3 *Ibid.*, Ian Mackenzie to King, 4 Sept. 1936; King Papers, Memo, 10 Sept. 1936, f. C109341; Fred Hatch, 'The British Commonwealth Air Training Plan, 1939-45', Ph.D. thesis, University of Ottawa, 1969, 29-30.

4 Public Record Office [PRO], Dominions Office Records, DO 114/85, Secretary of State for Dominion Affairs [SSDA] to High Commissioner, 13 May 1938.

5 External Affairs Records, Vol. 42, folio 243, Vol. 1, 'Precis of Conversations . . . 12 Aug. 1938'; PRO, Prime Minister's Office Records, Prem 1/397, 'Training of R.A.F. Pilots in Canada: Political Note', 11 Nov. 1938; Stacey, *Arms, Men and Governments*, pp. 83-4.

6 House of Commons *Debates*, 1 July 1938, pp. 4525-31.

7 Prem 1/397, 'Training of R.A.F. Pilots...'; PAC, C. D. Howe Papers, Vol. 48, file S-14-1(1), Memo, 'R.A.F. Training Scheme', n.d.

8 Prem 1/397, 'Training of R.A.F. Pilots...'.

9 *Ibid.*, att. to letter Sandford[?] to Sir H. Wilson, 28 July 1939.

10 PRO, Cabinet Records, Cab 66/1, W.P. (39)4, 4 Sept. 1939; King Papers, Black Binders, Vol. 15, file 53, High Commissioner to Secretary of State for External Affairs [SSEA], 4 Sept. 1939, f. C267860.

11 Vincent Massey, *What's Past is Prologue* (Toronto, 1963), pp. 304-6. PRO, Air Ministry Records, Air 20/333/IIIc/3/4, Note of Meeting... , 22, 23 Sept. 1939; *ibid.*, Street to Barlow, 24 Sept. 1939; Stacey, *Arms, Men and Governments*, p. 79.

12 There is ample evidence on this point including Massey's memoirs, the *Mackenzie King Record*, and the recollections of External Affairs personnel in this period. Interviews with C. S. A. Ritchie, Lester Pearson, and John W. Holmes, 1971.

13 Massey, pp. 304-5; Lester B. Pearson, *Mike. The Memoirs of the Rt. Hon. Lester B. Pearson*, Vol. I: *1896-1948* (Toronto, 1972), p. 151; Prem 1/397, Eden to Chamberlain, 25 Sept. 1939 and atts.

14 King Papers, Tel. Prime Minister [P.M.] to P.M., 26 Sept. 1939, ff. 224789ff.

15 *Ibid.*

16 King Diary, 26 Sept. 1939.

17 *Ibid.*, 27 Sept. 1939.

18 *Ibid.*, 28 Sept. 1939; King Papers, Memo re Emergency Council of Cabinet, 28 Sept. 1939, ff. C110723ff.

19 *Ibid.*, P.M. to P.M., 28 Sept. 1939, ff. 224801ff.

20 King Diary, 28 Sept. 1939. For Skelton's next shot at the proposal, see King Papers, Memo, Skelton to King, 29 Sept. 1939 and King's reply, 30 Sept. 1939, ff. C109479ff.

21 King Diary, 10 Oct. 1939; King Papers, Memo, Skelton to King, 7 Oct. 1939, ff. C267916-8 and docs on ff. C267928ff.; James Eayrs, *In Defence of Canada*, Vol. II: *Appeasement and Rearmament* (Toronto, 1965), pp. 106-7.

22 Air 19/83, 'Memo on the Incidence of Cost of the Air Training Scheme', 5 Oct. 1939. See also docs on Air 46/1, Air 46/2 and PRO, Foreign Office Records, FO 414/272 for further information on the U.K. side of the negotiations.

23 Air 20/405/IIIc/3/13, Note of 1st Meeting... , 10 Oct. 1939.

24 *Ibid.*, Note of Third Meeting... , 13 Oct. 1939.

25 King Papers, 'Dominion Training Scheme', 13 Oct. 1939. Additional Canadian material can be found in PAC, Ian Mackenzie Papers, file X-41. The Montreal *Gazette* estimated costs at $100 million for the first year. 16 Oct. 1939.

26 King Diary, 17 Oct. 1939.

27 Directorate of History, National Defence Headquarters, Ottawa, Air Vice Marshal E. W. Stedman Papers, Memo, 'BCATP', p. 2. The British were relatively optimistic after this meeting. See Air 20/405/IIIc/3/13, Notes of 6th Meeting... , 18 Oct. 1939; Air 8/280/1P3/574, Mission to Canada. . . . , n.d.; Air 20/338/IIIc/3/14, Riverdale to Wood, 19 Oct. 1939.

28 Air 20/405/IIIc/3/13. Notes of 7th Meeting . . . , 19 Oct. 1939.

29 Air 20/338/IIIc/3/14, Riverdale to Wood, 19 Oct. 1939.

30 Stedman Papers, 'BCATP', pp. 2ff.; *ibid.*, folders on Flying Training Scheme, estimates, 23 Oct., 16, 26 Nov. 1939; Hatch, 83ff.

31 Air 20/338/IIIC/3/14, Riverdale to Wood, 30 Oct. 1939 and atts.

32 Air 20/404/IIIC/3/7, 'Points for Tuesday's Meeting ... [31 Oct. 1939]'.

33 PAC, Privy Council Office Records, Cabinet War Committee Records, Memo re Emergency Council of Cabinet, 31 Oct. 1939.

34 Harold Balfour, *Wings Over Westminster* (London, 1973), p. 115.

35 Queen's University, C. G. Powers Papers, [U.K.] Notes of Meeting, October 31. The Canadian minutes are not essentially different. Memo re Emergency Council of Cabinet, 31 Oct. 1939. Cf. King Diary, 31 Oct. 1939, and Air 20/338/IIIC/3/14, Riverdale to Wood, 6 Nov. 1939.

36 King Diary, 31 Oct. 1939; Power Papers, Notes ... , 31 Oct. 1939; Memo re Emergency Council ... , 31 Oct. 1939; Air 8/280/1P3/574, Mission to Canada ... n.d.

37 King Papers, Memo for P.M., 1 Nov. 1939, ff. C109539ff. The British version is on PRO, Treasury Records, T160/1340, High Commissioner to SSDA, 1 Nov. 1939.

38 King Diary, 1, 3, 10 Nov. 1939; King Papers, Memo by Skelton, 2 Nov. 1939, ff. C268010ff.; Stacey, *Arms, Men and Governments*, p. 22. In connection with the 'free gift', Power noted that Britain at no time revealed details of costs of engines, equipment, etc. 'The suggestion has been freely made that at that time the economic planners of Great Britain had no desire to see Canada ... developing an aircraft industry of her own.' Norman Ward, ed., *A Party Politician: The Memoirs of Chubby Power* (Toronto, 1966), pp. 200-1.

39 King Papers, P.M. to P.M., 3 Nov. 1939, ff. 224807ff.

40 Air 20/404/IIIC/3/7, Notes of Meeting ... 3 Nov. 1939; Air 20/338/IIIC/3/14, Riverdale to Wood, 6 Nov. 1939.

41 *Ibid.*; Air 8/280/1P3/574, 'Air Mission to Canada ...'.

42 *Ibid.*; King Papers, 'Air Training Scheme Proposals', n.d., ff. C109455-6.

43 King Diary, 14 Nov. 1939.

44 Cabinet War Committee Records, Minutes, 14 Nov. 1939; FO 414/272, Note of a Special Meeting, 15 Nov. 1939; Toronto *Telegram*, 15 Nov. 1939.

45 Air 20/338/IIIC/3/14, Wood to Riverdale, 22 Nov. 1939.

46 Cab 67/2, W.G. (39) 105, 18 Nov. 1939.

47 Cab 65/2, Minutes, 25 Nov. 1939.

48 Cab 67/3, High Commissioner to SSDA, 25 Nov. 1939.

49 See the notes by King on his talk with Campbell on 25 Nov. 1939, which indicate that financial aspects still troubled him most of all. King Papers, 'Re: Air Training Scheme', ff. C109614ff.

50 Cabinet War Committee Records, Minutes, 27 Nov. 1939; King Diary, 27 Nov. 1939.

51 Cab 67/3, P.M. to P.M., 27 Nov. 1939; *ibid.*, High Commissioner to SSDA, 27 Nov. 1939; Air 20/338/IIIC/3/14, Riverdale to Wood, 30 Nov. 1939.

52 Eayrs, II, p. 111; King Papers, Memo, 'Priority of Air Training Scheme', 28 Nov. 1939, ff. C268121-5.

53 *Ibid.*, Statement, f. C109624; King Diary, 27 Nov. 1939. For King's views on the U.K. at this time, see Queen's University, Grant Dexter Papers, Memo, 30 Nov. 1939.

54 See Stacey, *Arms, Men and Governments*, pp. 24-5; Cab 65/2, Minutes, 2 Dec. 1939; King Papers, P.M. to P.M., 1 Dec. 1939, ff. C268144-5; Eayrs, II, p. 111.

55 Hatch, 104ff.; King Papers, Memo for P.M., n.d., ff. C268153ff.

56 Power Papers, Rogers to Riverdale, 8 Dec. 1939.

57 King Papers, Riverdale to Rogers, 9 Dec. 1939, f. C268164.

58 King Diary, 9-10 Dec. 1939; Stacey, *Arms, Men and Governments*, p. 26; King Papers, Memo by Heeney, 11 Dec. 1939, ff. C268210ff.

59 Cab 65/2, Minutes, 11, 13 Dec. 1939; Cab 67/3, W.G. (39) 148, 12 Dec. 1939; King Papers, Memo to P.M., 13 Dec. 1939, ff. C268219-21.

60 King Diary, 14 Dec. 1939; Power Papers, [U.K.] Notes of Meeting . . . , 14 Dec. 1939.

61 Proposal in *ibid.*, Riverdale to King, 15 Dec. 1939; King's reply in King Papers, P.M. to P.M., 16 Dec. 1939, ff. C268318ff.

62 King Diary, 15 Dec. 1939.

63 *Ibid.*

64 Air 8/264/1P3/575, Notes of Transatlantic Conversations . . . , 17 Dec. 1939; King Papers, Black Binders, Vol. 1, Comments by Colonel Ralston, 16 Dec. 1939; Power Papers, Riverdale to Rogers, 16 Dec. 1939; King Diary, 16 Dec. 1939, and press reaction in King Papers, ff. C268247ff.

65 Cab 65/2, Minutes, 18 Dec. 1939; Prem 1/397, Memo for Prime Minister [Chamberlain], 26 Dec. 1939.

66 *Ibid.*, High Commissioner to SSDA, 19 Dec. 1939. By way of contrast, see Campbell's bland comments in his memoir, *Of True Experience* (New York, 1947), p. 101.

67 Floyd Chalmers Papers (Toronto), 'Re Canada-U.K. War Financing Arrangements', November-December, 1941.

68 'The British Commonwealth Air Training Plan' (Ottawa, 1939). This is a pamphlet version of King's address on 17 Dec. 1939.

69 M. M. Postan, *British War Production* (London, 1952), pp. 229, 235. See also H. D. Hall and G. C. Wrigley, *Studies of Overseas Supply* (London, 1956), pp. 52-3; H. D. Hall, *North American Supply* (London, 1955), pp. 3ff.; J. Hurstfield, *The Control of Raw Materials* (London, 1953), p. 177.

70 E.g., King Papers, Skelton to Campbell, 15 May 1939, ff. 236987ff.

71 On the mission, see PAC, A. G. L. McNaughton Papers, Vol. 241, C.M.A. Mission files; King Papers, Memo by McNaughton, n.d., ff. C269932ff. On supply generally before 1939, see Stacey, *Arms, Men and Governments*, pp. 100ff.

72 Department of Finance, Ottawa, W. Clifford Clark Papers, file U-3-2, P.M. to P.M., 6 Sept. 1939.

73 King Diary, 6 Sept. 1939.

74 M. C. Urquhart, and J. A. H. Buckley, *Historical Statistics of Canada* (Toronto, 1965), p. 183.

75 Cab 67/1, W.P. (G) (39) 14, 19 Sept. 1939.

76 King Diary, 20 Sept. 1939.

77 Cab 67/1, W.P. (G) (39), High Commissioner to SSDA, 21 Sept. 1939.

78 *Ibid.*, (39) 18, 22 Sept. 1939.

79 *Ibid.*, (39) 45, 18 Oct. 1939.

80 FO 371/23966, High Commissioner to SSDA, 20 Sept. 1939.

81 See T160/1141, 'Canada's Sterling Balance', 30 July 1941, which indicates that the British estimated the deficit in fall 1939 at between £73-90 million. Cf. Hall, p. 229.

82 Stacey, *Arms, Men and Governments*, p. 30. estimates U.K. orders at $5 million as of 8 Dec. 1939.

83 Clark Papers, file U-3-3, 'Summary', n.d.; Hall, pp. 10ff.

84 Incredibly, discussions with the French did not begin until mid-May 1940. See PAC, Department of Finance Records, Vol. 2691, Towers to Ralston, 17 May 1940.

85 See R. S. Sayers, *Financial Policy, 1939-1945* (London, 1956), pp. 326-7.

86 *Ibid.*, pp. 333-4.

87 Clark Papers, file U-3-3, Financial Aspects of Negotiations with United Kingdom', n.d. [early Oct. 1939].

88 Stacey, *Arms, Men and Governments*, p. 11 cites Ralston saying on 21 Sept. 1939 that the $100 million war appropriation for the period to 31 Mar. 1940 set 'the limits within which expenditures can be made' and efforts should be made to spend less.

89 T160/1141, Osborne to Sir F. Phillips, 6 Oct. 1939. Osborne had been loaned to the Bank of Canada in its formative years by the U.K. Treasury.

90 Finance Department Records, Vol. 3440, National Income Statistics 1940-2, 'What Proportion of the National Income . . .', n.d. [Oct. 1939]; Sayers, pp. 330-1.

91 *Ibid.*, p. 328.

92 Cab 21/490, D.M.V. (C) (39) 1, 2 Nov. 1939. On the negotiations, see docs on Cab 99/1.

93 Cab 21/490, D.M.V. (C) (39) 12, 22 Nov. 1939.

94 See Pearson, I, p. 145.

95 Clark Papers, file U-3-3, Summary of Minutes of Meeting . . . , 1 Dec. 1939; Cab 21/490, D.M.V. (C) (39) 13, 1 Dec. 1939; Dexter Papers, Memos, 12, 29 Dec. 1939.

96 King Diary, 7 Dec. 1939.

97 King Papers, 'Canadian Economic Contribution', 1 June 1940, f. C246775. On wheat negotiations and problems, see J. W. Holmes, 'Bushels to Burn', *Behind the Head-lines*, No. 1 (September, 1940); D. A. MacGibbon, *The Canadian Grain Trade 1931-1951* (Toronto, 1952), pp. 100-1; and esp. G. E. Britnell and V. C. Fowke, *Canadian Agriculture in War and Peace 1935-50* (Stanford, 1962), pp. 200ff.

98 The whole National Income framework was Keynesian, of course. See Robert Lekachman, *The Age of Keynes* (New York, 1966), p. 145.

99 Copy of Crerar Memo on T160/1340; External Affairs Records, Vol. 67, file 388, SSEA to High Commissioner London, 8 Nov. 1939; Hall, pp. 12-13; Sayers, p. 330; T160/1140, Osborne to Phillips, 27 Oct. 1939. W. K. Hancock and M. M. Gowing, *British War Economy* (London, 1949), p. 369 provides comparative figures on war spending as a percentage of national income. In Graham Towers' view, the maximum Canada could spend in the first year of the war was 40 per cent of the national income. Finance Department Records, Vol. 777, file 400-16, 'Notes on Canada's War Potential', 31 Oct. 1939.

100 T160/1340, Treasury Note, n.d. and 'Note on Memo on Canadian War Finance', n.d. By January 1942 the Canadians had come to believe the national-income idea somewhat unsatisfactory. See Finance Department Records, Vol. 3440, National In-

come Statistics 1940-2, Towers to Clark, 6 June 1942. See also F. H. Brown *et al.*, *War Finance in Canada* (Toronto, 1940), pp. 65ff., which also seems to feel the Canadian national-income estimates were too low.

101 T160/1340, Note by Phillips, 1 Dec. 1939; External Affairs Records, Vol. 67, file 388, High Commissioner to SSEA, 14 Dec. 1939.

102 Cab 21/490, D.M.V. (C) (39) 11, 1 Dec. 1939; Clark Papers, file B-2-8-7-2-3, Towers to Ralston, 23 Jan. 1940; Stacey, *Arms, Men and Governments*, pp. 11-12; Hall, pp. 15, 229; Sayers, pp. 331-2.

103 Cab 21/490, D.M.V. (C) (39) 13, 21 Nov. 1939. In his memoirs, J. S. Duncan of Massey-Harris records that his firm was the first to get a British war contract—in December 1939. *Not a One-Way Street* (Toronto, 1971), p. 107.

104 Dexter Papers, Memo, 30 Nov. 1939; Sayers, pp. 328-9.

105 British policy at this time was to keep North American purchases 'limited to those materials unobtainable elsewhere'. Hurstfield, p. 181. Floyd Chalmers, in 1939 editor of *The Financial Post*, recalls conversations with British emissaries to Canada who were worried that orders in Canada would do nothing to solve British unemployment. Interview, 27 Sept. 1973.

106 Dexter Papers, Pearson to Dexter, 21 Aug. 1940.

3. Election
Victory and
European
Defeat

As he looked back on the year 1939, Mackenzie King was well satisfied with himself and his role. 'Unquestionably . . . the most important and eventful year of my life,' he noted on New Year's Eve, 'a year in which there have been many important decisions with respect to each of which wise judgement has been shown.' There was a tone of supreme smugness, but the list of achievements was impressive. The visit of the King and Queen in late spring had been 'outstanding', and certainly 'not a mistake'. The decision of Parliament to go to war also had been 'Outstanding and greatest of the achievements. . . . Every step that led up to that decision I personally engineered.' The Air Training Plan was still another triumph, as was the Quebec election result. 'Above all I think I may claim to be responsible in no small measure for the unity of Canada at this time.'

King's list went on and on. He had tried 'to save [sic] the war that now wages in Europe.' He had made important broadcasts, and he had helped his family with advice and money. Crucial changes had been made in the Cabinet. And there was one more achievement. The decision not to hold an election 'but to await developments in Europe,'—that, King noted, was 'all-important'.[1] And in a sense it was, for Canada had come very close to being in the midst of an election campaign when the war burst upon Europe. If that had happened the effects on Canada, on the Liberal Party, and on Mackenzie King would have been incalculable.

Throughout the last summer of the peace King had been looking for the best time to go to the people. All the ministers had been polled for their views on the prospects of success and on the state of the party organization in their provinces, and all had reported to the Prime Minister.[2] The responses were generally optimistic, but King was uncertain. As he wrote to Vincent Massey in London in mid-August, 'I, myself, would like to bring [the election] on at the end of the present month. Were the skies in Europe clear, I should have no hesitancy in so doing. I have had, however, to consider how appalling would be the consequences were Parliament to dissolve, and war to come on. It would mean that for seven weeks should war begin at the time of dissolution, there would not only be no Parliament, but no persons entitled to sit as representatives of the people.' Massey was asked for his estimate on the probability of war,[3] and so, very confidentially, was Neville Chamberlain.[4] The British Prime Minister's reply, sent on August 21, was entirely accurate: 'the situation has become decidedly more threatening and it certainly would be rash at this moment to forecast a date when an election could be held.'[5] The election was put off.

What the Liberals' fate would have been had the election been called is, of course, uncertain. Ian Mackenzie, at that time still the Minister of National Defence, had tried his hand at a draft platform for the election, which, as its title page might suggest, was uninspiring:

Carry on with King
Carry on for Canada
What is Your Alternative?
What Else Can You Do?
The Liberal Party's Policy to Meet
    The Challenge of These
    Restless Changing Times[6]

Mackenzie assessed his own province of British Columbia realistically enough, however, and his estimate was that the Liberals would take at least six of the seventeen seats there. His own seat, Vancouver Centre, Mackenzie rated as doubtful.[7] The Maritimes were in good shape, and T. A. Crerar, the Manitoba minister, believed that the Prairies were promising. Quebec, too, seemed to be relatively secure,[8] and this left only Ontario as a questionable area.

Questionable indeed. Mitchell Hepburn, the Liberal Premier, fought Mackenzie King at every turn, and as a result relations between the federal and provincial Liberal organizations had ceased. Contractors in

Ontario were warned against doing work for Ottawa if they hoped to keep their provincial jobs.[9] There had been suggestions that Hepburn was beginning to finance anti-King movements in Saskatchewan,[10] and earlier there had been evidence that the Ontario Premier was interfering with the raising of money for the federal party in Ontario.[11] The Ontario Liberal Association had seceded from the National Liberal Federation, and the NLF President, Senator Norman Lambert, had had no option but to create a separate federal organization in the province.[12] Mackenzie King professed puzzlement about Hepburn, even writing to Massey that 'The behaviour of the Ontario ministry is the most extraordinary thing I have known in our political history. I have yet to discover what it is due to,' King said, 'other than wounded vanity on Hepburn's part, and an unwillingness on my part to submit to dictatorship of any kind. This alone can account for Hepburn's readiness, in order to satisfy a personal grudge to destroy the Liberal Party, not in the Dominion only, but in the provincial field as well.'[13] That was an over-simplification, but clearly there were elements of personal pique in Hepburn's vicious opposition to the King government. The Premier had felt slighted when King had refused his nominations for the federal Cabinet in 1935, and he had bitterly resented what he saw as Ottawa's uncompromising unwillingness to assist Ontario in exporting hydro-electric power to the United States. As disagreement piled on disagreement, and as Hepburn found himself drawing closer to Maurice Duplessis in their joint opposition to Ottawa's intrusions into provincial areas, the breach widened irreparably. By the summer of 1939 it seemed clear that Hepburn and all the support he could muster would be thrown against the King government in a federal election.

The outbreak of the war postponed the battle. King and Manion had agreed before the emergency session of Parliament that there would be no general election until after a new sitting of the House of Commons began in January 1940. King informed his Cabinet of this on September 14: 'I said that Manion expected a short session and I had made it quite clear that there would be no extension of the term of Parliament.'[14] And although at the outset of the war the Conservative Party closed up its Ottawa offices entirely in a gesture of non-partisanship, the National Liberal Federation carefully maintained 'a small office to preserve contact with Liberal organizations throughout the country—having in mind a general election next year.'[15] King and his ministers were agreed that this was the wise course and subsequently instructed Senator Lambert to ensure that material was ready for the election that, as King wrote his organizer, 'may come at any time once Parliament has assembled.'[16] The money for the campaign was already largely in hand. Lambert had established a system of instalment payments to spread the contributions from corporations out over a wider time span, and he was scrupulous in exacting a 1.5 to 2 per cent cut of federal contracts from those firms lucky enough to get contracts from the government during the latter years of the depression.[17] The result of this preparatory work could be found in Senator Lambert's letter to King in July 1939: 'I can guarantee sufficient funds to meet the national expenses of a campaign.'[18]

All that remained now was to determine the date of the appeal to the people. King always kept the election in view; for example, when he spoke with Lambert on January 5, 1940, he 'said he hoped we would be ready for an early election; but [he] also hedged on possibility of serious offensive on Western Front.'[19] If the vote came in the midst of heavy fighting, King suggested, the result might be in doubt. Ten days later the Prime Minister spoke to Tweedsmuir and told the Governor General that he expected the forthcoming session, due to open on January 25, to continue into May and to be followed by a June election.[20] The next day the Cabinet discussed the coming election. The ministers heard Mackenzie King argue that 'we had no organization in constituencies and no financial provision for a campaign; that I thought we should not be too hasty.'[21]

King's slurs on the National Liberal Federation and its organizational efforts were habitual and almost always unfair. Under Lambert the party machine was efficient and as ready for an election as it could be, given the checks imposed on campaign preparation by the war. Attacks of this kind, word of which always reached Lambert from his cronies in the Cabinet, had prompted the party President to tell King in November that the forthcoming election was the last he would direct.[22]

But significantly King had no expectation of an immediate election in mid-January. The course of the war would have to be considered, and there remained a whole session of Parliament to get through. Nonetheless, as he recorded in his diary on January 18, Mackenzie King told his Cabinet that the Tories and Mitchell Hepburn were beginning to work up a campaign against the government. 'I pointed out the need for the Committee of the Cabinet to take in hand at once the question of political organization for a campaign. Said I would name the committee forthwith. That they must realize we must be ready at any time.'[23] Before the day was out, the Prime Minister would learn of the launching of the anti-King campaign.

I

Mitchell Hepburn had been fuming at what he considered to be Mackenzie King's inefficient war effort since September 1939. As early as October, after a meeting with the Prime Minister and members of his Cabinet, the Ontario Premier had told reporters in confidence that 'the situation at Ottawa would break your heart.... Mr. King apparently hasn't yet realized there is a war on.'[24] In December he wrote to W. M. Southam of the Ottawa *Citizen* about the 'most deplorable condition of affairs one could imagine' among the troops temporarily quartered at the Canadian National Exhibition grounds in Toronto. 'Men without uniforms, proper underwear and shoes.... Money should not be our main consideration.'[25] This presumably genuine concern, combined with Hepburn's undoubted desire to strike at Mackenzie King, led to a somewhat unprecedented state of affairs at Queen's Park.

There, on January 18, George Drew, Conservative Party leader and the Leader of the Opposition, had just ended a speech criticizing Mackenzie King's war leadership when Hepburn associated himself with the Opposition leader's words. The Premier, apparently on the spur of the moment and without consulting his Cabinet, then moved a resolution regretting 'that the Federal Government at Ottawa had made so little effort to prosecute Canada's duty in the war in the vigorous manner the people of Canada desire to see.' To ensure that the resolution would pass, Hepburn told his supporters that he would resign and bring on an election if he did not receive his party's support. At Hepburn's insistence the vote was recorded and the eighteen Conservatives present joined twenty-six Liberals in voting for the resolution. Ten Liberals voted against their Premier and for their Prime Minister.[26]

This extraordinary resolution at first rattled Mackenzie King. He went back to his office that night to prepare a statement and found none of his staff there. The Prime Minister flew into a rage—nothing annoyed him more than the inability or unwillingness of his staff to be available at all hours—and commented that 'This is the most important night since the war began. It is of such importance that on tonight's decision depends pretty much the whole future of the Government.' But as he would have done even if some assistance had been available, King himself began to draft his press release. His first sentence read 'The fullest opportunity to discuss Canada's war effort will be afforded when Parliament re-assembles,' but almost immediately upon drafting this he began to have second thoughts. By the time he had spoken to Ernest Lapointe and Norman Rogers on the telephone he had decided to delete it, 'having in mind that I might announce an immediate dissolution, and not give any pledge in advance of discussions in Parliament. My own thought is that we should not allow discussion to develop at all; make an immediate appeal. . . . At any rate, Hepburn has made an appeal absolutely necessary, and has made the issue that of the Government's conduct of the war.' The more he thought about it, the more King convinced himself that this course was correct:

> Hepburn's action has given to me and my colleagues and to the party here just what is needed to place beyond question the wisdom of an immediate election and the assurance of victory for the Government. What really has helped to take an enormous load off my mind is that it justified an immediate appeal, avoiding thereby all the contention of a session known to be immediately preceding an election.

The greatest relief of all, King added,

> is the probability of having the election over before the worst of the fighting begins in Europe. I have dreaded having to choose the moment for the campaign and specially to choose it at a time when human lives are being slaughtered by hundreds of thousands, if not by millions. In this way we can probably have the election over before the spring campaign in Europe begins.[27]

King had decided on an immediate election, but the way in which this would be brought about was unclear. On the 19th the Prime Minister turned over in his mind the prospect of having Parliament pass an Elections Act and an Active Service Voters Act and then seeking dissolution. This would avoid the estimates, the Unemployment Insurance question, the War Measures Act, and other contentious issues, all of which could be 'made as pledges on the part of the government as to what will be done if we are returned to power.' There were other advantages, too. 'We will also avoid the Union Government issue coming to the fore. Dr. Manion and his party will be taken so completely by surprise that they will not be able to get organized in fighting shape.'[28] These were important considerations, particularly the question of a coalition government, something King was determined to avoid at all costs.* But against these advantages there was that unfortunate promise to Manion about another session before dissolution, and there were scores of Members of Parliament who needed the indemnity they would receive from an extended session.

King outlined his thinking to the War Committee of Cabinet on January 22 with Lapointe, Crerar, Ralston, and Power in attendance. The only member raising questions was Ralston, who believed that the party had a good case and should present it to Parliament. He was, however, quickly brought around. The full Cabinet was not told of the plan at this time, and at its meeting after the War Committee had concluded, the Prime Minister simply asked for the ministers' reaction to the Ontario resolution. James G. Gardiner, the Minister of Agriculture and almost the only member of the Cabinet still on good terms with Hepburn, seemed to feel that the resolution should not be made an election issue. W. D. Euler agreed. Norman McLarty, the Minister of Labour, and C. D. Howe, the Minister of Transport, did not seem unduly concerned by the question. Only Mackenzie and Ilsley thought the Hepburn-Drew resolution important. King probably should have been concerned that his Ontario ministers were unenthusiastic about fighting Hepburn on this issue, but if he was he gave no sign of it. All he told his Cabinet was that he generally favoured an early dissolution.[29]

Out of necessity, King's staff had to be told more than the ministers. On this day King dictated for J. W. Pickersgill, the External Affairs officer seconded to his staff and one of those who assisted him with his speeches, a seventeen-page memorandum that was designed to serve as the basis for a statement justifying dissolution. This memo, impressive for its organization and its rationalizations, stressed that an election was required every five years and that the term of this Parliament was almost over. The people, King argued, have a right to their say, and if the election was delayed the campaign might be fought around the theme 'win the elections' rather than 'win the war'. If the election was put off, he added, Canada might find itself in a situation similar to that in 1916 when the life of Parliament had been extended for a year. And what

*During a visit by Anthony Eden, the British Foreign Secretary, to Ottawa in March 1943, King recorded Eden's quip that 'there was only one thing worse' than having a large number of parties in the House of Commons 'which was to have all parties in one government, which was perfect hell.' King agreed entirely: 'A government and an Opposition is the best thing.' King Diary, 31 Mar. 1943.

had that year brought? The Mackenzie-Mann deal on railways. Conscription. The War Times Elections Act. Union Government. This would not happen in this war. King stressed that there were issues a-plenty, and he saw Hepburn's resolution as essentially the same in its dire effect on the war effort as Maurice Duplessis' attempt to take Quebec out of the war. What would Hitler think of the Ontario resolution?[30] A further memo to Pickersgill a week later elaborated on these themes, with the Prime Minister arguing that he had to keep his eye on the main objective: 'namely, the psychological effect of a political campaign in Canada upon the course of the war in Europe... [it was] obviously desirable that I should limit political discussions as much as possible.'[31] King's capacity for finding a moralizing rationalization for his hard-headed political acts was boundless; on this occasion it had to be.

The following day the Cabinet met again, and the Prime Minister revealed a bit more to the ministers, once again stopping short of telling them that dissolution would come soon after Parliament reconvened. On leaving the Council chamber, 'I said au revoir to them all with a smile. Before we meet again announcement of intended dissolution will have been made.'[32] Dissolution was the sole prerogative of the Prime Minister, but Mackenzie King was carrying secrecy to near-absurd lengths. Over the next two days King worked privately on the Speech from the Throne to be used at the opening of the session. On January 25, the day the House was to meet, he wrote that 'I had not awakened this morning with the intention of dissolution today but the feeling has grown in me that this step should be taken at once.' The key moment, King added later, came while he was on his knees beside his bed praying. This 'feeling' required that King remove from the Speech any reference to a bill being introduced to permit the taking of the soldiers' vote overseas—'That would be a promise to the House.'* The Prime Minister then talked with Lapointe and persuaded him that an immediate dissolution was wise. 'I told him this was a matter which I had to decide myself.' Still, King was not entirely certain, although when he thought about the Opposition's reactions he became convinced of the soundness of his plan again. He called Lapointe a second time and 'told him I had now def-

---

*There was some confusion about the armed forces voters, but the way out was unwittingly provided by the Conservative leader in the Senate, Arthur Meighen, who remarked in the upper chamber that the provisions for the military vote could be arranged under the War Measures Act. King Diary, 25 Jan. 1940.

initely made up my mind that it was better to dissolve today. He said there would be an uproar and some protest. I said I would then move the adjournment of the House.' At twenty minutes past twelve King told Lapointe to inform the assembled Cabinet of the plan;[33] at last everything was in readiness.

Stunned consternation resulted when Tweedsmuir read the Speech. Even 'one of the Cabinet Ministers' wives,' the United States Minister reported, 'upon hearing the announcement . . . was apparently stunned by surprise.'[34] She could have been no more surprised than Dr Manion, who had some difficulty in getting the floor to complain that the Prime Minister had pulled 'a political trick. . . . [and was] sneering at the political traditions of Canada and the British Empire.'[35] Manion's complaint seemed entirely justified, and Mackenzie King's move was more clever than fair. King did not agree, of course. A few days before dissolution he had written in the diary that 'Nothing hurts me more than when the situation becomes personal and one's own position becomes misrepresented. That, of course, is the hardest cross to be borne in public life. It was the cross of all others, that Christ himself had to bear.'[36] To bear the cross was one thing but to drop it for the sword was another. Later King noted that 'The frank, chivalrous and wise thing to do was to announce the Government's intention from the Speech from the Throne, rather than seeking to take the Opposition by surprise by dissolving after political dissension had begun in Parliament itself.' The manner of dissolution was 'a feature to be admired' for the way in which it avoided political battles while the battle was on at the front.[37]

Most distressing about the affair was the way the nation's press reacted to this piece of unabashed trickery. There was almost no outrage, not even from those journals that a few days before had pontificated that the Ontario resolution did not remotely justify an election. The traditionally Tory press, desperately eager to get rid of the Roman Catholic Dr Manion, who was seen by Bay Street and St James Street as radical on economic questions and soft on French Canada, was surprisingly favourable to Mackenzie King. The Montreal *Gazette*, the voice of Montreal finance, observed that 'In the circumstances this exceptional procedure is not without justification. . . . A short campaign and a definite mandate will best serve the interests of the country.' There could be no doubt, in an editorial that failed even to mention Manion's name, that the *Gazette* did not expect that the Conservatives would win this 'definite mandate'.[38] King clearly had been helped by the simple fact that, as the American Minister noted in a despatch to Washington, the Hepburn-

Drew assault 'has not struck a very responsive chord throughout Canada. In fact, the very vehemence of this attack has caused a certain amount of resentment and a reaction favorable to the Canadian Cabinet.'[39] Certainly there was support for King's move from within the Liberal Party, one M.P. even telling the Minister that King had the most astute political mind in North America 'next to President Roosevelt'.[40]

The Liberal caucus on the day after dissolution confirmed this view by cheering King to the echo. The Prime Minister explained the reasons for his action and added that 'I thought that the best evidence that we had taken the right step was that all those who were opposed to us were condemning us for having taken it.' King went on to say that 'I would expect every man to be one hundred per cent loyal to myself and the ministry. There could be no other than Mackenzie King Liberals as candidates who would be recognized as such,' and any who did not choose to run on this basis should leave the caucus at once. None of the M.P.s moved, and King was gratified. No one, he wrote, ever 'had a parliamentary following more completely one hundred per cent behind him than I had this morning within the period of some twenty hours after I must have occasioned disappointment in the breast of every single member.' The Prime Minister told his Members of Parliament that the election would probably come on March 26 and that 'the chances were most of them would be back in the month of May and would get the indemnity that they had been looking for this year.'[41]

The Cabinet meanwhile was bolstering its political defences. On January 23 King had brought up the matter of the despatch of another infantry division overseas. 'I got unanimous agreement to say that the Second Division was being drawn for overseas service, the time of despatch depending on circumstances.' Such a move would help to convince the country that Canada was doing its utmost. Indeed Ralston, Lapointe, and Power 'wondered whether we should not say that our financial advisers were of the opinion that Canada could not stand more than what we were doing. I pointed out,' King answered, 'that that was one of the strongest reasons for an election. That there were things we could say after the election which we could not say on the eve of it.' Colonel Ralston, concerned with his Finance portfolio to the exclusion of everything else, thought that a decision to send a second division 'would be followed by a demand for a third and a fourth, etc. I agreed we can hold to [a promise of a second division] through the campaign. What we will require further later I do not know.'[42]

Another matter of concern to the Prime Minister had to be held over.

In King's view, organized labour had not yet received its due representation on the boards and committees that were beginning to proliferate in Ottawa. In particular, King told his ministers on January 27, labour had to be represented on the War Supply Board, the government's major purchasing agency until the Department of Munitions and Supply began to function in the spring of 1940. The problem, as C. D. Howe, the Minister responsible for the War Supply Board, put it, was that the Chairman of the Board, Wallace Campbell, the President of Ford of Canada, would resign if labour was given representation. 'I said I would prefer to put Labour on the Board,' King noted. 'Howe then explained that there were many millions of dollars in contracts involved, that to have Campbell resign at this moment or during the campaign, would be sure to precipitate a tremendous issue. . . . It seemed clear that politically it would be most unwise to have him leave, seeing he is a close friend of Meighen's', the former Conservative Prime Minister and still Mackenzie King's most feared and despised political opponent. 'Howe said he would be quite agreeable to having him dismissed the day after the campaign as he was a very arbitrary man.'[43] That careful calculation of political advantage was entirely typical of Mackenzie King.

So too was the way he worked to keep his Cabinet intact for the election campaign. Chubby Power, unhappy, talked of resigning. Lapointe was ill, disheartened, and thinking of leaving the government. Euler wanted a seat in the Senate. Not anxious to keep him, King promised Euler one of the first available Senate seats after the election.[44] Power was a different case. 'He said quite frankly he did not like feeling that he was welcome in the Cabinet part of the time doing all sorts of chores and the like, and part of the time, ready to be kicked out, he knew, because of his own behaviour.' Power drank too much, and there were periods when he was completely incapable of carrying on the work of his portfolio. But when sober he was one of the best of ministers, and in addition he was one of the very few members of the Cabinet with an interest in and talent for party organization and the mechanics of electioneering. 'What we could do without Power when it comes to matters of this kind,' King noted, 'I really do not know.'[45] Power had to be cajoled into staying, and he was. Dealing with Lapointe required yet another approach, and King met with his Justice Minister on February 1, with Colonel Ralston in attendance. The problems with the other ministers were thoroughly canvassed, and King led the discussion inevitably to the point that, as he recorded, 'We all finally came to the conclusion that we should seek to keep the Cabinet intact until the campaign was over.'[46]

Clearly no one feared that the government would be turned out. Neither was there any hope, at least in the Prime Minister's mind, of a sweep. Mackenzie King told the Governor General on January 27 that 'We would pull our own in the Maritimes and in the province of Quebec, and perhaps do better. In B.C., perhaps do better. In Alberta, perhaps do better. In Saskatchewan, not so well. Manitoba, doubtful. We would lose something in the Prairies. Gain in Quebec. Would probably lose several seats in Ontario. . . . we might lose 40 seats, but more probably 30.' Later in the conversation King revised his estimate of losses downwards to 20.[47]

King's election estimates were almost always sound, but in this instance he was being too cautious, perhaps overreacting in compensation for the high-handed way he had dissolved Parliament. In fact the government's position was very strong. Blessed with a huge majority from 1935, with some able ministers, a hefty party treasury and, in spite of his constant grumping, an efficient organization, King and the Liberals were certain of victory. The only way the election could be lost would be if gross errors were made in the campaign or if the war in Europe took a sudden and catastrophic turn for the worse. The war was out of King's hands, but mistakes could be prevented, and this was the Prime Minister's task.

The basic thrust of the campaign was laid down in a memorandum prepared on February 1, 1940, probably by Norman Lambert. The key point was that 'Our campaign must have the underlying basis of dignity and calmness suited to the primary fact that the whole nation is seriously engaged in the grim business of war.' The voters should be persuaded to re-elect the King administration because of the 'personal experience, ability and integrity of every member of the Cabinet,' because these men had done a 'strikingly satisfactory job' thus far in the war, and because their peacetime record has 'been of great practical value to Canada'. For puffery this was mild indeed. More frank was the admission that 'we shall blow both hot and cold on the subject of preparedness for war, showing that the Government in its wisdom and foresight did actually make great strides in the matter of preparedness while, at the same time, the Government had to fight against a Canadian public opinion which was definitely antagonistic to anything approaching military preparedness measures.' In a further shrewd judgement, the memorandum noted that 'We shall assume that only in the Province of Ontario does Canada's wartime effort almost completely overshadow all considerations of the normal functions of Government and the peacetime concerns of the people.' Elsewhere 'we assume that the war effort is of primary importance but that public opinion is also interested in the Government's peacetime measures and general policies for economic and social improvement.'[48] That assessment of the mood of the nation seemed accurate. The phoney war, the lack of fighting in Europe, and the suspicion that the belligerents were seeking to deal themselves out of the war inspired no one.

Or almost no one. The Conservative Party was badly divided on a wide range of questions, including the extent to which Canada's war effort should be pressed. But almost inexplicably in the light of his past careful attention to the mood of Quebec, Dr Manion found himself leading his party into the election committed to national government. The idea of coalition had been bruited around for years, sometimes as camouflage for the unification of the Canadian National and Canadian Pacific railroads, sometimes as a scheme to put down obstreperous labour, sometimes more idealistically as a device to bring the best men of the nation to fight the Depression, dictatorship, or other evils. Manion had opposed it earlier and so had King, who saw union government as a conspiracy between Hepburn, Drew, George McCullagh (the publisher of the *Globe and Mail*), and northern Ontario mining interests.[49] But now Manion and his caucus were determined to fight the election on a campaign for a government of the 'best brains' and as an earnest of their intentions the party's name was changed to National Government.[50]

This was a dangerous, even foolish course, for such a campaign inevitably stirred memories of 1917, conscription, and union government. Yet while Quebec had nothing but nightmares about this period, there were undoubtedly many in English Canada who believed conscription was necessary in any war and that only a coalition would or could impose and enforce it. Still, even on the most optimistic of calculations, the Tory chances were slight, something that makes Manion's positive euphoria at the outset of the campaign inexplicable. George Drew, the Ontario Conservative leader, visited him the day after the election was called and found him certain of a sweep and adamant in refusing any alterations in organization or tactics along lines Drew suggested. The result was that Drew returned to Toronto ready to work only for candidates he supported, not for the national campaign. Other Tories took similar attitudes, and before long the Conservative Party's disunity was apparent.[51]

The CCF were in no better shape. While not as openly divided as the Conservatives, the CCF suffered from what its historian has called 'the internal contradictions inherent in the party-movement'.[52] The split between those who had held out for a vote against the war and those who were determined to support the war effort had persisted since September 1939. The uneasy compromise that kept the party together satisfied almost no one in the caucus and probably very few in the country. To support an economic war effort but to oppose the despatch of troops was so obviously a halfway measure, so clearly a compromise, that even the limited public support for the CCF was likely to be shaken.[53]

II

'My present thought,' Mackenzie King wrote about his plans for the campaign, 'is to do nothing during the month of February at least, except broadcasting. Prepare a series of half-hour addresses, to be bound later in book form for the campaign. . . . In March, I might attempt some meetings. . . . I perhaps ought to pay the riding a visit, seeing I have not been there since the last election.'[54] A leisurely way to fight an election, it might seem. But Mackenzie King, after all, was in his 66th year, and his health had not been good in the recent past. Sciatica still bothered him, and he often suffered from pains in the eyes and feelings of generalized weakness.

Worse still, the preparation of speeches drained him completely, as he obsessively revised his texts, keeping careful watch over virtually every word. For his opening radio address of the campaign, scheduled for February 7, fully seven revisions were prepared over five days, all but one by the Prime Minister himself.[55] The starting point, almost invariably, was a long, dictated memorandum, often little more than points to be stressed or countered and intended ordinarily for Pickersgill, who would sketch out the first draft.[56] To flesh out the speech the Prime Minister's office maintained its own ready-reference file, a compendium of newspaper articles, Hansard speeches, pamphlets, and the like, all designed to bolster King's recollections of his record—and of the follies of the Opposition parties.[57]

The party and government record was important to Mackenzie King. The past had to be kept in mind, both so that its errors could be prevented from recurring and so that its glories could be remembered. On the day of his opening speech, King was thinking of Sir Wilfrid Laurier:

> I could not help thinking how strange it was that Sir Wilfrid had worked so hard for reciprocity and had been defeated in his efforts, and that 25 years later I had helped to bring his policies in that particular into their own. After all his efforts to maintain national unity, his life work in that particular seemed destroyed by the divisions which arose in the war and out of national government, and the steps taken then. It looks to me as if now it was going to be given to me to bring Laurier's policies in the matter of national unity into their own and that at a time of war, by forestalling in advance those steps which have led to the divisions and cleavages under Borden and his way of dealing with national affairs. If I can get the support of this country on a war effort, which is based on national unity . . . that . . . would establish Canada as a nation. . . .[58]

The theme of his radio speech was national unity and the dangers posed to it by the Tories' national-government scheme.

Mackenzie King asked his listeners to consider some questions. Shouldn't the running of the country be entrusted to those with experience? Should control be given to the inexperienced, to those bound by no common policies? Who would be in a Manion national government? What talents would its ministers have? Would there be representation of the two great races in such a government? Those were all good questions, and the Prime Minister hammered home the point when he enunciated the contributions his administration had made to national unity, contributions that could not have been achieved without his securing the consent of Parliament before Canada went to war. Nor could they have come by agreeing to send forces overseas before Parliament accepted participation or by committing Canada to fight in September 1938 at the time of Munich; nor, he added with telling impact, by forming a 'so-called "national" government that might enforce conscription or disfranchise many classes of Canadian citizens.' National government was just union government all over again.

Less convincingly, King also tried to deal with the dissolution of Parliament in this first address. 'It is perfectly true,' he admitted, 'that I have never failed to stress the supremacy of Parliament. But it has been the supremacy of Parliament over the government . . . not the supremacy of Parliament over the people. . . .' Surely no one could assume that the supremacy of Parliament meant 'depriving the people of their right to an early general election. . . .' If so, this 'shows how far some men have drifted in their thinking from any true conception of popular government, and how close they have come to sharing the mentality of dictators.'[59] The Prime Minister was generally pleased with this first broadcast, although as always he worried about his delivery and the fact that he had had to conclude with a rush to get everything into the allotted time.[60]

For the next week King virtually forgot about the election and devoted himself to a death-watch over the Governor General. On February 6 Tweedsmuir had been found unconscious in his bath and his condition worsened quickly until on February 11 he succumbed. King generally had liked Tweedsmuir although he found irritating his emphasis on titles and his penchant for referring to himself and his wife in conversation as His Excellency and Her Excellency. Still, in this difficult period King showed himself at his best, spending endless hours with Lady Tweedsmuir before and after the Governor General's death and even arranging for a floral wreath to be sent to Government House after everyone else had forgotten it. On February 11 Mackenzie King declared a unilateral political truce as a tribute, barring campaign speeches by Liberal ministers. The truce had to be unilateral as Dr Manion refused to go along with it, and the Tory leader annoyed King further by insisting on reading a tribute to Tweedsmuir over the radio in both French and English. This increased Manion's allotted time, and clearly the Prime Minister felt this was politicking. 'Perfectly horrible,' he noted with disgust.[61]

In fact, Manion was getting on Mackenzie King's nerves. 'I can forgive him much,' King noted on February 9, 'but I will never forget his saying at Brockville I felt an hereditary right in responsible government for which my ancestor had fought. . . . It was on a par with his remark concerning myself that he thought Mitch was right.' It was all typically 'low Irish' and Manion would 'learn a lesson in this campaign which he will never forget, and which it is pretty certain will end his public life. He will find his own political friends less sympathising with him or willing to do for him, than I myself had been.'[62] There was a terrible prescience in those comments.* In any case King showed no hesitation in tackling the Conservative leader head on, and in a radio

*After Manion was dumped as Tory leader he came to see King for a job and was made Director of Air Raid Precautions. At his funeral, as King observed, there were more Liberals present and participating than Conservatives. King Diary, 5 July 1943.

speech on February 23 he hammered the national-government issue yet again. Norman Rogers declared the speech 'devastating' and Arnold Heeney, King's principal secretary and soon to become secretary to the Cabinet, pronounced it 'shattering'. 'My own feeling,' King noted, 'is that the broadcast has completely destroyed Manion's appeal on the score of union government.' Then, reflecting again on poor Manion, the Prime Minister noted that his 'generalship has been as bad as it can be. He has left the ground of his own party to go on to strange and unknown territory, to form alliances with those who were his political enemies, who will not join with him. . . . I am sure it means, not only a humiliating defeat of his party, but the end of his leadership.'[63]

King was right, even though his repeated use of a sledgehammer to kill a mosquito should have aroused some sympathetic impulses among the electorate. Manion's national-government ship had rapidly foundered, and he could never answer the repeated Liberal demands that he name his proposed Cabinet. He was hampered further by flat pledges from the CCF leader, J. S. Woodsworth, and from the Prime Minister that none of their followers would join any national government.[64] But curiously, Manion seemed blissfully unaware of the perilous state of his campaign, and even well into February he still looked for victory.[65]

Manion expected 15 to 20 seats in Quebec, 'a tribute', Grant Dexter of the *Winnipeg Free Press* privately noted, 'to his capacity for self-delusion'.[66] Much more accurate were the Liberal assessments, which as early as February 8 put a rock-bottom figure of 50 seats as certain in the province. The Liberal organizer in the province told Dexter that they just might win 63 seats, or all except the seats held in English Montreal by two old Tories thought to be immune to every defeat but death. The only hope for the Tories was Camillien Houde, the Mayor of Montreal, who, if he became their leader and if he received about $20,000 for each constituency, might be able to win them some seats. Even this was unlikely, however,[67] for the Liberals had powerful weapons at hand. On February 22, for example, Ernest Lapointe compared the way French Canadians were being treated by his government with the way they had been maligned in the Great War years. The government had appointed a bilingual Canadian as Roman Catholic chaplain to the army and he had a French-Canadian deputy. 'Demandez aux autorités religieuses la différence entre ce système et celui qui existait pendant la Grande Guerre . . .'[68] The Province of Quebec, *La Presse* said with satisfaction, has reason to be pleased with the policies of the King government.[69] In another address Lapointe dealt with conscription, in Quebec as elsewhere a major issue. 'Le maintien de l'unité canadienne exige que notre effort militaire soit et reste volon-taire,' he said.[70] The Justice Minister was believed, too, when he said this, even by ordinarily suspicious isolationist Liberals.[71] Had he not pledged himself against conscription in March 1939 and in the war session of Parliament? Had Mackenzie King not said the same thing? Had Lapointe and his colleagues not promised to resign if conscription ever came about? The Liberals were against compulsory service overseas, and there could be little doubt of that.

The Conservatives' position was much less clear in the public mind. Dr Manion had come out against conscription in March 1939, even stealing a march of one day on the Liberals. During the election he repeated his pledges again and again, but without convincing anyone. Unfortunately in his autobiography, *Life is an Adventure*, written before he became party leader, Manion had stated his belief in conscription as the best and fairest way to raise men for war.[72] His party was full of Union Government veterans of the last war, all apparently still conscrip-tionist to the core, and all eager to demonstrate that conscription had not been an error in 1917. But Canada did not want conscription, not yet. Everywhere he went, Manion said after the election, Conservative candidates insisted that he repeat his opposition to compulsion.[73] Ground between the millstones of his party's past and his own, Manion had no chance.

Worse yet, no one seemed to take Manion seriously. The American Minister reported that the Doctor 'has a considerable amount of force-fulness,' but people throughout Canada 'generally regard him as somewhat too volatile and unstable in character, as not inspiring that degree of public confidence which should be demanded of a great leader in times of war.'[74] The British High Commissioner took a similar view, although Sir Gerald Campbell clearly felt Canadians faced a Hobson's choice in this election. 'Mr. King is unsatisfactory in the eyes of many people as a prospective war leader, but Mr. Manion is regarded as an even more unsatisfactory alternative.'[75] This latter view was generally confirmed when Manion began slinging epithets with abandon, attacking Norman Rogers as an 'irresponsible little falsifier . . . [an] unscrupulous little man' marked by 'his unfitness for office and by his contempt for the truth.'[76] That probably hurt him, and his wobbliness on conscription left him peculiarly vulnerable when Mackenzie King attacked him for leaving 'a peace promise' behind him everywhere he spoke. 'At no place,' the Prime Minister said, clearly enjoying the reversal of roles, 'has he enunciated a war policy. . . . Nearly every promise has been designed to influence unduly the community in which it has been made. Nearly every promise has been a promise to spend the taxpayer's money . . . or something which has nothing to do with the winning of the war . . .'[77]

Mackenzie King himself launched a brief Western swing at the end of February. On the 27th he spoke at Winnipeg at a great meeting, so warm that he noted in his diary that 'On every side today, I received evidences of a sweep. Manion is making a buffoon of himself. . . . I really believe that we are witnessing pretty much the extinction of the Conservative Party.'[78] At Prince Albert, his own constituency, he again met enthusiasm, something that rather surprised Mackenzie King who felt a mite guilty that this was his first visit to the riding since 1935.[79] The Prime Minister spoke to his constituents for a full two hours, the lengthy nature of his remarks being the single greatest flaw from which he suffered as an orator. In fact, according to observers, King was a 'very effective speaker on the hustings', a man who could 'bring the house down', particularly when he stuck to general subjects. Certainly Liberal Members and candidates were anxious to have him come to their areas to speak, a good indication of the value attached to Mackenzie King's coat-tails at election time.[80]

The Prime Minister no longer had any doubts about the outcome of the election after his Western trip. On March 1 in the midst of some general musings he noted that 'the major portion of the campaign is now over' and that his task now was to 'reserve my strength meanwhile for the task which will follow immediately thereafter'. In his mind the election victory he so confidently predicted would rank with Abraham Lincoln's in 1864, for Lincoln too had carried a democratic government to victory in the midst of a war. King's obsession with anniversaries and coincidences led him to note, as well, that it had been on March 1 that he had moved the dissolution of Parliament in 1921, a move that in his view had become the basis of the election campaign in that year. 'In 1925 made request for dissolution, the one refused by Lord Byng and which became the basis of the Liberal victory scored at that time. The campaign of today is based on the dissolution of January 25th and the grounds for it. All three,' King concluded, 'represent trust in the people and determination to maintain their fundamental rights in matters of government.'[81]

King's final major meetings took place in Montreal and Toronto. Both were great successes, particularly the Toronto meeting, highlighted by the appearance of Harry Nixon, a key member of Hepburn's cabinet who had resigned a few days earlier and then re-joined the provincial government. Mackenzie King was gratified at this support—'His manner, speech and all was really heroic'—and incensed at those members of Hepburn's cabinet who avoided the Toronto meeting. 'They will suffer for it all their lives,' he wrote. 'Their names in the history of the party and in the country's history will always have a question mark after them.'[82] Party loyalty at election times was a cardinal virtue for Mackenzie King, and he could even overlook Nixon's vacillation in grateful thanks for it.

But Hepburn's perfidy had had its effects on the party organization in Toronto. 'It is lamentable what lack of organization there has been in Ontario,' King noted. 'I am afraid it is going to cost us several seats. . . . the whole blame should be placed on Hepburn's shoulders. He has kept control of organization funds and machinery in his hands, and a completely new organization had to be set up by inexperienced men.'[83] The Prime Minister worried that party literature was 'devoid of anything broadly constructive and effective,'[84] and he felt frustrated and annoyed. But then poor organization was one of his perennial complaints, and King foresaw a majority of from 50 to 70 seats.[85] The organization that could produce that kind of optimism could hardly be so inadequate.

Nor was it, as the results of the election so clearly indicated. The King government was returned with 181 seats while the Conservatives lost their leader and won only 40, the CCF 8, Social Credit 10, and independents and others 6 seats. King had a majority of 117 over the combined Opposition, the largest ever to that point, and for the first time since 1917 a party had won a majority of the popular vote, fully 51.5 per cent.[86] In Quebec the government won 63.3 per cent of the popular vote and all but one of the provinces's 65 seats, a stunning proof of the effectiveness of Liberalism's hold on French Canada. Even more striking, in English Montreal the vote went heavily Liberal as well. Brooke Claxton, elected for his first time in the downtown seat of St Lawrence-St George, calculated that he received 58.4 per cent of the French-speaking vote and 56.9 per cent of the English-speaking vote.[87] D. C. Abbott, a classmate of Claxton's and like him a lawyer, won St Antoine-Westmount in Montreal, even carrying the Tory bastion of Westmount.[88] The disillusionment with Manion and a lingering resentment over the Duplessis election of October 1939 had swung many traditional Conservatives away from their party. The swing was helped by the Hepburn-Drew attacks,[89] and the Liberals took 50.8 per cent of the popular vote in Ontario and 57 of the 82 seats. In the Maritimes King won all but 7 of the seats, and only in the Prairies and in British Columbia did the government fail to win a majority in the popular vote. Even that did not seriously hurt the Liberals in terms of seats, for the party won 15 of 17 in Manitoba, 12 of 21 in Saskatchewan, 10 of 16 in British Columbia, and 7 of 17 in Alberta, that province still being infatuated with Premier Aberhart to whose Social Credit party it gave ten seats. Canada apparently had voted for stability, for a moderate war effort, for Mackenzie King.

The triumph immensely gratified Mackenzie King, who spent the evening of victory congratulating his ministers on their re-election. However he placed no call to Norman Lambert, the party organizer and fund-raiser whose work had greatly helped to produce the result.[90] Infuriated by this slight, Lambert told Chubby Power that that was it. Never again would he work for the party. Power passed this on to the Prime Minister who belatedly called Lambert on March 29 and invited him for lunch a few days later. The Senator was not particularly mollified, but King was more than a little annoyed at the organizer's attitude. 'I felt a little nettled at the unreasonableness of this attitude,' he grumbled. 'After all, it was their place to ring me up and congratulate me. It was scarcely mine, as Prime Minister, to be the first to congratulate them, though, naturally, they were in my thoughts for a word of very sincere thanks.'[91] If Mackenzie King was unloved by his subordinates, he had only himself to blame.

Mackenzie King was also unloved at the Foreign Office in London. There the election result was attributed to Manion's weaknesses and to the snap dissolution that had prevented Canadians from learning the true state of affairs with respect to the war effort. The result meant four things, one officer who had just returned from Canada, wrote:

(a) [King] himself—and in these matters he is largely the Government —will continue to remain lukewarm about any war measures which he cannot show to redound to Canada's own advantage.

(b) he will be as careful as possible, however, to refrain from letting any such lukewarmness become apparent: for if it did, it is still true that he would be thrown out at once.

(c) he will expect to be informed but in many cases preferably not *consulted* about war measures.

(d) on the other hand, he will very definitely expect to be *consulted* about anything bearing upon an eventual peace.*[92]

There were some shrewd comments in that minute, but the bitterness it displayed did not bode well for the future.

III

The future very soon would seem uncertain and perilous. In April Hitler seized Denmark and launched a daring and successful invasion of Norway. The next month, on May 10, the *Wehrmacht* assaulted Belgium, the Netherlands, and Luxembourg, and burst into France through the allegedly impassable and lightly defended Ardennes. The phoney war had ended.

In Ottawa, however, Mackenzie King's first thoughts after the election were to get away to the American south for a vacation and rest. The election had been a strain, and there were so many problems at hand. In Cabinet on April 2, for example, the Defence Minister and the Finance Minister had squared off on the question of consolidating the two infantry divisions—one still in Canada, one already overseas—into a corps, and King had supported Norman Rogers. 'Rogers,' he wrote later, 'fought violently for a Corps, asserting he thought he could maintain the stand of two divisions, whereas if this were not done we might have a third division on our hands. More than that he felt it might not be possible to raise voluntarily.' Ralston had resisted on financial grounds, but King had swung the discussion by arguing that Canadians wanted a corps and that this was owed to General McNaughton. The next day when the matter was settled on an interim basis, King again played a major role, although this time he also noted that it would have been better if Canada could have avoided an expeditionary force altogether.[93]

*The U.K. was anxious to consult Canada at the end of February 1940 about the neutrality problems that were arising with Norway. King learned of this in Winnipeg and talked with Lapointe and Crerar. 'We all took the view that we should not make any observations, to make it clear that it would be necessary to have Cabinet as a whole to consult with before expressing an opinion; also, that we are in a campaign and it would be inadvisable to have anything said about the Dominion attitude at this time which could be avoided.... Moreover, though we did not put this into the despatch, we all felt that, while Canada was at the side of Britain and France with our war effort and, particularly, as the matter referred to was distinctly a European one, it should be kept as between France and Britain themselves.' King Diary, 27 Feb. 1940.

The Prime Minister made much the same point after his return to Ottawa from his rest in Virginia and a visit with President Roosevelt. Britain had asked Canada to send troops to the West Indies. 'It will likely be opposed by Ralston and others,' King wrote in his diary on May 8, 'but I think it is better we should meet necessary requests of this kind and send men out there instead of having to meet pressure of sending others overseas. Let us watch the North American cause.'[94] Within two days, every eye was fixed on Europe's tragedy.

The one solace for Mackenzie King was that he had got the election out of the way before the German offensive. But now Parliament was set to meet for the new session on May 16, and the Conservatives could be expected to respond to aroused English-Canadian public opinion by aggressively pressing for coalition, for conscription, and for a greatly expanded war effort. The Tories' first chore had been to dump Manion rather unceremoniously and to select as leader in his place R. B. Hanson, a Fredericton lawyer. Slow and ponderous, Hanson led a caucus that was thin in able men, but there could be no doubt that in its demands for more action the Conservative Party was reflecting the sentiment of much of English Canada.[95]

Mackenzie King might be a satisfactory leader in peacetime, the Tories argued (something they would never have admitted previously), but certainly he was unable to meet the requirements posed by war. 'In this dreadful hour of crisis,' Colonel Alan Cockeram, the M.P. for York South, Ontario, intoned, 'when the very existence of everything we hold dear, hangs by a thread, I solemnly implore the Prime Minister, for the good of his country, to emulate the example of Mr. Chamberlain, who, with much less reason to do so than he has, resigned his office in the interest of sustaining public confidence in the ability and determination of the government to carry the war to a successful conclusion.'[96] Even in times of crisis the Tory vision of the world forbade criticism of England's leaders, no matter how inept and bumbling they might be.

The force of this and similar attacks mildly shook King, still basking in the triumph of March 26. He told the Cabinet on May 29 that elements in the country were trying to install J. L. Ralston, the Minister of Finance, as Prime Minister in his place. There were several reasons for this, King argued.

That they believed that Ralston being an ex-soldier would probably come to favour conscription, which was what they also wanted, and being associated with big business interests would work with them.

That they did not know Ralston who was incapable of sharing in views of the kind.[97]

But no one rose in Parliament to defend King against the attacks, and the next day King again recorded his worries. 'Each day,' he noted, 'brings us nearer the attack upon Britain which is liable to produce any kind of reaction in this country. It is going to be a terrific job of holding Canada together.' King added that 'I have remained perfectly calm. Have said nothing whatever in the H. of C. nor over the radio. Have just been too busy. . . . Besides,' he noted with an unusual stoicism, 'I have been determined to have my own men recognize that they must make the fight if they want to keep me as their leader. . . . They don't know the source from which their power has come, or the instruments to which they owe it.'[98] That day, however, the Minister of Agriculture, J. G. Gardiner, rose in the House and lambasted the Conservatives, accusing them of following 'the usual route taken by men who want to seek a way in by the back door.' There was considerable truth in that, and Gardiner went on to deliver a rousing defence of Mackenzie King. The group that sits behind him in the House, the Minister stated, 'is more national in its constitution and spirit . . . than any other government that could be created by any other person anywhere in the Dominion of Canada. . . . there is no man in Canada who can more effectively unite all the forces of this country' than the present Prime Minister.[99] That speech drew from the M.P.s 'quite the loudest demonstration in forty years,' or so Charlie Bishop* reported in the Ottawa *Citizen* on May 31.[100]

This speech pleased King immensely, but the next day he raised with Cabinet the possibility of bringing some businessmen onto a national security and defence committee. The ministers were not too keen on this idea, the Prime Minister noted, and there were 'very strong and sensible statements by both Gardiner and Cardin as to the folly of trying to please people that are opposed to us by bringing their friends into the government. Also that there was no greater folly than the limited horizon and capacity of many of the plutocrats, once, as members of boards of directors, they were divested of anything other than their money which gave them a seat at the table.' This satisfied King for the time being. 'I said I looked to Council and the party . . . to strike the serpent on the

---

*Bishop was not the most impartial of observers, and he had been passing tales of plots and conspiracies to King in the last few days. He was eventually rewarded with a Senate seat in April 1945.

head every time it is raised.'[101] For a time at least the national-government snake in the grass disappeared.

Another issue, conscription, was coming very much into view again as the front in France and the Low Countries deteriorated and finally collapsed. Just prior to the German invasion, M. J. Coldwell of the CCF could argue without fear of contradiction that people were opposed to compulsory service.[102] But a week later Hanson of the Conservatives could write in answer to an appeal that he and his party press for conscription that 'I have your stirring letter. . . . I have read and re-read it.'[103] The Canadian Legion, always ready to demand compulsory service, assailed the government in the sharpest possible terms for its bungling of the war effort. What was needed, the Legion leaders argued, were immediate steps to conscript the total manpower, industry, and wealth of the country.[104] Telegrams were soon beginning to come to the Prime Minister's Office demanding action.[105]

Characteristically King was cautious and wary. He announced a series of measures to accelerate the war effort, including an early despatch of the Second Division overseas and the formation of a corps in the field.[106] He persuaded the Cabinet to send a forestry battalion and railway construction engineers to Britain, and additional infantry to Iceland and the West Indies. But now King was realistically beginning to consider what might happen if Britain was knocked out of the war, for he stressed 'strongly the need of keeping our own defences strong; possible danger arising later on. Pointed out that up to a few weeks ago, our thoughts were all with respect to co-operation overseas. Today we would have to turn them into possibilities of internal troubles to be dealt with in Canada.'[107]

When he received word that the British had implemented a series of sweeping measures to control people, property, and almost every aspect of life, this too disturbed him. 'I saw clearly that instant demand would be made for similar so-called national service in Canada,' he recorded on May 22. 'I told my colleagues we might easily see the party divided into conscriptionists and non-conscriptionists. . . . That I certainly would resign before I would accept any move in the direction of conscription.'[108] The next day King learned that the First Canadian Division in England was being sent to France. 'I confess I began to feel a deep sadness as I thought of what this was certain to mean. In the light of developments as they are taking place, it was like sending our men into a fiery furnace to be devoured in whole, almost in their first encounter.'[109] This melancholy event, coupled with British telegrams seeking all possible aid from Canada, led King to mourn that the whole situation between Canada and Britain was now reversed. 'They had assured us they would be in a position to help us. It is really appalling how completely masses of people have miscalculated Germany's strength and been satisfied that they, of course, must win.' The British had promised to supply aircraft for the BCATP, he observed. 'Did not wish us to start a factory of our own for later production. Told us of great surplus they had, etc. Now they are in danger of having their own plants bombed. . . . They are behind in everything. It is an appalling day for Britain when she has to seek from one of her Dominions ships, ammunition, aircraft, additional land forces, etc.'[110] Worse yet, Canada had almost nothing to give.

Financial limitations still constrained what little Canada could offer. King told caucus on May 23 that he feared to announce that Canada's war effort would cost more than $1 billion a year. 'That we had to consider whether that would not occasion a run on the banks. The Governor of the Bank of Canada and officials there were fearful of just something of the kind which might create a very serious internal situation.'[111] Equally, Ralston was still keeping a tight watch on the money. 'I felt the only way to get Ralston to loosen up on the treasury was to let him know the inside information as I had it.' The Finance minister was 'well nigh stunned'[112] by the desperate nature of the Anglo-French position in France, and soon he was extending far greater financial assistance to Britain. 'These days,' he wrote to Graham Towers, 'we have to, and should, take chances.'[113]

At the same time Mackenzie King demanded that the British give Canadian firms some orders. A telegram from King to Prime Minister Churchill on May 18[114] drew only a non-committal reply that led King to escalate his language: '. . . I must express to you the sincere regret that is felt not less by the Canadian people than by my colleagues and myself that the resources and industry of Canada are not being afforded an opportunity to make anything like their full contribution to Britain's war programme, and that the authorities responsible for British purchases have not recognized the potential capacity of our industry to produce munitions.' That was certainly true, for the estimates of total British orders for munitions and supplies were still very low, only some $90 million.[115] King also hit out at the inefficiencies: 'Methods for United Kingdom purchases in Canada have been slow and cumbersome and are entirely inconsistent with conditions of today.'[116] The Prime Minister told a Canadian Manufacturers Association delegation the same thing on June 6. The delays in orders were caused by the 'British seeking to keep the contracts in their own hands.' And, he added, it was 'very clear from the experience of all, that the British Mission here . . . were real stumbling blocks. That the Treasury in London were responsible for delays, etc.'[117]

These representations to London had their effect in the new war situation, and on June 16 the British decided to divide their North American purchasing operations into two separate bodies, one in Canada and one in the United States. Most important, London agreed that its representatives should deal directly with the Department of Munitions and Supply in Ottawa, which would co-ordinate production. Considerations of price were largely shelved and the Canadian government essentially agreed to use its own judgement subject to an undertaking to absorb excess costs above agreed fair prices.[118] The Finance Department, too, agreed to accumulate sterling—in other words to absorb Britain's trade deficit with Canada—above the agreed upon limits.[119] The war of limited liability in the financial sphere had ended.

It was beginning to draw to an end militarily, as well. In caucus on June 5 Arthur Slaght, the Parry Sound, Ontario M.P. who was much too friendly with Mitch Hepburn for King's liking, suggested a national registration. Ernest Lapointe scotched this idea by noting the effects such a step, a precursor of conscription in the Great War, would have in Quebec.[120] But the idea was catching hold, as was the growing belief that with Britain in danger of being destroyed Canada was in danger of attack. 'Why send men overseas when they would be unarmed there?', M. J. Coldwell wrote a correspondent. 'Let them be trained and organized in Canada to defend North America.'[121] King, too, worried that 'an effort will be made to seize this country as a prize of war. We have, therefore, changed now to the stage where defence of this land becomes our most important duty.'[122] These defensive thoughts were recorded on June 16, the day France capitulated. Canada had become Britain's ranking ally.

The next day R. B. Hanson came to see King with three aims in mind: a national emergency should be declared; King should pass legislation putting at the disposal of the state all the manpower and material resources of the country; and a national government should be created to carry through these measures.[123] The Prime Minister was not particularly forthcoming to the Conservative leader, but when he went to the War Committee that night he found to his surprise that both Lapointe and Power had agreed 'that we should have a measure that would enable us to call out every man in Canada for military training for the defence of Canada.' King wrote that 'it was a relief to my mind, in that it amounts to what is right in the matter of mobilization of all resources.'[124]

King drafted the bill subsequently known as the National Resources Mobilization Act on June 18, and introduced it in the House of Commons that afternoon. The bill, he said, would 'confer upon the government special emergency powers to mobilize all our human and material resources for the defence of Canada.' For manpower, he hastened to reassure Quebec, 'it will relate solely and exclusively to the defence of Canada on our own soil and in our own territorial waters. It will enable the government to make the utmost efficient use of our manpower for the various needs of modern machine warfare. . . . The armed forces are only a part of the essential equipment of war. The skilled worker in the factory, the transport worker and the farmer . . . are as essential to the effective prosecution of the war . . .' King added that under the provisions of the bill, the government would have the power 'equally to call property and wealth, material resources and industry to the defence of Canada.' Once again the Prime Minister reiterated his pledges against conscription: 'no measure for the conscription of men for overseas service will be introduced by the present administration.' But a complete inventory of manpower was essential and a national registration would be taken as soon as possible. 'Let me emphasize the fact that this registration will have nothing whatsoever to do with the recruitment of men for overseas service.'[125]

Despite this unequivocal assurance from the Prime Minister, Quebec M.P.s in Ottawa and M.L.A.s in the legislature at Quebec City wobbled badly. The proposed bill seemed to be the first step to full conscription; a repetition of the Great War when registration had preceded the Military Service Act; and a first stage in dismantling the pledges made by King and Lapointe to Quebec. Certainly it was not the limited-liability war that had been promised the country September last. Half a dozen Members spoke against the bill with no real effect, King wrote that night; 'as Lapointe and I had taken our stand so strongly on no conscription overseas, and were prepared to give further assurances in that direction, we were able to keep our party steady.'[126] The NRMA passed into law on June 21. 'No one,' King wrote, 'will ever be able to say what service Lapointe and Cardin and Power have rendered in that Province, and what it has meant to Canada having a Liberal Government in office at this time.'[127]

That was partisan but true. Had a Conservative government proposed the NRMA, the reaction of French Canadians would have been much sharper. And certainly the pledges and promises of the Quebec ministers had had an enormous impact in assuaging Quebec's concerns. Still the extent of the concern that persisted despite the assurances is striking. The mistrust and fear of English Canada, of the federal government, was strong. But so too was the misunderstanding of the import of the events that were taking place in Europe. For the first time the fortunes of war posed a threat to Canada and Canadian interests, and there was every reason to prepare. In a sense, that Mackenzie King's government held back as much as it did that June was an indication of the Liberal party's sensitivity to the concerns of Quebec.

Mackenzie King had deliberately framed the National Resources Mobilization Act in the broadest of terms. Only section 3, which stated that the powers conferred on the government 'may not be exercised for the purpose of requiring persons to serve in the military, naval or air forces outside of Canada and the territorial waters thereof,'[128] was explicit. This was a fateful clause that would twice nearly bring down the King government before the war was over. But should the NRMA be limited only to military manpower? Some observers, and O. D. Skelton, the Under Secretary of State for External Affairs, was one, thought that the impression that the bill 'is merely old-fashioned conscription' should be corrected. 'I think it was made clear,' Skelton wrote to Mackenzie King, 'that the mobilization is intended to provide men for all kinds of war work of which service in the military forces is only one . . .'[129] Significantly, perhaps, even when casting his mind about, Skelton did not see the act being used for more than manpower purposes. There would be no conscription of wealth under the NRMA, no organization of industry. The King government would use the bill only for the mobilization of men.[130]

Parliament created a new department of government to administer the NRMA. The Department of National War Services came into existence on July 12 with James Gardiner, the Minister of Agriculture, holding the portfolio in addition to his primary responsibilities. Gardiner had been selected for the job on June 28 and the Saskatchewan minister began drafting the legislation to create the department immediately. Mackenzie King and Gardiner talked about the draft on July 3 and King was disturbed by Gardiner's plans for National War Services. 'He has drafted a measure which would make him almost as powerful as Hitler. I indicated wherein it will have to be considerably modified.'[131] The changes were duly made, and Gardiner set about his first chore—running the national registration.

The registration was held on August 19, 20, and 21 with the help of voluntary workers and by using the constituency and poll organizations that had served in the election of March 1940. All persons, male and female, over the age of 16 were obliged to register on forms distressingly similar to those employed in the national registration of the Great War. A special form was provided for single men between the ages of 19 and 45. The nearly 8 million cards went to the Dominion Bureau of Statistics where, among other things, researchers were surprised to discover the number of bank clerks and junior employees who had married secretly to avoid the wrath of their employers. Earlier, Gardiner announced that only those married before July 15 would be considered as married men in terms of the Act, and there had been a race to the altar in early July. Still, the registration showed 802,458 single men and childless widowers between the ages of 21 and 45.[132] Under P.C. 4185, these men became liable for military service as of August 27, 1940.

The solitary major event that marred the registration was a speech by the Mayor of Montreal, the ebullient and corpulent Camillien Houde. On August 2 the Mayor urged French Canadians not to register:

> I declare myself peremptorily against national registration. It is un-equivocally a measure of conscription, and the government recently elected, last March, declared through the mouths of all its political chieftains, from Prime Minister Mackenzie King to Premier Adelard Godbout of Quebec, and not excluding Messieurs Lapointe and Cardin, that there would be no conscription under any form whatso-ever. . . . Parliament, according to my belief, has no mandate to vote conscription. I do not myself believe that I am held to conform to the said law, and I have no intention of so doing, knowing full well what I am doing presently and to what I expose myself. If the government wants a mandate for conscription let it come before the people without this time fooling them.[133]

If Houde had expected to be hailed for his defiance of Ottawa, he was disappointed. The response in Quebec was muted to say the least, in part because Ottawa tried and largely succeeded in censoring the Mayor's remarks, and in part because the Mayor was promptly pitched into an internment camp where he stayed for four years.*[134] Extraordinarily, these draconian measures met with acceptance in Quebec, and almost no one tried to make a martyr out of Houde. Even *Le Devoir* said that he had acted the fool and received what he deserved,[135] and a *nationaliste*-circulated petition of support for the Mayor produced little response. Quebec really was prepared to accept home-defence conscription, and the American Minister, the able Pierrepont Moffat, attributed this to 'how much the Government here had learned from the mistakes of the past and how different was the spirit throughout Quebec during the present war.'[136]

The first home-defence conscripts reported for service on October 9, 30,000 strong. The term of service was only for thirty days, and the intent was to train 240,000 men in the first year. Of course thirty days' training was of little value militarily, and many of the officers running the camps saw their purpose as showing the conscripts a pleasant time and destroying the legends engendered after 'twenty years of pacifist debauchery'.[137] Worse, both instructors and equipment were in short supply. The Chief of the General Staff, General H. D. G. Crerar, later noted that 'Thirty days' training was all I wanted, initially, because all we could train with were U.S. rifles of last war vintage—and no ammunition!'[138] In fact Crerar was pressing for a more realistic scheme of four months' training even before the first NRMA men reached camp in October.[139] Others expressed similar views, including Gardiner who

*The Cabinet was united on the need for action and agreed that if the Mayor was given a day in court he would use it to 'speechify'. In these circumstances 'It was felt that if he were interned at once that would deprive him of this opportunity and would be most helpful in the end.' The RCMP was told to take him at night 'as there would be no opportunity for photograph displays, etc.' (King Diary, 3 Aug. 1940.) The arrest of Houde was by no means the worst of Ottawa's attempts to muzzle free speech and throttle dissent in the first year of the war. In October 1939 several Italian anti-fascists were arrested in Toronto on trumped-up charges, and one was held in jail until the following spring. In June 1940 the Communist party was banned at the same time as action was finally taken against fascist movements. Most shocking of all, the next month the Jehovah's Witnesses were proscribed, membership in this religious organization thus becoming a crime against the state. The suspicion existed and still exists that the Witnesses were banned because of pressure from the Roman Catholic hierarchy in Quebec. On civil liberties, see Ramsay Cook, 'Canadian Liberalism in Wartime: A Study of the Defence of Canada Regulations and Some Canadian Attitudes to Civil Liberties in Wartime, 1939-1945', M.A. thesis, Queen's University, 1955; M. J. Penton, 'The World War II Suppression of Jehovah's Witnesses in Canada: A Catholic Heresy Hunt?', a paper presented to the Canadian Historical Association meetings, June 1973; *Canadian Forum*, XIX (December, 1939); and the RCMP pamphlet, *Law and Order in Canadian Democracy* (Ottawa, 1949), esp. chapters XIII-XIV.

argued that putting men into industry was far more important than creating half-trained soldiers.[140] In the Senate Arthur Meighen constantly reiterated that there was no point in defending Canada for Canada's only defence was in Britain. There was, the former Prime Minister argued, a flaw in the logic of 'a contention that compulsion is not necessary to get men to fight outside this country but that we must apply compulsion to get men to fight inside their own domain.' Later he attacked the NRMA scheme as a 'colossal waste' that would produce nothing except 'half-trained . . . hothouse soldiers'.[141]

These partly justifiable criticisms had their effect, and by the end of October there was virtual agreement in Cabinet that the NRMA term should be extended to four months.[142] The final decision was made on January 28, 1941 and announced on February 20.[143] Two months later the government moved to keep the NRMA men on service for the duration of the war, thus freeing volunteers for service overseas.[144] Canada had two armies now, one for service in Canada and one for service overseas.

IV

The pressure of events meanwhile had forced Mackenzie King to consider changes in the Cabinet. There had been the attacks in the House of Commons in May and the demands for a 'war' prime minister, there had been calls for national government and for the inclusion of men of talent in the ministry. But King had shrugged most of this off, as well he might given the size of his majority. Still, the Cabinet was not too strong and some changes were necessary.

Several shifts had been made even before the new Parliament met on May 16. In April Mackenzie King put C. D. Howe in charge of the newly established Department of Munitions and Supply, and although Howe retained his Transport portfolio into July, this man of toughness and business savvy was very much in charge of the government's production and procurement programs. On May 9 J. A. MacKinnon, an Edmonton businessman who had been Minister Without Portfolio, succeeded W. D. Euler as Minister of Trade and Commerce. Although he had earlier importuned the Prime Minister for a Senate seat, Euler resisted his translation to the upper chamber and King was disgusted: 'His whole point of view was purely Euler and what would suit his convenience. I told him I needed a portfolio for MacKinnon and intended to make him Minister of Trade and Commerce.'[145] If King was tough in disposing of the stubborn Euler, he later regretted his weak surrender in elevating Pierre Casgrain, Speaker of the House from 1936, to the Cabinet as Secretary of State. The understanding was that Casgrain would be in the Cabinet only for a short time and would then go to his reward in the Senate or on the bench and, as King told his colleagues, Casgrain's elevation was a reward for his loyalty and that of his wife Thérèse. King was clearly far more impressed with Mme Casgrain— 'the ability lies with her'—but when the time came to dispose of her husband in December 1941 he would deal toughly with her.[146]

King's next appointment was more successful. The work of the Department of National Defence had multiplied, and Rogers had all he could do to cope. To give the administration of the air force and the British Commonwealth Air Training Plan to another minister was sensible, and King had the inspired notion of putting Chubby Power in charge. In spite of his weaknesses Power had more ability than most Cabinet ministers, and he proved an extremely successful Minister of National Defence (Air). The one difficulty was the muddy lines of responsibility in Defence. If both Rogers and Power were present, Rogers was *primus inter pares*; if Rogers was away, then Power was Acting Minister of National Defence; but only Power could speak for the air force.[147]

The Cabinet was weakened on June 10 when Norman Rogers was killed in an air crash. This was a shattering blow to Mackenzie King, who was closer to Rogers than to anyone else in the Cabinet with the possible exception of Lapointe. It was made worse by King's assuming the duty of breaking the news personally to Mrs Rogers, left a widow with two young sons, a task he handled with enormous concern and care for her feelings. 'Rogers was the best man I had in the administration, bar none, for this period of war. No loss could possibly be greater to the ministry,' King mourned. He 'had never failed me. I could not help using those words. . . . he was unfailing in his loyalty and devotion. He never thought of himself, but always of others—as beautiful a character as I have known.'[148]

Rogers' death made it essential to reconstruct the Cabinet now, and King moved Layton Ralston from Finance to National Defence. J. L. Ilsley transferred to Finance from National Revenue, and two new men were brought into the government. Colin Gibson from Hamilton, Ontario became Minister of National Revenue, and the M.P. from York North, William Mulock, the son of King's old mentor, Sir William Mulock, became Postmaster-General. At 42, Mulock was the youngest member of the Cabinet, but neither he nor Gibson added much in the way of strength to the administration.

King also looked outside Parliament for new men. He approached J. W. McConnell of Montreal, industrialist and proprietor of the Montreal *Star*, who refused outright. He conducted negotiations with J. S. Duncan of Massey-Harris only to see them collapse when Duncan tried to have his civilian salary guaranteed to him and then delayed too long in making up his mind.[149] He was refused by Tom Moore, President of the Trades and Labour Congress, by G. W. Spinney of the Bank of Montreal, and by J. M. Macdonnell of the National Trust Company.[150] It was all very disillusioning to King, and his only success in bringing in an outsider came on June 28 when Angus L. Macdonald, Premier of Nova Scotia, agreed to join the Cabinet. On July 12 Macdonald was sworn in as Minister of National Defence for Naval Services.[151] Macdonald's record in Nova Scotia had been an excellent one and one that fully lived up to his brilliant academic and legal reputation. But in Ottawa his success would be limited.

Mackenzie King made one final effort to give a more representative cast to his administration. On June 28 he spoke to the Conservative leader about bringing Opposition members into the War Committee, and he offered two posts to the Tories, one to Hanson himself and one to Grote Stirling, the Member for Yale, B.C. and Minister of National Defence in the last year of the Bennett government. Hanson considered the offer but cautiously decided in the end that all he would get would be responsibility without power, a position he announced in Parliament on July 11.[152] Mackenzie King was delighted with Hanson's decision and that of the other Opposition leaders:

Have succeeded in getting entire Opposition just where I want them. Blackmore said he or his party would not join a government that did not have Social Credit as the basis of its war finance. Coldwell came out openly that the party was a Socialist party. Would not join any other. Hanson said he was elected to oppose the government. Intended along with his party to do so. That places all three by their own declaration against national government, meaning thereby union government. All three have declined even to help share in responsibility by the indirect means of either consultation, advice or to the extent of obtaining information confidentially in the war effort of the government. That leaves the Liberal Party wholly and absolutely

responsible of itself and dependent on its majority from now on. . . .
To have established this in Parliament itself within the first couple
of months of its meeting is a great achievement.[153]

Still, the idea of national government would linger on.

Essentially the Cabinet as it stood in the summer of 1940 was the
Cabinet that would fight the war. The Minister of Justice, Ernest
Lapointe, remained the right-hand man, but his health had broken and
the war had sapped his spirit. 'The lines in his face are deeper,' Grant
Dexter noted in October 1940, 'and he has lost much weight, not only
about the waist but in his face. His shoulders sag more than I have ever
noticed them and there is a hurt look in his big brown eyes. Indeed, there
is an aura of sadness about Lapointe which is quite out of character.'[154]
Lapointe was now more of a symbol of the Liberal Party's commitments
to French Canada than a policy-making power within the government.
His senior colleague from Quebec, P. J. A. Cardin, was a strong figure
in the province, if not in the country at large, and as Minister of Public
Works and, after July, Minister of Transport as well, he controlled a
substantial amount of patronage. The two additional Quebec ministers,
Casgrain and Senator Raoul Dandurand, added nothing. Dandurand
was an octogenarian and government leader in the Senate, and although
King referred to him as 'a dear soul'[155] he was past rendering service to
the country or the party. French-Canadian representation was very weak,
particularly with Lapointe in ill-health.

Among the English-speaking ministers Ralston clearly enjoyed a
repute with King and with the country that far exceeded that of any
other minister. Enormously hard-working, the Colonel could be stubborn
in the extreme, and he suffered from the terrible inability to delegate
authority, a failing that chained him to his desk and gradually sapped
his strength—and judgement. Howe was another strong man, a businessman with a knack for choosing able subordinates and giving them their
heads. He was 'a man you could do business with,' but he was also seen
by many as lacking the 'social vision' to go with his great executive
ability.[156] Ilsley, the new Minister of Finance, was also a minister of great
ability, integrity, and first-class intelligence, and he inherited and built
up the most able group of civil servants in Ottawa—a group that ranked
with the very best anywhere. Power was first-rate, and Jimmy Gardiner,
the Minister of Agriculture and National War Services, had ability as
well, although this was tempered by a penchant for feuding with

colleagues and a strong partisan streak that made him a detestable figure to political opponents.

The rest of the ministry was not strong. T. A. Crerar, the Minister of Mines and Resources, was 'losing his grip'[157] in King's opinion, and seemed lacking in concern for and understanding of the needs and aspirations of the ordinary people of Canada. J. E. Michaud, the Minister of Fisheries and a New Brunswicker, was 'not much help', and Norman McLarty, the Minister of Labour, 'talks far too much' and suffered from the same failings that could be excused in Power because of his ability.[158] Ian Mackenzie was still a liability to the government because of his pre-war difficulties in National Defence, and the other ministers were still so green that judgements could not yet be passed upon them.

But for a government to have such men as Ralston, Howe, Ilsley, Lapointe, Cardin, and Power all at once was unusual. These half-dozen strong and able men more than compensated for the lacklustre ministers warming the lesser portfolios, and as the stars filled all the crucial portfolios, the King government that ran the war has to be judged as one of the strongest Cabinets Canada ever had—if not the strongest. When Louis St Laurent joined the government at the end of 1941 it would be stronger still. Of course King could grump about his men. 'I find Council very difficult when older members are away,' he moaned in July. 'Missed particularly Lapointe's presence and Rogers, both of whom usually support my point of view. Ralston does in some things but does not quickly see all sides of the question.'[159] But when Ralston and Howe were away, King missed their 'active and alert minds,' something he found lacking in Ilsley. 'Ilsley has a very narrow mind; has no vision with respect to international problems. Is of the old Colonial mind.' And, most scathing of all, 'Might better be a resident of Newfoundland than of N.S.'[160] No Prime Minister is ever satisfied with his colleagues, and this was certainly true of Mackenzie King, but for the war years, at least, King and Canada were well served.

1 Public Archives of Canada [PAC], W. L. Mackenzie King Papers, Diary, 31 Dec. 1939.
2 E.g., Queen's University, T. A. Crerar Papers, King to Crerar, 10 July 1939, and reply 25 July 1939; PAC, Ian Mackenzie Papers, file P-30, Mackenzie to King, 26 July 1939.
3 King Papers, King to Massey, 15 Aug. 1939, ff. 232076ff.; King Diary, 11 Aug. 1939.

4 King Papers, King to Chamberlain, 16 Aug. 1939.

5 *Ibid.*, Chamberlain to King, 21 Aug. 1939.

6 Mackenzie Papers, file P-16, Mackenzie to King, 18 Aug. 1939.

7 *Ibid.*, file P-30, Mackenzie to King, 26 July 1939.

8 Queen's University, Grant Dexter Papers, Memorandum, 28 June 1939.

9 Neil McKenty, *Mitch Hepburn* (Toronto, 1967), p. 168.

10 King Papers, Memo for Prime Minister [P.M.], 14 July 1938, f. C134984.

11 E.g., Queen's University, Norman Lambert Papers, Diary, 18 Apr. 1936.

12 *Ibid.*, Box 8, Memo re N.L.F., n.d.

13 King Papers, King to Massey, 15 Aug. 1939, f. 232078. There is excellent material on Ontario's problems with Ottawa, particularly with respect to hydro, in H. V. Nelles, *The Politics of Development* (Toronto, 1974) and in Christopher Armstrong, 'The Politics of Federalism: Ontario's Relations with the Federal Government', Ph.D thesis, University of Toronto, 1972.

14 King Diary, 14 Sept. 1939.

15 King Papers, 'Meeting of Executive Committee, N.L.F.', 19 Sept. 1939, ff. 228035-6.

16 *Ibid.*, King to Lambert, 18 Nov. 1939, ff. 229011-12, and Memo by Lambert, 20 Nov. 1939, ff. 229023-4.

17 P. Hippe, 'The Liberal Party of Canada', Ph.D. thesis, University of Wisconsin, 1956, 143ff.; McKenty, p. 168.

18 King Papers, Lambert to King, 24 July 1939, f. 228966; Lambert Diary, 14 Nov. 1939.

19 *Ibid.*, 5 Jan. 1940.

20 King Diary, 15 Jan. 1940. McKenty, p. 206, is wrong in his assessment of King's desire for an early election.

21 King Diary, 16 Jan. 1940.

22 Lambert Papers, Memo, 'The N.L.F.', n.d., and Memo, 20 Nov. 1939.

23 King Diary, 18 Jan. 1940.

24 Lambert Papers, Memo by Jack Hambleton of Toronto *Star*, encl. with H. C. Hindmarsh to Lambert, 6 Oct. 1939.

25 Public Archives of Ontario, M. F. Hepburn Papers, Supply Files (Private) 1939 H(2), 1 Dec. 1939; McKenty, pp. 201ff.

26 Toronto *Globe and Mail*, 19 Jan. 1940; McKenty, pp. 208-9; King Diary, 16 Jan. 1941, recounting an interview with Harry Nixon of Hepburn's Cabinet.

27 *Ibid.*, 18 Jan. 1940. Press reaction was heavily against using the Ontario resolution as an excuse for an election. *Winnipeg Free Press*, 20 Jan. 1940; *Globe and Mail*, 20 Jan. 1940; Montreal *Gazette*, 22 Jan. 1940. Cf. 'Why the Hurry?', *Canadian Forum*, XIX (February, 1940), 339.

28 King Diary, 19 Jan. 1940.

29 *Ibid.*, 22 Jan. 1940.

30 King Papers, Memo, King to Pickersgill, 22 Jan. 1940, ff. D53523ff. King's speech in House of Commons *Debates*, 25 Jan. 1940, pp. 2-9, generally followed this memo although with less partisanship.

31 King Papers, Memo, King to Pickersgill, 30 Jan. 1940, ff. D53552ff. This was

prompted by King's favourable response to Grant Dexter's article in Ottawa *Journal*, 30 Jan. 1942, which traced 'exactly the course of events in accordance with what was in my mind'.

32 King Diary, 23 Jan. 1940.

33 *Ibid.*, 25 Jan. 1940; Dexter Papers, Memo, 30 Jan. 1940; Norman Ward, ed., *A Party Politician: The Memoirs of Chubby Power* (Toronto, 1966), pp. 352-3; Public Record Office [PRO], Foreign Office Records, FO 800/398, Tweedsmuir to Lothian, 3 Feb. 1940.

34 U.S. National Archives, Department of State Records, 842.032/171, J. H. R. Cromwell to Secretary of State, 26 Jan. 1940.

35 House of Commons *Debates*, 25 Jan. 1940, p. 10; FO 371/25224, High Commissioner to Secretary of State for Dominion Affairs [SSDA], 2 Feb. 1940. Cf. J. W. Pickersgill, 'Mackenzie King's Speeches', *Queen's Quarterly*, LVII (Autumn, 1950) 425, which implies that King also felt uneasy.

36 King Diary, 23 Jan. 1940.

37 King Papers, Memo, King to Pickersgill, 30 Jan. 1940, ff. D53552ff.

38 Montreal *Gazette*, 26 Jan. 1940; Ottawa *Journal*, 26 Jan. 1940; 'Canada's War Effort', *Round Table*, March, 1940, 425; 'Backstage at Ottawa', *Maclean's*, 1 Mar. 1940, 10. But see criticism in *Globe and Mail*, 26 Jan. 1940 and Vancouver *Province*, 26 Jan. 1940.

39 State Department Records, 842.032/171, Cromwell to Secretary of State, 26 Jan. 1941; FO 371/25224, High Commissioner to SSDA, 2 Feb. 1940; Saskatchewan Provincial Archives, J. G. Gardiner Papers, Gardiner to Dr McCusker, 29 Jan. 1940.

40 State Department Records, 842.00/571, Cromwell to Secretary of State, 29 Jan. 1940.

41 King Diary, 26 Jan. 1940; Lambert Diary, 26 Jan. 1940.

42 King Diary, 23 Jan. 1940. See *ibid.*, 12 Feb. 1940, which indicates that pressures were building for a four-division corps.

43 *Ibid.*, 27 Jan. 1940. Floyd S. Chalmers Papers (Toronto), Memoranda, 26 Oct. 1939 and 2 June 1940 indicate something of Campbell's temperament and the successful efforts to dump him.

44 King Diary, 31 Jan. 1940.

45 *Ibid.*, 27, 29 Jan. 1940.

46 *Ibid.*, 1 Feb. 1940.

47 *Ibid.*, 27 Jan. 1940.

48 Queen's University, C. G. Power Papers, 'Memorandum re 1940 Election Campaign', 1 Feb. 1940.

49 King Diary, 13 Sept. 1939.

50 On this, see J. L. Granatstein, *The Politics of Survival* (Toronto, 1967) pp. 42ff.

51 Dexter Papers, Memo, 27 Jan. 1940; PAC, R. B. Bennett Papers, Macleod to Bennett, 30 Jan. 1940. For King's view of one who joined under the national government banner, see King Diary, 27 Jan. 1940: 'Deceitful double faced little prig, with no political sense or judgment, and endless affectation.'

52 Walter Young, *The Anatomy of a Party: The National CCF 1932-61* (Toronto, 1969), p. 95.

53 R. K. Pemberton, 'The CCF, The Election, and the Future', *Canadian Forum*, XX (May, 1940), 38-40.

54 King Diary, 27 Jan. 1942.

55 King Papers, Speech of 7 Feb. 1940 and revisions, 3-7 Feb. 1940, ff. D53809ff.

56 E.g., for 7 Feb. 1940 speech, see King Papers, 'Re the Prime Minister's Broadcasts', 31 Jan. 1940. ff. C185401ff. and 'Notes and Points for Speeches', 2 Feb. 1940, ff. C185421ff.

57 1940 Election files in King Papers, Vol. D84.

58 King Diary, 7 Feb. 1940.

59 *Mackenzie King to the People of Canada, 1940* (Ottawa, 1940), pp. 6, 10-11, 19.

60 King Diary, 7 Feb. 1940.

61 For King's responses to Tweedsmuir's illness and death, see *ibid.*, 6-16 Feb. 1940.

62 *Ibid.*, 9 Feb. 1940. For very different press comments on Manion's opening speech see *Winnipeg Free Press* and Halifax *Chronicle*, 10 Feb. 1940.

63 King Diary, 23 Feb. 1940.

64 Granatstein, pp. 44-7.

65 Dexter Papers, Memorandum, 7 Feb. 1940.

66 *Ibid.*

67 *Ibid.*, 8 Feb. 1940. On Conservative organization in Quebec, see Robert Rumilly, *Histoire de la province de Québec*, Vol. XXXVIII: *Ernest Lapointe* (Montréal, 1968), p. 104; Marc LaTerreur, *Les Tribulations des conservateurs au Québec de Bennett à Diefenbaker* (Québec, 1973) pp. 89ff.

68 Gardiner Papers, pamphlet, 'Je desire d'abord parler . . .'

69 *La Presse*, 9 mars 1940.

70 Rumilly, XXXVIII, pp. 111ff.

71 *Ibid.*, pp. 115-16.

72 *Life is an Adventure* (Toronto, 1936), p. 224.

73 Granatstein, p. 48. Cf. Gordon Graydon's comment in Toronto *Star*, 15 Feb. 1940.

74 State Department Records, 842.00/673, Cromwell to Secretary of State, 4 Mar. 1940. Cf. Scottish Record Office, Lord Lothian Papers, GD 40/17/405, 164-5, John Stevenson to Lothian, 28 Feb. 1940.

75 PRO, Dominions Office Records, DO 35/586, High Commissioner to SSDA, 16 Mar. 1940.

76 *Windsor Star*, 18 Mar. 1940.

77 *Mackenzie King to the People of Canada*, p. 77. Cf. King Papers, 'Campaign Promises by Dr. Manion', n.d.

78 King Diary, 27 Feb. 1940.

79 *Ibid.*, 29 Feb. 1940.

80 Hon. Paul Martin interview, 24 July 1971.

81 King Diary, 1 Mar. 1940.

82 *Ibid.*, 11-12, 14 Mar. 1940. For a good description of the Ontario problems, see McKenty, pp. 212ff.

83 King Diary, 23 Mar. 1940.

84 *Ibid.*, 19 Mar. 1940.

85 *Ibid.*, 22 Mar. 1940.

86 See J. M. Beck, *Pendulum of Power* (Toronto, 1968), pp. 238-9.

87 PAC, Brooke Claxton Papers, Vol. 27, 'Analysis of the Vote . . . 1940'.

88 Hon. D. C. Abbott interview, 29 Oct. 1971.

89 PAC, A. K. Cameron Papers, Vol. 5, T. A. Crerar to Cameron, 3 Apr. 1940.

90 For detail on Liberal fund-raising, see J. L. Granatstein, 'Financing the Liberal Party, 1935-1945', in M. S. Cross and R. D. Bothwell, eds, *Policy By Other Means* (Toronto, 1972), pp. 189-92. For Liberal literature and campaign data, see PAC, National Liberal Federation Papers, Vol. 801, 1940 election file.

91 King Diary, 29 Mar. 1940; Lambert Diary, 26-9 Mar. 1940.

92 FO 371/25224, Minute by P. Mason, 17 Apr. 1940.

93 King Diary, 2-3 Apr. 1940.

94 *Ibid.*, 8 May 1940.

95 Granatstein, *Politics of Survival*, chapter IV.

96 House of Commons *Debates*, 21 May 1940, p. 108.

97 King Diary, 29 May 1940.

98 *Ibid.*, 30 May 1940.

99 House of Commons *Debates*, 30 May 1940, pp. 349ff.

100 Ottawa *Citizen*, 31 May 1940.

101 King Diary, 31 May 1940.

102 PAC, CCF Records, Vol. 106, Coldwell to G. H. Williams, 8 May 1940.

103 W. D. Herridge Papers (Toronto), Hanson to Herridge, 15 May 1940.

104 Clifford Bowering, *Service* (Ottawa, 1960), p. 107.

105 E.g., King Papers, Memo, W. J. Turnbull to King, 23 May 1940, f. C744276, analyzing telegrams received.

106 *Ibid.*, Summary of Additional War Measures Announced by the Prime Minister', 20 May 1940, ff. C244224-5.

107 King Diary, 22 May 1940.

108 *Ibid.*

109 *Ibid.*, 23 May 1940. For the happier fate of the troops, see C. P. Stacey, *Six Years of War* (Ottawa, 1955), pp. 279ff.

110 King Diary, 23 May 1940. King had told his Cabinet of this possibility in January (*ibid.*, 29 Jan. 1940) and he was now worried that he would have to take the blame for the deficiencies. *Ibid.*, 3 June 1940.

111 *Ibid.*, 23 May 1940.

112 *Ibid.*, 27 May 1940.

113 Department of Finance (Ottawa), W. C. Clark Papers, file B-2-8-7-2-3, Ralston to Towers, 5 June 1940.

114 PAC, Department of External Affairs Records, P.M. to P.M., 18 May 1940.

115 King Papers, Memo, 'Canadian Economic Contribution', 1 June 1940, ff. C246775ff.

116 External Affairs Records, Tel. P.M. to P.M., 8 June 1940.

[117] King Diary, 6 June 1940. Cf. H. D. Hall, *North American Supply* (London, 1955), pp. 19ff.

[118] External Affairs Records, Tels SSDA to Secretary of State for External Affairs [SSEA], 16 June 1940 and reply 17 June 1940. For British supply organization in North America, see J. Hurstfield, *The Control of Raw Materials* (London, 1953), appendix 33, p. 484, and Hall, pp. 18ff., 218ff. Apparently the British Supply Board in Canada was recalled at the request of the Canadian government. King Papers, Memo for P.M., 26 June 1940, f. C240399.

[119] Clark Papers, file B-2-8-7-2-3, Ralston to Towers, 5 June 1940; Hall, pp. 230-1.

[120] King Diary, 5 June 1940.

[121] PAC, M. J. Coldwell Papers, Coldwell to Williams, 10 June 1940.

[122] King Diary, 16 June 1940.

[123] *Ibid.*, 17 June 1940; Granatstein, *Politics of Survival*, p. 60.

[124] J. W. Pickersgill, *The Mackenzie King Record*, Vol. I: *1939-44* (Toronto, 1960), p. 95.

[125] House of Commons *Debates*, 18 June 1940, p. 854.

[126] Pickersgill, I, p. 96. See esp. Lapointe's speech, 'Texte Complet des Discours sur la Mobilisation Générale . . . 23 juin 40' (Ottawa, 1940), with its absolute pledges. For description of the NRMA debate, see Bennett Papers, Notable Persons files, Hanson to Bennett, 4 July 1940; FO 371/25224, Campbell to SSDA, 24 June 1940; CCF Records, Vol. 110, Caucus minutes, 19, 21 June 1940. At Quebec City, René Chaloult introduced an anti-conscriptionist motion. See Rumilly, XXXVIII, pp. 164-5.

[127] Pickersgill, I, p. 97. Quebec press reaction to the NRMA was relatively favourable. Elizabeth Armstrong, *French Canadian Opinion on the War* (Toronto, 1942) pp. 15ff.

[128] *Statutes of Canada* (1940), chapter XIII, pp. 43-4.

[129] External Affairs Records, Vol. 107, file 687, Memo, 19 June 1940.

[130] E. L. M. Burns, *Manpower in the Canadian Army* (Toronto, 1956) pp. 116-17.

[131] King Diary, 28 June 1940, 3 July 1940.

[132] Raymond Ranger, *Report on the Operations of National Registration and Military Mobilization in Canada During World War II* (Ottawa, mimeo, 1949), pp. 9ff. (Copy in Directorate of History, National Defence Headquarters.) See also D. K. O'Brien, 'The Operation of Canada's National Registration in World War II', undergraduate paper, York University, 1974.

[133] Quoted in House of Commons *Debates*, 3 Aug. 1940, p. 2402 by Mr Hanson.

[134] King Diary, 3 Aug. 1940.

[135] *Le Devoir*, 7 août 1940; Armstrong, pp. 18-19.

[136] Harvard University, Pierrepont Moffat Papers, Vol. 17, Moffat to Elizabeth Armstrong, 24 July 1940.

[137] PAC, Ernest Lapointe Papers, Vol. 16, 'Survey of Conditions Prevailing in Military District 5, 9-22 Feb. 41'; Burns, p. 117; and Cameron Macpherson, 'The Birth of a Minority', an excellent York University paper, 1971, on the NRMA men.

[138] Directorate of History, National Defence Headquarters, H. D. G. Crerar Papers, 958C.009(D129), Crerar to Gen. Montague, 11 Dec. 1944, and *ibid.*, 958C.009(D13), Col. Burns to Crerar, 29 Oct. 1940. The Crerar Papers are now in PAC.

139 PAC, J. L. Ralston Papers, Vol. 38, Memo, 'The Canadian Army', 3 Sept. 1940;
PAC, C. D. Howe Papers, Vol. 48, file S-14 ND(1), Memo, 3 Sept. 1940.

140 Gardiner Papers, Gardiner to King, 14 July 1940.

141 Cited in Macpherson, p. 26.

142 King Diary, 23 Oct. 1940, 13 Nov. 1940.

143 Directorate of History, General Files, file 112.1013(D2), 'The Nature of the Canadian Army Effort in Mid-Summer, 1941 . . .' 18 May 1941; PAC, Privy Council Office Records, Cabinet War Committee Records, Minutes, 28 Jan. 1941; King Diary, 27-8 Jan. 1941; PAC, A. G. L. McNaughton Papers, Vol. 227, file CC 7/Crerar/6, Crerar to McNaughton, 4 Mar. 1941.

144 Ibid., 16 Apr. 1941; King Diary, 23 Apr. 1941.

145 Ibid., 7, 9 May 1940.

146 Ibid., 8-9 May 1940, 13 Nov. 1941, 15 Dec. 1941. Cf. Thérèse Casgrain, A Woman in a Man's World (Toronto, 1972), which is unrevealing on this matter.

147 On the difficult negotiations with Power, see King Diary, 17-20 May 1940. On the lines of responsibility, see Claxton Papers, Memoirs, Vol. 4, 818.

148 King Diary, 10 June 1940; King Papers, King to H.V. Cann, 12 June 1940, ff. 240627ff.

149 King Diary, 25-8 June 1940. Cf. the contradictory account in J. S. Duncan, Not a One-Way Street (Toronto, 1971), pp. 115ff.

150 King Diary, 25-8 June 1940.

151 Public Archives of Nova Scotia, Angus L. Macdonald Papers, Diary, 28 June 1940, 17 July 1940.

152 PAC, R. B. Hanson Papers, file P-100-N(NG), 3 undated memos; ibid., file P-100 (Parliamentary Work), Hanson to Sir E. Beatty, 11 July 1940.

153 King Diary, 12 July 1940.

154 Dexter Papers, Memo, 25 Oct. 1940.

155 King Diary, 29 June 1939.

156 Sir Stephen Holmes interview, 15 June 1971; 'Our Ottawa Letter', New Commonwealth, 8 July 1943.

157 King Diary, 22 May 1940.

158 Ibid.

159 Ibid., 15 July 1940.

160 Ibid., 5 Sept. 1940.

4. From Ogdensburg to Hyde Park and After

Mackenzie King was annoyed and frustrated. His bed-time reading in July 1940 was *Canada: America's Problem* by John MacCormac,[1] a *New York Times* reporter who had covered Ottawa from 1934 to 1939, and the book was full of the usual misrepresentations of King's role and influence. 'There is no allowance for judgment or reason over a period of leadership of 21 years. What has led to the greatest successes and everything is put down to either chance or instinct. Nothing conceded to vision or wisdom.' That galled King, but so too did MacCormac's comments on Mackenzie King's role vis-à-vis the Empire and the United States:

> [MacCormac] is also completely wrong in assuming that in matters concerning British and American relations, I have had in view aught else than maintaining as the foundation or the basis of the British Empire, complete self government of each of its parts, and the belief that on this basis not only would Canadian nationhood be attained to the full but that the British Empire itself would endure. He is quite wrong in assuming that I have had any North American view versus the British Empire view—the latter has been much more present to my mind and thought and desire than the former at all times in my life though I have believed that for the good of the world, it was important to cultivate between Canada and the U.S. and in a larger way the British Empire and the U.S., the best possible relations.[2]

King's fate seemed always to be misunderstood.

The Prime Minister was probably correct in the interpretation of his own motives on the subject of Canada's relations with the United States and Britain. He knew that many Canadians thought him vaguely disloyal to Britain and far too friendly towards the United States. He had even mentioned this to the American Minister in Ottawa at one point, offering the comment that to some of his compatriots he was known derogatorily as 'the American'.[3] But in the Prime Minister's opinion there was nothing wrong with this, for 'I regarded friendly relations as a blessing rather than otherwise.'[4] This friendship was intended to help Canada serve as the link between Britain, the Mother Country, and the United States, the lost colonies. If he could help tie the two great English-speaking nations together, this would be a factor of enormous importance and one that would redound to Canada's—and Mackenzie King's—credit. Today such efforts seem quaint and naive, but they did not in the 1930s, a few short years after bitter Anglo-American naval disputes and the end of the Anglo-Japanese alliance. Initially King's efforts at rapprochement were concentrated along economic lines; he shared with President Franklin Roosevelt the belief that a world economic conference could resolve some of the pressing social and economic problems that both believed were the cause of war. But this idea withered away, and Mackenzie King turned more directly to supporting political appeasement as his preferred method of averting war.[5]

So too did Roosevelt, although the President was far more willing than Mackenzie King to deliver harsh speeches aimed at the dictators. In August 1938 Roosevelt spoke at Kingston, Ontario and promised that 'the people of the United States would not stand idly by if domination of Canadian soil is threatened by any other Empire';[6] three months later in November he indicated that the United States would assume the responsibility for protecting the entire Western Hemisphere from attack. Such speeches were reassuring to Canadians, but they did create concerns of a kind. After Roosevelt's November remarks, for example, Mackenzie King noted that this 'amazing' speech forced him to be 'particularly guarded not to say a word that might be construed as failure to appreciate a generous attitude by the President. On the other hand, his remarks will be interpreted, in some quarters, as an effort to isolate North America. Jingos will wish to assert solidarity of British Empire.'[7]

Still, relations between the two men and the two countries were good. Trade agreements in 1935 and 1938 bound the North American economies ever more tightly together, and United States investment in Canada amounted in 1939 to $4.1 billion, fully 60 per cent of all foreign investment in the country.[8] In addition the military threat to the continent, still small but now perceptible, had led to secret conversations between the defence chiefs of Canada and the United States in January 1938, and although little of significance was accomplished, that consultation was a harbinger of closer co-operation.[9] On a more personal level, King and Roosevelt met regularly for chats about the state of the world. During these conversations King was almost always the listener, and he deferred to the President with somewhat embarrassing haste. Roosevelt had clearly taken the measure of the Prime Minister's vanity and desire to be on good terms, and the President was always ready to flatter his guest and pay him every courtesy. In May 1939, for example, a visitor to Laurier House brought King affectionate greetings from Roosevelt and added, as King recorded it, that 'there were few people in the world, when they met together, that were almost as one—like the President and myself. The President felt that way with me. Had a great affection for me.'[10] That mattered very much to King. But no man could be Prime Minister for almost fifteen years without being a careful judge of men himself, and King skilfully played up to the President. Both men were courteous and warm in an old-fashioned way, yet shrewd negotiators manoeuvring at all times. Possibly the two did genuinely like one another, but there can be no doubt that Mackenzie King was the junior partner in this relationship.[11]

The Prime Minister, of course, realized the political utility of maintaining close relations with Roosevelt. The American President had always been extremely popular in Canada, and some of this could be expected to redound to Mackenzie King's credit. The British, too, might be impressed by Canadian and American friendship. After the Royal tour in the spring of 1939, for example, King wrote to Roosevelt that George VI 'was also much impressed and pleased by the friendship which he saw I was privileged to share with you . . . and of what it obviously must have meant in the relations between our three countries, and was certain to continue to mean.' King said of the tour that 'I am convinced that nothing fraught with so great significance of good has happened since "the great schism of the Anglo-Saxon race".'[12] That Mackenzie King could feel this way about public relations frippery is revealing; that he could think Roosevelt might agree with him was foolish; but clearly in King's mind the tour had put him at the crucial linkage between the old world and the new, between Britain and America.

The coming of the war put the relationship to the test. King was pleased that Roosevelt recognized that Canada was neutral until the declaration of war on September 10 despite American legal opinion to the contrary,[13] yet he was more than a little unhappy about Roosevelt's initial attitude to the struggle. 'I came away from the radio feeling an almost profound disgust,' King noted after hearing the President's neutrality address on September 3. 'It was all words, words, words. America keeping out of this great issue, which affects the destiny of mankind. And professing to do so in the name of peace. . . . I was really ashamed of the attitude of the U.S.'[14] Still, Ottawa was exceedingly careful not to irritate American public or official opinion,[15] and restrictions on trade, currency, and personal movements across the border were almost invariably canvassed in Washington before implementation. The Prime Minister, wisely, tried to bend every effort to keep on good terms, even pressing Colonel Ralston, then Finance Minister, to be more accommodating during discussions about the St Lawrence Waterway early in 1940. King wrote that Ralston wanted the Americans to contribute more of the cost, but he 'conceded that the argument I had urged about the importance of keeping the goodwill of the United States at this time, and to co-operate with them on a matter which the President had so greatly at heart . . . was a strong reason why we should not take a stand which might risk all of this goodwill and lead the U.S. to become more nationalistic and self-dependent than ever.'[16]

The highpoints for Mackenzie King during the phoney war period were his meetings with Roosevelt. In April 1940 the Prime Minister went south for a rest at Virginia Beach, seizing the opportunity to visit the President at Warm Springs, Georgia and Washington. King worried about his absence from Canada during a period of Axis success in Scandinavia, but he reassured himself that 'there is real purpose behind my seeing the President and that I can do more in one week spent to that end than might be accomplished in months by remaining at Ottawa . . .'[17] In fact, on this trip very little of a policy nature was accomplished. King discovered, contrary to his earlier impression, that Roosevelt knew very little about the St Lawrence proposals, and the two men did little more than gossip about Winston Churchill's being 'tight most of the time'.[18] The one matter of consequence was Roosevelt's speaking 'of the dangers to the Atlantic Coast cities, of gas as well as bombs, etc. It was apparent to me from his conversation,' King wrote, 'that he felt a real concern about the inadequacy of the protection to our Canadian coasts. . . . He knew exactly from personal observation . . . much about the nature of the coasts . . .' Later Roosevelt would offer equipment to Canada 'at a nominal figure' and mention again that 'our inadequacy of defence represented a real danger to the United States.' King had to admit that 'we had done very little comparatively speaking' but he did suggest 'we were doing the best we could.'[19] That, in Roosevelt's view, was not good enough.

In general King hesitated before raising anything contentious with the President. He preferred to listen to Roosevelt's views and to draw him out, and King's diary is full of entries referring to the President's speaking 'without reservation' or 'giving his full confidence'.[20] King also could not fail to be impressed that Roosevelt devoted so much time to him. 'The President gave up the whole of the day to sharing its hours with me,' King wrote to a friend. 'We visited the [March of Dimes] Foundation [at Warm Springs, Ga], had long drives and long talks, most enjoyable and profitable.'[21] Such friendship should be worth something.

It would have to be after the Allied armies walked into the trap that Hitler had prepared for them. The complacency that had so distinguished Allied planning had proved false, and defeat stared Britain in the face. In London Winston Churchill became Prime Minister and for a time his speeches seemed to be the only defence that Britain had.

The defeat in France came as a heavy blow to Mackenzie King, and the pain was in no way eased by the appointment of Churchill as Prime Minister. King had regarded Churchill as an erratic war-monger since Chanak in 1922, and he had made no secret of his views. In March 1939, for example, he had told the Liberal caucus that Canada could not give Britain a blank cheque. Canadians might be prepared to follow Neville Chamberlain, he had said, but they might not follow Churchill or Duff Cooper, another anti-appeaser.[22] He had also discussed Churchill with George VI during the Royal tour, and the Prime Minister had been pleased to learn that Edward VIII's friend was no friend of George VI. The King had said he would never appoint Churchill to office unless it was absolutely necessary in time of war. ' I confess I was glad to hear him say that,' Mackenzie King had noted with satisfaction, 'because I think Churchill one of the most dangerous men I have ever known.'[23] With the beginning of the war, however, Churchill's return to the Admiralty led to a new beginning between the two men and to exchanges of telegrams after each other's speeches and triumphs. Churchill's message to King after the election of 1940 was particularly warm, signed, simply, 'Winston'.[24] But when King telegraphed congratulations to Churchill on his becoming Prime Minister, his words could have been interpreted in two ways: 'May you be given the vision and endurance so necessary to the duties of your high office and never more needed in the guidance of public affairs than at this critical hour.'[25] In King's view the vision and endurance were highly unlikely, although once he saw the way Churchill took hold and galvanized England, his criticism ceased almost completely.

Churchill, it seems clear, had no high regard for Mackenzie King, whom he saw as deficient in forthrightness and courage. To Churchill, Mackenzie King was a colonial who should, but didn't always, know his place and keep to it. But if he disliked King and his style, Churchill always carefully displayed a politesse equalling that shown by Roosevelt to King. Still, the word got around. R. B. Hanson, the Leader of the Opposition, told a reporter in Ottawa that 'he knew from friends that Churchill had no use at all for "the little son of a bitch" (his usual way of referring to the PM) . . .'[26]

The relationship between Roosevelt and Churchill, on the other hand, has been described as one of easy informality marked by a moratorium on pomposity and cant. 'They appraised each other through the practised eyes of professionals,' Robert Sherward wrote, 'and from this appraisal resulted a degree of admiration . . . that lesser craftsmen could not have achieved.'[27] Mackenzie King's place with the two giants was on the fringe, and certainly he was incapable of declaring a moratorium on pomposity and cant. But he was a professional too, at least as much so as Roosevelt and Churchill, and this must have won him some regard. He could not be an intermediary in the grandiose way he might have liked, but he realized that he could be 'a medium of communication . . . between Mr. R. & Mr. C. to have them understand each others [sic] point of view'.[28] This much he could do.

I

The task, as Mackenzie King soon discovered, was to avoid being misunderstood himself. At the urging of Rogers, Power, and Ralston in mid-May 1940, King decided to make a direct appeal to Roosevelt for training aircraft to keep the BCATP functioning now that it was certain that Britain would be unable to provide the aircraft she had agreed to find. To raise this matter with the President, King despatched to Washington Hugh Keenleyside, a first secretary in the Department of External Affairs. Keenleyside saw the President on May 19. Roosevelt was sympathetic, the first secretary reported, but unable to assist. More important than aircraft, however, was Roosevelt's expressed concern about the collapse in France and about 'certain possible eventualities which could not possibly be mentioned aloud'. Instructed to say the words 'British Fleet' to Mackenzie King, the envoy told the Prime Minister that he assumed 'this to mean that the [President] was anxious to have an understanding that the British Fleet would be transferred to this side of the ocean, in the event of an Allied defeat, rather than allow it to fall into German hands.'[29] That was exactly Roosevelt's intention.

Meanwhile King found himself pushed by the Prime Minister of Australia, Robert Menzies, to appeal for more assistance to Britain and France from the United States. Talking toughly, Menzies pressed the Americans to release 'every available aircraft' and to send 'volunteers of American airmen along similar lines to assistance rendered to Spain by German and Italian military volunteers during Spanish revolution.'[30] From London Vincent Massey, Canada's High Commissioner, suggested caution and the need to bend 'backwards in disciplining any desire to suggest in any way what the policy of the United States should be.'[31] Churchill felt otherwise and indicated that he had asked the United States for varieties of aid. 'If you,' he telegraphed to Mackenzie King, '... feel able to follow up our appeal by a personal appeal ... this would be very welcome to us.'[32]

Not unexpectedly, King responded cautiously to these pleas. To Churchill he indicated that he felt 'strongly that at the present moment any public appeal by outside governments would arrest rather than assist the formation of public and Congressional opinion favourable to action ...' He added that 'it would be equally embarrassing if information were to reach the public in any way as to personal appeals or discussions being made.' Moreover, 'as to making known the gravity and needs of the situation, particularly regarding air, I have been for some time in direct and personal touch, and am continuing to give close and direct attention to this aspect of the situation.'[33] This attitude was precisely the right one, for Roosevelt was upset by the tone of Menzies' initiative and by Churchill's support for it. Keenleyside later reported that the President 'felt there was, behind the argument, an implied—in fact, almost an explicit—threat. This might be expressed in these terms: "If you don't help us at once we will let the Germans have the Fleet and you can go to Hell." This attitude,' Roosevelt added, 'he could understand, and to some extent even sympathize with, but he did not feel that it was very helpful. In fact, if it were persisted in it would have the most deplorable effects—effects which would bear most heavily upon the authors of the threat themselves.'[34]

The fleet was central in Roosevelt's eyes. He saw Keenleyside again on May 25 and told him that he was afraid the French would surrender soon. It was unlikely that Britain would be able to withstand a subsequent German air assault. Should that occur, the President told Keenleyside, Britain would have to sue for peace, and the question of the terms would then be crucial. The President worried that the British might accept 'soft' terms and use the Royal Navy as a bargaining counter to get them, and this, in his view, would be unacceptable. The fleet had to be kept in action as long as possible and then dispersed to the Empire —even if that meant the occupation of Britain and destruction comparable to that visited upon Poland, Belgium, and France. The centre of Imperial authority should be transferred to Ottawa, perhaps, and the King given shelter in Bermuda. By then the United States would be ready to offer aid, the Royal Navy would have access to American ports, Europe would face a blockade, and the United States would control the Pacific. But if the fleet surrendered, Roosevelt warned, Japan would have a free hand in the Pacific, and Germany and Italy would absorb all the British colonies except those in North and South America.[35]

King was staggered when he heard this analysis from Keenleyside. 'I felt something of a sinking feeling as the President's message was narrated.' But the worst was yet to come. 'He wanted this picture to be given to Churchill,' King wrote, and he wanted the Canadian Prime Minister to get the concurrence of the Dominion Prime Ministers in such an appeal. For a moment, King added, 'it seemed to me that the United States was seeking to save itself at the expense of Britain. That it was an appeal to the selfishness of the Dominions at the expense of the British Isles. Each of them being secure by the arrangement. That the British themselves might have to go down. I instinctively revolted against such a thought. My reaction,' he wrote with some emotion, 'was that I would rather die than do aught to save ourselves or any part of this continent at the expense of Britain.'[36] Could he refuse Roosevelt's request? After thinking about the matter overnight and after calling Secretary of State Cordell Hull in Washington and questioning Keenleyside closely, the Prime Minister, stalling, decided that there was some confusion about what was intended. Did Roosevelt want him to present this view as the President's? Or was it an American view to be made known in a roundabout way? It was vital that he know what was required. Keenleyside again went to Washington to seek the answers, thus buying King some more time.

Keenleyside returned on May 29 to inform King that the President wanted him to make the approach to London,[37] and the Prime Minister spent a very trying May 30 drafting a suitable message to Churchill. The problem, he noted, was to 'try and meet the President's wishes so far as I could, of having the message appear to be from myself, while at the same time taking care to see that it was wholly his point of view that I was putting over and not my own.'[38] The telegram, sent the next day, was very carefully phrased:

> The United States, cannot, it is considered, give immediate belligerent aid. If, however, Britain and France could hold out for some months, aid could probably then be given. If further resistance by the fleet in British waters became impossible before such aid could be given, the President believes that, having ultimate victory for the allies and the final defeat of the enemy in view, it would be disastrous to surrender the fleet on any terms, that it should be sent to South Africa, Singapore, Australia, the Caribbean, and Canada. . . .
>
> Were this course adopted, the United States would assist immediately by opening its ports to the British fleet. . . . As soon thereafter as grounds could be found to justify direct and active American participation (and neither Mr. Roosevelt nor Mr. Hull believes that this would be more than a very few weeks) the United States would participate in a stringent blockade of the Continent of Europe. . . .[39]

In King's view, Churchill responded to this telegram in a superb speech in the House of Commons on June 4. 'We shall never surrender,' the British leader said resoundingly, 'and even if, which I do not for a moment believe, this island or a large part of it were subjugated and starving, then our Empire beyond the seas, armed and guarded by the British Fleet, would carry on the struggle, until, in God's good time, the New World, with all its power and might, steps forth to the rescue and liberation of the old.'*[40] A more personal reply to King came in a

*King admired Churchill's fervent oratory, but avoided trying it himself. Leonard Brockington, a lawyer, raconteur, and former chairman of the Canadian Broadcasting Corporation, had been brought into King's office to assist with speeches in 1940. In a conversation with Floyd Chalmers of *The Financial Post* in October 1940 he 'gave an example of the manner in which King shies away from anything of an emotional character. On the day that Italy declared war [June 10, 1940] King had to get up his speech very hurriedly for presentation to the House. It was the day that Norman Rogers was killed and things were very feverish. Brockington had written some notes out and had used the expression regarding Italy's entry into the war that it was a dagger driven into the back of a friendly neighbour. King had blue pencilled this saying that he couldn't go that far. Seven hours later in his national radio broadcast Roosevelt had used that expression and it had gone round the world.' Floyd Chalmers Papers (Toronto), Memo, 7 Oct. 1940.

telegram of June 5. 'We must be careful,' Churchill said, 'not to let Americans view too complacently prospect of a British collapse, out of which they would get the British fleet and the guardianship of the British Empire, minus Great Britain. If United States were in the war and England [were] conquered locally, it would be natural that events should follow the above course. But,' Churchill said darkly, 'if America continued neutral, and we were overpowered, I cannot tell what policy might be adopted by a pro-German administration such as would undoubtedly be set up. Although President is our best friend, no practical help has [reached us] from the United States as yet. . . . Any pressure which you can apply in this direction would be invaluable.'[41]

The contents of this disquieting message were passed to Roosevelt, again via the agency of Keenleyside, on June 6, along with a memorandum by King setting out his interpretation of Churchill's references to 'a pro-German administration'.[42] The President was alarmed and dismayed that Churchill should even raise such a possibility, and he was not at all soothed by King's gloss over the matter. Neither he nor Secretary Hull could understand the constitutional subtleties of the parliamentary system, nor could they promise much in the way of immediate aid.[43] They did, however, 'hope that Mr. K. will continue discussion with Mr. C. They hope and believe, that Mr. C. really means what he said to the House of Commons, and that his statement in the telegram to Mr. K. is not his final word on this all important matter.'[44]

It wasn't. King telegraphed Churchill on June 17 to suggest that the United States be given the opportunity of establishing bases in Iceland, Greenland, Newfoundland, and the West Indies, an idea that seems to have originated with the Canadian legation in Washington, and to ask that Canada's role be determined now if the worst should occur and the Royal Navy have to be dispersed.[45] The British lion, while weakened, had not lost its roar and Churchill let loose a blast at King on June 24: 'I have good confidence in our ability to defend this island, and I see no reason to make preparations for or give any countenance to the transfer of the British Fleet. I shall myself never enter into any peace negotiations with Hitler, but obviously I cannot bind a future government which, if we were deserted by the United States and beaten down here, might very easily be a kind of Quisling affair ready to accept German overlordship and protection. It would be a help if you could impress this danger on the President . . .'[46]

For Mackenzie King these sharp telegrams were heavy blows. He was near despair, his world of certitudes crumbling around him. Grant

Dexter of the *Winnipeg Free Press* wrote in a private memorandum of a conversation with Colonel Ralston at this time: 'Ralston had found King in his office at 2 a.m. working on this proposition [probably the telegram that was sent to Churchill at the end of May]. King had said that he was played out, finished and couldn't carry the load, or words to this effect. Ralston told me he said: "Chief, you've got to go through. The despatch you are working on may mean victory, the saving of civilization." King agreed.' Dexter, a confirmed skeptic, added his personal comment: 'Which indicates Ralston's position fairly well. Willie may be doing all he says but, in any event, he sure has J. L. buffaloed.'[47]

II

With Britain in danger of defeat, Mackenzie King now had to look to Canada's own defences. These were, in a word, negligible. Roosevelt had mentioned this to the Prime Minister during their April conversations, and the American Chiefs of Staff were acutely aware of the problem as well.[48] King, shrewdly, kept the parlous state of the Dominion's home defence before the President. On May 23, for example, the Cabinet War Committee accepted the Admiralty's request to send every available Canadian destroyer into British waters. Supporting the proposal, King insisted that the United States be informed. 'Let them see how completely depleted we were of defence on both coasts,' he wrote in his diary. The War Committee agreed that King should inform Roosevelt of 'the entire situation as a good neighbour. It was due to the U.S. who stood to suffer if our shores were wholly neglected. It was due to our own people to get from the U.S. all the help we possibly could.'[49]

King also put the problem directly to the newly appointed American Minister in Ottawa, the very professional J. Pierrepont Moffat. Shortly after his arrival, Moffat reported in a despatch on June 16, King suggested 'conversations between our Navy Department and naval and air officers from Canada'. There had been talks in 1938, King said. 'Of course, at that time both countries were at peace. Now Canada is a belligerent. Possibly a request for such limited staff talks, if made, might be exceedingly embarrassing to the President; this is the last thing he would wish.'[50] On June 17 the Canadian Chargé in Washington, Merchant Mahoney, called on Secretary of State Hull and made a formal request for such talks.[51] Pressed by the new war situation the United States would have to begin to think and plan for hemisphere defence.

Moffat indicated as much to the Prime Minister on July 5 when, as King recorded, he said that 'the U.S. had not, up to the present, distinguished as between Canada and other parts of the Empire. Moffat said he felt, however, that they were becoming not unaware of the fact that what was being done for Canada would increasingly be of immediate assistance to themselves.'[52] On July 13 King learned from Loring Christie, the Minister in Washington since the beginning of the war, that Mr Justice Frankfurter, 'Roosevelt's great friend', had suggested that the Prime Minister and the President should meet to draw 'a common plan of defence for North American continent including islands of the Atlantic'.[53]

Significantly the idea of closer ties with the United States began to be canvassed in public in Canada, too. In mid-July a group of influential men, mainly academics, younger politicians, and lawyers associated through the Canadian Institute of International Affairs, had drawn up a 'Program of Immediate Canadian Action'. Their concerns were fixed on the potential economic difficulties that Canada would face now that most of Europe was closed to her trade, but even more they urged the necessity for 'conversations with the United States aiming at a continental defence scheme'. Public opinion in Canada, they argued, 'is ready for a frank recognition by the government of the need for action.' Time was of the essence, and Canada had to take the initiative. 'If Canada allows this opportunity to go by default and the United States is consequently obliged to require us to cooperate, we might as a result be unable to maintain our independent identity.'[54]

Others reached the same conclusion. J. R. Baldwin, the Secretary of the Canadian Institute of International Affairs, who would soon join the civil service, wrote that Toronto opinion had shifted rapidly. 'A number of the traditional imperialists are now running for Washington,' Baldwin said. 'There is a real danger, I fear, that they will merely transfer their allegiance and colonial outlook to the United States.'[55] That was a problem in the eyes of supporters of a more independent Canadian foreign policy, but fear of what might happen in Europe goaded everyone to look for closer links with the United States. Bureaucratic opinion shifted rapidly to this view as well. The Bank of Canada had set up a committee in June to explore what steps would be necessary if, as it was euphemistically put, communications with the United Kingdom were cut. The results, the subsequent study indicated, would be simply catastrophic to the Canadian economy, with widespread unemployment as overseas trade disappeared at a stroke.

Graham Towers of the Bank told King that Canada would have to appeal to the United States for assistance and almost the only card that Canada held was that the 'United States will have to plan its defence on continental terms at least, and Canada will be an integral and necessary part of their plan.'[56]

The American export position was in much the same danger, and this awareness forced Washington planners to turn towards hemispheric thinking. Bruce Hutchison, the reporter for the Sifton newspaper chain, visited Washington early in June and had an astonishing conversation with A. A. Berle, the academic who had developed theories about large-scale corporations, who had served in Roosevelt's 'brain trust', and had then become Assistant Secretary of State. Berle's studies, Hutchison noted in a memorandum that was sent to the Prime Minister, 'now relate to the new American Empire. I can describe it as nothing else. He has been working, he said, on the re-organization of the economy of all North and South America, the new hemispheric concept.' Where, Hutchison asked, did Canada fit into this scheme?

> Well, [Berle said] it's a problem, but not as great as you might think. Don't forget that we are going in for huge armaments. This will provide a large employment for Canadians. Then there are such factors as the end of Scandinavian paper exports. You will get this business in the U.S. Wheat is the headache. But there, too, we will have to make concessions. You people still talk Manchester Liberalism. All right, we'll apply it to wheat. We'll say to the wheat producers, we can take so much wheat at a fixed price guaranteed by the government. You can produce more than that if you please, but you'll take whatever price the market will pay. In the end, your wheat men will get less and many of them will move into other industries. That has to come with us and with you, too. It was coming anyway. My feeling, in fact, is that the war has made it possible to settle many such problems, including the future of trade between the U.S. and Canada, which we could not settle in peace times. In these times Congress will be willing to do many things it would never do before.

'His whole assumption,' Hutchison concluded, 'was that Canada's economy would be merged with that of the U.S., but he did not foresee political union.'[57] Berle's scheme assumed a British defeat and a long war, of course.

Canadians by now accepted the idea of a long war, although few had yet brought themselves to consider seriously the possibility of British defeat.[58] The initiation of the Bank of Canada study indicated that preliminary planning for such a possibility was underway, but H. L. Keenleyside in the Department of External Affairs wanted something more. 'It is no longer any secret,' he wrote in a memo that proposed a sweeping reconstruction of Canadian policy, 'that the Government of the United States has been giving detailed and serious consideration to the possibility of re-organizing the whole economic life of the Western Hemisphere.' Canadians had not looked at this question at all, he argued, nor had they given much thought to the 'military necessity for a revision of our external possibilities'. It would seem improbable, Keenleyside said,

> that the United States in the chaotic and dynamic world that is likely to emerge from the present war, will be prepared to continue indefinitely to protect Canada without demanding a measure of active co-operation in return. It is a reasonable assumption that the United States will expect, and if necessary demand, Canadian assistance in the defence of this continent and this Hemisphere. Concrete steps such as the construction of the Alaskan Highway, the defensive development of the Pacific Coasts and the Maritime Provinces, the co-ordination of Canadian and United States war materiel . . . these are lines along which Washington is likely to require Canadian co-operation. If the United States is forced to defend the Americas against encroachments from across either Ocean, Canada will be expected to participate; thus the negotiation of a specific offensive-defensive alliance is likely to become inevitable.[59]

Keenleyside's memorandum was impressive prophecy.

Everything pointed in this same direction, including word from Washington. Loring Christie saw Roosevelt on August 15 and heard from him the good news that the United States would in all likelihood be able to supply destroyers to Britain in exchange for long-term leases on British bases in the West Indies and in Newfoundland. Roosevelt also told the Minister that he had the assurances about the Royal Navy that he wanted and, as Christie reported, the President indicated that 'he had been thinking of proposing to you to send to Ottawa 3 staff officers . . . to discuss defence problems. . . . He had in mind their surveying situation from Bay of Fundy around to the Gulf of St. Lawrence. They might explore question of base facilities for United States use . . .'[60] The very next day Roosevelt changed his mind and on the spur of the moment decided to invite Mackenzie King to visit with him during his inspection of U.S. Army troops near Ogdensburg, New York.[61]

Mackenzie King accepted the invitation without hesitation. Before leaving on the drive to Ogdensburg on August 17, he received a list of urgently needed war materiel from the Department of National Defence, a shopping list that he would do his best to fill. What was in Roosevelt's mind King did not know, beyond what he heard from Christie and what Roosevelt had said to him on the telephone—'the matter of mutual defence of our coasts on the Atlantic.'*[62]

Was King surprised at Roosevelt's suggestion of a Permanent Joint Board on Defence? If so, there is no indication in his papers or diary. The subject was raised and dealt with quickly. The two men agreed to establish the Board with equal representation from each country, its mandate limited to studying common defence problems and making recommendations to the two governments on ways to deal with them. About all that King queried, it seems, was the significance of making the Board permanent. 'I said I was not questioning the wisdom of it,' the Prime Minister enquired in that somewhat annoying way he had, 'but was anxious to get what he had in mind.' What Roosevelt was thinking of was 'to help secure the continent for the future'.[63]

The decision to set up the PJBD was an important one, its casual methodology notwithstanding. For the purposes of the war, the Ogdensburg agreement meant that the United States for the first time had signed what amounted to a joint defence pact with a belligerent. That had to count as a gain for the hard-pressed Allies. But for Canada the agreement marked the first realization of the changed shape of the world. Britain was in danger and no longer able to guarantee Canada's safety. In such circumstances it seemed prudent and wise to safeguard the Dominion by accepting the protection of the United States. No Canadian government could have done otherwise. But the lack of planning, the lack of understanding about what was involved, is striking. A few memoranda, some rumblings among pressure groups, a few casual

*During the Great War, when he was Assistant Secretary of the Navy, Roosevelt had talked of mutual defence to Sir Joseph Pope, the Under Secretary of State for External Affairs: 'He said,' Pope wrote on May 24, 1917, 'he considered the defence of our Atlantic ports a matter of common concern, and that we should pool our defensive resources etc., Halifax and New York, being the two most important points.' PAC, Sir Joseph Pope Papers, Vol. 46, Daily Journal, 24 May 1917. Prof. R. D. Cuff drew this to my attention.

conversations—that was all that preceded Ogdensburg. A shift of such magnitude, however necessary in the circumstances, deserved more careful consideration.

The rest of the discussion between President and Prime Minister was largely taken up with the destroyer deal and the offer of bases by Britain. For his part, King quickly indicated that Canada would not sell or lease bases, although his government 'would be ready to work out matters of facilities'. The prospect of annual manoeuvres by the forces of each country on the soil of the other was also raised and accepted. And King did try to get the supplies his National Defence people needed. 'I disliked taking advantage of all he had done and was doing to proffer a further request . . . but that I had promised our own boys . . .' Roosevelt was 'very nice' about the requests, but indicated there might be difficulty.[64]

The immediate official and public response to the text of the agreement, released by the Prime Minister and the President on August 18, was enthusiastic. A survey of editorials in thirty-seven newspapers found no opposition whatsoever,[65] and Dr Skelton was overjoyed. 'It was certainly the best day's work done for many a year. It did not come by chance,' the Under Secretary told his Minister, 'but as the inevitable sequence of public policies and personal relationships, based upon the realization of the imperative necessity of close understanding between the English-speaking peoples.'[66] The Cabinet agreed wholeheartedly. And at his first opportunity to report to Parliament on the agreement, King struck a similar note to Skelton's. The new arrangement 'is part of the enduring foundation of a new world order, based on friendship and good will. In the furtherance of this new world order, Canada . . . is fulfilling a manifest destiny.'[67]

Whose manifest destiny? That was the question troubling some Conservative politicians. R. B. Hanson, the Conservative leader, came to Ottawa from New Brunswick as soon as he heard of the agreement. But King mollified him, and he went home again. His suspicions soon were awakened anew by a letter from Senator Arthur Meighen, a man who saw dark conspiracies in everything that concerned Mackenzie King. 'Really I lost my breakfast when I read the account this morning and gazed on the disgusting picture of these potentates posing like monkeys in the very middle of the blackest crisis of this Empire,' Meighen wrote. 'We don't want Canadians to get the idea that we don't need to exert ourselves and this is just the idea they will get from this disgusting publicity. . . . King refused to have Canada sit on the Committee of Imperial Defence for fear it might entangle us in war. He has no objection, though, to such an arrangement with the United States. Neither have I for that matter,' the acidulous Meighen said. 'There is no danger of it entangling us in the war because there is no Spain left that the United States could lick . . .'[68] Hanson soon picked up this theme, and in a Labour Day address in Toronto he suggested that the agreement was 'window-dressing. . . . I am glad to know that the Government of the United Kingdom is aware of these discussions—otherwise, to me, it would have the appearance of casting off old and now embattled ties and taking on new and untried vows. I am not,' he added in a low blow, 'unaware of the inclinations of Mr. King in days gone by.'[69]

King could readily shrug off Hanson's speech, which met with a flood of editorial abuse,[70] but he could not ignore Winston Churchill's very similar reaction. In high enthusiasm after returning from his talks with the President, Mackenzie King had sent a full account to the British Prime Minister, much in the fashion of a small boy expecting the highest of praise from his father. Churchill had raised the matter in his War Cabinet on August 21. 'It was thought,' the Cabinet conclusions coolly stated,

> that Mr. Mackenzie King was putting himself into a difficult position from the point of view of Canadian politics, and that he would find it difficult to obtain approval for the arrangement by which the United States Army would be granted facilities for manoeuvres on Canadian soil. For this reason THE PRIME MINISTER thought that he should introduce one or two cautionary phrases in his telegram replying to Mr. Mackenzie King's account of his conversation with President Roosevelt.[71]

More specious and silly reasoning is difficult to imagine. But Churchill's brief telegram—'there may be two opinions on some of the points mentioned. Supposing Mr. Hitler cannot invade us . . . all these transactions will be judged in a mood different to that prevailing while the issue still hangs in the balance'[72]—was simply shattering to Mackenzie King who brooded on it for some time and then poured out his feelings to Cabinet and to the British High Commissioner.[73]

The High Commissioner, Sir Gerald Campbell, himself upset by Churchill's tone, told his colleague in Washington, Lord Lothian, that 'I would only say here that Winston Churchill's reply to Mackenzie King was somewhat dampening and was resented in consequence. . . . One thing which stood out was that this descendant of a rebel was fully convinced that at last he had rendered both Great Britain and Canada a service, and he was inclined to put the former before the latter.' Winston Churchill's wet blanket, Campbell concluded, 'threatened to bring him back rather abruptly to his general attitude of putting Canada first and Great Britain second.'[74]

The resentment lasted until a further telegram came from Churchill on September 12. This one, almost certainly sent in response to Campbell's pleas, was conciliatory and flattering, thanking King 'personally for all you have done for the common cause and especially in promoting a harmony of sentiment throughout the New World.'[75] Mackenzie King was overjoyed at this message, which gave him 'more pleasure than almost anything that has happened at any time. It made clear my part in bringing together the English-speaking peoples and an appreciation by Churchill of my own efforts in connection with the war; also, the significance of what I have striven to do on this continent.'[76] The Prime Minister would carry this telegram with him wherever he went for some time and on occasion it would be shown to journalists and political friends.

The PJBD established by King and Roosevelt at Ogdensburg soon became a functioning reality. The two countries each appointed four representatives and a secretary, with a civilian as the head of each delegation. O. M. Biggar, a distinguished lawyer and public servant, headed the Canadian section and Fiorello LaGuardia the American, while Hugh Keenleyside was the secretary on the Canadian side. The Board's initial meeting was held in Ottawa on August 26, and the agenda listed the defence of Newfoundland and of the east and west coasts, as well as the procurement of supplies.[77] Further meetings followed in Washington on September 9-10, in Boston on October 2, and in Halifax on October 4. Board members surveyed the defences on the coasts, created committees, and began to draw plans for the pooling of the defence efforts of the two countries in the event of any attack on North America.

The PJBD's military members produced two defence plans. The first, the Joint Canadian-United States Basic Defence Plan, 1940, was designed to meet the situation that would result if Britain were overrun and the Royal Navy lost control of the Atlantic. Strategic control of the Canadian forces was given to the United States by the Basic Defence Plan, subject to consultation with the Canadian Chiefs of Staff. The second plan, produced in the spring of 1941 and called ABC-22, was a by-product of the Anglo-American staff conversations of January 1941; it aimed at meeting Canadian-American defence requirements in a war that would see the United States join with the Allies to defeat the Axis powers. But when the Americans tried to secure agreement that ABC-22 should hand control over strategic planning to them, as had been the case with the earlier scheme, the Canadians this time balked. The Americans hoped to integrate the Maritimes, Newfoundland, the Gaspé, and British Columbia directly into their Northeast and Western Defense Commands, and their demands became the subject of heated debate in the PJBD and in the Cabinet War Committee in April and May 1941. The Canadians soon became convinced that the United States sought tactical control over Canadian forces, not just strategical control, and this was unacceptable. To LaGuardia, the American Chairman of the PJBD, such complaints were, as he said of another matter, just 'the usual difficulties because of pride and the little brother attitude'.[78] In fact they were fundamental, and the Canadians persisted until they won out. The upshot was a plan that called for the 'Coordination of the military effort of the United States and Canada [to] be effected by mutual cooperation,'[79] something far removed from the original U.S. goal. What was significant, however, was that the United States would even advance such a plan. While it made military sense to have common arrangements, it was too fast a step towards continental integration, too much a reversal of Canada's long struggle for autonomy for such measures to be accepted in any but the most dire circumstances.

III

The Ogdensburg Agreement can be seen in different ways: as Canada seeking security under the American wing; or as nothing more than the United States formalizing its hegemony over the Canadian Dominion. But unquestionably the agreement was precipitated by the events in Europe that altered the balance of power so decisively that spring of 1940. The Hyde Park declaration of April 1941, an economic arrangement between Canada and the United States, between King and Roosevelt, resulted from similar international factors largely beyond Canada's control.

The declaration grew out of Anglo-American financial diplomacy. The Roosevelt administration had been fairly successful in breaching the neutrality barriers erected by isolationists in the 1930s. The arms embargo had been repealed and destroyers swapped for bases without the intervention of Congress. But Britain still desperately needed American dollars and gold, and without hard cash could not secure munitions in the United States. The Chancellor of the Exchequer estimated on August 21, 1940 that British purchases in North America would amount to some $3.2 billion in the next year, as against total resources in foreign exchange and American securities of £490 million.[80] With prospective bankruptcy in sight, Lord Lothian, the Ambassador in Washington, was hardly exaggerating when he told reporters, 'Boys, Britain's broke. It's your money we want.'[81] The British plight was not immediately recognized by officials in Washington. Scepticism about the claims of hardship paralleled a belief in the opulence of Empire; President Roosevelt himself told Lothian that the British would have to liquidate $9 billion worth of assets in the Western hemisphere before a convincing case for aid could be made to the American people and Congress.[82]

The Anglo-American difficulties that eventually produced the Lend-Lease Bill had their parallels in Anglo-Canadian relations. London had been irritated by Canada's unwillingness to assume more of a financial burden in the early days of the war, and there had been the equally sharp comments in Ottawa about the British government's reluctance to place more than token orders in Canada. Both British orders and British pressures increased in the summer of 1940, and feeling mounted in Whitehall that Canada should begin to use her own gold reserves and direct investments in the United States to assist the cause. Furthermore British representatives began to demand that Canada hand over to Britain £70 million entrusted by the Bank of France to the Bank of England and stored in Canada, as well as an unspecified but very large sum of American dollars of the same origin. There was also £94 million that the French government had stored directly with the Bank of Canada.

Mackenzie King adamantly refused to turn the money over. Canada was a trustee for France, even a defeated France, the Prime Minister insisted, and he would not be moved. The British tried hard enough, even sending a very senior Treasury official to see the Prime Minister. Unfortunately King took an instinctive dislike to Sir Frederick Phillips, who 'looked like a thug', and the interview was frosty:

I told him [King recorded] that I thought the money was there on trust; that we were trustees, and had no right to allow the money to be used for any purpose other than that which might be sanctioned by the French Government. He said: but these are our American dollars. I told him I could not see wherein the American dollars belonged to the British....

He then said if we could not agree to this, they would have to possibly forego the purchase of the planes and go without planes. I told him I did not think he had any right to express the matter that way. That I was astonished, after all Canada had done and was doing to assist Britain in the war, that anyone speaking on behalf of the British Government should seek to place on our shoulders responsibility for the British not being able to get planes in the U.S. just because we were unwilling to allow all the laws of sacred trust to be violated....[83]

King's position was unquestionably correct legally, but the British case was compelling. 'This is not a war to be fought with kid gloves,' a Treasury memorandum noted. 'We are fighting not only for our existence but also for that of the French nation.... Our need of supplies is paramount, our resources for obtaining them otherwise than as gifts are rapidly disappearing...'[84] The gold, even so, was withheld.

Still, Canada was taking other steps to provide Britain with additional dollar supplies, among which the repatriation of Canadian securities held by British citizens was the most important. To March 31, 1941 the British deficit with Canada was $795,000,000. Of this amount, 31.4 per cent was met by Britain transferring gold to Canada, 26.2 per cent by the accumulation of sterling in London, and the remainder, 42.4 per cent, by debt repatriation.[85] The British wanted Ottawa to contribute more by way of sterling overdrafts, in effect a form of dollar loan, in part to reduce the pace at which Canadian securities were being redeemed. Moreover by late 1940 Britain's ability to cover her deficits with gold transfers had ended.

The deteriorating British position had very serious implications. The historian of British war finance noted that 'Whether the Dominion Government provided the United Kingdom with Canadian dollars in exchange for repatriated Canadian securities or for a sterling balance, the dollars had to be found by the Dominion Government either by taxation or by the sale of securities to the Canadian public.'[86] The problem for Canada was that the strain on the economy was already very great. Finance Minister J. L. Ilsley estimated in February 1941 that war expenditures in fiscal 1941 would run to $1.4 billion, with an extra

$400 million needed to cover the repatriation of securities from the United Kingdom and a further $433 million to pay for civil expenditures. In addition, Ilsley calculated that the provincial and municipal governments in Canada would spend $575 million, making a total of $2.8 billion in government expenditures at all levels, a figure well over half the total national income.[87] If the British position sagged even more, the demands on Canada would increase, and the result might be, as Mackenzie King gloomily feared, 'a greater burden than the people of Canada can be led to bear.'[88] All a far cry from the limited liability war of 1939; a solution to Britain's problems was now necessary in the Canadian interest.

Even under peacetime conditions Canada's economy was based on a 'bilateral unbalance within a balanced "North Atlantic Triangle".'[89] A chronic deficit with the United States had been balanced by a surplus with Britain and other trading partners. The war had curtailed Canada's markets, of course, and Britain was now financially strapped. In the meantime trade with the United States had increased, most of it as a direct result of war needs. In April 1941, the Deputy Minister of Finance, Clifford Clark, foresaw a deficit of $478 million in Canada's balance of payments with the United States, and by June Canadian officials were estimating that American imports had risen by $400 million per year over 1938 levels while Canadian exports to the United States had increased only half as much.[90] So long as Canada had to secure 30 per cent of the components required for British munitions orders in the United States, there was little prospect of a reduction in the deficit. Canada, therefore, faced the double bind of financing Britain's deficit while at the same time her own deficit of American dollars grew.

The King government had taken a series of actions in its efforts to right this balance. A Foreign Exchange Control order to prevent the export of capital had been issued in 1939, and simultaneous efforts were made to broaden exports, stimulate tourism, and increase gold production. The Foreign Exchange Control Board stabilized the Canadian dollar at 10 per cent below parity with the U.S. dollar. Further measures followed in the spring and fall of 1940, including a refusal of American dollar exchange for Canadian travellers to the United States. In December 1940 the government took its most serious step in a move that coincided with the end of British gold flows to Canada. The passage of the War Exchange Conservation Act prohibited importation of a long list of products from countries outside the sterling bloc. The measure, directed at the United States, was discussed by Cabinet in those terms. Simultaneously duties were lowered on imports from Britain while excise taxes were levied on automobiles and other articles that required high percentages of American components. These measures were expected to save $70 million in exchange, but the inexorable increase in the adverse trade balance continued despite these efforts.[91]

There were limits to what Ottawa could do in its efforts to cope with the exchange problem. In late October 1940 the U.S. Minister, Pierrepont Moffat, had informed Washington that 'Canada's biggest worry at the moment is financial—how to acquire more dollar exchange. The need,' Moffat said,

> is not yet desperate but the problem is rapidly becoming acute. It could, of course, be staved off if our legislation were amended and loans or credits granted to Canada, but there is some slight opposition to this prospect in financial circles here which argue that the future headache of servicing a large increase in Canada's foreign debt would be worse than any possible current headache. If loans or credits are not soon forthcoming then we must face the fact that Canada will have to take one or more of the following three measures: (A) Seizure against compensation and sale in New York of large blocks of American securities now held by Canadians; (B) Blocking in whole or in part the transfer to American owners of dividends from American companies; and (C) Selective purchasing from the United States under license, with strict rationing of non-essentials, among which are included American fruits and vegetables. There is much popular pressure in favour of number three . . .[92]

The third course was the one adopted, primarily because Ottawa officials were well aware of the reaction from financial circles in the United States to any attempt to implement a freeze on dividend payments. The first course had its own problems for a government determined to maintain Canadian investments in the United States. Estimates of the amount in question ranged from $275,000,000 to over $1 billion,[93] and while a sell-off *in extremis* might have been considered, the Department of Finance hoped to avoid any such course. The investments provided a cushion protecting Canada from some of the strains imposed by the nation's heavy foreign indebtedness and, among a host of additional reasons, there was the political difficulty involved in compelling Canadians to sell their holdings of American securities at what many investors would feel to be sacrifice prices.[94]

There was also, as Moffat observed, opposition to borrowing in the

United States. Ottawa officials believed 'it would be disastrous to face a future of making heavy interest payments to the United States year after year in perpetuity, or, alternatively, having a war debt controversy.'[95] That would not be good for Canadian-American relations. Nor, of course, were the interferences Ottawa had felt compelled to make with the flow of trade. These controls went against the trend towards liberalized trade between the two countries and would be certain to antagonize Cordell Hull, one of Canada's champions in Washington. They would also invite powerful opposition from American domestic interests, and this calculation certainly contributed to the decision to omit fresh fruits and vegetables from the December 1940 list of excluded imports. As Ilsley bluntly told the House of Commons, 'we had to weigh . . . the inevitable public reaction there would be in many of the agricultural districts of the United States, the embarrassment this restriction would cause . . . and the danger which would ensue not only to our own trade relations with the United States, not only to the market which our trade agreement with that country gives to so many of our primary producers, but to the whole trade agreement policy of the United States.'[96] That was pretty frank talk.

As the terrible year of 1940 drew to its close, Canadian and British calculations centred increasingly upon Roosevelt's proposed Lend-Lease Act. The bill was designed to speed up munitions production, to eliminate the need for cash payments on Allied orders, and to increase Roosevelt's freedom in foreign affairs. It empowered the President to order manufactured 'any defense article for the government of any country whose defense the President deems vital to the defense of the United States.' Such articles he could 'sell, transfer title to, exchange, lend, lease, or otherwise dispose of' to these governments.[97]

For the next three months Ottawa and London watched as this bill, introduced into Congress on January 10, 1941, made its way through the American legislative process. To Britain the Lend-Lease Act promised to be a god-send that would ensure eventual victory. Canadians agreed, although the government had to weigh the possibility that American generosity might end or at least severely limit British munitions purchases in Canada. C. D. Howe, the Minister of Munitions and Supply, raised this prospect in the Cabinet War Committee on February 18, telling his colleagues that he was 'gravely concerned' that Britain would shift orders for raw materials, food, and munitions to the United States where the terms would be easier. Ten days later Howe brought up the matter again, pressing this time for the despatch of a strong negotiating team to Washington to talk with both American and British officials. The diversion of orders from Canada to the United States, he warned, could have 'disastrous' results on the country's industrial program.[98]

The British knew well the impact Lend-Lease would have on Anglo-Canadian relations. Although junior ministers bemoaned Canada's accelerating drift out of the Empire and into the American orbit,[99] the Treasury clearly wanted Canada to use Lend-Lease to the fullest. This was made crystal clear in a memorandum prepared at Treasury in March 1941 for the newly named High Commissioner to Ottawa, Malcolm MacDonald. 'What we want Canada to do,' the brief bluntly said, 'is (a) to reduce her purchases in the United States to an absolute minimum . . . (b) to make use herself of the "Lease and Lend" Bill if the United States Government will agree to this, in order to obtain the maximum she can from the United States without payment. (c) In so far as Canada still has an adverse balance with the United States . . . to cover this with saleable Canadian marketable assets (e.g. United States securities etc.) held by Canada.' This prescription would be difficult for the Canadians to swallow. They would need heavier taxation, the Treasury argued, and have to accept some inflation. 'But clearly their objective should be to meet our needs so far as possible by saving and taxation and to reduce inflation to a minimum.' The brief concluded by noting that Britain had some cards yet to play with Canada:

> These are points of domestic policy on which we have no right to dictate to Canada, but it is as much in their interests as in ours to act along these lines, seeing that our only alternative, if we are unable to pay for our orders in Canada, is to place them instead in the United States in cases in which we should be able to obtain the goods under the 'Lease and Lend' Act.[100]

This slightly smug Treasury position was consistent with the British line throughout the war: Canada could do more. But the British now possessed a powerful weapon in Lend-Lease, and access to the $7 billion appropriation that accompanied it greatly improved their bargaining position with Canada.

What of Canada's attitude to Lend-Lease? Top officials in the Finance Department believed that Canada should steer clear of it. The British Treasury's representative in North America noted that Clifford Clark was opposed, despite his country's adverse balance with the United States and steeply mounting loans to Britain. Clark believed that acceptance of American aid would put Canada in a weaker position than Britain, separated by an ocean from American economic power, and he feared that the Americans later might drive a very hard bargain on tariffs.* Mackenzie King shared this reasoning. As he wrote in his diary on March 13, 'We do not intend to avail ourselves of the Lend-Lease Bill but to allow its advances wholly to Britain. There is, of course, a bigger obligation because of it all than appears on the face of it. I have no doubt,' the Prime Minister said, 'the U.S. would undoubtedly keep the obligations arising under the Lend-Lease Bill hanging pretty much over her head to be used to compel open markets or return of materials, etc. It is a terrible position for Britain to be in . . .'†[101]

Of course no one was certain that the Americans would permit Canada to get Lend-Lease aid except on severe terms. Ottawa had determined to resist demands to sell off Canadian-owned American securities. Planners also were fully aware that some Americans criticized Canada for not doing all she could to assist Britain. There was, for example, that matter of the French funds, and there were complaints that Canada charged the British for all purchases while the United States was expected to provide supplies free under Lend-Lease. The Secretary of the Treasury, Henry Morgenthau, personally told Clark that Canada would not be permitted to come under Lend-Lease unless 'steps had been taken to realize at least a portion of Canadian securities in the United States.'[102]

What Canada wanted was some way to have whatever benefits were available under Lend-Lease to solve her exchange problems while at the

*Clark estimated Canada's adverse balance with the U.S. at $400 million for the year from August 1940 and as much as $600 million for the year after that. Canada's remaining capital assets in the U.S. were $136 million in gold, $115 million in dollars, and $378 million in marketable securities. The British adverse balance was estimated at $1.2 billion, and some doubt was expressed at Canada's ability to carry on in the face of such deficits. Public Record Office, Foreign Office Records, FO 371/28792, Phillips to Treasury, 4 Feb. 1941; FO 371/28795, Phillips to Treasury, 4 Mar. 1941; R. W. James, *Wartime Economic Cooperation* (Toronto, 1949), p. 32. For an assessment of the conditions in which Lend-Lease might have been acceptable, see King Papers, Clark to King, 9 Apr. 1941, ff. 288032-3.

†The British historian, A. J. P. Taylor, noted that 'Lend-Lease enabled Britain to keep going, but the Americans drove a hard bargain. The American financial authorities stripped Great Britain of her gold reserves and her overseas investments. . . . As a condition of Lend-Lease, British exports were restricted. . . . Moreover, a postwar abolition of imperial preferences and controlled exchanges was dictated to the British. As an independent financial center, London ceased to exist. There was here a sharp contrast with Canada, whose mutual aid was given without strings or conditions.' A. J. P. Taylor, 'Daddy, What was Winston Churchill?', *New York Times Magazine*, 28 Apr. 1974, 84.

same time avoiding the kinds of sacrifices that were being demanded of the British both in the short run (liquidation of direct investments) and in the long term (weakening of the post-war bargaining position). The problem was to hit on a formula that obviated direct Lend-Lease aid, that did not add to Morgenthau's and Roosevelt's problems with Congress, and yet still reduced Canada's call on U.S. dollars. The ideal situation would be an arrangement whereby Washington agreed to buy some of her own war needs in Canada and also to supply under Lend-Lease the components Canada required for manufacturing munitions for Britain. And if, in addition, Washington could be persuaded to buy Canadian output for shipment to England under Lend-Lease, Ottawa would have access to British purchasing while avoiding the current requirement of financing it.

The War Committee heard one part of this formula on March 12. Clifford Clark reported that he had seen Secretary Morgenthau and suggested that the raw materials and components Canada required to manufacture munitions for Britain should be eligible for Lend-Lease on the British account.[103] Morgenthau was not too accommodating. When Canadian officials saw him again on March 18 and 19, he told them that if there were exchange problems Canada should begin to liquidate her securities. As for the question of bringing the British component of Canadian imports under Lend-Lease, that was a matter for Harry Hopkins to decide. Hopkins was the President's friend and confidant, and the man charged by Roosevelt with the administration of Lend-Lease.[104] This conversation convinced Clifford Clark that Morgenthau was the main obstacle to a favourable settlement, and he was increasingly of the view, as he told Grant Dexter on April 9, that 'a good deal of education was needed in the U.S. to prove to them that it was not in their own interest to put Canada through the wringer . . .'[105] This task of education would ultimately fall to Mackenzie King.

In the meantime the British agreed to maintain their orders in Canada. Clark had put the problem to the Cabinet War Committee on March 13: Canada had to find some way to finance British purchases or London might be forced to shift contracts to the United States where the terms seemed easier. His recommendation, Clark said, would be that Canada finance the British deficit with Canada upon the condition that the British undertake not to divert orders from Canada and that a suitable exchange rate for sterling be guaranteed.[106] Mackenzie King wrote that the Deputy Minister 'gave an exceedingly able and lucid account of the largest problem Canada has ever faced,'[107] not much of an exaggeration. On March 27 Ilsley presented the Cabinet with a draft telegram to London. This was duly sent and, after some hesitation in London, accepted.[108] The Canadian government had been blackmailed,* not too strong a word, into agreeing to finance Britain's deficit before arriving at a settlement of her own financial troubles with the United States. That settlement was now urgently required, especially since Congress had passed Lend-Lease on March 20.

At the Cabinet War Committee on March 21, Ilsley said that his Deputy Minister was convinced that only direct representations to President Roosevelt could produce immediate and sympathetic consideration of Canada's difficulties in retaining and financing British purchases in Canada. At this point Mackenzie King interjected to say that he was planning to go south in April.[109] It would be up to the Prime Minister personally to pry a favourable agreement out of the Americans, the kind of task that King relished. His friendship with Roosevelt would pay yet another dividend.

Mackenzie King left for Washington on April 15 and saw Roosevelt the next day. The first conversation was mainly about hemispheric military matters, the subject clearly uppermost in the President's mind. The United States would extend its patrols further out into the Atlantic, he said, and the President then proceeded to demonstrate that he was well briefed about the defence problems of the Labrador coast. Mackenzie King 'purposely refrained from discussing financial matters,' he recorded, 'as I saw how tired he was, and did not wish to introduce this subject until we got away when we could discuss it quietly.'[110] King also left this first conversation 'struck with the significance of the President's last remark as I was leaving, about the "good neighbour" policy, having been one of the great contributions we had made together to world affairs. . . . His emphasis . . . was quite marked.'[111]

The next day the Prime Minister saw Secretary of State Hull and Treasury Secretary Morgenthau in separate appointments. Hull was friendly and the two chatted about a wide range of subjects. When King turned to the business at hand he cleverly stressed the reciprocal nature of the arrangement he was suggesting, for reciprocity had always been a sacred totem to the Secretary. King wanted 'the components of

---

*In L. B. Pearson's view, Canadian officials could not bargain as toughly as they might have wished with the British because London was fully aware that the Canadian public would not go along. (L. B. Pearson Interview, 21 Oct. 1971.) This was surely true in this case, where Canada was put into an untenable financial position by the British before any agreement with Washington had been reached.

materials we were producing for Britain secured from America on the Lend-Lease American basis and that America would place orders with us for things that we could produce.'[112] Morgenthau was a more critical factor in the equation, much concerned with his difficulties with Congress. The Treasury Secretary told King that in order to get Lend-Lease passed he had had to make it clear that Britain was bankrupt. Canada, Morgenthau said, was not yet in that state and, as King recorded, 'he thought our situation was all right till the end of the year . . .' The Prime Minister had to disabuse Morgenthau of this attitude and then put to him his scheme for a virtual system of barter in war materiel. This interested the American and he said he would do 'anything possible . . . on this scale to help to get us purchasing power. . . . they would pay in dollars for things manufactured by us. I said it would go to purchasing American war materiel.' The two agreed that Clifford Clark would meet the Secretary the next day to discuss matters further. Mackenzie King also proffered a long defence of his position on the French assets, and he was convinced that this as well as his 'readiness to concede the necessity of his carrying Congress behind him' had saved the day.[113]

Matters seemed to be in hand at last. And on Sunday, April 20, just before he was to go to Hyde Park, Roosevelt's home on the Hudson River, King met with Clark and E. P. Taylor of the Department of Munitions and Supply. The Deputy Minister of Finance gave Mackenzie King a draft statement that expressed Canada's optimal demands, and the Prime Minister made some minor revisions to it.[114] He took this amended draft with him when he went off to spend a 'grand Sunday' with President Roosevelt.

It was indeed to be a grand Sunday, particularly for Canada and Mackenzie King. The conversation was warm and friendly, and Roosevelt again talked at length about hemispheric defence, aid to Britain, and American bases in Canada and Newfoundland. Later in the afternoon Roosevelt said that he had seen Morgenthau and had the Canadian situation explained to him. 'He thought,' King wrote later, 'perhaps it might be going a little too far to have something manufactured in Canada for the U.S. to Lease-Lend to England.'[115]

After a pleasant dinner the talk turned in earnest to the subject King had come to discuss. The Prime Minister had thought carefully about his approach and, as he explained it later in a somewhat idealized account to Grant Dexter, capitalized on Roosevelt's use of 'good neighbourhood' in their first conversation four days before.

Roosevelt had said to King [Dexter wrote after talking to the Prime Minister] that he didn't know much about the exchange situation: that he would like King to tell him about it and outline the policy which Roosevelt should follow. King hadn't bothered about the economics of it. He told Roosevelt that if he were in his place, he would have regarded [sic] only for the neighbourly phase of it. What the U.S. and Britain had done was one thing. Canada as the neighbour on this continent, the only one that really mattered, was another proposition entirely. If the U.S. insisted upon taking from Canada what few possessions she had in the U.S. it would only give voice to anti-U.S. sentiment in this country. Why not buy from Canada as much as Canada is buying from the U.S.—just balance the accounts. Roosevelt thought this was a swell idea.[116]

The President, much better briefed than this account suggests, was not the passive figure painted by King. But certainly Roosevelt looked at King's draft agreement and 'Said he thought it was first rate.'[117] There were only two changes requested by the President. As he had indicated earlier in the afternoon, he deleted any reference to the United States purchasing goods in Canada for subsequent Lend-Lease to Britain. The President also added aluminum to a list of war materials that Canada could supply to the United States. The amended draft was agreed to over the telephone by Morgenthau, and the Hyde Park Agreement was fact. It had all been incredibly easy.[118]

The six-paragraph statement expressed very simply the desire of the two men that 'in mobilizing the resources of this continent each country should provide the other with the defense articles which it is best able to produce . . .' The declaration anticipated that Canada 'can supply the United States with between $200,000,000 and $300,000,000 worth of such defense articles' over the next year, purchases that would 'materially assist Canada in meeting part of the cost of Canadian defense purchases in the United States.' The text also specified that 'In so far as Canadian defense purchases in the United States consist of component parts to be used in equipment and munitions which Canada is producing for Great Britain, it was also agreed that Great Britain will obtain these parts under the Lend-Lease Act and forward them to Canada for inclusion in the finished articles.'[119]

Justifiably proud of his triumph, Mackenzie King was showered with praise by his Cabinet ministers. C. D. Howe, his munitions plants now virtually assured of continuous full production, glowed. 'Said something

about being the greatest negotiator the country had or something about
the world's best negotiator,' King happily noted. 'Could hardly believe
so much could have been accomplished in so short a time. Said it
straightened out the most difficult problems they had had for months.'[120]
So it did. Significantly, King had secured the agreement without being
forced to make any major concessions. After all the long and frustrating
negotiations Clark and his colleagues had had with the Americans,
nothing tangible in the end was demanded of Canada.[121]

The agreement signed, the rest was housekeeping. As early as April
24, even before the modalities were clarified, the United States Army
began to honour the agreement.[122] Final details were arranged on May
14 when Clifford Clark and Sir Frederick Phillips of the Treasury signed
a brief memorandum in Washington that put on record Britain's
willingness to secure approximately $220 million worth of goods under
Lend-Lease for despatch to Canada. This would represent 'the actual
value of the "United States content" of Canadian war supplies to the
United Kingdom'. Morgenthau accepted this arrangement, and the
remaining details were worked out in the same amicable way.[123]

The Hyde Park Agreement did not solve all of Canada's financial
problems. Difficulties in maintaining British purchases in Canada
persisted until Canada itself adopted a variant of Lend-Lease in 1943.
And as the arrangements themselves worked out in practice, the positive
effects on Canada's balance of payments with the United States owed
less to the provision of components intended for Britain under Lend-
Lease than to increased American purchases in Canada. These rose very
fast, reaching $275 million in 1942, $301 million in 1943, and $314
million in 1944.[124] Additional American dollars flowed into Canada
after Pearl Harbor when the United States Army began heavy defence
expenditures in the Canadian North West and when American
investors, speculating on a revaluation of the undervalued Canadian
dollar, began sending large sums north of the border. The result was
that Canada's shortage of U.S. dollars was over by 1942 and, in fact, the
holdings grew so large by 1943 that controls had to be established to
keep the surplus within bounds.[125]

For Mackenzie King the lesson of this successful negotiation with
Roosevelt was very much the same as that he had drawn after the
Ogdensburg agreement eight months before. Beyond its immediate
significance, he told Parliament, 'the Hyde Park declaration will have a
permanent significance in the relations between Canada and the United
States. It involves nothing less than a common plan for the economic

defence of the western hemisphere.' Even more, the declaration was 'a further convincing demonstration that Canada and the United States are indeed laying the enduring foundations of a new world order, an order based on international understanding, on mutual aid, on friendship and good will.'[126] A new world order was being created and there could be no doubt about that. But Canada's place in it was that of a supplicant seeking favours.

IV

The Ogdensburg and Hyde Park Agreements had created closer ties than ever before between Canada and the United States by linking inextricably the defences and economies of the two nations. Ottawa wanted to go further still, and coincident with the discussions that preceded the Hyde Park declaration, negotiations were in process effectively to co-ordinate the war production of the two countries.

The idea of integrating production facilities was first discussed by the Permanent Joint Board on Defence in October 1940. A draft recommendation was then prepared, apparently by the Canadian side, calling for the appointment of 'supply' representatives to the Board.[127] Nothing was done immediately, however, in part at least because Keenleyside, the Canadian secretary on the PJBD, believed that such a move was premature before full studies were undertaken. Keenleyside was right, and he soon convinced Dr Skelton. The Under Secretary wrote to Mackenzie King just before Christmas 1940 that he had been thinking of this matter and talking about it with some others, most notably with Victor Sifton, the publisher and the newly appointed Master-General of the Ordnance. The questions that had to be examined, Skelton said, were these: 'Should Canada make a 50% increase in her steel capacity to meet the peak load in steel or arrange to get from the United States the additional requirements which would not be more than 2% of their capacity? . . . Should we attempt to build a factory which would take over a year to get into production five or six hundred advanced bombers and fighters in Canada, or should we concentrate on production of training aircraft and arrange with the United States for say a week's production of one of their factories when in full production?'[128] Those were real questions.

Various studies were soon under way, co-ordinated by Keenleyside.[129] A more formal study was launched with the approval of the Cabinet War Committee by R. A. C. Henry, a former Deputy Minister of Railways and Canals who had joined Beauharnois Light, Heat and Power Company, but returned on the outbreak of war to work for C. D. Howe.[130] Feelers were also put out in the United States,[131] and A. A. Berle in the Department of State was happy to forward them.[132] The result of this preliminary work was a formal recommendation, approved by the Cabinet War Committee on March 5, 1941,[133] that Joint Committees of Inquiry be established to study questions of integrating the continental economy. The goals were defined to be 'a more economic, more efficient, and more co-ordinated utilization of the combined resources of the two countries in the production of war requirements,' and the minimization of 'the probable post-war disequilibrium consequent upon the changes which the economy in each country is presently undergoing.'[134] This request was formally passed to the United States government on March 17.[135]

The very next day Berle was in Ottawa for further discussions on this and other subjects. In his diary he noted his conversation with Keenleyside:

They have proposed a study of economic pooling between the United States and Canada. Their plan is to have a joint study committee—three men on their side, three men on ours, and a couple of liaison men. In part this is to integrate our defence production with theirs: so that we may manufacture the things we can do best; they the things they do best, instead of trying to duplicate each other's production, buying, etc.

But the rest of it goes much further. Keenleyside realizes this is now one continent and one economy; that we shall have to be integrated as to finance, trade routes, and pretty much everything else; and in this I so thoroughly agree with him that it is refreshing. We talked long and happily about it—though much lies in the realm of dreams. This at least is a new order which can exist without hatred . . . and ought to lead to production without slavery.[136]

Berle and Keenleyside ran with the wind.

The United States officially accepted the proposal for the Joint Economic Committees on June 6, 1941, and the teams were named and announced shortly thereafter.[137] Curiously the Committees never amounted to much, and much of their work was swallowed up by the Materials Coordinating Committee,[138] the eventual product of that October PJBD recommendation. The Materials Coordinating Committee linked C. D. Howe's Department of Munitions and Supply directly with its American counterpart and became the most effective agency of co-ordination. The creation of a plethora of Combined Boards in 1942 effectively ended the work of the Joint Committees.[139]

The Joint Economic Committees were an abortive Canadian effort at co-ordination and integration. To seek to co-operate with the U.S. on economic matters as an equal was a sign of Canada's changing stature, particularly when Canada was the initiator of such discussions. But it was much more self-interest that motivated the government. Co-operation with the Americans would ensure access to scarce goods and an end to financial difficulties. If none realized that integration could also entail demands on Canada, the precarious war situation perhaps can be their excuse.

Much more nationalistic were Canada's efforts to secure military representation in the United States. Until Hitler's victories in May and June 1940, Canada did not even station military attachés in Washington. The Chief of the General Staff proposed the exchange of attachés on July 26 and, although there was some concern from the Cabinet War Committee about the American response to such a request, the Committee agreed. In the event the officers went south before the summer was out.[140]

Once the American members of the PJBD began pressing for strategic and tactical control over the Canadian forces in North America, attachés did not seem adequate military representation, and the Department of National Defence began to seek a mission that would provide 'direct communication between branches of the staff of each country'.[141] The need increased once Ottawa began to learn details of Anglo-American planning, and the Cabinet War Committee, increasingly feeling left out, became concerned 'to ensure that strategic discussion in areas of Canadian responsibility was adequately co-ordinated with that of the other two powers.'[142]

Typically, neither Britain nor the United States wanted to deal with Canada through a separate Washington mission. London was prepared to offer a Canadian military representative a place in its own mission, but the British military were adamant in their opposition to separate Canadian representation. All the hoary chestnuts were brought out again: it was important that the Commonwealth speak to the Americans with one voice; a separate Canadian mission would complicate business; Canadian interests would be better served if they were backed by a united mission; and there were probably not enough experienced Canadian officers for such duty.[143] The key opposition, perhaps prompted by the British military, came from the United States. The State Department, traditionally sympathetic to Canada and to Canadian interests in the United States, had no objections but the War and Navy Departments did. The military attachés and the PJBD were, in their view, quite sufficient, thank you.[144] Although Ottawa stood firm, and although Mackenzie King argued strongly for his point in discussions with Pierrepont Moffat, there was no success. The Americans insisted that so long as the Permanent Joint Board on Defence existed, nothing else was necessary,[145] and there would be no satisfaction for Canada until the middle of 1942. Yesterday's coup, it seemed, was today's drawback. More than a year of tenacious bargaining—and pleading—would be necessary to persuade the American government to permit the establishment of a Canadian Joint Staff Mission.

The difficulty in winning this simple-enough concession was only a sign of the dramatic shift in the attitudes of the United States Administration. After the military staff talks with the British at the beginning of 1941 and after the Lend-Lease Act was passed by Congress in March, the tenor of Washington opinion was far more concerned with global issues than with the hemispheric thinking that had dominated the American capital in the panicky weeks after the fall of continental Europe. From the bureaucracy's point of view, understandably enough, it was much more convenient administratively to deal with London alone than to cope with the variegated demands of a passel of Dominions. The results of this shift were felt particularly in Ottawa, of course. From being a vital link in the defence of the hemisphere, Canada had become only an appendage of limited importance. The Canadian government had made agreements of far-reaching importance on the assumption, the now faulty assumption, that American attitudes would remain constant. King and Roosevelt would still meet regularly and talk in a friendly way, but Roosevelt clearly could not spare much time for his friend. No longer would he find it necessary to pass messages to Churchill through the medium of Mackenzie King, particularly after his first meeting with the British Prime Minister off Newfoundland in August 1941, a meeting to which Mackenzie King was pointedly not invited. The new realities had intervened.

The suddenly distant Canadian position vis-à-vis the United States naturally concerned the Department of External Affairs. But the Department was severely weakened by the death of its creator, the Under Secretary of State for External Affairs, Dr O. D. Skelton. Skelton died of a heart attack on January 28, 1941 while driving his automobile on an

Ottawa street, and his death took from Mackenzie King a man who had been near to him since 1911 and his closest collaborator in policy-making since the mid-1920s.[146] Skelton's 'inborn frugality',[147] his care with public expenditures, had first won him a place in Mackenzie King's heart, and the policy attitudes the two men shared were very similar on most questions. In King's eyes, however, Skelton had been too anti-British, too nationalistic to be given his head.[148] The Doctor had also tried to dominate his thoughts and shape his course, King believed, and there had been occasional testy encounters between them. 'I had not meant to speak so sharply,' King wrote after one confrontation in June 1940, 'but I have so frequently been thrown off following my own judgment and wisdom in these matters by pressure from S. and the staff that I made up my mind I would not yield to anything of the kind.'[149] But this kind of tussling was infrequent, and King was well aware what he and the country owed to the Under Secretary. In a fulsome tribute for King, he lamented his own lack of the 'unselfishness and selflessness' that had characterized his friend.[150]

To succeed Skelton, King turned quickly to Norman Robertson. Only thirty-six, Robertson was a British Columbian who had attended Oxford and the Brookings Institution in Washington and who had joined External Affairs in 1929. Technically junior to men like Lester Pearson, Robertson was in Ottawa at the time of Skelton's death, available, and an officer in whom King already had confidence. There would be some difficulties for Robertson in adjusting to his new role* and some grumbling from those who had been passed over,[151] but Robertson would shortly become King's closest and most trusted adviser and an almost 'venerated' figure in British and American eyes.[152]

As Under Secretary, Robertson had to lead in formulating the Canadian response to the new American policy. In a long memorandum prepared in December 1941, shortly after Pearl Harbor brought the

---

*L. B. Pearson, back in Ottawa in May 1941 after serving in the High Commission in London, wrote to Vincent Massey that the two main obstacles to efficiency in the Department were 'the Prime Minister's insistence on dealing with one person and one person only, the Under Secretary, on every matter, great and small. Secondly, the necessity under the present system of getting the Prime Minister's approval for practically every step—diplomatic, administrative or political. . . . When the Prime Minister's approval has to be secured before a telephone extension can be installed and when the channel for securing that approval must always . . . be the Under Secretary, you will appreciate that any effective reform of Departmental organization and methods is difficult, if not impossible.' PAC, L. B. Pearson Papers, Vol. 1, Pearson to Massey, 27 May 1941.

United States into the war at last, Robertson brilliantly analyzed the current status of Canadian-American relations. Canadians, he said, 'have tended to take it for granted' that the United States 'will always regard Canadian interests as a close second to their own and appreciably ahead of those of any third country.' Now this was no longer the case.

> It is probably an inevitable consequence of the increasing involvement of the United States in the war and of its acceptance of leadership of the democratic cause that the President should tend more and more to deal directly with the Great Powers and find less time to spend on the specifically Canadian aspects of American international relations. Canada naturally loomed much larger in the American scheme of things when the President and both political parties in the United States were thinking primarily in terms of continental and hemispheric defence. Now that the world war is joined on both oceans, the United States is, not unnaturally, inclined to take Canadian concurrence and support entirely for granted.

The result had been a shift in the tenor of Canadian-American relations, a shift that Robertson believed to be 'rather abrupt and not too tactfully handled'. Part of the problem was caused by the scattering of responsibility for foreign affairs among new agencies and offices in Washington. Another cause was the growing pressure from the American government for the unification of Allied representation in the United States. Canadian matters were no longer always checked with the State Department, as they had been before the war; and indeed the Department was rapidly declining in influence with the President. Of course, Robertson said, contact between opposite numbers in the various agencies in Ottawa and Washington was close, and this was a useful aid to the speedy resolution of technical problems. But this gain was 'offset by the loss . . . of the preferred position Canada had gradually consolidated through long years of close and friendly collaboration with the President and the Department of State.'

Equally important was the shift in the American perception of power. Before the war, Robertson suggested, the United States had believed it could save the world by 'its example, by minding its own business, pursuing a fair and friendly policy toward its neighbours . . .' This era was over and 'we can see the United States turning everywhere to more direct and forceful methods of exerting its influence.' This had been shown, for example, in the way the Americans monopolized negotiations with Japan before Pearl Harbor put an end to efforts to avert war in the

Pacific. The effect of this 'new appreciation of the enormous strategic importance and strength of the United States' was a 'new sense of . . . "manifest destiny" and a corresponding disposition to take decisions and accept responsibilities. This change of attitude is very encouraging from the standpoint of the world in general,' the Under Secretary said, 'but it does imply quite an important modification of the special relationship in which Canada has hitherto stood with regard to the United States.'[153]

Robertson had painted an idealized picture of the pre-1941 Canadian-American relationship, but the broad outlines surely had been correct. So, too, was his analysis of the current difficulties. Paradoxically, once the Americans had entered the war and virtually guaranteed an eventual Allied victory, some of the warmth in Canadian feelings for the United States began to disappear. Canadians could rationalize away the slights and snubs from Washington—the war demanded sacrifices from us all—but the old relationship had seemed so close that the shock was sharp. The United States had been used by Mackenzie King as a makeweight to British power, and used effectively. But now American power was so great that it would be difficult to prevent its application against Canada and dangerous to call it into play except under the most carefully defined circumstances. Self-interest and the nationalism that had dominated Canadian policy thus far in the war would have to be exercised with even greater skill in the difficult years ahead.

---

1 *Canada: America's Problem* (New York, 1940), esp. chapters III, IV, VI, VII.

2 Public Archives of Canada [PAC], W. L. Mackenzie King Papers, Diary, 14 July 1940.

3 F. D. Roosevelt Library, F. D. Roosevelt Papers, PSF, Box 33, King to W. D. Robbins, 17 Dec. 1934, encl. with Robbins to Roosevelt, 18 Dec. 1934.

4 King Diary, 24 Oct. 1935.

5 J. L. Granatstein and R. D. Bothwell, ' "A Self-Evident National Duty": Canadian Foreign Policy, 1935-9', *Journal of Imperial and Commonwealth History*, III (Jan. 1975).

6 [United States Information Service], *Canadian-American Relations, 1867-1967* (3 vols, mimeo.; Ottawa, 1967), III, 34. For comment on this speech, see J. A. Munro, ed., *Documents on Canadian External Relations* (6 vols to date; Ottawa, 1972), VI, pp. 606ff.; PAC, External Affairs Records, Vol. 31, folio 163, Skelton to King, 15 Sept. 1938.

7 King Diary, 15 Nov. 1938.

8 M. C. Urquhart and K. A. Buckley, *Historical Statistics of Canada* (Toronto, 1965), p. 169. These figures had been higher at the beginning of the Depression.

9 King Papers, 'Memo to Minister on Conversations in Washington . . .', 26 Jan. 1938, ff. C112708ff.; Roosevelt Papers, PSF State Department, S. Welles to Roosevelt, 20 Dec. 1937; *ibid.*, PSF Welles, Welles to Roosevelt, 10, 14 Jan. 1938. A second meeting followed in November 1938. Directorate of History, National Defence Headquarters, 000.4 (D14), Memo, Gen. Anderson to Minister of National Defence, 23 Nov. 1938.

10 King Diary, 12 May 1939.

11 Nancy H. Hooker, ed., *The Moffat Papers* (Cambridge, 1956), p. 343, offers Pierrepont Moffat's assessment of the relationship.

12 Roosevelt Papers, PSF Britain—King and Queen, King to Roosevelt, 1 July 1939.

13 B. B. Berle and T. B. Jacobs, eds, *Navigating the Rapids, 1918-71: From the Papers of Adolf A. Berle* (New York, 1973), pp. 251-3.

14 King Diary, 3 Sept. 1939.

15 E.g., *ibid.*, 9 Sept. 1939, where King squelched a scheme that would have violated U. S. neutrality by recruiting airmen for the RCAF there.

16 *Ibid.*, 18 Jan. 1940. Cf. Berle and Jacobs, pp. 282-3 for a U.S. negotiator's comments on these talks.

17 King Diary, 20 Apr. 1940.

18 *Ibid.*, 23-4, 29 Apr. 1940.

19 *Ibid.*, 23-4 Apr. 1940.

20 *Ibid.*

21 King Papers, King to Leighton McCarthy, 24 Apr. 1940, f. 245645.

22 King Diary, 23 Mar. 1939.

23 *Ibid.*, 10 June 1939.

24 King Papers, Churchill to King, 27 Mar. 1940, f. 241585.

25 *Ibid.*, King to Churchill, 10 May 1940, f. 241587.

26 PAC, J. W. Dafoe Papers, Grant Dexter to George Ferguson, 21 Aug. 1940.

27 Robert Sherwood, *Roosevelt and Hopkins* (New York, 1948), pp. 363-4.

28 King Papers, Black Binders, Vol. 19, III, Misc. doc. 7 June 1940.

29 *Ibid.*, Memo by Keenleyside, 23 May 1940. See, on this whole period of negotiations, C. P. Stacey, *Arms, Men and Governments* (Ottawa, 1970), pp. 328-32; S. W. Dziuban, *Military Relations Between the United States and Canada 1939-1945* (Washington, 1959), pp. 11ff.

30 King Papers, Black Binders, Vol. 19, I, Menzies to King, 22 May 1940.

31 *Ibid.*, Massey to King, 23 May 1940.

32 *Ibid.*, Churchill to King, 24 May 1940. Most Churchill-King telegrams are printed in Public Record Office [PRO], Dominions Office Records, DO 114/113.

33 King Papers, Black Binders, Vol. 19, I, King to Churchill, 24 May 1940.

34 *Ibid.*, Keenleyside memo, 29 May 1940.

35 *Ibid.*, III, Keenleyside memo and atts, 26 May 1940.

36 King Diary, 26 May 1940; J. W. Pickersgill, *The Mackenzie King Record*, Vol. I: *1939-44* (4 vols; Toronto, 1960), p. 118.

37 King Papers, Black Binders, Vol. 19, III, Keenleyside memo, 29 May 1940.

38 King Diary, 30 May 1940.

39 Printed in Pickersgill, I, pp. 120-1.

40 Cited in *ibid.*, p. 121.

41 Quoted in W. S. Churchill, *The Second World War*, Vol. II: *Their Finest Hour* (6 vols; Boston, 1949), pp. 145-6. The telegram is in King Papers, Vol. 295, in a slightly different form, presumably because of decoding. Cf. Stacey, p. 331.

42 King Papers, Black Binders, Vol. 19, III, 'For Mr. Keenleyside . . .', 6 June 1940; Pickersgill, I, pp. 122-3.

43 Such aid as the U.S. could give is cited in PAC, C. D. Howe Papers, Vol. 5, Keenleyside to K. S. MacLachlan, 15 June 1940.

44 King Papers, Black Binders, Vol. 19, III, 'Report on discussion . . .', 7 June 1940.

45 *Ibid.*, Vol. 295, King to Churchill, 17 June 1940. The idea of bases appears to have arisen in conversation between Escott Reid of the Legation and Prof. W. Y. Elliot of Harvard, a member of the Business Advisory Council, which had passed a resolution advocating a transfer of bases. *Ibid.*, Black Binders, Vol. 20, file 77, Mahoney to Skelton, 24, 27 May 1940.

46 *Ibid.*, Vol. 295, Churchill to King, 24 June 1940. For a similar telegram to Lothian, the U.K. Ambassador in Washington, see DO 35/1003/WG11/1/1c, Churchill to Lothian, 9 June 1940. Lothian himself was not averse to considering the probability and consequences of defeat. See J. R. M. Butler, *Lord Lothian* (London, 1960), p. 286.

47 Douglas Library, Queen's University, Grant Dexter Papers, Memorandum, 7 June 1940.

48 S. Conn, *et al.*, *Guarding the United States and its Outposts* (Washington, 1964), pp. 7-9. Cf. U.S. National Archives, State Department Records, 842.20/150½, 'Decisions Required if Military Assistance is to be Afforded to Canada . . .', 5 July 1940.

49 King Diary, 23 May 1940; PAC, Privy Council Office Records, Cabinet War Committee Records, Minutes, 23 May 1940.

50 State Department Records, 711.42/195, Moffat to Hull, 16 June 1940.

51 Library of Congress, Cordell Hull Papers, folder 194, Memo of Conversation, 17 June 1940. For U.S. reaction to this see Stacey, p. 332 and Dziuban, pp. 14ff. See also Department of External Affairs, External Affairs Records, docs on file 703-40, part I.

52 King Diary, 5 July 1940.

53 King Papers, Black Binders, Vol. 20, file 77, Typed diary note, 13 July 1940.

54 Copy in University of British Columbia, Alan Plaunt Papers, Box 9, file 1. Among the group were Brooke Claxton, M.P., Prof. F. R. Scott, and Sen. Norman Lambert. The intent was to despatch the Program to as many public figures and opinion moulders as could be reached. Mr W. R. Young drew this to my attention. *Ibid.*, Box 8, file 20, Plaunt to J. R. Baldwin, 13 Aug. 1940. King's copy came from Claxton. King Papers, Vol. 286, Claxton to King, 23 Aug. 1940.

55 Canadian Institute of International Affairs, Edgar Tarr Papers, Baldwin to Tarr, 4 July 1940 and memos, 22 June 1940 and 4 July 1940; John W. Holmes interview, 22 July 1971.

56 King Papers, Towers to King, 15 Aug. 1940, ff. 25269ff; Department of Finance, W. C. Clark Papers, docs on file E-4-7-3.

57 King Papers, Black Binders, Vol. 19, Memo, 12 June 1940. There is a version of this memo in Hutchison's novel, *The Hollow Men* (New York, 1944), pp. 63ff. Another memo by Hutchison of an interview with Senator Pittman, Chairman of the Foreign

Relations Committee, was also influential. Copy in External Affairs Records, file 703-40, Part I.

58 See, however, the memo by Berle in State Department Records, 740.0011 EW 1939/4700, 12 July 1940, which indicates Christie was considering such a possibility.

59 External Affairs Records, Vol. 781, file 394, 'An Outline Synopsis . . .', 17 June 1940.

60 King Papers, Black Binders, Vol. 19, I, Christie to King, 15 Aug. 1940.

61 John M. Blum, *From the Morgenthau Diaries* (3 vols; Boston, 1964), II, p. 180.

62 Pickersgill, I, pp. 130-1.

63 *Ibid.*, p. 134.

64 *Ibid.*, pp. 133-5; Cabinet War Committee Records, Minutes, 20 Aug. 1940.

65 King Papers, Notes and Memoranda, Vol. 139, 'Press. . .'.

66 *Ibid.*, Black Binders, Vol. 19, file 77, Skelton to King, 19 Aug. 1940.

67 House of Commons *Debates*, 12 Nov. 1940, p. 57.

68 PAC, R. B. Hanson Papers, file S-175-M-1, Meighen to Hanson, 19 Aug. 1940. Cf. on Conservative reaction, J. L. Granatstein, 'The Conservative Party and the Ogdensburg Agreement', *International Journal*, XXII (Winter, 1966-7), 73ff.

69 Text in Hanson Papers, file S-802.

70 Granatstein, 'Ogdensburg Agreement', 75.

71 PRO, Foreign Office Records, FO 371/24259, Extract from War Cabinet Committee Conclusions, 231(40), 21 Aug. 1940.

72 Churchill to King, 22 Aug. 1940, in Cabinet War Committee Records, Documents.

73 *Ibid.*, Minutes, 27 Aug. 1940; King Diary, 26 Aug. 1940.

74 FO 800/398, Campbell to Lothian, 27 Sept. 1940.

75 King Papers, Vol. 286, Churchill to King, 12 Sept. 1940.

76 Pickersgill, I, p. 143.

77 External Affairs Records. Vol. 67, 'Record of Conversation . . .', 22 Aug. 1940.

78 Roosevelt Papers, OF 4090, LaGuardia to Roosevelt, 28 May 1942.

79 Stacey, pp. 349ff. See Cabinet War Committee Records, Minutes, 23 April 1941, 27 May 1941, 3 June 1941, etc., and also the press reports when Cabinet documents were made public. Toronto *Globe and Mail*, 20 Jan. 1972.

80 Corelli Barnett, *The Collapse of British Power* (London, 1972), p. 127.

81 Cited by David Dilks, 'Appeasement Revisited', *University of Leeds Review*, XV (May, 1972), 51.

82 Warren F. Kimball, 'Lend-Lease and the Open Door: The Temptation of British Opulence, 1937-1942', *Political Science Quarterly*, LXXXVI (June, 1971), 240-1; John M. Blum, *Roosevelt and Morgenthau. A Revision and Condensation of From the Morgenthau Diaries* (Boston, 1970), p. 341. Cf. Chalmers Papers, Memo of Conversation with Sir Edward Peacock, 1 Mar. 1941.

83 King Diary, 29 July 1940, 15-16 Aug. 1940.

84 PRO, Treasury Records, T160/1045, 'French Gold', n.d.; R. S. Sayers, *Financial Policy, 1939-45* (London, 1956), pp. 336, 557ff. King Papers, docs from C27201-48.

85 House of Commons *Debates,* 29 Apr. 1941, p. 2338; King Papers, Clark to King, 9 Apr. 1941, ff. 288021ff.

86 Sayers, p. 338.

87 H. D. Hall, *North American Supply* (London, 1955), p. 230. A later and probably more accurate estimate for fiscal 1941-2 puts the national income at $5.95 billion, war spending at $1.45 billion, aid to Britain at $1.15 billion, and civil expenditures at $1 billion. The total of public expenditures is therefore 60.5 per cent of national income. King Papers, 'Canada's War Effort', 4 Apr. 1941, ff. 288088ff. Cf. Clark Papers, file B-2-8-9-1, 'Canada's War Effort and Budgetary Position', 4 Mar. 1941; PAC, Ian Mackenzie Papers, file 2-29, Senior to Mackenzie, 28 Apr. 1941.

88 Pickersgill, I, p. 189; Grant Dexter Papers, Memoranda, 11, 25 Mar. 1941.

89 Sayers, pp. 322-3.

90 King Papers, Memo, Clark to King, 9 Apr. 1941, ff. 288014ff.; Louis Rasminsky, 'Foreign Exchange Control: Purposes and Methods', in J. F. Parkinson, ed., *Canadian War Economics* (Toronto, 1941), p. 120. The actual figures were worse even than these estimates. See Urquhart and Buckley, pp. 181-2.

91 House of Commons *Debates,* 2 Dec. 1940, pp. 610-12; *ibid.,* 29 Apr. 1941, pp. 2338-9; J. S. B. Pemberton, 'Ogdensburg, Hyde Park and After', *Behind the Head-lines,* I (April, 1941), 18; R. W. James, *Wartime Economic Cooperation* (Toronto, 1949), p. 18; King Diary, 28 Nov. 1940; PAC, Department of Finance Records, Vol. 3531, file B-04a, Robertson to Mackintosh, 17 June 1940; Clark Papers, docs on file B-2-8-7-2-2.

92 State Department Records, 842.00/601, Moffat to Secretary of State, 24 Oct. 1940; Chalmers Papers, Memo of Conversation with Towers, 26 Aug. 1940.

93 Urquhart and Buckley, p. 168. Cf. *The Financial Post,* 1 Mar. 1941; King Papers, Clark to King, 9 Apr. 1941, f. 288018. On the Canadian determination to hold these investments, see *ibid.;* Dexter Papers, Memo, 11 Mar. 1941; FO 371/28795, Phillips to Treasury, 4 Mar. 1941.

94 King Papers, Clark to King, 9 Apr. 1941. ff. 288023ff.

95 External Affairs Records, Vol. 35, 'United States Exchange Discussions', 20 Nov. 1940.

96 House of Commons *Debates,* 2 Dec. 1940, p. 556; Cabinet War Committee Records, Minutes, 27 Nov. 1490; King Papers, Robertson to King, 7 Apr. 1941, f. 287996; *The Financial Post,* 5 Apr. 1941; Department of Finance Records, Vol. 3568, file I-039 has data on the fruit and vegetable trade. If it had been cut off, estimates were that $7.5 million in exchange would have been saved.

97 The text of the act is in Edward Stettinius, Jr, *Lend-Lease, Weapon for Victory* (New York, 1944), pp. 335-9.

98 Cabinet War Committee Records, Minutes, 18 Feb. 1941, 26 Feb. 1941; *The Financial Post,* 18 Jan. 1941.

99 PRO, Prime Minister's Office Records, Prem 4/43B/2, Memo, Cranborne to Churchill, 5 Mar. 1941; T160/1340, L. S. Amery to Kingsley Wood, 10 May 1941.

100 T160/1054, 'Canadian Financial Assistance to this Country', n.d. [14 Mar. 1941], att. to MacDonald to Sir Horace Wilson, 17 Mar. 1941; Dexter Papers, Memorandum, 9 Apr. 1941.

101 Pickersgill, I, p. 189.

102 King Papers, Clark to King, 9 Apr. 1941, f. 288026. Clark's briefing papers for his Washington trip are in Clark Papers, file B-2-8-9-1.

103 Cabinet War Committee Records, Minutes, 12, 13 Mar. 1941.

104 *Ibid.*, 21 Mar. 1941; Hall, pp. 236-7.

105 Cabinet War Committee Records, Minutes, 21 Mar. 1941; Dexter Papers, Memoranda, 9, 18 Apr. 1941; Chalmers Papers, Memo of Conversation with Clark, 5 Apr. 1941.

106 Cabinet War Committee Records, Minutes, 13 Mar. 1941.

107 King Diary, 13 Mar. 1941.

108 Sayers, pp. 338ff.; Hall, p. 237; King Diary, 27 Mar. 1941; Clark Papers, Secretary of State for External Affairs [SSEA] to Secretary of State for Dominion Affairs [SSDA], 27 Mar. 1941; T160/1141, 'Canada's Sterling Balances', 30 July 1941.

109 Cabinet War Committee Records, Minutes, 21 Mar. 1941. King's briefing papers are in King Papers, ff. 287914ff.

110 Pickersgill, I, p. 190.

111 King Diary, 16 Apr. 1941.

112 Pickersgill, I, p. 190; Hull Papers, folder 196, Memoranda, 17 Apr. 1941; External Affairs Records, file 91-CY-40C, H. Wrong to Robertson, 25 Apr. 1941.

113 Pickersgill, I, pp. 190-2; King Diary, 17 Apr. 1941; External Affairs Records, Vol. 93, file 573(3), Robertson to King, 18 Apr. 1941. For Clark's meeting with Morgenthau, see Clark Papers, file B-2-8-9-1, 'Memorandum of Meeting with Morgenthau, April 18, 1941.'

114 Pickersgill, I, pp. 193-4. According to Hume Wrong, he, Clark, and J. C. Coyne, financial attaché at the Legation, had drafted the statement. External Affairs Records, file 91-CY-40C, Wrong to Robertson, 25 Apr. 1941.

115 Pickersgill, I, p. 197.

116 Dexter Papers, Memo, 21 Apr. 1941. King was also taking Clark's advice in taking this line. See Clark Papers, file B-2-8-9-1, Clark's 'Report on Visit to Washington, March 17-21, 1941'.

117 Pickersgill, I, pp. 198-202; Cabinet War Committee Records, Minutes, 21 Apr. 1941; Dexter Papers, Memo, 21 Apr. 1941. For an unhappy American official's reaction to the way the agreement was reached, see Harvard University, Pierrepont Moffat Papers, Vol. 19, J. D. Hickerson to Moffat, 30 Apr. 1941. For a postwar U.S. view, see Department of Finance Records, Vol. 778, file 400-16-3, H. Wrong to Clark, 17 Feb. 1948, enclosing 'Memo of Explanation relating to Hyde Park Agreement', 10 Nov. 1947, prepared in the State Department.

118 Pickersgill, I, pp. 198-202.

119 The text of the Agreement is in External Affairs Records, file 1497-40, SSEA to SSDA, 22 Apr. 1941.

120 Pickersgill, I, p. 202. Cf. Howe's detailed response to the terms of the declaration in King Papers, Howe to King, 25 Apr. 1941, ff. 288034Aff.

121 Press and public had difficulty believing Canada could have escaped so lightly. See *The Financial Post*, 26 Apr. 1941; *New York Times*, 21 Apr. 1941. Rumours were squelched in Parliament by Ilsley. House of Commons *Debates*, 29 Apr. 1941, pp. 2339-40. But cf. Clark Papers, file U-3-2-4-1(1), Memo by J. Coyne, 3 May 1941.

122 Stacey, p. 490.

[123] Memo, 14 May 1941 on State Department Records, 740.0011 European War 1939/11542; *ibid.*, Morgenthau to Hopkins, 15 May 1941; U.K. Treasury Records, T160/1335, Tel. British Supply Council in North America to Supply Committee, London, 26 July 1941 and atts. The difficulties remaining should not be underestimated. See on this Clark Papers, file B-2-8-9-1, Memoranda re Conference in Washington, 11-16 May 1941.

[124] J. de N. Kennedy, *History of the Department of Munitions and Supply* (2 vols; Ottawa, 1950), I, p. 475; James, pp. 34-5.

[125] *Ibid.*, pp. 35-6; W. T. G. Hackett, 'The "Bank", the "Fund", and the Canadian Dollar', in J. D. Gibson, ed., *Canada's Economy in a Changing World* (Toronto, 1948), pp. 119-20; C. D. Blyth, 'Some Aspects of Canada's International Financial Relations', *Canadian Journal of Economics and Political Science*, XII (1946), 303-4.

[126] House of Commons *Debates*, 28 Apr. 1941, p. 2289.

[127] External Affairs Records, Vol. 826, file 725, Keenleyside memo, n.d.; James, pp. 23ff.

[128] External Affairs Records, Vol. 826, file 725, Skelton to King, 23 Dec. 1940.

[129] *Ibid.*, Vol. 780, file 383, 'The Integration of War Industry in Canada and the United States', 27 Dec. 1940 and atts.

[130] *Ibid.*, Skelton to King, 10 Jan. 1941; Cabinet War Committee Records, Minutes, 20 Jan. 1941. See also the biography of Henry in Carolyn Cox, *Canadian Strength* (Toronto, 1946), pp. 53ff.

[131] External Affairs Records, file 1497-40, Reid to Keenleyside, 13 Jan. 1941.

[132] *Ibid.*, Vol. 780, file 383, Memo for File, 10 Feb. 1941; *ibid.*, file 1497-40, Memo on interview with Berle, 4 Feb. 1941.

[133] Cabinet War Committee Records, Minutes, 5 Mar. 1941; James, p. 23.

[134] External Affairs Records, file 1497-40, 'Memo on Economic Co-operation with the United States', 25 Feb. 1941.

[135] State Department Records, 842.20 Defense/71, Memo by Berle, 17 Mar. 1941 and atts.

[136] Berle and Jacobs, pp. 365-6. Keenleyside's memo of this meeting is much more cautious in phrasing. External Affairs Records, file 1497-40, 'Canadian-United States Industrial Integration', 18 Mar. 1941.

[137] *Ibid.*, Robertson to Canadian Minister, Washington, 28 Apr. 1941; *ibid.*, Wrong to SSEA, 6 June 1941 and atts; *ibid.*, Memo for Cabinet War Committee, n.d.

[138] James, p. 228.

[139] Reports of the Joint Economic Committees are in PAC, R. G. 25 F4, Vol. 1010; see also Queen's University, W. A. Mackintosh Papers.

[140] Cabinet War Committee Records, Minutes, 26 July 1940, 13 Aug. 1940.

[141] *Ibid.*, 23 Apr. 1941.

[142] *Ibid.*, 3 June 1941.

[143] Dominions Office Records, DO 35/1010 pt. III/WG 476/4/6, COS (41)374, 13 June 1941; Cabinet War Committee Records, Documents, MacDonald to King, 4 June 1941 and reply 6 June 1941.

[144] *Ibid.*, Minutes, 31 July 1941.

[145] *Ibid.*, 13 Aug. 1941, 2 Sept. 1941, 2 Oct. 1941; Stacey, pp. 354ff.; Dziuban, pp.

73ff.; State Department Records, 842.20/203, Moffat to Hickerson, 5 Sept. 1941.

146 Obituaries and appreciations of Skelton can be found in Grant Dexter, 'Oscar Douglas Skelton', *Queen's Quarterly*, XLVII, (Spring, 1941); W. A. M[ackintosh]., 'O. D. Skelton', *Canadian Journal of Economics and Political Science*, VII (1941); *The Times*, 30 Jan. 1941; Norman Hillmer, 'O. D. Skelton: the Scholar Who Set a Future Pattern', *International Perspectives* (October, 1973).

147 PAC, Brooke Claxton Papers, Vol. 224, Memoir Notes. Prof. R. D. Bothwell brought this to my attention.

148 E.g., King Diary, 14 Nov. 1938.

149 *Ibid.*, 14 June 1940.

150 Pickersgill, I, pp. 166-7.

151 See L. B. Pearson, *Mike: The Memoirs of the Right Honourable Lester B. Pearson*, Vol. I: *1897-1948* (Toronto, 1972), pp. 193-4; Dexter Papers, Memoranda, 11 Mar. 1941, 16 June 1942.

152 Interviews with Lord Garner, 16 June 1971; Sir Stephen Holmes, 15 June 1971; Charles S. Ritchie, 9 June 1971.

153 External Affairs Records, Vol. 810, file 614, Memo for P.M., 22 Dec. 1941; Memos by Keenleyside in *ibid.*, 27 Dec. 1941 and 14 Apr. 1942. For a U.S. view of the new sensitivity in Canada, see State Department Records, 711.42/237, 'Memo of Conversation with Robertson . . . 14 Feb. 1942'.

5. Financing the War at Home

A pall of frustration hung heavily over Canada in 1941. The war was going from bad to dismal and the people badly needed a victory against the Axis. The pressures of taxation, controls, and restrictions were beginning to get ordinary men and women down, and the only saving grace was that casualties were blessedly few. In 1941 for the first time the war began to hit home.

Ottawa, too, suffered under the impact of the war. The bureaucracy had expanded rapidly, and the capital city, bursting at the seams, was short of housing and office space. Money was tight, and the pressures on the national finances had become extreme. Canada's exchange problem with the United States had been largely solved for the time being by the Hyde Park agreement, but there were additional problems. The recommendations of the Rowell-Sirois Royal Commission on Dominion-Provincial Relations required consideration, particularly as their centralizing effects seemed tailor-made to meet the demands of wartime finance. The increasing rate of inflation had to be checked somehow lest Canada find itself in a price and wage spiral similar to that which had devastated the country during and after the Great War. And finally, Canada's fiscal relations with Britain had to be put into a better framework. The British needed this, but so too did Canadian business and labour. Hundreds of thousands of jobs were dependent on the war orders of the British government, and if Britain could no longer pay, those jobs would be lost unless someone met the bill.

These three separate but not entirely unrelated financial problems concerned the government more than any other questions in 1941. All

would be resolved by decisive actions emanating from the Department
of Finance, the department that dominated Ottawa intellectually during
the war. J. L. Ilsley, the Minister of Finance, was a dour Nova Scotia
Baptist with probably the sharpest mind and the finest oratorical style
in the government. Ilsley worried incessantly about everything, but he
would accept no advice from his Deputy Minister, Clifford Clark, that
he did not understand well enough to put before the Cabinet. Clark
himself was the power among the senior civil servants, and he had
gathered a group of advisers around him who, Brooke Claxton noted,
were 'hard to equal in any country or in any field'.[1] From these men—
Ilsley, Clark, W. A. Mackintosh, R. B. Bryce, Graham Towers, and the
rest—came the solutions to the fiscal problems that threatened to destroy
the Canadian war effort. The solutions were good ones, and out of them
came the war-induced prosperity that pushed the Gross National
Product to new peaks during the war.

I

Federal-provincial relations hinged around money and responsibilities.
The Royal Commission on Dominion-Provincial Relations had been
appointed on August 14, 1937 to conduct a 're-examination of the
economic and financial basis of Confederation and of the distribution
of legislative powers in the light of the economic and social developments of the last seventy years'. The government also had charged the
Commission with determining the measures that 'will best effect a
balanced relationship between the financial powers and obligations
and functions of each governing body.'[2] Under the chairmanship first of
Newton Rowell and, after his retirement because of ill-health, of Joseph
Sirois, the Commission held hearings in Ottawa and in the provinces
from November 1937 through to December 1938. From the outset there
were difficulties. Premier William Aberhart of Alberta declined to allow
his government to present a brief. Maurice Duplessis' Quebec was
predictably difficult—and the Premier was reportedly drunk and foul
at a dinner his government offered the visiting Commissioners. Mitchell
Hepburn presented an 'ill-tempered brief', and shortly after severed
completely Ontario's relations with the Royal Commission.[3] There
were scant prospects for general acceptance of anything the Commission
might recommend.

The Report of the Rowell-Sirois Royal Commission was delivered
to the government in the middle of February 1940 but was withheld

until after the general election had run its course.[4] The Commissioners proposed two plans, but their preferred course, Plan 1, was the only one considered seriously. The essence of its recommendations was as follows.

(1) Provincial debts (payments on which ran to $65 million each year) were to be assumed by the Dominion with adjustment for assets represented by the debt. Special provision would be made in Quebec to cover the provincial-municipal debt situation. Provinces and municipalities would retain their authority to borrow, but loans would have to be approved by a Central Financial Council if the province hoped to have these debt costs considered for purposes of future adjustment grants.

(2) The Dominion should assume the full burden of relief for the employable unemployed (some $50-60 million per year).

(3) The provinces and municipalities would retire from the fields of personal and corporation income taxes and succession duties (giving Ottawa about $65-75 million), and the existing system of subsidies to the provinces would be ended.

(4) Control of expenditures would remain the prerogative of individual provinces.

(5) The Dominion would pay to the provinces

(a) a sum equal to 10 per cent of the net income earned by mining and oil producing companies in the respective provinces;

(b) a national adjustment grant to enable the provinces to maintain social and educational services at a Canadian average without having to tax more heavily than the Canadian average;

(c) emergency grants in emergency situations.[5]

The recommendations of the Report went some substantial distance towards equalization, but the impact of its recommendations on the structure of Canadian federalism was very great indeed. In essence the Rowell-Sirois Report proposed to take power away from the provinces and give it to Ottawa in return for some subsidies. But for Ontario, Alberta, and British Columbia, the three provinces that would not be eligible for the Report's suggested National Adjustment Grants, the proposals were thoroughly unpleasant.*

---

*The National Adjustment Grant to a province was to be equal to the excess, if any, of the expenditure necessary to provide the average Canadian standard of government services over the revenue that would be derived from taxation of average

Nonetheless the initial press response to the recommendation was overwhelmingly favourable. A Department of Finance press analysis found only seventeen critical editorials out of a total of 160 from 88 different newspapers. The major objections seemed to be that the Report proposed no effective brake on reckless provincial spending, that its proposals tended towards centralization, and that none of this should even be considered in the midst of a war. The supporters of the Royal Commission's recommendations had a variety of motives, ranging from *The Financial Times'* delight that the holders of provincial bonds would benefit to demands that the needs of the war required immediate implementation of Plan 1.[6]

But what would happen to the Report? The events of May and June 1940 drove it from the public mind, and when Premier John Bracken of Manitoba wrote Mackenzie King in August to urge the immediate holding of a National Conference, the Prime Minister preached delay. 'With the war in progress,' King said with an evident lack of enthusiasm for the Report, 'it would certainly be felt by many that the government should await developments before seeking to bring the provinces as a whole into conference with the Dominion on matters so all important as those dealt with in the Commission's report.'[7]

If King was for delay because of the overriding demands of the war, the Ottawa bureaucracy was increasingly in favour of implementation for the very same reasons. In a memorandum to Finance Minister Ilsley on July 24, 1940, Graham Towers of the Bank of Canada argued the case for the Rowell-Sirois recommendations as a war measure. 'The need

---

severity. The object was to permit the poorer provinces to provide a level of social services equal to the Canadian average, but the result in monetary terms was as follows:

	Total Subsidies 1938	Proposed National Adjustment Grant
P.E.I.	$ 657,000	$ 750,000
N.S.	1,953,000	800,000
N.B.	1,567,000	1,500,000
Que.	2,592,000	8,000,000
Ont.	2,941,000	——
Man.	2,453,000	2,100,000
Sask.	5,620,000	1,750,000
Alta	1,776,000	——
B.C.	1,625,000	——
TOTAL	$21,184,000	$14,900,000

From A. M. Moore and J. H. Perry, *The Financing of Canadian Federation* (Toronto, 1966), pp. 13-14.

for greatly expanded Dominion revenues is clear,' Towers said, something about which Ilsley required no convincing. 'The need for developing an efficient taxation system which will yield the maximum of revenue with the least possible burden on the national income was never more urgent. . . . Reforms that were desirable yesterday are today essential; there can be no question of the urgent necessity of strengthening the Canadian economy both to make the maximum possible war effort and to face the post-war adjustments that will be necessary.' Equally important and pressing, some of the provinces were faced with the prospect of defaulting on their bonds, an unhappy prospect that could affect the Dominion's credit. The sole problem, Towers conceded, was 'whether it is now politically expedient and desirable to proceed.'[8]

Towers put the same case to the Prime Minister on August 15. He noted the increasing 'difficulties experienced by certain provinces in refunding their maturing obligations,' and he raised the prospect that Saskatchewan and New Brunswick might be forced to default in the autumn. 'It is hard to say how far the trouble would spread,' Towers argued, 'but I think it is safe to say that the repercussions would be very serious, and likely to have a bad effect on Dominion credit and on the Dominion's war financing.' The question of conflicting fields of taxation and the problem of responsibility for unemployment, still a major difficulty, were also acute, and the war made solutions essential. For example, Towers argued,

> Is it not likely that workers will face unemployment in the post-war period with much greater resentment—to put it mildly—than displayed during the depression years? In the interests of peace, order and good government the Dominion may well have to assume full responsibility. But if it does so without having made other arrangements along the lines contemplated in the Sirois Report, the financial situation will be chaotic. . . .

'If this were understood by the public,' Towers said, 'might not an effort to deal with the Report receive popular support; and, so far as the provinces are concerned, might action not be represented as the first constructive piece of work which provinces could do on the home front?'[9] This was powerful advocacy, but the Prime Minister's attention was wholly focussed on the war, not on finances. There was, therefore, a certain despondency evident when Towers told Floyd Chalmers of *The Financial Post* on August 26 that the 'first necessity was to achieve in the cabinet—and particularly in the mind of the P.M.—an earnest conviction that something should be done. . . . He thought King would get around to the subject soon,' Chalmers noted, 'but had had so much in his mind that he had probably not really thought of the matter.'[10]

The matter could not be delayed much longer. A memorandum to Ilsley on September 11, 1940 seems finally to have forced the issue. The unsigned paper outlined three courses: postponement of action until after the war; an immediate Dominion-Provincial conference; or the implementation of the essential recommendations of the Report immediately as a war measure with an undertaking to hold a conference after the war to modify details. The choice was a political one, of course, but if there was a preference in the memo it was for a Dominion-Provincial conference to be convened as soon as possible. Such a conference should be held while Parliament was recessed and it should be preceded by a campaign of public education, 'making clear that the Dominion has adopted the principles of the Report and that it is convinced of the urgency of adoption.'[11]

Ilsley brought the proposals to the Cabinet on September 19, and a Special Cabinet Committee was established with the Finance Minister as chairman.[12] The Committee met the following day and considered the options set forth in the memorandum of September 11. The ministers agreed 'that the Committee should recommend to Council that conversations should immediately be initiated with the individual provinces, with the object of exploring the possibility of obtaining agreement to the full adoption of the recommendations of the Report . . .' If results were unpromising, the Committee considered that 'every effort' then 'should be made to obtain agreement to a temporary application of the principal financial recommendations.' A full conference should follow these preliminary conversations.[13] The Finance Department's policy then was set: if possible, get the Rowell-Sirois recommendations adopted *in toto* and for all time; if this proved impossible, then secure agreement to Ottawa's assuming the fiscal powers recommended by the Royal Commission for the duration of the war.

In the course of the next few weeks Ilsley met with members of the New Brunswick government, the Premier of Prince Edward Island, Premier Godbout of Quebec, and with Mitchell Hepburn and some of his ministers in Toronto. In addition he wrote to some of the other provincial premiers. The net result of these preliminary soundings was predictable: Ontario was vehemently opposed to the implementation of the Report. According to Grant Dexter who had secured an account of Ilsley's conversation with Hepburn—a genuine strict constructionist in federal-provincial affairs—the Premier argued that the Royal Commission had been 'biased, unfair, out to get Ontario. Ontario would never accept its judgment.' He objected strenuously to what he saw as special treatment to Quebec municipalities, bailing out profligate spenders there 'at the expense of the Dominion taxpayers, the bulk of whom were in Ontario.'[14]

The Cabinet heard Ilsley's slightly mournful report on October 22, and the result was disappointing to those who had hoped a conference could be held soon. As Mackenzie King recorded,

> Discussed at length wisdom of having Dominion-Provincial conference on Sirois Report. Ilsley reported that Hepburn . . . had said that Ontario was unalterably opposed to the recommendations of the Commission and would fight it to the limit.
>
> I read a letter from Bracken strongly recommending conference. Council agreed that in view of Hepburn's opinion, it would be unwise to call a conference; also that we should not hesitate to let Parliament know of why holding of conference at this time was likely to be of little avail. I said there would be no agreement on the report till Hepburn and in all probability his government . . . would be removed. To this, the Cabinet agreed.
>
> If there had been possibility of agreement at a conference, we would probably have arranged for one forthwith notwithstanding the possibility of criticism of diverting our energies from the war effort.[15]

But when Ilsley's Committee came back to the Cabinet on November 1 with a renewed proposal for a conference and with draft invitations to the premiers, King and Lapointe, the members of the Cabinet most lukewarm about the Report and most reluctant to summon a conference, this time yielded. The warnings of impending financial disaster from Ilsley's Department could not be ignored; the pressing demands of Premier Bracken, supported by his fellow Manitoban, T. A. Crerar, could not readily be delayed further; and the federal government would be on much stronger ground if it could appear to the public as having been balked by provincial obstinacy.[16] In fact Ilsley, Clark, and Towers probably recognized that the conference was necessary, not so much to accomplish the adoption of the Rowell-Sirois recommendations, but more to prepare the public for decisive intervention by the federal government into provincial fields of taxation if the conference failed. Mackenzie King and Ernest Lapointe clearly did not grasp this, and both opposed holding a conference that was destined to fail. In part, too, both King and his lieutenant generally tended to support a policy of muddling through, and the drastic and direct Rowell-Sirois recommendations flew in the face of this. Only dire necessity could have persuaded the Prime Minister and the Minister of Justice to accept a conference in these circumstances, but the precarious financial state of the nation was such that they could not reject a Dominion-Provincial Conference out of hand.

The invitations were mailed to the provinces on November 2 and tabled in the House of Commons on November 7, an obvious move to put Hepburn and any other obstreperous premiers into the position of rejecting a conference publicly.[17] No premier chose to do so, although there was a marked lack of enthusiasm evident in some of the responses.[18]

The federal government's preparations for the conference, scheduled to open on January 14, 1941, now began in earnest. A 'central committee' of key civil servants began to collect information and prepare position papers. The chairman of this group was the Deputy Minister of Finance, Clifford Clark; other members included Dr Skelton, Prof. W. A. Mackintosh of Finance, Dr Sirois, and F. P. Varcoe, the Deputy Minister of Justice. The committee asked the provinces to supply financial data and it also began assessing the legal implications of implementing the recommendations of the Report.[19] There was something of an element of unreality about these preparations, however, for Mackenzie King and many of his ministers still expected the Conference to fail. 'I confess I have little hope of getting anything of the Dominion-Provincial Conference,' he wrote in his diary on December 6, 'nor am I personally satisfied that the Sirois report should be accepted holus-bolus. Financial interests are so strong behind it all that I feel a bit suspicious about a report not according more with democratic views that should be made to prevail once this war is over.'[20] King's suspicions about the 'financial interests' were widely shared, not least by Premiers Hepburn, Aberhart, and Pattullo, the three strongest critics of the report. 'Any time that the "Financial Post" of Toronto makes a recommendation,' Pattullo told King, 'suspicion is at once created.'[21]

Still, Ottawa needed more revenue and the Conference had to be held. The Cabinet, King noted, agreed.

All members . . . excepting Crerar expressed themselves as believing that the Dominion-Provincial conference . . . will amount to nothing. Ilsley said that it would last 3 days and would like to see the position of each province properly stated and the whole break up without too great friction.

I said in the preliminary speech, we would have to construct a mattress that would make it easy for the trapeze performers as they dropped to the ground one by one. I have never believed that the conference can succeed at this time of war. Were the government not to make the attempt, it would be blamed for whatever financial disasters will follow, as it certainly will, in the course of the next year or two.[22]

Financial disasters were much in King's mind at the end of 1940. The Cabinet War Committee had been discussing money problems frequently, and the strains on the country's finances were becoming very great indeed.[23]

As the conference drew nearer King worried about the preparations for it. 'As usual,' he noted grumpily, everything was left for him to handle, assisted only by his personal staff. The ministers avoided the work, and only Ilsley was helping out.[24] Worse, King was exceedingly unhappy with the outlines the Central Committee was providing for what he saw as the crucial opening speech of the conference. L. W. Brockington, one of the Prime Minister's personal assistants, forwarded the Committee's views. The opening speech should be about one hour in length and 'while it will inevitably contain a number of general remarks on the subject of national unity, Canadianism, the preservation of provincial autonomy, human values, the historic and economic importance of reconfederation and other cognate matters, it must deal with an analysis of the Commission's recommendations and particularly their application to war and postwar problems.' The financial implications had to be spelled out clearly, Brockington argued on behalf of the Central Committee, and both inflation and borrowing had to be rejected as ways to finance the war. Taxation was the only method, 'the most efficient and equitable way,' and 'a taxing authority with comprehensive national jurisdiction is an elementary essential.' There was no intention to force the provinces to accept the Report, Brockington noted piously, but it was hoped that 'representative Canadians will find it possible to sink petty differences and agree in the shadow of a national emergency such as the present.' The alternative, if the provinces refused to surrender certain taxes to the Dominion in return for a guarantee of provincial fiscal autonomy, was simply that of 'forcing the Dominion, regretfully, to take the taxes.'[25] There might have been grounds for thinking that the bureaucracy was using the war as a spur towards fiscal centralization.

This tough language appalled King, and he took the memo to Cabinet on January 9. He read the draft to his assembled colleagues and asked them to express their views. Whatever they decided, he said, they should assume responsibility for the opening statement with him. While in no way disagreeing with the need for increased federal resources, the Prime Minister's own view was that the speech had to be conciliatory, not dogmatic, dictatorial, or threatening. 'It was interesting,' Mackenzie King wrote later that day, 'how the point of view of the [civil service] intelligentsia by whom I am surrounded . . . was attacked from the entire Cabinet circle.' The government's tactics 'should be to draw all to make a very sympathetic approach to the provinces; get them in conference in right mood, and then allow developments to shape themselves as might be inevitable . . .'[26] Faced with this impasse, King turned, as he usually did, to Dr Skelton, and the Under Secretary, reliable as ever, agreed that a more conciliatory tone was necessary. Still, Skelton emphasized that 'the primary responsibility for trying to find a solution is the Dominion's,' and while his language was more gentle than that urged by the Central Committee, the thrust was much the same.[27] This should not have been surprising to King, for Skelton was a member of the Central Committee and his son, Alex, had played a key role both in the preparation of the Royal Commission's report and in the Dominion government's preparations for the Conference.

With King pressing for more flexibility, the drafting and re-drafting went on. On the 12th, after further discussions, King was still not pleased. 'I pointed out . . . that that was entirely the wrong way to go about effecting that end . . . ,' he noted. 'It is only the conciliatory approach that would get us anywhere in the discussion, and if we take the "take it or leave it" attitude, that attitude would be blamed for the failure of the conference. I felt from the start that the pressure of financial interests to have their own way is the greatest danger the conference faces . . . the velvet gloves will be even more necessary. . . . There never was a conference which required more in the way of tact,' he added, 'and the avoidance of certain attitudes than the forthcoming one.' To do anything else would be to play right into the enemy's hands. There was nothing 'Hepburn and Aberhart would like better than for the Federal Government and myself in particular to take an arbitrary and dictatorial position. Hepburn would run his provincial campaign on the effort of Ottawa to take from Ontario all its powers, privileges, rights, to sacrifice them to Quebec or to the Prairies.'[28]

In the end Mackenzie King got his way, and the final draft of the opening speech was ready for him to present to Cabinet on January 13. There was 'entire approval' of each section, he noted in the diary, and the whole text was 'exceedingly well received'. The response was so good that optimism started seeping into King's mind, almost in spite of himself. The conference, he told his diary, might be a true foundation on which to build for the future.[29]

The conference opened the next day in the Parliament Buildings. King's polished speech was generally well received. He justified the calling of a conference in wartime, and with no evident enthusiasm allowed that 'It is our considered view that the adoption of the commission's recommendations is necessary to put our country in a position to pursue a policy which will achieve the maximum war effort, and at the same time to lay a foundation for post-war reconstruction.' The recommendations were not immutable, King said, but the financial ones formed an integrated whole. Still, 'we do not approach the conference with our minds closed. We do not say "all or nothing" or "everything at once".' What we seek, Mackenzie King urged, 'is the largest possible measure of agreement to enable the federal and provincial governments so to cooperate as to make our Canadian system work with less friction and greater efficiency for the benefit of the people of Canada in all the provinces.' The crux of the problem, of course, was 'the financial relationship between the federal and provincial governments'. But Ottawa was approaching the problem in a spirit of conciliation and was acting in conference, he pointedly said, not with the arbitrary use of its constitutional power.

Mackenzie King then reviewed the Report's recommendations, stressing the federal government's opinion that they did not rewrite the constitution or centralize authority unduly. The problem 'facing us at present is to distribute the total burden more evenly, and to strengthen the parts of the foundation which bear the increased and increasing burdens.' The recommendations 'aim at rescuing autonomy from the perils of confused and overlapping jurisdictions, and making clear definitions between the functions of the federal and provincial governments.' The best way to maintain provincial autonomy, the Prime Minister said, is to maintain provincial credit.[30]

The conciliatory tone of the Prime Minister's speech was lost on Mitchell Hepburn. He had come to the conference, as he told Chubby

Power, 'with blood in my eye and dandruff in my mustache'.[31] He also came in the traditional role of an Ontario premier, defending provincial autonomy, provincial revenues, and provincial rights against the centralizing tendencies of the federal government. Hepburn was abusive in his remarks, objecting to any discussion of this 'highly contentious document' during wartime and attacking the Report as 'the product of the minds of three professors [Dr Sirois, Prof. H. F. Angus, and Prof. R. A. Mackay] and a Winnipeg newspaperman [J. W. Dafoe].' The Premier objected to having Ottawa take on responsibility for unemployment relief now that the war had gone a long way towards resolving that problem, and he charged that the Report was motivated by the desire of 'financial houses' to improve their bond holdings. Moreover, while Quebec got special treatment, Ontario got nothing. Ottawa, Hepburn claimed, could do whatever it wanted for war purposes under the War Measures Act, and no changes in Confederation were necessary. In a ringing peroration, the Ontario Premier said 'to me it is unthinkable that we should be fiddling while London is burning.'[32]

The other premiers were less flamboyant. Godbout of Quebec seemed willing to accept emergency measures but, he said, 'I do not think we should condition the permanent future of Canada on the war situation now prevailing.' Premier Macmillan of Nova Scotia objected to adoption of the Report but he was willing to talk about it, a view basically shared by McNair of New Brunswick. Bracken of Manitoba was the sole defender of the Report as it stood and to him 'implementation of the substance of the report was essential to national unity.' Pattullo of British Columbia—in T. A. Crerar's sharp phrase 'a compound of inordinate vanity and . . . thickheadedness'—was flatly opposed, while Campbell of Prince Edward Island was discursive but ultimately in favour of adoption. So too was Patterson of Saskatchewan. 'With all the arts of the successful demagogue' Premier Aberhart attacked the Report in Social Credit terms, arguing that the 'large corporations and financial institutions' would be the only ones to benefit from the Report. The solution, the Alberta Premier predictably urged, was 'to overhaul the monetary system'.[33] After this discouraging beginning the conference adjourned for the day.

Efforts the next morning to strike an agenda and to start committee study of the Report collapsed, as T. A. Crerar wrote later, 'in the god damnedest exhibition and circus you can imagine.'[34] When the delegates met again in the afternoon everything was confusion. After some argument, Ilsley was permitted to deliver the speech that he and his Deputy

Minister had drafted for delivery to the conference's finance committee. The Finance Minister's speech was a clear reflection of his Department's views and as such it was somewhat in advance of the Prime Minister's. The federal government needed the money to fight the war, Ilsley knew, and his language was tough. The Report had to be adopted, he told the conference. Canada had to have an equitable tax system and the danger of the national credit being damaged by provincial difficulties had to be averted. There was also the need for a basic standard of 'decency and justice' throughout the country and the necessity to begin preparations for postwar reconstruction. Neither could be accomplished without fiscal reform. These were his positive arguments. Then 'at the risk of some misinterpretation,' Ilsley warned the premiers that the Dominion would 'undoubtedly have to invade provincial tax fields such as succession duties' and 'increase its rate in such fields of progressive taxation as the income tax.' Moreover it might become necessary to cease paying the present 40 per cent cost of unemployment relief, to stop helping the provinces meet their maturities, and possibly to begin gas rationing, a step that would strike directly at provincial revenues.[35] The velvet glove that Mackenzie King and the Cabinet had carefully drawn on had been removed by the Minister of Finance.

The conference dragged to its close after Ilsley's speech, but not without an extraordinary final performance from Mitchell Hepburn. 'If you want to do something as a war measure go ahead and do it,' he shouted. 'But don't smash this confederation and stir up possible racial feuds in your efforts.' Ontario would never accept the Rowell-Sirois recommendations, for if it did 'We shall be left in the hands of a bureaucracy established in Ottawa. . . . I myself will not sell my province down the river for all time to come, and allow our social services to remain a victim of the dictatorial methods of a bureaucracy to be set up in Ottawa.'[36] The other premiers had a chance to speak and King then met with his ministers privately, returning only to announce that there was no point in continuing further. As he closed the conference, King noted that by holding it the federal government had at least avoided the controversy that would have arisen if Ottawa had invaded provincial revenue fields without discussion. He regretted the lack of agreement, the Prime Minister said, but he was grateful for the support the premiers had indicated for the war effort. Such support eased his mind about the steps that would have to be taken.[37]

Initially Mackenzie King's response to the meeting was that while to outward appearances it was a failure, 'in reality it has served the purpose we had in view, of avoiding attack for not having called the Conference, and particularly what would have followed, invasion of provincial sources of revenue. We have now got the pledge of the provinces to let us take their revenues if we need them—a tremendous achievement.' And, as was his wont, King gave credit where it was due: 'Had I gone the length those financial men and intelligentsia around me would have wished; saying that the whole thing was to be taken or nothing, I would have played completely into the hands of Hepburn, Pattullo and Aberhart. As it was, I had enough in what I said, to save the situation, and put us in our true position.'[38]

But a few days later King was being plagued by inconsistent second thoughts. In a conversation with Skelton, one of the last King would have with the Under Secretary before his death, the Prime Minister 'pointed out how our government had been forced through the Finance Department, E[xternal]. A[ffairs]., etc. into the recent conference on the Sirois report when both Lapointe and I were . . . absolutely opposed to anything of the kind at this time, and that we could have accomplished much more by waiting for the right moment and not deliberately creating new situations and problems.' The conference's failure, he added later, 'has given the enemies of the government a chance to disclose divisions in the Liberal ranks and to claim we have erred in judgment in trying to do such other things as changing Constitution etc. in time of war. I wonder what would have been said if I had made the kind of speech that was written out for me emphasizing we were re-creating Confederation . . .'[39]

The Rowell-Sirois Report had been shelved. That was clear. The blame was spread around by the newspapers, but most was affixed to 'Canada's three saboteurs', Hepburn, Aberhart, and Pattullo, although the Prime Minister came in for his share of attack for his unwillingness to provide a forceful lead.[40] Yet the conference did serve the purpose of putting the three premiers in the apparent position of blocking rational consideration of change, and Ilsley did establish the case for Ottawa's need for more revenue.

All that remained was to get the money, but Ilsley and Clark had no firm ideas on how to proceed. Ottawa would have to move into the provincial taxation fields and implement some wartime version of the Rowell-Sirois recommendations, but this would be difficult. Walter Gordon, the scion of Clarkson, Gordon of Toronto and a Special Assistant to Clark at this time, had been convinced from the first that the conference would fail and he had told this to his chief. After the meeting's collapse, Gordon was informed by Clark 'that as I had been so smart in predicting the failure of the conference, I could take on the job of finding an alternative solution to the problem of financing the war effort.' Gordon took Clark at his word and, according to his own recollection, came to the Deputy Minister soon after with a proposal:

> My premises were that as long as Hepburn was around, we should not expect cooperation from the provincial governments; that, however, a large majority of the people in English-speaking Canada was behind the federal government in the war effort and probably was prepared to accept some of the burden this implied; that if this public support was to be retained, the federal government must bounce back from its failure at the conference with tax proposals the provinces would have no option but accepting. I argued that the tax proposals should be confined simply to financing the war effort and not [be] mixed up with social objectives no matter how overdue or desirable these might be. I suggested these social aims would have to be pursued after the war was over, although I acknowledged that a little something could be done to alleviate the financial difficulties of the poorer provinces in the plan I would put forward.

Gordon's plan was simple. Ottawa should impose the heavy taxes it needed to finance the war effort and should promise to give to any province that agreed to surrender its own income, corporation, and succession taxes an annual payment equal to its previous revenue from these fields. Agreement was to be voluntary, Gordon said, but provinces that failed to accept this arrangement would saddle their citizens with onerous double taxation. 'I argued,' Gordon recalled, that

> that would be the responsibility of the provincial government in question, not of Ottawa. It was my submission that a scheme along these lines would work and that every province would have to accept it if the federal government was firm enough. The situation would become chaotic, however, if the federal government were to get cold feet and start making special deals with individual provinces.[41]

This clever scheme of blackmailing the provinces made its way successfully through the Department of Finance and to the Cabinet on March 26, 1941, when the 1941-2 budget was under consideration. The options were essentially two: Gordon's scheme; or increasing the sales tax and defence tax substantially with lesser increases in other areas. In the end the Cabinet decided to accept Gordon's proposal and to do so without advance word to the provinces. Mackenzie King and Ernest Lapointe argued that 'we should do what we were going to do in the Budget without a word in advance, as at our last conference we had been told we had the power to do this and should do it, and must exercise that power. The Cabinet became one in that view.' What was now being done, Mackenzie King concluded in reference to Gordon's scheme, 'will last until the year after the war which may mean that, at that time, the provinces will have come to see that the Sirois Report is, after all, what is best for them as well as for us.'[42]

The Ottawa position was duly announced as a 'temporary wartime expedient' in the budget speech on April 29 and, as Gordon had foreseen, the provinces after some bitter complaints were soon forced to capitulate. The Dominion-Provincial Taxation Agreement Act, 1942, assented to on May 28, 1942, formalized the arrangement.[43] Plan 1 of the Rowell-Sirois Report was now dead, but the needs of the war had been met.

II

Those needs also forced the government to intervene massively in the economy. The pressures of inflation were such by the middle of 1941 that the government faced a situation not dissimilar to that which had arisen during the Great War when the cost of living had skyrocketed. The difference between 1917 and 1941 was the economic sophistication that could now be found within the Department of Finance, the Bank of Canada, and the Wartime Prices and Trade Board.

From the beginning of the war the King government had imposed controls on the marketplace. There were very few objections to such controls, in part because similar ones had been exercised in the earlier war, and in part because there were signs of hoarding even before war was declared by Canada.[44] The key board, established on September 3, 1939, was the Wartime Prices and Trade Board.[45] Under the control of the Minister of Labour, the WPTB had sweeping powers to control the price, supply, and distribution of the necessities of life, but in its first two years of life the Board played a relatively minor role. Only six administrators were appointed to control wool, sugar, leather, coal, oils and fats, and rents, and only sixty-four orders were issued by the WPTB, of which fifty-one dealt with rents.[46] Closely associated with the WPTB was the Wartime Industries Control Board, another appointed body with jurisdiction over the supply of basic materials such as oil, steel, metals, and timber. The WICB saw its task in the early part of the war as the achievement of voluntary co-operation to control prices, increase production, and achieve equitable distribution.[47]

Another aspect of the control system established at the outset of war was the regulation of foreign exchange. A Foreign Exchange Control Board was created on September 15, 1939, and immediately had to deal with the complex and pressing task of stopping the drain of foreign exchange from Canada. In addition various export and import controls were established, including a War Exchange Tax of 10 per cent on all non-Empire imports. The export control system was formalized by P.C. 2448 in April 1941, which gave the Minister of Trade and Commerce the power to grant or refuse permits to export goods. Import controls fell to the Minister of National Revenue, who had a wide range of orders in council at his disposal. The War Exchange Conservation Act of December 2, 1940 was another weapon, and one that prohibited entirely certain classes of imports. The intent was to conserve American dollar exchange, and the Hyde Park agreements of April 1941 eased the pressure in this area.

Control of the economy was also exercised through taxation. The provinces vacated certain tax fields early in 1942, and the federal government increased the rates in a wide spectrum of existing and new taxation areas. Excise, sales, and retail purchase taxes were increased or imposed, and the War Exchange Tax also produced substantial sums while at the same time serving to deter unnecessary imports. The rates of personal income and corporation taxes were also substantially raised,[48] and the normal rate of corporation tax went from 18 to 40 per cent. All profits in excess of 116 ⅔ per cent of standard profits (the average of profits from 1936 to 1939) were taxed at 100 per cent, but the corporations would get a 20 per cent postwar rebate. The object, as Finance Minister Ilsley said in a speech at Edmonton on September 3, 1941, was to ensure 'that if any company does increase its profits because of war conditions, the Treasury will derive nearly all the benefit.' No great fortunes, he added too optimistically, 'can be accumulated out of wartime profits.'[49] In addition, in an effort to soak up excess capital and to help finance the all-consuming war effort, the government sold vast sums of war bonds and war savings stamps.[50]

But nothing had yet been done on a major scale to control wages and prices. This was an entirely different problem in scope, far more difficult to manage and demanding a huge bureaucracy to administer. Many Canadians also seemed to feel that such sweeping controls, once imposed, could never be removed. J. M. Macdonnell, the President of the National Trust Co., expressed this fear in November 1939 when he suggested that the civil servants 'will feel that the controls they have operated during the war are to some extent at any rate to be maintained in peace. They will find a considerable number of the community, particularly the Socialists, who will agree with them . . .'[51]

But the necessity for more sweeping controls was becoming apparent, pressures from the business community notwithstanding. In fact some controls were positively heartening to manufacturers and employers, as when the government passed an order in council on December 13, 1940 setting guidelines that in effect put a ceiling on wage increases in war industries.* The intent, as Mackenzie King noted, was to prevent 'that vicious spiral of previous years'. In the Prime Minister's view the order also 'secured to labour its standards both of living and of nominal wages —practically the highest point they have reached in our country's history.'† Yet the inflationary spiral continued despite the wage-increase controls. The cost of living rose only 4 per cent in 1940, but in the first three quarters of 1941 the index increased by 7 per cent. The big jump in prices (from 104.6 to 107.8 on the cost of living index between April and June 1941)[53] seriously frightened the government, and officials began thinking of ways to damp down inflationary tendencies.

---

*The government had preceded this order with P.C. 2685 of June 19, 1940, which met some of organized labour's complaints by urging that employers pay fair and reasonable wage rates and by suggesting a bonus system for temporary adjustments to wages. More important still, this order recognized labour's right to organize and bargain collectively, and it ordered disputes to be settled by negotiation or with the conciliation services of the government. P.C. 2686 of June 19, 1940 also set up the National Labour Supply Council with substantial labour representation, both orders being a direct response to labour's complaints as presented to Mackenzie King on June 13, 1940. See Richard Clarke, 'Labour and Wartime Wage Control', graduate paper, York University, 1974.

†The initial labour response to the wage controls established by P.C. 7440 of Dec. 13, 1940 was favourable, but within a few months complaints were very loud. Employers were taking advantage of every loophole and the cost-of-living bonus system established by the order was being interpreted by employers—and the government conciliation boards—as voluntary not mandatory. P.C. 4643 of June 27, 1941 rectified this, but labour complaints continued. Richard Clarke, 'Labour and Wartime Wage Control', graduate paper, York University, 1974.

According to Grant Dexter, the Winnipeg reporter with access to everyone and everybody in Ottawa, the WPTB asked for stiffer controls in May 1941. By this stage the Canadian Manufacturers Association, traditionally an agency for the regulation of competition, was telling the Cabinet that it supported price controls,[54] and the bureaucracy was no longer forcing the pace. But no one, neither the CMA nor the WPTB, apparently contemplated a total freeze on wages and prices. This idea emerged from the Bank of Canada in June and was then considered by the WPTB, from which it received a divided verdict. The difficulties inherent in such a policy seemed overwhelming to the Board.[55] Initally there was agreement on only one point: the WPTB had to be taken from the Department of Labour and put where it belonged—in Finance.[56] The Cabinet agreed that it was the best of sense to unify fiscal and anti-inflationary policy under one minister, and there was agreement too on extending the WPTB's jurisdiction to include all goods and services. 'Finance would be held responsible in the end for inflation,' King quoted Ilsley as saying, and all agreed that the responsibility should be his.[57]

This was crucial, for Ilsley leaned towards a total freeze on prices and wages. The question was thoroughly canvassed within the Finance Department and the Bank of Canada in the late summer of 1941, and opinion soon coalesced around the belief that only a complete freeze could check inflation. Everyone recognized the political pressures such a freeze would produce, however, and this tended to temper enthusiasm.[58] Nonetheless Ilsley warned a gathering of businessmen at the Seigniory Club at Montebello, Quebec on September 18 that 'We have the agencies established and empowered to achieve price stability. . . . I can assure [you] things will not be allowed to drift.'[59]

The Cabinet met to hear Ilsley's proposals on October 3. Graham Towers of the Bank of Canada, Clark, the Deputy Minister of Finance, and Hector McKinnon of the WPTB were in attendance. 'I, myself, took strong issue with the attempt to do everything at once which is the view that Towers and Clark so strongly hold,' King wrote about this meeting. The civil servants were not judges of opinion. 'They seem to think that we can at one stroke, legislate to have prices kept where they are and wages, the same.' This was foolish, King said. 'That we would all be made ridiculous in the end trying to do by Order-in-Council something that the economic forces of the world would defy with impunity.'[60] It was far more sensible to take a piecemeal approach, the Prime Minister argued, and in this view he was essentially supported by the WPTB chairman.[61] The Cabinet deferred its decision, but before the meeting adjourned King told an anecdote that he attributed to Churchill:

> You know, Mackenzie [the British Prime Minister had said], flying in a bomber is a great way for a politician to travel. It is dramatic. It is very rapid. But the only point you should bear in mind is that you must have some place to land.

That, said King, is what the proposals for a freeze brought to mind. It would be dramatic and everyone would cheer. But three months later, if and when the economy was in chaos, the government would be cursed.[62]

Dramatic action of this kind frightened the Prime Minister. He had the highest regard for the permanent officials in Finance, but he sometimes thought that they were too close to the financial interests. 'It is not safe to trust bankers . . . with human nature and human force,' he confided to his diary on October 3. His conversation on October 18 with John Blackmore, the Social Credit leader in the House of Commons, was similar. Blackmore had told him that he was in favour of price controls because they could be seen as a move towards Social Credit. 'I told him it looked as though we were falling over into his camp; also I thought he and his party might have, before the next election comes, to join with us in putting some of the financial interests in their places.'[63]

Despite King's doubts, Ilsley was still sanguine about getting his price and wage control policies through Cabinet. 'He said it was 50 to 1 for acceptance,' Dexter wrote on October 9, 'and McKinnon must get right on with organization.' But as the days passed the Finance Minister grew gloomier. J. G. Gardiner, the Minister of Agriculture, bitterly fought any attempts to take responsibility for controls on agricultural products away from his jurisdiction, and King was still adamant.[64] The opposition was not unfounded. No other democratic nation had introduced such sweeping controls as those proposed by Ilsley, and even the economists were divided in their assessments of the effects of a freeze. Could full utilization of resources be achieved under such controls? No one knew.[65]

The key Cabinet meeting was held on October 10. Surprisingly, Mackenzie King found himself alone in his opposition to the freeze. Equally surprising, the Prime Minister gave in very quickly and accepted Ilsley's proposal, even indicating 'how I thought approach should be made as to announcement of policy, making clear it was not intended as a cure-all; that the problem was a most difficult one to deal with. Later appealing to the public to co-operate with the government to save an appalling situation that might develop, stressing influence of foreign conditions, making very difficult any real solution, and leaving the way open for making clear the methods that would have to be adopted to effect adjustments which time and experience would occasion. Making clear,' Mackenzie King told his colleagues, 'it was only a trial of what seemed the best thing to do.'[66] The intention at this stage was still only to issue a press release announcing the implementation of the policy at some near date.

The immediate problem was to find someone to lead the now enormously powerful WPTB. One of the earliest suggestions was Donald Gordon, the Deputy Governor of the Bank of Canada, but Towers refused to permit his deputy to leave. The Governor's stubbornness led to other names being canvassed, including H. R. MacMillan of British Columbia, the timber controller, and Walter Gordon. Eventually, however, on Ralston's suggestion, King intervened directly with Towers and pried Donald Gordon free. 'We let Towers know that we felt the Bank and the Finance Department were mainly responsible for the policy,' King recorded of his conversation with Towers on November 7, 'and that they owed it to the Government to help to see that it did not suffer through inadequate administration at the start.'[67] The choice of Gordon was an inspired one, and after McKinnon resigned as Chairman of the WPTB on November 19, the new administrator quickly built up an awesomely efficient organization.[68]

There was still a long way to go before the policy could be announced. On October 15 Mackenzie King met with Tom Moore of the Trades and Labour Congress, A. R. Mosher of the Canadian Congress of Labour, and with several other leaders of organized labour, and informed them of the government's intentions. He stressed the dangers that inflation posed to living standards, and in a successful effort at mediation he gradually won pledges of co-operation from the union men. The leaders were combative, critical of the government's labour policies, and angry about the short notice on wage controls. But King won them over by agreeing that the government had been slow to implement its labour policies: 'I had to confess that, as Prime Minister, I had difficulty in getting anything done as I wished to have done because of the bureaucracy by which I myself was surrounded; that I shared their impatience about the lack of readiness in carrying out the government's policies . . .'[69] King was always willing to fix blame elsewhere, but certainly the Prime Minister was correct when he told his Cabinet later that 'It was folly to attempt any step of the magnitude proposed without having Labour's cooperation.'[70]

Mackenzie King announced the government's price and wage control policy in a national broadcast on Saturday, October 18. The Prime Minister began by stressing the importance of the proposed steps: 'It will affect the daily lives of each one of us. It will require the co-operation and support of all. It will help to intensify the effort of this country in war. It will help to prevent a repetition of distress and depression after the war.' The situation in 1941 was much the same as that in 1916, King said, except that the country was spending 40 per cent of its national income now while in the Great War the country had never devoted more than 10 per cent to the war.[71] 'The government must have the goods to build and maintain our war machine. . . . The same gallon of gasoline cannot be used in an army tank and a pleasure motor car.' Therefore, he said, 'the government has decided to halt the rise of prices; to undertake the control of all prices; and, where necessary, to take other steps to control civilian consumption in fair and equitable ways.'

This was no panacea, Mackenzie King warned, echoing his words in Cabinet, but it was necessary. On and after November 17 (later changed to December 1), 'no person may sell any goods or supply any services at a price or rate higher than that charged by him for such goods or services during the four weeks from September 15 to October 11. . . . Except in cases where minimum prices are fixed, prices will be free to fall below the ceiling.' The freeze, the Prime Minister added, would apply to rentals, to utility rates, to transportation, laundering, undertaking and embalming, and the supplying of meals and refreshments.

This was only one aspect of the policy. Wages were also included: 'It is obvious that the prices of finished goods cannot be controlled successfully unless the cost of production is also controlled.' The government had taken steps towards a war industries' wage policy in December 1940 and, while this had worked well, it had put non-war industries in difficulties. 'The government has therefore decided to extend its wartime wage policy to cover all industry. . . . Henceforward no employer in Canadian industry or commerce may, without permission, increase his present basic wage rates.' A cost of living bonus, to be determined by the government, would ensure that wages kept in line with prices. For agriculture, King held out special promises. The price ceiling would be applied, but 'total agricultural income will be supported, where necessary, by government action.' The government would also make supplementary payments to farmers in the spring-wheat area and cover transportation costs on feed grain for Eastern farmers. The prices for farm goods would be determined on the basis of maximum market prices during the four weeks ending October 11.[72]

King's speech had been largely drafted for the Prime Minister by J. W. Pickersgill of his office, assisted by Grant Dexter of the *Winnipeg Free Press*. The agricultural paragraphs were mainly based on memoranda supplied by Gardiner, the Minister of Agriculture,[73] and seemed to satisfy that sometimes difficult Saskatchewan representative. The cost of living bonus, to be fixed in due course at 25¢ per week for each percentage point rise in the cost of living index for those earning more than $25 per week and at one per cent of the weekly wage rate for those earning less than $25 per week, was perhaps less well thought out than other parts of the package. The bonus itself tended to contribute to the inflationary spiral, for it was a commitment by the government that if price controls failed wages would keep pace. In addition the freeze did not attempt to grapple with inequities, and the index by which the bonus was determined was a nation-wide one that favoured, for example, the worker in low-cost rural New Brunswick more than the plant foreman in expensive Toronto.[74] On the other hand, it was time that the National Policy began working in reverse, and the past inequities weighed heaviest outside of central Canada and always had.

In the month between King's speech and the date the price and wage measures were to go into effect, there was enormous activity in Ottawa. There was, of course, some consternation among businessmen, farmers, and labour, although the business response was rather mild. Earlier in the year there had been rumblings against any price-control measures, in part on the grounds that any interference with the economy was a mistake. The less interference the easier the transition to peace. Some businessmen also argued that since the United States had no controls and since Canada was so dependent on the Americans, it would be exceedingly difficult to maintain the ceilings.[75] Once the plan was announced, however, there was little carping. The Toronto *Telegram* reported on October 25 that 'Toronto's industrial leaders are of almost unanimous opinion that it is most radical and far-reaching—but vitally necessary in the present emergency.' The influential *Financial Post* said much the same thing on November 1: 'Businessmen generally support the plan. They find in it features that are undesirable but accept rigid controls as a drastic measure to prevent inflation.' Of course many

Canadian industries had always arranged prices to limit destructive competition, and about all the freeze did was to shift the locus of decision-making. The shift was not all that great either, since the government's controllers were brought in directly from the industries they were expected to regulate.

There were exceptions to the favourable business response to the ceilings. Retail grocers claimed that the freeze would ruin them and flooded the Prime Minister's Office with telegrams.[76] C. L. Burton of the Robert Simpson Co., 'perhaps the most influential retailer in the country,' Pickersgill noted to Mackenzie King,[77] was another protester. In a long letter to King on November 18 he objected that freezing prices on the base period September 15—October 11 was unfair because 'most of the goods sold in the specified period were produced, manufactured and distributed for sale several months earlier on the basis of then prevailing lower costs.'[78] There was some truth in that argument.

Labour was more obstreperous. Wage control hit directly at the unions because it removed one of the real incentives workers had for joining a union, namely the increased wages that union bargaining power could secure.[79] The public complaints of labour, however, fixed more on the lack of consultation in working out the freeze policy, a charge that did not ring true because of the Prime Minister's meeting with union leaders on October 15 and the fact that the freeze had not been finally accepted by Cabinet until October 10. Tom Moore, the President of the Trades and Labour Congress, called the freeze a step towards 'the establishment of a totalitarian state' and claimed that consultation had been minimal despite the government's pledges to recognize the unions as the representatives of the working force. Moreover wage stabilization was unjust so long as wages were too low, as they were, and the government should fix the minimum wage at $25 a week. And, Moore asked, why were stock dividends not pegged?[80] The TLC would call a conference, he said, to consider the wage and price controls.[81] A. R. Mosher, the President of the Canadian Congress of Labour, was also critical. 'The proposed legislation leaves no avenue open for the free process of collective bargaining.'[82]

Farmers were equally unhappy. H. H. Hannam, the President of the Canadian Federation of Agriculture, complained to Mackenzie King that the freeze discriminated against agriculture because 'the economic returns to farm people in the four weeks prior to October 11 were somewhat below a parity position with other groups in the nation . . .' Farmers had to overcome the effects of ten years of depression, Hannam argued, and rising farm prices would have redressed the balance. At the very least the government should find some more scientific way of fixing the base price than merely looking at four weeks. The government was not very forthcoming, but King did agree to arrange meetings for Hannam in Ottawa.[83] These talks, held in mid-November, largely mollified Hannam.[84]

Agriculture received short shrift because the government basically believed that it had caught up with other sectors of the economy. Certainly this was the view of W. A. Mackintosh, the Queen's University economics professor who was serving as special assistant to Clifford Clark, the Deputy Minister of Finance.[85] As Mackintosh wrote to a friend, 'the price rise from about May of this year to September was very rapid, and it was to a large extent concentrated in agricultural prices. This meant that for the first time there was a practical possibility of dealing simultaneously with all prices and wages, and accomplishing it with some justice.' Justice, clearly, was capable of different definitions.

Mackintosh also dealt in his letter with some of the difficulties facing the government. One objection to the freeze, he said, is that 'instead of keeping prices down so that people can buy what they want at fixed prices, it would be better to allow rising prices to force curtailment of purchases.' But inflation could not be accepted, Mackintosh maintained, because those on low incomes would bear the brunt. The government has not yet made clear 'that a necessary part of its prices and wages policy is a rigorous curtailment of supplies whether that is accompanied by formal rationing to the consumer or not.' As for labour's complaints about the freeze ending collective bargaining, Mackintosh was not convinced. 'In my own view the limitation was not imposed by the wages order, but by the facts of the case in which the government is the sole purchaser of the output of a large number of plants.'[86]

In fact, while Mackintosh was writing, the whole question of the freeze was up in the air. There would be a freeze, but what kind? The Bank of Canada and Clifford Clark favoured an unyielding, concrete ceiling, Grant Dexter wrote, while the WPTB favoured a 10 per cent leeway so that hardships could be adjusted. Unfortunately many of the controllers and administrators hired by the Board to enforce the ceiling were lobbying for the flexible policy. Dexter recorded that he had been asked to visit a Château Laurier suite where C. L. Burton of Simpson's and his son, one of the administrators, were holding court and urging the press to give publicity to the flexible ceiling. The argument advanced was much like the one Burton had put to the Prime Minister:

raw materials prices had risen so fast that a freeze would force secondary manufacturers to produce at a loss. The result would be to throw the wholesale and retail trades into confusion. When Donald Gordon heard of this lobbying he was, Dexter said, horrified, and he read the riot act to his employees, informing them that they were now civil servants and had better act as such.[87]

But the retailers' complaints had had their effect, and the chairman of the WPTB tried to deal with them when he met with a large number of Canadian publishers on November 27 for an off-the-record briefing.[88] Gordon put heavy emphasis on the dangers posed by inflation and on the duty of the press to inform the public of these dangers. Inflation, he said, 'was a useful servant in promoting the production of goods at the beginning of the war, but now, when practically all our productive resources are being used to the full . . . the inflationary technique can become a fearful master unless it is curbed.' The 'fearful master' had to be checked and only 'heroic measures' could do this. 'Any alternative,' Gordon argued, 'in the form of selective control or an attempt at a gradual stop is doomed to failure for the simple reason that the spiral of inflation feeds on itself.' The contention that the freeze would cause ruin was 'ridiculous. It is based upon a conception of the price ceiling policy and its administration which assumes an unimaginative bureaucratic application which will disregard the very difficult adjustments which have to be made. . . . Can anyone honestly believe that the alternative of a chaotic inflation is preferable to making an attempt at such adjustments?'

The WPTB chairman then turned directly to the complaints of the retailers:

The problem can be stated very simply. Here is a retail price. When that retail price was figured out, the cost of manufacturing, processing and delivering the goods to the retailers was so much and since then the cost of replacing the goods has risen very rapidly. Consequently, if retailers' prices are to be held, everyone back from the retailer to the primary producer must accept a lower price—must accept his share of the added cost so that the retailer may receive his replacements at a cost which will enable him to absorb only his own additional costs in the form of labour or other overhead and still sell the goods at a reasonable profit.

When you think of it, surely that cannot be an impossible problem to solve.

What Gordon was proposing became known as the 'squeeze'. Companies that retailed goods could not be expected to bear the burden of the freeze alone, his message went, and the effects had to be rolled back down the line in the direction of the wholesaler, manufacturer, and primary producer too. If the squeeze was too great to be borne at some point on this chain, then a subsidy might be offered. The total squeeze on leather footwear, for example, was eventually determined to be 15 per cent, of which 4 per cent was divided between wholesaler and retailer, 4 per cent borne by the manufacturer, and the remaining 7 per cent paid in subsidy by the government to the manufacturer.[89] Without the squeeze and the rollback in prices, the only alternative would have been for the retailer to pass the increased costs on to the consumer, a course many businessmen favoured. The government could not accept this, however, since such increases in the cost of goods would be reflected on the cost of living index, thus forcing wages up through the bonus and accelerating the inflationary spiral.[90]

Donald Gordon's logic was impeccable. He ended his address to the publishers by assuring them that each industry and business had been asked to supply competent administrators to the WPTB. Each was now represented by competent men 'in most instances nominated by the industry or business itself'. The regulators would be the representatives of the regulated. Interestingly, this was a direct reversal of pre-freeze WPTB policy. The administrators before the freeze, Kenneth Taylor, the Secretary of the WPTB since 1939, wrote, 'have been deliberately chosen from outside the industries they direct. . . . this is the preferable policy. It has avoided jealousies and the inevitable suggestions of bias or favouritism within the industry . . .'[91]

Those charges would now be heard, but not from within the audience listening to Donald Gordon. The freeze seemed to load the dice for the benefit of large industry and business. Grant Dexter, writing after the freeze had been in effect nearly a year, summed up the process in a private memorandum:

the only people who got hurt in the squeeze were the consumers and the little fellow who was not worth salvaging in the view of Prices and Trade. The price ceiling, in the main, was held. The manufacturers' and retailers' costs were brought into line by several methods—quality was reduced, particularly in textiles; the number of lines was cut down, models were standardized. These benefitted the manufacturers greatly, since the old price remained. They passed along part of their winnings to distributors and retailers, though I am told that the small retailer often lost out. There have been no complaints worth mentioning; everybody is happy. Where the consumers could not be squeezed, the lads got subsidies. . . . In a word we have been getting an inverted inflation. The quality is cut but the price remains constant—a process which, no doubt, is capable of considerable expansion. . . .

It is suggested . . . that we are witnessing a great trustification, cartelization, of Canadian industry, competition is being knocked out. Behind all this front stage tragedy of the nation being stripped for total war . . . nothing very much has happened or is happening. Nobody's been hurt, except the consumer and the little guy. The big chaps are managing to bear it all bravely.[92]

The big fish ate the small fish, and the process of consolidation and rationalization under way in Canadian industry since the turn of the century merely accelerated.

In terms of checking inflation, however, the freeze was completely successful. The cost of living had risen by 17.8 per cent from August 1, 1939 to October 1, 1941, but from October 1, 1941 to April 1, 1945 the percentage increase was a mere 2.8 per cent. The cost of fuel and light actually dropped by almost 5 per cent, and the cost of clothing and home furnishings was virtually stable. Only food rose in price. Rationing also played its part. In 1942 coupon rationing was adopted for sugar, tea, coffee, butter, and gasoline, but at no time did the shoe pinch very tightly. At its lowest point the butter ration was still six ounces per week per person, and the meat ration, depending on cut, was never lower than one to two-and-a-half pounds per week per person. The gasoline ration, reduced to its lowest point in April 1943, still permitted non-essential users to draw 120 gallons per year, enough for 2,160 miles of pleasure driving.[93] All in all, the Canadian experience with controls on inflation and rationing was unquestionably the most successful of that of any of the belligerents.

III

Under the leadership of C. D. Howe, meanwhile, the country's war production was rapidly approaching undreamed of peaks. The beginnings had been slow. In the four-month period ending October 31, 1939, the total of contracts placed was only $41.3 million,[94] and the subsequent two months added merely an additional $19.7 million.[95] The value of war contracts for 1939 and 1940 was just over $500 million, a substantial enough sum but only 5 per cent of the grand total of Canadian war production from 1939-45. The big jump in production came in 1941 when the nation's factories produced $1.17 billion, a figure that was more than doubled in the following year to $2.46 billion.[96] The growth in national income was extraordinary and all the predictions of the economists were outstripped; the depression was over at last.

On the negative side, too much Canadian production was directed at the British market for comfort. The scare that the government had received at the end of March 1941 when it seemed possible that Lend-Lease might steal away British orders to the United States was a salutary one; thus while Canadian officials outwardly were confident that war production destined for Britain would continue to make up the bulk of Canadian orders, there were still some doubts.

In the British view, Lend-Lease offered attractive provisions that could not be 'offset to any extent by considerations of retaining Canadian goodwill.'[97] To C. D. Howe, the British seemed to believe that 'while Canada was presently granting credits, Canada's obligations would have to be refunded at the termination of the war and that consequently as much business as possible should be placed in the United States.'[98] The potential effects of such a British policy were enormous, and not simply in the short term. J. B. Carswell, the Department of Munitions and Supply's liaison man in Washington, saw Anglo-Canadian trade and commercial relations in decline and U.S.-U.K. relations in the ascendancy. Canada had to adopt something similar to Lend-Lease, Carswell argued in July 1941, or 'I can see . . . our pre-war business with the United Kingdom and the Empire disappearing and going to the United States.' British and American industrialists were already thinking about postwar markets and 'I suggest that we need to do a little thinking along the same line ourselves.'[99] Howe agreed, and as he wrote the Finance Minister a few days later, he was 'beginning to doubt the wisdom of accumulating sterling balances in London that will never be paid, and at the same time, attempting to operate the supply situation under present financial handicaps.' What had to be done, Howe said, was to arrange the transfer of all Canadian securities held in Britain to Canada and to acquire ownership of all British capital investments in war plants and machinery in Canada. In return, Canada could make a substantial contribution to British purchases in Canada as a gift, probably as much as half so that only enough sterling balances would be built up to cover Canadian commitments in Britain. 'I believe,' he added, 'that the time to be generous with Britain is now ... rather than in the post-war period when our people will be in a less generous mood.'[100] Although Howe did not mention it, there was also the difficulty caused for Canada by a popular feeling in the United States that Canada, part of the British Commonwealth, was setting stiffer terms to Britain than the non-belligerent Americans. The Prime Minister had dealt with this question in a speech in New York City on June 17, 1941, when he denied that Canada insisted on cash on the barrelhead. That charge, Mackenzie King told his American audience, 'overlooks the fact that the whole of Canada's direct war effort is a contribution which is neither leased nor lent, but is an out and out freewill offering—a gift to the hard-pressed people of Britain, gladly and proudly made.'[101] That was not a particularly convincing rejoinder.

Howe continued working to ensure that British orders were not diverted.[102] His appointees on the British Supply Council in North America were arguing the Canadian case, as were his representatives in London. A telegram to London in mid-August gave the Minister of Munitions and Supply's view that 'Canada will not exact more onerous terms of settlement post-war than will be obtained from United States . . .'[103] The result was yet another British assurance that there would be no switching of orders to the United States, an assurance that was finally transformed into a binding arrangement in October.[104]

This settlement of Canadian difficulties with London was a welcome but temporary one. Clearly, as C. D. Howe had seen, a longer term arrangement for financing British purchases in Canada was necessary. At the end of August 1941, therefore, Howe again approached Ilsley with suggestions for rationalizing matters. Hyde Park was working well, he told the Finance Minister, and there were no longer any problems with American exchange. There was even no pressing need for new munitions orders. The considerations affecting a new financial arrangement with the British were then three: would it please the Canadian people? would it eliminate American criticism that Canada charged Britain for goods the U.S. handed over free? and would it avoid an unpleasant postwar situation? A suggestion that Clifford Clark had made—that Canada should fix a sum for her aid to Britain each year— was unsatisfactory, Howe claimed. It would inevitably be either too small or too great. The amount of aid should be limited only by Canada's productive capacity, less essential domestic requirements and less the amounts needed to balance Canada's accounts with the United

States. Howe then turned to British investments in Canada, a subject on which he was insistent. The British investment in Canadian munitions capacity was about $250 million and this could be taken over and covered from Canada's sterling balances in London. There was also no objection that could be raised, the Minister stated, to repatriating Canadian securities held in England. 'I see no reason why we are not justified in wiping out Canada's indebtedness to Britain under the generous terms that we are now offering should the war continue.'[105]

Negotiations with London were proceeding on this and other fronts. One point that worried the Canadians was the relatively low prices for food that farmers were receiving from Britain. In late August 1941 the British suggested that Canada should enact a Lend-Lease act of her own, and the Canadians countered by suggesting that in return for British readiness to pay more for food the Canadian government would compensate the British handsomely in other directions.[106] But despite speedy British agreement to this proposal,[107] the negotiations bogged down in Ottawa and nothing was decided by late October. The British High Commissioner, Malcolm MacDonald, was somewhat discouraged—'the much brighter prospect . . . has somewhat faded';[108] in the meantime the British trade deficit continued to grow frighteningly. The Canadian estimate of its size for the fiscal year beginning April 1, 1941 was $1,159 million, and according to the High Commissioner there was still no organized Canadian policy relating to the repatriation of Canadian securities. In June, MacDonald reported, the Canadians had asked for the repatriation of £31 million in Dominion bonds, but 'there seems no likelihood of any further requests by Canada for the repatriation of securities held in the United Kingdom.'[109]

The Canadians finally turned to a discussion of proposed financial aid to Britain in December 1941. The Cabinet War Committee discussed the matter on December 15 and 16, and the full Cabinet went over the ground again on December 18. The mood was apocalyptic, primarily because the demands of the armed forces for their next year's program were large, so large that Ilsley had told his colleagues in the War Committee that they were beyond the capacity of the country.[110] Mackenzie King shared this view, and he wondered how Canada could afford to give huge sums in aid to Britain at the same time. After the Cabinet meeting on December 18, he recorded his feelings in a disouraged entry in his diary:

Long discussion on financial relations with Britain—problem very involved. I found myself more in sympathy with Dandurand, Cardin, St. Laurent and MacKinnon than with Ralston, Power, Macdonald and Howe with respect to matters that require most careful consideration and grounds on which whatever action was taken should be put. The latter group seem to favour the idea of making good fellows of ourselves and presenting Britain with a Billion Dollars, writing off the debt to England, which is payable in sterling, but assuming it in dollars to our public debt. This is a means of recovering some other bad debts which might otherwise be lost and making a gesture to offset the United States Lease-Lend.

I told the Cabinet they better realize the Lease-Lend had strings attached to it and one of them was the end of British preference so far as Canada was concerned. We would probably get it both ways if we gave up all our bargaining strength; that there was no more cold-blooded body on earth than the British treasury and I was afraid there would be many heartbreaks from now on through Britain and the United States taking everything in their own hands and ignoring Canada. Nevertheless, I was ready, like Cardin, to join in on any financial matter which might seem to help the entire war situation . . .

King added that 'It does seem to me, particularly in matters that come from the Bank of Canada . . . that too much of our policy is being dictated purely in British interests and not sufficiently in our own.'[111] It was a bargaining situation to King, and he strongly pressed Ilsley a few days later 'not to give to the British Treasury in advance the intimation, as he wished, of what we were proposing to do in making a virtual gift of a billion dollars to Britain but to allow me to hold this card in making pleas which I might have to make with Churchill and Roosevelt alike for some recognition of what Canada is doing in discussions pertaining to our right to participate in at least the direction of our own part of the war effort, and not have it taken altogether out of our hands.' Ilsley and the Cabinet accepted this position.[112]

King broached the billion-dollar gift to Churchill during his visit to Ottawa at the year-end, although not in the tough bargaining manner that he had initially proposed. The Cabinet approved it on January 2, 1942 as part of the 1942-3 war program amounting in all to $3.5 billion. The billion dollar gift was, as King noted in his diary, 'a tremendously generous one'[113] but there were strings attached, something that disturbed the British mightily.

The Bank of England's man in Ottawa reported on the major

problems. Canada, he said, proposed 'that their sterling holdings as at 30th November 1941 be transformed into a Canadian dollar loan secured by a pledge of the Canadian dollar securities owned by British holders.' The securities would not actually be called in but they would have to be available if required. In addition, 'Canada makes no suggestions about the duration of the loan but propose that no interest be charged during the war period: they also propose that during this period an amount equal to the estimated income from British-held Canadian dollar securities be applied annually in reduction of the loan. It is further suggested that Canada might buy the British interest in Canadian war plants for about $225 million . . .' The chief objection to this proposal, the banker said, was that it 'resuscitates the whole notion that the U.K. should strip herself of all overseas assets,' something that the Americans had pressed for before introducing Lend-Lease. Britain should resist pledging securities to Canada. 'We must surely maintain that H.M.G.'s undertaking to another member of the British Commonwealth does not need to be supported by collateral. Moreover,' he added in a plaintive note on the difficulties of dealing with the colonies, 'such an arrangement would create a most awkward precedent...'[114]

The Chancellor of the Exchequer, Sir Kingsley Wood, responded to the Canadian proposals in precisely the same way: the suggestion 'that the U.K. Government should give collateral security in respect of a loan to us by another Empire Government comes as a shock to me.' It was true, Kingsley Wood admitted, that the United Kingdom had given collateral to the United States' Reconstruction Finance Corporation for a loan, but the United States was a foreign country and a non-belligerent at the time. 'It may be that the Canadian proposal has been formed a little unthinkingly on this model or indeed it may be a try-on, but it is quite unprecedented for any British Empire Government to give collateral to another Empire country. It would surely be seriously damaging to the Imperial conception; it would certainly reflect seriously on our credit and set a dangerous precedent both for ourselves and other Empire countries which may borrow either during or after the war.' And, he added, if Canada demanded terms of this kind, so would South Africa and India.[115]

A further Treasury study of the Canadian proposal found two underlying principles behind it. One was to avoid cancellation of the British debt to Canada 'lest this engender a feeling that the U.K. could not pay and could not stay the financial course'. The other was 'to make a really generous contribution'. Of the latter there could be no doubt: 'a stupendous contribution for one country, with a population of 11,000,000, to make to another in time of war, a vast additional burden to be assumed voluntarily by a country unable as yet to foresee how much of her potential resources will require to be drained to meet her own more personal needs.' Moreover, this was a gift and 'clearly one better than the "Lease-Lend" aid of the U.S. where, God knows, there are plenty of conditions from which there will probably be precious little freedom for many years after the war.' The sticking point was the securities. This smacked very much of 'scraping the barrel'. But there was the positive side that this might forestall a possible demand in some later phase of the war for British-owned Canadian dollar securities to be repatriated.[116]

The British War Cabinet considered the Canadian offer on January 8 and 12. The printed conclusions of the meeting on January 12 bluntly state that the Cabinet recognized 'that the offer was a very generous one, but agreed that the proposal that H.M.G. should pledge Canadian securities held in this country as collateral for the Canadian dollar loan into which our existing sterling debt was to be converted was both without precedent in relations between any British Empire Governments and that its adoption would be likely to involve serious difficulties.' The problem, the British saw, was that the Canadian government 'did not accept, and indeed, did not appear to appreciate at all, our view that it was entirely wrong for one Empire Government to ask collateral security from another. They had expressed great disappointment at our reaction, and had said they could not get agreement to a free contribution of 1,000 million dollars to cover our future expenditure in Canada unless we agreed to give collateral security . . .' The result left the British in a spot. 'We clearly wished to avoid a breakdown in the discussions, for it would be sure to become known to the public that the Canadian offer had been made and that we had regarded it as unacceptable. Though our refusal . . . was very fully justified, no doubt the effect on Canadian public opinion . . . would be such as we would certainly wish to avoid.'[117]

A compromise had to be found. The War Cabinet surmised that the Canadians were most concerned that the British might sell or pledge Canadian securities to the United States. 'We could meet them on this by what was often called a "negative pledge", i.e. an undertaking that Canadian dollar securities owned in this country would not be sold nor pledged except in agreement with the Canadian Government.' Further, the Cabinet agreed that 'we could undertake that if any securities were sold, the proceeds would be applied to reduce the amount of the loan.'[118]

This compromise was tentatively accepted by the Canadian Cabinet in mid-January 1942—while Mackenzie King was absent. He was not amused:

> Council agreed while I was away that we should accept a second proposal which the British have made but which does not turn over their securities to us outrightly. They say that to do this would embarrass them with South Africa and India. I was holding out on the score that when these two countries give them a billion dollars, they can talk about not returning securities. However, I learned later that while they have agreed to not let proceeds of any Canadian securities be kept for other than our account, the British Government desires to have the fact that they are keeping Canadian securities entirely for us as a means of meeting settlement later on, entirely a secret.

King could not see why South Africa and India should not get their securities too. 'It is the financial control which London exercises over different parts of the Empire, and which is carried out in the special interests of Britain which, in my mind, needs very careful looking into.'[119]

King succeeded in undoing the decision of his colleagues, and in the course of this reversal the discussion got very hot. Malcolm MacDonald wired London that the Deputy Minister of Finance told him that 'Discussion on these revised proposals—was extremely protracted and keen, and opposition was so strong that Clark who attended this part of the meeting thought they were going to be defeated.' The view, as a result, seemed to be that British amendments to the Canadian proposal would not be able to be carried through Cabinet. MacDonald added that 'I am conscious that the Ministers' goodwill regarding these proposals is getting a bit frayed...'[120]

After further discussions a mutually acceptable arrangement was reached. A memorandum prepared in London laid out its dimensions:

> The Canadian government have gone a considerable way to meet us. They no longer ask us to pledge our Canadian Dollar Securities as security for the loan, but they ask us to give what is sometimes called a 'negative pledge'. We are also asked to agree that if we give collateral

security to any other part of the Empire we would, in that event, also give collateral security to Canada in respect of the present loan. That seems quite reasonable. Also Canada reserves the right to require the pledge of collateral security if we repatriate from any other part of the Empire securities other than securities of an Empire government or guaranteed by an Empire government. This is more difficult . . . the underlying idea is that if we were to vest gold-mining shares or other industrial shares or business interests which belong to us in other parts of the Empire Canada would reserve the right to ask us to pledge as security for the present loan the Canadian Dollar Securities which we own. . . . It is not our policy that the other Empire Governments should strip us bare and take over from us our business interests. . . .

We should very much like to get rid of [this clause] altogether, but it is clear that we should not succeed in this.[121]

The bargaining had been tough, but as the *Economist* observed on January 31, 1942 it was still 'the most generous financial transaction between Governments that the war has yet produced'.

The official announcement of the Canadian gift to Britain was made in the Speech from the Throne that opened the 1942 session of Parliament on January 22, and the act conferring the $1 billion gift was assented to on March 27. The public response was generally favourable in English Canada but substantially less so in Quebec. *The Financial Post* realistically noted that 'What we are doing is writing off the "bills to Britain" now instead of leaving them for post-war negotiation. . . . The alternative would have been squeezing Britain, with disastrous consequences not only to her but to our primary producers who will want to hold their British markets after the war . . .'[122] The Toronto *Star* put it all in terms that the man on the street would grasp: the gift would cost each Canadian $87.[123] Some Canadians didn't want to pay. A Canadian Institute of Public Opinion poll at the end of February found only 53 per cent in favour of such gifts to Britain and 35 per cent against.[124] Soon picked up by the anti-conscriptionist Ligue pour la défense du Canada, then rapidly engaged in mobilizing Quebec against the conscription plebiscite, the gift was trumpeted as yet another example of Canada's subservience to Britain. The opposition forced a shift in the tenor of editorials supporting the gift. *The Financial Post* now argued that 'We could, of course, refuse to ship Britain any munitions, food or equipment that she could not pay for in cash. That would mean a billion dollars less taxes and borrowing in Canada; and a billion dollars less income for our workers and farmers.'[125]

The gift, therefore, came to be viewed as less of a contribution to Britain than as an investment in full employment in Canada. That made it no less generous than before, but the government soon began to appear eminently hard-headed and practical. The *Economist* on April 25 characterized the Canadian policy as 'a mixture of idealism and what Mr. Coldwell, the Cooperative Commonwealth Federation leader, called "hard-boiled business".' Perhaps that was the proper mixture. And how fortunate that the gift also satisfied what the *Economist* called 'the Canadian feeling that Canada should exceed in generosity the terms granted by the United States in its Lend-Lease Act. There is no doubt that the Canadian proposal does so.'[126]

In the financial sphere, Canada was now fighting a total war—her dollars were being mobilized. The same thing was certainly true for production of munitions and foodstuffs. The problem that would fill all Mackenzie King's waking hours for the first six months of 1942 was that too many Canadians felt that was not enough. The symbol of total war was military manpower, and military manpower could be mobilized only with conscription.

---

1 Public Archives of Canada [PAC], Brooke Claxton Papers, Vol. 221, Draft Memoirs, Vol. 4, p. 813; Taylor Cole, *The Canadian Bureaucracy* (Durham, 1949), pp. 269-270.

2 P.C. 1908, 14 Aug. 1937.

3 PAC, W. L. Mackenzie King Papers, 'Mr. Hepburn and the Federal Government', n.d., ff. C121491ff.; H. V. Nelles, 'Premier Hepburn and the Ontario Opposition to the Rowell-Sirois Report', University of Toronto graduate paper, 1966, 16-21; Richard Alway, 'Hepburn, King and the Rowell-Sirois Commission', *Canadian Historical Review*, XLVIII (June, 1967), 113ff.

4 King Papers, King to Bracken, 29 Jan. 1940, ff. 239738-9 and att. memo, Pickersgill to Heeney, 2 Feb. 1940; *ibid.*, Heeney to A. Skelton, 3 May 1940, 252072-3.

5 R. M. Burns, 'The Royal Commission on Dominion-Provincial Relations: The Report in Retrospect', in R. M. Clark, ed., *Canadian Issues: Essays in Honour of Henry F. Angus* (Toronto, 1961), p. 147; King Papers, Memo, 6 Jan. 1941, ff. C182997ff.; PAC, Department of Finance Records, Vol. 3443, 'Summary of Recommendations . . .', n.d.; A. M. Moore and J. H. Perry. *The Financing of Canadian Federation* (Toronto, 1966), pp. 13-14.

6 Department of Finance Records, Vol. 2701, file 300-1(2), 'Newspaper Comment on the Royal Commission Report', 15 June 1940.

7 King Papers, Bracken to King, 23 Aug. 1940 and reply, 23 Sept. 1940, ff. 30769ff.

8 Department of Finance Records, Vol. 2701, file 300-1(2), 'Sirois Report and the War', 24 July 1940.

9 King Papers, Towers to King, 15 Aug. 1940, ff. 252092ff.; cf. R. M. Fowler, 'Confederation Marches On', *Behind the Headlines*, No. 4 (December, 1940), 13.

10 Floyd Chalmers Papers (Toronto), Memo of Conversation with Towers, 26 Aug. 1940.

11 Department of Finance Records, Vol. 2701, file 300-1(2), 'Memo on the Report of the Sirois Commission', 11 Sept. 1940.

12 King Diary, 19 Sept. 1940; Department of Finance Records, Vol. 2701, file 300-1(2), Heeney to Ilsley, 23 Sept. 1940; PAC, Department of External Affairs Records, Vol. 6, file 31(4), Heeney to King, 23 Sept. 1940. Other members of the Committee were Crerar, Cardin, Ralston or Power or Macdonald, Mackenzie, Gardiner, and McLarty or Gibson.

13 *Ibid.* The report of the Committee was approved by Cabinet on 24 Sept. 1940. Department of Finance Records, Vol. 2701, file 300-1(2), Ilsley to Towers, 25 Sept. 1940.

14 Queen's University, Grant Dexter Papers, Dexter to Dafoe, 25 Oct. 1940; Memorandum, 17 Oct. 1940.

15 King Diary, 22 Oct. 1940; the Bracken letter is in King Papers, 18 Oct. 1940, ff. 239754ff.

16 King Diary, 1 Nov. 1940; PAC, C. D. Howe Papers, Vol. 54, file S-25, 'Report of the Cabinet Sub-Committee . . .', n.d.; Christopher Armstrong, 'The Politics of Federalism: Ontario's Relations with the Federal Government, 1896-1941', Ph.D. thesis, University of Toronto, 1972, 586.

17 E.g., King Papers, King to Bracken, 2 Nov. 1940, ff. 239760ff.

18 The letters from the premiers are printed in *Dominion-Provincial Conference Tuesday January 14, 1941 and Wednesday January 15, 1941* (Ottawa, 1941). Cited hereafter as *Proceedings*.

19 King Papers, 'The Central Committee', 5 Jan. 1941, ff. C183010-3.

20 King Diary, 6 Jan. 1940.

21 King Papers, Pattullo to King, 31 Oct. 1940, ff. 248368-9.

22 King Diary, 13 Dec. 1940.

23 E.g., PAC, Privy Council Records, Cabinet War Committee Records, Minutes, 24 Oct., 22 Nov., 27 Nov. 1940.

24 King Diary, 7 Jan. 1941.

25 King Papers, Memo, 7 Jan. 1941, ff. C183014ff.

26 King Diary, 9 Jan. 1941.

27 King Papers, 'Provincial Conference', 10 Jan. 1941, ff. C183032ff.

28 King Diary, 12 Jan. 1941; Pickersgill, I, p. 160.

29 King Diary, 13 Jan. 1940.

30 *Proceedings*, pp. 1-10; King Papers, ff. C183079ff. Cf. D. V. Smiley, 'The Rowell-Sirois Report, Provincial Autonomy and Post-War Canadian Federalism', *Canadian Journal of Economics and Political Science [CJEPS]*, XXVIII (February, 1962), 57.

31 Neil McKenty, *Mitch Hepburn* (Toronto, 1967), p. 227.

32 *Proceedings*, pp. 10-16.

33 *Ibid., passim.* The Crerar quotes are from Queen's University, T. A. Crerar Papers, Crerar to Dafoe, 16 Jan. 1941.

34 *Ibid.,* and Armstrong, 593.

35 *Proceedings,* pp. 71-5.

36 *Ibid.,* pp. 79-80.

37 *Ibid.,* pp. 103-7. Notes for this speech were prepared by Pickersgill. King Papers, ff. C182979ff. Crerar Papers, Crerar to Dafoe, 16 Jan. 1941.

38 King Diary, 15 Jan. 1941; Pickersgill, I, p. 162. King had largely accepted Pickersgill's advice about tactics. See King Papers, 'Re Dominion-Provincial Conference', 15 Jan. 1941, ff. C183109ff.

39 King Diary, 18 Jan. 1941.

40 Department of Finance Records, Vol. 22, file 101-85-15, 'Review of Press Comment . . .', n.d. The quote is from Vancouver *Province.* For Conservative views on the Conference, see PAC, R. B. Hanson Papers, file C-700. For Ontario and B. C. reaction, see Alway, 136-7; PAC, Ian Mackenzie Papers, Vol. 19, files 31-89 and 31-89A and Vol. 41, file G-64(2).

41 Denis Smith, *Gentle Patriot: A Political Biography of Walter Gordon* (Edmonton, 1973), p. 23. There is some doubt about Gordon's sole responsibility for this idea.

42 King Diary, 26 Mar. 1941. For a different view, see PAC, J. W. Dafoe Papers, Dexter to Dafoe, 13 May 1941.

43 For Hepburn's reaction, see Armstrong, 602ff. The 1942 Act is printed in C. P. Stacey, *Historical Documents of Canada,* Vol. v: *The Arts of War and Peace 1914-45* (Toronto, 1972), pp. 279-81. See also J. A. Maxwell, 'Recent Developments in Dominion-Provincial Fiscal Relations in Canada', *Occasional Paper,* No. 25, National Bureau of Economic Research (New York, 1948), 11-13; and Moore and Perry, pp. 17-19.

44 External Affairs Records, Vol. 111, file 705, Robertson to Skelton, 1 Sept. 1939.

45 Established by P.C. 2516, 3 Sept. 1939.

46 Pauline Jewett, 'The Wartime Prices and Trade Board: A Case Study in Canadian Public Administration', Ph.D. thesis, Radcliffe College, 1950, 12-13; K. W. Taylor, 'The Wartime Control of Prices', in J. F. Parkinson, ed., *Canadian War Economics* (Toronto, 1941), pp. 47ff. A list of WPTB personnel as of June 1940 is in King Papers, N. McLarty to King, 26 June 1940, ff. 246276-9.

47 For the timber controller's assessment of his role, see Dafoe Papers, Dexter memo 'of address by H. R. MacMillan . . . Nov. 2, 1940'.

48 According to opinion polls of 15 Apr. 1942, the public would have been willing to accept higher rates of personal income taxes. See *Public Opinion Quarterly,* vi (Fall, 1942), 481.

49 'Speaking of Money and War: Extracts from a Series of Addresses by Hon. J. L. Ilsley . . .' (Ottawa, 1941), address of 3 Sept. 1941. The excess-profits tax was resented by business, of course. E.g., see King Papers, President, CMA to King, 5 Dec. 1940, f. 241978. For an early effort to evade blame for its imposition, see Chalmers Papers, Memo of Conversation with C. F. Elliott, Commissioner of Income Tax, 6 Oct. 1939. Cf. *The Financial Post,* 19 Apr. 1941.

50 This section is based on E. J. Spence, 'Wartime Price Control Policy in Canada', Ph.D. thesis, Northwestern University, 1947, 15-22.

51 Quoted in *The Financial Post*, 18 Nov. 1939. Poll data of 18 July 1942 indicates widespread satisfaction with controls, fully 50 per cent believing they should be retained in peacetime. *Public Opinion Quarterly*, VI, (Winter, 1942) 655. Cf. George Davidson, *et al.*, *Canada in Transition* (Toronto, 1944), pp. 34ff., which argues for continued controls.

52 King Diary, 13 Dec. 1940. (P.C. 7440.)

53 R. W. James, *Wartime Economic Cooperation* (Toronto, 1949), p. 60.

54 Cabinet War Committee Records, Minutes, 5 May 1941; King Diary, 5 May 1941.

55 Dexter Memo, 9 Oct. 1941; K. W. Taylor, 'Canadian Wartime Price Controls', *CJEPS*, XIII (1974), 84.

56 Department of Finance, W. C. Clark Papers, file W-2-2, Memo by W. A. Mackintosh, 6 June 1941; Jewett, 15ff.

57 Pickersgill, I, p. 268; Taylor, *CJEPS*, 84n.; Cabinet War Committee Records, Minutes, 13 Aug. 1941.

58 Dexter memo, 9 Oct. 1941; Jewett, 18-20; Clark Papers, file W-2-2, Memos, 29 Sept., 7, 8 Oct. 1941; and particularly Privy Council Records (R. G. 2-18), Vol. 8, file W-32, Memorandum on Prices and Wages Policy', n.d.

59 'Speaking of Money and War . . .', address, 18 Sept. 1941.

60 King Diary, 3 Oct. 1941.

61 Dexter memo, 9 Oct. 1941. For a discussion of the problems in deciding between total and partial controls, see Taylor, *CJEPS*, 85ff.

62 Cited by Dexter memo, 9 Oct. 1941.

63 King Diary, 3, 18 Oct. 1941.

64 Dexter memo, 9 Oct. 1941.

65 Spence, 49.

66 King Diary, 10 Oct. 1941.

67 *Ibid.*, 7 Nov. 1941. Gordon was mentioned as the leading possibility by Dexter. Memo, 9 Oct. 1941.

68 Jewett, 34ff., details the manoeuvring.

69 King Diary, 15 Oct. 1941.

70 Pickersgill, I, p. 270.

71 Other estimates put Great War peak expenditures as high as 15 per cent. Spence, 50 n.

72 W. L. M. King, *Canada and the Fight for Freedom* (Toronto, 1944), pp. 30ff. See also *Price Control in Canada* (a WPTB pamphlet), December 1941.

73 King Papers, Gardiner to King, 14 Oct. 1941, ff. 48876ff.; Pickersgill, I, p. 269.

74 R. E. Moffat, 'Canadian Price Control since 1939', *Annals*, CCLIII (September, 1947), 128.

75 'The Price Ceiling', *Canadian Banker*, XLVIII (January, 1941), 153-4.

76 King Papers, Vol. 24, tels.

77 *Ibid.*, World War II Prices and Wages file, Pickersgill to King, 25 Nov. 1941 (recently discovered King Papers).

78 *Ibid.*, Burton to King, 18 Nov. 1941, ff. 46386ff.

79 J. C. Cameron, 'The Development of the Dominion Government's Labour Policy', *Canadian Banker*, L (1943), 62.

80 Toronto *Globe and Mail*, 21 Oct. 1941.

81 H. N. Drennon, 'The Industrial Relations Policy of the Canadian Dominion Government, 1939-1948', Ph.D. thesis, Duke University, 1951, 175ff.

82 Toronto *Globe and Mail*, 21 Oct. 1941. Cf. 'Freezing Injustice', and 'Holes in the Ceiling', *Canadian Forum*, XXI (December, 1941), 261ff.

83 King Papers, Hannam to King, 25 Oct. 1941 and King's reply, 28 Oct. 1941; Gardiner to Hannam, 31 Oct. 1941, ff. 49760ff. Cf. V. C. Fowke, 'Economic Effects of the War on the Prairie Economy', *CJEPS*, XI (1945), 373ff.; J. F. Booth, 'The Economic Problems of Canadian Agriculture in the War and Post-War Period', *CJEPS*, VIII (1942), 446ff. Gardiner would later argue that the freeze lost Saskatchewan for the Liberals. Jewett, 46.

84 King Papers, Hannam to King, 17 Nov. 1941.

85 Interestingly, Mackintosh, Clark, and O. D. Skelton had all written on Great War price policy. See W. C. Clark, 'Should Maximum Prices be Fixed?', *Queen's Quarterly*, XXIV (April, 1918); O. D. Skelton, 'Canadian Federal Finance—II', *Bulletin of the Departments of History and Political and Economic Science in Queen's University . . .*, No. 29 (October, 1918); W. A. Mackintosh, 'Economics, Prices and the War', in *ibid.*, No. 31 (April, 1919).

86 Queen's University, W. A. Mackintosh Papers, Mackintosh to J. M. Macdonnell, 5 Nov. 1941.

87 Dexter Papers, Memo, 10 Nov. 1941. See also Privy Council Records (R.G. 2-18), Vol. 8, file W-32, 'Major Problems Involved in a Price Ceiling', n.d.

88 The briefing was subsequently printed by the King's Printer and given limited circulation. Copy in Queen's University, Donald Gordon Papers.

89 Taylor, *CJEPS*, 89; Spence, 181ff.

90 Jewett, 29ff.

91 Taylor in Parkinson, p. 54.

92 Dexter Papers, Memo, 29 Oct. 1942; Crerar Papers, Crerar to Dafoe, 1 Dec. 1942; Moffat, 126; J. T. E. Aikenhead and P. K. Haywood, 'Practical Problems of the Retail Price Ceiling', *CJEPS*, VIII (1942), 433ff.

93 See Wartime Information Board, *Canada at War*, No. 45 (1945), 142ff. For flash-backs to war controls, see Toronto *Telegram*, 1 Nov. 1969; Toronto *Star*, 19 Oct., 17 Nov. 1973.

94 Defence Purchasing Board, *Contracts Awarded 14 July-31 October 1939* (Ottawa, 1940).

95 War Supplies Board, *Record of Contracts Awarded, 1 November-30 December 1939* (Ottawa, 1940).

96 *Canada at War*, No. 45, 79.

97 Howe Papers, file S-5(1), J. B. Carswell to Howe, 16 July 1941.

98 *Ibid.*, Howe to Ilsley, 15 Aug. 1941 and atts; *ibid.*, E. P. Taylor to A. B. Purvis, 23 July 1941.

99 *Ibid.*, Memo, Carswell to Howe, 16 July 1941.

100 *Ibid.*, Howe to Ilsley, 21 July 1941.

101 Clipping from Montreal *Star*, 18 June 1941, in King Papers, f. D53428.

102 E.g., Beaverbrook Library (London), Lord Beaverbrook Papers, Box 22, file 7, Tel. British Supply Council to Supply Committee, 4 Aug. 1941.

103 Howe Papers, file S-5(1), tel. Howe to Banks, 13 Aug. 1941.

104 Clark Papers, file U-3-2-4A, High Commissioner Ottawa to Clark, 16 Aug. 1941; *ibid.*, Carswell to G. K. Shiels, 17 Oct. 1941.

105 Howe Papers, file S-5(1), Howe to Ilsley, 25 Aug. 1941. Howe argued the same in Cabinet War Committee Records, Minutes, 15 July 1941. Finance Department estimates put total British holdings in Canada at $1,385 million as of 1941. Clark Papers, file R-6-2, Memo, 10 Sept. 1941.

106 Public Record Office [PRO], Treasury Records, T160/1141, W. A. W. Clark to R. Culhane, 30 Aug. 1941 and encl. draft Secretary of State for Dominion Affairs [SSDA] to Chancellor of Exchequer, n.d.; Cabinet War Committee Records, Minutes, 15 July 1941, and especially 'Report of the Economic Advisory Committee on Means of Utilizing Canada's Accumulating Sterling Balances', 12 July 1941 in *ibid.*, Documents; H. D. Hall, *North American Supply* (London, 1955), p. 240; R. S. Sayers, *Financial Policy, 1939-1945* (London, 1956), pp. 341ff.

107 *Ibid.*, p. 342.

108 T160/1340, Tel. High Commissioner Ottawa to SSDA, 27 Oct. 1941.

109 *Ibid.*, T160/1335, High Commissioner to SSDA, 28 Oct. 1941; Hall, pp. 239-40. The deficit estimates were increasing rapidly. In August the Canadians estimated the deficit at $900 million. King Papers, 'Report of Economic Advisory Committee . . .', 8 Aug. 1941, ff. C246336ff.

110 Cabinet War Committee Records, Minutes, 4 Dec. 1941.

111 King Diary, 18 Dec. 1941.

112 *Ibid.*, 23 Dec. 1941.

113 *Ibid.*, 2 Jan. 1942.

114 T160/1252, Cobbold to Waley, 6 Jan. 1942; Sayers, pp. 343ff.

115 T160/1252, Draft memo by Chancellor of Exchequer, n.d.

116 *Ibid.*, 'Canada's Financial Proposals vis-à-vis United Kingdom', 4 Jan. 1942.

117 PRO, Cabinet Records, Cab 65/25, War Cabinet 4(42), 12 Jan. 1942.

118 *Ibid.*; and *ibid.*, E.C. 3(42), 8 Jan. 1942; PRO, Prime Minister's Office Records, Prem 4/44/9, W.M. (42) 3rd concls, item 4; 4th concls, item 8, 8 Jan. 1942.

119 King Diary, 19 Jan. 1942.

120 T160/1252, Tel. High Commissioner Ottawa to SSDA, 20 Jan. 1942.

121 *Ibid.*, Memo, 'Canada', n.d.

122 31 Jan. 1942.

123 T160/1252, 'Press Comment . . .', 4 Feb. 1942.

124 *Public Opinion Quarterly*, VI (Summer, 1942), 312-13.

125 T160/1252, 'Recent Press Opinion . . .', 26 Mar. 1942; Sayers, pp. 346-9.

126 Clipping in Department of Finance Records, Vol. 778, file 400-16-21.

6. The Conscription Crisis of 1942

Through almost two years of war, Mackenzie King had been remarkably successful in damping down the fires of controversy at home. He had managed the Quebec election well, and he had skilfully brought the country into the war. Hepburn's pretensions had been checked, along with Dr Manion's, by the triumphant election of 1940. The war effort was gaining momentum every day; production was increasing; and the armed forces, though not all heavily engaged, were gathering their strength.

Overseas the war was not going well. Defeat followed defeat. North West Europe was gone, the Balkans lost, the Middle East and the Suez Canal teetering. The Russians seemed unlikely to last out the winter, and still the United States maintained its formal neutrality. The Japanese, still at peace, intensified their tough talk the more economic pressures were put upon them. But no one in Canada seemed to doubt the eventual outcome of the war. We always won, didn't we? And the Americans would be in it eventually, thus ensuring victory. Complacency remained very strong.

Not everyone shared it. In the Cabinet the Minister of National Defence, Colonel Ralston, worried about the shortage of recruits for overseas service. The decline in volunteers had forced the Cabinet in April 1941 to agree to keep NRMA conscripts on duty in Canada for the duration, thus freeing men for service overseas. None objected to this action, and the Cabinet also decided to launch the first large-scale national recruiting campaign. The drive would begin on May 11, 1941, a rather late date in the war for the first major organized effort to raise men, and itself an indicator of the degree of complacency. At the same time, Ralston was beginning to beat the drum just a little for conscription.

A single-minded man, Colonel Ralston fought very hard for the interests of his department. As Minister of Finance he had resisted expenditures and fought against escalating costs because his officials believed that Canada was being asked to do too much too fast. Now, as Minister of National Defence, he was fighting for the interests of his staff and acting to protect the interests—and lives—of his soldiers overseas. Reinforcements were not yet in short supply, but they likely would be once the Canadian troops overseas went into battle, and preparatory action should be taken as soon as possible. Emotionally, Ralston was a conscriptionist. A front-line soldier in the Great War, a supporter of the Union Government of 1917, a convinced believer in the virtues of Empire, he could be nothing else. Still, as he told the Cabinet War Committee on April 23, 1941, 'Conscription for overseas was impossible from the point of view of national unity; otherwise it might be the proper policy to meet the whole situation.'[1]

With the first part of that statement Mackenzie King could agree; with the second he could not. The Prime Minister was neither emotionally nor intellectually opposed to conscription, but as an unsuccessful Liberal candidate in the election of 1917 and as Laurier's heir he was very aware of its potency as a political weapon in the hands of his opposition. When the matter came up again in the War Committee on April 30, he told his colleagues that 'The present government could have no thought of conscription for overseas service, under any circumstances.'[2] The lines were beginning to be drawn.

All this was profoundly disturbing to the Prime Minister, particularly since the recruiting drive had not yet been launched and since there were still almost no Canadian army casualties. He raised the matter again in the War Committee on May 9 when he insisted that his colleagues 'decide against countenancing conscription in any current discussion. All were agreed to that,' Mackenzie King wrote later that day, 'Ralston merely asking that conscription . . . not be barred wholly should situations later arise. Lapointe stated he, of course, would not stay in the government. Gardiner also stated he would have to leave if there were conscription. . . .'[3]

Meanwhile the recruiting drive began, its aim the enlistment of

32,000 volunteers. The nation's eleven military districts were each assigned a quota:

M.D.			
1	(London)		2,840 men
2	(Toronto)		6,631
3	(Kingston)		2,342
4	(Montreal)		4,367
5	(Quebec)		1,734
6	(Halifax)		2,116
7	(Saint John)		1,478
10	(Winnipeg)		2,603
11	(Victoria)		3,105
12	(Regina)		2,711
13	(Calgary)		2,507
			32,434 men[4]

The posters were in place, the recruiting sergeants ready; but the volunteers were slow in coming. In the Cabinet War Committee on May 20, after the campaign had been under way for a few disappointing days, Ralston, supported by Chubby Power and other ministers, argued that Canadian troops be given the opportunity for battle action. 'It was unfortunately true,' the minutes record the Minister of National Defence as saying, that the absence of action 'accounted for the degree of apathy evidenced by the public as regards the war effort and prevented enthusiasm being aroused in regard to the recruiting campaign.'[5] This argument appalled Mackenzie King; his ministers were willing to sacrifice lives for publicity purposes.[6] Still, King knew that conscription sentiment was emotional, not rational, and if conscription was to be averted the recruiting drive had to succeed. The result was a decision in Committee, confirmed the next day,[7] to send a telegram to Churchill reaffirming the Canadian government's willingness to send its troops wherever they might best serve.

The Prime Minister decided he could best assist the recruiting drive by going on a speaking tour through the Western provinces beginning on June 24. Speeches were always nerve-wracking for the Prime Minister, and he knew that he would face hostile audiences in much of the West. On June 10 Ralston had told him that 'certain communities, particularly Vancouver and others, were deliberately refusing to help in recruiting.'[8] Organized opinion in the West seemed to be all out for conscription and all out against Mackenzie King. It was all the fault of 'the Tories', King believed, who were as usual seeking to stir up prejudice against him. 'They are going out of their way to create a wholly erroneous impression as to my personality. It is part of the detraction and belittlement I have had from the beginning of my political career.'[9]

For his opening speech in Calgary there was a good turnout. Many of the crowd had probably been lured to the grandstand at the Exhibition Grounds by handbills, issued by the 'Calgary Committee for Conscription', found wrapped around milk bottles the morning of June 27. King's speech went very well, all things considered, but the press coverage reflected the biases of the pro-conscriptionist newspaper publishers across the country. The *Globe and Mail* quoted taxi drivers, cigar-store clerks, and local newspapermen as demanding conscription, and the refrain continued and intensified as Mackenzie King's small entourage made its way through the west.[10] The derogatory coverage of the Prime Minister's tour was exceeded only by deliberate efforts to paint the recruiting campaign a failure. The Calgary *Herald* on June 19 pointed out that the campaign 'is lagging dismally', and a few days later a columnist in the same paper declared that 'We might as well face up to the facts. . . . The recruiting drive has flopped; it has flopped loudly and dismally and openly. Every Canadian knows that.'[11]

But in fact that campaign did not flop. The results of the drive were announced on July 16, a few days after Mackenzie King's return to Ottawa. The objective had been exceeded by 7 per cent. All told, over 48,000 had volunteered, but medical examinations had reduced the number accepted to 34,625. Even better, only three of the military districts—London, Victoria, and Montreal—had failed to exceed their quotas. Quebec City had produced 122 per cent of its requirement, something better than Toronto's 115 per cent.[12]

But such recruiting drives only confirmed the die-hard conscriptionists in their beliefs. Conscription was the only way to fight a major war. Conscription equalized suffering, taking rich and poor, French and English. And above all conscription had been used in the Great War. To suggest that voluntarism could produce a great army in a new and greater war was to countenance the possibility that the Borden government had acted in error in 1917. And that was something that Conservatives and some old Unionist Liberals were not prepared to do.

One such Conservative was Arthur Meighen. The draftsman of the Military Service Act of 1917, twice Prime Minister, a towering and commanding figure, and the one man whom Mackenzie King both loathed and feared, Meighen was the rallying point for those who believed that no government led by Liberals, subservient to Quebec, could ever run a war effort befitting a great nation. By May 1941, having barely contained himself thus far in the war, Meighen was ready to press the Conservative Party towards an open and frank endorsement of conscription. 'That the time has come,' he wrote to a friend in May, 'I have no question, and the Party cannot too soon take up its true position to suit me.'[13] In August Meighen wrote to another crony, Murdoch MacPherson of Regina, Saskatchewan, an unsuccessful candidate for the Tory leadership in 1938 and one of the first Conservatives to declare for conscription: 'I am steadily moving to the conviction that we ought to move faster . . . and that the Conservative Party has to take this thing in hand as its own mission, that it must choose its leader and choose him soon and get into action on strong British total war lines without delay. . . . I believe that whatever is done should be done this Fall.'[14]

Some Conservatives did not share Meighen's impatience; many of them, responsive to their constituents' mood, were in the party's caucus. R. B. Hanson, the Leader of the Opposition, was one of those who believed that the party should go slowly. After his return from a trip to England, in fact, he had told a gathering of the party faithful at the august Albany Club in downtown Toronto on October 29, 1941 that if he declared for conscription the results would be dismal. 'Immediately the Conservative party in Parliament nailed conscription to its masthead, we'd consolidate all those forces that have been opposed to us since 1917 and they would be marshaled [sic] against us.' To make conscription a political issue, Hanson said, would only defeat the purpose of its sponsors.[15] This was a courageous speech, but it was not the one his audience had come to hear, and it reinforced the views of those who believed that a change of leadership in the party was essential. The means were at hand, too, for a party conference was scheduled for November 7 and 8 in Ottawa. The longed-for successor was, of course, Arthur Meighen.

The Ottawa meeting of the Conservative Party achieved its end after some bitterness and confusion. Meighen himself was one doubtful factor. As he told the delegates, he was 67 years old and dreaded the task. He was also concerned about the opposition that had been expressed to his return to the party leadership and at one point he actually refused the draft outright: 'I wouldn't dream of accepting this terrible responsibility. I therefore shall not.' But after he left the meeting, a unanimous vote was squeezed out of the delegates and a committee despatched to Toronto to see the former Prime Minister. 'Reflections over Sunday and Monday,' Meighen wrote to a close friend, 'compelled me to change my mind. I became convinced, and certainly my wife became convinced, that I would lose what respect and regard the people felt for me if in the full light of day and with an appeal which had by that time reached Coast-to-Coast dimensions, I refused to try to do the one thing I can do, if indeed, there is anything I can do, entirely well. . . .'[16]

Once his decision was reached, Meighen came out forthrightly and squarely. In a declaration that the *Globe and Mail* melodramatically headlined 'I Shall Answer the Call', Meighen threw down his challenge:

> A Government on a strictly party basis is in office and exercising despotic powers. This state of affairs in a war of life and death is anomalous. Such a Government . . . cannot bring the whole nation to its maximum endeavour. . . .
>
> This nation is in the throes of a crisis. . . . That Britain is doing its mightiest few will dispute. . . . Who will dare to say that Canada is even in sight of a total war? . . .
>
> I shall, therefore, urge with all the power I can bring to bear compulsory selective service over the whole field of war. . . .[17]

There could be no doubt about the new Conservative policy. Its aims were conscription and national government, and Mackenzie King was now in a fight for his political life and, as he saw it, for the preservation of the unity of Canada.

I

In some notes he made on November 13, the day Meighen's acceptance of the leadership was announced, Mackenzie King's view of the present situation was very clear:

Issue

Conscription	)	1917 all over again
	)	same leader
National	)	same cry—
Government	)	support allied forces
		non-party government

Yet King was convinced that 'Meighen could not form [a] national government.' A national government meant all the parties. 'Will Liberals unite under Meighen? Will C.C.F. unite under Meighen? Will Social Credit unite under Meighen?' No, it was impossible. 'In reality Tory party to control [,] ulterior policies to be enforced.'[18]

King put these ideas to his Cabinet that same day and to the Liberal caucus the day following. It was characteristic of King to seek to consolidate his position with Cabinet and caucus before a struggle, and well he might. To both, the Prime Minister argued that the whole political situation had changed with Meighen's return. Before Meighen, the Tories had been ostensibly for co-operation with the government; now, with Meighen, the Opposition was directly challenging the administration. And, as he told his supporters, 'the one advantage I saw in Meighen coming in and directly opposing the Government was that it would give all members of the House a chance to fight in the open for our policies.' In Cabinet there was a suggestion that the government should stand on the ground that conscription was unnecessary. King agreed, but he suggested that the possibility of an election on the question should be kept in the background. 'It was necessary to put the fear of the Lord into the Tories, who did not want to face the people and who knew that the people generally were against conscription for overseas; also, to keep some of our people in line.' This last was important and King told the caucus that 'the only thing that could destroy the Liberal party was itself, because a house divided against itself falls. How I had seen Sir Wilfrid's colleagues, one by one, leave him to join forces opposed to him.'[19] This was the Prime Minister's great fear, and the reason for the extraordinary care and speech-making he lavished on his caucus. All were Liberals, yes, and the party had a huge majority; but the conscription issue was a powerful one and the sole question that could destroy his majority and the government with it. The English-Canadian Liberal Members of Parliament had to be kept in line.

Quebec demanded attention as well, particularly after the death of Ernest Lapointe on November 26, 1941. Lapointe and King had been genuine friends for more than twenty years. They shared the same attitudes on most policy and personality questions, and they had worked well together and in their own spheres. Perhaps the secret of the relationship of Prime Minister and Minister of Justice was that King always left Lapointe paramount in Quebec. Lapointe had been failing badly since the beginning of the war, but his effective and massive intervention in the October 1939 Quebec election had been a demonstration of the power he still wielded. His death deprived Mackenzie King and Canada of his counsel at a crucial moment in the war and in domestic politics.

Another French Canadian had to be brought into the Cabinet to fill the gap as soon as possible. Cardin almost automatically assumed Lapointe's mantle as the senior Quebec minister, but because of his long organizational involvement and his open activities as a patronage broker in the Montreal region, he lacked Lapointe's stature as a spokesman for the province. There was not a single additional *Canadien* of stature in the government; moreover, the important Quebec City area had no French-Canadian representative at all. The Prime Minister's first choice as a replacement for Lapointe was Premier Adelard Godbout, but the Quebec Liberal leader demurred—his friends advised him against leaving the province.[20] Another name suggested by Chubby Power and others was Louis St Laurent, a corporation lawyer without previous political experience. When King learned that Cardin was agreeable, he called St Laurent to Ottawa. The two men met on December 5. King could be extremely persuasive on such occasions, but St Laurent had already made up his mind to enter the Cabinet if asked. This war, unlike the Great War, posed a threat to Canada; no one could shirk war service in such a situation; and besides, as St Laurent said many years later, 'I was the best man in Quebec' for the job.[21] So it proved. St Laurent had been a great lawyer, and he brought to a Cabinet that badly needed strengthening the facility for making his solution to a problem seem to be the only solution. Very quickly the new Minister of Justice established bonds of affection and confidence with the Prime Minister and his colleagues.

Meanwhile the discussions in Cabinet were coming more and more to focus on conscription, in part at least in response to the Meighen campaign. Already Mackenzie King had hinted that a plebiscite on conscription might be necessary if the pressures continued to mount,[22] and T. A. Crerar, the Minister of Mines and Resources, had told Grant Dexter that Mackenzie King was contemplating a plebiscite and 'will take the position that if conscription carries, he will retire and some other leader will have to come forward to carry it out.'[23] This idea lay dormant but not forgotten while the Cabinet turned to a consideration of the defence program for 1942-3.

The Army General Staff, supported by Colonel Ralston, pressed for the further expansion of the army overseas. As the country's program had developed, there were already three infantry divisions, an army tank brigade, and miscellaneous corps and army troops in Britain.[24] The military, operating on the principles that the war had to be fought and won in Europe and the more troops the better, hoped to expand this force into a five-division army of two corps, an army that would undoubtedly require an extraordinary effort to maintain at full strength with reinforcements once the hard fighting began. The difficulty, as a Cabinet manpower study clearly demonstrated, was that only 609,000 men were left in Canada who could conceivably be called to the colours. Of that number untold thousands were required to fill jobs in industry while the navy and air force programs would take at least 175,000. An army of five divisions, as well as a large navy and air force, was more than Canada could support without the most severe and draconian methods of mobilizing the population.

The manpower squeeze was complicated by the belief of the Department of National Defence that there were relatively few potential airmen among French Canadians. The *Québecois* were seen by the military planners as lamentably unprepared for technical duties; a classical education had its benefits, but an aptitude for aircraft maintenance was not one of them.[25] This posed a problem for Ralston because the army would have to absorb those French Canadians, a fact that was drawn to the Minister's attention by the Master-General of the Ordnance, the publisher Victor Sifton. 'When [Sifton] pointed out that after deducting 200,000 English speaking for the air force and navy,' Grant Dexter wrote in a confidential memorandum, 'this would leave 400,000 for the army but they would have to take one French Canadian for every English-speaking Canadian, Ralston protested. The army would not have masses of Quebeckers under any conditions: they would not be able to do anything with them. There is only limited room in our army for these men. They can't speak English. We have no French C officers to handle them. Their fighting ability is questionable etc. etc. Ralston said,' Dexter reported, 'that conscription was necessary to get more men from the English-speaking provinces.'[26] Hearsay evidence like this must be taken lightly. However Ralston was speaking to a close aide, and he may have been reflecting the views of his generals as well as his own. Certainly no one would have dared to say any such thing in public.

Ralston first brought the army program to the Cabinet War Committee on December 2, 1941, but the matter was carried over for detailed discussion on the following day. Mackenzie King spent most of the morning reading the report. 'I was impressed . . . by the care with which it was prepared with a view to getting War Committee's consent to [a two-corps] Canadian Army overseas,' he recorded, 'rather than a [single] Canadian Corps.' The whole thing 'is based on the assumption that recruiting as of a certain period can be maintained up till March, 1943, this notwithstanding that it is known that there has been already increasing difficulty in keeping recruiting up to earlier standards, and that it is bound to become more difficult as time goes on.'[27] The next day, before going to the Cabinet War Committee, King took the unusual step of dictating his 'Personal View with respect to 1942-43 Proposed Programme of the Army':

> If the military authorities can give reasonable assurance that, by any plans that can be devised, or arrangements made short of conscription for overseas service, and the Minister of Finance is prepared, along with other commitments, to assure the War Committee that in his opinion it would be possible to have the armed forces overseas so increased without creating in itself a situation which will make impossible the raising, by taxation, war loans or other means, the revenues necessary for the purpose, I shall be prepared—subject to approval of the steps to be worked out for the purpose—to support the programme. Otherwise until Parliament itself has decided to adopt conscription for overseas service, or the people, by a referendum, or a general election, have approved the policy of conscription, to limit my support of the proposed programme to the extent that may be necessary to bring it within the limits of what it may reasonably be assured, can be secured without resort to conscription.
>
> In other words, it would be impossible for me . . . to sanction in advance any programme which would be in the nature of committing the country by the government itself to a policy of conscription for overseas service.[28]

King offered this view to the Cabinet War Committee. 'I made it clear,' he wrote, 'that I would not support a programme which would necessitate conscription. . . . Ralston took the position he could not say whether conscription would or would not be necessary but that if it was, he thought the govt. should support it in a referendum or in the House.' Shortly thereafter the Chief of the General Staff, then General Kenneth Stuart, was brought into the Cabinet room. King asked him if this was the last demand the army would make. Stuart replied that it was. 'He did not think there would have to be a further demand on Canada so far as the army was concerned.' Could the program be carried out without conscription? Stuart's answer, as recorded by the

Prime Minister, was 'that the programme had been worked out so as to fit into the government's policy of voluntary enlistment for overseas. That is what the staff had aimed at, had worked for, and what he believed could be accomplished in that way.' To himself, King had to 'confess these statements . . . impressed me very much. . . . I still feel that the same energy, money and manpower, applied to industry and other branches would in this war serve a greater purpose, but we have to deal with conditions as they are.'[29] King was snapped back to reality the following day, however, when the Chief of the Air Staff, Air Marshal L. S. Breadner, answered the same question by saying 'quite frankly . . . that he did not think [the RCAF program] could' be implemented without conscription.[30] The whole question, the War Committee agreed, would go the full Cabinet for discussion on December 9.

In the intervening few days the entire complexion of the war irrevocably altered. The Japanese assault at Pearl Harbor on December 7 brought the United States into the war at last, but the devastation wrought on the American Pacific Fleet virtually ensured that Japan would have a free hand for some time. The entry of the United States meant eventual victory for the Allies, that seemed certain, but now that Canada was at war with Japan* it at once increased the pressures for a greater Canadian war effort and re-directed its focus. Clearly Canada had to do more in a war that was now truly a world war. Equally, the Japanese military threat to the Pacific coast† demanded

*The first direct military effect of the Pacific war on Canada came with the fall of Hong Kong on Christmas Day, 1941. At the request of the United Kingdom, Canada had despatched an understrength brigade to the crown colony in the late fall. All the Canadians, along with the island's other defenders, were killed or captured by the Japanese.

†The threat to the Pacific Coast was not only external, or so many British Columbia citizens believed. There were more than 20,000 Japanese Canadians living in the coast province, and resentment and discrimination against orientals had long been a part of B.C. life. As early as July 1940 the Attorney-General of B.C. was suggesting that plans be made to intern the Japanese in a crisis (University of British Columbia, Duff Pattullo Papers, Wismer to Lapointe, 2 July 1940), and the report of a federal Special Committee on Orientals in British Columbia in December 1940 recommended a new registration of all Japanese. The Pearl Harbor attack increased the pressures for drastic action. The naval and military commanders in the area recommended the removal of the Japanese because of the growing tendency to vigilantism in the province (PAC, Ian Mackenzie Papers, file X-81, extracts from letters, 27, 30 Dec. 1941), and in a series of escalating orders Ottawa acceded. On January 14, 1942 males between 14 and 45 years of age were ordered evacuated to the interior; on February 26 the evacuation policy was extended to cover all Japanese living in security areas. 'It is the government's plan,' the Vancouver minister, Ian Mackenzie, said, 'to get these people out of B.C. as fast as possible. Every single man,

that substantial numbers of Canadian troops be kept in Canada. What did this do to the conscriptionists? The home-defence army now could be seen as a wise precaution and the conscriptionists as zealots who were willing to sacrifice Canada to save Britain. The question had become immensely more complicated.

The Cabinet had to consider the effects of the Japanese war as it debated the war program. The meetings on December 9 and 10 were long, and King asked each minister to give his views on conscription. Dandurand, Crerar, Cardin, Power, Gardiner—all flatly opposed compulsion. Crerar, a member of the conscriptionist Union Government of 1917, was firm: supplies were needed more than men; it would be a mistake to send too many men overseas; men were needed in Canada now that the war in the Pacific had begun. Cardin was eloquent as he argued that Quebec's war effort was from the head, not the heart as was English Canada's, and therefore finer in quality. No leader could be found, he said, who could persuade Quebec to accept conscription. C. D. Howe, more interested in production than anything else, was firmly in the middle. He didn't like the idea that the question should be decided on past pledges, but on the other hand he believed more could be done without conscription. It might become necessary, but every effort should be made to avoid it. The key proponents were Ilsley, Macdonald, and Ralston, all three Nova Scotians. Ilsley believed in conscription, he said, and while he would like to avoid the issue if possible, the door should not be closed to it. Macdonald was all for conscription on theoretical

woman and child will be removed from the defence areas of this province and it is my personal intention, as long as I remain in public life, to see they never come back here.' (Vancouver *Province*, 4 Apr. 1942.) The government also confiscated the property of the Japanese and sold it off at sacrifice prices. The culmination of government policy came on August 4, 1944, when Mackenzie King announced that although there had been no sabotage by Japanese Canadians, any Japanese found disloyal would be deported at the end of the war along with any who wished to leave. Those adjudged loyal could remain but they would be forbidden from concentrating in one area of the country. (House of Commons *Debates*, 4 Aug. 1944, p. 5948.)

There is no defence for such governmental actions, and the only exculpatory remarks possible are that many rational people feared a pogrom against the Japanese in British Columbia early in 1942. Also worth noting is that public sentiment in Canada as a whole seems to have supported the government's response. A poll on December 22, 1943 found 54 per cent wanting to deport all Japanese after the war. In January 1945 a similar survey found only 33 per cent in favour of complete deportation with 41 per cent agreeing that loyal Japanese could remain. (*Public Opinion Quarterly*, VIII (Spring, 1944), 160 and IX (Spring, 1945), 106.) The best account is F. LaViolette, *The Canadian Japanese and World War II* (Toronto, 1948).

'Mackenzie King himself was lukewarm about sending troops overseas', but political pressures demanded otherwise. In December 1939 the first troops left Halifax.

The election victory of 1940 'would rank with Abraham Lincoln's
in 1864, for Lincoln too had carried a democratic government to
victory in the midst of war.' The Prime Minister signing autographs
in Ottawa on election day.

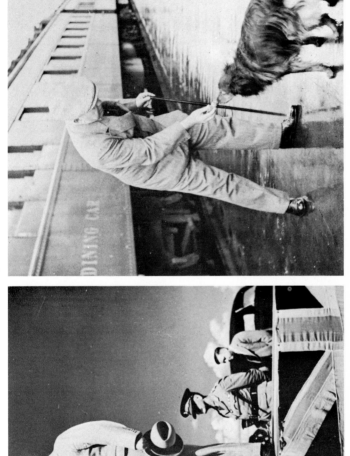

Mackenzie King 'enjoyed the perquisites of power. . . .' The Prime Minister finds a friend on the station platform alongside his train during his western swing, 1941.

'The Prime Minister decided he could best assist the recruiting drive by going on a speaking tour through the Western provinces. . . .' Mackenzie King addressing troops, summer 1941.

The 'Tories,' King believed, were 'going out of their way to create a wholly erroneous impression as to my personality.' Mackenzie King on his tour of the west in the summer of 1941.

'Lapointe and King had been genuine friends for more than twenty
years. They shared the same attitudes . . . they had worked well together. . . .' The Prime Minister leads the mourners at Lapointe's
funeral, November 1941.

'King had regarded Churchill as an erratic war-monger . . . although once he saw the way Churchill took hold and galvanized England, his criticism ceased almost completely.' King and Churchill leaving the House of Commons in Ottawa, December 1941.

'This honest, honourable and simple soldier. . . .' Colonel Ralston was Minister of National Defence from 1940 to 1944, a strong man worn down by responsibilities.

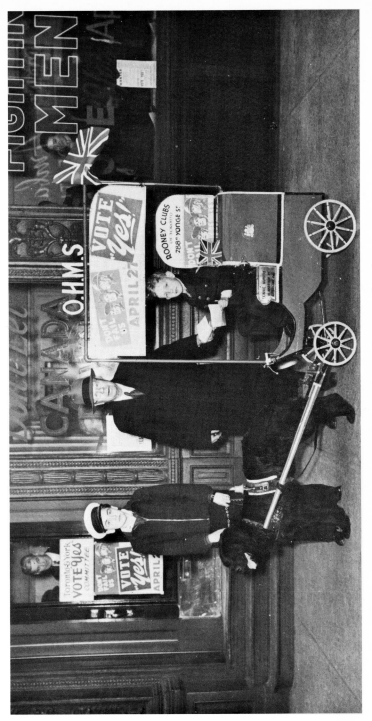

'. . . most "Yes" publicity consisted of ministerial speeches and advertisements placed by patriotic brewers, distillers and manufacturing firms.' In Toronto, additional methods were used to get out the vote in the conscription plebiscite of 1942.

'The King government that ran the war has to be judged as one of the strongest Cabinets Canada ever had . . .' The members of the Cabinet War Committee, 1943. Seated left to right: C. G. Power, T. A. Crerar, Mackenzie King, J. L. Ralston, J. L. Ilsley. Standing left to right: A. L. Macdonald, J. E. Michaud, C. D. Howe, L. S. St Laurent.

'There were few people in the world, when they met together, that were almost as one—like the President and myself.' President Roosevelt addresses the crowd outside the Parliament Buildings. August 1943.

'Again and yet again Mackenzie King resisted the Churchill line' at the Commonwealth Prime Ministers' Meeting, May 1944. The Prime Ministers from left to right: King, Smuts (South Africa), Churchill, Fraser (New Zealand), Curtin (Australia).

Norman Robertson became 'King's closest and most trusted adviser.' Robertson with the Prime Minister in London, May 1944.

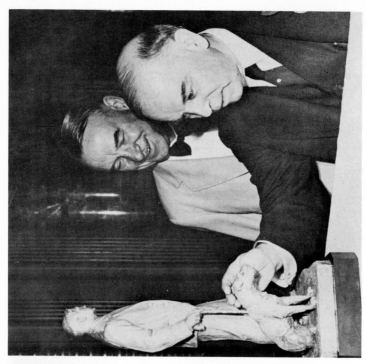

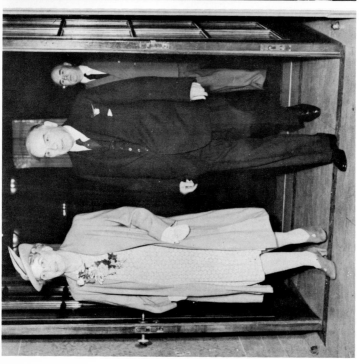

'. . . the twentieth anniversary of his assuming the leadership of the Liberal Party . . .' Mackenzie King entering the Château Laurier dining room with his sister, and receiving a statuette of himself and his dog, Pat.

'King, his government, and his country had survived.' A cartoonist's view of the conscription crisis of November 1944.

'The war . . . irrevocably altered Canada's role in the world and its perception of its place in a constellation of Great Powers.' Mackenzie King at the San Francisco Conference of 1945, with Norman Robertson seated behind him.

'Canada had emerged from the war proud of her part. . .' Victory celebrations in Ottawa, 1945.

'We come now with a series of measures which . . . will help to make our country more prosperous than it has ever been before,' King told the voters in 1945. But this Toronto Liberal candidate found that the promise of 'Jobs' did not win him his seat.

grounds. The Navy minister believed that the burden of sacrifice should be borne equally, and he warned that he would support conscription instantly the moment he felt it was necessary. The Minister of National Defence was almost apologetic as he made his remarks. He had tried to avoid raising the question, but as the responsible minister it was his duty to say what was necessary to win the war. The war could not be won by defending Canada in Canada. If the time came and if there was a danger of Canada being unable to support the men overseas without conscription, then he would support it and, the implication was clear, he would resign if his advice was not taken.[31]

Mackenzie King concluded this parade of views by giving his. The unity of Canada would be disrupted by conscription, and it would hurt the war effort. 'I suggested that it might be well to consider how public feeling might change in Canada, if our people began to see their sons slain in Britain and Europe while the Americans were defending their own country at home, after all we had done.' That had to be thought through, the Prime Minister said. Later Mackenzie King 'mentioned that it might serve to illustrate what I had in mind if I pointed out to the younger men present what I believe the future might reveal in regard to conscription, as the past had done in reference to myself. I said that my future was in the past.' What he meant by this, King said, was that the verdict of history would be the same as it was of 1917, 'more particularly when we had not only the light of past experience to warn us against it, but until today, the deep resentment felt as a consequence of what had happend.'[32]

The subject of a referendum on conscription was raised at one point during the meeting. King made clear that if one were held 'I, for one, would speak very strongly against supporting conscription.' Later he added that a referendum would create divisions: 'as someone had said, we would be no further along if the referendum went against conscription.'[33] For the moment at least, this idea was not yet ripe.

King spent several hours over the next few days worrying about the Cabinet meeting and talking about it with some of his ministers. Ralston was the key, Mackenzie King decided. 'He has been living too closely to the matter, and I think has committed himself so strongly to all proposals that he sees no way of modifying any of them. He seems to me to be quite overwrought and is liable to either break or tender his resignation, if he does not get his own way.' Part of the difficulty, he was convinced, was that Colonel Ralston was too much under the influence of the generals and too affected by his visits to England. Another unfortunate influence was that the three defence ministers were too often together and not enough in the company of other ministers. 'It tends to bring the military end too strongly to the fore.' It would have been different if Norman Rogers had survived, King mused, perhaps forgetting that Rogers had begun to press strongly for more divisions just before his death. 'It is not as though an extra division from Canada will mean the turning of the balance one way or another.' The trouble was that Ilsley, Macdonald, and Ralston, anglophilic English Canadians, didn't see this. 'They still have the kind of attitude toward Britain that Fielding and others of the Maritimes have had.'[34] There was some substantial truth in that, and Cardin pointed it out to King the next day when the two talked. The now-senior Quebec minister had been deeply concerned by the Cabinet discussion. 'Feels that some of our colleagues do not at all comprehend the Canadian situation, and that their action will destroy both the govt. and the party. I am fearful of both consequences.'[35]

Some way had to be found to cool the question for a time. One suggestion, apparently proposed to King by J. T. Thorson, who had entered the Cabinet as Minister of National War Services in June 1941, was for a Cabinet committee to study the manpower question. Ralston agreed to this, and King named Thorson, St Laurent, and Gibson to work on the matter.[36] Another method might yet be a plebiscite. This option was put forcibly to King by one of his secretaries, J. W. Pickersgill, on December 16:

> To my surprise, he stated that he believed that, if presented to them in a proper light, Quebec would accept conscription. . . . I said I could not believe that, though I did believe a referendum might be the only way out of the situation. Pickersgill seemed to think it might be wise to lose no time in the holding of it, to have it over even before Parliament met. I doubt the wisdom of that, though I do think that it might well come as a part of government policy to be set out in the Speech from the Throne. If that is to be done, I shall have to keep this in mind until the very last moment. It would cut the ground out from any amendment to the Address which the Tories might move favouring all-out conscription, for it would be a reference to the people themselves rather than to their representatives.[37]

This thought was strengthened the next day when King learned that the Manitoba legislature had passed a resolution calling on Ottawa to introduce conscription as part of an all-out war effort. Undoubtedly recollecting the way he had used the Ontario resolution in January 1940, King wrote that 'the minute I saw it I felt I had at last just what I wanted. It gives me the best of reasons for an immediate referendum. The framing of the latter is something that will have to be done with care but I can see wherein if a referendum is taken before Parliament re-assembles, we will be free from all that discussion in the House.'[38] King took this idea to the Cabinet on December 18, where its reception was generally favourable. Angus Macdonald wrote in his diary that the Prime Minister had said 'this government must be kept in power for the good of the country. Therefore let us take a plebiscite and be guided by it.' The original question as suggested by Mackenzie King was 'Are you in favour of the Government's *having power* to send men beyond Canada?' Another suggestion of King's was simpler: 'Are you in favour of conscription?'[39] Other ministers were soon trying their hand at question-framing, most notably Ian Mackenzie who sent proposals to Chubby Power who in turn had been delegated to investigate the mechanical problems involved in holding a plebiscite.[40] The advantages seemed so obvious. The plebiscite would effectively squelch the Tories in Parliament and, since the writs had been issued for four by-elections to be held on February 9, and since Meighen was certain to run in one of them, the referendum would 'remove that issue from the contest.' That would help scuttle Meighen. It would also help St Laurent, who was to run in Quebec East, and the Minister of Labour, Humphrey Mitchell, appointed to the Cabinet on December 15 after years of service in the trade union movement and on government boards, who would seek election to the House in Welland, Ontario at the same time. The referendum would also create delay and help to keep the party united.[41]

The one flaw in this reasoning was Cardin's continued opposition to the idea of a referendum on conscription. The Works and Transport Minister feared that his province could only see a vote on the question as a sign that King was preparing to implement conscription; this might have disastrous electoral results, particularly in the two by-elections scheduled there. The Prime Minister tried to persuade Cardin otherwise but failed. 'It was clear to me,' he wrote, 'that, all circumstances considered, it would be best to defer final decision till we have a party caucus when Parliament re-assembles.'[42] The matter was effectively shelved until the new year.

The question came up again on January 5 when Ralston's army program was finally approved provided, as King noted, 'that we believed conscription was unnecessary; that the programme represented an all-out effort; that we believed this programme could be carried out without resort to conscription.'⁴³ His hand had been forced on this, King believed, because he was convinced that Ralston and Macdonald would resign if the program was not approved. 'Indeed,' King wrote of a conversation with Power, 'they had been talking along these lines, and even going further, getting out unless colleagues from Quebec would agree to a referendum.' That had to be avoided, King wrote, because the loss of the two defence ministers at this stage would 'create a panic with respect to Canada's war effort.'⁴⁴ That judgement was probably correct, but King's troubles—and the nation's—would have been infinitely less if he had forced the two dissident ministers out then and if he had rejected their demands for a grossly oversized military establishment, one far beyond the capacity of the country to support readily along with all her other commitments.

The plebiscite suggestion still remained, although King continued to waver badly. In a crucial memorandum that he wrote on January 8, the Prime Minister tried to work out his 'Position re Conscription'. The whole problem had been 'Made a political issue by Meighen . . .' and one course would be to 'Let Parliament decide—(Straight issue), Meighen vs. King . . .' There were alternatives to this course, although a general election was 'out of the question'. A referendum was possible and it could take two forms. One, simply put, would remove the restrictive clause in the National Resources Mobilization Act that limited conscription to home service, but that, King observed, was 'likely to be defeated'. The second course was better:

> to give govt. authority (it has power now) at its discretion if need arises to apply conscription at some time in future, to meet an emergent situation, in other words, release govt. from any restrictions (express or implied in carrying on the war). . . .
>
> If not carried—would end matter. Ministers who not satisfied, to take responsibility and resign.
>
> If carried:
> (i) would not lead to immediate conscription as govt. has declared no need for.
> (ii) Might not lead to conscription at any time, as views of majority of Govt. would continue to govern, and probably govt. would find ways and means of holding together to prevent division in country which would destroy war effort, (possibility: e.g., call up large numbers of

men—mere possibility of its enforcement, would bring in necessary recruits).

(iii) Unless convinced of necessity and desirability I would not agree to conscription.

(iv) I would, if majority thought otherwise, step aside, and ask Governor General to send for member of Ministry. . . .

(v) I would do all in my power to assist Ministry. . . .[45]

King's reasoning was subtle but direct, and the conclusions he reached in that memorandum guided him in the weeks ahead.

The problem with Quebec's reaction to the plebiscite was also starting to ease. As T. A. Crerar first noted, the trend now seemed to be in favour of a vote. J. E. Michaud, the Minister of Fisheries, told him that 'a few weeks ago he had had a talk with the Cardinal [Villeneuve] and that the Cardinal feels strongly about the war and the need for an Allied victory; that he expressed the opinion on the conscription issue that, if the Government got released from its pledge by a referendum and, after this release, if King were to announce that the Government was prepared to put in conscription should it prove necessary to maintain our forces overseas, he would support it.' But as Michaud also added, it would not be sufficient simply for the government on its own to decide that if the voluntary system failed conscription would be necessary. 'It would be necessary to show Quebec clearly what the view was of the rest of Canada on the matter; that they attach a great deal of importance to the pledges which have been given.'[46] Cardin attached great importance to those pledges, too, and he was the key figure now. He and King talked on January 15, and Crerar and Cardin discussed the plebiscite on January 16. To both, Cardin indicated the necessity to keep the Liberal party in power and prevent a national government under Meighen from taking office. Quebec, he believed, might even support a referendum given the alternative of Meighen, and in wartime, after all, he reflected, governments had to have the power to do what might become necessary.[47] Cardin had been brought into line.

After some last-minute wavering and haggling about the wording, King decided to use the Speech from the Throne on January 22 to announce his decision. It was important, he wrote, to include 'a reference with respect to bringing about a release from the commitments made with respect to conscription so as to let the issue be fought out on the floor of Parliament and so deprive our opponents of an obvious weapon which they are using effectively, namely that the necessities of the war should override any past promises. What I was aiming at above all else was to keep faith with the people.'[48] The phrasing in the Speech as delivered by the Governor General said that 'My ministers accordingly will seek, from the people, by means of a plebiscite, release from any obligation arising out of any past commitments restricting methods of raising men for military service.' The plebiscite form was used primarily because it was advisory, while a referendum was generally considered to be binding. The date set for the vote was April 27 and the wording of the question to be put to the electors was neatly, if obliquely, phrased along the lines of the wording in the Speech: 'Are you in favour of releasing the Government from any obligations arising out of any past commitments restricting the methods of raising men for military service?'[49] The task now was to sell the question to the people, particularly those in Quebec.

II

The first selling job had to be to the Liberal caucus. On January 22 Cardin did his loyal best to persuade the Quebec Members that the government should be freed from its pledges. Quebec had done a good job in the war, he began, directing his remarks first at the English-speaking M.P.s. 'You English-speaking people are influenced not only by your judgment but by your sentiments; the call comes to your hearts from the Motherland from which you came. The French-Canadians have not that call; our decision comes from our minds; it arises from our judgment alone.' Then, speaking to the *Québecois*, he insisted that 'I am going to vote for the release, and I am going to urge my fellow French Canadians to do the same thing.' It was, T. A. Crerar wrote to his friend J. W. Dafoe in Winnipeg, 'an eloquent and moving appeal'.[50] Cardin's reasoning, expressed later to another Quebec M.P., was that he was voting to release the government because 'il vaut mieux avoir la conscription avec King qu'avec un autre—Hanson ou Meighen.'[51]

Cardin had made the statesmanlike decision, much as other Quebec leaders had been forced to do by the needs of the majority. But whether other French Canadians would or could go along was unclear. The American Minister reported to Washington that a number of French Canadians had told him that 'We think that M. Lapointe would have agreed to this plebiscite';[52] his own view, however, was that the government was waiting too long to take the vote. 'This will allow the sores of national disunity to fester and if the present bitterness on the part of Ontario toward French Canada continues,' Pierrepont Moffat suggested, 'there may be as much disunity resulting from a plebiscite as there would have been by completely ignoring Quebec.' His own sympathies were with the conscriptionists, he said, but 'their tactics, however, are so short-sighted, so uncooperative and so insulting to anyone who happens to hold a different point of view that one's feelings of sympathy are obscured.'[53] Some of the anti-conscriptionists were less than wise, too, among them Premier Godbout of Quebec. In a speech at Montreal on January 26, Godbout was provoked by *nationaliste* hecklers into saying that he was against conscription for overseas service and that 'le service obligatoire pour outre-mer, dans le moment, serait un crime.'[54] The Premier implied that Mackenzie King shared his view, too, and the speech was deeply embarrassing to the government and to Godbout himself, who could only apologize and say that as he had blurted this out he could not remember his exact words.[55]

Among those particularly troubled by the Godbout blunder were Ralston and Macdonald, and the two defence ministers came to see King on January 31. Ralston began the interview by saying that the plebiscite entailed delay, and he wanted to be able to say in a speech that he was making a few days hence that if conscription became necessary before the plebiscite, it would be invoked. Macdonald's notes of the interview give King's reply:

> P.M. said the question had to be viewed as a whole. It was a mistake to urge conscription just for conscription's sake. We must be sure we would get more men under conscription than without it. We must fill the needs of industry, farming, home defence, as well as the needs of the armed forces. . . . Conditions in this country might get so bad that no-one could govern the country. If you had to use machine guns, what would be the use of conscription? He had denied the Godbout statement. Surely his colleagues would believe him.

This was not the problem, the unhappy ministers assured King. What did concern them was what would happen if the plebiscite carried. Mackenzie King replied that the decision would be made then 'considering everything', a phrase that he elaborated upon by indicating that 'everything' meant the whole country, not Quebec alone. This was not a satisfactory response for Macdonald, at least, and although he did not press the point, he left the interview shrewdly convinced that King's response to the plebiscite results would likely be that 'Conscription might give you a few more men here and there, but it would create a terrible situation in the country and consequently will not be worthwhile.'[56]

Why the two ministers were so insistent is not clear. There was as yet no shortage of men, and Ralston knew this. A few days earlier General Stuart had told him that 'raw manpower has not been and is not today the limiting factor either in the wartime expansion of the fighting formations . . . or in respect to the extent of our reinforcing organization. I can say, therefore, that, even if compulsory overseas service was introduced tomorrow, I would not recommend an increase in the present Army Programme.'[57] The reasons for their attitude then have to be judged as largely symbolic. They believed King tricky and felt he could not be trusted; he would wiggle out of every commitment that was not nailed down. And, although the need for men was not yet pressing, unless the commitments were made now they would never be honoured later. In addition, conscription was the touchstone of a total war effort, the *sine qua non*, and without it Canada's war would remain half-hearted.

That was an attitude that Arthur Meighen shared. The Conservative leader was seeking election to Parliament in the Toronto constituency of York South, a safe seat that had been opened for him by the resignation of the sitting Conservative, Lt.-Col. Alan Cockeram. Despite the hard blow the plebiscite announcement had dealt it, Meighen's campaign was still pitched around conscription and national government, needless to say, and he followed the traditional campaign practice of speeches, tea parties, advertising, and impressive (and bipartisan) committees. There was no Liberal candidate in the field against him, ostensibly because of the tradition that party leaders not be opposed in by-elections.[58] This left Meighen opposed only by a local CCF schoolteacher, Joe Noseworthy, but the fight was more difficult than anyone expected. The constituency had a very heavy working-class population that had suffered from unemployment as much as any other group in the country during the Depression. This evil memory made Noseworthy's campaign talk of social security very effective, and the CCF tactic of blanket canvassing was bringing the message home to the voters. Then, too, although most of the official Liberal leadership in the constituency were conscriptionists and serving on Meighen's committees, former National Liberal Federation president and party bagman, Senator Norman Lambert, had given the CCF some small financial assistance, and Arthur Roebuck, a Toronto Liberal M.P. with his own scores to settle, had taken to the radio to broadcast denunciations of Meighen and, more particularly, of Premier Mitch Hepburn who was supporting him. The result of these disparate factors, combined with the notorious flightiness of electors in a by-election, was a shattering defeat for Meighen by some 5,000 votes. The CCF had begun its upward climb— this was its first victory ever in Ontario—and the effectiveness of social welfare as an issue and of blanket canvassing as a technique had been established. The Tories had lost their leader, and Meighen's pro-conscription and national-government campaign had been dealt its death blow. For Mackenzie King it was almost a miracle that he should be spared the scourge of Meighen and, as he told the CCF leader, M. J. Coldwell, 'if titles were in order, I'd make you a K.C.B.'[59] King's happiness was increased by the victories St Laurent and Mitchell had scored in their constituencies. It was a striking endorsement both of the government's policies and of Mackenzie King himself.

The day after the by-election triumphs T. A. Crerar wrote that 'the time between now and the taking of the plebiscite offers some time for passions . . . to cool. I expect the debate will collapse in a few days.'[60] Crerar was correct in his assessments of English-Canadian opinion, for what else could conscriptionists do except to support the plebiscite? But in Quebec, his prediction was as wrong as could be. There, as Brooke Claxton observed, feeling was as strong as ever:

> 99.9% of the people in Quebec are against conscription and have been right along. Recently a Gallup Poll on this matter showed a vote of two to one against in Quebec. I thought then and know now that it was much higher. Despite active searching I do not think that I have found a French Canadian who is in favour of conscription. You hear talk in places like Westmount, Toronto, Hamilton and Winnipeg about French-Canada being in favour of conscription but you cannot run anyone who is to earth and you certainly cannot get them out into the open.[61]

Mackenzie King found this to be true when he tried to persuade four Quebec M.P.s to take a position. None wanted to appear favourable to the plebiscite and 'all [were] dead against conscription.'[62]

The ground was ready in Quebec for the emergence of one of the war's most effective pressure groups, La Ligue pour la défense du Canada. The LPDC's origins are somewhat obscure. André Laurendeau, its first secretary, indicated that the idea of an organization to mobilize opposition to the conscription plebiscite occurred to several people simultaneously. The Quebec historian, Robert Rumilly, credits the idea to a group of young men who met Abbé Groulx, Quebec's leading clerical nationalist, and who were encouraged by him to see Laurendeau and Paul Gouin, leader of the late l'Action Libérale Nationale. Whoever the founder, the LPDC was organized and given its name at a meeting in Gouin's home, probably before the end of January 1942.[63] Its goal was to bring together representatives of large public organizations and to achieve at one and the same time close links with them and full freedom of action. This was, surprisingly, accomplished, and the nominal directors of the Ligue were officers of L'Union Catholique des Cultivateurs, the Montreal Catholic Labour Council, the Montreal Société Saint-Jean-Baptiste, the Voyageurs de Commerce, and various youth movements. The presidency was given to Dr J.-B. Prince, 'un veteran du bourassisme',[64] but in fact the real leadership was exercised by Maxime Raymond, the independent and isolationist Liberal Member of Parliament for Beauharnois-Laprairie, Georges Pelletier, the publisher of Le Devoir, and André Laurendeau, then the editor of L'Action Nationale, a small nationalist and isolationist monthly.[65] As secretary of the Ligue, Laurendeau was responsible for its day-to-day functioning, and much of its success was directly attributable to his energy.

The LPDC manifesto was published in the January issue of L'Action Nationale and widely circulated throughout the province in leaflet form. The argument was simple, direct, and compelling. Why should you vote 'No' in the plebiscite?, the voter was asked. 'Parce que nul ne demande d'être relevé d'un engagement s'il n'a déjà la tentation de le violer, et parce que, de toutes les promesses qu'il a faites au peuple du Canada, il n'en reste qu'une que King voudrait n'être plus obliger de tenir: la promesse de ne pas conscrire les hommes pour outre-mer.'[66]

Maxime Raymond offered his detailed criticism of the plebiscite in Parliament on February 5. He began by noting the scope of the war program proposed by the government in the Speech from the Throne—the loan of $700 million to Britain, the gift of $1 billion to Britain, the war budget of $3 billion, and the plebiscite. It was a 'national war effort extended to the country's utmost capacity,' too much in fact for a country still 'in the development stage'. Worst of all was the plebiscite, the violation of the pact, of the compact made on September 9, 1939 and renewed in the election of 1940. Was it not Ernest Lapointe who had told the House and the country that he was 'authorized by my colleagues in the cabinet from the province of Quebec . . . to say that we will never be members or supporters of a government that will try to enforce [conscription]. Is that clear enough?' Lapointe's words had been very clear, as was his next paragraph, also recited by Raymond. 'Provided these points are understood,' King's lieutenant had said, 'we are willing to offer our services without limitation and to devote our best efforts for the success of the cause we all have at heart.' The meaning of Lapointe's pledge was clear, Raymond argued: 'Participation without conscription'. The pact existed, the plebiscite was a violation of it, and he would resist it. The pledge against conscription had been offered to Quebec, but now the government was asking all Canada to release it from its promise to French Canada.[67] All the LPDC arguments were there in the Raymond oration.

The task of La Ligue pour la défense du Canada was now to proselytize, and its tactics were those of a classic pressure group. Public meetings were held, hats were passed, and memberships were sold at $1 each. A flood of leaflets circulated through the province and into New Brunswick and northern Ontario. The press releases were circulated—but only rarely printed. The organization, created by Laurendeau, was smooth and efficient, unusually so for such an *ad hoc* organization; more impressive yet, this efficiency was largely achieved without money. To judge by the LPDC account books, individual contributions were small, averaging only about $2, and some meetings produced little or no revenue.[68] At one stage Laurendeau was reduced to writing pleading letters to newspapers, urging their editors in the interest of fairness to give the LPDC some coverage. There was no way the Ligue could hope to match the government's lavish advertising budget, he wrote to Ottawa's *Le Droit*. 'La Ligue est trop pauvre. . . .'[69]

Worse, much of the press in Quebec was actively hostile to the aims of the Ligue. Nothing had been expected from the Montreal *Gazette*, the *Star*, or the Quebec *Chronicle-Telegraph*, of course, but the reaction of the French-language press must have been a surprise. The whip was cracked over the editors, dependent in war circumstances more than ever on government advertising, and they generally toed the line; some press attacks against the Ligue were scurrilous.[70] Only *Le Devoir* was enthusiastically campaigning for a 'Non' vote. Similarly the radio was closed to the LPDC except for such time as it could purchase on individual private stations. In a decision forced upon it by the government, the Canadian Broadcasting Corporation decided that only recognized political parties would have free access to the airwaves during the plebiscite campaign. This tactic meant that only the parties in Parliament, all calling for a 'Yes' vote, would be heard. The government had effectively shut out the LPDC.[71]

Curiously, none of these tactics worked against the Ligue. Its meetings were very often large and enthusiastic, and chapters sprang up throughout the province, often assisted by the Société Saint-Jean-Baptiste. In Montreal a poll-by-poll organization covered much of the city,[72] and leading *nationaliste* figures began to jump on the bandwagon. One such was René Chaloult, M.L.A., who introduced a motion in the Legislature in Quebec City calling for a 'Non' vote. The Alberta and Manitoba legislatures had urged positive votes, he argued impeccably, so Quebec could express its opinion too. The motion embarrassed the Godbout government, and for a time the Liberal Cabinet seemed on the verge of a split. But after pressure was brought to bear on the malcontents, the Liberals hung together and defeated Chaloult's motion.[73] In Ottawa the independent-minded Jean-François Pouliot, M.P., a persistent disruptive force in the Liberal caucus, moved a six-month hoist on the plebiscite bill, an effort that the government handily crushed, there being only thirteen votes in support. Ironically, two of Pouliot's votes came from Toronto Tories who wanted conscription immediately without benefit of a plebiscite.[74]

All these efforts served to keep the anti-conscriptionists' pot boiling. The LPDC stepped up its advertising as the date of the plebiscite drew closer, and again and again Ernest Lapointe, in his grave for four months, dominated its pamphlets. 'Jamais, Jamais . . . a dit M. Lapointe,' was the title of a Georges Pelletier article in *Le Devoir* on February 21. *L'Aiglon*, 'L'organe Libéral Dorchester-Bellechasse', published in St Joseph-Beauce, put in headline type that 'L'Honorable Ernest Lapointe a dit: La Conscription Jamais Votons NON.' Another popular theme was to stress that men were needed closer to home. 'Souvenons-nous de Hong-Kong,' one leaflet warned, drawing attention to the slaughter of Canadian troops there in December 1941. 'Souvenons-nous de l'Australie.' Nor were Mackenzie King's past promises forgotten, and *L'Action Nationale* quoted the Prime Minister extensively. Like nothing before or since, the plebiscite seemed to unite the nationalist intellectuals of the province with the people.[75] Only the federal politicians and their press and radio were out of step.

Certainly there can be no doubt that French-Canadian opinion was united. The Canadian Institute of Public Opinion, then a new organization, demonstrated repeatedly that Quebec was against conscription and becoming more so. In the middle of March, 79 per cent were opposed to conscription; on April 11, 74 per cent, and at the end of April, just before the plebiscite was to be taken, a stunning 81 per cent of those questioned indicated their opposition. The polls also demonstrated that in Canada at large those of high income were more favourable to conscription than those earning less, while rural voters were less enthusiastic than city residents.*[76]

From the government's point of view, the task of countering the efforts of the LPDC in Quebec was organizational. How was the plebiscite, this educative process for conscription, going to be run? Would there be a great national advertising campaign? Massive speakers' organizations? Inexplicably, nothing was decided until the end of March, a lapse that is puzzling even though the plebiscite bill did not win the approval of the House of Commons until March 4. Norman McLarty, the Secretary of State since his shift from the Labour portfolio on December 15, 1941, had suggested the creation of a publicity machine to Mackenzie King on March 6, but his plans were not ready for discussion by a Cabinet committee until March 25. One advantage, McLarty told the Prime Minister, was that Parliament had allocated

*In a poll on April 4, 1942 the Canadian Institute of Public Opinion asked respondents if they would vote 'for or against freeing the government from any pledges it had made restricting the methods of raising men for military service?' The results:

By Income bracket

	Upper	Middle	Lower
Vote to free	72%	70%	54%
Vote against	20	21	34
Undecided	8	9	12

Urban vs Rural

	Farm	Small Town	City
Vote to free	57	59	68
Vote against	29	30	23
Undecided	14	11	9

Public Opinion Quarterly, VI (Fall, 1942), 488.

$1,500,000 for advertisements to get out the vote,[77] but the government could not spend public money to encourage a 'Yes' vote. As a result a public subscription fund had to be set up to spread the 'Yes' message, and the donations were made tax deductible.[78]

Mackenzie King was appalled by the shambles that McLarty had created. At a Cabinet meeting on April 1, an appropriate enough day, he complained that 'all we had was evidence of what the opponents were doing.' McLarty was working on the wrong lines 'in talking of establishing a national committee, instead of getting men to organize non-partisan [sic] committees and taking effective steps toward that end. He seems incapable of getting men around him to work in an efficient way.' But what could be done? 'I felt it useless to try and take on a load myself,' King wrote in his diary; 'the matter would just have to go as best it could. I do not recall an occasion when I felt Cabinet as a whole more incompetent.'[79] Ten days later, McLarty having fallen ill in the meantime and the Postmaster-General, W. P. Mulock, having taken his place at the head of the publicity drive, King was still frustrated. The Cabinet committee in charge of publicity had produced nothing, he wrote. 'Tonight I spent an hour with Mulock telling him what I thought should be done. I had to cancel altogether a pamphlet McLarty had prepared of fifty questions re plebiscite because of worth-less character of some of the questions and embarrassment which would have come from others. It seems impossible to have anyone take intelligent grasp of the situation.'[80] The inevitable result of the government's mismanagement was that most 'Yes' publicity consisted of ministerial speeches and advertisements placed by patriotic brewers, distillers, and manufacturing firms.

In Quebec the plebiscite organization was even less satisfactory than in the rest of the country. The plan had been that the Quebec ministers would take care of their province, but there was no co-ordination of the Quebec campaign with that in the rest of the country. Worse, only the Cabinet ministers were actively campaigning, almost none of the French-speaking M.P.s taking part at all.[81] Such as it was, the 'Yes' campaign in the province tried to stress that Mackenzie King could be trusted: 'N'oublions pas que le Gouvernement en général et que tout particulièrement notre premier ministre, dont le sain canadienisme est bien connu, n'ont aucun intérêt à demander au Canada des sacrifices qui ne seraient pas nécessaires.' 'AYEZ DONC CONFIANCE EN M. MACKENZIE KING ET VOTEZ OUI le 27 AVRIL 1942.'[82] But with almost no one willing to speak for Mackenzie King and his policy, the 'Oui' campaign began to seem more and more futile. Cardin was discouraged about the outlook, and the Prime Minister began to fear that as many as 80 per cent of the Quebec electorate would refuse to release the government from its pledges. 'The people don't like conscription for overseas,' he recorded on April 3, 'they are prepared for it for defence within and around shores of Canada,—but they are coming to have less and less confidence in the wisdom of the British Govt.'[83] Perhaps, but in Quebec at least it was a lack of confidence in the Mackenzie King government that was at issue.

The results of the plebiscite on April 27 were, as F.-A. Angers described them in *L'Action Nationale*, 'Un Vote de Race'.[84] In general French Canada voted 'Non' and English Canada voted 'Yes' and there can be no doubt of this. In Ontario the government position was supported by 82.3 per cent of the electorate, in Prince Edward Island by 82.4 per cent, and in all the other provinces except Quebec by substantial majorities. Alberta and New Brunswick were the lowest 'Yes' provinces with 70.4 and 69.1 per cent respectively. In Quebec, by contrast, only 27.1 per cent voted to release Mackenzie King from his pledges against conscription. What is striking is that in English-Canadian constituencies that voted 'No' and in Quebec constituencies that voted 'Yes', the population mix was different from that prevailing in the overall area. In Quebec only nine constituencies had a 'Yes' majority. All were Montreal area ridings, all had English-speaking majorities, and five were represented by English-speaking M.P.s. Of the eight constituencies outside Quebec voting 'No', six were heavily French-Canadian and were represented by French-speaking M.P.s, and two were populated by large numbers of Ukrainians, Germans, and other ethnic groups.* French Canadians, wherever they lived in Canada, had voted against conscription, and they had been joined to a substantial extent by non-Anglo-Saxon voters. The simple fact seemed to be that many people living in Canada still thought of themselves as Ukrainians or Germans or Irish, not as Canadians. The war was a war for England, not Canada. Why then increase your burdens by voting for conscription? Frank Scott, the perceptive McGill law professor, hit the nail on the head: 'British

*Quebec 'Yes' ridings: Cartier, Jacques-Cartier, Laurier, Mount Royal, Outremont, St Ann, St Antoine-Westmount, St Louis-St George, Verdun. The extra-Quebec 'No' ridings: Prescott, Russell (Ontario); Provencher (Manitoba); Gloucester, Restigouche-Madawaska, Kent (New Brunswick); Vegreville (Alberta); and Rosthern (Saskatchewan). See *Canada Gazette*, 23 June 1942, for plebiscite results.

people everywhere', he wrote in *Canadian Forum*, 'would do well to reflect on one fact that this war has brought strikingly to light, namely, that the non-British people who are supposed to "enjoy" the blessings of the British Empire do not seem to appreciate those blessings as much as we have been taught they did.'[85]

The plebiscite had been a triumph for La Ligue pour la défense du Canada and for Quebec nationalism. It had been a defeat for Mackenzie King, and one that left his major problem still unsolved. His task now was to take sufficient action to satisfy the conscriptionists in Cabinet while still not alienating a newly united Quebec. Squaring the circle would be simpler.

III

'My belief is that we shall never have to resort to conscription for overseas,' Mackenzie King wrote in his diary during the long wait for the plebiscite results on April 27.

> We will repeal the clause in the National Resources Mobilization Act, which limits the government's power to the confines of Canada. I will announce that we intend to extend the application of the provisions of the N.R.M.A. to cover the coasts of Canada, possibly going the length of using Canadians anywhere in the northern half of this hemisphere. I doubt if we shall ever have to go beyond that.... All we shall have to be sure of is reinforcements of the army at present in Britain. If there is any pressure on the part of our men to enforce conscription, just for the sake of conscription, I will fight that position to the end. Quebec and the country will see that I have kept my promise about not being a member of the government which sends men overseas under conscription. The only exception I will make in that will be that our own men need additional numbers which could not be obtained voluntarily, but I do not think this will be the case....[86]

That was as clear a statement of intentions as Mackenzie King could make, and to a substantial extent he would try to carry it out.

But the results of the plebiscite had shocked him. To his colleagues he said that 'the govt. appeared to be safe. That while we were not claiming the results as a vote of confidence in the administration, there could be no doubt that the vote was such in large part.' There seemed to be more truth in the first part of that statement than in the latter. The Prime Minister also warned his Cabinet 'not to interpret the vote as a vote for conscription'.[87] That was the difficulty, however. Everyone did seem to draw that conclusion, not least Colonel Ralston who responded quickly to King's comments by suggesting that the Prime Minister was minimizing the importance of the results, which were a clear go-ahead signal. After all, the Finance Minister chimed in, what other purpose had the plebiscite had?

King then suggested that the limiting clause, section 3, of the NRMA should perhaps be repealed at least insofar as North America was concerned, much as he had indicated to himself on April 27. To his surprise this dissatisfied the hard-line ministers. Angus Macdonald argued that it would be a mistake to take two bites at the cherry and that the government would be in difficulties later if it had to send troops to the United Kingdom or Europe. And according to his diary, Macdonald told the Prime Minister that 'if I had thought the discussion was to take this turn and if this view was the prevailing view I should have taken a different course on the plebiscite question and I should have to think carefully over what my future course would be.' St Laurent, the Minister of Justice, and Michaud, the Minister of Fisheries, entered the debate at this point, according to Macdonald's diary, arguing that if section 3 was repealed conscription would have to be enforced immediately. Not so, Macdonald replied. The moral right had been given by the people yesterday, he argued, but just when it had to be exercised was another matter. There was the beginning of a way out in that remark, but no one seems to have grasped at it, and the discussion continued fruitlessly for some time. Macdonald's last notation for the day held out little hope for an amicable settlement: 'Mitchell [the Minister of Labour] said majorities had rights as well as minorities.'[88]

The difficulties ahead were now evident. 'It looks to me as though the plebiscite had really helped the all-out conscription movement,' King wrote in some despair on May 1, 'mostly because of Quebec not having voted to trust the government, as it is clear they have interpreted the vote to be on conscription. If they had voted to trust the government, knowing that it was known what their views were, they would have been helping the situation against any interpretation of the ballot being for conscription outright.'[89] If King had genuinely believed that the vote was about an abstract question of releasing the government from its pledges, he had fooled himself. If he believed that a 'Yes' vote from

Quebec would have made it easier to resist conscription, he was mis-
interpreting the national mood and that of his Cabinet. The demands
to go all the way immediately would have been well-nigh irresistible.

As it was the demands were becoming hard to resist. T. A. Crerar, for
one, was still against conscription, but he wrote the Prime Minister on
May 1 to suggest that section 3 be deleted from the NRMA and the
amendment be accompanied by a declaration that conscription would
be employed if necessary 'to maintain effectively Canada's war effort'.
This, Crerar argued, was 'a compromise which our French-Canadian
friends could, and should, accept. One thing is certain: if the need for
conscription arises, it will have to be applied, if not by the present
Government then by another which would succeed it.'[90] But Crerar
was a moderate. On May 1 King learned that his Ontario ministers had
met the day before and agreed to try to carry the Ontario M.P.s with
them in demanding all-out conscription at once. This provoked sharp
exchanges between the Prime Minister and some of the ministers,
particularly C. D. Howe. The Quebec members and ministers were just
as restive, although against conscription.[91]

In this situation King decided to follow the line that had been
suggested first by Macdonald and then Crerar. He would amend the
NRMA by deleting section 3 but 'stating the Government's policy to be
only the extension of application of conscription for the present . . . to
the Western hemisphere . . . making some pledge which would bring
us back to Parliament before we actually enforce conscription. In that
event,' he wrote, ' I can always have my colleagues understand that they
will have to find another leader if there is an attempt to bring conscription into force where that is not necessary.'[92]

But when he presented this proposal to Cabinet on May 5, Ralston
objected strenuously to returning to Parliament before enacting conscription. That would tie the government's hands, and what would
happen if an emergency arose? At this stage this point did not seem
particularly critical to the Prime Minister. The only difference, he
noted, was 'whether, in stating the Government's policy, I should say
that we would, when we felt it necessary to enact conscription, do so by
Order-in-Council and then come to Parliament for approval, or whether
we should advise Parliament of our intention to proclaim conscription
for overseas for certain reasons, and then make that a question of
confidence.'[93] The positions soon hardened, however, with Ralston and
Macdonald pressing increasingly hard for Cabinet's right to implement

conscription without a new debate in the House. The same question dominated discussion the next day when Ralston indicated that 'he had come to Council in the morning feeling that he might have to break with his colleagues in the matter of not agreeing to a second discussion on the plebiscite.' Arthur Cardin joined in to say that as he had lost the confidence of his compatriots in the province of Quebec, perhaps he too should resign. This day and the next Cardin urged that section 3 not be repealed, but on May 8 King told his colleagues that he would give notice to Parliament of his intention to delete the clause from the National Resources Mobilization Act, agreeing after more discussion that 'my position would be that we would make no commitment either for or against going to Parliament first or later, and would decide it in the light of circumstances at the time; that would be part of our decision and that was what I meant by responsibility to Parliament.'[94]

For Cardin this was the signal to withdraw from the government, and when he came to see Mackenzie King on May 9 he brought his letter of resignation with him. The two men had a long discussion, but Cardin, thinking of what had happened to the French-speaking ministers in Borden's government in 1917, was adamant: 'He did not want to be like Blondin or other men who had to walk across the city of Montreal accompanied by a policeman.'[95] That was probably a genuine reason, but Louis St Laurent told Grant Dexter that Cardin 'was the vainest man [he] had ever known. Cardin . . . had thought that if he made a speech or two asking for a Yes vote, the people of Quebec would obey him. The shock of the No vote was terrific. He felt deserted, abandoned and such was his vanity that he had resigned, no doubt with the clear hope of resuming the leadership of French Canadians.'[96] Cardin was to be disappointed in that hope, too.

The resignation of the senior Quebec minister left effective French-Canadian representation in the Cabinet at its nadir. Only St Laurent held a senior portfolio, and the Minister of Justice was still largely untried and an unknown quantity to his province.[97] King worried about this, of course, but he tried to use this weakness in the Cabinet in the only way he could, arguing with the conscriptionists. Cardin had left, he said on May 11, because of 'the effort to have the Cabinet decide that it would enact conscription by Order-in-Council first, and go to Parliament after, instead of going to Parliament, stating we intended to enact the Order, and asking for a vote of confidence before so doing in order that an action so all-important might have the backing of Parliament. [Cardin] felt it was useless to try to resist further what seemed to be a determination to have conscription at any price, when he knew his own province and many parts of the Dominion would not agree to it being so forced, and that any attempt at its enforcement would be disastrous.' Then King turned directly to the attack:

> I added it was obviously clear that the Government could not carry on without Ministers from a Province which represented one third of the population. . . . That I did not think any Government could enforce conscription in the light of what the plebiscite revealed to be the feeling of the entire French Canadian population, including those in other provinces than Quebec. . . . unless the House of Commons were united in backing a step of the kind. . . . I gave them to understand I myself would not head an Administration charged with such a task.[98]

Nothing was yet resolved, beyond the agreement of May 8.[99]

The same day Bill 80, the bill to amend the NRMA, was introduced in the House of Commons. Obviously it posed different problems for each of the parties. The Conservatives' difficulty was one of tactics. After much squirming,[100] the Tories had finally united around the belief that conscription was necessary,[101] but there seemed to be insuperable obstacles to drafting an amendment to Bill 80 that would, as House Leader R. B. Hanson said, not 'challenge directly the principle of the Bill and leave the impression in the country that we were opposing it.'[102] The upshot was a Conservative decision to vote for passage of the Bill, a decision that pleased no one. Hanson estimated that there might be as many as sixty Liberal bolters plus the CCF and Social Credit against the Bill. 'If we were to vote against the Government the thing would be very close—I have an idea the Government might be defeated.' But to do this would make an election necessary, delay conscription, and possibly see the battered Conservative Party wiped out. The only option for the Conservatives, therefore, was to vote for Bill 80.[103]

The CCF moved through an equally tortuous course towards a decision. At a special party caucus on May 12, the M.P.s decided to demand the conscription of wealth and industry. If this failed, then the CCF Members would vote against Bill 80. This course had the advantage, in addition, of belatedly showing Quebec that the English-Canadian CCF was concerned with its interests. 'Show trust in Quebec,'

Frank Scott had written to the party's National Secretary, David Lewis, 'press the conscription of wealth, and we have the French.'[104] Soon there was wavering in the caucus, nonetheless,[105] partially attributable to the government's tough budget, brought down in May, which imposed stiff new taxes. From the CCF point of view the budget was a good one, but as Lewis argued in a memorandum that was designed to firm up the caucus, it was not good enough. There were no moves towards social security or to maximum production through conscription of industry and the limitation of profits. In addition, Bill 80 was the climax of government rule by order in council, and the government still sought control over life but not over property. The 'vested interests', he said, 'must not be placed above human life and rights.'[106] The waverers returned to the fold.

The Liberals, the sole party with substantial French-Canadian representation in Parliament, faced the largest problem. At a party caucus on May 12 Mackenzie King addressed himself directly to his Quebec Members, many of whom 'were deeply concerned and seemed to be facing a discouraging situation.' The Prime Minister went laboriously over the reasons for the plebiscite, offered an interpretation of the results, and briefly recounted the Cabinet's difficulties in deciding on the course to be followed. Bill 80 had been introduced in Parliament, he said, to avoid an 'agitation through the country that we were bowing to Quebec and not getting a free hand when we had asked the country in the plebiscite to give us a free hand.' When he was asked if the government would return to Parliament before putting conscription into force, Mackenzie King replied 'that I did not wish to get rid of one commitment in order to make another.' Who knew what conditions would be when or if conscription became necessary? Why give the Opposition a weapon in advance? But, he said, 'I thought they knew my attitude well enough toward Parliament to realize the position I would take.'[107]

That was as far as King could go given his promise to Cabinet on May 8. Whether it would be far enough to keep the Quebec M.P.s from bolting was uncertain. Brooke Claxton wrote to a friend in Montreal that 'four members from Ontario, two from New Brunswick, and fifty-five from Quebec may conceivably vote against repeal,' enough to defeat the government if the Opposition united.[108] In his darker moments the Montreal M.P. believed this to be a real possibility. 'The fools from the province of Quebec are not deliberately doing anything,'

Claxton wrote to J. W. Dafoe. 'They are being led by a handful of disgruntled and frustrated demagogues to divide Canada, ruin their province, and put King and themselves out of public life.' The *nationalistes*, he said, harking back to 1911, 'are again turning over the reins to a group of Tory imperialists. This time—Ralston, Macdonald and Company.'[109] Claxton's bitterness unquestionably had been fueled by the 61-7 vote in the Quebec legislature on May 20, demanding that Ottawa maintain the voluntary system.[110]

The Liberal caucus met again on May 27. The Quebec M.P.s remained unanimous in their view, and the English-speaking remainder was still divided in its attitude. The Prime Minister spoke again, and just before he concluded he said that 'if conscription is necessary, Parliament must decide the matter.' He, Mackenzie King, would not take the responsibility. This came as a shock to the Minister of National Defence for Naval Services because, as Macdonald wrote in his diary, 'His last words were taken by many to mean that after the repeal of Section 3, there would be a further debate in Parliament on the question of conscription. . . . His last statement is at variance with the understanding arrived at in Council about two weeks ago, when he introduced his Bill for the repeal of Section 3. It was then understood,' Macdonald maintained correctly, 'that there was no commitment whatever as to either going to Parliament or not going to Parliament.'[111] Characterized (somewhat harshly) by his fellow clansman, Malcolm MacDonald, as 'charming and incidentally successful but rather "lightweight",'[112] Macdonald complained by letter to King.[113] King, naturally, argued that his words had been misconstrued: 'I had not gone further than make clear that responsibility to Parliament would have to be my guide,' he told the Nova Scotian; '. . . I had made no commitment on the part of the government.'[114] Insignificant in itself, this incident was another blow to the trust between the Prime Minister and his ministers.

Meanwhile Mackenzie King suffered his usual mental agonies in preparing his speech for the second reading of Bill 80. On June 9, the day before he was to speak, he decided finally to omit anything bearing on the question of whether Parliament would debate conscription a second time. 'I felt an immense relief once this was cleared up in my own mind,' he recorded.[115] His speech on June 10 was over two hours long and in it he made his instantly famous statement that his policy was 'not necessarily conscription, but conscription if necessary',[116] a description that was in fact exceedingly accurate. But if King thought he was clear in what he omitted from his speech, many others were thoroughly confused. Both Grant Dexter of the *Winnipeg Free Press* and the American Minister understood him to promise not to return to Parliament for a second debate on conscription.[117] The debate in the House of Commons would go on for another month; the debate in Cabinet would last as long.

When the Cabinet met on June 12, King once again raised the crucial question of another conscription debate. 'I thought it was absolutely necessary that when the time came, if it did come, to put conscription into force, Parliament's approval should be given. That we had lost considerable support already through not making perfectly clear how this was to be done.' A debate could be avoided, King said in answer to Ralston, by telling the House that it had 'a day or two—at the most—to express its approval or disapproval of the Government's action. If they approved, well and good. If they did not, then the Ministry would resign.' Ralston and Macdonald still objected, and King said that if such an eventuality arose he would see the Governor General and ask him to call on one of the Cabinet to become Prime Minister:

> I said to them I would like you to consider the position exactly as I see it now. We are sitting here. The House is in session, will be in session again this afternoon in an hour or two. Does anyone suppose that if that action had to be taken today, with the knowledge of what is owing to Members in the House of Commons, that I could sign an Order to put conscription into force and go an hour later and tell the House that this had been done, and ask for confidence in my action? . . . I said I would never do that.
>
> There was complete silence in the Cabinet. . . . I could see that all my colleagues excepting Ralston and Macdonald were solidly with me.

King had made his position perfectly clear at last. 'If it is agreed that Parliament will approve the Government's action before any action is taken I will . . . stay on and do my best. . . . I shall never be at the head of a Government that will enforce conscription without having Parliament share that responsibility with me.'[118]

For Ralston this was completely unsatisfactory. This honest, honourable, and simple soldier genuinely believed that to go back to Parliament in a time of crisis when men would be desperately needed could cause unnecessary casualties. This was enough for him, enough to justify every effort to prevent King from following such a course. What Ralston neglected in his overriding concern for the soldier at the front, of course, was that he was dealing with a hypothetical situation while King was dealing with actual difficulties. The fragile relationship between English Canada and Quebec was never far from King's mind; it scarcely entered Ralston's. Mackenzie King was aware that delay might endanger the lives of infantry; but he was even more aware that haste now would endanger the life of the nation. In his view, and correctly so, the nation was more important. Two strong men were about to clash directly.

The Defence Minister came to King after the conclusion of Cabinet and said, 'Mr. King, I think I will have to resign.' King was not surprised at this and he was, in fact, prepared to contemplate this eventuality.[119] Still, he tried to persuade Ralston that their differences did not justify such irrevocable action. Ralston, however, argued that the Prime Minister's policy seemed to be devoted to pacifying Quebec. 'It would mean the whole business over again and having the country run by Quebec, to have another debate.' After further discussion, Ralston left with the matter still undecided. Mackenzie King was convinced that Ralston would not resign, at least not on the grounds he was arguing. Such abstruse procedural points 'would never stand in the light of day.' Clearly King was right. The point at issue was important, but scarcely important enough to warrant a resignation or to justify upsetting the war effort and the country at large. Ralston was trying to put pressure on him, King knew, but he also realized that the pressures on Ralston to serve the state in its time of need were greater still.[120]

Even so, the pressure for strong action was growing. 'The Maritimers', Grant Dexter noted privately on June 16, 'fomented revolt over the weekend.' Angus Macdonald was the most bitter:

> . . . I talked with Angus [Dexter said]. He is becoming fatalistic. No use trusting King—a twister and wobbler who does not mean ever to have conscription. He will stand by Ralston. Ilsley will too, he thinks. They must really make King straighten out or force the issue now. He is certain that King means to keep dodging until cornered and then to have a general election. . . . I do not doubt his sincerity.[121]

But, as Dexter noted at the same time, he was getting suggestions that Ralston was looking for 'a good way out. He is running into very heavy weather ahead. The army is too large.'[122]

Whatever his motivation, when Ralston met the Prime Minister on June 15 the two men went over the same ground and again reached no conclusion. According to King's account, Ralston sounded as if he intended to resign, and the Prime Minister had decided to accept this resignation 'rather than yield to his request that an Order-in-Council be signed before obtaining a confidence vote from the Commons.'[123] Ralston's version, recorded by his friend and colleague, Macdonald, was that King's attitude was 'Take it easy. Wait. Do nothing at least until this debate is over.'[124]

So the debate in the Commons went on. Most of the ministers spoke on Bill 80, each carefully carving out his own territory and expressing his own view. The splits in the government were readily apparent and, as Dexter wrote, 'Our ministers now do their fighting in the house and not in the cabinet.'[125] For King, as he saw it, part of the task was to avoid being sustained in his policy only with the support of the Conservatives. On June 16 he calculated that the party might only survive if the Speaker cast a tie-breaking vote. This would never do: 'I thought . . . our men should know that I would not seek to carry on the govt. if I had not the confidence of my own party to enable me to do so independent of any other.'[126] It was the Quebec M.P.s who were causing all the difficulties, and King was not always charitable in understanding the difficulties the Members faced. Aurel Léger, the Acadian M.P. for Kent, New Brunswick, came to see him on July 2: 'It was somewhat pathetic to hear how he was trying to decide for or against the government. He had first decided to stay with us. Then, talked with members of his constituency and received a few letters, which caused him to go the other way.'*[127] But when Ernest Bertrand, the M.P. for Laurier, supported the government King was simply delighted. Joseph Jean (Montreal-Mercier) opposed Bill 80, but 'in a very nice way' and this too impressed King. Both men would be made Cabinet ministers, Bertrand in the fall of 1942 and Jean in the spring of 1945.[128]

The crisis had reached it apogee. At Cabinet on July 7 Mackenzie King told his ministers that he intended to wind up the debate that day. Angus Macdonald recorded what followed.

*It is worth noting that Catholics in English Canada were troubled by the Bill 80 affair. Archbishop McGuigan of Toronto wrote Angus L. Macdonald on 4 July 1942 that 'You and Mr. Power, as Cabinet ministers, have, without making any allusion to religion, made it clear that the Quebec mind is a racial and not a religious attitude. You have thus done a great service to the English-speaking Catholics throughout the whole of Canada.' Public Archives of Nova Scotia, A. L. Macdonald Papers, file 36-116.

On the question he said that if a majority of Liberal Members did not vote for the second reading he would have to go to the Governor General and advise either dissolution of Parliament or that the Governor General should call upon someone else to form a Government. He doubted if a dissolution would be wise at this time. A general election would be a bad thing for the country.

On the question of going back to Parliament he announced that what he had in mind to say was that the Government should come to a decision and then report to Parliament. If Parliament were not in session it should be called immediately. Upon meeting Parliament he would ask for a vote of confidence.

Ralston said he did not know if he could go along with such a policy or not, and Mr. Crerar asked what would happen when he reported to Parliament; would there be a long debate. Mr. King said, 'No.' He would call 'closure' and have a two-day debate. The P.M. said that he intended to declare that he was stating only his own personal opinion as one member of the Government.

Ralston said he did not know whether that would work or not. People would interpret any statement made by the Prime Minister as the statement of the Government. The P.M. then said he could do no less in view of his high regard for Parliament. The weight of opinion in the Cabinet would seem to incline itself to an acceptance of the P.M.'s suggestion, though Ilsley, Howe and I questioned the wisdom of the course proposed. Howe said that if we endorsed conscription and then went to Parliament, we would make it much easier for those opposed to conscription to support us. They could say, 'The thing is done now, and there is nothing to do but support the Government.'

On the P.M.'s method, they would feel it their duty to oppose conscription to the end and would vote against it. . . . Ilsley said that while we talked of closure now, we would not have closure at the time, but that the debate would go on as the present debate has gone on, for a week.

Dr. King, McLarty, MacKinnon and MacKenzie [sic] expressed themselves in favour of the P.M.'s view. Gibson asked what would be wrong with deciding on conscription and putting it into effect before going to Parliament. The P.M. said that some members might feel that that was an insult to them under the rights of Parliament. He felt that if he went to Parliament today and asked for a vote of confidence, he would get it, but if he went to Parliament today and announced that he had put in conscription, he doubted whether he would get it.

We left at 2:45 without any more definite conclusion in our minds.[129]

That night, before King made his speech in the House of Commons, Ralston came to turn in his letter of resignation.*[130] 'When I began to speak,' King wrote in his diary, ' I had his letter in my folder. . . . Was rather amused that in speaking, the resignation was actually in the House on my desk. . . . It was the thing that might have embarrassed anyone whose mind was not definitely set, regardless of consequences, knowing that one was absolutely in the right.'[131] The Prime Minister's long speech ended the debate on Bill 80, and in the vote that followed the government was handsomely sustained with a majority of 104. Only eleven French Canadians voted against the Bill, although others abstained. The CCF voted against, the Conservatives for. [132]

The next morning Mackenzie King spoke for a long time with St Laurent. Since his maiden speech in the House during the Bill 80 debate, St Laurent had risen rapidly in King's estimation.[133] The Justice Minister advised King to see Ralston alone and to argue that his resignation would provoke an election with dangerous consequences for the country. It was not that St Laurent admired the Defence Minister's views, not at all.

---

*Ralston's letter of resignation was polite but firm: '. . . I feel that our views are so definitely conflicting that I should tender my resignation. . . .' The letter went on to give Ralston's interpretation of the meaning of the plebiscite result and of Bill 80, then added: 'But this morning in Council you made clear that . . . you do not intend to put compulsory service overseas actually into effect until you go back to Parliament again for approval. . . . With great respect, I fail to see what good purpose can be served by such a proceeding. . . . I am convinced that the course you propose would be taken as vacillation at a time when decision was needed and that it would do serious injury to our war activities in lowering morale and keeping alive the spirit of disruption and bitterness.' PAC, J. L. Ralston Papers, Vol. 85, Ralston to King, 7 July 1942.

The Prime Minister's reply to this letter, written on July 11, rehearsed Mackenzie King's interpretation of the course he was proposing: 'A reading of my speech in the House . . . will, I think, make wholly clear that I am as strongly opposed, as you are yourself, to a second debate, or to any course which will involve delay in enforcing conscription for service overseas once the government has decided that that step is necessary and expedient.' He concluded his letter by praising Ralston's services and hoping that 'you would be justified in withdrawing your letter. If you do not feel that you should withdraw the letter, I hope you will be willing to allow its existence, at least for the present, to be a matter of confidence between us. . . .' Ibid., King to Ralston, 11 July 1942.

Ralston and those who felt like him [King recorded in his diary about his conversation with St Laurent], did not consider the strictly Canadian point of view at all; that the atmosphere in which Ralston worked was that of not paying any consideration, other than that of regarding the whole of the war effort as something that should be thought of, only in terms of ignoring any opinion other than that which the military mind regarded as worthy of consideration. . . . the setting up of a military dictatorship and ignoring wholly the civil power. . . . an imperialist point of view which, politically, would ignore any distinct Canadian attitude altogether. . . . at the bottom of everything lay the desire to get me out of office. . . .[134]

Meanwhile Macdonald had definitely decided to remain in the government, and the Nova Scotia minister was trying to persuade Ralston to do likewise. So also was Grant Dexter, and even the angry Ilsley doubted that Ralston had grounds for resignation.[135] But King was hearing from others who believed Ralston should be let go. T. A. Crerar argued that his letter should be accepted because 'he saw only one side of things and was not given to considering the social problems as they should be viewed.'[136] This was a remarkable comment from Crerar, a genuine nineteenth-century free-enterprise Liberal.

Ralston was feeling the pressure, too.* He talked with Chubby Power on July 9 and, as Power recorded, 'He appeared to be in state of great perturbation, and more incoherent than I have ever seen him before.'[137] Ralston said that 'he was not sure that he had very strong grounds on what might be considered a matter of procedure, but he had pointed

---

*The conscription debate was not the only matter that had weighed on Ralston's mind. From January until June he had been deeply worried by the Royal Commission inquiry into the Hong Kong disaster. The inquiry had been established in response to charges by George Drew, the Ontario Conservative leader, that the soldiers sent there had been untrained, and that this proved that the voluntary system had failed. (Toronto *Daily Star*, 13 Jan. 1942.) As the responsible Minister, Ralston was directly concerned in this affair, and the Royal Commission, headed by the Chief Justice, Sir Lyman Duff, probed deeply into command arrangements. The result, as released in the *Report on the Canadian Expeditionary Force to the Crown Colony of Hong Kong. . . .* on June 4, was that there had been no serious mismanagement. The Quartermaster-General's branch of National Defence Headquarters, however, was censured for a lack of initiative in moving the Canadian troops' vehicles too late for loading with the expedition. The Conservatives, after a good deal of internal dissension, pressed the matter to a vote of censure in the House of Commons on July 28, 1942; the motion was turned back easily, 130 to 34. For a sketch of the inquiry and the Conservatives' difficulties, see J. L. Granatstein, *The Politics of Survival* (Toronto, 1967), pp. 119ff.

out to the Prime Minister that his objections were mostly to Mr. King's attitude generally on this question of Conscription, and that he felt there was too much procrastination, and backing and filling, and the matter should be brought to a head sometime.' However, Ralston hesitated to provoke the break, and he was afraid of the effects an election might have. To Power, his colleague's reasons were not sufficient, although he did tell Ralston that if Macdonald went, he would go too. But two days later Power told Ralston that 'I did not believe I could go with him.'[138]

Under all this pressure Ralston finally gave in. His diary entry said it all: 'Finally decided, in view of [King's] assurances as to expediting action after decision and freedom to act, and to avoid appearance of quitting in midst of pressing activities, would not press.'[139] On July 13 Power and Macdonald helped Ralston draft a letter to the Prime Minister setting out his terms. 'It is pretty stiff,' Power noted, 'but I think King will accept it. It leaves Ralston free to take any stand he likes on the question of a Vote of Confidence prior or anterior to the decision of the Cabinet to impose Conscription for Overseas, and states that in view of Mr. King's assurances that when the decision is made matters will move swiftly and expeditiously he agrees not to press his resignation for the moment.'*[140] Mackenzie King accepted Colonel Ralston's terms; the letter of resignation, however, was never withdrawn.

For Mackenzie King the successful resolution of this crisis and the final passage of Bill 80 on third reading in the House were great victories. He had kept his government together, except for Cardin's resignation, in the face of terrific pressures. He had put the issue in such a way that Ralston could garner no real support even from his two close friends and colleagues in the Department of National Defence. Parliamentary procedure, even for ministers versed in its nuances,

---

*Ralston's letter, dated July 13, 1942, was much as Power described it. The Minister noted that 'In our discussions since the writing of my letter you have assured me that you would see to it that there would be no delay in obtaining Parliamentary action when a decision is made, and you have told me that you consider that any debate should be curtailed to not more than two days.' In the light of these assurances and 'the understanding indicated in your letter [of July 11] that I will not be bound to the course you have outlined, nor limited in any way in my right to take at any future time whatever course of action I may feel necessary and in the national interest, I am prepared not to press my resignation for the present.' The Prime Minister's reply, sent on July 15, offered King's thanks for Ralston's 'consenting not to press your resignation for the present. I sincerely hope the occasion may not arise when you will feel it necessary to give the matter a further thought.' Copies in PAC, J. L. Ralston Papers, Vol. 85.

hardly seemed sufficient justification for a resignation in the middle of the war. He had been assisted by the military situation, too. There was no need for conscription: casualties did not justify it; recruiting, while slowing, was still adequate; and the Chiefs of Staff had time and again assured the War Committee that the military program could be implemented without it. Second, the approach of the war towards Canada—the Japanese occupation of the Aleutian Islands, the shelling of Estevan Point by a Japanese submarine, the sinking of ships in the St Lawrence—tended to create a genuine justification for keeping troops in Canada. And, finally, the Hong Kong debacle was, or seemed to be, an object lesson on the need to think very carefully before despatching troops abroad.

Above all, in this crisis King had demonstrated an astonishing resilience and toughness. Ralston, seven years younger, came near to cracking under the strain while King was still fresh and alert. On July 10 he noted that 'Ralston looked an ashen grey in colour and his face terribly set with lower jaw protruding as though he was going through a terrific strain. I think he has felt that I would yield and that my position is perhaps stronger than he had realized.'[141] Indeed.

But beyond simply outlasting Ralston and keeping the government intact, what was King's purpose? To the Minister of Mines and Resources, T. A. Crerar, it was clear: '. . . King has never had but one point in his mind. He is determined to bring in conscription without losing Quebec—without forfeiting national unity.'[142] That was a shrewd assessment, for on July 24 King wrote in his diary that 'If we can only keep off putting conscription into force, we will have little trouble when the time comes for that to be necessary.'[143] But how to judge necessity? That was the question asked by Field Marshal Sir John Dill, the British representative on the Joint Chiefs of Staff in Washington. King's answer was clear.

I said if today there were an offensive and there was need for more reinforcements, I would say that at present it was necessary. That I would certainly agree that if, in January or February, there was not all the reinforcements that were needed, and could not be got without conscription, that at that time it would necessary. That, as a matter of fact, with conscription in Canada, and men being trained and volunteers enlisting for overseas in numbers required, it seemed to me wrong to try simply to get an order through before any necessity had arisen.[144]

The question of necessity would return to haunt King, but certainly in his conversation with Dill he did not sound like a man prepared to resist conscription to the death.

Significantly, King's fight in June and July had convinced Quebec Liberals that he was indispensable. Some Quebec Members had voted against King, but they all recognized that they needed him. St Laurent told Grant Dexter that 'provided that the need for conscription could be reasonably proved, Quebec would accept it under King. The members would vote against but would then support the law and would not lose face with their constituencies.'[145] A poll in late August 1942 tended to confirm this regard for the Prime Minister when it found that fully 50 per cent of French Canadians believed that Mackenzie King was the greatest living Canadian,[146] a substantial tribute and one that was offered in spite of the plebiscite.

King's single error in this long, arduous struggle concerned Colonel Ralston. Crerar had been right in his assessment of the Minister of National Defence—Ralston was too inflexible. The resignation, once offered, should have been accepted at once. That he chose to put the unity of the Cabinet as his first goal, however, cannot really be held against King. But the price of that unity would be high indeed and it would be paid in full in October and November 1944.

---

1 Public Archives of Canada [PAC], Privy Council Records, Cabinet War Committee Records, Minutes, 23 Apr. 1941.

2 *Ibid.*, 30 Apr. 1941; J. W. Pickersgill, *The Mackenzie King Record*, Vol. I: *1939-1944* (Toronto, 1960), p. 220.

3 PAC, W. L. Mackenzie King Papers, Diary, 9 May 1941.

4 King Papers, 'Reports on Recruiting . . . ,' ff. C244254ff. Districts 8 and 9 had ceased to exist athough the numbering was not changed.

5 Cabinet War Committee Records, Minutes, 20 May 1941.

6 King Diary, 20 May 1941.

7 Cabinet War Committee Records, Minutes, 20, 21 May 1941. In fact the telegram was not sent by King as had been agreed. See C. P. Stacey, *Arms, Men and Governments: The War Policies of Canada, 1939-1945* (Ottawa, 1971), pp. 41-2.

8 Pickersgill, I, p. 222.

9 *Ibid.*, p. 224.

10 See the superb analysis of press coverage during King's trip in Fergus Glenn, 'The Conscription Build-Up', *Canadian Forum*, XXI (October, 1941).

11 *Ibid.*

12 Jean-Charles Harvey, *French Canada at War* (Toronto, 1941), pp. 9-10.

13 PAC, Arthur Meighen Papers, Meighen to H. R. Milner, 14 May 1941. On this Conservative material, see J. L. Granatstein, *The Politics of Survival* (Toronto, 1967), pp. 74ff.

14 Meighen Papers, Meighen to MacPherson, 7 Aug. 1941.

15 Toronto *Telegram*, 30 Oct. 1941.

16 Meighen Papers, Meighen to H. Clark, 14 Nov. 1941.

17 Toronto *Globe and Mail*, 13 Nov. 1941.

18 King Papers, Notes, 13 Nov. 1941, ff. C244474ff.

19 Pickersgill, I, pp. 282-3.

20 *Ibid.*, pp. 270-1; Queen's University, C. G. Power Papers, Memo, 'Appointment of . . . St Laurent to the King Cabinet 1941', n.d.

21 Louis St Laurent interview, 6 Nov. 1971.

22 King Diary, 14 Nov. 1941.

23 Queen's University, Grant Dexter Papers, Memo, 18 Nov. 1941.

24 See Ralston's report to Parliament in House of Commons *Debates*, 5 Nov. 1941, pp. 4112ff.

25 Dexter Papers, Memo, 20 Nov. 1941; PAC, Ralston Papers, Vol. 144, 'Potential Manpower Reserve', n.d.; *ibid.*, 'Manpower Committee Minutes', 16 Dec. 1941—9 Jan. 1942.

26 Dexter Papers, Memo, 9 Dec. 1941. See on French Canadians in the military, J.-Y. Gravel, 'Le Québec Militaire, 1939-1945', in J.-Y. Gravel, ed., *Le Québec et La Guerre* (Montréal, 1974), pp. 84ff.

27 King Diary, 2 Dec. 1941.

28 King Papers, 3 Dec. 1941, ff. C244478ff.

29 King Diary, 3 Dec. 1941; Cabinet War Committee Records, Minutes, 3 Dec. 1941.

30 King Diary, 4 Dec. 1941.

31 *Ibid.*, 9-10 Dec. 1941.

32 Pickersgill, I, pp. 308-9.

33 King Diary, 10 Dec. 1941.

34 *Ibid.*, 11 Dec. 1941.

35 *Ibid.*, 12 Dec. 1941.

36 *Ibid.*

37 *Ibid.*, 16 Dec. 1941.

38 *Ibid.*, 17 Dec. 1941.

39 Public Archives of Nova Scotia, A. L. Macdonald Papers, Diary, 18 Dec. 1941.

40 *Ibid.*; Power Papers, Mackenzie to Power, 19 Dec. 1941; King Diary, 19 Dec. 1941; King Papers, ff. C256616ff.

41 King Diary, 19 Dec. 1941; Dexter Papers, Memo, 22 Dec. 1941.

42 Pickersgill, I, p. 316.

43 *Ibid.*, p. 335.

44 *Ibid.*, p. 334; King Diary, 5 Jan. 1942.

45 King Papers, 8 Jan. 1942, ff. C244522-4.

46 Queen's University, T. A. Crerar Papers, Crerar to Dafoe, 8 Jan. 1942.

47 King Diary, 15 Jan. 1942; Crerar Papers, 'Memorandum dictated by Minister . . . January 16 . . .'

48 King Diary, 19 Jan. 1942.

49 The wording of the question was approved in Cabinet on 20 Jan. 1942. King Papers, Memo by Heeney, f. C257021.

50 Crerar Papers, Crerar to Dafoe, 23 Jan. 1942. For a report of a less harmonious caucus, see Macdonald Diary, 28 Jan. 1942.

51 Fondation Lionel-Groulx, Fonds Bloc Populaire Canadien, Hon. Cardin file, pen note, n.d.

52 Harvard University, Pierrepont Moffat Papers, Vol. 47, Memo of Conversation with M. Philippe Brais. . . . , 24 Jan. 1942.

53 *Ibid.*, Memo of Conversation with Mr J. W. McConnell . . . , 24 Jan. 1942.

54 Robert Rumilly, *Histoire de la Province de Québec*, tome XXXIX: *Le plébiscite* (Montréal, 1969), p. 184.

55 King Diary, 27 Jan. 1942; Dexter Papers, Memorandum, 27 Jan. 1942.

56 Macdonald Diary, 31 Jan. 1942, 'Conversation Ralston and I had with P.M. . . .'; copy in Ralston Papers, Vol. 53; King Diary, 31 Jan. 1942.

57 Ralston Papers, Vol. 148, 'The Influence of Compulsory Service . . .', 25 Jan. 1942.

58 This 'tradition' had been honoured by King in 1938 when Dr Manion was seeking election in a London, Ontario, by-election.

59 On the by-election, see J. L. Granatstein, 'The York South By-Election of 1942', *Canadian Historical Review*, XLVIII (June, 1967); Granatstein, *Politics of Survival*, pp. 102ff.; M. J. Coldwell interview, 6 July 1963; U.S. National Archives, State Department Records, 842.00/626, Moffat to Secretary of State, 7 Feb. 1942 and *ibid.*, 842.00/650, 14 Feb. 1942.

60 PAC, J. W. Dafoe Papers, Crerar to Dafoe, 10 Feb. 1942. An opinion poll on 14 Feb. 1942, however, found 54 per cent opposed to the decision to call the plebiscite. *Public Opinion Quarterly*, VI (Summer, 1942), 312. For criticism of the plebiscite, see King Papers, Notes and Memoranda, Vol. 140, Plebiscite file #2, 'Criticisms of the Plebiscite', n.d., and editorials in virtually every Conservative newspaper on 23 Jan. 1942.

61 PAC, Brooke Claxton Papers, Vol. 53, Claxton to J. M. Macdonnell, 18 Feb. 1942.

62 King Diary, 3-4 Feb. 1942.

63 Rumilly, XXXIX, p. 187.

64 André Laurendeau, *La Crise de la conscription 1942* (Montréal, 1962), p. 82.

65 *Ibid.*

66 Fondation Lionel-Groulx, Fonds de La Ligue pour la défense du Canada, pamphlet files.

67 Fondation Lionel-Groulx, Fonds Maxime Raymond, pamphlet of speech, 5 février 1942.

68 Fonds LPDC, livre de caisse 1942; 'souscription' files; Montreal file, J. P. Cloutier to Laurendeau, 6 mai 1942.

69 *Ibid.*, 'Presse' file, Laurendeau to C. L'Heureux, 17 avr. 1942.

70 M.-A. Gagnon, *Jean-Charles Harvey, Précurseur de la révolution tranquille* (Montréal, 1970), p. 194; Rumilly, XXXIX, p. 218; Laurendeau, p. 97; King Diary, 19 Mar. 1942. Cf., *ibid.*, 12-13 May 1942. On *La Presse*, see Pierre Godin, *L'information-opium: une histoire politique du journal La Presse* (Montréal, 1973) pp. 104ff.

71 F. W. Peers, *The Politics of Canadian Broadcasting* (Toronto, 1969), pp. 328-31; King Papers, Notes and Memoranda, Vol. 141, Plebiscite file no. 3, Pickersgill to King, 2 Mar. 1942. The Radio Broadcasting Censor, R. P. Landry, objected to the use of radio for plebiscite speeches, but he was assured that the policy was that of the government. Directorate of History, National Defence Headquarters, file 951.059(D2), Landry to T. C. Davis, 13 Apr. 1942 and reply 13 Apr. 1942. For Laurendeau's complaint, see Fonds LPDC, radio files, Laurendeau to Frigon, 4 avr. 1942.

72 L.-A. Frechette, 'A Chacun ses responsabilités', *L'Action Nationale*, XIX (avril, 1942), 220-1; Fonds LPDC, Montreal file, E. Simard to Laurendeau, 20 avr. 1942.

73 Rumilly, XXXIX, pp. 212ff; Laurendeau, pp. 96-8; King Diary, 13 Mar. 1942.

74 Rumilly, XXXIX, p. 214; King Diary, 26 Mar. 1942.

75 E.g. from Fonds LPDC, pamphlet files; PAC, L.-P. Picard Papers; and *L'Action Nationale*, XIX (janv., fév.-mars, 1942).

76 Figures as published in *Public Opinion Quarterly*, VI (Fall, 1942), 488-9.

77 King Papers, McLarty to King, 6 Mar. 1942, ff. 71365-7, and 25 Mar. 1942, 71369ff.

78 Queen's University, Norman Lambert Papers, Diary, 27 Apr. 1942.

79 King Diary, 1 Apr. 1942.

80 *Ibid.*, 10 Apr. 1942.

81 Moffat Papers, Vol. 47, Memo of Conversation with T. C. Davis, 21 Apr. 1942.

82 Picard Papers, leaflet.

83 King Diary, 3 Apr. 1942.

84 *L'Action Nationale*, XIX (mai, 1942) 299-312.

85 'What did "No" Mean?', *Canadian Forum*, XXII (June, 1942).

86 King Diary, 27 Apr. 1942.

87 *Ibid.*, 28 Apr. 1942.

88 Macdonald Diary, 28 Apr. 1942.

89 King Diary, 1 May 1942.

90 Crerar Papers, Crerar to King, 1 May 1942; Dexter Papers, Memorandum, 6 May 1942.

91 Pickersgill, I, p. 366.

92 *Ibid.*

93 *Ibid.*, p. 367; Dexter Papers, Memo, 6 May 1942.

94 Pickersgill, I, pp. 368-9.

95 King Diary, 9 May 1942.

96 Dexter Papers, Memorandum, 11 May 1942.

97 Moffat Papers, Vol. 43, Memo of conversation with G. O'Leary, 11 May 1942.

98 Pickersgill, I, pp. 371-2.

99 St Laurent apparently thought King had secured agreement on returning to Parliament, or so Dexter told Macdonald. Macdonald Diary, 13 May 1942.

100 PAC, R. B. Hanson Papers, file P-450-C, Hanson to J. A. Clark, 6 May 1942; Granatstein, p. 118.

101 Queen's University, Herbert Bruce Papers, Bruce to Meighen, 12 May 1942; Hanson Papers, file S-815 #2, Memo for caucus and att. notes, 12 May 1942; Rodney Adamson Papers, (Port Credit, Ontario), Diary, 12, 19 May 1942.

102 Hanson Papers, file S-175-M, Hanson to Meighen, 14 May 1942.

103 *Ibid.*, file S-175-J, Hanson to Sen. G. B. Jones, 16 June 1942.

104 PAC, M. J. Coldwell Papers, Memo by D. Lewis on Bill 80, 30 June 1942; M. S. D. Horn, 'The League for Social Reconstruction: Socialism and Nationalism in Canada, 1931-45', Ph.D. thesis, University of Toronto, 1969, 477.

105 Queen's University, G. M. A. Grube Papers, Grube to Noseworthy, 4 July 1942.

106 Coldwell Papers, Lewis memo, 30 June 1942.

107 Pickersgill, I, p. 374; Macdonald Diary, 12 May 1942.

108 Claxton Papers, Vol. 44, Claxton to H. A. Kidd, 14 May 1942.

109 Dafoe Papers, Claxton to Dafoe, 21 May 1942. This view was shared by Pierrepont Moffat. See State Department Records, 842.00/640, Moffat to Secretary of State, 21 May 1942.

110 Rumilly, xxxix, pp. 260-4; State Department Records, 843.00/642, Moffat to Secretary of State, 23 May 1942.

111 Macdonald Diary, 27 May 1942.

112 Public Record Office [PRO], Dominions Office Records, DO 35/586, High Commissioner to Secretary of State for Dominion Affairs [SSDA], 4 Aug. 1942.

113 Macdonald Diary, letter of 28 May 1942 attached.

114 Pickersgill, I, p. 379; Macdonald Diary, 4 June 1942.

115 Pickersgill, I, p. 380.

116 House of Commons *Debates*, 10 June 1942, p. 3236.

117 Dexter Papers, Memorandum, 16 June 1942; Moffat Papers, Vol. 47, Memo, 11 June 1942.

118 Pickersgill, I, pp. 383-4; Macdonald Diary, 12 June 1942.

119 So were other ministers. 'CDH[owe] referred to Ralston in front of T.A.C[rerar]. in talking to P.M. "as making no difference whether he stayed or not".' Lambert Diary, 31 May 1942.

120 Pickersgill, I, pp. 384-6.

121 Dexter Papers, Memorandum, 16 June 1942.

122 *Ibid.*

123 Pickersgill, I, p. 387.

124 Macdonald Diary, 16 June 1942.

125 Dexter Papers, Memo, 16 June 1942.

126 King Diary, 16 June 1942.

127 *Ibid.*, 2 July 1942.

128 Pickersgill, I, p. 390.

129 Macdonald Diary, 7 July 1942; Pickersgill, I, pp. 392ff.; Ralston Papers, Vol. 85, Diary Notes, 7 July 1942; 'Backstage at Ottawa', *Maclean's*, 15 Aug. 1942, 15.

130 Letter in Ralston Papers, Vol. 85.

131 Pickersgill, I, p. 395; Ralston Papers, Diary Notes, 7 July 1942.

132 The Tories were jubilant at the CCF vote, which they saw as halting the slide to the CCF, particularly in Saskatchewan. Meighen Papers, M. MacPherson to Meighen, 9 July 1942. But Jimmy Gardiner was afraid that the CCF vote had been calculated to win support in Saskatchewan and Quebec. Saskatchewan Archives, J. G. Gardiner Papers, T. H. Wood to Gardiner, 9 July 1942 and reply, 15 July 1942. On the CCF decision, see Walter Young, *The Anatomy of a Party: The National CCF 1932-61* (Toronto, 1969), pp. 230-1; Dominions Office Records, DO 35/586, High Commissioner to SSDA, 4 Aug. 1942.

133 Dexter Papers, Memorandum, 17 July 1942.

134 King Diary, 8 July 1942; Pickersgill, I, p. 397; Dale Thomson, *Louis St. Laurent, Canadian* (Toronto, 1967), p. 125; Ralston Papers, Diary Notes, 8 July 1942.

135 Macdonald Diary, 8-9 July 1942.

136 King Diary, 9 July 1942.

137 Power Papers, Memorandum for the Record, entry 12 July 1942.

138 *Ibid.*; Norman Ward, ed., *A Party Politician: The Memoirs of Chubby Power* (Toronto, 1966), pp. 136ff.; Pickersgill, I, pp. 400-1. Quebec *nationalistes* did not fear the prospect of the resignation of the Defence ministers. Pelletier, the editor of *Le Devoir*, thought it might produce a government 'moins coco'. Fondation Lionel-Groulx, Fonds Georges Pelletier, Pelletier to L. Richer, 17 juillet 1942.

139 Ralston Papers, Diary Notes, 10-13 July 1942.

140 Power Papers, Memo for Record.

141 Pickersgill, I, p. 402.

142 Dexter Papers, Memo, 17 July 1942.

143 King Diary, 24 July 1942.

144 *Ibid.*, 12 July 1942.

145 Dexter Papers, Memorandum, 21 July 1942.

146 Poll of 26 Aug. 1942 in *Public Opinion Quarterly*, VI (Winter, 1942), 657.

7. Public Welfare and Party Benefit

'I have been thinking a good deal in the last 48 hours about the future,' Mackenzie King wrote in his diary early in January 1943 after his trip to Brockville, Ontario, for the funeral of Senator George P. Graham, a former Cabinet colleague. Ian Mackenzie, the Minister of Pensions and Health, 'said to me that he thought what should be done,'

> what he would like to see done and what he believes the party would like and be best for the country would be for me to lead the party through another general election. To make the post-war program of social reform, and the peace conference, the main subject of appeal. That it would be a natural rounding out of my life-work. . . . old age pensions; unemployment insurance, etc. We could now add: health insurance. In other words, make a complete programme of social security. My whole record of public life would back up the sincerity of my appeal. Also framing of peace would make a strong appeal. . . . I agreed with him that nothing could more completely please me if I had the physical strength and endurance; that I was not anxious to stay on were I to become, in any way, impaired in health or lose mental vigour.

At the very least, King told himself, he should stay until the war was won, and certainly he would not want to retire before August 1944, a date that would mark his quarter-century of leading the Liberal Party.[1]

That conversation with Mackenzie was a crucial one for King, and one that marked the beginning of a new period for the Prime Minister. The issues discussed would dominate King's thinking—and the country's—to an increasing extent through 1943 and 1944. Everyone in government, in the civil service, and in industry seemed afraid that the dislocations that would accompany the reconversion to peace would be marked with massive unemployment and popular unrest. People would not willingly accept a return to the conditions of the 1930s, not after the relatively prosperous wartime years. Social welfare legislation, fundamentally conservative in intent, could help damp down this unrest; it could cushion the shocks of peace; it could help re-elect the Liberal Party and thus maintain the free-enterprise economy against the assaults from the left. These were vital factors in Mackenzie King's view because he expected that the political balance after the next election, whenever that might be, was certain to be delicate. He told J. W. Pickersgill on January 8th, 1943 that 'The chances were that there would be 4 parties; not one of which would be able to command a majority in the House. The party with which others would be least apt to ally themselves would be the Conservative party . . . some kind of a coalition between the C.C.F. and the Liberals. The situation might very easily be similar to what it was when I took office in 1921 with the Liberals being the party with the largest following.'[2]

That was not an unlikely assessment of events. Certainly there seemed no prospect of a great surge of support for the Liberal government on the scale of that in 1940. After the plebiscite and the wearying fight over Bill 80, after three and a half years of war, the government was tired and not a little dispirited. Canada's record in the war was highly creditable, but it had not been dramatic. The armed forces had yet to win the chance for heroics on a large and sustained scale, and there was little opportunity for posturing inherent in the enormous Canadian production of war materiel. Even such achievements as the billion dollar gift to Britain tended to reinforce the image of Canada as a producer/banker, not as fighter.

The government suffered from this image. It suffered as well from a too strong emphasis on 'winning the war first' in all its propaganda. The people didn't need or want such exhortatory speeches, Brooke Claxton noted in a memorandum in late 1943, for they were well aware of the needs of the time and of the possibilities of suffering and loss.[3] What was required now, the Montreal M.P. and King's parliamentary assistant*

---

*The first parliamentary assistants were named on April 29th, 1943 and additional ones were appointed shortly thereafter. They included, in addition to Claxton, D. C. Abbott (to the Minister of Finance), Lionel Chevrier (to the Minister of Munitions and Supply), Paul Martin (to the Minister of Labour), and Joseph Jean (to the Minister of Justice).

said, was to focus people's attention on the postwar period, on the better world that victory would bring. Morale was slumping, he told Mackenzie King. 'At the time when the Canadian people are beginning to realize and take pride in the immense job that has been accomplished in the war, large sections of the population are feeling uncertain and critical because they do not see action in dealing with post-war reconstruction.'[4] This was not simply his impression, Claxton said. The Wartime Information Board, the government's propaganda arm, reported that when asked 'Are there any of these things that you would like to know more about?' people overwhelmingly selected 'Plans for After the War' from out of a list of twelve items.[5] Earlier the Wartime Information Board had reported to the Prime Minister that its opinion sampling found the public's reaction to the coming of the postwar period to be 'something akin to dread'. The people wanted 'great changes' once the war was won, and paradoxically, of course, the people wanted the changes now. At the very least, the public had to learn how the government intended to create this better world, this world fit for heroes.[6]

If the Liberals had been slow to learn this lesson, the CCF and the Tories had not. The CCF had been pressing hard for social security for years and their efforts had received a substantial boost from their success in the York South by-election of February 1942. If the people were concerned about such questions, it was a tribute to the effectiveness of the CCF campaign for them. The Conservatives, too, seemed to have accepted the result of York South and come to terms with the new reality. After drifting aimlessly into the summer of 1942, some moderate and progressive men had seized the party reins. At a conference at Port Hope, Ontario in the early days of September, a forward-looking platform had been drafted. The leading figure in the Conservative revival was J. M. Macdonnell, the President of the National Trust Company and one of the men whom King had asked to join the government in 1940. In articles and speeches the Toronto Conservative called for a 'New National Policy' with social security as its goal; the state, he wrote, had to provide every citizen with employment at a wage that 'will enable him to live in decency'. In a speech to the Toronto Conservative Businessmen's Club in June 1943, he was more explicit still: 'I would say: "would you rather adopt a policy which will retain the largest amount possible of free enterprise or—hand over to the C.C.F.?" In plain words I would say—"Half a loaf is better than no bread".'[7] Macdonnell and other 'Port Hopefuls' took their new Conservatism to the party's

Winnipeg convention in December 1942 and succeeded in getting it adopted. The Conservative Party was now officially committed to social security, full employment, collective bargaining, and medical insurance. More, the party had a new leader in John Bracken, the long-time Liberal-Progressive Premier of Manitoba, and at Bracken's insistence the party had a new name too, one that reflected the import of the new policy. As the Progressive Conservative Party, the Tories would set out to defeat both the CCF and its socialism and Mackenzie King and his policies of delay and evasion.[8]

I

Only the Liberal Party seemed left out of the trend to reorganization and to advanced policies. The party machinery was in bad condition, no doubt of that. After the election of 1940, in fact, the National Liberal Federation virtually ceased to exist. The Cabinet had discussed the future of the Federation in January 1941 and had named Senator A. N. K. Hugesson of Montreal to be President. But Hugesson was unable to make the machine function at all, and matters drifted again until the beginning of 1943 when the Cabinet's newly created committee on organization appointed Norman McLarty, the Secretary of State, to take over the NLF in addition to his ministerial duties. McLarty studied the organizational weaknesses of the party—in three provinces there was no organization left—but he was unable to get further than re-opening an office and getting mailing lists in hand.[9] Severe shocks would be needed to wake the slumbering Liberal Party.

If the party was moribund, the bureaucracy of the civil service was not, and there was substantially more preparatory activity in Ottawa for postwar reconstruction than critics realized. The most important step, far and away, was the final passage of the Unemployment Insurance Act in the late summer of 1940. This was a measure that had been in the works for several years, but Mackenzie King had refused to press ahead with it because of objections from New Brunswick, Alberta, and Quebec to any cession of their powers to the Dominion. With the change of government in Quebec, however, and with personal pressures exerted on the two other recalcitrant premiers, by early January 1940 King had finally secured provincial consent from all provinces except Alberta to a constitutional amendment giving Ottawa power to operate the unemployment insurance plan.

This was important because, in King's view, the scheme had to be started in good times. 'Authorities in the field of unemployment insurance', he wrote to the premiers on January 16, 1940, 'are generally agreed that the most favourable time for its establishment is a period of rising employment, during which a fund can be built up out of which benefits can subsequently be paid.'[10] Premier Aberhart of Alberta received an additional note informing him that New Brunswick and Quebec 'advised me that they realized the great importance of having immediate steps taken to meet post-war conditions of unemployment, and are now prepared to give their consent to an amendment.' Aberhart would soon be brought into line.[11]

There was rather more difficulty with the Cabinet. On January 16 the unemployment insurance proposals drew general support, King noted, 'but Ralston, Howe and Ilsley were outspoken about it. Ralston, on the score that we needed the money for the prosecution of the war, that we had spent enough on socialistic legislation in what we had done for unemployment relief, housing, etc. . . . looked like an election appeal.' This kind of backwards-looking conservatism infuriated Mackenzie King who observed that 'Howe has very much the employer's mentality. Ilsley is just blind with prejudice. Ralston has set his whole mentality in the direction of keeping down expenditures. . . . He has been closely associated with large corporations and is out of touch with the social trend.' He disliked fighting with Ralston, the Prime Minister added, but he would have the satisfaction of knowing that if the measure was adopted 'it is due to the fact that I have taken a definite stand in Council.'*[12]

The Unemployment Insurance Bill finally passed through the House and Senate in the summer of 1940. On August 1, Mackenzie King patted himself on the back:

> This is really a great achievement for the Liberal Party. We inaugurated social legislation [with] the old age pensions measure. Set out to get a federal measure of unemployment insurance. Got the

---

*Although King was thinking of postwar needs when he pressed for the measure, unemployment was still a terrible problem in the first year of the war. A report from the Economic Advisory Committee, the key body of senior civil servants that exercised a watchdog role on all war-finance measures, reported that 612,000 people were on direct relief as of March 1, 1940 with a further 160,000 fully employed on direct relief. The situation was worst in Quebec—in Hull 23.3 per cent of the total population was on direct relief as of December 1939, and in Chicoutimi the figure was an incredible 35.3 per cent. The one ray of hope was that unemployment in the country had decreased by 104,000 since April 1939. King Papers, Report of Economic Advisory Committee, 2 May 1940, ff. 232126ff.

B.N.A. Act amended to give power to the federal government to legislate; got consent of all provinces of Canada to this end, and have now got the bill through both Houses. It will be law in a few days. For all time to come, that will remain to the credit of the Liberal Party under my leadership. It was when I was nominated leader that the party for the first time committed itself to this particular reform.[13]

It was a great achievement, but it had been a long wait since 1919.

Other measures of reconstruction planning were being undertaken by the Cabinet Committee on Demobilization and Re-establishment that had been set up on December 8, 1939 under the chairmanship of Ian Mackenzie. This Cabinet group was primarily charged with the task of re-integrating the members of the armed forces into civilian society, but because ministers were always busy with departmental chores, relatively little was accomplished. The committee's major achievement, it seems, was to establish the General Advisory Committee on Demobilization and Rehabilitation, a committee of civil servants, on August 10, 1940. Within a year of its founding the Advisory Committee had begun to propose the revision and amendment of existing legislation to provide benefits to servicemen and to begin the task of drafting the various schemes for war gratuities that would eventually make the Canadian program of veterans' benefits the best anywhere.[14]

For the first four years of the war Ian Mackenzie was at the heart of the entire planning process for rehabilitation and demobilization. The British Columbia minister had not been a success as Minister of National Defence, and the inefficiencies in the department's contracting procedures had embarrassed King and the government. The Prime Minister's friendship saved Mackenzie's political career, and in September 1939 he had been transferred to the Department of Pensions and Health, a less demanding portfolio than National Defence. Still, Mackenzie was no fool, and he wanted to make a success of his new portfolio. He could see that the public would want a brave, new world with the peace, and his department, with its mandate to oversee pensions and health, seemed a logical place to begin work to reconstruct society.[15]

In early 1941, therefore, Mackenzie was instrumental in getting the Cabinet to authorize the formation of still another Committee 'to examine and discuss the general question of post-war reconstruction, and to make recommendations as to what Government facilities should be established to deal with this question.'[16] In March Mackenzie convened a meeting of a group of men with a view to forming them into a

Committee on Reconstruction. Attending Mackenzie's gathering were Principal F. Cyril James of McGill University, Principal W. S. Wallace of Queen's University, Tom Moore of the Trades and Labour Congress, J. S. Maclean of Canada Packers, and Dr Edouard Montpetit of the Université de Montréal. Principal James, an Englishman who had been educated in the United States and who had taught at the University of Pennsylvania for a dozen years before coming to McGill in 1939, was named chairman.[17]

At its first meeting on March 22 the Committee on Reconstruction tentatively laid out the areas it was to study. Such questions as the effectiveness of wartime controls and the desirability of their continuing in peacetime would be looked at, as would measures of physical reconstruction, trade, and the conversion of industry to peacetime uses.[18] The Committee soon secured the right to hire a small research staff and to draw on public funds for travel and secretarial help,[19] but its status remained unclear. In July 1941 Principal James wrote to Mackenzie demanding a broader role for his committee, the right to pursue research in the United States and the United Kingdom, and access to government departments. Matters had been brought to a head, James complained, by the appointment of the Joint Economic Committees established by the Canadian and American governments on June 20, 1941 as a by-product of the economic integration facilitated by the Hyde Park agreement. The Joint Economic Committees' mandate included studying steps necessary to reduce postwar economic dislocation. To James and to Mackenzie, who was embarrassed to admit that he had never heard of the Canadian-American bodies, the JEC were threats to the status of the Committee on Reconstruction.[20] James' complaint and the Minister's subsequent representations to Cabinet resulted in a new order in council on September 2, 1941 that put the Committee onto firm foundations at last. It was to report to the Cabinet Committee on Demobilization and Rehabilitation on the economic and social implications of the transition from war to peace.[21]

The Committee on Reconstruction had already acquired as its research director Leonard C. Marsh,[22] a young British-born economist who had worked for Sir William Beveridge at the London School of Economics and who, in his ten years at McGill, had demonstrated both an interest in and a capacity for research into social problems. Marsh, like many other young academics in the 1930s, sympathized with the CCF, and he was a member of the League for Social Reconstruction, the party's intellectual prop.[23] Under Marsh's direction the Committee on Reconstruction began a fairly extensive research program in areas such as agriculture, resources development and conservation, construction, housing, employment, and women's postwar problems.

Principal James himself prepared the first draft of the 'memorandum', the basic document that set out the Committee's conception of its role and purposes. 'The central problem of postwar reconstruction', this memorandum, written in May 1941, stated, 'is the finding of adequate employment opportunities for the returning soldiers, as well as for the men and women who will no longer be required in the munitions factories.' The Committee's biases were frankly stated: 'It is unanimously assumed . . . that our ultimate aim is the maintenance of individual liberty and the preservation of democratic institutions. Even though satisfactory reconstruction policies may require some restriction of economic liberty during the period immediately following the war, such restrictions should be as few as possible and so designed that they will facilitate the restoration of maximum individual liberty in the shortest possible time.' Proper timing of reconstruction measures was going to be important too. Underlying everything James' memorandum said was the expectation that rapid inflation at first, then recession at best and depression at worst would follow the war, exactly as had occurred after the Great War. Again and again this was stated as certainty: 'If, for any reason, reconstruction should not proceed smoothly during the postwar recession the country would inevitably be confronted by rapidly mounting unemployment and widespread dissatisfaction.'[24] Principal James feared for the worst, and he expected a repetition of the pattern of events from 1919 to 1921. There had been great social unrest at that time—the Winnipeg General Strike was one example—but the Great War had not taken place after a decade-long depression like this war. The Canadian people might not be willing to return to distressed economic conditions with the peace; this made skilfull reconstruction policies a vital necessity.

The work of the Committee continued throughout 1942. In March the House of Commons established its own Special Committee on Reconstruction and Re-establishment before which James Committee members frequently appeared, as Principal James put it, 'as a means of testing out many ideas that had been developed . . . , of familiarizing many Members of Parliament more effectively with what was going on, and of providing a channel for suggestions, proposals and ideas that they were able to put forward.'[25] In October the Committee on Reconstruction filed a report with the Minister of Pensions and Health, 'the first concrete report' on reconstruction. The major recommendation was that planning for the postwar period should be the responsibility of a Minister of Economic Planning, a recommendation with which Ian Mackenzie concurred.[26] But this proposal was frowned on by the Economic Advisory Committee, the group of senior civil servants that played a crucial role in all economic questions. The committee of mandarins argued that such a ministry would be unsuccessful and inexpedient, and to ensure that no similar proposals emerged from the Committee on Reconstruction it proposed making the James Committee responsible not to Mackenzie but to the President of the Privy Council, Mackenzie King in other words, the minister to whom the Economic Advisory Committee also reported. If James could not get the support of Ian Mackenzie behind his proposals before they went to Cabinet, his Committee would be effectively circumscribed if not completely emasculated. Under a new order in council in January 1943,[27] the changes were formalized and, in addition, James' Committee henceforth became known as the Advisory Committee on Reconstruction, a significant change in status. At the same time, to make the humbling of the James Committee complete, the Economic Advisory Committee established its own reconstruction planning body under Professor W. A. Mackintosh, a mandarin of great influence and ability.

But if the Committee had been gutted in the bureaucratic infighting, it did not yet seem aware of it, for it was soon involved in what was unquestionably its most important activity: the preparation of the Report on Social Security for Canada, the Marsh Report.* The genesis of the Report is found in a note that Principal James jotted down after meeting Ian Mackenzie on December 19, 1942, just two and a half weeks after the release of the Beveridge Report in England, a report that promised Great Britain a wholesale revision of the social order. 'IM wants to present a general Social Security plan to Parliament in

---

*After the Marsh Report, the James Committee continued its work, still under assault from the civil servants. Its final report was sent to the Prime Minister in September 1943, and not published until the new year. The Advisory Committee's recommendations were explicitly free-enterprise in tone, including the end or reduction of corporation and excess-profits taxes. Very few of its proposals were adopted, although the enormous sweep of its research studies had turned up good ideas. (See *Report of the Advisory Committee on Reconstruction* (Ottawa, 1944); Department of Finance, W. Clifford Clark Papers, file E-3-5, 'Main Recommendations of the Report . . . ,' 17 Nov. 1943; King Papers, Vol. 59, King to James, 11 Oct. 1943.) Part of the difficulty from which the James Committee suffered was King's dislike for Principal James: 'I said James was an ass of a fellow,' he told the Governor General. King Diary, 8 Aug. 1943.

February,' James wrote. 'He says he has a Health Bill ready. . . . I said if all the data were ready in skeleton form we would consider the matter at the meeting on the 8th [January]—but I doubt if it will be ready. IM said he would see that it is ready.'[28] The task of preparation fell to Marsh, a man whose training and research fitted him for the task. Two days after the Minister's instruction, Marsh had already been to see Mackenzie's secretary with an outline of the proposed study.[29]

The next month was extraordinarily busy for Marsh. He gathered together a group of five or six experts[30] in the field of social security measures and holed up with them in the Château Laurier in Ottawa. Drawing on his and their extensive backgrounds, Marsh would prepare an outline for each brain-storming session, and the discussion became the basis for the report, the first draft of which was transmitted to Principal James on January 17, 1943, less than a month after it had been requested.[31] The Committee chairman sent a copy to the Prime Minister who asked that the report be given to the parliamentary Committee on Reconstruction and Rehabilitation as well as to the proposed Committee on Social Security.[32]

The Marsh Report was presented to the House of Commons Committee on Reconstruction and Rehabilitation on March 15 and was scheduled for presentation to the Social Security Committee a few days later. Somehow the press violated an arrangement not to release the material until its unveiling before the second committee, and as a result the Marsh Report burst upon the public on March 16.[33] The initial response was cautious. The Montreal *Gazette* thought the ideas useful, but expensive. The Toronto *Star*, noting that the Marsh proposals would cost far less than war expenses, was delighted, but the Toronto *Telegram* objected that 'The scheme outlined is an Utopian dream absolutely impossible of realization within the next generation.' Some Quebec journals worried about provincial rights, but on balance the national response was favourable.[34]

What had Marsh wrought? The Marsh Report set out in a coherent form the main features of the existing measures of social legislation, suggested ways of improving them, and laid down the principles that had to be considered if a comprehensive scheme for social security was to be undertaken in an effective manner. In his first section Marsh laid out the maxims that set the tone for his detailed chapters.

Provision for unemployment, both economically and socially, is the first and greatest need in a security programme designed for the modern industrial state.

The basic soundness of social security is that it is underwritten by the community as a whole.

One of the necessities for economic stability is the maintenance of the flow of purchasing power at the time when munitions and other factories are closing down. . . . In this perspective, a wide and properly integrated scheme of social insurance and welfare provision of $100,000,000 or $500,000,000 is not to be regarded with the alarm which, with inadequate understanding, it might otherwise occasion.

Children's needs should be met as a special claim on the nation, not merely in periods of unemployment or on occasions of distress, but at all times. This is the basic case for children's allowances.

There was no hectoring tone, but there was a clearly evident educative thrust, aimed at the politicians and the press as much as at the public.

Turning to 'Employment' Marsh then set out the three areas in which programs had to be readied to combat unemployment at war's end. The first was occupational re-adjustment, a means of training workers for new jobs and placing them in tasks that properly fitted their talents. Next was unemployment insurance, and finally a national reserve program of public employment projects. Like everyone else, Marsh assumed that a recession would follow the war and he believed that a works program, adequately planned and financed, could break the boom-bust cycle. Ottawa would have to assume a large role in working out the timing of such schemes with the provinces.[35]

The Report then looked at 'The Universal Risks: Sickness, Invalidity, Old Age'. Marsh's first suggestion was for a national health insurance scheme. Coincidentally on the day the Marsh study was released, Ian Mackenzie had unveiled just such a scheme, the product of years of study by the officials in his department and the result of consultation with the medical profession. Mackenzie was distinctly unhappy at the way his 'concrete proposal' was forgotten in the barrage of publicity that greeted what he called 'an excellent, if hasty, survey of possibilities'.[36] But Marsh had worked closely with Mackenzie's departmental officials preparing the health insurance scheme, and he had carefully written his proposals so that they would complement and reinforce those put forward by the Minister. Marsh wanted health insurance that was universal, with graduated levels of assistance depending on income, and he looked to both sickness cash benefits and maternity benefits for employed female workers. He also wanted universal, contributory old age pensions of $45 a month for married couples, and he challenged the orthodox view that 'insistence on the responsibility of children for their [aged] parents is socially sound.'

Under 'Family Needs' Marsh crusaded for children's allowances, describing them as 'a clear part of the policy of a national minimum— of the direct attack on poverty where it is bound up with the strain imposed by a large family on a small income'. Children, Marsh proclaimed, 'should have an unequivocal place in social security policy.' The allowance suggested was to average out to $7.50 per month per child. Marsh also tried to establish minimum standards of living for families. Carefully canvassing the existing literature and assuming efficient management of household funds, Marsh estimated that a family of five with three children under 12 required $122.85 each month. In emergency this minimum could be reduced to $94.54 a month but a cut of this kind, he said, forced crowded housing and ended any prospect of savings. As Marsh demonstrated, two thirds of the male heads of urban families and three quarters of rural families fell below the desirable minimum as of 1941. One third of urban families and half the rural families in the country fell below the reduced minimum, and this at a time when rents of $40 a month were common in large cities. The figures as presented were simply shocking. Marsh concluded his Report with this comment:

> Finally, the obvious but vital point must be made that social security payments are not money lost. The social insurances . . . are investments in morale and health, in greater family stability . . . in human productive efficiency. They demand personal and community responsibilities; but in the eyes of most of the people who are beneficiaries, give a more evident meaning to the ideas of common effort and national solidarity. It has yet to be proved that any democracy which underwrites the social minimum for its citizens is any the weaker or less wealthy for doing so.

As Marsh knew, the chief complaint about the proposals in his Report would be their cost. His estimates were rough, admittedly so, but it was evident that costs would be high, probably about $900 million each year on social-security measures, exclusive of employment maintenance projects. This worked out to between 10 and 12½ per cent of the National Income, assuming, as Marsh did, that the postwar figure would be roughly double that of 1939 or about $7 billion. Marsh contemplated a Dominion postwar budget of approximately $2.2 billion, of which $1 billion would be for works projects, $500 million for Dominion participation in his proposed social-security schemes, and the remainder for other responsibilities of the federal government. $400 million would have to be raised through contributory methods to support the social insurance plans. The expense was great, but the potential rewards were enormous.*[37]

There were severe criticisms, of course. Walter Gordon, back in Toronto with Clarkson, Gordon, Accountants, was appalled. 'I was interested in reading Mr. Marsh's . . . statement,' he wrote to his friend W. A. Mackintosh in Ottawa, 'that while it took a full two months to get his one billion dollar a year plan on paper, that all the thinking was squeeezed into a period of one week.' This was fascinating, Gordon said. 'Having in mind the "pie in the sky" era to which we are all looking forward, I presume this means . . . say thirty hours per one billion dollars. . . . As I see it, if Marsh can figure out ways of spending a billion dollars in thirty hours he could have tossed off a five and a half billion dollar budget in one hundred and sixty-five hours.'[38] Pie in the sky, indeed. A more thoughtful and less flippant response was that of the CCF. Marsh's report, *Canadian Forum* intoned, was 'the price that Liberalism is willing to pay in order to prevent socialism.' Still, the Report's proposals were worth implementing.[39] The Conservative response was not unexpected, despite the party's move to the left after Port Hope and Winnipeg that should have given progressive Conservatives more influence. The author of the official Tory reaction was Dr Charlotte Whitton, a very formidable lady indeed, but perhaps rather old-fashioned in her approach to the new social-welfare realities. In her book, *The Dawn of Ampler Life*, with its introduction by John Bracken, Miss Whitton portrayed the effects of Marsh's proposals as debilitating to the national moral fibre. The costs predictably terrified her, and the net effect of the Whitton book was to suggest that

---

*In retrospect, what is striking is the way Marsh—and everyone else—underestimated the extent to which National Income would soar. In 1943 it was $8.8 billion; by the end of the war it was $9.6 billion, and by 1948 it had reached $12 billion. By 1955 National Income was over $20 billion. Of course government expenditures kept pace. In 1945 social-welfare costs (excluding the substantial sums for veterans benefits, health and education costs) were $250 million; in 1948 $386 million; in 1955 $853 million. The growth in the economy and the growth in welfare costs both exceeded expectations. M. C. Urquhart and K. A. H. Buckley, *Historical Statistics of Canada* (Toronto, 1965), pp. 130, 207.

the Progressive Conservative Party was still more conservative than progressive.[40]

II

The Liberal government's response was muted. The stirrings of reconstructionist sentiment had been apparent for some time, but the demands of the war were still too pressing for attention to be diverted to post-hostilities planning on a major scale. The CCF victory in York South and the apparent transformation of the old Tory Party at Port Hope and Winnipeg were signs that public interest was focussing on the coming peace, but the Liberal Party did little and said less.

The Cabinet and its members seemed either uninterested or hostile at the beginning of 1943 before the Marsh Report was released. The exception was Mackenzie, whose Associate Deputy Minister, Walter Woods, had proposed the creation of a new Department of Health and Social Security on January 7 'with a view to broadening, centralizing and integrating our national Social Security legislation'.[41] Mackenzie, although not accepting the proposal completely, did forward it to the Prime Minister,[42] and a few days later the subject of social security was raised in Cabinet. 'I pointed out,' King wrote later,

> the need for social security legislation at this session. If not legislation, full consideration of a full programme. Ilsley at once objected to what it would involve in the way of expenditures. Howe was for providing plenty of work; Crerar for giving opportunity of work. The mind of the Cabinet, at any rate, does not grasp the significance of the Beveridge Report.
>
> Mitchell did say that unless something was done on that line, the government would be through. . . . I get very fatigued when I encounter a strong opposition to what seems to me the obvious and right thing for a liberal party to pursue. Little by little, the effect the war is having on some members of the government [is] to make them so reactionary as to cause the party generally to lose ground right along to the C.C.F. What is worse, to lose in a way that would make the government very unstable after another general election.[43]

There was at least one more supporter of social security in the Cabinet, in addition to Mackenzie.

Mackenzie King's personal commitment to social security was undoubted. In his jottings in his diary throughout this period he came back again and again to his 1918 book, *Industry and Humanity*. 'Everything I wished to say,' he wrote about his difficulties in preparing a speech on social security in early March 1943, 'is in my "Industry and Humanity". But the mere fact that it is so personal to myself . . . makes it difficult for me to get public utterance which might appear to be putting myself forward and reforms which have been initiated by myself. I must get over that,' he concluded, 'and identify social security with my life work.'[44] To some extent he did, and on March 5, 1943 King responded to criticism directed against him by reading a few paragraphs from his book in support of unemployment insurance, workmen's compensation, widows' pensions, maternity and infants' benefits. 'To save the spirit of men from being crushed,' King read, 'is quite as important as to prevent their bodies from being broken or infected.'[45]

But in a curious way, once the Marsh Report had been made public King's cautious nature re-asserted itself. Probably he was set off by Ilsley who wrote him on March 17 that it was important to make clear that the Marsh Report and the health insurance proposals presented by Mackenzie* were not intended legislation, nor even government proposals.[46] The result was a new note of hesitancy in King's comments to the Liberal caucus.

> . . . I said I would never allow an appeal to the people on social security measures at a time of war with a view to bringing them to support the government because of what it would pay out of the public treasury. They must realize the real nature of what was involved in a social security programme. It was a social revolution—a levelling down of those who were privileged. . . . That this could not

*The Economic Advisory Committee had objected strenuously to Mackenzie's health insurance scheme, and the latter wrote in a white heat to King of the 'stalling by a financial group of two years' work . . .' So angry was he that Mackenzie said 'If it is not possible to introduce this bill at the present session, I shall have to consider the matter very seriously,' a veiled threat to resign. Mackenzie argued that Canada had given $1 billion to the U.K.—'Now, when it is sought to help the health of the Canadian people, financial arguments are brought forward to retard the legislation.' The matter came to Cabinet on January 22, Deputy Minister of Finance Clifford Clark being brought in to speak against it. The bill, nonetheless, was sent to the House of Commons Social Security Committee for consideration, but years would go by before such a measure was enacted. PAC, Ian Mackenzie Papers, file 567-27(4), Mackenzie to King, 20 Jan. 1943; King Diary, 22 Jan. 1943; I. J. Goffman, 'The Political History of National Hospital Insurance in Canada', *Journal of Commonwealth Studies*, III (1965), 136ff.

be done in a day, but would take years. What was needed was a proper basis on which to construct a new order. . . . It was wrong to think of increased outlays on anything that could be avoided until victory was won. Important, however, to keep everything in readiness for the peace.[47]

A few months later King was sharper still in his comments about social security. It was the soldier overseas who deserved consideration: '. . . we had no right to be complaining about increasing old age pensions and all these local matters when these men were offering their lives. They were entitled to first consideration. I said members did not understand human nature if they believed people of the country generally, farmers, workmen and others were to be swept off their feet by a lot of promises of this and that.'[48] King would shortly change his mind about raising old age pensions, and he would lead the Cabinet in forcing the Finance Minister to accept the increase.[49]

Nonetheless he had shifted his position on social security, a shift that seems to have taken place around the time that the Marsh Report was issued. Social security was King's area, his own special field of expertise ever since *Industry and Humanity*, and now the Marsh Report had come along and pre-empted the field with specifics. Apart entirely from the political difficulties that these proposals created within the Cabinet and caucus, Marsh's Report must have posed difficulties for King himself. Clearly, therefore, such proposals had to be impractical in wartime. They might be possible in peacetime, but certainly not now.

Only major alterations in the political situation could persuade King that his attitude of January 1943 was the correct one, that social-security measures had to be passed now if the government was to survive. Soon those political shifts would be apparent. On August 4, 1943 the Liberal government in Ontario was routed by George Drew and the Conservative Party. Mitch Hepburn had been succeeded as premier by the lacklustre Gordon Conant and then, after a leadership convention, by Harry Nixon. Nixon's only virtue as a political leader was that he had been a solitary King loyalist in the provincial administration, but this helped him not at all in the provincial election and Liberalism was destroyed. Drew won 38 seats, and Nixon was reduced to the leadership of a 15-seat Liberal rump. The surprise of the election, however, was the CCF success in moving from no seats before the election to 34 after. The socialists won 400,000 votes, led the military vote, and captured virtual control of industrial Ontario and the north. This result did not surprise Mackenzie King—after years of Hepburn, it was a wonder that any Liberals could get elected. But he was shocked by the results in four federal by-elections on August 9. All former Liberal seats, Cartier in Montreal fell to Fred Rose, a Communist running under the party's wartime banner as a Labour-Progressive Party candidate; Stanstead in rural Quebec was lost to the nationalist Bloc Populaire Canadien, the party formed from the coalition that had shaped La Ligue pour la défense du Canada; and Selkirk, Manitoba, and Humboldt, Saskatchewan were captured by the CCF. The defeats were decisive, indicating both the extent of the growing support for the left in the country and the growing tide of resentment against the government in Quebec. The 'good-bye elections', as Grant Dexter called them,[50] had shaken the government, and it was no comfort that the Conservatives had been afraid even to run candidates in the contests.[51] The next month the surge of CCF support* was graphically confirmed when the Canadian Institute of Public Opinion reported that the CCF had the support of 29 per cent of the population, the Liberals and Tories trailing with 28 per cent each.

The effect of these hammer blows was profound. The Liberal Party had to be reorganized. The government had to confront the need for social-welfare legislation. If these steps were not taken the government would inevitably be defeated, possibly by the CCF, and the effects on Canada would be incalculable. Chubby Power, never a smug, satisfied Liberal, wrote to J. W. Dafoe in Winnipeg that 'it would appear as if we would have to "pull up our socks" if we are not to have a debacle Federally such as has occurred Provincially.'[52] This thought was much on Ian Mackenzie's mind too. On August 19 he wrote to King to remind him of their conversation at the beginning of the year. 'I believe it was partly as a result of that discussion that you decided to include in the Speech from the Throne the very encouraging paragraphs relating to social security,' Mackenzie said. Work had gone on in Parliament, in the departments of government, and in the James Committee, but 'generally speaking the instructions given were to go slow. . . .' There were those disturbing political events of a few days ago, however,

*The string of CCF successes culminating in Ontario in 1943 had begun with the British Columbia provincial election of October 1941, when the party had captured 33.4 per cent of the popular vote, more than the Liberals or the Conservatives, and 14 seats. The socialist strength was enough to force the two old parties into coalition. After the B.C. success, York South established the party federally.

Mackenzie said, 'so disturbing as to make very clear the duty of the government to give anxious and sustained attention to the situation.'

What was needed, the Minister argued, was a broad program of social security. A Dominion-Provincial conference on the subject should be held in late 1943, and health insurance should be proceeded with quickly. But improvements had to be made to the old-age pension legislation, to veterans' allowances, to government organization.

> I feel very strongly that these are some things we cannot delay. We should begin in the near future the shaping of our policy on—
> 1. Reconstruction and its various phases;
> 2. Social Security and its various phases;
> 3. The incomplete phases of rehabilitation.
> ... Then, as I recommended to you once before, we should jump to the country immediately after the European armistice, on two issues—
> 1. Canada's policy at the Peace Conference table. . . .
> 2. The most sweeping policy of national social reform yet attempted in Canada along Liberal lines. For this we are not ready. For this we should be getting ready.[53]

How much influence Mackenzie's pleas had on the Prime Minister is unclear, but certainly his suggestions were very similar to the Liberals' general election platform of 1945.[54]

The preparations, in fact, began almost immediately. A meeting of the Liberal parliamentary whips was scheduled for September 22, to be followed by a full caucus on September 24, and a meeting of the National Liberal Federation on September 27 and 28.[55] The Cabinet, in preparation for these party gatherings, was also getting ready. A subcommittee established to look at grievances quickly produced a report recommending a wide range of immediate remedies. Among the courses suggested, for example, were fuller explanations of the reasons behind the government's restrictive policy on beer production and sales, an end to taxing of overtime work, and a patronage-oriented insistence that public works announcements be released by ministers and Members of Parliament from the province and area concerned.[56]

The NLF had had to be reconstituted for its meeting. The body was declared to consist of seven voting members from each province, the members being found from within the party organization and the provincial Liberal executive. The Members and Senators could attend, of course, but only the seven members in a provincial delegation could vote. The sessions were to be private, except for a dinner on the first night at which Mackenzie King was to speak.[57]

The orchestration extended to policy, too. One who realized the need for preliminary consideration of the issues of policy that would come before the NLF was J. W. Pickersgill, the member of Mackenzie King's office staff who was gradually becoming one of the Prime Minister's key advisers. In a long memorandum to King, Pickersgill set out his diagnosis of the party's problems.

> The Liberal Party should . . . stick firmly by its wartime controls which have protected the standard of living of the less fortunate in the community but, at the same time, it should seek by positive, concrete measures to remove this fear of the future. . . .
>
> . . . In terms of purchasing power, wages are as remunerative, generally speaking, as they have ever been. The real hardship—and the greatest single cause of poverty—is the fact that wages which give a decent living to a married man without children, and something more than a decent living to a single man or woman, are wholly inadequate to support children. . . . Probably three-quarters of labour's real grievances on the score of wages could be removed by the immediate establishment of children's allowances paid by the State. . . .

Pickersgill went on to recommend a floor under farm prices after the war, greater efforts to counter malnutrition, a comprehensive housing policy, and a public development program.

> From a political standpoint, [he added] parties in opposition can afford to rest on their promises; that is really all they have to offer. From a party in power, promises are useless. . . . The voters know that a government in office has the power to act and they are going to judge it largely on the concrete, tangible evidences of action. . . .
>
> But, once the war is won, the voters are not going to vote for a political party merely because it did a good job in winning the war. They are going to vote for the party they think is most likely to do what is needed to provide the maximum employment and a measure of social insurance in the future. The record of the government will help it only if that record is joined to a program already partly carried out; a program which is a tangible proof of continuing action.
>
> The suggestions made above can all be carried out immediately.

They are all essentially more progressive than the programs of the
Conservatives or the CCF. To carry them out promptly, and with a
vigorous and sustained publicity program, would put the Liberal
Party, where it should be, once more in the van of progress.[58]

Pickersgill's memorandum very skilfully put together most of the
ideas then current in Ottawa; more important, Pickersgill put them in
a form that would appeal to Mackenzie King. With the assistance of
Brooke Claxton, King's parliamentary secretary and the other livewire
in his office, he had drafted the basic outlines of a new Liberal platform
and one that would go before the NLF.[59] The Pickersgill-Claxton
recommendations were progressive in that they called for the extension
of the welfare state; the proposals were in no way radical, however. All
that the suggestions did was to raise the national mean somewhat
higher, to give the protection of the state to those in the population
who needed it most. In that sense the recommendations were genuinely
conservative, for Pickersgill, Claxton, and many others, including
Mackenzie King, realized that unless society proved more accommodating to those ordinary people who had suffered through the depression,
its way of life would be changed drastically. The Liberal Party, as
it had been for much of its life, was again becoming the progressive-
conservative party.

Before the National Liberal Federation meeting, the Members of
Parliament and Senators met in caucus on September 24. Mackenzie
King began, as Senator Norman Lambert noted, 'by raising particular
hell about the way the members of the party had allowed him to be
abused by Hepburn and others during the past 6 years: that he had to
have an organization; and that he would quit if he didn't get it.'[60] The
choice was between an election now or the immediate creation of an
organization.[61] What annoyed him particularly, the Prime Minister
told his members, was that the party seemed afraid even to refer to him.
At the time of the last Victory Loan, for example, the phrase 'our
leaders' was meant to refer to Churchill and Roosevelt, not to the
Prime Minister of Canada. Such slurs, intended or not, had to end.[62]
All this was familiar stuff to the caucus members.

So too were the complaints the M.P.s ventured about government
policy. Controls were too tight, patronage was lacking, there wasn't
enough beer available to working men. Some wanted social-security
legislation now and there were heated debates on the government's
policy. The caucus continued the following day, and King wrote that

'It was clear that the members were all wanting to have things done for others; whole families to have pensions now, etc. More and more of expenditures and have less and less of taxation. One felt as one listened,' he added a bit cynically, 'how easily an audience could be swayed by false doctrine.' But was this false doctrine? Not entirely, for although King once again told his party that the social-security reforms should wait until peacetime, he did agree that the government had to have everything in readiness. It was, he wrote that night, a 'Chance to enlarge the opportunity for people in different homes'.[63]

The NLF meetings began two days later with the striking of committees to report on a wide range of questions, including organization, finance, and (carefully prepared in advance) resolutions.[64] The meeting was a meeting like the others. There were the usual speeches and toasts, the jockeying for position and place, the *pro forma* resolutions. Such things were expected, and all the traditions were honoured.

For Mackenzie King, whose task it was to open the meeting with a speech and to address the dinner on September 27, it was a particularly trying experience. He had learned just before his first appearance at the meeting that his nephew Lyon, the father of two young children and a surgeon on the destroyer HMCS *St Croix*, had been lost in the sinking of the ship. King had always cast a paternal eye on his nephews, their families and their problems, and he was severely shaken.[65] He 'found it difficult to be at all lighthearted in meeting the members . . .', he wrote. 'I made my remarks mostly in reference to the war and how serious the present situation was, and what terrible fighting there still would be. . . . I told members above all else to keep uppermost in their minds the lot of the men and women who are giving their lives . . . that we may continue to enjoy the freedom that we have here.'[66]

In the evening King delivered a formal address, unusual in that it was the first biting, partisan address that he had made since the 1940 election campaign. The speech, as well, had the usual quota of slightly embarrassing references to himself that King seemed to feel such occasions demanded. 'The continuing confidence of the members of the Liberal party of Canada in my leadership of the party is something for which I am profoundly grateful. I believe I am right,' he told the delegates, 'when I say that no leader of a political party living today, in any country, has been accorded over so long a period of time so continuous an expression of the confidence and regard of his political supporters.' Thus launched, King briefly sketched out the history of the Liberal Party under his leadership, particularly the great victories of 1935 and 1940. 'We were told,' he said of the last election, 'that while I might be all right as a leader of the government in times of peace, I was not the one to lead a government at a time of war.' The people had given their answer. 'I challenge any responsible citizen to say that Canada's war effort has not been magnificent.' Surely this had to mean something to the Canadian public? 'Is it to be said that we have lost the country's confidence because we have performed so well the one task that matters most; done so well in the one thing that is, and will remain, the supreme task of any government until the war is won?'

To King, the cause of this discontent was obvious. Ontario voters were not unhappy with Ottawa but with the Hepburn government and 'the manner in which public affairs had been conducted in that province in the preceding six years.' The August by-elections, he argued, were lost because of a lack of organization, not because of government policy. This was his central point. The other parties had not ceased their organizational efforts because of the war. The Tories had devised a secret plan to split the government over conscription, a plan that had been stopped in York South in February 1942. That having failed, they had held meetings and a convention, selected a new leader, and begun organization across the nation. 'I am not saying that the Progressive Conservative party has not a perfect right to do as it pleases with respect to its own affairs. All that I wish to make clear is . . . its course has been quite the opposite to that followed by the government and its supporters.' The CCF was the same, Mackenzie King said, excoriating the socialists for their present enthusiasm for the war in contrast to their lukewarm policy in 1939. The CCF were sabotaging price controls, they were fostering the notion of a painless war effort, they were 'boring into the labour organizations of the country in order that through the medium of organized labour they may further their political ambitions and aims.' The third opposition group, the Bloc Populaire Canadien, also drew his fire. 'Its self appointed leaders who are a small group of malcontents are indifferent to the good name of Canada and to the security of Canada. They pretend that Canada is in no danger in this war. They talk as though Britain and not nazi Germany was the real enemy. . . . The Bloc Populaire is the only party I have ever heard of whose platform and policies are contained in the single word "non".'

Clearly the Liberal Party had to re-group and re-arm to oppose the desires and goals of the opposition parties. Not that he wanted an election now. The party had to be ready to move ahead, to deal with the problems of peace. 'The task of Liberalism,' King said, in a ringing peroration, 'will not be finished when the war is won. That great moment will but mark a place of new beginning. The future of the Liberal party will not be found in defending the privileges of the few or in arousing the prejudices of the many. . . . In meeting the problems of the post-war period, the task of Liberalism will remain the preservation and extension of freedom.'[67]

Even though it completely lacked specific proposals, this tough speech was music to Liberal ears. 'It was like the old days,' King wrote later that night after he had shaken hands with the party faithful, 'each one was saying that the last speech was the best of all. It seemed to have pleased the party very much that I had spoken out so strongly.'[68] Liberal reorganization seemed in hand.

The platform was also essentially ready. To the Prime Minister reading the resolutions a day later, 'It was really more like a digest of laws and compendium on the whole problem, than a programme or platform.'[69] But it was more, a supremely political document. The resolutions made the appropriate noises of perseverance until victory, of support for the armed forces, the Commonwealth, the monarchy. The measures of joint defence with the United States should be maintaind into the peace. Generous benefits to help re-establish the returning soldiers were pledged, and the delegates came down on the fence in supporting 'both public and private enterprise' and in believing that both would have to be expanded to provide full employment, social security, and a rising standard of living. Labour was praised for its role in creating the nation's wealth and promised the full support of the government in its battle for collective bargaining once the war was over. But it was in the area of social security that the NLF made its mark: 'The Liberal Federation believes that a programme of social security should include social insurance and assistance against the consequences of economic and social hazards.' The delegates expressed their support for a 'national scheme of social insurance' to include insurance against privation resulting from unemployment, accident, ill-health, old age, and blindness. They recommended an improved old-age pension scheme. And they urged 'consideration of children's allowances as a contribution' to a 'healthy nation with good family life and adequate support for the raising of children.'[70]

The NLF meeting left the party and the government further ahead on the road to social welfare and somewhat ahead in preparing for the election, whenever that might come. But how much further ahead? To Grant Dexter of the *Winnipeg Free Press*, not very much. The government was full of burnt-out men, he wrote to Dafoe in Winnipeg on November 1, 1943. 'They are finished. . . .' The 'very encouraging flurry of optimism' after the September meetings had seeped away. 'They are back where they were and I can see no disposition to stand up to the C.C.F., to contest the field. . . . The Cabinet has lost the will to step outside the line of war policy already grooved.'[71] That was the truth, and men like Pickersgill knew it. In the same month he sent to the Prime Minister a long list of questions about postwar policy: 'Is the government going to base its policy on full employment? . . . Is a single agency to be charged with social security planning and administration? . . . Will any positive advances be made in social security at the next session? . . . Will legislation be introduced to establish: a floor under fish and farm prices; children's allowances . . . health insurance; contributory old age pensions?'[72] Mackenzie King gave no immediate answers, but although he and his Cabinet were tired and some ministers were very discouraged, there was at last some prospect of a major effort to create a coherent social-security program.

III

Something had to be done, and Mackenzie King's mind turned first to the establishment of a Reconstruction Department that could deal with the need to find work for demobilized veterans and with the necessity for a concrete program that would deal with all aspects of the postwar economic situation and, in particular, with housing.[73] The Prime Minister talked with Power and C. D. Howe in November and December 1943 about this and found the two ministers enthusiastic. The Cabinet was generally in favour of the idea, too, although Ilsley questioned its necessity and Crerar delivered a long harangue against welfare, increasingly his response to such proposals.[74] Ian Mackenzie, perhaps interested in carving out his own niche, wrote to King that the Ministry of Reconstruction should also deal with social security. 'In my opinion,' he argued, 'they should be so combined, as the functions of the two are complementary.'[75]

Mackenzie's suggestions were only part of the deluge that fell on King in the next few weeks in response to a request that ministers forward their suggestions for a postwar program. Mackenzie's reply was among the most detailed, for he urged the establishment of a Department of Veterans Affairs and a series of concrete social-security measures. Many of the Cabinet favoured family allowances; all favoured efforts to create employment after the war, housing programs and the like. *Laisser-faire* seemed scarcely in evidence.[76]

C. D. Howe's position was important. Howe was already being touted as the logical man to lead any Reconstruction Ministry,[77] and he argued that the essential point in reconstruction was to ensure that the war-enhanced prosperity* was maintained by providing jobs. 'Doubling of our productive capacity,' he said, 'was brought about by a working partnership between Government, industry, the producer and the worker. Government set the tasks and gave financial support where needed. The same partnership . . . should be organized to undertake conversion from war to peace.' The problem of reconversion was not all that difficult, the Minister of Munitions and Supply claimed, because food would be in short supply throughout the world for some years after the war and agriculture could absorb 300,000 men. Forestry and mining could take an additional 200,000. Many war plants could be converted with little difficulty to peacetime production, and the construction industry should be able to employ many workers displaced by the drop in industrial production. Howe indicated that he supported a good pension system for workers at age 65 and health insurance. But he could not accept family allowances, which 'tend to encourage idleness and thus defeat our objective of maintaining production at its present level.'[78]

The comments of Finance Minister Ilsley were equally significant. He was clearly concerned with the budget, and he knew that the national debt would be swollen after the war: carrying charges would be substantial; there would be large expenses on defence, on social security, on housing, and on reconversion of industry. 'In view of all these things,' he said to King, 'it is quite probable that Dominion expenditures may at least in certain years approach $1½ or $2 billion. . . .' Could the country support such a sum? 'I am convinced (as are my advisers) that it is quite impossible for the Dominion Government to manage annual expenditures and national debts of the magnitude indicated, if we have to go back to our pre-war taxing system.' This was the key in Ilsley's view: '. . . unless the Dominion retains exclusive control in the present income and corporation tax fields (and preferably also secure control of the succession duty field) we will find it quite impossible to solve Canada's post-war economic and financial problems.' The policy

*One indication of this war prosperity was the extraordinary rise in chartered bank deposits from $2.5 billion in September 1939 to $5.75 billion in mid-1945. E. P. Neufeld, *Bank of Canada Operations and Policies* (Toronto, 1958), p. 114.

prescription was still essentially that presented by the Rowell-Sirois Royal Commission. Ilsley insisted that an arrangement had to be reached with the provinces because 'trying to carry out hastily conceived plans by means of grants-in-aid will prove ultimately destructive both of efficiency of administration and of the possibilities of obtaining a settlement [with the provinces] at a later date. . . . we must work out a program on the basis of existing financial and constitutional arrangements at least as satisfactory as those we have at present.' Ilsley's program included 'the establishment of a minimum of social security legislation, including family allowances, unemployment assistance, increased old age pensions, and, possibly health insurance.' In addition, construction projects that would create jobs were essential, particularly in housing, natural resources, and rural electrification. In conclusion Ilsley argued that industry would have to be encouraged to invest large sums in the immediate postwar period, and he believed that legislation would be necessary to secure credits to assist this investment.[79]

Those views were perhaps less Ilsley's than those of his civil servants,[80] but they were important, and the Prime Minister read Ilsley's memo to the Cabinet on January 6, 1944. Mackenzie King noted that it brought 'home to the Ministers the many matters that have to be settled. . . . As we proceeded Members began I think to appreciate what an appalling series of problems there are before the government . . . and how exceedingly difficult the whole matter of reconstruction and post-war reorganization is going to be.'[81] The Cabinet at last was getting down to serious consideration about social security, and the differences between 'progressives' and the 'old guard' would shortly become apparent.

On January 11, 1944 the Cabinet did approve the establishment of three new departments: Reconstruction, National Health and Welfare, and Veterans Affairs.[82] At about the same time consideration was being given to the Speech from the Throne that would open the 1944 session of Parliament on January 27. This would probably be the last full session before an election, or so many of the ministers believed, and care and attention would be required in shaping the party's and the government's program.

Mackenzie King himself finally got down to serious concentration on the Speech on January 22. 'It has been a very difficult job working out the programme,' he wrote that night of his labours with his aides,

but if it is worked out, I can claim it as my own because we have had to decide some things together which I have never been able to get Council yet fully to agree upon. . . . I feel by having it in printed form before I see my colleagues . . . that it will be much easier to get final agreement. . . .[!]

. . . we have . . . a programme of social legislation that really rounds out what I have worked for through my life, namely, gaining recognition of the fact that where the State, through organization of industry, etc. being what it is, gives great opportunities to a few, and robs the many of many opportunities, it should become the duty of the State to work out some scheme of social justice which will see that opportunities are widened for the many and that at least for all there should be a minimum standard of life. . . .

The doctrine of national minimum standard of life which I have set forth in my Industry and Humanity in 1918 as part of the post-war policy, I have now worked into the words of the representative of the King, to be spoken from the Throne as government policy. That makes life worth while. There will be a great fight over this by wealthy classes and even many of them, middle classes, will be up in arms, but at least the great numbers of people . . . will see that I have been true to them from the beginning of my public life.[83]

When the draft was presented to the Cabinet on January 24, however, some ministers were sharply critical. Ilsley, for example, notwithstanding the position he had argued in his memorandum on social security a few weeks earlier, was shocked. Some people would say the government was 'seeking to outdo the CCF. We might as well join the Tories.' Crerar and Gardiner, the Minister of Agriculture, objected to points in the draft, but King cut them off. The Prime Minister, however, did intervene to block a definite promise being made for legislation on health insurance on the grounds that the provinces would have to agree first to permit Ottawa to keep some of the revenue fields it had taken over for war purposes: 'I pointed out that nothing was to be gained by promising something that we could not implement without taxation the people would not agree to bear, and insisted on agreement being reached with the provinces first of all.'[84]

The Speech from the Throne on January 27 was a landmark in the development of the social-security state in Canada. The 'post-war object of our domestic policy is social security and human welfare,' the Governor General read. 'The establishment of a national minimum of social security and human welfare should be advanced as rapidly as

possible.' The government pledged itself to guarantee 'useful employment for all who are willing to work', to upgrade nutrition and
housing, and to provide social insurance. It said that its postwar planning was concentrating on three fields—demobilization, rehabilitation,
and re-establishment of veterans; reconversion of the economy; and
insurance against major economic and social hazards—and it announced
that new departments of government were to be created. A promise was
given that family allowances would be introduced, and the King government pledged that it would seek agreement with the provinces for
health insurance and for a national contributory old-age pension scheme
'on a more generous basis' than at present. In addition, harking back
to Pickersgill's memorandum of the late summer of 1943, the Speech
stated that it was the government's policy to keep the price ceiling
intact and to provide a floor price for farm staples.[85] It was one of the
most promising of Throne Speeches, and one that was firmly based on
the Marsh Report, on the Pickersgill memorandum, on the National
Liberal Federation resolutions and, yes, on *Industry and Humanity* too.

Certainly King believed this. When, for example, one of the officials
of the Health League of Canada told the Prime Minister that he had
been reading his *Industry and Humanity* and could see everything the
government was doing laid out there, King was delighted.[86] A birthday
telegram to Ian Mackenzie—'we are sharing in an epochal reform, one
with which through time the names of the Mackenzies will be irrevocably associated'—[87] expressed this pride of ownership again. And in a
speech in the House of Commons in July, King again waxed proud
about his and his government's achievements:

> . . . so far as this administration has power to have it so we intend to
> see if we possibly can that the new order expresses a new social
> concept altogether of industry as being in the nature of social service
> and the obligations and rewards that grow out of that conception.
> . . . we must have a wholly new conception of industry as being in
> the nature of social service for the benefit of all, not as something
> existing only for the benefit of a favoured few. . . .[88]

At root of all the proposals now being advanced by the government was the fear of postwar unemployment, depression, and possible
disorder. 'What would happen when the boys and girls came home and
war production ceased?', C. D. Howe later recalled thinking. 'There
were misgivings and fears. Memories of the depressed thirties were in

everyone's mind.'[89] This view had been expressed again and again in Cabinet and departmental discussions since 1940; now it was beginning to be expressed in public. J. R. Beattie of the Bank of Canada delivered a paper to the Canadian Political Science Association in 1944 and sent a copy to the Premier of Manitoba, Stuart Garson. 'It seemed so important to put the view that properly designed and executed social security proposals can create employment just as much or perhaps even more per unit of expenditure than public works . . . ,' Beattie told Garson. '[B]usiness has an overwhelming interest in accepting social security and helping to make it work, in view of the practical alternatives.'[90]

Some businessmen were still confused and dubious, and the government responded by issuing a White Paper on Employment and Income on April 12, 1945.* The White Paper had been suggested early in March by Prof. W. A. Mackintosh, who was concerned with the need for 'a single coherent statement, in simple language for laymen, of what had already been done and what could be expected in respect of postwar reconstruction.'[91] Within a few days Mackintosh had shown a draft of his proposal to his minister, C. D. Howe, and was circulating it widely throughout the senior levels of the bureaucracy.[92] A copy was shown to the Prime Minister at the end of March and a few days later it went before the entire Cabinet, having first been accepted by a Cabinet Committee consisting of Howe, Ilsley, and St Laurent.[93] On April 12, barely five weeks after Mackintosh had suggested it, the White Paper was tabled in Parliament.[94]

The White Paper flatly stated 'the maintenance of a high and stable level of employment and income' to be 'a major aim of government policy.' To achieve this, the government moved a very substantial distance in the direction of Keynesian economics: 'The Government will be prepared, in periods when unemployment threatens, to incur deficits and increases in the national debt resulting from its employment and income policy, whether that policy in the circumstances is best applied through increased expenditures or reduced taxation. In periods of buoyant employment and income, budget plans will call for surpluses. The Government's policy will be to keep the national debt within

*The White Paper was very similar in tone and content to those issued at the same time by Britain and Australia. In the United States, the Employment Act of 1946 had similar intent. See Robert Lekachman, *The Ages of Keynes* (New York, 1966), p. 177; A. E. Holmes, *United States Fiscal Policy 1945-59* (London, 1961), p. 38.

manageable proportions and maintain a proper balance in its budget over a period longer than a single year.'[95] Before the war, budget deficits had been akin to sin; in 1945 they were simply an economic tool.

The White Paper also promised an end to wartime controls as soon as practicable, and it laid out the government's intention to foster exports. In addition, the government promised to help private industry convert to peacetime production. Tax breaks and special depreciation allowances were proffered and, in a pledge that must have gladdened every heart on Bay Street, the government proposed 'not only to reduce taxation as rapidly as possible but to develop its fiscal policy so as to encourage the increase of private investment to a high and stable level.'[96]

The government's assistance to business and industry combined with the social-security legislation to form an attractive—and expensive—package. In a speech to the Board of Trade in Vancouver, Ian Mackenzie was explicit as he enumerated the benefits to the economy from the series of government acts. Unemployment insurance had been established at the beginning of the war so it could be used to prevent postwar hardship, and the fund now had $250 million in assets. The National Housing Act was designed to create $1 billion in new construction, and the public appropriation for it was $275 million. The Industrial Development Bank was authorized to assume liability up to $75 million. The public appropriation to maintain farming and fishing floor prices was $200 million and $25 million respectively. An Export Credit Corporation had been authorized to issue insurance on exports up to $100 million. Family allowances would put at least $200 million into the economy each year, a total of a $1 billion over the next half-decade. The War Service Gratuity to veterans would amount to $752 million, and other veterans' benefits including education, clothing, land-settlement grants and the like, would amount to an additional $449 million. The total of these measures, Mackenzie told his presumably bedazzled audience of businessmen, would be $3,126,000,000 for 'maintaining our national economy during the post-war period'.[97] It really was true, as Brooke Claxton told a CCF friend, 'You socialists have schemes, but I have the bills right here in my pocket.'[98]

IV

One of these bills was family allowances, the scheme that Mackenzie had indicated would pump $200 million into the economy each year. That was a substantial sum of money at any time, and it was also some 40 per cent of the prewar federal budget. The family allowances bill alone amounted to something in the nature of a social revolution in Canada; equally important, it was a sure sign of a radical change in fiscal thinking.

The idea had been considered before the war. In fact, as a memo prepared for Mackenzie King demonstrated, the Prime Minister himself had referred to family allowances on numerous occasions in *Industry and Humanity*.[99] Family allowances had been suggested in the House of Commons in 1929 by J. S. Woodsworth and forwarded to the Select Standing Committee on Industrial and International Relations, which eventually reported that 'as this proposal is new in Canada, and requires more careful consideration, no immediate action shall be taken. . . .'[100] The question was examined in Quebec four years later and rejected again: 'It would be impossible and dangerous to extend family allowances to the whole population and to make them a state institution.'[101]

But the war legitimized many previously disadvantageous ideas. The CCF had endorsed family allowances at its national convention in 1942, and the measure was also suggested by a private Member in the House of Commons in 1943.[102] More significantly, the Marsh Report put substantial stress on the idea of regular monthly payments to families with children as part of 'the direct attack on poverty where it is bound up with the strain imposed by a large family on a small income.' Most important of all, family allowances came to the Cabinet in a confidential report from the National War Labour Board in August 1943. Under its chairman, Hon. C. P. McTague, a Justice of the Ontario Supreme Court, the NWLB had recommended that a family allowance be paid to each worker with children as an alternative to loosening wage controls. In McTague's view, family allowances were the best way of putting money into the hands of those who needed it while still maintaining the necessary anti-inflationary policy. He had canvassed the idea with the Deputy Minister of Finance, with Graham Towers of the Bank of Canada, and with Ilsley; all agreed with his reasoning, and all, McTague recalled later, believed the economy could support the cost.[103] As a result, McTague's report argued that 'substandard wages are indefensible at all times' but if, in wartime, the government could not see its way clear to removing wage controls, 'then we can think of no other solution for the case of the head of the family who is receiving a substandard wage, than a system of family allowances.'[104]

Organized labour's representative on the NWLB, J. L. Cohen, K.C., rejected this recommendation and submitted a minority report. It was not family allowances that were at fault, Cohen argued in an able statement, but the use of them as a device to keep down wages. More-over such a recommendation tended to give tacit support to the idea that wages need provide only subsistence; labour would never accept this view.[105]

The two reports, which dealt with a host of other matters including recommendations for a Wartime Labour Relations Code that supported collective bargaining,* were discussed by the Cabinet in September. The ministers accepted collective bargaining—'The main gain so far as labour is concerned,'[106] Mackenzie King said—but there was more difficulty about other matters, not least family allowances. 'There was a considerable debate as to whether the cost of living situation should be met by paying subsidies to large families,' the Prime Minister noted on September 14 after a Cabinet meeting, '—to families based on the number of children, or in some other way. The Quebec members all favoured the former, while Mitchell [Minister of Labour] was against any attempt on the score that his officials thought the matter too difficult for administration. I find the sentiment of labour swinging toward that course,' he added, 'on which I think a real policy may be founded for dealing with social security matters.'[107] Significantly, the Economic Advisory Committee was largely in support of the idea, although it foresaw difficulties in administration and observed that the 'Public is completely uneducated in the matter and there is room for racial controversy.' That last point was crucial, for English Canadians might see family allowances as a devious way of giving government money to French Canadians and their large families. Still, the advantages were great. Family allowances would benefit everyone, including farmers. They 'would meet the problem of the low paid family man without adding to business costs and thus make the stabilization policy

---

*The King government's response to organized labour's demands for full protection came in P.C. 1003 of 17 Feb. 1944. This order set out the right of employees to join and form unions, prohibited unfair labour practices, established machinery for defining and certifying bargaining units, required compulsory collective bargaining and conciliation, and affirmed the right to strike. In a sense this was labour's Canadian Magna Carta, and the union movement thereafter was no longer an alien force on the outside looking in. The order in council, in addition, had been produced through consultation with organized labour, and this process of negotiation as well as its result helped the government politically by tending to neutralize labour's leftward thrust. In this sense, P.C. 1003 was another of the King government's efforts at re-establishing the political balance. See the accounts in H. D. Woods, *Labour Policy in Canada* (Toronto, 1973), pp. 86ff.; Stephen Purdy, 'Another Look at Order-in-Council P.C. 1003', York University graduate paper, 1973.

easier than under any comparable increase in wage rates.' And most important, family allowances would fit into the social security program 'and would be invaluable in post-war problems'.[108]

Curious as it may seem, Mackenzie King then had second thoughts about family allowances. At a Cabinet meeting on October 1 the Prime Minister pointed out that 'to tell the country that everyone was to get a family allowance was sheer folly; it would occasion resentment everywhere. Great care had to be taken in any monies given out from the Treasury as distinguished from exempting portions of income already earned.'[109] King's innate conservatism about public funds incredibly blinded him to the great gains that could be won by family allowances. The Prime Minister persisted in this view until he had a chance conversation with J. W. Pickersgill. The young private secretary had been raised and educated on the pension paid to his mother, the widow of a Great-War soldier. He told King this, and as Pickersgill recalls it, suddenly King realized that a pension differed only in amount, not in principle, from family allowances. That pension had saved a family; so, too, could family allowances save families from destitution and permit other boys to get an education. The characteristic intuitive flash, prompted by Pickersgill, was enough, and King changed his mind completely.[110] His task now was to carry the issue through Cabinet, Parliament, and with the public.

Surprisingly, perhaps, the Prime Minister and others discovered that the key officials in the Department of Finance did not oppose family allowances, which they saw as putting money into the hands of those who needed it—and those who would spend it. 'Clark is completely sold on family allowances,' Grant Dexter learned, '. . . the only effective way to deal with slum clearance. You have to give the boys the money to buy the houses you intend to build for them. That is a little crude, but it has the idea.'[111] Exactly. In a Cabinet memorandum early in January, Clark argued that without family allowances the federal government would have to pay enormous sums 'to make possible municipally constructed and municipally managed low-rental housing projects. . . . With children's allowances on anything like an adequate scale, it should be possible to avoid such a program.'[112]

Pickersgill used the same argument in a memorandum that he circulated on January 12, the day before an important Cabinet meeting that would consider family allowances. 'Children's allowances,' he argued, 'would place income where all or most of it would be spent on better housing, food and other necessaries. By enabling large families to pay higher rents, children's allowances fit in naturally with a slum clearance programme . . .' In addition, the Prime Minister's assistant argued that family allowances would 'lead to better fed children and an expanded farmers' market.' Most important, perhaps, 'the economic problem after the war will not be to produce what we need, but to find markets for what we must produce if we are to avoid unemployment. The provision of children's allowances would almost certainly result in a considerable net addition to the home market both for food and manufactured goods.'[113]

There were other advantages and liabilities too. Pickersgill argued that family allowances were a natural Liberal program that was certain to be opposed by 'some of the more reactionary elements in the Conservative party' with 'resulting division' that will 'help the Liberals'. The CCF, painted by Pickersgill as just another special interest group, would be similarly disturbed because 'many of their trade unionist allies are not keen . . . because they will weaken the argument for higher wages.' Some would claim that this was appeasement to Quebec. 'But that is already being said about the government to the people who are influenced by this argument,' Pickersgill claimed. 'It is more likely to work the other way and to help to recover some of the ground the government has lost in Quebec.'[114] Clifford Clark dealt with this argument as well in his memorandum when he suggested that 'the payments to Quebec would not be very much larger than those to Ontario,' the numbers of children under fourteen in Quebec being almost exactly proportional to the population ratio. There would be the 'trash' argument, he said; 'that in some cases the allowances will not be spent for the welfare of the children at all but for unwise purposes by a "no good" father or mother, and also that they may tend to promote greater idleness or unproductivity on the part of shiftless workers or farmers. They might in some cases', Clark admitted, 'but such bad effects should be far more than offset by the opposite kind of effect on those recipients who for the first time are given "hope" and the ambition to better themselves and improve the lot of their children.'[115]

Clark attended the decisive Cabinet meeting on January 13, 1944 and made a presentation along the lines of his memorandum to Cabinet. His performance was superb, and Mackenzie King clearly thought it had swung the decision. The Prime Minister himself had spoken strongly in favour of the measure: 'I said quite frankly that I thought the

Creator intended that all persons born should have equal opportunities. Equal opportunity started in days of infancy and the first thing, at least, was to see that the children got the essentials of life . . .' King then read to the Cabinet 'a brief statement of the arguments which Pickersgill had written out and gave them as my own convictions—as a summary of the convictions which I held. . . .'[116] In his diary Angus L. Macdonald noted the long discussion on family allowances, adding that the measure was approved, 'Howe dissenting'.[117] T. A. Crerar, too, would have opposed the measure, but he had been absent during the Council meeting.[118]

Family allowances were mentioned in the Speech from the Throne, but a draft bill was not prepared until early June. Under its terms the payment would be $5 per month for children up to 5 years of age, $6 for those from 6 to 9, $7 for those from 10 to 12, and $8 for those 13 to 15 years of age. Those rates would be reduced by $1 per month for the fifth child, by $2 per month for the sixth and seventh, and by $3 a month for the eighth and any additional children, the assumption being that the expenses of child-rearing decreased after a certain point. The detailed proposals came to the Cabinet on June 15, 1944 when King told his ministers that payments would not begin until July 1, 1945. 'This would make certain they would not come into force until after the elections were over . . . ,' King wrote in his diary. 'I did not like the idea of spending public money immediately before an election. . . . people were likely to be more grateful for what they were about to receive than anything they might have been given in advance.' The Cabinet agreed, although Crerar was still opposed to the entire scheme, joined now by Macdonald and Ilsley who seemed finally to have come around to opposing the views of his deputy minister.[119]

Mackenzie King's temper by this time was getting short. At the Cabinet War Committee on June 14, Howe said the Prime Minister had grumped that 'Some of those who are against giving something to the poor are all for giving millions to England.'[120] Howe thought the slur was aimed at him; Ralston believed Ilsley the intended victim. A few days later Grant Dexter said that the Prime Minister had told him he 'was the only radical in the Cabinet. Some of his colleagues still think they can go out and shoot a deer or bison for breakfast.' This was aimed at Crerar, Dexter believed.[121] Certainly Ilsley, Howe, and Crerar were the core of the opposition within the Cabinet to family allowances.

Opposition in the caucus still had to be silenced. On June 29 King seized on what he believed to be a critical attitude towards the family allowances on the part of George Fulford, a wealthy Member from Brockville. 'George', the Prime Minister said,

> you were blessed with a father and mother who gave you every advantage, from the moment of your birth. Had the best of nourishment, the best of education and care. All advantages, where his father had been distinguished as a Senator, and all of these things combined brought you here as a member of Parliament carrying on their work. I said what would have been your chances had the positions been reversed, and you had been one of the men, bringing up a poor family, that was struggling for its existence but doing honourable work. Unable, however, to provide the children with what they should receive. Would not you today have been in the position of some of these people you have been talking to, and might not some of their sons be in your position. I said if equality of opportunity meant anything, it meant that every man, every child, should have his chance....[122]

That was effective advocacy, and the caucus gave the Prime Minister 'a great ovation when I finished. They told me that if I would get out in the campaign and say to the people what I had said to Caucus, we would sweep the country.'[123]

The inevitable general election was much in the air, particularly after the Saskatchewan election on June 15. The CCF had won an enormous victory, taking 47 of 52 seats, and winning two thirds of the overseas vote. Coming after the Ontario election of 1943, the federal by-elections of August 1943, and the opinion-poll results of September, this was enough to frighten even the sturdiest of Liberals. The only consolation for the caucus was that the Conservatives were even more terrified, their candidates having failed to win a single seat and all having run third and lost their election deposits. The 'Progressive' Conservative label did not seem to assist the party much in the Prairies, the territory that John Bracken had been expected to deliver to Conservatism.[124]

The reaction of many Conservative Members of Parliament to family allowances, as a result, seemed almost instinctive. To such men as Dr Herbert Bruce, a Toronto M.P., the family-allowance bill was aimed at Quebec where the higher French-Canadian birth rate would lead to federal monies being used in 'bonussing families who have been unwilling to defend their country'. It was, Bruce said, 'a bribe of the most brazen character, made chiefly to one province and paid for by the rest,' a charge that led to his expulsion from the House for a day.[125] John Bracken himself called the measure a 'political bribe',*[126] and the Premier of Ontario, George Drew, attacking the constitutionality of the bill, warned that 'one isolationist Province' must not be permitted 'to dominate the destiny of a divided Canada. . . .'[127] Charlotte Whitton, the Conservatives' social-welfare expert, even argued that the 'erratic, irresponsible, bewildered of mind, and socially incapable, feebleminded and mentally affected parents are definitely the progenitors of many of our largest families,' and that 'payments of cash grants would perpetuate this menace. . . .' Worse, they would extend 'the uneven rate of natural increase' of Canada's newer racial stocks at the expense of the apparently less fertile native stock.[128] Not all the Conservatives felt this way, however. Such Members as John Diefenbaker and Howard Green supported the idea of family allowances and they were instrumental in persuading their colleagues not to oppose the bill on second reading in the House of Commons.[129] But if the public had the impression that the Conservative Party was less than enthusiastic about social welfare, there was good reason for this.

The vote on second reading, in fact, was 139-0, an incredible demonstration of the perceived political potency of family allowances. But that vote was also a tribute to the effective defence of the bill offered in the House by the Liberals, a defence that was organized and orchestrated by Brooke Claxton. The result, Claxton said to a close friend, had been 'overwhelming', and he was convinced that the case made in Parliament had actually changed minds, 'probably the first time in the history of political institutions that that has happened'.[130] The House campaign probably played some part in shaping the public mind as well. Certainly the people generally supported the idea of family allowances. The Canadian Institute of Public Opinion reported in a poll taken on August 2 that 57 per cent of a national sample and 81 per cent of Quebec respondents favoured family allowances. Predictably, too, the higher the age group the greater the opposition to the baby bonus, but fully 72 per cent of those in their twenties thought the allowances a 'good idea'.[131]

As his reward for shepherding the bill through Parliament, Claxton

*According to polls taken on October 14, 1944, 29 per cent of those questioned thought family allowances 'a political bribe' while 34 per cent believed them to be 'a necessary law'. A very realistic 16 per cent thought the measure both necessary and a bribe. But fully 87 per cent of those questioned had heard of the family-allowance bill. *Public Opinion Quarterly*, VIII (Winter, 1944-5), 582.

was brought into the Cabinet on October 13, 1944 as the first Minister of National Health and Welfare. His task would include setting up the administration for the distribution of family allowances and publicizing the virtues of the plan. This he did with a will, sending Liberals across the country pamphlets, speeches, and good, hard statistics. Family allowances alone, Claxton calculated later, raised the expenditure on health and welfare from 2.2 per cent of federal revenues in 1943-4 to 10.3 per cent in 1945-6, a remarkable jump.[132] One chart[133] also showed how much each part of the country would receive from the baby bonus, compared with its share of the tax burden.

	Total Federal Tax Collected		Estimated Distribution of Family Allowances	
Maritimes	$109 million	4%	$28 million	11%
Quebec	905	34	84	33
Ontario	1235	47	75	29
Prairies	185	7	54	21
B.C.	206	8	15	6
	$2640	100%	$256	100%

It seemed very clear from that chart that Ontario was subsidizing, not Quebec, but the West and the Maritimes. And, despite the large families in French Canada, Quebec was actually paying in taxes a shade more in percentage terms than would be received from the family allowances.

Perhaps this was at the root of the constitutional challenges thrown at Ottawa by the Quebec government. Premier Adelard Godbout, elected in 1939 with the assistance of the federal party, was very mild in his response to the measure. 'May I also remind you,' he wrote to Mackenzie King after the scheme was mentioned in the Speech from the Throne, 'that family allowances are, like other elements of social security, within the field of provincial jurisdiction. . . .'[134] That reasoned opposition could be treated gently, but the problem was compounded for the Mackenzie King administration by the return to power of Maurice Duplessis—always a hard-line autonomist—and his Union Nationale party in the provincial election of August 8, 1944. The UN received only 38.2 per cent of the popular vote while the Liberals drew 42.4 per cent, but Duplessis' men won 48 seats, eleven more than Godbout's. The one consolation for the Liberals was that the Bloc Populaire

Canadien, led provincially by André Laurendeau, won only four seats and 16.3 per cent of the vote.*[135]

Godbout's defeat had been unexpected, but Mackenzie King was strangely placid as he contemplated Duplessis' return: 'I realized there would be some decided advantages, strange as it may seem, in having an Opposition Government in office in Quebec.' In addition, recent provincial elections had demonstrated that Bracken was in a worse position than the government. He had been destroyed in Saskatchewan, and Duplessis had carefully disassociated himself from the Progressive Conservative Party in this election. The CCF had made no gains in Quebec, and therefore had no chance to become a national party. And the Bloc Populaire, he added, 'can get nowhere as a party. Their following will probably recognize this and their influence will gradually disappear.' That was not a bad analysis, one that King concluded with the comment that 'the situation has made clearer than ever that I am in a better position to keep our country united and to form an administration than any of the other leaders.'[136]

King's benign acceptance of the Liberal defeat in Quebec undoubtedly reflected the pleasurable glow of the night before. It had been the 25th anniversary of his assuming the leadership of the Liberal Party, complete with a gala (if austere wartime) dinner at the Château Laurier thrown for him by the party. The evening was a splendid one, and King, carried away, spoke for about an hour instead of the 15 minutes he had intended. He made it clear that if the five-year life of Parliament permitted, there would be no election until after the war was over, and he stated his intention of running again in his constituency of Prince Albert, even though Saskatchewan was now lost to the Liberal cause. 'I made clear too that the issue would be the new order of things which the social programme based on "Industry and Humanity" contains.'[137] Mackenzie King's greatest achievement, that social program would be the best of all issues on which to fight, for with it the Liberal Party had moved firmly onto the left-centre side of the road. The Tories

---

*The Quebec result demonstrated the fallibility of opinion sampling. A poll on July 8, 1944 had predicted Liberals—37 per cent, UN—14 per cent, and Bloc Populaire—27 per cent. On July 29 the prediction was Liberals—40 per cent, UN—29 per cent, and Bloc Populaire—25 per cent. On August 5, a few days before the election, the polls reported the Liberals—35 per cent, the UN—32 per cent, and the Bloc—27 per cent. The results of the vote, however, gave Liberals 42.4 per cent, the UN 38.2 per cent, and the Bloc 16.3 per cent. *Public Opinion Quarterly*, VIII (Fall, 1944), 444-5.

could have the right, the CCF the left. Mackenzie King and the Liberal Party would hold to the centre and prevent the polarization of Canadian politics along class lines.

---

1 Public Archives of Canada [PAC], W. L. Mackenzie King Papers, Diary, 7 Jan. 1943.

2 *Ibid.*, 8 Jan. 1943.

3 PAC, National Liberal Federation [NLF] Papers, Vol. 603, Claxton to Sen. Robertson, n.d.

4 King Papers, Claxton to King, 5 June 1943, in newly discovered King Papers, World War II—Reconstruction file.

5 Wartime Information Board Memo, n.d., att. to *ibid.*

6 PAC, Wartime Information Board Records, Vol. 7, file 2-16, D. B. Rogers to King, 20 Jan. 1943, encl. WIB survey #21, 16 Jan. 1943. Similar attitudes prevailed in the armed forces according to *ibid.*, John Grierson to King, 9 Oct. 1943. I am indebted to W. R. Young for bringing these files to my attention. There was general confirmation of the WIB data in Gallup polls. See *Public Opinion Quarterly*, VI (Fall, 1942), 482. By 1943 a flood of literature was beginning to reach the public. See, e.g., J. J. Heagerty; *Canada Plans Health Insurance* (a *Canadian Affairs* pamphlet, 1 Dec. 1943). L. C. Marsh and O. J. Firestone, *Will There be Jobs?* (*ibid.*, 1 Oct. 1944); G. F. Davidson, *Canada Plans Security* (*ibid.*, 15 Nov. 1944); and J. F. Close, 'One Million More Jobs', *Behind the Headlines*, V (1945).

7 J. M. Macdonnell, 'The Conservatives and a New National Policy', *Saturday Night*, 25 July 1942, 6; Queen's University, J. M. Macdonnell Papers, Vol. 52, Address, 12 June 1942.

8 For an account of Port Hope and the Winnipeg convention, see J. L. Granatstein, *The Politics of Survival* (Toronto, 1967), chapter VI.

9 For details on Liberal organization problems, see J. L. Granatstein, 'Financing the Liberal Party, 1935-45', in M. S. Cross and R. D. Bothwell, eds, *Policy by Other Means* (Toronto, 1972), pp. 192-3. The Cabinet committee consisted of Power, Mackenzie, McLarty, and Mulock.

10 Cited in T. M. Cane, 'A Test Case for Canadian Federalism: The Unemployment Insurance Issue, 1919-40', M.A. thesis, University of Western Ontario, 1972, 110. See also PAC, Ian Mackenzie Papers, file CNS-40.

11 Cane, 110.

12 King Diary, 16 Jan. 1940.

13 *Ibid.*, 1 Aug. 1940.

14 Wartime Information Board Reference Paper #12, 'Post War Planning in Canada', 30 July 1943; see also Robert England, *Discharged* (Toronto, 1943); Walter Woods, *Rehabilitation (A Combined Operation)* (Ottawa, 1953); and Walter Woods, *The Men Who Came Back* (Toronto, 1956) for detailed accounts of war gratuities and benefits.

15 Based on a reading of Mackenzie Papers.

16 P.C. 1218, 17 Feb. 1941.

17 King Papers, Mackenzie to King, 24 Mar. 1941, ff. 261797-8.

18 Minutes, att. to *ibid.*, Mackenzie to King, 31 Mar. 1941, ff. 261799ff.

19 *Ibid.*, Mackenzie to King, 27 May 1941, ff. 261837ff; McGill University, F. Cyril James Papers, Box 324, James to King, 24 Sept. 1943.

20 *Ibid.*, Box 334, James to Mackenzie, 16 July 1941, and Notes of Conversation with Mackenzie, 30 July 1941.

21 P.C. 6874, 2 Sept. 1941. For the Committee finances, see James Papers, Box 326, Budget files.

22 King Papers, Minutes of Committee on Reconstruction, 31 May 1941, ff. 261870ff.

23 On Marsh see Toronto *Star*, 13 Apr. 1943, and Montreal *Standard*, 20 Mar. 1943. I am much indebted to Dr Marsh for a long correspondence that was extremely helpful to me.

24 Copy in King Papers, Mackenzie to King, 2 June 1941, ff. 261851ff.

25 Queen's University, Principal W. S. Wallace Papers, Remarks, in Minutes of Proceedings of Special Joint Meeting, 4 Dec. 1942.

26 King Papers, Mackenzie to King, 5 Oct. 1942, f. 27869. The report is in Department of External Affairs, External Affairs Records, file 1843-A-40C.

27 P.C. 609, 23 Jan. 1943; James Papers, Box 334, James to Mackenzie, 6 July 1942; King Papers, Report of Economic Advisory Committee . . . 28 Nov. 1942 (in recently discovered materials, Reconstruction file); External Affairs Records, file 1843-A-40C, Part I, contains much material on the James Committee and its difficulties, as well as Economic Advisory Committee minutes.

28 James Papers, Box 334, Note of conversation, 19 Dec. 1942.

29 Mackenzie Papers, Vol. 79, file 567-27(3), Memo for Mr Mackenzie, 21 Dec. 1942. Among his publications, Marsh had written *Health and Unemployment* (Toronto, 1938), an apposite study for his new post.

30 There was a reasonable literature on social security: A. Brady, 'Reconstruction in Canada: A Note on Policies and Planning', *Canadian Journal of Economics and Political Science [CJEPS]*, VIII (1942); Harry Cassidy, *Social Security and Reconstruction in Canada* (Toronto, 1943); C. A. Ashley, ed., *Reconstruction in Canada* (Toronto, 1943); and F. C. James, 'The Impact of the War Upon Social Progress', *Educational Record* (July, 1942).

31 James Papers, Box 337, Marsh to James, 17 Jan. 1943.

32 King Papers, Vol. 59, James to King, 8 Feb. 1943, and reply, 13 Feb. 1943; James Papers, Box 331, James to Marsh, 17 Feb. 1943.

33 See Toronto *Globe and Mail*, 19 Mar. 1943; James Papers, Box 335-6, James to King, 15 Mar. 1943.

34 Montreal *Gazette*, 17 Mar. 1943; 'Pros and Cons Across Canada', Montreal *Gazette*, 24 Mar. 1943; PAC, Department of Finance Records, Vol. 3588, file S-12, WIB Press Survey, 15-22 Mar. 1943. For more academic discussion, see S. K. Jaffary, 'Social Security: The Beveridge and Marsh Reports', *CJEPS*, IX (1943), 571ff.

35 L. C. Marsh, 'What's Happened to the Marsh Report?', CBC National Talks, 8, 15 Apr. 1951. Texts in Dr Marsh's possession.

36 Mackenzie Papers, file 567-27(4), Mackenzie to J. W. McConnell and other publishers, 17 Mar. 1943.

37 References throughout to *Report on Social Security for Canada* (Ottawa, 1943), *passim*.

38 Finance Department Records, Vol. 3588, file S-12, Gordon to Mackintosh, 26 Mar. 1943.

39 *Canadian Forum*, XXII (1943), 292.

40 C. Whitton, *The Dawn of Ampler Life* (Toronto, 1943).

41 King Papers, Vol. 62, Woods to Mackenzie, 7 Jan. 1943.

42 *Ibid.*, Mackenzie to King, 8 Jan. 1943.

43 King Diary, 12 Jan. 1943.

44 *Ibid.*, 3 Mar. 1943; 17 Feb. 1943; 6 Mar. 1943.

45 House of Commons *Debates*, 5 Mar. 1943, p. 1020; *Industry and Humanity* (Toronto, 1918), pp. 346-7.

46 King Papers, Vol. 59, Ilsley to King, 17 Mar. 1943. For Mackenzie's response see *ibid.*, Vol. 62, Mackenzie to Ilsley, 18 Mar. 1943.

47 King Diary, 24 Mar. 1943.

48 *Ibid.*, 9 June 1943.

49 *Ibid.*, 23 July 1943.

50 Queen's University, Grant Dexter Papers, Memorandum, 1 Sept. 1943. See also Myer Siemiatycki, 'Communism in One Constituency: The Communist Party and the Jewish Community of Montreal, with particular reference to the election of Fred Rose to Parliament in 1943 and 1945', York University graduate paper, 1974.

51 J. W. Pickersgill, *The Mackenzie King Record*, Vol. I: *1939-44* (Toronto, 1960), p. 566.

52 PAC, J. W. Dafoe Papers, Power to Dafoe, 9 Aug. 1943.

53 King Papers, Mackenzie to King, 19 Aug. 1943, ff. 87540ff.

54 Cf. King Diary, 2 Sept. 1943.

55 King Papers, Vol. 62, McLarty to King, 2 Sept. 1943; Vol. 56, King to Crerar, 2 Sept. 1943.

56 E.g., *ibid.*, Vol. 62, McLarty to King, 21 Sept. 1943.

57 Toronto *Globe and Mail*, 18 Sept. 1943.

58 Printed in J. W. Pickersgill, *The Liberal Party* (Toronto, 1962), pp. 32ff.

59 King Papers, Memo, Claxton to King, 21 Sept. 1943, ff. C209825ff.

60 Queen's University, Norman Lambert Papers, Diary, 24 Sept. 1943; King Diary, 24 Sept. 1944.

61 Public Archives of Nova Scotia, A. L. Macdonald Papers, Diary, 27(?) Sept. 1943.

62 Pickersgill, I, pp. 577-8.

63 King Diary, 25 Sept. 1943; King Papers, Memo of caucus proceedings, 24 Sept. 1943, ff. C208503ff.; Toronto *Globe and Mail*, 25, 27 Sept. 1943.

64 PAC, Brooke Claxton Papers, Vol. 31, Claxton to G. Ferguson, 5 Oct. 1943.

65 Cf. Mrs Margery King Papers (Toronto), King to Mrs King, 6 Oct. 1943. I am indebted to Prof. Michael Cross for securing this material for me.

66 Pickersgill, I, p. 583.

67 NLF Papers, Vol. 861, transcript of meeting 27-8 Sept. 1943, 140-70.

68 King Diary, 27 Sept. 1943.

69 *Ibid.* 28 Sept. 1943.

70 NLF Papers, Vol. 861, transcript; 'The Task of Liberalism', (Ottawa, 1943).

71 Dexter Papers, Memo, 1 Nov. 1943, 23 Dec. 1943; King Diary 27, 29 Dec. 1943.

72 King Papers, Memo, 23 Nov. 1943, f. C209679.

73 Pickersgill, I, p. 632.

74 King Diary, 16 Nov. 1943.

75 King Papers, Mackenzie to King, 17 Nov. 1943, ff. 87662ff.

76 Copies of the Minister's replies are in *ibid.*, Notes and Memoranda, Vol. 141.

77 Pickersgill, I, p. 632.

78 King Papers, Howe to King, 17 Nov. 1943, ff. 84594ff. Cf. the comments of George Orwell on capitalism's inability to produce the goods in S. Orwell and I. Angus, eds, *The Collected Essays, Journalism and Letters of George Orwell*, Vol. II: *1940-43* (London, 1970), pp. 99ff.

79 King Papers, Ilsley to King, 4 Jan. 1944, ff. 104015ff.

80 Dexter Papers, Memo, 23 Dec. 1944; King Diary, 6 Jan. 1944.

81 *Ibid.*

82 *Ibid.*, 11 Jan. 1944. The names of the departments were not finally decided until much later.

83 *Ibid.*, 22 Jan. 1944.

84 *Ibid.*, 24-5 Jan. 1944; Dexter Papers, Memo, 12 Feb. 1944.

85 House of Commons *Debates*, 27 Jan. 1944, pp. 1-2. See also C. A. Pearson, 'A New Social Order: Liberal Party Philosophy, 1944-47', M.A. thesis, Carleton University, 1967.

86 King Papers, Vol. 71, Dr Bates to King, 27 June 1944, and reply, 30 June 1944.

87 *Ibid.*, Vol. 82, King to Mackenzie, 26 July 1944.

88 House of Commons *Debates*, 28 July 1944, pp. 5534-5.

89 Cited by W. A. Mackintosh, 'The White Paper on Employment and Income in its 1945 Setting', in *Canadian Economic Policy Since the War* (Ottawa, 1966), p. 13.

90 Public Archives of Manitoba, Stuart Garson Papers, Beattie to Garson, 10 July 1944. The public was perhaps less afraid than the politicians. A WIB opinion survey (#68, 28 July 1945) showed only 27 per cent of a national sample preferring a return to the *status quo ante bellum*, with a full 42 per cent believing social security desirable. Wartime Information Board Records, Vol. 4.

91 Mackintosh, p. 15; W. A. Mackintosh, 'Canadian Economic Policy from 1945 to 1957—Origins and Influences', in H. G. J. Aitken, *et al.*, *The American Economic Impact on Canada* (Durham, 1959) pp. 56-60.

92 Mackintosh, 'White Paper', p. 15; Department of Finance, W. Clifford Clark Papers, file E-3-5, Mackintosh to Clark, Robertson *et al.*, 27 Mar. 1945.

93 King Papers, Heeney to King, 30 Mar. 1945, in newly discovered King Papers, World War II—Reconstruction file; Mackintosh, 'White Paper', p. 16.

94 House of Commons *Debates*, 12 Apr. 1945, pp. 808ff.

95 *Employment and Income with Special Reference to the Initial Period of Reconstruction* (Ottawa, 1945), pp. 21, 23; Mackintosh, 'White Paper', p. 18.

96 *Employment and Income*, p. 11.

97 Mackenzie Papers, file 1-36, address, 8 Feb. 1945.

98 M. S. Horn, 'The League for Social Reconstruction: Socialism and Nationalism in Canada, 1931-1945', Ph.D. thesis, University of Toronto, 1969, 542n.

99 King Papers, Extracts, n.d., ff. C187579ff.

100 House of Commons *Debates*, 13 Feb. 1929, pp. 85-90; *Report . . . of the Select Standing Committee on Industrial and International Relations . . . May 31, 1929* (Ottawa, 1929), p. iv. Both cited in Patricia Oxley, 'Family Allowance Furor', graduate paper, York University, 1971, 2-3.

101 Cited in *ibid.*, 3.

102 *Ibid.*

103 Hon. C. P. McTague Interview, 1 June 1965.

104 *Report of the National War Labour Board Arising out of its Public Inquiry into Labour Relations and Wage Conditions . . .* (Ottawa, 1943), p. 15; cf. King Papers, N. Robertson to King, 8 June 1943, ff. C187885-6.

105 *Report of the National War Labour Board . . .*, p. 27; Dexter Papers, Memo, 3 Sept. 1943.

106 Pickersgill, I, p. 590.

107 King Diary, 14 Sept. 1943.

108 External Affairs Records, file 1843-A-40C, Pt. II, Summary of Discussion for Economic Advisory Committee, 17 Sept. 1943.

109 Pickersgill, I, p. 591; Dexter Papers, Memo, 2 Oct. 1943.

110 Hon. J. W. Pickersgill interview, 13 Aug. 1971; Bruce Hutchison, *The Incredible Canadian* (Toronto, 1952), pp. 327-8.

111 Dexter Papers, Memo, 23 Dec. 1943. Not all the civil servants favoured the plan. See A. K. Eaton, *Essays in Taxation* (Toronto, 1966), pp. 134ff. for the views of one who did not.

112 'Children's Allowances', copy in Mackenzie Papers, Vol. 30.

113 Claxton Papers, Vol. 62, Memo, Pickersgill to Claxton, 12 Jan. 1944.

114 *Ibid.*

115 'Children's Allowances'.

116 Pickersgill, I, p. 634.

117 Macdonald Diary, 13 Jan. 1944.

118 *Ibid.*, 20 Jan. 1944.

119 *Ibid.*, 15 June 1944; King Diary, 15 June 1944; J. W. Pickersgill and D. F. Forster, *The Mackenzie King Record*, Vol. II: *1944-45* (Toronto, 1968) pp. 27-8.

120 Macdonald Diary, 15 June 1944.

121 *Ibid.*, 20 June 1944.

122 Pickersgill, II, p. 35.

123 *Ibid.*, pp. 35-6.

124 For comment, see documents in PAC, John Bracken Papers, Vol. 47; in PAC, CCF Records, Vols 66-7; in Queen's University, T. A. Crerar Papers, Crerar to Dexter, 17 June 1944; in *Maclean's*, 15 July 1944 and 1 Aug. 1944; and S. M. Lipset, *Agrarian Socialism* (New York, 1968), *passim*.

125 House of Commons *Debates*, 31 July 1944, p. 5677; Queen's University, H. A. Bruce Papers, Bruce to Graydon, 20 July 1944; H. A. Bruce, *Varied Operations* (Toronto, 1958), p. 328.

126 Toronto *Star*, 24 June 1944.

127 Toronto *Globe and Mail*, 10 Aug. 1944; see Oxley, 39-41.

128 Cited in *ibid.*, 13.

129 A. R. Adamson Papers (Port Credit, Ont.), Diary, 26 July 1944; PAC, Gordon Graydon Papers, Vol. 22, Social Security file, Caucus Notes, n.d.; Granatstein, *Politics of Survival*, pp. 168-70.

130 Claxton Papers, PARC Box 269199, Claxton to T. W. L. MacDermot, 2 Aug. 1944; King Papers, Claxton to King, 6 July 1944, f. C188050.

131 *Public Opinion Quarterly*, VIII (Fall, 1944), 446.

132 Claxton Papers, Vol. 176, 'Health and Welfare Expenditures . . .', 26 Nov. 1945.

133 Macdonald Papers, file 5-81, Claxton to Macdonald, 15 Feb. 1945.

134 King Papers, Vol. 77, Godbout to King, 4 Feb. 1944, and Vol. 58, Godbout to King, 1 Dec. 1943.

135 For a good analysis of Quebec voting, see Kenneth McRoberts, 'Contrasts in French-Canadian Nationalism: The Impact of Industrialization Upon the Electoral Role of French-Canadian Nationalism, 1934-1944', M.A. thesis, University of Chicago, 1966, 146ff. For the Duplessis attack on family allowances, see correspondence and memos in King Papers, ff. 123170ff.; Oxley, 41ff.

136 Pickersgill, II, pp. 42-3.

137 *Ibid.*, pp. 45-6.

8. A Nation on the World Stage

The Cabinet War Committee's deliberations were sombre, Mackenzie King recorded in his diary on July 15, 1942, when the ministers were 'discussing [the] procedure to be taken vis-à-vis the U.S. because of Churchill and Roosevelt having decided to plan the war themselves and ignore Canada. . . . ' This was important, not least because Canada's ability to get some of the supplies it needed was directly affected. Chubby Power, King noted of his pugnacious Air Minister, 'wanted to fight by withholding radio direction finders, aluminum and other substances that the U.S. wanted from Canada. Later seemed to be arguing that the matter should be taken up with Churchill and the President. I pointed out that both of these were extreme measures until we at least knew the exact situation. . . . I suggested Power himself should go to Washington and talk with his opposite number whomever he might be.' But Power said there was little use: 'No one there would talk to him.'[1]

A minor incident soon resolved, of course. And yet the Cabinet discussion in July 1942 was not untypical of others that regularly took place throughout the war. Notwithstanding Canada's very substantial contribution to the Allied war effort in terms of men, munitions, money, and raw materials, the nation did not receive influence commensurate with its participation in the war. There were a wide variety of reasons for this failure, not least Mackenzie King's unwillingness to fight as hard as he should have to get a greater role for Canada. Still, the most compelling reason for it is the simplest—the United States and Great Britain preferred to concentrate power in their control, not to share it with lesser powers.

I

One such example of Great Power indifference concerned the Combined Boards, those bodies announced by Roosevelt and Churchill on January 26, 1942, to ensure complete co-ordination of the Anglo-American war effort, including the production and distribution of war supplies. Initially a Combined Raw Materials Board, a Combined Munitions Assignment Board, and the Combined Shipping Adjustment Board were formed, followed in June 1942 by the Combined Production and Resources Board and the Combined Food Board. The latter two were to concern Canadians most, but all the Boards posed the problem of just how Canada would fit into this Anglo-American system.

Canada's position concerned the government from the moment it knew of the establishment of the Boards. In his first words to the Prime Minister about the Boards on January 28, the Under Secretary, Norman Robertson, felt constrained to point out that no one could commit Canada without its consent. 'They will have to consult Canada whenever Canadian cooperation is required,' he said, pointing out that what was needed was to work out the ways in which consultation could take place.[2] From Washington Hume Wrong, the second in command of the Legation, defined the ways Canada could claim recognition.

> The principle, I think, is that each member of the grand alliance should have a voice in the conduct of the war proportionate to its contribution to the general war effort. A subsidiary principle is that the influence of the various countries should be greatest in connection with those matters with which they are most directly concerned.

That was a principle that would eventually become an axiom of Canadian war and postwar policy, but Wrong's notable good sense was probably missing when he suggested that Canada should seek 'representation on all or most of the combined bodies in collaboration with the United Kingdom or as part of a general Commonwealth representation.'[3] That was not the way to Mackenzie King's heart.

Hume Wrong may have been correct, however, when he wrote to his friend, L. B. Pearson, in Ottawa that Canadian policy was largely responsible for the fact that Canada was being ignored by the British and Americans in the Combined Boards set-up:

> Mainly for reasons of internal political balance the Government has hitherto adopted in these matters what may unkindly be called a

semi-colonial position. With the entry of the United States into the war we are not as well placed to influence the conduct of the war as we were when the United States was neutral. Canadian influence can be greatest when there is a divergence of policy between the United Kingdom and the United States. Now that they are partners, we become only a junior member of the partnership. If we had sought earlier to undertake more extensive political responsibilities, it would be easier now to maintain our status. We have tended, however, to be satisfied with the form rather than the substance.[4]

Still, what was to be done? Grant Dexter of the *Winnipeg Free Press* saw some confidential memoranda on February 9 and, as he recorded, the External Affairs view was that the Boards 'overlooked or ignored' the special relationship between Canada and the United States. The problem was complicated from Canada's point of view because the British expected Canada's liaison with the Boards to take place in London, something that made the Canadians unhappy. 'We might often wish to line up with the U.S. but being members of the U.K. side of the committee,' Dexter noted, 'we could not do so.' A possible course might be to remain aloof from the Boards, but neither this nor any other course except representation on the Boards seemed particularly palatable. Dexter wrote that his sources said Mackenzie King was convinced that Canada could not force its way onto the joint committees, while C. D. Howe was most concerned about the effect the Combined Boards would have on the existing Canada-United States economic structure. 'He thinks it is silly to even talk about approaching Washington via London and his line is that Washington and London must come to us.' And, Dexter said, Howe was willing to bargain toughly. If Canada needed steel and couldn't get it from the Boards, it would simply divert men from copper, zinc, and aluminum production into steel and let the Anglo-American war effort run down. 'Asked if he would go through if his bluff is called,' Dexter noted, Howe 'chuckled and said he'd see when the time comes.'[5]

After a visit to Washington, however, Howe convinced himself that the Boards posed no problem for Canada. The system could be made to work, for the Americans involved were the same men who had established the systems that already worked so well between Canada and the United States. Munitions ordered by Britain in Canada would be counted as part of the United Kingdom pool, while United States orders in Canada would go into the American pool.[6] The pragmatism of the businessman was very much in evidence. The War Committee as a whole, however, tended to prefer a closer and more formal relationship with Washington than with the United Kingdom on the Munitions Assignment Board, partly as a response to the obstacles that London was throwing in Canada's way. In the British view, Canada should be represented 'like the other Dominions' at the London end only,[7] not at Washington at all, a view that simply neglected the special requirements of the Canadian-American continental relationship and the rather substantial difference in the Canadian war effort when compared with that of all the other Dominions lumped together. At the Cabinet War Committee meeting on March 18, as the Prime Minister wrote, 'we are all of one mind that our relationship should be with the U.S. who are quite prepared to give full representation on boards there, than with London [where] there seems to be a feeling that we cannot be represented without creating embarrassment to other Dominions, etc.'[8]

But in fact when Canada tried to secure representation on the Munitions Assignment Board in Washington, difficulties developed there too. Mackenzie King approached Roosevelt directly on this point on April 16, and won what he believed was the President's approval.[9] But matters were baulked by Harry Hopkins, Roosevelt's friend and the chairman of the Washington MAB. His suggestion was that Canada should apply instead for representation on the Combined Production and Resources Board, then in process of formation. In the end, after lengthy and troubled conversations and after an offer of three-quarters membership on the MAB was made and rejected, Canada followed the original Hopkins suggestion. The Americans were not all that co-operative, although as Professor Stacey notes, much of the difficulty sprang from disputes among ministers and departments in Ottawa, most noticeably between Howe's Munitions and Supply and Ralston's National Defence.[10]

The eventual result saw the government establish the Canadian War Production and Assignments Board in Ottawa with representation from both the United States and the United Kingdom. In the view of the United States Army's official historians, the Canadian Board was more useful as a link with the Department of Munitions and Supply and National Defence than as an agency for making allocations of munitions on any strategic basis. American observers noted that Canadian needs always received priority and the remainder of Canadian munitions production was allocated on the basis of contractual obligation, not strategic necessity.[11]

The effect of the American and British treatment of Canadian claims was to rouse King to anger. He told R. H. Brand, the British Ministry of Food representative in the United States, that he was in difficulties because of the 'embarrassing position that Canada was being placed in through no representation on Boards that are of vital concern to us. I said I was anxious not to be difficult in any way, but had to safeguard the national position, particularly in the light of precedence [sic] being established even before post-war matters received attention.'[12] A few days later on July 30, 1942 he made the same point to Sir Frederick Leith-Ross* of the British Treasury: '. . . we felt that we were not getting the representation to which our country was entitled on boards dealing with economic and military matters that I thought our people expected in view of the fact they had been in the war for nearly 3 years while the Americans had not been in a year as yet. . . . Also of the fact that we were one of the large producing countries . . . had provided Britain with a gift of a billion dollars . . .'[13]

The Combined Food Board was one of the new bodies on which Canada felt entitled to representation, and a demand to this effect was made in London and Washington on July 14.[14] The thrust of the argument, largely based on a memorandum drafted by John Deutsch, a special assistant to Norman Robertson, was that 'Next to the United States, Canada is by far the most important contributor of foodstuffs to the common pool of the United Nations.'[15] The initial response from London was cool, arguing on the one hand that the Combined Food Board would only make recommendations and on the other that Canadian membership 'would not make for technical efficiency'.†[16]

This kind of two-faced argument was not calculated to please Ottawa, and for one of the few times in the war the Canadian officials began to talk tough. Telegrams from British officials in Ottawa to London made clear that there was little possibility of a further billion dollar gift to

---

*Leith-Ross did not impress King who wrote that he 'struck me as one of the types of Englishmen who antagonize by their mere appearance and manner. "Tranquil consciousness of effortless superiority." He seemed to think that because Mr. Eden thought a certain course was desirable . . . that ought to be sufficient. I felt like saying we were not beholden in any way [to] Mr. Eden.' King Diary, 30 July 1942.

†The real reason for British reluctance to allow Canada onto the Combined Food Board was expressed by Lord Woolton, the Minister of Food: 'If we give way to the Canadians there is a danger that all the United Nations are going to be represented on the Food Board at Washington. This will mean that the centre of gravity will move from London to Washington, and the Combined Food Board will determine the food policy of this country.' R. J. Hammond, Food, Vol. 1: The Growth of Policy (London, 1951), p. 242.

the United Kingdom unless the Whitehall attitude changed, and Graham Towers of the Bank of Canada was reported to have said that London's CFB position treated Canada 'as a small boy to be relegated to the sidelines'.[17] The High Commissioner also threw his weight behind a more flexible position with regard to Canadian claims,[18] but these representations notwithstanding the British stood firm. At a crucial meeting in Ottawa on September 16 between British officials and Canadian ministers, the surprised British won despite all the Canadian threats. The only sweetener offered to Canada was British support for Canadian membership on the Combined Production and Resources Board and a British statement that the CFB would in no way alter the existing arrangements protecting Canada's food exports to Britain.[19] Mackenzie King was satisfied that everything had been settled 'without any recriminations',[20] but the whole episode fitted neatly Lester Pearson's complaint that Canadian policy was all too often 'the strong glove over the velvet hand'.[21]

The offer of membership on the Combined Production and Resources Board, made on September 16, 1942, had been the product of much heart-searching in London. A Foreign Office minute on September 7 worried that there was no guarantee that Canada would settle for the CPRB if it was offered and drop its pressure for membership on the Food Board. Was this 'merely the thin edge of the wedge?'[22] Indeed it was, but the alternative—a Canada-United States Production and Resources Board as suggested by C. D. Howe—was even worse. On administrative grounds it would delay matters[23] and on high political grounds, as Malcolm MacDonald warned from Ottawa, it would 'lead [to] the Dominion and the United States becoming steadily more closely associated to our possible prejudice. Surely we wish to put some check on this process.'[24] London worried about this—and also about future cash gifts from Canada. Clement Attlee, the Secretary of State for Dominion Affairs, was said by his officials to share 'the view that Canada's claims are special and strong. Evidence is accumulating daily to show that failure to meet Canada over this matter is likely to have serious effects upon the spirit of co-operation which has been so excellent hitherto.'[25] The result was the British offer of September 16. The Americans had no objections to this, Harry Hopkins earlier having suggested CPRB membership as an alternative to membership on the Munitions Assignment Board. Perhaps it really was, as Professor Stacey suggests, that everyone except the Canadians recognized that the CPRB would not be a very important body.[26] And certainly the Canadian position was that membership on the Board did not in any way derogate from Canada's primary responsibility—the supply of Canada's own armed forces from Canada.[27]

The Canadian case for membership on the Combined Food Board was renewed in early 1943, much as the Foreign Office had feared it would be in September last. There were, Canadian officials believed, certain difficulties in transacting business because Canada was not a member of the CFB.[28] The claim was advanced in meetings with British officials in March who, naturally enough, urged that Canada not press its claims. But this advice was rejected for a variety of reasons, eventually transmitted to the British in a long memorandum on April 13, 1943. The CFB now dealt extensively with commodities of great concern to Canada, a change from the state of affairs in 1942 when the Board dealt mainly in commodities that Canada merely imported. In addition Canada was already represented on most of the CFB commodity sub-committees—'The special position of Canada has thus already been recognized and the addition of a full Canadian member to the Board is the logical completion of what has already been done.' The memorandum by Norman Robertson also argued that public opinion demanded representation, and the Under Secretary rebutted the argument that if Canada won membership other states would demand similar treatment. These British objections, he noted, were the same ones 'advanced from the first against Canadian membership' and Canada could not accept them because 'it can be urged that if the present situation continues, the Food Board will gradually lose its influence and authority because it is constituted on too narrow a base.'[29]

In fact, Canada was close to winning its point. The British Food Mission in the United States seemed agreeable to Canadian membership now for practical reasons, and the Ministry of Food in London grudgingly prepared to accept Canadian membership.[30] In the course of the summer the American government too became convinced that a reorganization of the CFB was desirable, and although the theoretical basis of the Canadian claim was in no way conceded,[31] Canadian representation on the CFB won American support as well.[32] Canada accepted membership on October 27, 1943, a satisfying conclusion to a battle that had lasted more than a year.

II

At much the same time as the struggle for representation on the Combined Boards was under way, Canada was fighting to gain representation on the directing council of the great relief organization that the Allied powers were creating to administer matters in liberated Europe, the body that eventually became known as the United Nations Relief and Rehabilitation Administration. Discussions among the various Allied governments on this score had begun as early as August 1941,[33] and in the next month an inter-allied meeting pledged to make available food, raw materials, and other necessities to help rehabilitate Europe.[34] As originally envisaged, this inter-allied committee would have had all belligerents as equal members, but because of objections to various aspects of the scheme from the Soviet Union, consideration of relief lapsed until the spring of 1942.

American proposals at that time called for a United Nations Relief Council to be composed of representatives of the United Nations and of other friendly governments, the Council to be run by an Executive Committee composed of the Big Four powers. The British soon asked for Canadian concurrence in principle with this new plan, and in discussions in External Affairs and in the Cabinet War Committee at the beginning of June 1942, the government position was formulated: Canada agreed in principle but reserved the right to raise the question of Canadian representation at a later date. The grounds for this eventual claim were clear: 'Canada's probable post-war position as a major supplier of needed foodstuffs'.[35] Once again, Canada was forced to begin a struggle for what the government believed to be fair representation.

The British position, as expressed to the Canadian government by British officials in Ottawa and by officers at Whitehall in the summer of 1942, was very familiar. Canada's representation on the directing body of UNRRA would create problems, both because other states—Australia and Brazil were usually cited—would demand representation and because 'the Americans might not like the British side over-weighed by Canadian representation.'[36] This was a view guaranteed to infuriate Canadians, but the British were generally willing to be accommodating in other directions, primarily because of gratitude for the Canadian cash gift—and hopes for more. The Foreign Office view, usually expressed by Gladwyn Jebb, was that Canada should be brought onto the Combined Food Board instead of onto the Relief body,[37] but as we have seen that course created problems of its own.

The whole question of Canadian representation was thrashed out at a meeting of British officials in London on September 16, 1942. The High Commissioner in Ottawa, Malcolm MacDonald, was not present, but his views had been set down in a telegram. The Canadians would settle for nothing less than full representation on UNRRA, he warned, and the Ottawa position was based on four main props: too much executive power was concentrated in British and American hands; a judicious widening of membership and sharing of power would be justified; a belief that Canada's contribution in certain fields—munitions and food, for example—was such as to warrant proper consideration; and a fear that when the Canadian people learned how badly Canada was being treated there would be a row that would prejudice the war effort and aid to Britain.[38] Those arguments received substantial weight at the officials' meeting, as N. B. Ronald, the Foreign Office's representative, noted.

> I argued that there was really no analogy between this and the Combined Boards. The latter had already been set up and additions to their membership were in effect in the gift of the U.K. and the U.S. The Relief Policy Committee, however, was very far from realization: it was a piece of machinery proposed for the operation of a project, the general lines of which had not yet been agreed to by anyone. Furthermore, membership would anyhow not be in the gift of the U.S. and the U.K. but a matter for consideration by an as yet unknown number of Governments. I found myself in a minority of one. Their anxiety about a renewal of the 'free gift' of dollars made the Treasury anxious to meet Canada. The Dominions Office as usual were all out to appease Canada and brushed aside my question of how they would deal with a possible Australian claim also to be accorded a Director's seat. . . . The Ministries of Food and Production . . . were all in favour of meeting Canada . . . in order to be able the better to resist her claims in other directions.[39]

The Dominions Office rationale for its support of Canada's claim was probably much as Ronald described it, inter-departmental pecking order and pique aside. But Dominions Office memoranda were more perceptive than Ronald was willing to concede: 'It is true that Mr. Mackenzie King . . . has so far shown little desire to participate in higher strategical decisions and that even now it is on bodies dealing with questions of supply . . . that he is primarily pressing for a full measure of Canadian representation. In questions of food and relief,' one such memorandum argued, 'Canada's contribution and practical interest are great, and it is doubtless felt that Canada cannot afford (as she might in purely strategical matters limited to the war period) to surrender her claims to a voice in the formation of policies which will ramify into the post-war period.' The Dominions Office also noted the Canadian claim that Canada could contribute more in relief than China and Russia certainly, and possibly more than Britain. Finally, and most important, 'Canada's position is essentially different from that of other smaller powers in that her contribution to the war effort is far and away greater than theirs.' This was crucial, and the Dominions Office view, firmly stated, was that unless Canada's wishes were met on UNRRA, further cash aid was doubtful, a matter of importance because Canada's aid from April to June 1942, for example, was two-fifths that of the United States. 'In other words, Canada's contribution to us in the way of free supplies is, per head of population, five times as great as that of the United States.'[40]

The Foreign Office, however, remained largely in charge of high policy and, as a Dominions Office official told MacDonald in Ottawa, 'Right from the start the Foreign Office have taken a line which involved squeezing Canada off the Committee. . . . the Cabinet decided that the balance of advantage lay in confining membership' to the Great Powers.[41] This attitude even led the Foreign Office to attempt to block an American move to expand the directing committee to seven members.[42] But when this move failed, the British changed position and supported expansion while the Russians vehemently opposed it, now supported by the Americans.[43] The British switch did have the salutary effect, as MacDonald reported from Ottawa, of improving the prospects for further Canadian aid to the United Kingdom.[44]

The Canadian position by this time had crystallized into a statement of what would shortly become known as the functional principle. Hume Wrong had come close to formulating this early in 1942 during the initial discussions about the Combined Boards, and Loring Christie of the Department of External Affairs had played with functionalism in his brilliant policy memoranda before the war. But the first explicit statement of the principle came in a memorandum sent to the Prime Minister on January 18, 1943 by the Under Secretary, Norman Robertson.

While experience between the wars has shown the great practical difficulties of applying to membership in international bodies the legal concept of the equality of states, we are confident that no workable international system can be based on the concentration of influence and authority wholly in bodies composed of a few great powers to the exclusion of all the rest. It is not always the largest powers that have the greatest contribution to make to the work of these bodies or the greatest stake in their success. In international economic organizations such as the Relief Administration representation on such bodies can often be determined on a functional basis and in our view this principle should be applied whenever it is feasible.[45]

This statement of principle was approved by the Cabinet War Committee on January 21 and sent to Washington and London.

The functional principle did not meet with immediate acceptance, of course. In Washington, Dean Acheson, the Assistant Secretary of State responsible for economic policy in the Department of State, was prepared to see Canada serve on the important Committee on Supplies of UNRRA but not on the directing committee.[46] This position was firmly rejected by the Canadian government in a tough memorandum to the United States on February 9: 'The Canadian Government and people are ready to do their full share in the task of organizing and providing post-war relief. They do not feel they can do so if effective participation in the formulation of policy is to be restricted to the four greatest Powers, two of which will themselves be major recipients of relief.'[47] The Americans, according to Lester Pearson in Washington, were generally convinced that the Canadian position was strong, but they argued that it was the Russians who were blocking Canadian participation, not them.[48] The result was another Canadian note delivered to representatives of the four Great Powers on February 26: 'the Canadian position has been further reviewed. . . . [Canada] will not find it possible to participate in the activities of the proposed Organization unless Canada is afforded in some way a position in the direction of its work which is commensurate with the contribution to international relief which Canada undoubtedly will be expected to make.'[49] That was as tough a position as Ottawa had taken on any question during the war.

The hard line produced some results. On February 26 Pearson reported that the Big Four were willing to compromise, guaranteeing Canada the post of Chairman of the Supplies Committee and the right to sit with the directing committee whenever supply matters were discussed. The External Affairs' response held that this was acceptable,[50] but the Cabinet War Committee on March 3 refused to agree, with Ilsley, St Laurent, Power, and the Prime Minister all arguing that as the compromise left the general principle of four-power control unchanged it should be refused.[51] Pearson communicated this reiterated demand for full membership to Acheson on March 4. 'He said,' Acheson observed, 'that he thought the underlying reason for the War Cabinet's decision was its belief that the form that this organization took would furnish a pattern for further economic organizations and that Canada must insist upon having a larger part or else it would be excluded from such participation on all other similiar organizations.'[52] A letter from Mackenzie King to the Canadian Minister in Washington, Leighton McCarthy, made the same point: 'We cannot accept the idea that our destinies can be entrusted to the four larger Powers and we have advanced the principle that representation on International bodies should depend on the extent of the contribution which each country would be expected to make to their work.'[53] That was the functional principle, neatly put.

The Canadian stand clearly had an impact. In Washington, Gladwyn Jebb of the British Foreign Office told Pearson that the solution might be for Canada to take Britain's place on the policy committee of UNRRA, a suggestion that frightened the Canadians: 'The idea that Canada might represent the whole Commonwealth . . . savors of outworn constitutional doctrine.' The Americans and others would argue that Canada was merely a spokesman for the United Kingdom and, as the sensibly nationalistic Robertson wrote to the Prime Minister, 'I should favour having both Canada and the United Kingdom on the Central Committee and not either Canada or the United Kingdom.'[54]

But on March 31 Anthony Eden came to Ottawa for a visit. In his conversation with Mackenzie King the subject of UNRRA was discussed, of course, and Eden argued strenuously for the first compromise position of membership on the Supplies Committee and representation at the policy committee when supplies were discussed. 'As practically all questions related to supplies,' King recorded Eden's argument, 'this meant Canada getting the largest possible recognition. He felt this went as far as it was possible to go in reconciling views of Russians, Americans, etc.' Later Eden told King that 'if we did not accept the position as now proposed the whole business would have to fall through.'[55] Eden's arguments converted King, who was also being worked on by Lester Pearson, for on April 7 the War Committee accepted the compromise. There were strong objections from Power and Ilsley, but King prevailed.

I said to my colleagues that in considering the matter, we would have to consider how the Canadian people would view the rejection of a proposal of the kind with its possible consequences and repercussions as against refusing to participate at all because not given full recognition. . . .

Before going into the Cabinet, I had felt the only thing for us to do was to accept. We would have gained nothing by refusing . . . [except] the ill-will of the four great powers. . . . The whole business is very involved and is one of the cases where it is clearly impossible for a lesser power to really do other than be largely governed by the views of the greater powers. . . .

This was one of the cases where, as Prime Minister, I would have had to decide regardless of what the others might have said in discussion. I felt the right decision has been made and was relieved to have Howe and Ralston support the proposal where, earlier, they had been opposed to so doing.[56]

On balance King's judgement was sensible. Face was involved for everyone, and great powers were less willing to lose it than Canada.*

Canada contributed to UNRRA 1 per cent of her national income in November 1943, followed by a second and similar contribution in August 1945. Lester Pearson, named the Canadian representative to UNRRA, was elected Chairman of the Committee on Supplies, Chairman of the General Committee, and Chairman of the Committee on General Policy at the 1944 meetings of UNRRA in Montreal.[57] The Canadian role was a major one, even though it turned out that the Chairman of the Supplies Committee did not have a vote when he sat with the Big Four representatives on the Steering Committee. Ultimately Canadian pride was assuaged by elevation to the Steering Committee, on motion by the United States in mid-1945.[58]

The experience with UNRRA had been revealing. Canada had argued firmly for its rights and lost, despite its best efforts. But that functional principle on which Canadians had stood was worth reiter-

---

*Involvement in international affairs had its rewards, of course. Brooke Claxton returned from the UNRRA conference in Atlantic City in late 1943 in a state of near euphoria. 'I was impressed more than ever with the opportunity of Canada to affect the main movement of events,' he wrote to J. W. Dafoe. 'It happens that we are almost the only country whose best interest is served by being objective. That is recognized by a good deal of the other nations. They also recognize our tremendous capacity demonstrated by our contributions during the war.' PAC, Brooke Claxton Papers, Vol. 223, Claxton to Dafoe, 10 Dec. 1943.

ation, and Mackenzie King propounded it for the first time in public in a speech in Parliament on July 9, 1943.

> . . . authority in international affairs must not be concentrated exclusively in the largest powers. . . . A number of new international organizations are likely to be set up as a result of the war. In the view of the government, effective representations on these bodies should neither be restricted to the largest states nor necessarily extended to all states. Representation should be determined on a functional basis which will admit to full membership those countries, large or small, which have the greatest contribution to make to the particular object in question. . . .[59]

This would remain a guiding principle of Canadian policy through the war and beyond.

III

During the debates over Canada's place on the Combined Boards and in UNRRA, one of the key Canadian bargaining positions was the nation's willingness or unwillingness to give further financial aid to Britain. The billion dollar gift of early 1942 was a generous donation, made no less so by the fact that it served to keep Canadian factories working at full blast and prevented a war-debt controversy after the war. The gift was a testimony to Canada's wealth and stature, a tribute to Britain, and a conscience offering. But whether more aid would be given or whether it would or could be offered on such a grandiose scale was by no means certain.

This was a crucial matter to British officials in Ottawa and London, primarily because the $1 billion was being spent far faster than anyone had anticipated early in 1942. In July a Dominions Office paper noted that 'Instead of lasting into 1943 as was originally hoped the gift seems likely to run out about the middle of October.' One possible suggestion to stretch out the billion dollars was that Canada could undertake to pay all the costs of her RCAF squadrons serving in the United Kingdom, something that under the terms of the Air Training Plan agreement of 1939 had not been done. This idea, first raised during the discussions preceding the billion dollar gift in late 1941, interested Air Minister Power, primarily because the process of Canadianizing the RCAF on which he was working would be facilitated immensely if Canada paid the complete costs for her airmen. The idea was likely to appeal to the British, too, because the money involved was estimated at $150-250 million, or enough to extend the life of the gift six to ten weeks. Another proposal, also mooted in 1941, was that Canada could take over all British investment in munitions plants in Canada. Other suggestions were that Canadian exports to the British Isles could be cut or that Britain could get more goods from the United States under Lend-Lease, two proposals unlikely to win much support in Ottawa.[60] One course that could no longer be followed was the repatriation of government bonds. The Dominion, the Deputy Minister of Finance said, 'has wiped out its debt to British investors,' although there was still approximately $1 billion of stocks and bonds outstanding for provincial and municipal governments and for private corporations.[61]

In the British Treasury's view, the ideal state of affairs with Canada would be 'if our relations . . . were placed on a reciprocal aid basis'. S. D. Waley, the Under Secretary of Treasury, argued that 'we should cease to make any claim for the equipment and maintenance of Canadian Forces and they would supply munitions, raw materials and food for the sterling area without any monetary charge. It would no doubt help if Canada were regarded as contributing defence articles and food, and the money side were eliminated.' Of course, Waley added, there might be difficulties from the Canadian side and 'it is unfortunate that we have been making so much difficulty about Canadian representation' on Combined Boards and in UNRRA.[62] It was indeed, and Waley's man in Ottawa wrote to his chief in November 1942 that Clifford Clark held firmly to the view 'that the Ministers will not be ripe in any way to discuss the main question of our future financial relationships . . . until this whole wretched question of Canadian representation . . . is really out of the way.'[63] But something would have to be done and soon. British assessments of the total of their orders placed in Canada for the period from October 1, 1942 to the end of December 1943 were $1.5 billion from the Ministry of Supply and a further $232 million from the Ministry of Aircraft Production, a total far beyond Britain's ability to pay.*[64]

---

*A complicating factor was the belief of some Canadian officials that Britain was not doing her share in the war. General McNaughton, for one, was bitterly critical of 'traditional' British industry, and he argued that a 25-pounder gun could be built in Canada in 40 per cent of the time it took in Britain. (Queen's University, Grant Dexter Papers, Memo, 6 Mar. 1942.) Another critic was C. D. Howe who returned from a trip to Britain in October 1942 to tell Mackenzie King that 'business as usual'

The Anglo-Canadian financial negotiations began on December 11, 1942 when a British team met with Clifford Clark. At this first meeting Clark indicated that he expected the $1 billion gift to last to the end of 1942, and he was optimistic that the government would agree to assume ownership of British munitions plants in Canada and pick up the costs of the RCAF overseas. The Canadians hoped that Britain could pay in gold from the end of 1942 to mid-February to cover their purchases in Canada. Clark said he had not determined how best to help Britain in 1943 but, the British note recorded, 'He mentioned that he did not think it would be practicable . . . to produce a further monetary Gift to the United Kingdom though it might be feasible to make a Gift to the United Nations though the latter would probably need to be expressed other than in currency.'[65] Clark reaffirmed this view at the next meeting, adding that he felt 'it would be necessary for the Gift to take some other form, for example, that the Canadian Government should take an omnibus War Appropriation and from it should supply munitions and possibly food in kind to the various nations.' Clark had no idea, he said, how this could be worked out.[66]

In fact, Clark was simply stalling until his suggestions could be considered by Cabinet, initially on December 23. The basis of discussion was a long memorandum prepared in the Department of Finance and dated December 15, 1942. The paper first laid out the position. As of December 15, the British had used up $968 million of the gift and only enough for two more weeks remained unallocated. In the seven months ending October 31, 1942, Britain had spent just over $1 billion in Canada, of which $621 million was for munitions, $188 million for foodstuffs, and $91 million for raw materials. The best Canadian estimates were that the British trade deficit with Canada in fiscal 1943-4 would be about $1,170 million, and there was in addition the problem of helping other countries in the sterling area to purchase in Canada.

What was to be done? The recommendations were numerous. First was the suggestion that, as Britain now had built up her American dollar reserves thanks to the presence of large numbers of American troops in Britain, the United Kingdom should pay some $150 million

---

was the philosophy he found there. 'He thought we, in Canada, were doing infinitely more for the war effort. . . . The nation as a whole was working harder. Moreover our taxes were higher than theirs. He felt we had gone altogether too far.' (King Diary, 21 Oct. 1942.) The British view of Canada, predictably, was much the same. H. D. Hall and G. C. Wrigley, *Studies of Overseas Supply* (London, 1956), p. 64.

in gold or American dollars to cover its purchases in Canada until new legislation was passed. That would solve the immediate problem although, the Department of Finance warned, it might provoke the Americans into getting tough with Canada and accusing the Dominion again of demanding cash on the barrelhead.[67] The long-run problem could be met in a variety of ways. One was to purchase the British interest in munitions plants, something that everyone would likely accept. Another method was for Canada to assume full responsibility for equipping and maintaining a specified number of RCAF squadrons, probably 35 in all. This would amount to $322 million per year, and this too would command support everywhere. A related solution would be for Canada to accept financial responsibility for all RCAF personnel overseas, a proposal that would cost $58 million each year on the present RCAF strength but one that would increase markedly as aircrew strength rose. In addition Canada could help the British by increasing some purchases in the United Kingdom and by covering several minor British activities in Canada.

More important were the remaining options. Canada could accumulate sterling, much as it had done before the $1 billion gift. In March 1942 the sterling accumulation had amounted to $1,086 million. But there were fundamental objections to this scheme, most notably the argument that 'it is not in Canada's long-run interests to build a huge international debt of this sort.' Another method would be to repatriate the remainder of Canadian securities held in the United Kingdom. 'A good many people,' the memorandum noted,

> would argue that we should take back all or most of these securities and investments. . . . They contend that it is only straight common-sense for us to pay off our debts to Britain. . . . They say that the U.K. would do this if she were in the same position. Some of them allege that it is important to eliminate the power and influence of British business interests in Canadian business circles. Some of them would go on to argue that the present conditions give a fine opportunity for the Government to get control of the C.P.R. [U.K. holdings included $335 million in C.P.R. securities] looking to its ultimate amalgamation with the C.N.R., and also to make a step toward the socialistic state by acquiring a substantial Government interest in such large and profitable concerns as C.I.L., International Nickel and Imperial Tobacco.

Against this course of action it is argued that the provision of our

war supplies, foodstuffs, etc., to the U.K. is part of our fair and reasonable contribution to the joint Allied war effort and that for us to
charge our Allies for them—and particularly for us to charge them
what the traffic will bear—is to exploit our position unreasonably. . . .
It is maintained that if we build up a reputation for hard bargaining
during the war, it may cause other countries to bargain sharply with
us . . .

And, the Department of Finance argued, trade follows investment, and
to repatriate additional securities might hurt Anglo-Canadian commerce
after the war.

Another solution might be to give Britain $1 billion. This was simple,
direct, and good publicity. But 'it would appear that a gift of this type
would be politically less popular today than it was a year ago, particularly as Britain is no longer the centre of the military stage.' In the
Department's view, it would be easier 'to get approval of a gift to all
the United Nations than a gift to Britain alone.' The suggested method
was that Canada should donate her surplus production—everything that
remained after the needs of the Canadian forces had been met—to the
Allies. Such a scheme would, in a Rooseveltian phrase, eliminate the
dollar sign, and place Canada 'on a plane of generosity, statesmanship
and leadership indubitably as high as that which the U.S. reached as a
result of Lend-Lease legislation'.[68]

This skilful memorandum posed choices and alternatives with deft-
ness, even raising the threat of the socialist hordes on the one hand
as a contrast to statesmanship, wisdom, and international repute on
the other. The Cabinet War Committee struck a sub-committee to
consider the recommendations, and its report was presented for consideration on January 13, 1943. Predictably the course recommended by the
Department of Finance was approved by the sub-committee and accepted
in principle by the War Committee. Mackenzie King, however, was unhappy. 'I agreed strongly with Macdonald that we were taking on, I
thought, more than the nation was capable of carrying and told [Ilsley]
I thought this measure would meet much more opposition in Parliament than he believed.'*[69] But a few days later when the Deputy
Minister of Finance came to the Cabinet War Committee to make a
presentation on the proposals, King 'was surprised at the unanimity, and

*'I fully realize,' a British Treasury official noted, 'that in proportion to her popu-
lation and resources Canada is doing far more for us than the United States is doing.'
PRO, Dominions Office Records, DO35/1218, Tel. Phillips to Munro, 26 Jan. 1943.

doubly so at the favourable attitude of the Quebec members in the light of the opposition there was last year.'[70]

The new Canadian scheme had two prongs. The first, covering the period until the end of March 1943, called for the interim deficit, estimated at $385 million, to be met by a cash payment to Canada and by Canada's purchasing the British interest in munitions plants to the tune of $205 million. The adverse balance for the remainder of 1943 was calculated to be some $1,155 million. Part would be met by Canada's assuming responsibility for 35 RCAF squadrons. The remainder of the deficit, another billion dollars, would be met by a new Canadian gift. But to overcome the confusion that had resulted about the first gift being in terms of money, it would be made clear that the new gift was in goods. In addition, while the first billion had been to Britain alone, the second 'in form . . . is to be to the *United Nations*'.[71]

The scope of the new proposal was awesome, as a Dominions Office official noted.

> To make this new gift she will have to supply to other countries (mostly the U.K.) goods to the value of about one-third of her budget expenditure. It is as if the U.K. were to give away goods to the value of about £1,700 millions in one year. In actual magnitude the gifts will be smaller than the U.S. contribution to other countries in the form of lend lease. But lend lease has only amounted to 13% of the total U.S. war effort since March, 1941, which is the same as saying not more than 10% of her total budget expenditure. Per head of population the Canadian gifts will cost Canada about five times what lend lease costs the United States. Canada's income tax is already as high as ours; it may have to go higher. To sum up, Canada is devoting as large a proportion of her national income to defence expenditure as any other country; in no country is the proportion of defence expenditure which is given away in the form of free supplies anywhere near so high as in Canada.[72]

Perhaps it was too much. Certainly this was Angus L. Macdonald's view. The Navy minister complained bitterly about new gifts to Britain 'before having monies available for our own services,' a reaction to the financial constraints that Ilsley's Department was placing on Canadian defence spending. In the Finance Minister's view, the Canadian budget could under no circumstances go beyond $5.5 billion, and the new gift to the Allies cut deeply into the available total. King agreed with Ilsley that $5.5 billion not be exceeded, and he hit out at the proposals to give more aid to Britain. 'Now all have seen that we have gone the limit,' he wrote.[73] A few days later on February 24, there was another 'very tense' scene in the Cabinet War Committee with the three defence ministers pressing for more and Ilsley tenaciously resisting, supported by King. The Prime Minister noted again that 'The hardest thing to defend will be the billion dollar expenditure for materials for the United Nations, when there is not enough money to provide for our own forces first. . . . Between the demand now for men as well as for money, we have reached a ceiling that pretty well settles the question of any attempt at further conscripting of men for overseas service.'[74] As it was, King reflected a few days later, the budget resolutions amounted 'pretty nearly to a revolution in the order of things as they have been in the past, where strata of society were based on differences of wealth.'[75] Taxes would be going up.

The Mutual Aid agreement of 1943 put Canada's aid to Britain and the Allies on a comparable basis with aid from the United States under Lend-Lease. But, as expected, the bulk of Canadian Mutual Aid went directly to the United Kingdom, a total of $722,821,000 in fiscal 1943-4. The Soviet Union and Australia received substantial sums, too, while China, India, and the West Indies also received help.[76]

But as it always did, the new appropriation began to run out, and still sensitive to public opinion[77] and to worries about high taxation, Mackenzie King once again geared up to resist the demands of the profligate spenders. On September 8, 1943 he told the War Committee that 'The Minister of Finance would not be able to again propose to Parliament any billion dollar loan to Britain. That such money as we could raise by taxes here would have to go toward meeting domestic problems as, for example, what was required for subsidies, wages, etc.'[78] King's tightfistedness was understandable, considering the sagging fortunes of the Liberals in opinion polls, in by-elections, and in provincial elections. And King must also have reflected bitterly that his government's manpower policy was held up as proof that Canada was doing too little while the critics (in Cabinet and out) somehow neglected the enormous financial and manufacturing contributions Canada was making to the war.

Certainly King returned to this theme time and again. In October he told his colleagues 'that I thought the time had come when we should consider the Canadian people themselves. Not necessarily meeting every request that came from Britain in the light of all that we had done, specifically anything that involved extra taxation and subsidies on top of rationing our own people. I was in favour of doing all necessary to win the war,' he said, 'but we had to keep a fair balance.'[79] A few days later he worried that if taxes were not lowered the government would be defeated and the CCF elected.[80] But despite the Prime Minister's grumbling and that of some of his ministers,[81] the appropriations for the fiscal year 1944-5 contained provision for yet another $887 million in Mutual Aid. The clinching argument was that unless Canada helped Britain now, the United Kingdom would be unable to trade with Canada after the war. Moreover, as Norman Robertson argued to King, 'it is impossible to discontinue production in Canada of supplies for export . . . without causing grave dislocation at home,' the result being that even if Mutual Aid was cancelled 'we should have to finance the same amount of domestic production' in any case.[82]

In fact the British were beginning to think of ways to reduce their dependence on Canada. 'If Canadian dollars are scarce,' one official noted, 'the United Kingdom must be able to cut down its imports from Canada, and must retain the right to decide for itself which things come first.' Wartime purchases should be kept up, but after the war 'In certain cases the Canadian position should be satisfactorily met by the proposed long-term contracts, tapered off when suitable. . . . But in other cases we are apparently looking to switch pretty completely from Canadian to European sources of supply as soon as we can.' This was a very natural thing to do in the British self-interest, but it is 'essential that we should take the Canadians fully into our confidence. . . . this is the least we can do.'[83] Indeed.

From the British point of view, the problem was that the $887 million Mutual Aid appropriation for 1944-5 did not appear large enough to cover British purchases. Waley, the British Treasury Under Secretary, wrote that the appropriation 'has placed us in a position of the greatest difficulty. We cannot cover the deficit by paying gold and U.S. dollars to Canada because our gold and U.S. dollar reserves are already quite insufficient in comparison with our liabilities. . . . It would be no solution to ask Canada to hold large amounts of sterling as this would only postpone the difficulty. . . . The solution which the Canadians seem most likely to have in mind is that they should make us a cash loan,' an undesirable course because Britain did not want to borrow to cover its war expenditure and, in any case, 'if there were any question of a loan, we should be pressed to give our commercial investments to Canada as collateral.' One solution might be to have Canada pay all the costs of her forces in Britain, including costs for advanced RCAF training and stores, expedients that could produce $370 million to cover non-recurrent costs and an additional $220 million each year.[84] After visits to Ottawa by Lord Keynes, the great economist and the chief adviser to the Treasury,* and after further consultations, Canada eventually agreed in August 1944 to assume all the costs, as the British desired.[85] This converted the deficit at one stroke to a surplus of $200 million. Mackenzie King as usual eventually supported the measure. The British, he wrote, 'are now in a very desperate position and if we are to get the markets in Britain which we shall wish to have and need to have later on, we shall have to assist at this time in meeting the situation.' It was a generous agreement, he added, and 'it leaves Canada in the position that we have paid for everything that relates to any contribution made to the war.'[86]

That was the best position to be in, particularly as the British increasingly negotiated in a cold and ruthless way. Mackenzie King complained of this to the Governor General on December 1, 1944, noting 'their icy, hard-as-steel way of getting money'.[87] But again, as always, King agreed to a new Mutual Aid appropriation, a sum that eventually reached $670 million by September 1945.[88] Difficult as it is to say, the British simply regarded this as their due, and in February 1945 they were threatening to reduce trade with Canada and other non-sterling areas because of their financial problems. The Prime Minister, concerned that this 'might easily bring about a severe depression in this country,' again prepared to recommend further aid.[89]

The final settlement came in the spring of 1946. Owed $425 million under the Air Training Plan cost-sharing arrangement, Canada waived that debt. The British paid $150 million under a claims agreement and all other claims, both ways, were wiped out except for the interest-free loan of $700 million, negotiated in 1942. All in all, the British Treasury noted, Britain had received free of charge from Canada a gift of $1 billion, $2,043 million in Mutual Aid and the $425 million BCATP debt, a total of $3,468 million. 'The past has been satisfactorily liquidated,' the Treasury noted. 'Our debt to Canada arising out of the war is free of interest for the time being and of reasonable dimensions, and

*Apparently Canadians held their own with Keynes. 'Almost alone, outside the ranks of British and Americans,' Keynes' biographer noted, 'the Canadians seemed capable of understanding the international monetary problems as a whole.' R. F. Harrod, *The Life of John Maynard Keynes* (London, 1951), pp. 541-2; PRO, Dominions Office Records, DO 35/1014/WR106/1/30, Clutterbuck to Duff, 16 Nov. 1942.

during the war we were never, from shortage of finance, prevented from securing all Canada could let us have for the war effort.'[90]

From the Canadian point of view, matters were perhaps less satisfactory. Graham Towers had exaggerated when he told the Canadian Manufacturers Association in 1943 that 'Never from the start of the war to the present day have so-called financial considerations limited or determined the scope of our war effort.'[91] But that was close enough to the truth to be taken as gospel. The effects of this unparalleled generosity were an enormous increase in Canada's national debt, a jump of $10.5 billion to an overall total five times greater than it had been in 1939. The war had cost Canada $18 billion from 1939 to 1945, and almost one-fifth of that had been given freely to Britain.[92] Canada's debt to her past was also satisfactorily liquidated.

IV

The Canadian government's concern over the shape of the postwar world had been demonstrated time and again in the discussions about financial aid to Britain and the Combined Boards and UNRRA. The Mutual Aid bills were assistance to the hard-pressed Mother Country, yes, but they were no less an effort to keep the British market open to Canadian products after the war. The concern over functional representation had a similar postwar motive in the desire to ensure that Canada's new strength in the world would be appropriately recognized in whatever international bodies were created after the war. Canada was looking to the peace.

So was everyone else. As early as the UNRRA negotiations in March 1943, as we have seen, the British had suggested that Canada might serve on the directing committee of the relief organization in lieu of Britain and as a representative of the whole Empire. This was old doctrine in new garb, smacking as it did of a common foreign policy and redolent of old battles fought and won by Mackenzie King in the 1920s. Was Canada once again to be forced to fight against the discredited idea of the diplomatic unity of the Empire?

Certainly some officers in the Department of External Affairs were afraid of this. In Ottawa Hume Wrong circulated an important memorandum in March 1943 in which he argued that Canada should insist on the functional principle being part and parcel of any institutionalized United Nations. And, moreover, member states of the Commonwealth should keep each other informed, but 'they should not directly represent' each other.[93] This was a starting point for a Canadian policy towards international organizations, and another step was taken in July 1943 when an inter-departmental body, the Working Committee on Post-Hostilities Planning, was set up.[94] By December the Committee had been granted higher status as the Advisory Committee on Post-Hostilities Planning. Its membership was to consist of the Under Secretary of State for External Affairs as Chairman, the Chiefs of Staff, the Secretary to the Cabinet, the Deputy Minister of Finance, and other high civil servants.[95] This high-powered committee would soon be needed, primarily because of the disturbing speech that Lord Halifax, the British Ambassador in Washington, delivered in Toronto in January 1944.

In the course of a long address to a Board of Trade dinner on January 24, Halifax argued for unity of policy.

> I suggest that in the years of peace it was a weakness, which we should try to cure, that the weight of decision on many problems of defence was not more widely shared. . . .
>
> I do not mean that we should attempt to retrace our steps along the path that led from the Durham Report to the Statute of Westminster. To do so would be to run counter to the whole course of development in the Commonwealth. But what is, I believe, both desirable and necessary, is that in all the fields of interests, common to every part of the Commonwealth—in foreign policy, in defence, in economic affairs, in colonial questions and in communications—we should leave nothing undone to bring our people into closer unity of thought and action. . . .
>
> Today we begin to look beyond the war to the reordering of the world which must follow. We see three great powers, the United States, Russia and China, great in numbers, areas and natural resources. . . . If, in the future, Britain is to play her part without assuming burdens greater than she can support, she must have with her in peace the same strength that has sustained her in this war. Not Great Britain only, but the British Commonwealth and Empire must be the fourth power in that group upon which, under Providence, the peace of the world will henceforth depend.[96]

Halifax's speech was not anything new or startling. He was repeating sentiments that, while not quite platitudinous, were wholly common. What was shocking—to Mackenzie King—was Halifax's choosing to offer them at a Toronto dinner attended by John Bracken, the Progressive

Conservative leader, and by Premier George Drew, the Tory leader in Ontario. That lent a partisan cast to the evening, as did the Ambassador's presenting his speech in ultra-imperialist Toronto.

Certainly King was appalled, 'simply dumbfounded. It seemed such a complete bolt out of the blue, like a conspiracy on the part of the Imperialists to win their own victory in the middle of the war.' King added that 'it has fallen to my lot to have to make the most difficult of all the fights. This perpetual struggle to save the Empire despite all that Tories' policies will do.' Worse, King convinced himself that Halifax's speech had been co-ordinated with Churchill, and he was 'deeply concerned and very hurt that Halifax should have made a speech of the kind in Canada without having let me know what he intended to say. . . . The whole thing, a complete frame-up.'[97] Despite King's instant conspiracy thesis, Churchill and the British government had not known of Halifax's text, although it had been forwarded to London in advance of delivery in the usual way.[98] Churchill himself complained to the Dominions Secretary that Halifax's remarks were 'in effect an interference in Canadian politics, turning markedly against Mackenzie King,'[99] and after the British Prime Minister raised the question in the War Cabinet, Eden, the Foreign Secretary, drew the difficult chore of writing to Halifax: 'I rather think that the Cabinet, and in this case particularly the Dominions Secretary, would have liked to have been consulted beforehand as regards the line you were proposing to take.'[100] That was close to a reprimand, made mainly because of a concern for Canadian sensitivities. Certainly the Foreign Office itself agreed with Halifax. 'The speech may not be popular with some Canadians,' Gladwyn Jebb minuted, 'but it seems to me excellent none the less.'[101]

Not to the Prime Minister of Canada. In his lengthy address in the Throne Speech debate on January 31, Mackenzie King told the Members of Parliament that Halifax's conception of the postwar world was predicated on the wrong premises, at least for Canada.

Could Canada, situated as she is geographically between the United States and the Soviet Union, and at the same time a member of the British Commonwealth, for one moment give support to such an idea? . . . What would seem . . . to be suggested is that the prime Canadian commitment should be to pursue in all matters of external relations . . . a common policy to be framed and executed by all the governments of the Commonwealth. I maintain that apart from all questions as to how that common policy is to be reached, or enforced, such a conception runs counter to the establishment of effective world security, and therefore is opposed to the true interests of the Commonwealth itself.

. . . Collaboration inside the British Commonwealth had . . . a special degree of intimacy. When, however, it comes to dealing with the great issues which determine peace or war, prosperity or depression, it must not in aim or method, be exclusive. . . . Our commitments on these great issues must be part of a general scheme, whether they be on a world basis or regional in nature.[102]

The debate in Canada over Halifax's remarks had barely been started when King's House of Commons speech effectively squelched it. Some right-wing Conservatives talked Empire, but they were soon virtually disavowed by their party leader, and even the newspapers of Toronto took moderate positions.[103] The war had changed the world and Canada with it.*

Lester Pearson summed up the resulting state of Canadian policy in a letter from Washington on February 1, 1944. Canada's two goals in the postwar period should be to influence British and American policy 'when it appears to be going in the wrong direction' and to seek a meaningful role in the postwar international organization. Both goals could be attained, the new Minister in Washington said, by 'achieving . . . a very considerable position as a leader, if not *the* leader, among a group of states which are important enough to be accepted' as such by the Great Powers.[104]

Mackenzie King took this line at the Commonwealth Prime Ministers' meeting in May 1944. Again and again Churchill and some of his ministers tried to structure a Commonwealth bloc under British direction as a necessary part of the postwar world. Again and yet again

---

*Perhaps the change was more apparent than real. A Canadian Institute of Public Opinion survey on March 25, 1944 found that Canadians were undecided whether Canada should share in an Empire foreign policy or make her policy alone:

	Decide Herself	Common Policy
Total	47%	46%
Quebec	70	21
Rest of Country	39	55
Age 21-29	58	37
Age 30-49	48	45
Age 50+	39	54

Public Opinion Quarterly, VIII (Summer, 1944), 303.

Mackenzie King resisted the Churchill line, also attacking the British Prime Minister's desire for regional councils within the yet-to-be-formed general international organization: 'it would be unwise in our ideas for a world organization to overemphasize the idea of a *bloc*,' King said, 'and it might be wiser to concentrate on how the most effective co-operation could be worked out.'[105] In his formal statement to the Conference on May 11, Mackenzie King insisted that 'an effort should be made to give the smaller Powers a larger share in the direction of the many functional organizations which will be set up.' Turning to joint Empire representation on world bodies, King was blunt: 'Frankly I do not think representation . . . for the "British Commonwealth and Empire" as such is feasible or really desirable. Representation of the United Kingdom, on the other hand, is indispensable.' The important point, he argued, was not to rouse suspicion in the world that the Empire was a bloc, not to turn the clock back to where it had been before the 1926 Imperial Conference when the idea of the Empire as a single contracting unit was ruled out.[106] King's powerful speech effectively routed the centralists, and Grant Dexter summed up King's victory somewhat too fulsomely: 'There was nothing to fight. He found agreement everywhere. . . . The conference came to a complete acceptance of Mr. King's position naturally, inevitably and harmoniously. . . . He won without a struggle, and he emerged from the conference with greatly enhanced prestige.'[107]

The Canadian position would be sustained as the United Nations Organization took shape the following year. The concept of a Commonwealth bloc was even more unworkable in 1944 and 1945 than it had been in the 1920s, and the incredible thing is that the British were so foolish even as to raise it. Defeat had been inevitable from the first, the tactics employed were clumsily amateurish, and certainly there was no prospect whatsoever that Mackenzie King would consider ideas he had repeatedly rejected in the past. It would have been much better for Britain to adopt a different tack. J. J. S. Garner at the High Commission in Ottawa had been convinced that 'we would be wise to proceed by "frequent informal and personal consultations and contacts at all levels" in our relations with the Dominions, rather than any endeavour to bind them by formal undertakings to do this or that.'[108] And Garner's superior, Malcolm MacDonald, offered much the same advice to the Secretary of State for Dominion Affairs.

[It would be wrong for] you in London [to] feel more annoyed at the

Canadian attitude and more apprehensive about it than the deeper facts warrant. Canada's co-operation with us . . . is absolutely assured, provided we don't create too many difficulties for her by saying or doing things which upset responsible French-Canadian opinion, and which appear to suggest an infringement of Canadian national sovereignty. Also, we must be careful not to suggest that we want Canada to side with us in a process of 'ganging up' against the United States.[109]

The men on the scene were far more perceptive about Canada than those insulated from reality in Whitehall and Downing Street.

V

The question of Canada's relationship with the United States was similarly under constant review during the latter years of the war, and the Canadian government was generally careful to stay as far away as it could from American-British quarrelling. But Canada's problems with the United States were in many respects more difficult than those with London, primarily because of the proximity of the United States. The Atlantic Ocean after all provided a splendid buffer against Imperial centralization, but the 49th parallel offered no shelter at all against the United States. That had been advantageous at times, of course, but it could pose problems, particularly after the Americans entered the war and began military construction operations in Canada to provide road, air, and supply links to Alaska.

The Alaska Highway, in particular, impressed Mackenzie King with the potential dangers this new American influence posed for Canada. The road, he told Malcolm MacDonald in March 1942, 'was less intended for protection against the Japanese than as one of the fingers of the hand which America is placing more or less over the whole of the Western hemisphere.'[110] To another visitor he said much the same thing, adding that it was 'clear to my mind that America has had as her policy, a western hemisphere control which would mean hemispheric immunity . . . from future wars but increasing political control by U.S.'[111]

Clearly some Canadian response was necessary to preserve and enhance Canadian control in the North West Territories, and this was forcibly impressed on King by MacDonald. The High Commissioner returned to Ottawa at the end of March from a trip to the Territories, heartened by the pace of development, but also appalled at the absence of any Canadian presence. He told Norman Robertson that 'for most practical purposes, the Canadian Government's representative in local contacts with the American forces in the Northwest is the Secretary of the Alberta Chamber of Commerce and Mines whose offices are in Edmonton and who acts as an unofficial representative of the Department of Mines and Resources.' The American presence had been allowed to grow in a fit of absence of mind, Robertson reported to the Prime Minister, and a good, competent Canadian staff would have to be sent to the area, 'capable of collaborating with and controlling the American development activities'.[112]

The American presence was substantial. Nearly 15,000 Americans were in the North by the end of 1942, and the United States was spending money freely—$130 million for the Alaska Highway, $140 million for an oil-distribution system based on Norman Wells, N.W.T., and millions more for weather stations, air strips, and general improvements. All these helped open up the Territories, but what offended Canadians was the way 'The Americans . . . have apparently walked in and taken possession as if Canada were unclaimed territory inhabited,' Vincent Massey complained from London, 'by a docile race of aborigines.'[113]

Action would be necessary immediately to re-establish the Canadian hold on the territory. H. L. Keenleyside in the Department of External Affairs surveyed the entire situation in a balanced report on April 9, 1943 and recommended a range of actions that included more publicity for Canadian efforts in the North, 'matter-of-fact' statements by government officials that 'there is no question of complete Canadian control over all Canadian territory and facilities,' and the appointment of prominent and able men to what he called a Canadian North West Commission.[114] This last suggestion was picked up and modified by the Secretary to the Cabinet, Arnold Heeney, who suggested to the Prime Minister that a Special Commissioner be appointed.[115] Mackenzie King soon acted upon this idea and Brigadier W. W. Foster, an army officer who had impressed King during his speech-making tour of the West in mid-1941, was named to the post, with headquarters in Edmonton. In a secret letter, Foster was instructed to ensure 'that the natural resources of the area shall be utilized to provide the maximum benefit for the Canadian people and to ensure that no commitments are to be made and no situation allowed to develop as a result of which the full Canadian control of the area would be in any way prejudiced or endangered.' To do this, Foster was ordered to ensure that all American requests for new or expanded projects were referred to the Canadian government.[116]

There would be difficulties aplenty in the ensuing years, but the fit of absence of mind was over.[117] In the end the King government decided to pay the United States for the construction costs expended for all airfields and other facilities of continuing value built in Canada by the United States, one method of ensuring sovereignty. There was also a clear willingness, expressed in the final version of a Post-Hostilities Committee paper on Canadian-American postwar defence relationships, for Canada to accept full responsibility for all future defence measures on Canadian territory.*[118]

The experience in the North West Territories seemed symptomatic of the American attitude in other areas too. In the North Atlantic, for example, the United States Navy showed a singular lack of tact in trying to send advisers to help the Royal Canadian Navy conduct convoy operations in the area. Admiral L. W. Murray, in command in Newfoundland, raged at such a suggestion—his staff had been doing this work for three and a half years, he wrote to the Chief of the Naval Staff in Ottawa in March 1943, while the Americans had no operational experience that could compare.[119] In other areas the same attitude could be detected. W. A. Mackintosh in the Department of Finance, one of the creators of the Joint Economic Committees of 1941 and no anti-American, wrote to a friend in September 1944 that 'In economic as well as in political thinking the United States is veering toward imperialism.'[120]

Escott Reid, a young officer in the Department of External Affairs who had served in Washington early in the war, expressed the same fears. Back in Ottawa again, he wrote to the Under Secretary to note that some Canadians feared that Canada was becoming an adjunct of the United States 'without the formalities of annexation' simply because the Americans were becoming more insistent on demanding and getting their own way. To many Americans their participation in the war 'is a favour which the United States is conferring on humanity and which carries with it the right to run things their own way.' This was particularly true of recent dealings, Reid said. Before the war the patronizing 'Good Neighbour' attitude had not been displayed to Canada, but now

---

*An earlier version of this paper was tougher: 'Canada will not be willing to permit the United States to provide and maintain defence installations in Canadian territory. Canada will itself provide, maintain and operate all such installations, with the possible exception of facilities installed by international agreement in special cases.' Department of External Affairs, file 7-CB(s), C.P.H.P. (44) Report 4 (final), 16 June 1944.

it was and one reason for this change was just plain aggressiveness. One example Reid cited dealt with an argument over wheat sales. The American Embassy in Ottawa had told the Deputy Minister of Trade and Commerce 'that if we did not sell the wheat at the low price demanded by the United States they would be forced to announce publicly that because of Canada's decision the United States would have to cut down on wheat shipments to the United Kingdom and the U.S.S.R.' The message was clear, Reid said: Canada would have to be prepared for 'energetic, aggressive and at times inconsiderate policies on the part of the Administration in Washington and as close neighbours we may see more of this than most other people.'[121]

The Americans could be aggressive, it was true. But they could also be very helpful in a variety of ways. For example, when in the spring of 1942 Canada and the United States were talking about trade with Latin America, there was some worry in Ottawa that the war would give the United States an opportunity to shut Canada out of the market and to stop Canadian firms from getting raw materials, such as steel, that exporters needed. This was needless concern, the Deputy Minister of Trade and Commerce learned from his officials. The Americans 'assumed that it was Canada's right to export as in the past,' and they were quite agreeable to seeing steel diverted from war purposes to the export trade.[122] Another case concerned Canada's holdings of American dollars. The Hyde Park agreement of April 1941 had worked so well that by the end of 1943 Canada held 650 million American dollars, some $300 million above agreed limits. The Americans worried about this, but they were prepared to co-operate, and if agreed measures to reduce Canadian holdings of U.S. dollars could be implemented, then Canada could retain everything acquired after that date. The Cabinet War Committee agreed to this on March 22, 1944, and most of the extra American dollars were used to pay for tanks destined for the Canadian Army overseas.[123] In more political terms, President Roosevelt could help his great and good friend, Mackenzie King. In March 1945 the State Department told Roosevelt that Mackenzie King, coming to Washington for one of his regular visits, 'is seeking to rebuild his prestige and thus may want to meet the press here and capitalize on his friendship with you.'[124] The result was that the President ensured that Mackenzie King was with him when he met a press conference, and Roosevelt told the reporters that the Canadian Prime Minister was under consideration for the chairmanship of the United Nations Conference on International Organization, scheduled to open in April at

San Francisco.[125] That was a nice gesture, and King was properly grateful: 'Before coming away I thanked the President for what he had said in the afternoon at the conference. He said if there was any way he could help me in my election he would wish to do it. To come and see him at the White House. . . . That I would always be welcome.'[126]

In the final analysis, then, suspicions of the United States were outweighed by other considerations. In the first place the United States would definitely take a greater interest in Canadian defence preparations than she had before the war, primarily because 'Canada lies astride the overland route between the United States and the USSR.'[127] Any deterioration in Soviet-American relations would be embarrassing to Canada, post-hostilities planners realized, but in the event of any such difficulty Canada knew where it would stand. The logic of this position demanded increased Canadian-American defence co-operation, and the Permanent Joint Board on Defence continued into the peace.

The logic of economics also demanded collaboration, and this was recognized by a joint Canadian-American decision, announced on May 21, 1945, to 'consider and deal with the problems of the transition from war to peace in the same spirit that was manifested in the Hyde Park Declaration.' In effect this agreement committed both countries to the relaxation of their wartime control apparatus in concert in an attempt to minimize the problems of reconversion both faced.[128] And although this renewal of Hyde Park did not in itself have great practical consequences, when rearmament would begin in the late 1940s it was one of the economic links that could be cited to justfy industrial mobilization planning and the placing of American contracts in Canada.[129]

Most important of all, public opinion in Canada was very well disposed to the United States. At the meeting of the Canadian Institute of International Affairs at Kingston in late May 1945, this continental friendship was very much in evidence. The CIIA's membership comprised virtually everyone in Canada interested in foreign policy in a serious way, and its meetings were considered important enough that both the British High Commission and the American Embassy sent representatives. The Canadian desk officer at the State Department in Washington, J. Graham Parsons, also attended and addressed the delegates. His remarks and the reaction they created were reported to London by a British observer.

There was a high degree of acceptance of the proposition that Canada's future political alignment would be with the United States, and only secondarily with the British Commonwealth. . . . The view . . . was tactfully encouraged by Mr. Parsons. . . . He said that Canada's views and wishes exerted an influence on the United States administration out of all proportion to Canadian power, and added that on commercial policy Canada already enjoyed a consideration accorded to great powers alone. The enormous gratitude of the company at this remark could not be concealed, and it apparently occurred to no one that it might be a bit exaggerated and of questionable validity in relation to the future.[130]

The report on the meeting by the Second Secretary of the American Embassy in Ottawa was not dissimilar, but this officer noted that the conference participants were concerned about Canada's need for capital now that Britain, in financial trouble itself, could no longer supply Canadian requirements. This would be no problem: 'what better source than that just across the border'?[131]

The war, then, irrevocably altered Canada's role in the world and its perception of its place in a constellation of Great Powers. The suspicions of Britain that had existed before the war in the minds of Mackenzie King and his advisers had not disappeared. In some respects those suspicions were stronger than ever, a not incomprehensible reaction to a series of difficulties with the United Kingdom that ran from financial negotiations, to the British Commonwealth Air Training Plan, to membership on the Combined Boards and UNRRA, and to Lord Halifax's unthinking intrusion into Canadian domestic politics. The admiration for the British war effort, the close ties built up during the war by the Canadian troops in England, the links of sentiment and race—these could not entirely outweigh the suspicion that Britain would try to use Canada when it served her interests. Towards the United States, the feeling was somewhat different. King had begun the war feeling very close to his friend Franklin Roosevelt and very sympathetic to his policies, although this was tempered by dissatisfaction at the American reluctance to join the war before Pearl Harbor forced them in. This friendship with the President had great benefits for Canada, ensuring the nation's physical safety and its economic security. But there were disadvantages too, as the American military presence in the North West demonstrated very sharply. Mackenzie King and many of the officers of the Department of External Affairs as a result had a healthy mistrust of the benevolence of the United States,[132] balanced to an appreciable extent by the realization that the United States was now an active power in the world and that the world could never be the same again.

Canada had emerged from the war proud of its part and loyal to the senior partners with whom it had fought. The links with both Britain and the United States were stronger on a personal level in 1945 than they had ever been before. But for the first time, perhaps, government officials had an awareness that as a small power in a world dominated by giants Canada would have to be very careful indeed. If suspicions of the great powers are one mark of a small country's nationalism, Canada emerged from the war in 1945 much more nationalistic than it had been in 1939.

---

1 Public Archives of Canada [PAC], W. L. Mackenzie King Papers, Diary, 15 July 1942.

2 King Papers, Memo, Robertson to King, 28 Jan. 1942, ff. C243537ff.

3 Department of External Affairs, External Affairs Records, file 3265-A-40C, Wrong to Robertson, 20 Jan. 1942. The credit for the functional approach is generally given to Wrong. L. B. Pearson interview, 21 Oct. 1971.

4 External Affairs Records, file 3265-A-40C, Wrong to Pearson, 3 Feb. 1942.

5 Queen's University, Grant Dexter Papers, Memo, 9 Feb. 1942.

6 PAC, Privy Council Records, Cabinet War Committee Records, Documents, Howe to Heeney, 5 Mar. 1942.

7 Public Record Office [PRO], Dominions Office Records, DO 114/112, Secretary of State for Dominion Affairs [SSDA] to Canadian Government, 18 Feb. 1942, p. 17.

8 King Diary, 18 Mar. 1942. This was passed to the U.K. Tel. encl. with Massey to SSDA, 23 Mar. 1942, on DO 114/112, p. 21. See further docs in *ibid.* for U. K. response. Cf. U.S. National Archives, State Department Records, 711.42/237, [Moffat] Memo of conversation with Robertson, 19 Feb. 1942, and King Diary, 21 Mar. 1942, for King-MacDonald talk on this.

9 *Ibid.*, 16 Apr. 1942.

10 C. P. Stacey, *Arms, Men and Governments: The War Policies of Canada 1939-45* (Ottawa, 1970), pp. 168-71. See docs on External Affairs Records, file 3265-B-40C, particularly two minute sheets bearing on the King-FDR talks, and dated 29 May 1942. Not until Sept. 1942 did Howe and Ralston reach agreement, but by that time External officials had become convinced that Canada's best course was to have nothing to do with the MAB. This was eventually acceded to by Cabinet. Docs on *ibid.* and Cabinet War Committee Records, Minutes, 7, 21, 28 Oct. 1942.

11 R. M. Leighton and R. W. Coakley, *Global Logistics and Strategy* (Washington, 1955), pp. 254-5.

12 King Diary, 27 July 1942.

13 *Ibid.* Cf. Leith-Ross' account in his *Money Talks* (London, 1968), p. 298.

14 DO 114/112, Massey to SSDA, 14 July 1942, pp. 8-9. The decision to seek membership had been reached on 11 June by the Cabinet War Committee. See

Minutes, 11 June 1942. For details on this matter, see External Affairs Records, file 3265-D-90C. Cf. R. J. Hammond, *Food*, Vol. I: *The Growth of Policy* (London, 1951), p. 241.

15 See draft memo on External Affairs Records, file 3265-D-90C and DO 114/112, Massey to SSDA, 14 July 1942.

16 *Ibid.*, Tel. to Canadian Govt, 18 July 1942, p. 9; PRO, Foreign Office Records, FO 371/31543, Minute by N. B. Ronald, 16 Sept. 1942.

17 *Ibid.*, Tel. Phillips to Treasury, 31 Aug. 1942.

18 *Ibid.*, MacDonald to SSDA, 9 Sept. 1942.

19 Minutes of Meeting, 16 Sept. 1942 in PAC, C. D. Howe Papers, file S-27-1-3; FO 371/31543, Tel. MacDonald to SSDA, 16 Sept. 1942; King Diary, 16 Sept. 1942; Hammond, p. 242.

20 King Diary, 16 Sept. 1942.

21 King Papers, Memo, 18 Mar. 1943, ff. C241878ff.

22 FO 371/31543, Minute by J. E. Coulson, 7 Sept. 1942.

23 *Ibid.*, Tel. Sinclair to Lyttelton, 4 Sept. 1942.

24 *Ibid.*, Tel. MacDonald to SSDA, 9 Sept. 1942.

25 *Ibid.*, J. J. S. Garner to Moore, 9 Sept. 1942.

26 Stacey, pp. 175-6. Canadian membership was announced on 10 Nov. 1942. Text in DO 114/112, pp. 27-8.

27 See Howe Papers, file S-27-1-3 (35), Howe to Heeney, 30 Oct. 1942 and reply, 12 Nov. 1942; Cabinet War Committee Records, Minutes, 28 Oct. 1942. On the CPRB, see External Affairs Records, file 3265-E-40C.

28 See *ibid.*, file 3265-4-40C, Memo of 16 Dec. 1942; Cabinet War Committee Records, Documents, Memo, 10 Feb. 1942.

29 Memo of 13 Apr. 1943, enclosed with MacDonald to SSDA, 14 Apr. 1943 on DO 35/1221.

30 *Ibid.*, Tel. British Food Mission to Ministry of Food, 9 Apr. 1943; Minute on *ibid.*, by C. R. P., 30 Mar. 1943; Hammond, pp. 246-7.

31 External Affairs Records, file 3265-D-40C, Deutsch to Prime Minister, 29 Sept. 1943.

32 Stacey, pp. 176-7; S. M. Rosen, *The Combined Boards of the Second World War* (New York, 1951), pp. 232-3; Docs on DO 35/1212. For discussion of the working out of arrangements with the Boards on which Canada served and those on which it did not, see PAC, Wartime Prices and Trade Board Records, Vol. 62, 'History of the London Office' and 'History of the Washington Division of the WPTB', two historical reports by A. F. W. Plumptre.

33 PAC, Department of Trade and Commerce Records, file 34221-1, Tel. SSDA to Secretary of State for External Affairs [SSEA], 21 Aug. 1941.

34 External Affairs Records, file 2295-G-40, copy of Cmd. 6315.

35 *Ibid.*, SSEA to Massey, 6 June 1942. See on UNRRA negotiations, L. B. Pearson, *Mike: The Memoirs of the Rt. Hon. Lester B. Pearson*, Vol. I: *1897-1948* (Toronto, 1972) pp. 250 ff.

36 King Diary, 30 July 1942.

37 FO 371/31543, draft letter, July 1942; *ibid.*, Minute, 4 Aug. 1942 and 10 Aug. 1942.

38 FO 371/31543, Tel. High Commissioner to SSDA, 9 Sept. 1942.

39 *Ibid.*, Minute, 16 Sept. 1942.

40 *Ibid.*, Memos, 5 Sept. 1942, 5 Dec. 1942.

41 DO 35/1014, Minute, 2 Oct, 1942. Cf. *ibid.*, 'Official Committee on Post War Commodity Policy and Relief', 12 Oct. 1942. J. W. Holmes interview, 27 July 1971.

42 DO 35/1014, Minute, 2 Oct. 1942.

43 External Affairs Records, file 2295-G-40, Memo, Robertson to King, 18 Jan. 1943.

44 DO 35/1014, Tel. High Commissioner to SSDA, 11 Nov. 1942.

45 External Affairs Records, file 2295-G-40, Memo, Robertson to King, 18 Jan. 1943. Functionalism was much in vogue at the time thanks to the writing of David Mitrany, *A Working Peace System* (London, 1943). See A. J. Miller, 'Canada at San Francisco: A Reappraisal of the Influence of the "Functional Concept" ', a paper in the CIIA Library, Toronto.

46 *Foreign Relations of the United States, 1943*, Vol. I (Washington, 1963) pp. 864-5; External Affairs Records, file 2295-G-40, Pearson to Robertson, 27 Jan. 1943. Acheson's position was suggested by Pearson. See Pearson, I, p. 252.

47 *Foreign Relations*, I, pp. 866-7. This memo had been approved by Cabinet War Committee on 4 Feb. 1943.

48 External Affairs Records, file 2295-G-40, Robertson to King, 11 Feb. 1943.

49 *Ibid.*, Robertson memo, 26 Feb. 1943; *Foreign Relations*, I, p. 881; Cabinet War Committee Records, Minutes, 24 Feb. 1943.

50 External Affairs Records, file 2295-G-40, Robertson memo, 26 Feb. 1943.

51 *Ibid.*, W. C. Clark to Robertson, 3 Mar. 1943; Cabinet War Committee Records, Minutes, 4 Mar. 1943; Pearson, I, pp. 252-3.

52 *Foreign Relations*, I, pp. 881-2.

53 External Affairs Records, file 22-V(s), King to McCarthy, 1 Mar. 1943.

54 *Ibid.*, file 22-D(s), Memo, 17 Mar. 1943.

55 King Diary, 31 Mar. 1943; Cabinet War Committee Records, Minutes, 31 Mar. 1943; Pearson, I, p. 254.

56 King Diary, 7 Apr. 1943; Cabinet War Committee Records, Minutes, 7 Apr. 1943; Pearson, I, p. 253.

57 Docs on Trade and Commerce records, files 34221-2 and 34221: E.

58 Docs on FO 371/51367.

59 House of Commons *Debates*, 9 July 1943, p. 4558.

60 PRO, Treasury Records, T160/1252, 'Financial Relations with Canada', July 1942, encl. with Liesching to Waley, 3 July 1942; PAC, Department of Finance Records, Vol. 3437, Memo, Clark to Ilsley, 13 Aug. 1942.

61 *Ibid.*, Vol. 778, file 400-16-21, Clark to M. Campbell, 27 Aug. 1942.

62 T160/1252, Waley to Phillips, 11 Aug. 1942.

63 *Ibid.*, Munro to Waley, 17 Nov. 1942.

64 PRO, Cabinet Records, Cab 92/45, J.W.P.S. Working Committee (42)8, 24 Oct. 1942.

65 T160/1252, Memo by Munro, 11 Dec. 1942.

66 *Ibid.*, 14 Dec. 1942.

67 Department of Finance Records, Vol. 3437, Memo, 23 Dec. 1942, and Ilsley to M. MacDonald, 24 Dec. 1942 indicate that the money was paid just as the Cabinet was considering the Finance recommendations.

68 PAC, J. L. Ralston Papers, Vol. 45, file 493-22, Memo, 15 Dec. 1942. See also R. S. Sayers, *Financial Policy, 1939-45* (London, 1956), pp. 349ff. and docs on Department of Finance Records, Vol. 3437; Cabinet War Committee Records, Minutes, 23 Dec. 1942.

69 King Diary, 13 Jan. 1943; Cabinet War Committee Records, Minutes, 13 Jan. 1943.

70 King Diary, 22 Jan. 1943. Cf. PAC, Ian Mackenzie Papers, file 567-29(4). Mackenzie to King, 20 Jan. 1943 indicating the Pensions Minister opposed further aid to Britain.

71 DO 35/1218, Minute, 26 Jan. 1943.

72 *Ibid.*, Minute, 26 Jan. 1943; Sayers, pp. 350ff.

73 King Diary, 19 Feb. 1943.

74 *Ibid.*, 24 Feb. 1943.

75 *Ibid.*, 26 Feb. 1943.

76 Canadian Mutual Aid Board, *Final Report* (Ottawa, 1946), p. 34.

77 For public reaction, see Department of Finance Records, Vol. 405, file 101-106-4.

78 King Diary, 8 Sept. 1943; Cabinet War Committee Records, Minutes, 8 Sept. 1943.

79 King Diary, 19 Oct. 1943.

80 *Ibid.*, 21 Oct. 1943.

81 *Ibid.*, 4 Jan. 1944.

82 King Papers, Memo, 31 Dec. 1943, ff. C250975-6.

83 T160/1376, Clutterbuck to Robinson, 24 Apr. 1944.

84 *Ibid.*, Waley to Eady, 9 May 1944; Sayers, pp. 355ff.

85 *Ibid.*, pp. 357-8; Ralston Papers, Vol. 45, file 493-22, Heeney to Ilsley, 15 Aug. 1944; T160/1376, 'Mutual Aid from Canada', n.d.

86 King Diary, 14 Aug. 1944.

87 *Ibid.*, 1 Dec. 1944.

88 *Ibid.*; Mutual Aid Board, *Final Report*, p. 34.

89 Cabinet War Committee Records, Minutes, 14 Feb. 1945; docs on Department of Finance Records, Vol. 3437 (Trade Policy) and Vol. 4369, file U-3-11.

90 DO 35/1220, Memo, 30 Aug. 1946; Sayers, pp. 361ff.; House of Commons *Debates*, 11 Apr. 1946, pp. 762ff.

91 Mackenzie Papers, file 4-1, address of 10 June 1943.

92 T160/1340, address by Towers, 20 Mar. 1945.

93 External Affairs Records, file 22-D(s), Memo, 19 Mar. 1943.

94 *Ibid.*, docs on file 7-AB(s), part I. For detailed and excellent accounts of Canadian policy and policy-making on UNO and post-hostilities planning, see James Eayrs, *In Defence of Canada*, Vol. III: *Peacemaking and Deterrence* (Toronto, 1972), chapter II.

95 Cabinet War Committee Records, Minutes, 16 Dec. 1943; docs on External Affairs Records, file 7-AQ (s).

96 Quoted in J. L. Granatstein, *Canadian Foreign Policy Since 1945* (Toronto, 1969), pp. 13-14. See on Halifax's speech, Eayrs, III, pp. 201 ff.

97 J. W. Pickersgill, *The Mackenzie King Record*, Vol. I: *1939-44* (Toronto, 1960), p. 636; King Diary, 25 Jan. 1944. Cf. Charles Ritchie, *The Siren Years* (London, 1974), p. 163.

98 FO 371/38553, Minute by N. Butler, 2 Feb. 1944.

99 DO 35/1204/WC 75/9, Minute to Cranborne, 31 Jan. 1944.

100 FO 371/38553, Eden to Halifax, 10 Feb. 1944.

101 *Ibid.*, Minute 2 Feb. 1944.

102 House of Commons *Debates*, 31 Jan. 1944, pp. 41-2. See the draft by Wrong in King Papers, ff. C160273ff.

103 J. L. Granatstein, *The Politics of Survival* (Toronto, 1967), pp. 171ff. Both L. B. Pearson and J. W. Holmes believed Halifax's speech played right into King's hands. Interviews, 21 Oct. 1971 and 27 July 1971.

104 External Affairs Records, file 7-V(s), Pearson to Robertson, 1 Feb 1944.

105 PRO, Prime Minister's Office Records, Prem 4/42/5, Confidential Annex, P.M.M. (44) 9th Meeting, 9 May 1944. See also British documents on Cab 99/27-8. The British documents and the Canadian ones are in King Papers, Notes and Memoranda, Vols 322-3 and External Affairs Records, file 7-V(s). Cf. Eayrs, III, pp. 205ff.

106 Prem 4/42/5, P.M.M. (44) 12th Meeting, 11 May 1944. For comment see Edgar Tarr Papers (Toronto), Tarr to D. Skelton, 11 May 1944, Pearson, I, pp. 267-8. For grumpy British views on Dominion pretensions, see Cab 21/851, Memo, Bridges to Churchill, 10 May 1944, with Churchill's pen comments.

107 Grant Dexter, *The Commonwealth Conference May 1944* (Winnipeg, 1944), pp. 17-18. This was not the U.K. House of Commons view. See King Papers, Wrong to Robertson, 26 June 1944, f. C232543.

108 DO 35/1204/WC 75/23, Garner to Costar, 4 Feb. 1944.

109 DO 35/1204, extract, MacDonald to Cranborne, 12 Feb. 1944. The Ottawa advice was, as usual, neglected. See Eayrs, III, pp. 209ff. for his account of the British Commonwealth Relations Conference of 1945.

110 King Diary, 21 Mar. 1942.

111 *Ibid.*, 18 Mar. 1942.

112 External Affairs Records, file 52-B(s), Memo, 30 Mar. 1943 and MacDonald's 'Note on Developments in North-Western Canada', 6 Apr. 1943; King Diary, 29 Mar. 1943.

113 Eayrs, III, pp. 349-50.

114 External Affairs Records, file 5221-40C, Memo, 9 Apr. 1943.

115 *Ibid.*, file 52-B(s), Memo, 13 Apr. 1943.

116 *Ibid.*, file 5221-40C, letter to Foster, 20 May 1943.

117 On this complicated subject, see the External Affairs files already cited; all files prefixed 463; Brig. Foster's files (PAC, R.G. 36-7); PAC, R.G. 24, Records of Canadian-American Operations in the North West, 1942-5; and records in Directorate of History, National Defence Headquarters, particularly files prefixed 112.3M2 and 181.009.

118 This document is printed in Eayrs, III, pp. 375ff.

119 PAC, Adm. L. W. Murray Papers, Vol. 1, docs on North West Atlantic Command; and Vol. 4, taped recollections; W. G. Lund, 'The Royal Canadian Navy's Quest for Autonomy . . . 1941-43', a paper presented to the Canadian Historical Assn, June 1974.

120 Department of Finance Records, Vol. 3597, file DO3c, no. 1, Mackintosh to C. H. Herbert, 29 Sept. 1944.

121 PAC, External Affairs Records, Vol. 110, file 702, Memo, 29 Feb. 1944.

122 Department of Trade and Commerce Records, Vol. 263, file 34302, J. M. Evans to Wilgress, 6 Mar. 1942 and reply, 10 Mar. 1942.

123 Cabinet War Committee Records, Minutes, 8, 10, 22 Mar. 1944.

124 Roosevelt Library, Hyde Park, F. D. Roosevelt Papers, file PSF Canada 1-45, Memo, Grew to Roosevelt, 8 Mar. 1945.

125 FO 371/50684, Tel. Washington to Foreign Office, 15 Mar. 1945.

126 King Diary, 13 Mar. 1945; J. W. Pickersgill and D. F. Forster, *The Mackenzie King Record*, Vol. II: *1944-45* (Toronto, 1968), p. 335. Cf. Ritchie, p. 187.

127 Eayrs, III, pp. 375-80; External Affairs Records, file 7-AD(s), part II, 'Post War Defence Arrangements . . .' This document was finally approved by Cabinet War Committee in July 1945.

128 Press Release, 21 May 1945, in King Papers, ff. C161691ff.

129 Denis Stairs, *The Diplomacy of Constraint: Canada, the Korean War and the United States* (Toronto, 1974), p. 103.

130 FO 371/50365, Notes on Annual Conference . . . , att. to Holmes to Stephenson, 15 June 1945.

131 State Department Records, 842.00/6-145, Atherton to Secretary of State, 1 June 1945 and encl.

132 For a contrary example, see S. D. Pierce and A. F. W. Plumptre, 'Canada's Relations with War-Time Agencies in Washington', *Canadian Journal of Economics and Political Science*, XI (1945), esp. 410-11. For an American view, see State Department Records, 711.42/3-2245, L. Clark to Secretary of State, 22 Mar. 1945.

9. The Second Conscription Crisis

The second Quebec Conference between President Roosevelt and Prime Minister Churchill and their staffs took place in Quebec City in September 1944. On the outside for most of the meetings, Mackenzie King nonetheless felt obliged to stay on hand, and on September 14 he took advantage of his presence in the old city to deliver a speech to a closed meeting of the Reform Club, the Quebec *rouge* elite. Three months after the invasion of Normandy the war was going well, and it seemed clear that it would soon be over. King believed that conscription would not now be necessary, and he told the assembled party faithful so.

> I had maintained the position that there would be no conscription unless it were absolutely necessary [King wrote in his diary about his remarks]. That I never believed it was necessary. Now men saw for themselves those who had served had done so voluntarily.[1]

King's record of his remarks hardly made them seem controversial, but others had different accounts of his extemporaneous comments. Angus L. Macdonald, sitting near King at the head table, recorded that the Prime Minister said 'Have you had conscription? . . . If you have not had it up to now, is it likely that you will ever have it when the war in Europe is nearing its end?'[2] And Grant Dexter, piecing the story to-

334 | CANADA'S WAR

gether from those present, produced the most dramatic phrasing of all.

> Come what may, he would hold the country together. There would
> be no conscription for overseas service. He would honour Lapointe's
> pledge to the uttermost. There had never been a shadow of doubt in
> his mind. No ministry of which he was the head would ever, under any
> circumstances, have imposed over-all conscription. Never. He knew
> that Quebec's trust was in him. Fail them, he would not. So there had
> been plebiscites, Bill 80's and what-not. But, please note gentlemen,
> there had been no conscription and there never would be. Trust
> Willie. The cheering, I am told, was right from a thousand tummies—
> shook the Château [Frontenac]. . . .[3]

But if the faithful cheered, the conscriptionist ministers of 1942 did
not, and on the next day Colonel Ralston came to see the Prime
Minister.

> He then said: I have something I want to speak of which unfortu-
> nately is disagreeable [King wrote]. . . . he understood that I had said
> yesterday . . . that I would not stand for conscription or be at the head
> of a government that would. He said he had been one of the team and
> had wondered whether I was changing our policy. That it made a
> pretty hard time with him in dealing with his staff and others in
> trying to squeeze out the numbers that they need for reserves. That
> there might be a holocaust when they try to get into Germany. . . . I
> told him I had made no statement of the kind. That what I had said
> was that I had mentioned that conscription would not be resorted to
> unless it was necessary. That now it was apparent the war was going
> to end soon and that it would be to the glory of the men overseas to be
> able to say they had enlisted voluntarily. . . . what I had said about
> there being no conscription to be feared was that we would certainly
> not have conscription for any participation with Japan. . . . I would
> not certainly be head of any government that sought conscription
> against Japan. He said he had not thought of that difference.[4]

Ostensibly the matter was smoothed over. But Ralston and Macdonald
both were once again deeply suspicious of the Prime Minister on the
conscription question. As Dexter, always equipped with the best sources
in Ottawa, noted, 'So nothing much happened, except that the Col. hates
his guts more than ever.'[5] Exaggerated, perhaps, but the relationship

between the Minister of National Defence and the Prime Minister had been strained severely once more.

I

Since the plebiscite and the long Cabinet dispute over Bill 80, there had been little talk about compulsory service. The problems with manpower were still present, and still nearly unresolvable, but the Cabinet had managed to avoid further serious divisions on this topic.[6] After D-Day, however, the political wars had begun in earnest.

The first shot had been fired on June 19, 1944 by Hon. C. P. McTague, the National Chairman of the Progressive Conservative Party and the recently retired head of the National War Labour Board that had recommended family allowances. Speaking to his own nomination meeting at Guelph, Ontario, McTague demanded that the government pass an order in council at once to make home-defence conscripts under the National Resources Mobilization Act available for service anywhere. To do otherwise, McTague argued, could 'only be construed as deference to the will of the minority in the Province of Quebec as voiced in the plebiscite.' Significantly, McTague made it very clear that he spoke for the party, not as an individual.[7] To John Bracken, sitting on the platform behind McTague during his speech, this must have come as a shock. Apparently he had not known in advance what McTague was going to say, and he had been trying to build bridges into French Canada. But confronted with these remarks, the Conservative leader had no choice: 'One point in Mr. McTague's remarks I wish to support and endorse. . . . In this time of national emergency surely there will be no Canadian who will find it in his heart to deny that appeal. Certainly it receives the endorsement of this party, and, I would like to think, of the great majority of people in all other parties as well.'[8]

Quickly other Conservatives began to pick up the cry. George Drew, the Ontario Premier, told the Winnipeg Canadian Club on June 21 that 'Those who wear the Canadian uniform must be ready to wear it anywhere.'[9] Richard Hanson, Conservative House of Commons leader from 1940 until Bracken's selection, told Parliament much the same thing. The home-defence army of 75,000 men had been 'held immobilised, neither in the war nor out of it; neither in industry nor agriculture nor out of them, and costing the Dominion $150,000,000 each year.' This was a 'foul blot on Canada's national effort and unity,' Hanson claimed.[10]

The Tories clearly sought for a viable national issue after the Saskatchewan provincial election had seemingly demonstrated that Bracken's progressivism provided little political muscle. But the partisan nature of their complaints aside, their case had some merit. In abstract terms nothing could justify keeping one fairly large segment of Canadian manpower both home and safe and out of productive labour. This did discriminate unfairly; this did tend, in a horrible phrase, to deny equality of sacrifice. But what kind of a concept was 'equality of sacrifice'? And wasn't the retention of the NRMA troops in Canada justified by political necessity? That there was a need for it could scarcely be denied; but that the Liberal Party and Mackenzie King were the beneficiaries in Quebec also could not be denied. Most important, however, in the early summer of 1944 there seemed no shortage of rein-forcements overseas. The army had suffered heavy casualties in Italy and in Normandy, but the flow of reinforcements seemed adequate. Certainly this was Ralston's view. The voluntary system was doing its job, he said, and the NRMA troops were doing useful work in Canada. But if 'the sending of these N.R.M.A. men is necessary to maintain the army overseas, then I shall be for sending them.'[11]

Who were the NRMA soldiers, the Zombies as they were popularly and disparagingly known? According to a mimeographed, anonymous letter sent to Members of Parliament in 1944, the Zombies were the children of immigrants, the victims of prejudice, the prewar un-employed.

> Let us be 'honest and frank'. Give me a chance to tell you why I am a 'Zombie'. Assure me that all Canadians, who have honestly tried to abide by the laws of this country, will have equal rights, equal opportunities for education in every field and enterprise. Assure me this with deeds not promises.[12]

That letter was written in English, of course, pointing up the often forgotten fact that the NRMA were not all French Canadians. The data are somewhat unclear, but estimates produced in the Department of National Defence in November 1944 put the number of French-speaking and both French- and English-speaking NRMA troops at 26,362 or 44 per cent of the total of 59,679 soldiers. Another calculation showed that 22,824 had been enrolled in Military Districts Nos 4 and 5, the Quebec army commands, amounting to 38 per cent of the total

NRMA strength. The best estimate, therefore, was that only 35 to 40 per cent of the NRMA were French Canadian,[13] just a few percentage points higher than the proportion of French-speaking Canadians in the total population.

The refusal of the NRMA men to enlist in the overseas army tormented the military and the government. Brigadier W. H. S. Macklin, the commander of 13 Canadian Infantry Brigade, a largely NRMA formation stationed in British Columbia, grappled with the question in a memorandum in May 1944. A very able and intelligent officer, Macklin had tried to persuade his men to volunteer for overseas service, but his success had been limited. In his report, Macklin tried to appraise the difference between the volunteer and the Zombie, unconsciously revealing the blinkered vision from which even officers of good will suffered.

The volunteer feels himself a man quite apart from the N.R.M.A. man. He regards himself as a free man who had the courage to make a decision. He seldom takes the trouble to analyze the manifold reasons put forward by those who won't enlist. He lumps them all together as no more than feeble excuses masking cowardice, selfishness, and bad citizenship. In many cases no doubt he is right. . . . The volunteer is conscious of his position. He is proud of it. He is anxious to work. He salutes his officers and speaks to them with self-confidence. The N.R.M.A. soldier slouches at his work. He tends to become sullen. He nurses his fancied grudge against 'the Army'. He hates 'the Army'. He has little self-respect and therefore little respect for his officers. . . .

. . . As regards the English-speaking N.R.M.A. soldiers who refuse to volunteer they vary all the way from a large number who have no patriotism or national feeling whatever, to a few intelligent men who, I believe, honestly think that by holding out they will some day force the Government to adopt conscription which they feel is the only fair system.

The great majority are of non-British origin—German, Italian, and Slavic nationalities of origin predominating. Moreover most of them come from farms. They are of deplorably low education, know almost nothing of Canadian or British History and in fact are typical European peasants, with a passionate attachment for the land. A good many of them speak their native tongues much more fluently than they speak English and amongst them the ancient racial grudges and prejudices of Europe still persist. Here again the process of converting these men into free citizens of a free country willing to volunteer and die for their country will be a matter of education, and I think it will be slow. At present there is negligible national pride or patriotism among them. . . . They do not know what they are fighting for and they love nothing but themselves and their land. This fact must be recognized.

A separate report dealt with French-Canadian NRMA soldiers. They were said to be influenced against volunteering by the work of 'secret societies' and by being 'strongly attached to women's apron strings'.

A number are determined never to sign active in protest against the repeated attempts to have them sign, against the jibes and taunts suffered over the years from Active personnel and the public. . . . They are members of a fraternity. They have developed a fixation. They want to follow home sentiment and feel they would be letting down those people who fought so hard to keep them in Canada.[14]

Whether these views were correct is another story. The solidarity of the NRMA had largely been created by the treatment they had received, the prejudice created by a system that in wartime perverted the normal societal values. 'The Zombie,' one student of the NRMA has written, 'had once been the kid next door who had been "proud as punch" to earn his lance-corporal's stripe at the training camp; now statistics would be compiled to show that he was of partial Serbo-Croatian descent, spoke a foreign language in the home, had no great love for England, and was happier on a farm than on a battlefied.'[15] The government's policies had created the problem, but if reinforcements could only keep up with casualties it might yet escape the consequences.

Throughout the early summer of 1944, therefore, a close watch was kept on the manpower situation. At a meeting of the War Manpower Committee of the Cabinet on June 21, Chubby Power indicated that the RCAF would halt its recruiting at least until October and reduce its Canadian establishment by 10 per cent. The Navy minister, however, had been enlisting men at a higher rate than predicted, and Angus L. Macdonald said that he would like to keep this rate up for at least three months more.[16] Recruiting was undoubtedly becoming more difficult as the available manpower became used up, but throughout the spring and summer of 1944 between 3,500 and 5,100 men volunteered each month, while from 1,000 to 3,000 NRMA soldiers 'converted' to active force volunteers.*

Overseas, too, there seemed to be no serious problems. Lieutenant General Kenneth Stuart, the Chief of Staff at Canadian Military Headquarters in London since December 1943, visited the front in July and seemed pleased with what he had seen. He flew to Ottawa and on August 3 he reported to the War Committee of the Cabinet, offering unequivocal assurances: 'General Stuart reported that although the Army had been fighting for some twelve months in Italy and two months in France, the reinforcement situation was very satisfactory. At present there were reinforcement personnel available for three months at the intensive battle casualty rate.'[17] Mackenzie King recorded these comforting words, too, noting that Stuart 'was most emphatic about there being no doubt of ultimate success and the possibility of the war being over sooner than we expected. He made clear that we had plenty of reserves.'[18]

Stuart's statement to the War Committee was the triumphant justification of Mackenzie King's policies. He had fought the war and won it without conscription. Moreover Canada had done this without a great racial split and with a war effort that had won praise from everyone. It was a splendid achievement, King believed. Still in this frame of mind he had spoken in Quebec City, but already the signs of impending difficulty were becoming apparent.

'The need for trained reinforcements in the Canadian Army is urgent,' Major Conn Smythe, the Toronto hockey magnate, charged on September 18. Wounded in Normandy and returned to Canada for convalescence, Smythe said that 'The reinforcements received now are green, inexperienced, and poorly trained. . . . Many have never thrown a grenade. Practically all have little or no knowledge of the Bren gun. . . . Large numbers of unnecessary casualties result from this greenness.' He was giving out this information, the owner of the Toronto Maple Leafs said, so that relatives of the men overseas could ensure that no further casualties were 'caused to their own flesh and blood by the failure to send overseas reinforcements now available in large numbers

---

*The advertising aimed at the NRMA was cloying and sentimental: 'We're proud of you son. Yes we're proud to see that G[eneral] S[ervice] badge on your arm, the badge that means service on any fighting front in the world. We didn't want you to go, no parents do. But something bigger than we had ever dreamed of has called you. And we're proud our boy has risen to meet that responsibility. . . . you put your country's interests ahead of your own . . .' Toronto *Star*, 8 July 1944.

in Canada.'[19] A routine denial was issued by the Department of National Defence the next day.

A few weeks later George Drew amplified and repeated Smythe's charges in an address to the Canadian Corps Association in Toronto on October 5. There was a shortage of reinforcements, Drew said, 'while 80,000 men wearing the same uniform are kept here in Canada in the sixth year of war, performing no real military duty of any kind.' Colonel Ralston bore 'the heaviest load of guilt for this shameful situation,' the Premier claimed, giving vent to one of the very few direct attacks launched at Ralston to this time, and the Department's counter-statement to Smythe on September 19 was 'the most contemptible of all the contemptible excuses invented by guilty men to hide their guilt.'[20]

More important than Smythe's, Drew's attack had about it echoes of Premier Hepburn's assault on Ottawa almost five years before. It was also less than fair for its direct attack on the chief proponent within the Cabinet of taking every action possible to reinforce the serviceman overseas. In fact on September 22, over C. D. Howe's objections, Ralston had insisted on keeping the NRMA force in being as a source of reinforcements. Ralston, King wrote that day, 'is quite determined to keep these men until he is sure we do not have to have conscription which means, in his mind, practically until the war is over.'[21] A few days later the Defence minister went overseas on one of his regular inspection tours. He was at the front when Drew launched his assault.

The first news Ralston had of the Drew speech came in a flurry of cables from Ottawa, messages that had been the subject of earnest consultation in the Prime Minister's office and with Army headquarters. Arnold Heeney, the Secretary to the Cabinet, had checked with General J. C. Murchie, the Chief of the General Staff since early May, and had learned that while his information was 'five or six weeks old,' the General was not alarmed, saw no justification for Drew's charges, and believed the Canadian position to be better than either the British or American.[22] The telegrams, sent to Ralston on October 9, Thanksgiving Day, relayed the text of Drew's speech and added King's comment: 'For obvious reasons I have refrained from entering into controversy with Drew. Unfortunately there is no one else who can reply with sufficient authority except yourself. . . . To meet Drew's point I believe the public must be assured that reinforcements are available in adequate numbers and have been available long enough to have time to receive proper training.'[23]

Ralston did not get King's wire until October 13 when he returned to London from a visit to the front in Belgium. He replied ominously that while the training situation was satisfactory he was unhappy about reinforcements: 'On that point I regret to say that conditions and prospects of which I have learned will, I feel, necessitate reassessment in light of the future, particularly regarding infantry involving, I fear, grave responsibilities.'[24] Nevertheless, Ralston did send a statement that began, 'There has been no overall deficiency of reinforcements. . . . The Army went into battle with its full quota behind it. On 23 Sep 44, the Army in both theatres was up to 100% of its full authorized War Establishment. This does not include the reserves of reinforcements in the UK and Canada. These figures refer to fit men, ready for battle.' But, he added, 'the main problem that has faced us for some time past has not been one of the total available number of reinforcements. It has been a problem of the distribution of these as between the different arms of the service. . . . Our experience in battle showed that, in all arms except the Infantry, we had allowed for more casualties than were actually occurring. Conversely, in the Infantry, we had more casualties than had been forecast.'* Ralston's statement went on for three more pages, providing facts and data to support his analysis.[25] But while his press release served temporarily to silence Drew, Ralston had pointed directly to the difficulty.

The Minister's statement probably put the best face possible on the situation. In Italy senior officers and N.C.O.s had complained to him about shortages of reinforcements and about the poor training many replacements had received. But other officers were not unduly concerned, and investigation of specific cases generally demonstrated that most reinforcements had at least been in the army for substantial periods of time.[26] Still, the complaints of the officers and men—and the widespread feeling that the NRMA troops would be the first demobilized and thus the first to get good jobs—[27] had hit at Ralston's strong Baptist conscience and strengthened his resolve not let down his boys overseas. Projections and forecasts made at his request by Canadian Military Headquarters in London shook him even more. By early 1945, as a memorandum General Stuart sent to him on October 11 showed, there

*The casualties suffered by the infantry were very heavy, but it should be borne in mind that in the five divisions and two brigades of Canadian troops serving overseas late in 1944 there were only 34,000 infantry all told. This figure, checked and approved by both the Minister of National Defence and the Adjutant General, is a revealing one. PAC, A. G. L. McNaughton Papers, Vol. 256, file 903-92, Brooke Claxton to R. Emmans, 12 Dec. 1944.

would be an overall surplus of 13,000 reinforcements but a shortage of 2,000 infantry. The situation was even more precarious because the men to be despatched from Canada in December would require refresher training in the United Kingdom; because some recovered casualties would not be ready to return to action by the end of 1944; and because the distance to Italy meant that troops despatched after November 30 would not arrive in time to see action before the new year. According to this report, there had been 34,000 casualties suffered to the end of September 1944. The projection was for 29,000 additional casualties to the end of 1944, a drop of 11,000 from the headquarters' original estimates. The result was Canadian Military Headquarters' prediction that 'we can on a basis of available reinforcements now in sight maintain the present Canadian Army to December 31. In about two months time the position for the future will need reassessment in the light of circumstances.'[28] This memorandum had largely shaped Ralston's telegram to King and his statement.

For Mackenzie King, Ralston's telegram served only to confirm his worst fears. He had told Louis St Laurent as early as September 28 that he was afraid the Minister of National Defence might return from Europe, like Sir Robert Borden in 1917, with a demand for conscription.[29] Now he was more than ever convinced that this was the case.

> ... considering all aspects of the situation more harm than good would be done with any attempt to force conscription at this time. I could not bring myself to being the head of a Government which would take that course—a course which might, after five years of war in Europe, and preparation for a year and a half of another war in the Pacific—lead to spurts of civil war in our own country. It would be a criminal thing, and would destroy the entire War record. . . . This is going to be a trying experience for me. Indeed, Ralston has been a thorn in my flesh right along. However, I have stood firm before and shall do so again.[30]

The final battle between the Prime Minister and his Minister of National Defence was about to be joined.

II

Ralston returned to Ottawa on October 18, accompanied by General Stuart and a memorandum dated October 15. This paper, prepared by Stuart, was more pointed than the General's original effort of October 11.

. . . Until about two months ago, I was satisfied with the general reinforcement position both in respect to First Canadian Army and 1 Cdn Corps in Italy.

There were three main reasons for my optimism; the general situation, our overall reinforcement holdings and my expectation, based on 21 Army Group [the Army Group of which First Canadian Army formed part] forecast of activity, that casualties for balance of 1944 would be intense and normal in alternative months.

Stuart reiterated that there would be a shortage of 2,000 infantry by the end of December, but he added that 'nothing is certain' in war and that the position might be worse.

I say this because of what has actually happened in the last two months. Our casualties in infantry have been greater than was anticipated for two main reasons. The first was that we anticipated infantry casualties of 45% of total casualties; they proved to be 75% of casualties. The second was that forecasts must also be based on anticipated scale of activity. We used Army Group scale of activity with intense and normal casualties alternating monthly. Actually since 'D' day our casualties in 21 Army Group have been at an intense rate continuously.

. . . The only solution that I can see is to find an additional 15,000 infantry to add to our reinforcement pool on or before 31 Dec 44, and to ask that replacements sent monthly from Canada in 1945 shall be increased to 5300, of which 4300 should be infantry.

. . . I recommend, therefore, if the numbers required cannot be found from General Service personnel in Canada, that the terms of service of N.R.M.A. personnel be extended to include overseas service in any theatre.[31]

What must be remembered is that Stuart's memorandum referred to anticipated shortages, not to existing ones. Equally important, the estimates were just that, estimates of expected casualties. Even some of the data presented as hard facts were dubious. On October 30, for example, Stuart had to tell his Minister that he was wrong in stating that casualties since D-day had run at intense rates. In fact, he apologized, 'Our casualties since "D" day have been above normal but under the intense rate.'[32] The difference was substantial: intense casualties were 20 per cent of strength; normal were 6 per cent.[33] And again it must be noted that it was Stuart himself who had told the War Committee on August 3 that everything was rosy. It was Stuart who had passed so little information back to Ottawa in the intervening two months that the Chief of the General Staff could say on October 9 that he had no information to support Drew's claims of shortages. Such errors of omission and commission as had taken place had occurred at Canadian Military Headquarters in London.*[34]

Whatever the mistakes, whatever the blame, Ralston believed immediate action essential. He told Mackenzie King this just after his arrival back in Canada on October 18, reiterating the arguments that Stuart's memorandum made. The troops overseas were concerned about the Zombies staying at home while their casualties increased because of a lack of reinforcements, and Ralston said that he had seen men leave hospitals to return to the front. 'He did not wish to be emotional,' King recorded him as saying, 'but this had affected his feelings as to the necessity of easing the situation.' He intimated further that he would be prepared to resign if his wishes were not met.[35]

King responded by reminding Ralston of the protracted debates that had preceded every increase in the army overseas. Each time the Cabinet had been assured that there were enough reinforcements. In addition, King argued, the war was almost over—'the people of Canada would hardly understand why we should resort to conscription at this time.' The results would be serious. 'We would have to weigh the probable moral advantage it might serve to send some of the N.R.M.A. men overseas against the very grave situation to which it would give rise. That I thought it would be much better if the necessity demanded to reduce the size of our army overseas.'[36]

The issues, much as they had been raised by Ralston and King, came before the War Committee on October 19 in a dramatic meeting. General Maurice Pope, in attendance, wrote later that 'I think that I was really frightened officially for the first and only time in my life.'[37] There were grounds for his fears, for it was instantly clear that Ralston's issue had all the potential force needed to split the Cabinet wide open.

---

*Victor Sifton, Master-General of the Ordnance from 1940 to 1942, wrote to Ralston on March 1, 1944 to argue that 'a good many of your difficulties have arisen because a small group of G.S. officers were determined to keep things in their own hands and in consequence recommended appointments of men who either were sympathetic to them or who they felt sure they could dominate. This has now produced the inevitable result, a lack of capacity in key positions. . . . Politically, I should think your first trouble will come from reinforcements.' PAC, J. L. Ralston Papers, file 646-32, Sifton to Ralston, 1 Mar. 1944.

St Laurent said that while he had every sympathy for Ralston's position, it was too late in the day to change government policy. Howe, Michaud, Macdonald, and Power all asked for time to consider the question. Macdonald, it was clear, would stay with Ralston; Michaud and Power would almost certainly side with King; and Howe was probably the only War Committee member whose position was genuinely undecided.[38] After the initial exchanges, General Stuart was brought into the meeting. Mackenzie King began by asking him to explain his remarks to the Cabinet War Committee in early August. Stuart's reply, as King recorded it, was that 'he had made a mistake. . . . I said to him that having given us the wrong information and having made a mistake, I hoped he would, as I know he would, do all he could to help the government out of the present situation.'[39]

The next day, before the War Committee met, Mackenzie King talked with the Minister of Justice about the growing crisis. He was greatly reassured to learn that St Laurent's position remained essentially the same as his: conscription was acceptable if it was necessary to win the war, and only in those circumstances. Ralston was using necessity in a different way, St Laurent believed, as meaning necessary to provide reinforcements. King then said that 'I had about come to the conclusion that if Ralston persisted in his attitude and tendered his resignation, I would accept it and invite [General A. G. L.] McNaughton to come into the Cabinet. That I felt pretty sure McNaughton would accept.'[40] Later King spoke with Malcolm MacDonald, the British High Commissioner, and decided to seek Churchill's advice on the probable duration of the war. Eventually he would despatch General Pope to Washington to see President Roosevelt on much the same kind of mission.[41]

Meanwhile the search for alternatives was under way. Chubby Power tried to cool matters by urging the Prime Minister to seek Macdonald's and Ilsley's help in keeping Ralston in the government.[42] King's chief advisers—Heeney, Pope, and Under Secretary of State for External Affairs Norman Robertson—sought alternative ways of finding reinforcements. Among their suggestions were disbanding some units, reducing physical standards, and combing out General Service volunteers from units in Canada. They also believed that some results might come from a 'new determined drive to obtain the maximum number of volunteers . . . from N.R.M.A. personnel in Canada'. To do this, 'concerted political support' was essential and financial incentives should be offered. If those expedients failed, then infantry battalions could be reduced from four companies to three with the extra men being used as reinforcements.[43] J. W. Pickersgill, on the other hand, produced an analysis of the numbers and locations of both NRMA and General Service troops in Canada, and he was convinced that reinforcements could most likely be found from among the GS personnel.[44]

The Army staff, too, did its homework. General Murchie told Ralston in a memorandum on October 23 that he expected the war to last into 1945. His estimate was that 15,000 additional infantry would have to be despatched from Canada before the end of December, followed by a continuing draft of 4,000 each month.[45] The Adjutant General, Major-General A. E. Walford, estimated that perhaps 5,500 additional volunteers could be found for overseas service by withdrawing men from the training stream, by remustering specialists and non-commissioned officers to infantry, by lowering the minimum age from 19 to 18½, and by accepting a slightly lower medical standard.[46] Murchie also considered the possibility of converting more Zombies. Some 9,000 NRMA had volunteered in the last six months, he said, but a strong resistance had built up among the remaining home defence conscripts. 'It is possible that an intensive campaign to induce volunteering at this stage may only increase that resistance,' he counselled with the voice of despair. As for reducing the fighting strength of infantry battalions or reducing the strength of the First Canadian Army by a division, that was 'a matter of government policy'. But, the CGS warned, 'it would be essential that the field commanders be consulted' before any such decision. The only feasible course, in Murchie's view, was to use the NRMA as reinforcements. 'On purely military considerations' this course would meet the needs of the front 'without disruption of the organization and fighting efficiency of the Canadian Army.'[47]

The entire Cabinet met on October 24. For most of the ministers this was the first they had learned of the reinforcement shortage. The shock must have been profound when, after detailing the situation as he and his staff officers saw it, Ralston declared that 'I must say to Council that, while I am ready to explore the situation further, as I see it at the moment, I feel that there is no alternative but for me to recommend the extension of service of N.R.M.A. personnel to overseas.'[48] Mackenzie King, who believed that 'there is something inhumanly determined about [Ralston's] getting his own way, regardless of what the effects may be on all others,'[49] then launched into a long speech of his own. His refrain by now was familiar to all the War Committee members: the war was almost over; conscription would divide the country in the moment of victory; it was the army that had made the errors; and he had agreed in 1942 to consider conscription only if it was necessary to win the war. There were the purely political considerations, too.

> . . . we all had an obligation to those who had sent us to Cabinet Council, to those whom we were representing as Ministers and that as the Leader of the Party and of the Government, I had to consider what was owing to the Party. That all I would say was that if we were driven to the extreme indicated, the Liberal Party would be completely destroyed and not only immediately but for indefinite time to come. That the only party that would gain would be the C.C.F. who would be handed, in an easy fashion, complete control of government. I doubted if even extreme Tories would like to see that particular result.[50]

Those remarks were intended only to caution the conscriptionists, few of whom were among the progressive ministers on social security questions, for example. The threat of the CCF might help tilt the balance.

The Prime Minister then opened the floor to his colleagues. Gardiner, the Minister of Agriculture, was the most vehement of the majority of the ministers who opposed conscription. T. A. Crerar, however, sounding for the first time in the war as if he favoured sending the NRMA men overseas, surprised King who later glowered that 'Crerar was anything but helpful.'[51] The Quebec ministers, of course, unanimously opposed conscripting the home-defence soldiers for overseas service. With no decisions reached except for an agreement on lowering the age limit for overseas service, the Council adjourned.[52]

The Cabinet met again the next day, October 25, for a long and fruitless session as positions hardened quickly. The highlight of this sitting, however, came when Ralston stated that there were 120,000 General Service volunteers in Canada. 'My God,' Chubby Power expostulated, 'if that is the case, what are you talking about getting more men under conscription?' King called this revelation 'astounding'.[53] This question was then searched through by the three Defence ministers and the army staff. In his personal record of the crisis, Power noted that he had never before realized that the medical standards for infantry were so high or that men over 38 years of age were not permitted to serve overseas. He added of this inquest that General Stuart was 'a little uncooperative' and that he was unable to get him to say 'that it was extremely likely that the Canadian troops would be withdrawn from the line' after their present difficult and bloody fighting in the Scheldt estuary ended.[54]

The report of the ministers' study came before the War Committee on October 27. 'The result,' King wrote, 'was that it was apparent that the army could be kept up to strength and with all necessary reinforcements up to the end of the year.' None had doubted that. 'In the new year, the reinforcements would be short, only some 700 could be raised in January and 3,000 by the first of February. This is without any conscription. . . . it seemed to me that none of the Defence Ministers were too sure of the figures they were dealing with.'[55] This should not have been surprising, for General Stuart himself was unsure of the numbers—or so the Governor General told Mackenzie King.[56] What did seem clear after this discussion was that there were 120,000 GS men in Canada—and a further 90,000 in England. What, ministers wanted to know, were these men doing? The army had the answers.[57]

	Suitable for Infantry	Not Suitable for Infantry but Not Below PULHEMS 2*	Over- or Under-age; PULHEMS 3, 4, 5	TOTAL
Operational	4,000	1,000	6,000	11,000
Non-Operational	8,000	1,000	45,000	54,000
Depot Appraisal – Replacement & Rehabilitation	—	500	6,500	7,000
	12,000	2,500	57,500	72,000
Training Stream	30,000	11,000	9,500	48,000
	42,000	11,000 [sic]	67,000	120,000

*The PULHEMS system was a method of assigning medical categories to soldiers. PULHEMS stood for Physique, Upper extremities, Lower extremities, Hearing, Eyesight, Mental capacity, and Stability. The PULHEMS standard for infantry was 1111221. C. P. Stacey, *Arms, Men and Governments: The War Policies of Canada 1939-1945* (Ottawa, 1970), p. 451n.

Large numbers were in training. Larger numbers still had high PULHEMS scores, an indication that under the army's system of grading both health and mental stability they were unfit for front-line service, at least as infantry. Of those in the training stream, the expectation was that 11,000 infantry would have embarked for the United Kingdom by the end of the year, with a further 10,500 scheduled to sail between the new year and the end of May 1945. A still further 9,500 officers and men, not of the infantry, were to have been despatched over the same time period.*[58]

The huge numbers in Britain and Canada were explicable. The situation had been caused as a result of the long inactivity of the Canadian Army between 1939 and 1943 and because the Army had been split, with part serving in Italy and part in North West Europe, a split that had necessitated a build-up of the army's supply and services 'tail' and a consequently low 'teeth-to-tail' ratio. Canada, General E. L. M. Burns later wrote, was simply too large a country with too small a population to maintain an overseas army split between two theatres, a largely self-contained base organization for each, a large administrative and training organization in the United Kingdom, an even larger organization in Canada, as well as a large commitment of home-defence troops.[59] Very few of these men could be pried loose, and many of them, most of them, were genuinely unfit or ill-trained for infantry service. With unlimited time, many could have been re-trained, but there did not seem to be time to spare. The fault, therefore, was not a shortage of men, but a lack of flexibility in their management and use.[60]

Still the ministers were dubious. Even Macdonald, conscriptionist though he was, worried: 'I thought Stuart's estimates of infantry casualties for the period September 23—December 1 must be considered accurate,' he wrote after the War Committee meeting on October 27. 'The unknown factors are the length of the war and the number of our casualties, with a third, perhaps, the amount of men we can draw from the General Service men in Canada.'[61] Dr J. H. King, government leader in the Senate, was less convinced of the credibility of the army position even than Macdonald. Ralston's position was 'terrible', he said

*Of the men in the United Kingdom, 35,631 were 'non-effectives', sick or wounded men, men on courses, on loan to British forces, or men listed as Prisoners of War or missing. The number of reinforcements in the U.K. was 18,065, of whom 6,657 were infantry. The remainder presumably was necessary to run the large training and administrative operation necessary for the Canadian Army. C. P. Stacey, *Arms, Men and Governments: The War Policies of Canada, 1939-1945* (Ottawa, 1970), p. 452.

to the Prime Minister. 'To think that we had the numbers of men that we had in the Army altogether; there were only a very small number in the fighting line, and that out of 130,000 [sic] General Service men in Canada alone, we could not find 15,000.'[62]

Mackenzie King generally shared this point of view. Convinced that Ralston would resign unless he got his way he was fully aware of the difficulties this would cause his government. On October 26 he had talked with the Defence Minister, appealing to him as 'a soldier . . . as a Minister of the Crown' to stay in the government. Ralston was adamant: 'he had thought the matter out and owed it to what he had talked over with himself.'[63] On October 30 the two men met again. Again King stressed the necessity to keep the country united. What would happen, he asked Ralston, if we went to Parliament to get conscription or a vote of confidence? There would be delay, argument, or worse. 'The main point,' the Prime Minister argued, sounding not unlike Ralston arguing against taking conscription back to Parliament in the acrimonious Cabinet disputes of 1942, 'was to get the men and that would not be helped by a discussion throughout the country on conscription.' Ralston kept saying that 'he was anxious not to impose . . . any additional burdens on me,' King wrote, but 'he did not see how he could possibly stay on unless his words could be implemented.'[64] The Cabinet meeting on October 30 did not ease matters any.[65]

The Prime Minister went home after this anxious and dispiriting day to find a telegram from George Fulford, the Brockville Liberal M.P., with whom he had had words in the caucus during the debate on family allowances. Fulford argued vehemently for sending the NRMA men overseas, and the telegram, King wrote, 'caused me to feel exactly what the conspiracy is, because I believe it has come to that.'

> It is not merely a question of conscription. The same men who are for conscription are the same identically as those who opposed most strongly the family allowances and other social reforms in the budget: Ilsley, Ralston, Howe, Macdonald, Crerar and Gibson? [The query perhaps indicates that King was doubtful about Gibson's position.] It is perfectly plain to me that in pretty much all particulars my position is becoming identical to that of Sir Wilfrid Laurier's where his supposedly strongest colleagues left him, one by one. . . .[66]

It all came clear to King. Conscription of the NRMA men would solve nothing. It would have no influence on the outcome of the war, and it would cause terrible disunity at home.[67] If others could not see this they must have an ulterior motive—to block his great social-welfare reforms by dividing the country on a spurious conscription issue, knowing the potential for racial strife inherent in that question. 'What would probably happen,' King wrote,

> would be that we would have a real Tory party composed of conscriptionists of the different parties who also were seeking to preserve their wealth and perhaps a combination of Liberals and Progressives and Labour who will make up a real Liberal party. For my part I shall certainly become a member of the latter, rather than the former and do what I can to save Liberalism and the lives of the many. . . .[68]

There was a certain logic behind King's reasoning. The coincidence of Cabinet members who supported conscription and who were cool on social-welfare questions was striking, and King was a man who constantly remembered the break-up of the Liberal Party over conscription in 1917. Given his memories of the Great War, given his understanding of the limited social vision of some of his colleagues, of the Opposition, and of the business community, his instant conspiracy thesis must have rung true to King. That there was no hard evidence for it does not seem to have disturbed him. The conspiracy was necessary to King for it could justify his accepting Colonel Ralston's resignation. If the Minister wanted to leave the Cabinet he should now be permitted to go; this would make it harder for the 'conspirators' to operate. At this point in his thinking, Mackenzie King's thoughts turned once more to General McNaughton.

In 1944 McNaughton was an enormously popular figure in the country and with the troops. He had been relieved of his command of the Canadian Army overseas at the end of 1943, but the public had been told only that it was because of ill-health, not because McNaughton, in the eyes of his superiors, did not seem likely to be able to handle troops in operations. Since his return to Canada early in 1944, McNaughton had been on leave, resting, re-establishing himself, keeping his options open. He had in fact been approached in oblique ways by members of the Progressive Conservative Party, including C. P. McTague, who raised with him the prospect of his heading a committee to study 'economic post-war reconstruction policy'. This convoluted scheme seems to have been largely designed as a device to counter socialism in Canada and to provide Conservative leader John Bracken with a high-powered group of advisers. Implicit throughout (at least in the General's mind) was an understanding that McNaughton could succeed Bracken as leader.[69] Others, including the CCF, were seeking McNaughton too. Mackenzie King was well aware of his popularity in the country, and in a conversation the two men had on September 23, the General indicated that he had been approached with offers. Perhaps this was behind King's suggestion of the Governor Generalship, the position scheduled to come free in the spring of 1945. The General decided to accept this post,[70] and on October 14 King learned of this. McNaughton, therefore, was much on the Prime Minister's mind throughout October.

On October 31 the Prime Minister arranged to see the General. He outlined the situation to McNaughton and found him at one with his views. 'He was strongly of the belief that the conscription issue in Canada would work irreparable harm,' King noted, and McNaughton agreed that if Ralston resigned he would enter the Cabinet as Minister of National Defence. His first acts, the General said, would be to sack Generals Murchie and Stuart. In his own memorandum of this meeting, McNaughton wrote, 'National emergency not political at P.M.'s disposal if required.'[71] Mackenzie King had prepared the fall-back position he would need if Ralston remained obdurate and resigned.

Meanwhile the Colonel was making his own preparations. In a draft letter of resignation, dated October 31, the Minister rehearsed the situation that had caused the crisis, and he concluded:

I realize and have realized ever since the war began, the grave possibilities of division on this question. I have done everything I could up to the very last minute to avoid it and to maintain a volunteer army. Those efforts have not been successful because of unexpectedly greater Infantry casualties. I think our pledges to our fighting men as well as our assurance to the people of Canada make it necessary for us to take this step, serious though it is.

The Government as a whole (certain colleagues excepted) has rejected my advice and recommendation for reasons which, with respect, I do not think are sufficient nor consistent with the Government's policy and procedure as announced to the House of Commons.

Since I am in disagreement with the Government on this vital matter of policy, and particularly in a field for which I would be directly responsible, I beg at once to tender my resignation. . . .[72]

Whether this letter was written before or after the Cabinet meeting of October 31 is unclear, but certainly Ralston was correct in assuming that the majority of the Cabinet opposed his recommendations to send the NRMA overseas. The Prime Minister's estimate at the Cabinet table put thirteen ministers with him and eight with Ralston,[73] although Macdonald, Ilsley, Mulock, and Gibson indicated that they were prepared to resign on this question. The Prime Minister then asked Ralston if he was prepared to form a government. He was not. Macdonald gave the same reply, but Ilsley, although the nervous strain of his responsibilities weighed heavily on him, said he would need some time to consider the question. 'It is pretty clear,' King wrote of this response, one that flew in the face of King's belief in his indispensability, that 'he has it in mind he may be the one to be asked to form a Government. If he does, heaven help him and help the Government for he will go all to pieces in no time.'[74]

The sense of finality lay heavily over the Council chamber. Mackenzie King thanked the ministers for their support over the years they had served together, and it was agreed that matters would be finally resolved on the next day, November 1. That night King definitely decided that he would not resign, at least not until Parliament had a chance to reject his government's position. 'I think the right procedure would be to carry on, not accept some of the resignations of Ministers until Parliament assembles, and if that cannot be done, to fill up the positions with new Ministers.'[75] His every instinct was to hold power, in part because it was psychologically and emotionally essential to him, in part because the delay involved in bringing Parliament together might produce an easing of the situation at the front or even a German collapse.

Shrewd observers of the situation were also trying to determine what would happen. That evening Angus Macdonald talked with Grant Dexter and Bruce Hutchison, two sympathetic Sifton-chain reporters. The newsmen believed that McNaughton would be made Minister of National Defence and that there would be a great—and necessary—house-cleaning in the Department. How, they wondered, 'is it that in this war the Army, with some 40,000 casualties out of a total force of 400,000, is now so short of reinforcements that it has to resort to conscription whereas in the last war we had some 200,000 casualties out of, say, 500,000, and did not have to invoke conscription until the last year of the war?' That was a good question. The reporters also believed that if Ilsley and Macdonald followed Ralston out of the government, King could not carry on. 'They also think that King will put on conscription,' Macdonald wrote, 'rather than let us and perhaps Howe and Crerar and Mitchell break from the Government.'[76]

The next morning King again saw General McNaughton and formally asked him to become Minister of National Defence. 'I said I think this should be done immediately. Every hour is important. Ralston will probably tender his resignation this afternoon. I will take it to the Governor General. Ask him to accept it and will return to the Cabinet. . . . I will,' King said, 'at the same time tell the Governor General I propose to recommend your appointment.'[77] McNaughton, for his part, was eager. In his view, Stuart had turned to advocacy in support of the conscription of the NRMA men. 'Surely this was outside his province. . . .' McNaughton's note of this conversation went on: 'I was not prepared to say that conscription was necessary for the efficient prosecution of our part in the war. This did not mean that the present Army Establishment had to be kept up as it was. Changing from the Volunteer System to Conscription was a very serious step. We needed to know that it was really necessary before we took it. If it was necessary we should be able to convince the public . . .'[78]

King's preparations for this crucial Cabinet meeting continued. He visited the Governor General and told him of his plans. He spoke to several ministers, bolstering the flagging, reassuring the supporters, and urging the potential bolters to be calm and to wait.[79]

The Prime Minister had prepared as best he could, but whether McNaughton or anyone could persuade NRMA men to volunteer for overseas service was much in doubt. There were 68,489 NRMA soldiers on strength as of September 27, 1944, of which 8,743 were on extended leave. Only 16,000 were trained infantry. Perhaps an additional 26,000 could be remustered to infantry, but this required time.[80] Certainly the officers commanding the NRMA were dubious. Major-General George Pearkes, V.C., commanding on the Pacific Coast, told Ralston on November 1 that at most 2,000 or 3,000 could be persuaded to convert in a three-week campaign, and of that number only 1,500 would be infantry. The NRMA men wondered why they should go overseas now, Pearkes said, and they wanted only to return to civilian life. Nor would it do any good to threaten them with conscription. If this were done, they would simply hang back and wait, their general attitude being 'If the Government tells us to go, we will go.' If it didn't, they wouldn't.[81] McNaughton would have a tough job persuading the NRMA to convert.

First, the question of Ralston had to be settled. When the Council met at 3 p.m. on November 1, Ralston seemed 'extremely mild and moderate,' King noted, and the discussion picked up where it had left off the day before. Again the talk was of numbers, appeals, volunteers, but Ralston avoided saying that conscription would have to be adopted. At 5 p.m. King slipped from the room to call McNaughton, telling him that the discussions were taking longer than he expected. According to his note, McNaughton said that 'If it can be done peacefully without a Cabinet split all the better. . . .' King 'was not to consider himself under any obligation to me.'[82]

Fair enough, but Ralston was not co-operating. He seemed prepared to allow time for an appeal to the troops, to bend over backwards to avoid a split.[83] But King had made his plans on the expectation that Ralston would press his resignation; that he did not made the Prime Minister suspicious.

> . . . here is a scheme to make the situation still more difficult for me. We will be met tomorrow by some condition of things which will mean going over the same ground again to no effect. . . . I am convinced now that what was intended was that . . . all these things would be united together . . . and then everything limited down to the smallest point, which would then go to show that I was not willing even secretly among ourselves to give an undertaking.

'The moment that I sensed this,' King wrote later, 'I felt that the time had come to speak out.' Ralston was not saying what King hoped he would. The Prime Minister, quickly deciding on his course, then forced the break.

> I then said I thought we ought to, if possible, reach a conclusion without further delay. . . . After what had been said last night I realized some way would have to be found . . . to save the government and to save a terrible division at this time. . . . That I had been asking myself was there anyone who could do this. . . . If there was, I thought it was owing to the country that such a person's services should be secured. I said I believed I had the man who could undertake that task and carry it out. I then mentioned General McNaughton's name. . . . I said that he believed he could get the reinforcements that were necessary. . . .
> I then said that the people of Canada would say that McNaughton

was the right man for the task, and since Ralston had clearly said that he himself did not believe we could get the men without conscription, while McNaughton believed we could, and that he, Ralston, would have to tender his resignation . . . that I thought if Ralston felt in that way he should make it possible for us to bring McNaughton into the Cabinet at once—the man who was prepared to see this situation through. I said that in regard to a resignation from Ralston, he had tendered his resignation to me some two years ago and had never withdrawn it. . . .[84]

There is one other detailed account of this moment, found in Macdonald's diary. The Navy minister's version is somewhat different.

. . . the Prime Minister said, 'Well, in these matters as in so many others, everything depends on how much heart a man puts into his efforts. I have to tell Council that two years ago Colonel Ralston submitted his resignation to me. This resignation has never been withdrawn, and this fact has been on my mind during these two years. I cannot be accepting resignations every day. Consequently, I have had to look around and see whether there is in all of Canada another man who could carry out our policy. I believe there is such a man, and that man is General MacNaughton [sic]. I have asked General Mac-Naughton if he would be prepared to accept the portfolio of Minister of National Defence and MacNaughton said that he would. I believe that MacNaughton will have the confidence of every man, woman and child in this country. He knows the situation, and he believes that re-inforcements can be had without making resort to N.R.M.A. men.' The Prime Minister said that he felt that way himself. . . .

It was now obvious that Colonel Ralston's term as Minister of National Defence was over, but the Prime Minister said, 'I feel that I should accept Colonel Ralston's resignation.'

(This is Crerar's view of what the Prime Minister said. I am not sure, however, that King did not say, 'I feel, Colonel Ralston, that you should submit your resignation.')[85]

Both accounts agree that Ralston's behaviour in the face of this stunning, brutal event was faultless.[86] The Minister said that he would, of course, hand in his resignation, that he had done his duty faithfully, and that he hoped the new Defence Minister would be successful. He then shook hands with his colleagues and after a few additional words left the Council chamber for the last time.[87] King then told his dazed ministers that 'it was one of the hardest things I had to do in my life, but that it was the only course I could see for me which would serve to meet the war situation.'[88] Colin Gibson, the Minister of National Revenue, sitting next to Macdonald, viewed it differently: 'This is the most cold-blooded thing I have ever seen.'[89]

It was indeed; it was also a terrific gamble. All the conscriptionist ministers could have risen to their feet and followed Ralston from the room, leaving the government in ruins. But King had shrewdly assessed his ministers and he counted on their willingness to wait and see if McNaughton could produce the men.[90] He was right. No one followed the departing Colonel from the room, although there was later a good deal of grumbling in ministerial offices. Macdonald, for one, believed that he could not stay 'very much longer and work with the Prime Minister'. He and Ilsley wondered why King had wielded the axe the way he had. The two Nova Scotians concluded that it had been done 'to frighten others who might be thinking as Ralston thinks' and 'so that the whole matter might be veiled under the oath of Cabinet secrecy.' But Macdonald felt that Ilsley would stay in the Cabinet, and T. A. Crerar, he noted, took a certain glee in Ralston's sacking on the grounds that this would teach the General Staff a lesson.[91]

III

The Prime Minister called McNaughton as soon as the meeting ended at 6.30 p.m. and told the General that 'all [were] relieved' that he was to take over. McNaughton's response expressed his 'willingness to help solve difficulties in the emergency and my confidence we could win through. My satisfaction at the turn of events, which enabled me to serve under him personally.'[92] On November 2 the new Minister was brought to the Cabinet, welcomed warmly, and settled in Ralston's chair. The crisis was resolved. To the press, the Prime Minister said only that 'Everything speaks for itself.' 'For days on end,' the Acting High Commissioner in Ottawa reported to London, 'everything went on "speaking for itself" except the Prime Minister and Colonel Ralston.'[93]

The crisis atmosphere gradually eased over the next few days. The mood was one of relief primarily, mixed in CCF circles with a tinge of regret that only the Liberals seemed to be defending national unity in the face of the conscriptionists.[94] Of course King was still under attack from some of those who remained in the Cabinet, T. A. Crerar in particular starting a long and difficult correspondence demanding answers to a series of questions.[95] Ralston, too, engaged the Prime Minister in an exchange of letters,[96] and there were some demonstrations in Cabinet, most notably from Angus Macdonald.[97] But the feeling that the crisis had passed was pronounced, and it was noticed among others by Macdonald himself.[98] Was this a sign that Ralston had been pressing too hard, too soon?

The key event in Cabinet was the establishment on November 3 of a Recruiting Committee, consisting of McNaughton, Mackenzie, Mulock, Major-General L. R. LaFlèche, the Minister of National War Services, Gibson, Claxton, and Gardiner. The Committee would consider how best to appeal to the NRMA, using high and patriotic means, the resources of the church and the Canadian Legion, as well as government organs like the Wartime Information Board.[99] The Committee also collected all the available information on the NRMA men. From March 1941, they learned, 150,000 had been enrolled in the home-defence army. Of this number 42,000 had gone active, 33,500 had been released, 6,000 had transferred to the navy or air force, and 8,676 were on extended leave. Of the balance of 59,679, 6,000 had been NRMA since 1941, 25,000 since 1942, 17,000 since 1943, and 10,000 from earlier in 1944. A total of 42,000 were felt to be eligible for infantry. French Canadians numbered no more than 37 per cent.[100]

How could these men be persuaded to volunteer to serve overseas? The Committee believed that some way had to be found to provide them with a face-saving way of converting, some way to make them identify with the men overseas. The great appeal of McNaughton was believed to be the government's trump card and the Committee felt that he should go to see the troops. He should offer the men a deal, a pledge that they would suffer no discrimination and would be treated like volunteers. The Prime Minister, the Committee said, should make a national broadcast on November 8, with a pitch that was friendly but intense. The recommendations were basically accepted by the full Cabinet on November 7.[101]

By that date, however, the careful planning had begun to go awry. The problem was McNaughton. The general had ventured out of

National Defence Headquarters on November 5 to speak in Arnprior, Ontario and on the next day to address a Legion meeting in Ottawa. To his horror and astonishment, he met with jeers and catcalls, something that he had never expected and certainly not from his comrades of the Great War. Had he lost touch with opinion in Canada? Could he produce the men? Certainly he would not make any more speeches, nor would he travel outside of Ottawa. McNaughton's confidence was badly shaken.*[102]

At the time it seemed that English-Canadian opinion was in what Brooke Claxton saw as a 'highly emotional state'.[103] Ministers—along with rank and file Members of Parliament and leading Opposition figures—received mail and form-letters demanding conscription, resolutions from clubs, associations, Legion groups, and even some union locals.[104] The press in English Canada was unfailingly conscriptionist and occasionally vicious, and the Montreal *Gazette* said the Mackenzie King government, 'hoping for a political advantage, . . . risks a military disaster'.[105] The *Globe and Mail* argued much the same line, stating in an editorial on November 7 that 'the Government is wickedly sacrificing young men's lives to retain its governing power in Quebec.'[106] A Wartime Information Board survey prepared on November 18 calculated that 'There are no English-language papers which oppose conscription on principle. The division is between those which believe conscription is necessary now, and that the government is avoiding it in an unjustified attempt to placate Quebec, and those which believe that the government will introduce conscription when it becomes necessary.' The survey also reported that with one qualified exception, all French-language newspapers are opposed on principle to conscription.'[107]

While newspapers can shape opinion, however, they may not necessarily reflect it, and the opinion polls taken in November and December 1944 and later tend to indicate that the firestorm of opinion reported by and represented in the press may not have been entirely accurate. For example, when the Canadian Institute of Public Opinion asked voters which party they supported, the results were revealing.[108]

*McNaughton wrote a friend on February 10, 1945 that 'what existed in the Home Defence Army at the end of October last was none of my making. I had to take conditions as I found them. . . . This Home Defence Army was in a sad state of demoralization. It was neither fit to go to the front nor were there sufficient loyal dependable forces available to compel obedience if that course had been adopted.' PAC, A. G. L. McNaughton Papers, file 870-94, McNaughton to W. Griffin, 10 Feb. 1945.

	Liberal	PC	CCF	Bloc Pop. Can.
Jan. 1944	30%	29%	24%	9%
Mar.	34	30	22	8
June	35	30	21	7
Sept.	36	27	24	5
Nov.	36	28	23	5
Jan. 1945	36	28	22	6

The poll data suggested that the Liberals were not hurt by the conscription crisis and that neither the Progressive Conservatives nor the Bloc Populaire Canadien, to cite the two extremes on the manpower question, gained at the government's expense. Polls directly on the conscription question provide some evidence to indicate that the 1944 crisis did not arouse Canadians as much, for example, as had the Dieppe raid and its heavy casualties in August 1942. At that point 62 per cent of a national sample supported conscription while only 32 per cent opposed it; this was the highest level supporting conscription reported during the war by the Canadian Institute of Public Opinion. On November 13, 1944, in the midst of the crisis, only 57 per cent supported conscription; six weeks later on December 30, 60 per cent supported compulsion.[109] Opinion was polarized on racial lines undoubtedly, but a good many Canadians must have agreed with Professor J. A. Corry of Queen's University when he wrote to his Member of Parliament that 'in a country with one big solid minority such as we have in Canada, I think democracy demands the consent of that minority on big issues.'[110] Others too must have shared the attitude of *Canadian Forum* that public opinion was being manipulated by a fanatic, unscrupulous press campaign.[111] And certainly some Members of Parliament, even some from Ontario, thought their constituents unhappy about conscription at this stage of the war.[112]

Nonetheless when he went to the Cenotaph in Confederation Square for Remembrance Day ceremonies on November 11, Mackenzie King was reportedly asked 'What about the Zombies?' by the assembled veterans,[113] and his radio address on November 8 did not win any noticeably enthusiastic response. The Prime Minister had said that the NRMA men would not be demobilized since 'they will continue to be a potential ultimate reserve of reinforcements whose compulsory employment in any theatre may, in the light of developing circumstances, have to be reconsidered.'[114] That was aimed directly at the Zombies, reminding them that they would be held in service until the volunteers were demobbed. Their best course, King's message flatly said, was to volunteer.

The best course for the conscriptionist ministers was less clear. Ralston and his friends in the Cabinet held some conversations about the prospects for a conscriptionist party, but Ralston showed no desire to take the lead.[115] Part of the difficulty was that many people who might normally be conscriptionists could not persuade themselves of the need for conscription at this point in the war. Macdonald found this in his riding executive in Kingston, Ontario: 'It seemed to me,' he wrote on November 13, 'that there is here as elsewhere doubt as to reality of need.'[116] This was Jimmy Gardiner's view, too. In an interview with a reporter for the *Winnipeg Free Press*, the Minister of Agriculture argued that it was ridiculous to talk of a crisis in an army of 450,000 when it couldn't find 15,000 men out of the NRMA. 'Everyone knew there was no overall shortage of reinforcements. It was true there was some unbalance. . . . But whose fault was that—only the army chiefs themselves.'[117]

Probably the blame was the army's. But now it was being pressed to make one supreme effort to persuade the NRMA to convert. On November 14 McNaughton met with the senior commanders and urged them to pull out the stops. All agreed, but there was neither enthusiasm for the task nor optimism about the results—only 'hardened cases' were said to remain among the NRMA men. The District Officers Commanding, in fact, made it clear that they 'felt strongly that they would be unable to provide any number approaching 15,000 men by 31 Dec. 44. They wished to go on record as stating that after examination of the facts as given they were of the opinion that the numbers stated could not be produced . . . but would use every effort to secure the maximum results.'[118]

Almost certainly the officers were correct. Brooke Claxton received a letter from a friend, a major stationed at Camp Petawawa, Ontario, enumerating the NRMA soldiers' reasons for not converting to active service. First, there was no chance of conscription with both King and McNaughton against it. French Canadians worried they would be posted to English-speaking units. The high-powered salesmen with their 'go active' pitches were creating resentment, and the feeling was developing that McNaughton's appointment 'stinks to high heaven', and that the General had entered the Cabinet only out of a desire to hit back at Colonel Ralston in payment for a long series of slights, incidents, and fights.[119]

The gloom began to settle in once again. 'It is beginning to look,' Angus L. Macdonald wrote on November 14, vindication fairly leaping off the page, 'as if this appeal will not succeed any more than other appeals.'[120] That unfortunately was becoming clear to everyone. Mc-Naughton could point to lower casualties than expected since the beginning of November, but he had to cite lower NRMA conversion figures too. On November 20 he told his Cabinet colleagues that while there were more than 1,000 volunteers off the street in the last week for which detailed figures were available, the rate of NRMA conversions was low, ranging from 151 to 280 men in each of the weeks of October. The result of all this was that while McNaughton could predict a reinforcement surplus of 700 at the end of December, for each month thereafter a substantial deficit would exist, increasing progressively from 2,375 at the end of January 1945 to 9,500 at the end of May. The projections for May, Macdonald observed, were 'within 700 of that which we estimated at the end of October'. Those figures, Macdonald noted, 'seemed to me to strike the Cabinet with even more force than the figures . . . at the end of October.'[121]

The Cabinet's difficulties were complicated further because Parliament, summoned by Mackenzie King on November 13, was to meet on November 22. To call Parliament, King reasoned, might help block further resignations. As he told Chubby Power, in hospital in Quebec City recovering from appendicitis, 'I could not go on this way any longer. That I did not want to get into the position where I would be blamed for having let matters run too long without consulting Parliament and up to a time which made [it] impossible to get the necessary aid to the soldiers overseas. I said I was seeking a vote of confidence.'[122]

Between the 13th and 20th of November, however, the Prime Minister received contradictory advice from different quarters. Chubby Power advised that the Quebec M.P.s seemed to favour dissolution and wanted the Prime Minister to go to the country on the conscription issue. Power himself urged King to strike a deal with the Governor General, ensuring that he would get dissolution if defeated in the House on the conscription question. Ian Mackenzie believed the government would fall on a straight vote on conscription in Parliament. The Prime Minister himself spent a good part of November 17 trying to frame a motion to present to the House, fiddling with ways of avoiding any mention of reinforcements at all and simply seeking support in carrying on the war effort.[123] His own views were clear, nonetheless, as an extraordinary memorandum he wrote showed:

Re: Conscription

1. Keep men overseas and what will be best for them *foremost*.
2. Remember your authority and power comes from Liberal members in H. of C. and through them from the people.
3. Have said no conscription, conscription *if necessary* to be interpreted by speech 1942—see necessary and advisable in light of all the circumstances.
4. Have said *no election* while war is on and *until* end of term.
5. Make others take responsibility for bringing on an election in wartime.
6. The King's Government must be carried on—do all possible to this end.
7. May mean turning over govt. to those who are most needed for that purpose.
8. Keep in mind Liberal Govt. now 2 wings (1) Voluntary enlistment (2) Conscription. This division will disappear with end of war.
9. Be careful *who you take into government* and about attempting to carry on without men needed in Defence Departments—Finance, munitions—remember what it means to administer a war and conduct an election at the same time over months.[124]

Clearly King intended to continue in power as long as he could. But if he was beaten in the House of Commons, or if the important ministers began to resign, he seemed to favour turning power over to another rather than provoking an election.

Meanwhile the crisis of numbers went on. McNaughton foolishly compounded the difficulties by talking optimistically to the press, a development that led four officers to protest to the Chief of the General Staff that the recruitment drive had no chance of success. In Vancouver General Pearkes encouraged his staff officers to talk to the press and express their own views—all of which pointed to the complete failure of the drive to get enough men.[125] Yet McNaughton told the Prime Minister on November 19 that everything would come out all right. 'He said to me,' King wrote, 'that he had to handle these officers very carefully. That if he began to oppose them, he might have a revolt on his hands and a situation which would be very difficult to manage.' McNaughton had to ensure that the generals would co-operate in getting the needed men.[126]

The conscriptionist element in the Cabinet had become increasingly impatient, however, and the Cabinet meeting on November 20 had

364 | CANADA'S WAR

concluded with Macdonald, Ilsley, Crerar, and others pressing vigorously for a date to be set after which conscription would follow if men
were not found from the NRMA. The date most often mentioned was
December 1. McNaughton tried to resist this drift in the discussion by
emphasizing the difficulties that could arise in trying to enforce conscription. The men who would have to maintain order in the country
should opposition arise were themselves NRMA, he said. There might
be bloodshed. This had little effect.[127]

After the end of the meeting King took St Laurent, Gardiner, Mackenzie, and McNaughton back to his office for further discussion. He
seemed to be moving in the direction of accepting a deadline, but he
was firm in reiterating that he would never serve in a conscriptionist
government. His final thoughts for the day, as set down in his diary,
were unequivocal on this score:

> More and more I come back to my firm convictions that the thoughts
> I had when the matter first came up were the right ones and that I
> should stand firmly against agreeing to conscription and not follow-
> ing the voluntary enlistment, because I doubt if it would help to get
> the men, and secondly the great possibility of making the situation
> worse for the present and for all time to come in Canada. There is
> another reason. It is that I should not myself take any step which
> will prevent the men overseas getting reinforcements they need by
> becoming responsible for a dissolution before all methods have been
> tried. I am sure that those who have been responsible for this plot
> when they begin to administer carrying out conscription will find
> they have made a fatal error and that instead of helping the men
> overseas they will help to prejudice Canada's entire war effort. . . .[128]

Again his thoughts pointed to resignation before an election.

The next day King met the Cabinet at 4 p.m. He told the ministers
that he had been thinking matters over carefully and that he realized
there were sincere and irreconcileable differences. Then, reading notes
he had prepared beforehand, King said:

> I would ask the public appeal for the trained men for service overseas
> to be continued until . . . (three weeks as a minimum). If at the end
> of that time, the requisite number of men are not available I will
> then make way for some other member of the Administration to take
> over, which will leave the Administration free to pass immediately an

order in council under amendment to the N.R.M.A. Act [sic] making its provisions applicable to men called up under provisions of the Act. (By this means there will be no necessity of the government going back to Parliament for a vote of confidence as the stipulation in that regard related exclusively to myself and it was based on the need for a vote of confidence because of it being assumed that I would not have my heart in the enforcement of the Act.)

I shall not take any step which will prevent the men who are fighting overseas from obtaining needed reinforcements by any method that is feasible.

I have taken the only method that I believe possible.

It is for those who believe in a different method to be given the opportunity.[129]

The reaction to King's statement was something close to consternation. Gardiner said he would follow the Prime Minister. Howe said King was essential for the postwar period. Macdonald, as he wrote later, responded that 'the position which he had stated would place his successor in a very difficult position. I believed that if he resigned, most of the Cabinet would go with him, and I felt that most of the Liberal caucus would be behind him.'[130] St Laurent said he would leave with King, a position shared by the other French-Canadian ministers, La-Flèche, Bertrand, and Fournier. King was amused by this: 'The effect of so many of the men coming instantly to my side caused Angus Macdonald to say that it was apparent the Government was not for conscription.'[131] Macdonald then said that 'I thought the best thing for us who were strongly for conscription, such as Ilsley and Crerar, was to leave the Cabinet. It would save embarrassment to what was apparently the majority of our colleagues. Ilsley thought this was right.'[132]

At this point Gardiner suggested that if Mackenzie King agreed to remain as Prime Minister 'we would announce that if the voluntary system failed at the end of the test period, 8,000 Zombies would be sent over. The question would be reviewed with regard to the second 8,000, but we would send the rest home and would have no more conscription of any shape, no more call-up.'[133] The Cabinet briefly canvassed Gardiner's suggestion but Power and St Laurent both objected to it and the argument turned elsewhere.[134] Later that evening Ian Mackenzie, increasingly taken with Gardiner's idea, called on Power, saying that he had come to believe that St Laurent would

366 | CANADA'S WAR

accept this proposal and so would most of the other ministers, except possibly those from Quebec. Power, however, remained adamant.[135]

King had stood firm this far. He would not countenance conscription and he would turn over power to a conscriptionist rather than cause an election to prevent the troops from getting needed reinforcements. The conscriptionists for their part, aware that they were in a numerical minority in the Cabinet, were prepared to withdraw, leaving their anti-conscriptionist colleagues to carry on, presumably under King. As King had indicated a few days earlier, however, he was fully aware of the enormous difficulties involved in carrying on without men like Ilsley, Macdonald, and the remainder of the hard-liners. Those were the factors in his mind in the morning of November 22 when McNaughton called him on the telephone.

The National Defence Headquarters staff were convinced that the voluntary system could not produce the needed men, the Minister of National Defence said. Although there had been every sign that this was coming for days past, McNaughton, 'a highland chief' who valued the loyalty of his subordinates above all else,[136] took this advice like 'a blow in the stomach'.[137] He had asked the Chief of the General Staff to give him this word in writing,[138] McNaughton told the Prime Minister, and he had also received the resignation of the District Officer Commanding in Winnipeg. If the army commanders resigned one after the other, the military machine would run down like an unwound clock.

This call from the General greatly affected the Prime Minister. 'Instantly,' he wrote,

> there came to mind the statement I had made to Parliament in June [1942] as to the action the government would necessarily take if we were agreed that the time had come when conscription was necessary. It was apparent to me that to whatever bad management this may have been due, we are faced with a real situation which has to be met and now there is no longer thought as to the nature of the military advice tendered, particularly by General McNaughton. . . . it will be my clear duty to agree to the passing of the order in council and go to Parliament and ask for a vote of confidence, instead of putting before the House the motion that I have drafted. . . . This really lifts an enormous burden from my mind as after yesterday's Council it was apparent to me that it was only a matter of days before there would be no Government in Canada and this in the middle of war

with our men giving their lives at the front. A situation of civil war would be more likely to arise than would even be the case were we to attempt to enforce conscription.[139]

The decision for conscription had been taken. General Pearkes' mischievous action on November 20 in allowing his officers to talk with the press had already created a feeling in King's mind that the system was breaking down. McNaughton's foolish optimism of the last week, followed by his 'body blow' advice, also contributed to King's state of mind as did the resignation of the Winnipeg military commander. All were symptoms of trouble, but there was no revolt of the generals.[140] Some senior officers probably had not tried very hard to persuade the NRMA to volunteer; some felt a deep loyalty to Colonel Ralston. But when the Chief of the General Staff told the Minister of National Defence that he and his principal officers were agreed that the voluntary system had failed, the CGS acted properly and constitutionally, although there can be no doubt that such collective advice was unusual and a form of pressure.

But for the Prime Minister, only a revolt could suffice. He had to find some way of making his *volte-face* appear credible, and only extreme urgency could justify his course both to himself and to his ministers. The tactic now was to win some time. First, the House of Commons had to be faced and the Ralston-King resignation correspondence presented. Caucus had to be attended to, soothed briefly, and sent packing with the advice that an emergency Cabinet meeting was necessary. Then key ministers had to be cautioned to do nothing until they heard what the Prime Minister had to say in Council. Above all, St Laurent and Power, the two key figures in Quebec, had to be persuaded that King's new course was the proper one.

St Laurent came to see Mackenzie King first. Told of McNaughton's telephone call, St Laurent was very disturbed by the thought of a 'Palace revolution'. To accept conscription would be to lose Quebec in the next election, he feared, but he would stand by the Prime Minister.*[141] Power was next, coming in to see King about five minutes

---

*St Laurent's formulistic view of the switch, as propounded to Power on December 14, went as follows: 'The Big Interests were bound to destroy King because he had embarked on a programme of Social Legislation, and had not been favourable to the C.P.R. or to the Banks. That Family Allowances were considered by the Interests to be a drain on financial resources. . . . the Toronto Group were not so

before the scheduled Council meeting at 8 p.m. To Power, King did not fly the kite of military revolt, something that the Associate Minister of National Defence would not have been likely to accept. Instead King argued that General McNaughton had advised him that the voluntary system had failed. Power was unimpressed: 'I could not follow fully what he had in mind,' Power wrote, 'but I told him I was unable to agree. I said I thought St. Laurent would follow him and my other colleagues from Quebec. I said the only thing I could do was to go out quietly and make no fuss about it.'[142]

At roughly the same time that King was explaining his somersault to St Laurent and Power, the Cabinet conscriptionists were meeting in T. A. Crerar's office. Gathered there were Crerar, Howe, Mulock, Gibson, Macdonald, and Ilsley. 'Mulock was prepared to resign,' Angus Macdonald wrote,

> and had a letter of resignation written. Crerar also had a letter written. Gibson and Howe said they had made up their minds that we would have to decide by tonight on a definite policy, and that policy would have to be conscription. . . .
>
> . . . Our discussion . . . turned mainly on what time limit should be fixed. Crerar thought that the 30th November would be long enough. Ilsley, I think, felt that McNaughton had spoken of the 2nd December as being the end of a week, and a date at which he could appraise the value of the appeal.
>
> I urged them to try to keep to the main point tonight and not be drawn off by discussions on very minor and irrelevant points. I felt, as I said yesterday in Cabinet, that the appeal had already failed, and that any further extension of the time would have no real effect, but might help the Quebec Ministers. I felt that all present were firm in their resolution. As to what the consequences of our resignations would be I am not sure.[143]

T. A. Crerar's account of the meeting is also significant:

> At luncheon at the Rideau Club . . . Howe called me aside and told me that he was going to break with the Prime Minister at caucus. He

---

much in favour of Conscription itself but in using it as an instrument to destroy King. . . . King had no alternative but to cede and hand the reins of power over to people who would destroy all Social Legislation, or accept Conscription.' Queen's University, C. G. Power Papers, Notes, 14 Dec. 1944.

had thought the matter over and had finally come to the conclusion that the only course was to send the NRMA men as reinforcements. I said to him, 'You have definitely reached that conclusion?' and he said that he had. I saw Gibson a few minutes later and told him of Howe's decision . . . and he told me that Mulock was also of the same mind. . . .

At the conclusion of caucus Macdonald spoke to me and said that he thought those of us who felt alike should meet to discuss our course. . . . I suggested that we might meet in my office in the House of Commons. I spoke to Gibson and Howe, and Gibson said he would speak to Mulock. . . . When we gathered I said that we were in a serious situation; that the action we were contemplating might bring about the downfall of the Government; that we should not be influenced by any false modesty, but should face the responsibility involved with a possible fall of the Government as men capable of seeing our duty and doing it. I said, further, that whatever action was taken should be taken together; not necessarily that we should send in a joint resignation but that our several resignations should go in at the same time. . . . Ilsley arrived shortly afterward and agreed with this.[144]

King did not learn of this meeting until early in January when Grant Dexter told him of it. 'This makes clearer than ever that the hand of Providence was in the success I had,'[145] he wrote, and perhaps he was right. At the very time that a bloc of ministers planned to submit their resignations, King forestalled them.

The Cabinet gathered at 8 p.m. on November 22. 'P.M. was late in arriving,' Macdonald wrote in his diary.

When he got in, he began by saying that he felt that the Caucus and the meeting of the House had shown that most of the Party were behind the Government. However, our first duty was to the men overseas. We must do nothing which would jeopardize their safety in any way. He had been talking to MacNaughton [sic] this morning and MacNaughton felt the voluntary system had failed and that we must have reinforcements for overseas.

MacNaughton then said that he was a believer in the voluntary system and had been. He had assumed office hopeful that the voluntary system could produce results. He had hoped to enlist the support of various individuals and agencies . . . but that support had not been

forthcoming. There had been sabotage by some of these elements. . . .
He referred again to the British Columbia incident. . . . He also felt
that we had to get 16,000 men overseas to form a pool and get them
over as quickly as possible.

How this could be done was in doubt. Gardiner returned to his previous
suggestion of an order in council specifying a strictly limited number of
men. Macdonald argued that 'we had better pass the Order in Council
in general terms, without any limitation or restriction, and then say
informally or at least not in the Order that, at present, we were sending
only 16,000, that being the number now needed.' The Cabinet made
no decision on method, and the Prime Minister expressed the hope that
Cabinet would stand together. At last Power spoke up. He had already
told the Prime Minister that he could not support conscription, and
now he told his colleagues. Gardiner said that he agreed with Power
and that, perhaps he should go, too.[146] King replied, as Macdonald
wrote later, that he hoped there would be no resignations 'and he said
if there were to be many, he did not think he could carry on. He was
willing to fight his foes, but not his friends.'[147]

IV

Clearly King had handled the matter brilliantly thus far. He had held
off the conscriptionists for more than a month, fighting them for every
inch. He had clearly established to Quebec and to the French-speaking
ministers that he opposed conscription—and he had fired Colonel
Ralston as a testimony of faith. When he reversed himself on November
22, it was done only with the government on the verge of breaking
up and on military advice that the men were needed and could not be
found any other way. He could and did claim necessity. How much
better, too, that he could cite to St Laurent the prospect of a generals'
revolt. That threat justified his step and made it necessary to preserve
civilian supremacy in the state.* And what timing that his changed
stand on conscription could come as the conscriptionists were plotting
to resign en masse, a move that would have brought down the govern-

*Did King believe this? In a memo he wrote in 1949, he again cited St Laurent
referring to revolution and said the Army threats of resignation 'compelled the
govt. to yield'. King said he told the Justice Minister the country could not be
allowed to know the army was opposing the government. King Papers, Notes and
Memoranda, Conscription file No. 6, Memo, 29 Dec. 1949.

ment. The switch, too, came in such a way that it disarmed the Opposition, already building up to a full head of steam.[148] The timing had been brilliant, but King had had more than his fair share of luck.

The Prime Minister's task now was to keep Quebec in line. After telephone calls to a number of newspaper publishers, to Cardinal Villeneuve, to Liberal leader Godbout, and to other key figures in the province, King went off to his party caucus. It was 11.45 a.m. on November 23. The Prime Minister began his remarks by tracing events since mid-October, the appointment of McNaughton, the difficulties faced by the appeal to the NRMA men, and the subsequent failure to get the men. 'He then went on to talk of a United Cabinet,' Power wrote later, 'and suggested that it was evident by the fact that all members of the Cabinet were sitting around the table.' This was a not uncharacteristic tack of Mackenzie King's, one that banked on the difficulty of interrupting him and on the embarrassment such a step might cause. Power was not a man to be intimidated, however. 'I felt bound to interrupt him there and to say that I had already told him personally, which was not a Cabinet secret, that I could not follow him in this course, and read the note which I had sent him.'[149] Much of the rest of caucus was taken up by a long statement from Ralston, now vindicated. The Quebec Members, stunned by events, gave little reaction.

At Cabinet, Chubby Power made his farewell and left. Ralston had gone because he wanted conscription, Power because he opposed it. The remaining ministers settled down to dealing with a draft order in council that would send up to 16,000 NRMA men overseas. The recruiting campaign, in other words, would continue so that additional men could be despatched if possible; in fact, if the requisite number of volunteers could be found, no conscripts at all need be sent.* This was the slimmest of possibilities, but King characteristically kept the option open.[150]

---

*Between 9 Nov. and 4 Dec. 1944, 2,701 NRMA converted to General Service, and there were 3,236 enlistments from the public and 360 from the reserve army for a total of 6,297. After 23 Nov. 1944 there was a large jump in NRMA conversions. (PAC, Brooke Claxton Papers, Vol. 101, Memo of Enlistments (G.S.) . . .) The public response to the government position, British observers noted, was bewilderment: some papers said 'Conscription Introduced' while others believed 'Voluntary System to be Maintained'. PRO, Cabinet Office Records, Cab 66/60, Tel. High Commissioner to Secretary of State for Dominion Affairs, 7 Dec. 1944, printed on W.P.(45)7, 5 Jan. 1945.

King told Parliament of the government's new policy that day, and the next General McNaughton, not a Member of Parliament, appeared by special arrangement. Poor McNaughton had been preparing a speech justifying the volunteer system and, assisted by Pickersgill and Claxton, he had been forced to revise it hurriedly between the Cabinet decision and his parliamentary debut.[151] McNaughton was badgered and harangued by the Tories, eager for blood and delighted to attack a man who had come very close a few months before to joining with them, but the General bore it well. Clearly the viciousness of the attacks helped solidify the Quebec Liberals, many of whom, while restive in the extreme, could understand that little would be gained by voting against King.[152] Still, on November 24 Alphonse Fournier, the Minister of Public Works, wrote to King to suggest that he should leave the government. It was Fournier's estimate, too, that up to 60 per cent of the Quebec M.P.s would cross the floor of the House. The remainder, he believed, would remain in the Liberal Party but vote against the government.[153]

In fact Fournier was wrong, and he himself remained in the government along with all the French-Canadian ministers.[154] Nor did the predicted schism in the ranks of the backbenchers come about, in part at least because of King's great speech to the House on November 27. Turning his back to the Opposition benches, King appealed to his own followers and quoted Laurier's speech to Parliament on March 13, 1900.

If there is anything to which I have devoted my political life, it is to try to promote unity, harmony and amity between the diverse elements of this country. My friends can desert me, they can remove their confidence from me, they can withdraw the trust they have placed in my hands, but never shall I deviate from that line of policy. Whatever may be the consequences, whether loss of prestige, loss of popularity, or loss of power, I feel that I am in the right, and I know that a time will come when every man will render me full justice on that score.[155]

It was one of King's greatest performances. Blair Fraser, the *Maclean's* reporter, said on the Canadian Broadcasting Commission that night that 'as a speech it was a magnificent performance. . . . three hours without notes, except for two or three prepared bits and a sheaf of quotations, and his voice never flagged from beginning to end. Apart from everything else, for a man 70 years old it was a remarkable feat of energy and endurance.'[156] The next day the caucus of Quebec members received the Prime Minister in a friendly fashion,[157] and when the vote of confidence in the government finally came on December 7, King was sustained with a majority of 73. Nineteen French-speaking Members from Quebec voted with King.[158]

The crisis was finally over. Only 2,463 NRMA were actually posted to units of the First Canadian Army, and of that number 69 were killed, 232 wounded, and 13 made prisoners of war.[159] The estimates of need that had provoked the reinforcements crisis in the first place proved, as estimates often do, to be wrong, as the Canadian troops fortunately suffered fewer casualties than had been expected. Fortuitous circumstances at the front—the transfer of the Canadians from Italy to North West Europe, for example—had kept casualties down, and even without the extra reinforcements produced by the order in council, the reinforcements pool overseas on April 27, 1945, Colonel Stacey calculates, would have been 8,500 strong.[160]

Whatever the numbers, King, his government, and his country had survived. The army overseas did not go short of necessary reinforcements. Quebec was unhappy, but not implacably hostile. English Canada fumed but it had got its way.* And the government, the government of national unity, had survived. But for Mackenzie King, looking back at the harrowing period from mid-October, the primary motive was relief.

> Certainly I shall never have another task comparable to the one of the past six weeks. Over and over again, I have thought . . . that some day the world will know some of the things that I have prevented. I doubt if they will ever know what has been prevented at this time. I must make increasingly clear to the world that prevention of

---

*A poll on December 9, 1944 asked respondents if they approved the government's decision to send NRMA men overseas or if they would have preferred greater efforts to get volunteers. Fully 50 per cent approved while 33 per cent wanted greater efforts to persuade volunteers. The poll provided additional data:

	UK origin	French	Other	Age 21-9	Age 30-49
Approve	66%	8%	55%	46%	49%
Volunteers	16	77	29	40	33

Public Opinion Quarterly, VIII (Winter, 1944-5), 591.

wrong courses of evil and the like means more than all else that man can accomplish. That lesson surely should be the one that comes out of the war.[161]

That is not the most inspiring of political creeds. But even if one concludes that both the conspiracy against social welfare and the military revolt were figments of King's imagination, he had prevented other occurrences. There was no reinforcement shortage in the end, for one thing. The government, though weakened by the resignation of one pro- and one anti-conscriptionist, had stayed together, thus preventing a government of reaction from taking power or an election at the climax of the war. The essential unity between French- and English-speaking Canadians had held together, at least in the Liberal Party, and the sundering of racial peace had been prevented. What had been prevented was important, but in the election of 1945 that was shortly to come, King's emphasis would be on what he had accomplished. That, too, was important.

---

1 J. W. Pickersgill and D. F. Forster, *The Mackenzie King Record*, Vol. II: *1944-45* (Toronto, 1968), p. 84.

2 Public Archives of Nova Scotia, Angus L. Macdonald Papers, Diary, 14 Sept. 1944.

3 Queen's University, Grant Dexter Papers, Memo, 22 Sept. 1944.

4 Public Archives of Canada [PAC], W. L. Mackenzie King Papers, Diary, 15 Sept. 1944; Pickersgill, II, pp. 84-5. Cf. Macdonald Diary, 14 Sept. 1944 and added note of 21 Sept. 1944—King 'is surely inaccurate' in claiming he referred to Japan.

5 Dexter Papers, Memo, 25 Sept. 1944.

6 For detail on Canadian manpower policy, see PAC, National Selective Service Records, Vols 36-7, 5th, 6th, 7th Reports on National Selective Service Operations; United States National Archives, Office for Strategic Services files, doc. no. 41307, 'Canadian Manpower Problems', prepared by J. W. Tuthill, U.S. Legation, Ottawa, 4 Aug. 1943.

7 Extract from McTague speech in Progressive Conservative Party, *Speaker's Handbook 1945* (Ottawa, 1945), war policy, sec. 1.

8 *Public Opinion* [Conservative Party newspaper], Jan. 1945, 20; J. L. Granatstein, *The Politics of Survival* (Toronto, 1967), pp. 177-8; Queen's University, H. A. Bruce Papers, Bruce to C. G. McCullagh, 21 June 1944; PAC, John Bracken Papers, Vol. 16, Jean Morin to Bracken, 21 June 1944.

9 Toronto *Globe and Mail*, 22 June 1944.

10 *Ibid.*, 4 July 1944.

11 Montreal *Gazette*, 11 July 1944; PAC, J. L. Ralston Papers, Box 46, file 133, Speech attacking McTague, n.d.

12 PAC, R. B. Hanson Papers, Overseas Reinforcements Correspondence, 1944, anon., 18 Nov. 1944.

13 PAC, A. G. L. McNaughton Papers, Vol. 255, file 897-24, Memo, Adjutant General to Minister, 13 Nov. 1944.

14 Ralston Papers, Vol. 50, 'Mobilization of 13 Brigade on an Active Basis', 2 May 1944 with atts; National Defence Headquarters, Directorate of History, file 112.21009 (D209), 'Trends in the Thinking of Army Units', Sept. 1944. For a recent view, see Dennis Braithwaite in Toronto *Star*, 7 Dec. 1973.

15 Cameron Macpherson, 'The Birth of a Minority: The Army System and the Zombie Myths', undergraduate paper, York University, 1970, 53. The best fictional accounts of the system employed against Zombies is in Ralph Allen, *The High White Forest* (New York, 1964) chapter VI; for Quebec attitudes, see Roch Carrier, *La Guerre, Yes Sir!* (Toronto, 1970).

16 Ralston Papers, file 614-11, Minutes, 21 June 1944; Dexter Papers, Memo, 22 June 1944. The Ottawa *Citizen*, 21 Oct. 1944, reported that of 1,200 surplus airmen in Toronto, 130 had agreed voluntarily to transfer to the army while the rest were demobbed to await their call-up.

17 PAC, Privy Council Records, Cabinet War Committee Records, Minutes, 3 Aug. 1944; Ralston Papers, Vol. 44, Extracts, att. to Breen to Ralston, 29 Aug. 1945; *ibid.*, Vol. 88, Stuart to Chief of General Staff, 2 Aug. 1944; Macdonald Diary, 3 Aug. 1944.

18 King Diary, 3 Aug. 1944. But see the following accounts, all of which indicate reinforcement difficulties at an earlier stage; John Swettenham, *McNaughton*, Vol. III: *1944-66* (Toronto, 1969), pp. 20ff.; Col. Dick Malone, *Missing From the Record* (Toronto, 1946), p. 144; and esp. Charles Stacey, *Arms, Men and Governments: The War Policies of Canada, 1939-45* (Ottawa, 1970), pp. 425, 434-5.

19 Montreal *Gazette*, 19 Sept. 1944; Stacey, p. 440.

20 Toronto *Globe and Mail*, 6 Oct. 1944. Drew had written King to demand an investigation of Smythe's charges. King Papers, Black Binders, Vol. 7, file 25.

21 King Diary, 22 Sept. 1944; Macdonald Diary, 22 Sept. 1944; Cabinet War Committee Records, Minutes, 22 Sept. 1944.

22 King Papers, Black Binders, Vol. 7, file 25, Heeney to King, 9 Oct. 1944. A memo prepared for the Chief of the General Staff and forwarded to the War Committee on 10 Oct. 1944 showed 10,000 reinforcements available at 30 Sept. 1944. *Ibid.*, Memo, Acting/Adjutant General to CGS, 10 Oct. 1944. Moreover, CCF leader M. J. Coldwell, on 12 Oct. 1944, was assuring his Ontario colleague E. B. Jolliffe that General Simonds had told him on a recent visit overseas that reinforcements were satisfactory. PAC, Coldwell Papers, Vol. 17.

23 Tel., 9 Oct. 1944, in Ralston Papers, Vol. 59, and King Papers, Black Binders, Vol. 7, file 25.

24 *Ibid.*

25 Ralston Papers, Vol. 43, Statement, n.d.

26 Stacey, p. 441. But cf. Malone, p. 151; Ralston Papers, Vol. 26, Diary by Minister's Military Secretary, 27, 29, Sept. 1944. But Ralston's diary also shows few complaints overall and almost none in North West Europe.

27 This was not true. The Cabinet had agreed that NRMA men would only be

directed to civilian employment as the situation permitted. Macdonald Diary, 22-3 Sept. 1944; Pickersgill, II, pp. 113-14; PAC, C. D. Howe Papers, Vol. 53, Heeney to Howe, 25 Sept. 1944.

28 Directorate of History, Canadian Military Headquarters Files, 1/COS/20, Chief of Staff to Minister, 11 Oct. 1944. Almost exactly the same state of affairs existed in the American army. See Stephen Ambrose, *The Supreme Commander: The War Years of General Dwight D. Eisenhower* (Garden City, 1970), p. 540.

29 Pickersgill, II, p. 114.

30 King Diary, 13 Oct. 1944. All the reports from overseas seemed to indicate Germany was collapsing. E.g., Ralston Papers, Vol. 43, Secretary of State for Dominion Affairs [SSDA] to Secretary of State for External Affairs [SSEA], 14 Oct. 1944.

31 *Ibid.*, Chief of Staff to Minister, 15 Oct. 1944.

32 *Ibid.*, 30 Oct. 1944.

33 King Papers, Black Binders, Vol. 7, file 25, Memo, General Pope to King, 16 Oct. 1944.

34 See Swettenham, III, pp. 26ff. which blames Stuart for the crisis. Stuart was no friend of McNaughton. Swettenham, III, pp. 29-30, also cites a telegram from Stuart on 27 Aug. 1944, which hints at reinforcement problems. Cf. Power's assessment of Stuart. Norman Ward, ed., *A Party Politician: The Memoirs of Chubby Power* (Toronto, 1966), pp. 152-3.

35 Pickersgill, II, pp. 125-6; Power, p. 151.

36 Pickersgill, II, pp. 126-7.

37 Maurice Pope, *Soldiers and Politicians* (Toronto, 1962), p. 247.

38 Accounts in Cabinet War Committee Records, Minutes, 19 Oct. 1944; Macdonald Diary, 19 Oct. 1944; Queen's University, C.G. Power Papers, Box 3, Notes of Discussions on the Conscription Crisis, 19 Oct. 1944; Pickersgill, II, pp. 133-5.

39 *Ibid.*, pp. 133-4. Stacey, p. 443, sees this meeting as a grilling of Stuart; I do not.

40 Pickersgill, II, pp. 135-6.

41 King Diary, 20-1 Oct. 1944; R. M. Dawson, *The Conscription Crisis of 1944* (Toronto, 1961), pp. 21-2; Pope, pp. 252-4. Apparently the crisis was not raised in the U.K. War Cabinet, or at least not long enough to make it into the minutes. Public Record Office [PRO], Cabinet Records, Cab 65/44. Pope's meeting with Roosevelt is reported in detail in Stacey, pp. 466-8. Stacey, pp. 448ff., puts substantial emphasis on King's telegram to Churchill and subsequent events in the War Committee that show Mr King guilty, in Col. Stacey's phrase, of 'essential dishonesty'.

42 King Diary, 21 Oct. 1944; Power Papers, Notes, 21-2 Oct. 1944.

43 King Papers, Black Binders, Vol. 7, file 25, Memos, Heeney to King 20 [?], 23 Oct. 1944.

44 *Ibid.*, Memo, 19 Oct. 1944, in newly discovered King Papers, W.W. II Reinforcement file.

45 Ralston Papers, Vol. 43, CGS to Minister, 23 Oct. 1944.

46 Directorate of History, file HQS 9011-9-1, Adjutant General to Minister, 23 Oct. 1944. Pope, p. 248, notes that 150,000 men had already been discharged from the armed forces.

47 Ralston Papers, Vol. 43, Murchie memo, 23 Oct. 1944.

48 *Ibid.*, unheaded remarks to Council, 24 Oct. 1944.

49 Pickersgill, II, p. 138; Pope, pp. 248-51.

50 Pickersgill, II, p. 146. See Bruce Hutchison, *The Incredible Canadian* (Toronto, 1952), pp. 346-7, for a good account.

51 Pickersgill, II, p. 148.

52 *Ibid.*, pp. 144-7; Macdonald Diary, 24 Oct. 1944; Power Papers, Notes, 24 Oct. 1944; Ralston Papers, Vol. 85, 'Notes for the Record . . .', 26 Dec. 1944 [a document prepared by T. A. Crerar].

53 Power and Macdonald put this revelation at a War Committee meeting the next day. Power Papers, Notes, 26 Oct. 1944; Macdonald Diary, 26 Oct. 1944. But the Cabinet War Committee Minutes do not refer to it. King Diary, 25 Oct. 1944 and Pickersgill, II, p. 152 cite it on the 25th.

54 Power Papers, Notes, 26 Oct. 1944.

55 Pickersgill, II, pp. 164-5; Cabinet War Committee Records, Minutes, 27 Oct. 1944; Power *Memoirs*, p. 154; Hutchison, p. 348.

56 Pickersgill, II, p. 161.

57 Directorate of History, file HQS 9011-9-1, Brig. Spencer to Minister, 27 Oct. 1944.

58 PAC, Brooke Claxton Papers, Vol. 101, Memo of 30 Oct. 1944, from HQS 9011-7-8. Copy in Ralston Papers, Vol. 63. Cf. Macdonald Diary, 30 Oct. 1944.

59 E. L. M. Burns, *Manpower in the Canadian Army* (Toronto, 1956), *passim*.

60 Directorate of History, file 112. 3H1.001 (D 10), Statement of Gen. McNaughton, 12 Feb. 1964.

61 Macdonald Diary, 27 Oct. 1944.

62 Pickersgill, II, pp. 168-9. See Stacey's fine account, pp. 451ff. There was some resentment against Ralston among Liberal M.P.s. Paul Martin interview, 24 July 1971.

63 Pickersgill, II, pp. 158-9.

64 *Ibid.*, pp. 171-2.

65 Macdonald Diary, 30 Oct. 1944; Ralston Papers, Vol. 43, aide-mémoire, 30 Oct. 1944; Pickersgill, II, pp. 172-4.

66 King Diary, 30 Oct. 1944; Stacey, pp. 453-4.

67 Arguments advanced by Pickersgill, 29 Oct. 1944. King Papers, ff. C244828ff.

68 Pickersgill, II, p. 175.

69 McNaughton Papers, Vol. 267, Progressive Conservative Party file, and particularly McTague to McNaughton, 10 Aug. 1944; M. Brown to McNaughton, 17 Aug. 1944; McNaughton to Henry Borden, 30 Aug. 1944; Borden to McNaughton, 1 Sept. 1944; and McNaughton memo, 27 Sept. 1944.

70 Pickersgill, II, pp. 118-21; McNaughton Papers, Vol. 267, Memo, 13 Oct. 1944.

71 Pickersgill, II, p. 177; McNaughton Papers, Vol. 267, Appointment to Cabinet file, Memo, 31 Oct. 1944.

72 Ralston Papers, Vol. 43.

73 Pickersgill, II, p. 179.

74 *Ibid.*, p. 181.

75 *Ibid.*, pp. 181-2.

76 Macdonald Diary, 31 Oct. 1944. There is a confused account of this day in John Hawkins, *The Life and Times of Angus L.* (Windsor, N.S., 1969), pp. 230-1. See also Claxton's memo to King, 1 Nov. 1944, in King Papers, f. C244843.

77 Pickersgill, II, pp. 182ff.

78 McNaughton Papers, Vol. 267, pen notes, 1 Nov. 1944; Swettenham, III, pp. 43-4.

79 Pickersgill, II, pp. 182ff.

80 Ralston Papers, Vol. 43, att. to aide-mémoire, 30 Oct. 1944.

81 *Ibid.*, Notes on telephone conversations, Ralston-Pearkes, Macdonald-Pearkes, 1 Nov. 1944.

82 McNaughton Papers, pen notes, 1 Nov. 1944.

83 Macdonald Diary, 1 Nov. 1944.

84 Pickersgill, II, pp. 188-92.

85 Macdonald Diary, 1 Nov. 1944; cf. Dexter Papers, Memo, 6 Nov. 1944.

86 Cf. Brian Heeney, ed. *The Things that Are Caesar's: The Memoirs of a Canadian Public Servant* (Toronto, 1972), pp. 70-1.

87 For Ralston's subsequent actions, see Ralston Papers, Vol. 85, Diary, 1 Nov.-7 Dec. 1944; *ibid.*, resignation papers. His parliamentary assistant, W. C. Macdonald, resigned with him. King Papers, Black Binders, Vol. 8, file 28, Macdonald to King, 2, 15 Nov. 1944.

88 Pickersgill, II, p. 194; Stacey, pp. 456ff.

89 Macdonald Diary, 1 Nov. 1944. Other accounts are Crerar's 'Notes for the Record . . .' in Ralston Papers, Vol. 85; Power Papers, Notes (although only second hand for this event as Power was in hospital with appendicitis from 27 Oct.); and Dexter Papers, Memo, 9 Jan. 1945, based on a conversation with King. The Prime Minister argued that Ralston had resigned, not been fired.

90 Pickersgill, II, p. 195. Cf. Malone, p. 156.

91 Macdonald Diary, 3 Nov. 1944; Macdonald Papers, Macdonald to W. A. Macdonald, 25 Nov. 1944; Ralston Papers, Vol. 47, Crerar to Ralston, 2 Nov. 1944.

92 McNaughton Papers, Vol. 267, pen notes, 1 Nov. 1944.

93 Cab 66/59, Tel. High Commissioner to SSDA, 11 Nov. 1944, printed on W. P. (44) 719, 8 Dec. 1944.

94 PAC, CCF Records, Vol. 150, D. Lewis to S. Knowles, 6 Nov. 1944; Coldwell Papers, F. R. Scott to Coldwell, 2 Nov. 1944.

95 E.g., Queen's University, T. A. Crerar Papers, Crerar to King, 3 Nov. 1944; copies of all Crerar-King correspondence in Ralston Papers, Vol. 50.

96 Printed in House of Commons *Debates*, 22 Nov. 1944, pp. 6506-9.

97 Macdonald Diary, 3 Nov. 1944.

98 *Ibid.*, 5 Nov. 1944.

99 *Ibid.*, 3 Nov. 1944, Pickersgill, II, p. 203.

100 Crerar Papers, Memo, Heeney to Cabinet, 6 Nov. 1944.

101 Claxton Papers, Vol. 101, Minutes of meeting, 6 Nov. 1944; McNaughton Papers, Vol. 255, file 892-10; King Papers, Black Binders, Vol. 7, file 25, LaFlèche to King, 6 Nov. 1944 and atts; Swettenham, III, pp. 51-2.

102 McNaughton interview, 23 Mar. 1966; Stacey, p. 463. See especially McNaughton Papers, Vol. 266, Drew to McNaughton, n.d. [16 ? Nov. 1944]. Cf. Swettenham, III, p. 52.

103 Claxton Papers, Vol. 101, Memo to Prime Minister, 9 Nov. 1944.

104 E.g., see Bracken Papers, Vol. 34; Claxton Papers, Vol. 101; Coldwell Papers, reinforcements files.

105 Montreal *Gazette*, 13 Nov. 1944.

106 *Globe and Mail*, 7 Nov. 1944.

107 King Papers, Notes and Memoranda, conscription file #6, Wartime Information Board Survey #50, 18 Nov. 1944. See also PRO, Dominions Office Records, DO 35/1118, Review of Dominions Press, Series E, No. 215, 18 Jan. 1945; Claxton Papers, Vol. 101, WIB Surveys and Field Reports.

108 *Public Opinion Quarterly*, IX (Spring, 1945), 88-9.

109 *Ibid.*, VIII (Spring, 1944), 153; (Winter, 1944-5), 591.

110 Macdonald Papers, file 26-15, Corry to Macdonald, 23 Nov. 1944.

111 *Canadian Forum*, XXIV (December, 1944), 196.

112 Paul Martin interview, 24 July 1971.

113 Macdonald Diary, 11 Nov. 1944. But King Diary, 11 Nov. 1944 reports 'not the slightest disturbance'.

114 Cited in Cab 66/59. High Commissioner to SSDA, 11 Nov. 1944, printed in W.P. (44) 719, 8 Dec. 1944.

115 Macdonald Diary, 11-12 Nov. 1944; Dexter Papers, Memo, 6 Nov. 1944.

116 Macdonald Diary, 13 Nov. 1944.

117 Dexter Papers, Chester Bloom to V. Sifton, 10 Nov. 1944.

118 King Papers, Black Binders, Vol. 7, file 25, 'Minutes of a conference of GOsC . . . a.m., 14 Nov. 1944'; *ibid.*, 'p.m., 14 Nov. 1944'; Macdonald Diary, 15 Nov. 1944; McNaughton Papers, Vol. 271, Minutes of Minister's Morning Conferences . . . ; Swettenham, III, pp. 54-5; Stacey, pp. 463-4.

119 Claxton Papers, Vol. 101, Major Stott to Claxton, 16 Nov. 1944; cf. Swettenham, III, pp. 55ff.

120 Macdonald Diary, 14 Nov. 1944.

121 *Ibid.*, 20 Nov. 1944.

122 Pickersgill, II, pp. 212-13.

123 Power Papers, Notes, 15 Nov. 1944; Pickersgill, II, pp. 218-19; King Papers, Conscription file, drafts by Pickersgill, St Laurent, Mackenzie, n.d. (in recently discovered files).

124 King Papers, Memo, n.d., ff. C244028-9.

125 Montreal *Gazette*, 21 Nov. 1944; Saskatchewan Archives, J. G. Gardiner Papers, Pearkes file, Gardiner to Editor, Winnipeg *Tribune*, 24 Feb. 1945; Stacey, pp. 468-9.

126 Pickersgill, II, pp. 219-20.

127 *Ibid.*, pp. 221-2; Macdonald Diary, 20 Nov. 1944.

128 Pickersgill, II, p. 224.

129 King Papers, Notes, n.d., ff. C244030-2; Pickersgill, II, p. 226.

130 Macdonald Diary, 21 Nov. 1944.

131 Pickersgill, II, p. 227.

132 Macdonald Diary, 21 Nov. 1944.

133 Power Papers, Notes, 21 Nov. 1944; Macdonald Diary, 21 Nov. 1944.

134 Power *Memoirs*, p. 162.

135 Power Papers, Notes, 21 Nov. 1944.

136 The phrase is C. S. A. Ritchie's. Interview, 9 June 1971.

137 Pickersgill, II, p. 229; Swettenham, III, p. 59; Dexter Papers, Memo, 9 Jan. 1945.

138 The letter from the CGS is printed in Stacey, p. 471.

139 Pickersgill, II, p. 229.

140 On the military revolt: Swettenham, III, pp. 59-60; Pope, pp. 257ff. and esp. the note on pp. 259-61; Macdonald Diary, 7 Feb. 1945; Stacey, p. 471. The only academic proponents of the revolt theory are Dawson, pp. 83ff. and James Eayrs, *The Art of the Possible* (Toronto, 1961), pp. 93-5, who considers that widespread resignations were a certainty, as a minimum.

141 Dale Thomson, *Louis St. Laurent, Canadian* (Toronto, 1967), p. 150; Hutchison, p. 375; Dexter Papers, Memo, 9 Jan. 1945.

142 Power Papers, Notes, 22 Nov. 1944.

143 Macdonald Diary, 22 Nov. 1944.

144 Notes for the Record . . . , in Ralston Papers, Vol. 85; Dexter Papers, Memo, 23 Nov. 1944.

145 King Diary, 9 Jan. 1945.

146 Gardiner Papers, Gardiner to King, 23 Nov. 1944.

147 Macdonald Diary, 22 Nov. 1944; Pickersgill, II, p. 233; Power Papers, Notes, 22 Nov. 1944.

148 PAC, Arthur Meighen Papers, M. G. O'Leary to Meighen, 22 Nov. 1944 and reply, 23 Nov. 1944; Coldwell Papers, Memo re Reinforcements Overseas, by Andrew Brewin, n.d. [22 Nov. 1944?].

149 Power Papers, Notes, 23 Nov. 1944; Macdonald Diary, 23 Nov. 1944; Queen's University, Norman Lambert Papers, Diary, 23 Nov. 1944; Pickersgill, II, p. 237.

150 House of Commons *Debates*, 23 Nov. 1944, p. 6529; Dexter Papers, Memo, 23 Nov. 1944; Crerar Papers, Memo, 24 Nov. 1944.

151 Swettenham, III, pp. 61-3.

152 Dexter Papers, Memo, 23 Nov. 1944 anticipated this effect and 'Backstage at Ottawa', *Maclean's*, 1 Jan. 1945, 14 reported it. Charles Ritchie, *The Siren Years* (London, 1974), p. 187.

153 King Papers, Black Binders, Vol. 8, file 28.

154 Fournier's decision to stay has been attributed to St Laurent's pressure. Thomson, p. 154. Joseph Jean, St Laurent's parliamentary assistant, also resigned. King Papers, Black Binders, Vol. 8, file 28, Jean to King, 1 Dec. 1944.

155 House of Commons *Debates*, 27 Nov. 1944, pp. 6617-18.

156 Copy in King Papers, ff. C245035ff. This view was shared by the U.K. High Commissioner. Cab 66/60, Tel. High Commissioner to SSDA, 7 Dec. 1944, printed on W.P. (45)7, 5 Jan. 1945.

157 Pickersgill, II, pp. 247-8.

158 Quebec opposition was sharp, nonetheless. See: Quebec *Official Gazette*, 30 Nov. 1944, with a Legislature resolution condemning conscription; Fondation Lionel-Groulx, Fonds Raymond, 1945 election file, notes, n.d.; Fondation Lionel-Groulx, Fonds Bloc Populaire Canadien, Raymond to R. Benoit, 1 Dec. 1944; Robert Rumilly, *Histoire de la Province de Québec*, tome XLI: *Duplessis reprend les rênes* (Montréal, 1969), pp. 156ff. For a different view, see Grant Dexter, *The Conscription Debates of 1917 and 1944* (Winnipeg, 1945). For press response, see Gardiner Papers, J. G. Fogo to Gardiner, 12 Jan. 1945 and encl. 'Review of Editorial Attitude of Daily and Weekly Newspapers . . .'

159 Directorate of History, file 133.009(D1), Casualty Statistics (compiled 1949).

160 Stacey, pp. 481-2 concludes that conscription was militarily justified.

161 Pickersgill, II, pp. 271-2.

10. The Election
of 1945

The life of Parliament would run out in the spring of 1945, and Mackenzie King naturally enough worried about the proper time to go to the people. On January 16, 1945 he learned that the prospects were that the Canadian Army overseas was faced with six weeks of heavy fighting. 'This,' he wrote in his diary,

> adds a very great bearing on the wisdom of avoiding another campaign on conscription between now and the time that this fighting is over. We have all the reinforcements that are needed. If Parliament were sitting at the time, there would be discussion from day to day there which would be most embarrassing. . . . Indeed the campaign might well take the shape of Parliament having to dissolve with the issue being carried to the country which is what the Tories want and no doubt accounts for their anxiety to have an election brought on sooner rather than delayed.

An election fought on conscription would not be to Mackenzie King's liking. It was far better to wait until victory was won, for then 'the force will have gone out of the conscription issue before the time for election comes . . . and the real problem of the electors, namely, peace negotiations, post-war problems, and our social legislation will come more clearly before the electorate before the vote is taken.'[1] The campaign thrust should be on the future, not on the sometimes unhappy events of the past. The election should be focussed on the leader and the team best capable of creating a new social order for Canada.

I

The Prime Minister had long held to the view that it would be best to hold the election after the war in Europe was over, despite advice to the contrary. In July 1943, for example, Chubby Power had sent him a long memorandum on the advisability of an early election. The national war effort was too large, Power argued, the strain too great. The period of patriotic exultation was almost over 'and the burden of taxation is being felt more and more'. In some ways the most political of King's ministers, Power argued in addition that manpower needs would gradually aggravate the situation, particularly in Saskatchewan, Quebec, and rural areas generally 'where the Liberal party usually draws its greatest support'. How to justify a wartime election? Power was equal to this: the coming year would see heavy fighting, a factor that made an election then undesirable. Shortly thereafter peace would come, bringing in its train terrific problems of reconstruction, and an election would disrupt the smooth transition from war to peace. But a government blessed with a renewed mandate in 1943 would be in a position to grapple with these challenges, and it would be a 'virile, active, strong Government with authority and prestige'. Those were only his own views, Power said, and he knew that Ian Mackenzie, for one, disagreed with them. But he believed that the party had a better chance in 1943 than later.[2]

Power's letter interested the Prime Minister, particularly its frank admission that Canada had gone too far in its war effort. The election question worried him somewhat, but he was firm in his resolve.

> Were I looking at the matter purely from the point of view of winning an election, I would feel there might be much to be said for an appeal this year. On the other hand, I do not believe the Canadian people wish an election any sooner than it is necessary to have one. . . .
>
> As long as there is the prospect of the war ending by the autumn of 1944, I think I shall hold off for that length of time, be the consequences what they may.[3]

His judgement was confirmed by the narrow Conservative victory in the Ontario election and the Liberal losses to the CCF and the Labour-Progressive Party in federal by-elections in August. The September 1943 Gallup Poll, showing the CCF just ahead of the Liberals and Conservatives, was yet another reason for delaying an election, as well as the necessity for rebuilding the dormant and decayed National Liberal Foundation. The September 1943 meeting was a first step towards this end.

Power was not yet convinced. In a memorandum to the Prime Minister sent at the beginning of 1944, the Air Minister argued that 'The next session will decide the election. The attitude and conduct of the government and its members right from the beginning of the session and throughout is more important than anything else.' The Prime Minister should create a series of Liberal caucus committees, Power said, and he attached a list of 50 M.P.s 'who normally can be counted upon to be active and to render good service'. This was not many in a party that had close to 200 Members of Parliament in its ranks, to be sure, but if the good Members could do their job and study the Tories, the CCF, reconstruction, war achievements, anti-inflation policy, and the like, they would produce information of value—and, equally important, they would feel that they were doing something useful. This last was the burden of Power's suggestion. The Prime Minister should mend fences in the party caucus, talk to the disgruntled, and turn back to politics once again. The party had to be readied for the coming election.[4]

This advice Mackenzie King accepted. At a caucus on February 2, 1944 he told his Members that this was almost certain to be the last session before the election, and he announced the establishment of a number of caucus committees. He also added that the war had to be won before major reconstruction measures could be put into effect.[5] By the end of February the caucus committees were getting ready to report.

The party machine was also being refurbished. Money was being collected, in large part by C. D. Howe.[7] And in May 1944, without consulting Sen. Wishart Robertson, President of the National Liberal Federation, the Cabinet named J. Gordon Fogo, a Halifax lawyer who had been serving in the Department of Munitions and Supply, as party chairman. As such, Fogo was clearly the Cabinet's choice to run the election, and before long the National Liberal Federation formally withdrew, leaving the field to Fogo's campaign committee.[8]

The preparations took place while the party's standing in the opinion polls was beginning to improve,[9] but unfortunately this trend was not particularly noticeable in Ontario, the province with the most seats. A very extensive opinion survey was conducted for the National Liberal Federation by Cockfield, Brown, the party's advertising agency, in May and June 1944. The survey, one of the first of its kind in Canada, looked at 43 seats, and estimated that if an election were held in 1944 the Liberals would lose ten seats to the CCF and six to the Conservatives. The party stood to gain only two seats from the Conservatives, and the projected results in the 43 seats would be 18 CCF, 13 Conservative, and 12 Liberal.[10] An accompanying analysis of opinion in 19 Ontario ridings showed Liberalism stronger among women than men, but age did not appear to be a factor, Liberal support being consistent among all age groups. The party was strongest in rural areas and strongest, too, among farmers and well-to-do business or professional men. The report also noted that the Liberal Party had lost more ground to the CCF than the Conservatives and, in addition, that Liberalism had lost more to the Tories than it had gained from them. The political situation was in flux, but the Liberal Party in Ontario was not in good shape.[11]

The survey also tested, like breakfast cereal names, a series of political slogans. The best seemed to be 'Work-Progress-Unity', the only problem being that Conservative voters felt this described their party nicely. The favoured slogan among convinced Liberals was 'Bring Victory Home', while other slogans such as 'Let's Stay Prosperous', 'Keep Moving Forward', and 'The Liberal Party Gets Things Done' did not score well in this test. What this meant was difficult to determine, except that the winning slogan seemed to suggest that victory was being won over fascism and could be won over troubles at home too. The implicit message, perhaps, was that reconstruction policies were the keys to winning an election.[12]

Very few Liberals, however, seemed optimistic about party chances. Angus Macdonald for one was deeply pessimistic and unconvinced that the government deserved re-election. 'It looks to me,' he wrote in his diary on June 22, 1944,

as if this government would be badly defeated when it appeals to the Country. It has been weak at all points where pressure has been exerted—on Conscription, on labour matters, on financial concessions to this or that group. . . .

The P.M. talks of the importance of having a Liberal Government in office—for the good of the country. This government seems to have lost any appeal it ever had. The P.M. is responsible for this, more than any other member of it. He is naturally a compromiser. The service vote is heavily against us and much of this—probably almost all of it stems back to him. Yet it is true that some members refer to him as our greatest asset.[13]

Chubby Power was equally pessimistic in a letter he wrote to his son overseas. The lack of patronage, the suspension of Liberal organization, the high taxes, and the manpower muddle—all these things put the government in difficulty, and some people even believed it could run third in the election. But Power didn't put the blame on King for all of this. In fact, he noted that 'The Country generally, and almost unanimously agrees that the King Government has done a wonderful war job. Production, care and maintenance of troops, anti-inflation policy, finances, etc., no patronage, no graft, efficient administration . . .' About all that Mackenzie King was personally blamed for, but not by Power, was the conscription situation. 'They say he is afraid to offend Quebec.'[14]

But Quebec was offended—and Saskatchewan too. The results in the provincial elections in those two provinces during the summer of 1944 were further blows at the Mackenzie King government. The return of Maurice Duplessis to power and the victory of the CCF under Tommy Douglas in the West were omens of catastrophe. Saskatchewan, hitherto the preserve of Jimmy Gardiner's organization, now seemed lost, and even the solid Liberal Quebec that had been the prop of the Liberal Party in the twentieth century seemed in jeopardy. The Prime Minister responded to these shattering losses by organizing a full-scale inquest into the state of the party.[15] 'I intend to follow from now on the practice of getting some of these matters on record,' King said in his diary, 'that the responsibility may be appropriately placed in relation to possible future happenings. It is really shameful the little attention any of the ministers with the possible exception of Gardiner and Power, have given to organization matters.'[16] That sounded ominous too, as if King was trying in advance to fix the blame elsewhere.

The Cabinet got down to political study in the week of September 5. The key document before the ministers was an appraisal, riding by riding, from the National Liberal Federation. The party's possibilities were sketched out by province.[17]

	GOOD	FAIR	SMALL	NEGLIGIBLE
N.S.	10	2		
N.B.	6			
P.E.I.	3	1		
P.Q.	37	12	7	9
Ont.	19	25	27	11
Man.	4	8	1	4
Sask.	(no estimates available yet)			
Alta	4	8	5	
B.C.	6	2	5	3
	89	58	45	27

To everyone's surprise, things did not seem as black as the ministers had feared. King himself observed that 'Taking it all together, the outlook seemed brighter than I had anticipated it would be. Ontario and Quebec are the parts that are in poorer shape.'[18] Even so, the results of the NLF estimates promised a minority government at best.

More hopeful perhaps was the party's organizational readiness in terms of campaign themes and media preparation. H. A. Kidd, Cockfield, Brown's man with the party, had been working in Ottawa on the campaign with Brooke Claxton and J. W. Pickersgill since December 1943 when his agency had been retained by the National Liberal Federation. Two full-dress campaigns were prepared, the most expensive one being budgeted at about $150,000.[19] Whether this would be enough was unclear, and Postmaster-General Mulock, for one, complained bitterly to King about this 'third class publicity' proposal. It was 'inadequate and will almost certainly result in the failure of the party to reach the people with the consequent result that we will be defeated.'[20] According to the Cockfield, Brown representative, Mulock's complaints were founded on his support for a competing advertising agency, not on his response to the media presentation that had been shown the Cabinet. This presentation had stressed the theme 'Vote for a New Social Order', the pitch that eventually was used in the election. The sample advertisements and billboards were shown to the ministers and, according to Kidd, the response was total silence. Later Kidd learned that the advertisements, heavy with type and deliberately stressing programs rather than personalities, had in fact been greeted with moderate enthusiasm.[21]

More time was spent worrying about Quebec than about the advertising for the coming election. Some ministers were hopeful about finances,[22] but there were severe organizational problems in the province, particularly in the Montreal area where no one had taken hold since P. J. A. Cardin had resigned in May 1942. Curiously, at this very time in September and October 1944, talks were in train, led by Power, to bring Cardin back into the Liberal Party. Although St Laurent was agreeable, some of the ministers worried what English Canadians might think if the anti-conscriptionist former Public Works Minister came back; the matter died when King refused to consider it.[23] This refusal to rebuild the party with Cardin's aid almost guaranteed a fragmentation of the vote in Quebec, and Power foresaw the Liberals winning only 14 of the 24 seats in his Quebec City area. The rest, he wrote to the Prime Minister, would go to 'Pouliot independents [friends presumably of the fractious and difficult Liberal M.P. for Temiscouata, Jean-François Pouliot], Cardinites—thinly disguised Union Nationale, to Bloc Populaire.'[24]

The one optimistic note about Quebec, some Liberals felt, was the inadvertent help being given by George Drew. His attacks on the Liberal government and particularly his vicious comments about family allowances, won Francophone supporters for the Liberal Party with every speech. Early in October Power even told Grant Dexter that the Bloc Populaire was finished as a viable political force. The BPC's chief organizer, he said, had come to see him in an effort to get a Liberal nomination for himself. Dexter recorded Power as saying 'that dissolution cannot be unduly postponed. To hell with the war. It is all over but the cleanup. He wants dissolution by Nov. 15 at the latest.'[25]

The dissolution of the government was in full flow by that date, although not of the kind that Power had sought. He himself would be one of the casualties of the conscription crisis, as would the brief flower of Liberal optimism. 'We had every reason to be optimistic about the political situation in this province,' one of Jimmy Gardiner's organizers wrote from Saskatchewan, 'up to the time that the conscription crisis developed at Ottawa.' Everything was now confused, the organizer added.[26] Not just in Saskatchewan. Enthusiasm in the National Liberal Federation offices dwindled away to nothing, and the press became increasingly hostile to the government, seeing it as a corpse ready to be laid out.[27] For Mackenzie King the lesson was clear. The election would have to wait until victory in Europe. In a letter to an acquaintance in mid-January, he argued that 'I have done my best to avoid the hatreds engendered by the enmities of political strife being added to the anxieties and hatreds of war. At the risk of losing power altogether, I have succeeded in staving off anything of the kind to within three months of the expiration of the present term of Parliament. If,' he concluded, 'within the next few months, while men are giving their lives at the front, a war-time election becomes inevitable, the responsibility therefore will rest upon others.'[28]

II

When he referred to 'responsibility' the Prime Minister had in mind the forthcoming by-election in Grey North, Ontario, set for February 5, 1945. The by-election had been called to give the Minister of National Defence, General McNaughton, a seat in the House of Commons, and the sitting Member, W. P. Telford, was readily prevailed upon to retire to clear the way for the General.[29] The government's hope had been that McNaughton might receive an acclamation,[30] but the Conservatives had dashed this expectation. The Tories, still bitter about the conscription crisis, saw in English-Canadian resentment their best hope, and the Grey North by-election gave them a good chance to test the sentiment of rural Ontario about conscription.[31] Their candidate, Garfield Case, the Mayor of Owen Sound, chose to fight the by-election on that issue alone. 'We do not feel that this riding,' Case said, 'should be made a "guinea pig" to try to prove to the men overseas that Ontario is satisfied with a half-hearted, piecemeal, manpower policy.'[32] There would also be a CCF candidate in the race, too, although the leadership of the party had apparently tried to dissuade the local organization from running anyone.[33] But once the constituency decided to go ahead, the CCF put all its resources behind the party candidate, Air Vice Marshal A. E. Godfrey. 'We will let the voters decide whether they prefer to go back to the hungry thirties with the old parties,' the CCF statement of its decision read, 'or go forward with the C.C.F.'*[34] Like McNaughton, Godfrey was an outsider, a businessman with a steel company in Gananoque, Ontario, and he apparently had a personal

---

*The CCF could not count on the united support of organized labour, much of which was given to McNaughton. The Communist-dominated United Electrical Workers supported the Liberal, as did the official Labour-Progressive Party newspaper in Toronto, the *Canadian Tribune*. LPP policy since May 1944 in fact had been to elect as many Communist candidates as possible in the coming general election, all pledged to co-operate with a re-elected Liberal government. The enemy of the LPP, it seems clear, was the CCF, for in the democratic socialist movement was its greatest challenge. See Gad Horowitz, *Canadian Labour in Politics* (Toronto, 1968), pp. 90ff. On the background for this see I. M. Abella, *Nationalism, Communism and Canadian Labour* (Toronto, 1973), pp. 76ff.

score to settle with General McNaughton who had refused to intercede to gain him an extension of service with the RCAF.

The Minister of National Defence, of course, was the focus of public attention in this his first try at politics. He told his nomination meeting in Owen Sound on December 16 that he was running in North Grey only for the short session of Parliament to come before the expected spring general election. In that election, he said, with a certain disarming naïveté, he would run in his native constituency of Qu'Appelle, Saskatchewan. He was a new boy in politics, McNaughton admitted, and he seemed to believe that his record of service to the country would help get him elected. Referring briefly to conscription in his first speech in the riding, the Minister said that while there had been a shortage of men, there was no shortage now. He had seen the situation through to 'a solution which ensures our efforts for the future'.[35]

But McNaughton's campaign got off the tracks from the start. He made the mistake of coming to Owen Sound in a private railway car, radio-equipped so that he could keep in touch with his department. However necessary the private car, it created an unfortunate impression, an impression that worsened when McNaughton's press of work promised to keep him out of the riding until the new year.[36] More damaging still, rumours that the General was a Roman Catholic spread. Such things mattered in fiercely Orange Grey county, and although McNaughton was a good Protestant he was married to a Catholic, and he refused to make any compromises. He would attend midnight mass with his wife on Christmas Eve, he said, exactly as he had done in the past.[37] Adding fuel to local bigotry was the Rev. T. T. Shields of Toronto, a tireless crusader against the whore of Rome and its agents in Canada: Mackenzie King, Quebec, and General McNaughton. It was Quebec that had prevented conscription, the Reverend told a large Owen Sound crowd on January 4. 'The Roman Catholic hierarchy is determined to keep its followers at home, to BREED their kind, while our men are allowed to go overseas to be killed or wounded, so that the balance of the population will be more easily adjusted.' Stooping very low even for his ilk, Shields remarked darkly that 'It is a singular fact that General McNaughton has adopted the theory promulgated by the Church to which his wife belongs. You can draw your own conclusion. . . . I give you my final word,' Shields said, 'in my humble opinion a vote for McNaughton is a vote for the Roman Catholic hierarchy and for the further enslavement of Canada.' With only 4.7 per cent of the riding Catholic, with a number of Orange lodges, this kind of hatred may have been effective.[38]

Certainly it distressed Mackenzie King. 'The whole attitude of the Tories,' he said, instinctively attributing the sins of the bigot to his opposition, 'is the most unpatriotic thing I have known in my experience in public life, encouraging class hatred, race hatred, religious hatred—everything that can make for intolerance and this while we are in the midst of war and men are sacrificing their lives to save the freedom of the world.'[39] Perhaps the proper course was to dissolve Parliament before the by-election could be held, King thought, thus avoiding an embarrassing defeat for McNaughton. God knew he had been unable to get his ministers working to help the General. On December 29 he had told his Cabinet ministers for Ontario to get to work for the Defence minister, but on January 3 they had come to Cabinet with a report that 'incensed' King. 'It began by suggesting I should speak in the constituency or make a couple of records. McNaughton should spend a couple of weeks in the constituency. Hepburn should be called in to help. . . . Nothing about what Ontario Ministers would do.' The Prime Minister spoke very strongly to his ministers, lashing them to a major effort. 'This one constituency alone would be a test of all general elections.'[40] In the end King got his way, as he usually did. Mulock was despatched to the riding to run McNaughton's campaign along with Gordon Fogo, the national campaign chairman, and eventually $14,000 would be spent on the by-election.[41]

Still, the Prime Minister would have to intervene, and on January 12 he released a message to the electors. There was only one issue in the by-election, the citizens of Grey North were told, that of providing a seat in the House of Commons for the Minister of National Defence.[42] The Premier also had a second message in draft for release a week later. This message would make clear that controversy would provoke a dissolution. As he wrote in his diary, King was determined that 'If on [the official] nomination day, candidates are put into opposition to McNaughton, we will then the following day dissolve.'[43]

But there was no way of stopping the Tories, already scenting victory. By mid-January the Conservative campaign was beginning to shift to counter the CCF, Conservative estimates being that McNaughton was running a poor third.[44] That was probably correct, for McNaughton's— and the government's—prestige slumped after he felt obliged to tell the nation on January 20 that while 8,300 NRMA soldiers had arrived overseas, fully 6,300 more were Absent Without Leave somewhere in Canada. How then could McNaughton be portrayed as a man who could manage the war effort? The desertions, one Conservative spokesman said, were the 'withering fruit' of the government's manpower policy.[45]

Mackenzie King released his second letter to the electors on January 23. The Prime Minister had worked over his text endlessly, and the final version bitterly attacked the Opposition parties for hindering the war effort with 'unwarranted and unworthy' activities in the by-election. The government, he warned, would have to consider 'whether any useful purpose could be served by attempting to hold another session of the present Parliament.'[46] This barely veiled threat to dissolve did not deter either Case or Godfrey, both of whom duly filed their nomination papers and formally signified their intention to remain in the race. After considering whether he should cancel the by-election, dissolve Parliament, or withdraw McNaughton from the race, Mackenzie King finally decided to let events take the course they would. The last word from Grey North was promising for McNaughton, or at least more promising than before.[47]

The tide of the by-election would not turn in McNaughton's favour, however. On January 31 Conservative leader John Bracken, fresh from a visit to the battlefields, came to the constituency to press the party's hard line on conscription. The leader's appearance was necessary to counter a series of inexplicable revelations about candidate Case—one that he had allegedly been a draft evader in the Great War and a second that he had recently written a private letter to a 'friend' stating his aversion to conscription.[48] Bracken took the initiative and hit hard, homing in on the issue of 'reinforcements'. He had gone overseas to learn the truth, Bracken said, and he found that the soldiers felt betrayed by General McNaughton. The question before the electors was a simple one, therefore: 'Do you or do you not approve as Minister of National Defence a man whose recent course of action is held in complete contempt by the men overseas?'[49] The next day Bracken focussed on the AWOL NRMA soldiers, a by-product of the government's 'cowardly partisan policy'. Then he lashed out at McNaughton.

Let him tell you why some of those men arrived in Britain without their rifles which they were expected to have. Let him tell you about how they threw their rifles . . . their ammunition overboard. Let him tell you the truth, which is a condemnation of the complacency, the lack of leadership and the inept mishandling of the entire manpower problem in this nation.[50]

This was a devastating charge, and one that was soon picked up by the international press, repeated in the United States Senate, and broadcast throughout the world.[51]

The Bracken charge at last roused McNaughton's anger. There was a rumour that one soldier had thrown his kit overboard, he said, but there was no confirmation of this report. In any case there was only one man involved in the rumour, not hundreds, and it was scurrilous of Bracken to impugn the honour of all the NRMA soldiers. (The Cabinet considered the question and after some difficult discussion decided not to bring Bracken before the courts or before a judicial inquiry.[52] Before too long the Tories knew that Bracken was wrong and the General was right and, although the by-election was over by that time, the party offered no correction.)[53] But the vigour of McNaughton's counterattack —plus the Liberal money and organizational talent poured into Grey North—began to be felt. An opinion poll taken a few days before Bracken's intervention had shown McNaughton and Case neck and neck;[54] now a final push might put the Liberals over the top.[55]

Bracken feared this too, and he pulled out all the stops in an address on February 3. The Prime Minister's cowardly manpower policy had provided only a 'driblet of reinforcements', the usually mild-mannered and fair-minded Conservative said, and had failed to make French Canadians 'bear a fair share of sacrifice in time of war.'[56] 'Equality of sacrifice' had been a demand of the conscriptionists of the Great War, but that was one line of approach that few had used in this war. Now Bracken, a man who should have known better, was dipping into the same barrel of vituperation as that of such men as Rev. Shields. He was also killing his and his party's chances in Quebec.

The result of the election was a Conservative victory. Garfield Case won 77 of 127 polls and a majority of 1,236 over McNaughton and 4,215 over Godfrey. The basic issues had probably been two: reinforcements and local representation, and although some observers felt that the constituency's desire to have a local man as its representative in Ottawa was the stronger,[57] the press and the Conservative Party's leaders convinced themselves that reinforcements and conscription had been and would remain winning issues.[58]

McNaughton felt badly burned by his experience of political warfare and although he made a brave show of it he was shattered.[59] So was the Prime Minister. His party seemed to be in ruins, and while he consoled himself with the thought that the Tories had stolen the election with rum, religion, and skulduggery, there was no joy in Laurier House the evening of February 5.[60] But after a few days King gradually begun to recover his normal optimism, his talent for turning defeat into a forerunner of victory. After all McNaughton was an outsider, a parachuted candidate who had no ties to the riding and only intended staying there for a few months. In addition there was more to Canada than rural Ontario, and the Orange cast to the Tory campaign could not fail to have been noticed in the rest of the country and particularly in Quebec. As he wrote to Telford, the Member who had resigned to make way for McNaughton, 'I am convinced in my own mind that we can make the defeat in Grey North the cornerstone of victory in the general elections.' Certainly there was still unhappiness over reinforcements, but peace would cure that.[61] If the Conservatives continued to ride the conscription horse, flogging it unmercifully all across the country, the gains for Liberalism might be very great indeed.

III

But in order to capitalize on the Conservatives' errors, King would have to restore the divided Quebec party to health, and this was a task that he soon took on. When Chubby Power wrote him on January 17 about a matter concerning the RCAF, King seized the opportunity to invite the former Air Minister in for a chat.[62] 'Mr. King began the conversation with the usual compliments,' Power noted on January 29, and then talked politics at length. He seemed to be expecting an election in May, Power gathered, fearing that if it was held in April there 'would be no roads. I said that might be an advantage rather than otherwise.' But the main discussion centered on Quebec, where the optimism of fall 1944 had been dissipated by the conscription crisis. At least 20 Liberal Members of Parliament could not decide what to do and were looking to Power to lead them, the ex-minister had told Angus Macdonald in December,[63] and he indicated as much to King. 'I told him I had thought of promoting a wing of the Liberal Party to be called "The Canadian Liberal Alliance." He argued very strongly against this saying that a separate movement or group, or wing of the Liberal Party would be difficult to handle since the men in it would lose any sense of responsibility and might tend to drift away. I agreed,' Power wrote, 'that there was a good deal in what he said but that on the other hand the members who had voted against him were not ready as yet to sneak back into the Party. They had considerable support from their electors and thought they had done the right thing.' After further conversation the two parted on good terms 'with King saying that he was sure I would be back with him soon.'[64]

That was not at all certain, as King discovered when he and St Laurent met with Power again on February 20. The pressures on Power to return to the fold had been continuous if largely unsuccessful through February,[65] and this meeting was undoubtedly expected to bring Chubby back once and for all. The conversation began inauspiciously, however, when Power read a memorandum he had prepared that called for Independent Liberals in Quebec to 'face the issue boldly and proclaim they are the authentic Liberals, inheritors of the Laurier-Lapointe tradition, that the King Government had abandoned that tradition.'[66] This was too much for the Prime Minister, who objected that he had neither abandoned that tradition nor supported conscription and, as Power noted in his diary, 'Both King and St. Laurent made speeches at me.' Power's account went on:

> The principal argument took place on the question of a distinct and separate organization, though there was no objection to our calling ourselves Independent Liberals if we so desired and to making the statement which he proposed to do explaining wherein we differed from the Dorion-Independent Group,* in that we proposed to support Liberals in other provinces, and would not support any Government other than Liberal.
>
> Mr. King got quite angry at the idea of a distinct organization and said that if the people in Quebec were ashamed of him he should resign. St. Laurent said he thought that such an organization would do harm to those who had supported Mr. King in a contrary vote, and King said he could not abandon those who had stuck by him. For some time the situation became fairly tense and I was obliged to say I did not care, that I was prepared to get myself elected in Quebec-South and pay no attention to any organization. . . . We finally got

---

*The Dorion Group was a collection of isolationist Liberal-nationalists and displaced Conservatives under the leadership of Frédéric Dorion, an Independent who had been elected to the House in a November 1942 by-election. See *Le Devoir*, 29 janvier 1945; Fondation Lionel-Groulx, Fonds Bloc Populaire Canadien, Dorion file.

around to the point that unless we got together in some way, and agreed on something, that our chances of success in the district were very slim....

Power felt that the Prime Minister and Minister of Justice were afraid of the effect on the rest of the country if it appeared that all the seats in the Quebec City area, except St Laurent's own, were being contested by independent rather than regular Liberals. That, Power recorded, 'would be a serious blow to the Liberal Party chances since people in other Provinces would argue since King had no support in Quebec he could not possibly be successful.'[67] Mackenzie King, too, had his own suspicions of Power. 'It seemed to me that Power was anxious to create a certain wing which he himself would control. . . . An effort, in other words,' the Prime Minister feared, 'to try to wrest leadership in Quebec from St. Laurent to himself.'[68] The upshot, nonetheless, was that St Laurent and Power agreed to discuss candidates between themselves. Power would establish his headquarters at the Château Frontenac to give advice to his friends: 'in other words,' as Power wrote, 'to act as Organizer for them'.[69]

Power had succeeded in keeping some of his options open, and if he could strike an arrangement with the men around P. J. A. Cardin in Montreal, he could exercise enormous influence in the province and the party. In the days after his meeting with King and St Laurent, he had several conversations with representatives of the former Works Minister. The result of these meetings confirmed Power's view that the Liberal organization in Quebec was split apart, and he became partially convinced that a group of men were working to make C. D. Howe the Prime Minister in place of Mackenzie King. He learned too that Cardin had been in negotiations with the Dorion independents and while it sounded ominous for the fortunes of the King-St Laurent party, Power was not fooled: 'I got the impression of a great deal of insincerity and a vast amount of bluff as to their power and prestige.'[70]

Meanwhile the inexorable preparations for the undeclared election continued. Representatives of the political parties met in early February with Canadian Broadcasting Corporation officials to arrange for free-time broadcasting. A ratio of time was supposed to be derived for each party from a complicated mix of seats in Parliament, popular vote, number of candidates in the last election, and the standing of parties at the time of the preceding dissolution. The difficulty, as Gordon Fogo, the Liberal Party Chairman, wrote, was that this formula gave the

Liberals 60 periods of air time while the Conservatives got only 27, the CCF 8, and Social Credit 4. This would be difficult to defend, Fogo admitted, so he had settled for 21 Liberal periods as against 15 Conservative, 14 CCF, and additional free time for other groups qualifying as national parties.[71]

Simultaneously Fogo was fending off attempts to break up the advertising team he had assembled for the election. Advocates for agencies other than Cockfield, Brown were demanding a share of the billings, claiming that there had been earlier promises to this effect.[72] But Fogo adamantly insisted that the existing arrangements did not lend themselves to a distribution of advertising among several agencies. 'Moreover,' he argued, the fee arrangement with Cockfield, Brown 'is not intended to show them any ultimate profit.'[73]

The Liberal Publicity Committee began regular meetings early in February as well. Most meetings involved Fogo and the advertising agency representatives, but on occasion Brooke Claxton or J. W. Pickersgill, the link between the Prime Minister's Office and the Liberal campaign, participated.[74] The discussions usually were concerned with printing dates, paper allocations, and national publicity planning, and only rarely were issues discussed in any other context than how to present them.[75] The final advertising budget, exclusive of French-language advertising, amounted to $143,000.[76]

The party literature was pitched around the theme 'Building a New Social Order for Canada', the slogan that appeared on all of the key Liberal campaign flyers. These flyers, each featuring a Cabinet minister* and a different policy area, stressed the government's past and future: 'Liberalism and Labour—A Record of Achievement'; 'New Housing Plan'; 'Liberal Family Allowances'.[77] The thrust, while not de-emphasizing Mackenzie King, deliberately aimed to increase confidence in the party program, a response to a Canadian Institute of Public Opinion survey in August 1944 that found voters most influenced by party policy.[78] French-language advertising stressed Mackenzie King substantially more than did the English-language material.[79]

No date had yet been fixed for the election. King had thought in January of May 7, but when he realized that this would clash with the

---

*This may not have been wise. A poll demonstrated in early 1945 that other than Ilsley, Howe, McNaughton, and Macdonald, few Canadians could identify any ministers. Asked to identify those ministers doing a good job, 28 per cent named Ilsley, and 5 per cent cited Howe. No other got more than 3 per cent. *Public Opinion Quarterly*, IX (Spring, 1945), 88.

great money-raising campaign of the Victory Loan, he turned his attention to June as the most likely month for the test. In fact King was shopping for a date and had not made up his mind. He did believe that it was best 'to see the date fixed at a time subsequent rather than prior to the termination of the war in Europe.' The reason was very clear—conscription had to be eliminated as an issue. 'The main purpose of the campaign,' he wrote to the Premier of Nova Scotia, 'would be to have the people pronounce upon the government to conduct the business of Canada during postwar years, not to discuss controversial issues of the past.'[80] This view was certainly shared by Claxton, who wrote to King after a swing through the Maritimes in February that 'The best issue for us is: "Who do you want to finish the war and make the peace?"' The Liberals could win, he said, providing the reinforcement question was defused, providing the Cabinet offered positive leadership, and providing the campaign of publicity was more active.[81]

But the Liberals also had something else going for them—a feeling that John Bracken, the Progressive Conservative Party leader, was neither very effective nor able to control the reactionaries in his party. Bracken had deliberately chosen not to enter the House of Commons since his selection in December 1942, a failure that severely hurt him in the country, and the party's inability to win in Saskatchewan had hurt the Progressive Conservatives seriously.[82] This assessment was widely shared by Liberal campaign planners,[83] and there were even reflections of it in opinion polls taken for the Conservatives. Rodney Adamson, the Conservative M.P. for Toronto York West, was told by his private polls that the majority in his riding was not concerned with the removal of government controls on business but was vitally interested in social legislation of various kinds.[84] A Liberal campaign that reinforced these themes would probably be very effective.

This was Mackenzie King's instinctive feeling, too. On March 2, thinking about the coming San Francisco United Nations Conference, he mused that it 'may give me in the eyes of the people, the greatest opportunity of leadership I have thus far had. It will change the whole trend of the campaign from the conscription issue in a general election to leadership in peace in the post-war world. I cannot but believe that the end of the war in Europe will come in a fashion which will make this possible.'[85] When the 1945 session of Parliament opened on March 19, these ideas had crystallized in his mind, and he explained to the Liberal caucus two days later that 'the campaign would be fought on the peace issue and the social issues. I spoke of Sir Wilfrid's attitude on conscription, and made clear that I thought everyone was entitled to vote as he thought best on that issue. It was not a thing that was permanent.' Conscription in King's view was finished 'and we could go right on with outlook of the future forgetting the differences of the past and uniting to win the election.'[86]

The Quebec situation was still confused, and Power continued with his plans to run as an independent Liberal. He was in fact prophesying the defeat of St Laurent and of General LaFlèche, two ministers who had stayed with King in the conscription crisis. His guess on the election result, he told Angus Macdonald on March 20, was 80 Liberals and 70 Conservatives.[87] Power's election manifesto was also ready. The section headings—'Nous Sommes Des Libéraux' and 'Nous Sommes Canadiens'—conveyed something of the flavour, as did Power's explanation of why independent Liberalism mattered. The Liberal Party had abandoned its role as interpreter and moderator during the conscription crisis. 'Pour ces motifs, et parce que la mésure adoptée n'était alors ni nécessaire, ni opportune, nous nous sommes opposés au gouvernement et au parti officiel, et, advenant pareilles circonstances, nous continuerons à soutenir la contre-partie.'[88]

By April, however, the war seemed certain to be over in a matter of weeks and the Quebec rebellion in the Liberal Party had begun to run out of gas. Power's friends split on the course to be pursued, and Power himself said that if his law firm prospered he would leave politics. At a meeting with the Prime Minister on April 11 he indicated he would consider a seat in the Senate if it was offered to him, gratuitously adding that although a tide was running towards Mackenzie King 'he could not even come anywhere near winning'.[89] A few days later, after conversations with Cardin, Power told Mackenzie King that Cardin had the support of Premier Duplessis and would sweep Quebec.[90] The former Works Minister announced the formation of Le Front National on April 27, an attempt to gather all independents under his banner. Power, at least, would not link up with Cardin.

Another complicating factor in this already fluid situation was the near coincidence of the Ontario provincial election with the national contest. George Drew's Progressive Conservative minority administration had demonstrated its capacity to survive for a year and a half, but on March 22 the Opposition had finally toppled it. Drew announced his election on April 12, his chosen date being June 11. At a Cabinet meeting on the 12th, C. D. Howe suggested that the federal election should be held the same day as Drew's, a move that would eliminate any harmful effects to the Liberals if, as many feared, Drew won a great sweep. The strategy session was interrupted when the Cabinet received word of President Roosevelt's death, but that day King definitely decided to accept Howe's suggestion[91] and told Parliament the next day. On April 15, not to be outmanoeuvred, Drew advanced his election date one week to June 4, an action that annoyed King and one that he thought would make it impossible for the soldiers overseas to vote in the provincial election.[92] Of course, having the two elections so close together was not without its opportunities. *Saturday Night* commented that 'with a dual campaign, with national and provincial issues inextricably inter-mixed, inevitably Mr. Drew will be forced into the Dominion campaign and anything that he will say, and particularly anything that will be said against him, will have national prominence. And it will undoubtedly be manoeuvered by the Liberals that there will be much to be so prominent.'[93]

The Ontario stage was complicated by the return of Mitch Hepburn. On December 6, 1944 the Liberal caucus at Queen's Park had unanimously selected the former Premier as party leader once again. Harry Nixon, the choice of the Liberal convention in 1943, moved Hepburn's selection himself.[94] For Mackenzie King the return of his old antagonist was worrisome, even though Hepburn seemed only a shadow of his former self. Still, on March 2 King was struck by a newspaper article that reported that the Ontario Liberal leader had now repented of all his attacks on the Prime Minister in the past. 'I had waited long for this confession,' Mackenzie King said in his diary, 'but he has found he has had to make it in the hope of getting back into a strong position in the party. I have never asked for anything from him.'[95] Nor could he bring himself to do so. But when Hepburn called him on April 14, the day after the election date was announced, King told the Ontario Liberal that he had instructed his party members to co-operate: 'We would all work together. . . . it would certainly be helpful to have his forces and my own working together against a common enemy.'[96] Unfortunately, Hepburn's tattered crew was not much of a gain.

Ontario would be the key in the election, Mackenzie King knew, and he worried about the inadequacies of Cabinet representation from that province. His entire Cabinet worried him in fact, and through the early months of 1945 he had considered on various occasions what should be done. Crerar was going to resign and wanted the Senate; Michaud hoped for the bench; Macdonald, unfriendly to the Prime Minister and unhappy in Ottawa, wanted to return to Nova Scotia politics; McLarty from Windsor, Ontario had to be replaced; General LaFlèche would be happy with a diplomatic appointment; and W. P. Mulock, very ill in Toronto, wanted to retire from politics. With six ministers moving out of the government, King had ample scope to re-build with younger men.

This he did. The Ontario slots he filled with young and able men, defying hallowed convention as he did so. His new ministers were J. J. McCann from Renfrew South, an Irish-Catholic medical doctor who became Minister of National War Services; Lionel Chevrier, the Member for Stormont, a French-Canadian Catholic who became Minister of Transport; and Paul Martin from Windsor, another Ontario Franco-phone but one who had been educated at English-language institutions and who lived in English-speaking Ontario. All three new ministers were Catholics and this worried King but he decided he had no option.[97] In fact, as the Liberal Party traditionally drew its support largely from Catholic voters, this probably hurt the government not at all. The New Brunswick vacancy left by Michaud's departure, King filled from outside the House of Commons, turning to David MacLaren of Saint John, a man who was strongly supported by Michaud. MacLaren was named Minister of National Revenue. Crerar's place in the government was filled by J. A. Glen, the Speaker of the House since the beginning of the 1940 session. Glen, the Member for Marquette, Manitoba, took Crerar's portfolio as Minister of Mines and Resources.

The Quebec situation was difficult for King, with St Laurent hard put to suggest new members. Of one M.P. there was no question what-soever. On April 16 King spoke with D. C. Abbott of Montreal-Westmount and told him that he would be brought into the Cabinet. Along with Claxton this meant two English Protestants from Montreal and while this too was not desirable in terms of balance, King believed it necessary simply because both Abbott and Claxton were so able. Joseph Jean, also from Montreal, was brought into the government as Solicitor-General. Jean had opposed King's conscription policy but he had done so in what the Prime Minister viewed as a non-harmful way and he deserved his reward, especially, as St Laurent said, since it would hold out hope for other less-than-brilliant members of the party caucus that they also could aspire to a place in the Cabinet.[98] For King, how-ever, the important point was that Jean's appointment rewarded those with faith in his leadership. Others like Power and Cardin, he com-plained in his diary, were 'trying to control the whole following in Quebec on lines not of standing up for me but using me when it suits them or throwing me to the wolves when it suits them to do so.' He intended to 'trust the people,' the Prime Minister said, and 'it will be interesting to see if the Province of Quebec does not find before the campaign is over, that it is desirable to fall in line with those who have faith in myself. If they don't, they will be sorry for generations to come.'[99]

In mid-April 1945 few except the Prime Minister could have expected Quebec to fall into line. The independentist campaigns continued, and Liberal observers feared that Cardin would do well. The one advantage in the situation, as Brooke Claxton could not fail to note, was that if the independents ran well on their anti-King, anti-conscription platform, this 'should help us elsewhere'.[100] One difficulty was that there was no Liberal leadership in the province. Louis St Laurent was at the United Nations Conference on International Organization with the Prime Minister, and none of the other Quebec ministers had much of a following. Good leadership would win seats for the party, Claxton urged, for while the Liberals were not strong neither was anyone else.[101] In fact the Liberals, the established party, the old rock around which political loyalties had been constructed, were gradually beginning to gather back the wayward. Fogo noticed this trend on May 5,[102] and Chubby Power, said to be in a state of 'benevolent neutrality',[103] admitted as much to his friend Angus Macdonald on May 9. Chubby now gave the Liberals 40 seats in the province, a gain of at least 15 over a month ago,[104] and the decision by Cardin to withdraw from the leadership of his Front, less than two weeks after launching it, greatly increased King's chances. The end of the war in Europe on May 8, finally ending the conscription crisis once and for all, also helped the Liberals,[105] giving them a full month between V-E Day and the election date to solidify their support. With the campaign about to begin, the Liberals were in better shape than anyone would have dared to forecast in the black days of late November 1944.

IV

Mackenzie King made his first national address of the campaign from Vancouver on May 16. Fresh from the United Nations Conference on International Organization at San Francisco, King was in good spirits. For a man who had led the country through six wearying years of war, for a man of over 70 years of age, he was in excellent health. Pickersgill, his aide and travelling companion at this time, could still recall 25 years later the energy with which King tackled the business of preparing his first broadcast.[106]

King's radio address began by telling the electorate that the war situation had prevented him from visiting all parts of Canada as much as he would have wished. 'I have felt it my duty to be on the bridge of the ship of State as much as possible when rough weather threatened, and, particularly, while we were in the midst of the storm.' More felicitously, King said that 'in appealing to you for a renewed expression of your confidence, I am able to do so in terms, not of promise, but of performance.' The people now would have to decide either to allow 'the affairs of our country in its national and international relations' to be carried on by 'the tried and trusted administration which you know' or turned over 'to unknown and untried hands.'

> It is for you to decide whether you wish this change from the known to the unknown to take place before the present world war is at its end. It is for you to decide whether you wish a change to be made before the conferences which are to settle the terms of peace are held. It is yours to decide whether you wish another government to take over before there is brought into being the mighty instrument which is now being forged at San Francisco for the maintenance of world security and peace.

The theme was clear: Mackenzie King was the only man with sufficient experience to lead the nation in this troubled time. And in making his remarks around this theme, King was closely following a line suggested a few days earlier by Pickersgill. There should be no hesitation, the aide had suggested, 'in playing up your personal position. This is one of the biggest issues in the campaign, and one of the easiest to turn to the advantage of the Liberal cause. It is so easy to say that, after holding for so long the highest position in the gift of the Canadian people, after guiding the country through the principal phase of the greatest war in history. . . . you can have no unfulfilled ambition but one: to place your experience at the service of the people. . . .' This would be very effective, Pickersgill urged, especially if it were coupled 'with just a hint . . . of a yearning for leisure.'[107]

King must have believed this for, after warning the electorate not to determine their vote on the basis of one issue alone, an oblique reference to the reinforcements issue, he then suggested that the voters raise questions to the parties seeking their vote:

First of all you might ask: Who is its leader? What experience has he had in national and international affairs?* To what extent has he participated in the proceedings of the Canadian Parliament? You might also ask: Who would be the Ministers in a Cabinet to be formed by each of the parties seeking office?†

The Prime Minister concluded this skilfully drafted speech, with its sharpened barbs carefully concealed by platitudes, by stressing his life-long goals.

My life's interests, I need not tell you, have been with the cause of peace and with the promotion of human welfare and social reform. It is because I see close at hand, unparallelled opportunities to further these great ends that I should like to serve in another Parliament.[108]

John Bracken's speeches, by contrast, were hard and biting. The Tories had a good social-welfare platform, shaped and moulded over a three-year period, but Bracken and his advisers, bemused by the Grey North result, still believed that there was a sense of outrage in English Canada over conscription, and it was to this theme that Bracken returned again and again. First he pledged that conscripts would finish the war with Japan, and then he hit squarely at King's 'cowardly man-power policy; a policy by which he defied the wishes of the majority of this nation, in order to try to keep the political support of a minority which had kept him in power so long, and whose votes he again wants.'[109] At Calgary a week later he asked if Canadians 'Are to con-

*This was a good tack, or at least the polling data suggested so. A poll on Feb. 23, 1944, admittedly a year earlier, showed that 42 per cent believed King the best man to represent Canada at the peace table, while 24 per cent thought Bracken the best, and only 6 per cent Coldwell. *Public Opinion Quarterly*, VIII (Spring, 1944), 143.

†This line, too, was probably effective, for when the Trades and Labour Congress endorsed the Liberals on May 19, 1945, their statement of support concluded: 'Certain obligations were accepted by Government as to what will be the procedure when the time arrives to go forward to . . . peacetime economy. . . . [It] must be given the opportunity to redeem them. . . . [It] must be given the opportunity of keeping faith with the people. . . . There is a danger that a new group, put into power at this time, would institute policies that might have no relation whatever to the pledges that an overwhelming number of people . . . have put their faith in.' (Gad Horowitz, *Canadian Labour in Politics* (Toronto, 1968), p. 105.) For an analysis of the effects of labour's divisions on the electoral results in one city, see Ian MacPherson, 'The 1945 Collapse of the C.C.F. in Windsor'. *Ontario History*, LXI (December, 1969), 197ff.

tinue a system whereby one part of Canada sends forty-six percent of its available manpower and another sends twenty-two percent. Are we to have fastened on this country for all time to come a system that exempts a third of the population from its fair share of Canada's burden of defence?'[110] In Vancouver Bracken called the government's manpower policy 'one of irresolute and feeble compromise,' all based on its 'frantic desire to satisfy Quebec'.[111] The Tories were making no efforts to woo French-Canadian voters, that was sure. Whether or not English-speaking voters were any longer interested in reinforcements was moot.

The Liberals didn't think so. Brooke Claxton's message to his Montreal electors in St Lawrence-St George stressed six points: 'Finish the Job; Re-establish Veterans; Jobs and Opportunities; Social Security; World Trade; The Rest of the World.'[112] That was looking ahead. Mackenzie King pressed this view directly in a speech in London on May 30.

Remember, from now on, it is with the future, not with the past that you should be concerned. . . . All [the Progressive Conservative] criticisms about the details of policies in the past, all their harpings on alleged mistakes or shortcomings of the present government in the conduct of the war, all they have to say about what they call the manpower muddle, is just so much political dust thrown in your eyes to conceal their own very obvious political limitations.[113]

But for all this, most of the Prime Minister's speeches were concerned with Liberal policy rather than with responses to the Opposition. In Edmonton on May 18 his message was international co-operation, a pitch intended to solidify support for the United Nations and to attack Social Credit's policies in this area. At Prince Albert, his own constituency,* King talked of social legislation.

I am happy to say that so far as the present administration is concerned, we have not waited until the war is over to plan what we were

*There had been serious thought given to where King should run, Prince Albert being buried in the heart of CCF Saskatchewan. Some believed the seat could only be won if King spent a week in Prince Albert, clearly an impossibility; others feared that if King left, this would hurt the cause elsewhere. The upshot was King's decision to stay. Queen's University, T. A. Crerar Papers, Memo of Caucus Proceedings, 6 [?] Apr. 1945; King Diary, 5 Apr. 1945; King Papers, Vol. 96, King to C.L. Burton, 21 Apr. 1945.

406 | CANADA'S WAR

going to do to meet the situation that is already before us. We have
already placed on the statutes of Canada, law after law to deal with
the situations that will have to be met through the coming years. We
do not come before you making promises. . . . We come now with a
series of measures which . . . will help to make our country more
prosperous than it has ever been before.[114]

The key point in this social welfare package, of course, was family allowances, and it is fair to say that the great measure was the keystone of the
Liberal campaign. The Speech from the Throne closing the fifth session
of Parliament had pointed up the baby bonus and announced that
registration for it would begin on February 1, with payment of the first
cheques beginning in July 1945.[115] The registration kept the measure
before the public and, although there were reports of people worrying
that signing up for family allowances might lead to investigations of
their income-tax status, there were no real difficulties.[116] By May 30,
1945, in fact, fully 95 per cent of those interviewed by the Canadian
Institute of Public Opinion had heard of the scheme, most in favourable
contexts.[117] Delighted with the response, the National Liberal Federation sent out reams of material stressing the benefits the baby bonus
would bring to each constituency. Every month, a letter sent to Ontario
candidates on March 29, 1945 said, family allowances would pour
$132,981 into Cochrane, Ontario, $153,891 into Welland, Ontario, and
similar sums across the province, a total of more than $6 million in
all.[118] The party was careful not to emphasize the money alone. 'Liberal
Family Allowances are simple justice to children . . . ,' one bulletin to
candidates noted towards the end of May, 'one of the Four Freedoms for
which we have been fighting.'[119]

The effect of this on the Tories was pronounced, and the party was
forced to spend much time explaining that Bracken's references to
'political bribes' did not mean that he was against the principle of the
measure, not at all. In fact, Conservatives should be careful about this
issue, one party official warned, lest it foster the 'Tory reactionary cry'.[120]
It was too late; the image had been reinforced and established for a year
and more.

In Winnipeg Mackenzie King's message was full employment and
national unity, including some sharp digs at the Conservatives' inability
to field candidates in Quebec. Until nomination day, King told his
audience, the Tories had only three or four candidates when suddenly

'27 candidates were produced, like rabbits out of a hat.'*[121] In London the theme was government planning, and in Montreal on June 2 the Prime Minister talked of national unity and his party's role in Quebec.

It is just thirty-six years ago today that I was invited by Sir Wilfrid Laurier to become a member of his Cabinet. . . . I have had, in the office of Prime Minister, to go through most of the experiences and many of the trials which Sir Wilfrid encountered in the years he was in office. I am proud indeed to say that . . . I never failed him once. . . .

I saw Sir Wilfrid defeated by an unholy alliance between the Nationalists of this province and the Tories of the other provinces of Canada. I saw all that grew out of that ignoble and treacherous plot. I need not give you the record. It will be for all time a blot of shame on the pages of our country's history.

But the question I wish to put to you . . . is whether you, the people of the province of Quebec, intend to allow the tactics of 1911 to be repeated successfully in 1945, and to have Mackenzie King in 1945 suffer the fate of Sir Wilfrid Laurier in 1911?[122]

King's final address on June 8 was his most political speech of the campaign, a straight, all-out attack on John Bracken, his relative newness as a Tory, his refusal to seek a seat in Parliament, his subservience to 'special interests'. Worse, as King said (in a paragraph for which his party's own advertising agency took credit):[123]

It is now perfectly clear that there has been a highly financed campaign of modern publicity, with special write-ups in the press, endless photography in the magazines; with radio, films, posters and what not, to sell John Bracken, the new leader of the Progressive-Conservative party, by the same methods that are used in selling a new breakfast food, or a new brand of soap. For two and a half years, Mr. Bracken has appeared everywhere, except in Parliament.[124]

It was a good hit, and so was King's closing appeal to the voters.

The choice on Monday next is not between a Liberal majority and a

*In the end the Conservatives ran 31 candidates under their party label in Quebec, and they could count on the support of perhaps 10 additional independents. See J. L. Granatstein, *The Politics of Survival* (Toronto, 1967), chapter VIII for details.

majority for some other party. No party but the Liberal party has the remotest chance of securing a majority in the next House of Commons.* The choice, therefore, is between a Liberal majority, and no majority for any party. I appeal, therefore, to men and women of all parties . . . to take the only course which will ensure a continuance of strong and stable government in Canada in these very critical years.[125]

King delivered his appeal for a Liberal majority in the teeth of George Drew's massive election victory in Ontario. This was clearly a boost for the Conservatives and a blow to the CCF who had been confident of great results in the province. For the Liberals, the results were difficult to interpret. The provincial party had been savaged by Drew in 1943 and few had expected it to come back; but a majority government had resulted in Ontario and this might be a good Liberal omen for the federal results. The check to the CCF might also help Liberal candidates elsewhere.[126]

The Prime Minister responded to the Ontario result with the hope that 'the cry Drew in the Province and Mackenzie King in the Federal field, may still hold good. I believe it will. Not as largely as if both votes had taken place simultaneously. On the other hand, the result in Ontario should, I think, ensure us the elections in the Federal field. It has demonstrated that the C.C.F. have lost their power. . . .' The effect, King estimated, 'will be that in Vancouver the Tories will be strengthened. In Alberta, the Social Credit will lose some seats and we will gain some. In Saskatchewan the C.C.F. will lose some seats and we will gain some. . . . In Ontario. . . . We will lose a dozen seats. The Tories winning in Ontario should help us; give us pretty nearly solid Quebec. I cannot see that a Tory victory in Ontario will help the Tories in the Maritimes. We shall hold our own there. . . .' All in all, King estimated that he would get a majority: 'I shall indeed be greatly surprised if a week from tonight, the Liberals have not carried in the

*According to M. J. Coldwell's mss memoirs, the CCF leader was approached by Grant Dexter, acting as King's emissary, in Spring 1945. The message was that King felt none would get a majority, that he hoped Coldwell would support him and join a coalition under him. Coldwell replied that coalition was impossible, and Dexter returned a few days later with a further offer—that King would recommend Coldwell as his successor when he retired. The CCF leader remained unmoved. (PAC, M. J. Coldwell Papers, Vol. 42, Memoirs No. 27, pp. 4ff.) There is no evidence of this in either the Dexter or King Papers.

Dominion an over-all majority of at least twenty and possibly forty seats.'*27

King's surprise would be pronounced. On election day, June 11, the Liberals were reduced to the barest majority, winning—depending on estimates of the loyalties of independents—from 125 to 127 seats in a House of Commons of 245 seats. The Conservatives won only 67 seats, however, while the CCF garnered 28. In terms of the popular vote, the Liberals took 41.3 per cent, the Conservatives 28.5, and the CCF 14.7. The Bloc Populaire Canadien won only a tiny 3.5 per cent of the popular vote and elected just two Members. Quebec had been the key; there the King party won 53 seats and 50.8 per cent of the popular vote while the Conservatives, collecting a pathetic 8.4 per cent of the vote, could elect but two Members. In Ontario, Liberals won 34 seats, a drop of 23 from the 1940 election, while Bracken got 48 and the CCF, incredibly, failed to elect any Members despite getting more than a quarter of a million votes. In the West the Liberals held on to 19 seats, a drop of 25, while in the Maritimes they kept 19, the same number they had received in 1940.[128]

The election-night casualties included General McNaughton in Qu'Appelle, Saskatchewan and D. L. MacLaren in Saint John, the only two ministers to go down to defeat. But there were some narrow squeaks. Jimmy Gardiner hung on as one of only two Liberals in what used to be a solid Saskatchewan, winning his seat by a handful of votes. Douglas Abbott in Montreal-Westmount had a similar narrow victory, and the Prime Minister himself alternated between joy and despair on election night. The early returns had him trailing, King recorded, but 'when I really felt I was defeated, I felt a little outbreak of perspiration for the moment, but that . . . soon passed away. It was like a tiny shock.'[129] But later that evening King learned that the Canadian Press had declared him elected. It was a personal victory for King and a national victory for the party. To win re-election after six years of war, after conscription crises, after controls, rationing, and hardships was a great achievement. The victory belonged to King too, for it was the Prime Minister who had pressed on in the face of the many difficulties, the Prime Minister who had pushed through the great social-reform program that more than anything else secured the Liberals their

*Election eve polls suggested the Liberals would get 39 per cent of the vote, the Conservatives 29 per cent, the CCF 17 per cent, and the Bloc Populaire Canadien 5 per cent. *Public Opinion Quarterly*, IX (Summer, 1945), 234.

majority. After it all, King's primary response was one of relief. He went to Kingsmere the day after the election.

> I sat quietly for a short time in the sunroom, in my heart thanking and praising God for his goodness. The relief of mind that I experience is indescribable. It brings with it peace of heart as well. . . . almost as if I had had a bath after a dusty and dirty journey, with the storm of lies, misrepresentations, insinuations and what in which I have had to pass during the past few weeks—I might even say over most of the years of war. One could go back and say almost over one's public life. I felt a real vindication in the verdict of the people and the sense of triumph therefrom.[130]

Mackenzie King had fought his last general election.

V

For the Tories the defeat was a bitter one. Sold like soap, John Bracken had failed to attract consumers outside of Ontario, and when he met Mackenzie King by chance on election night the meeting was strained. 'He put out his hand to shake hands and extended congratulations,' King recorded. '. . . He then said to me "we shall be seeing more of each other soon". . . . We have got him now where we want him. He is like a fly having buzzed around outside and caught with the glitter at the end into the spider's web.'[131] King was right. Bracken was in Parliament at last, exactly where the Prime Minister wanted him. He would not last long enough to fight another election.

Most striking in the Liberal victory was the result in Quebec. The party's 53 seats was a huge increase over what even the most optimistic had predicted earlier. Partly this was due to the collapse of the Cardin Front National a month before the election;[132] partly it was a product of Chubby Power's election-eve decision to adhere very closely to the official party line;[133] partly it was a last-minute panic by Liberal independents who needed the support the organization could offer.[134] But there were other reasons too, and they were summed up in a letter sent by the American Consul in Montreal to his Ambassador. The tone is patronizing, but the reasoning is probably sound.

1. Jean Baptiste is a solid fellow. He does not cut off his nose to spite his face. . . .

2. Jean Baptiste's political philosophy is progressing from reaction-ism through conservatism to liberalism. He is not headed for radicalism.

3. The political leaders of the Province . . . judged to a nicety just how much support was necessary in order to allow Mr. KING to barely win.

4. Quebec will be in a position to do so but may refrain from blatantly exerting very much pressure on the new government in Ottawa. The pressure boys, Bloc Populaire and Independent, were not elected.

5. Quebec is afraid of Ontario. . . .

6. The Bloc Populaire is dead. It died during the last provincial election but it was disinterred for a marriage with Camillien HOUDE. . . .*

7. Half of the Quebec voters supported the two established political parties. The other half, divided between the parties or loyalties, does not appear to present a serious threat to the existing political organization of the province or of the Dominion. . . .

Quebec and Mr. King have saved each other. There is little cele-brating over the rescue since Quebec's part was not altogether voluntary.[135]

Quebec and Mr King had saved each other. That summed up the result of the election very neatly.[136]

Elated by his victory though disappointed at its size, Mackenzie King learned on June 14 that he had in fact lost his Prince Albert riding, thanks to the delayed military-vote results. To the Prime Minister it seemed 'cruel it should be my fate, at the end of the war, in which I have never failed the men overseas once, that I should be beaten by their vote.'[137] But even here there was victory in defeat for the Liberal Party as a whole won a plurality in the military vote, with the CCF a close second and the Conservatives far behind. Because of some ominous hints of rampant socialism among the troops overseas, few had expected any such result, particularly the Tories who had made substantial efforts at cultivating the military. The striking statistic in the soldier

*Houde, the Mayor of Montreal who had been interned for his comments about the government's national registration in August 1940, had been released in 1944. He was made deputy leader of the Bloc Populaire by Maxime Raymond, its leader. He lost his own race, but Raymond and one other BPC candidate were elected.

vote was not the 342,907 men and women who voted,* but the approximately 400,00 who did not.[138] General H. D. G. Crerar, the commander
of the First Canadian Army in North West Europe, had told a friend
in March that 'There is a general feeling of resentment . . . and no
political party, or person or political life in Canada, stands high at
present in the eyes of the Canadian Army Overseas.'[139] That effect
presumably had led many soldiers and airmen to pass up the opportunity to vote for or against the government or the Opposition. The
Prime Minister, of course, had no difficulty in finding a seat for himself.
His choice was Glengarry, a safe Eastern Ontario seat that eventually did
its duty.

What had won the election for the Liberals? Certainly it was not the
party's policy on conscription. From Vancouver, Ian Mackenzie told
the Prime Minister that conscriptionist feeling was still strong in British
Columbia, and he attributed the Liberal losses there to this. The
Minister of Trade and Commerce, J. A. MacKinnon, said the same
about Alberta.[140] But this was resentment lingering over the crisis of
November 1944, not a desire for conscription to fight the Pacific war.
Douglas Abbott recalled that 'even in Westmount no one wanted conscription for the Pacific,'[141] a typical reaction. No, what had won for
the government was a combination of factors. A. Davidson Dunton, the
General Manager of the Wartime Information Board, put together
the results of all the WIB's surveys and opinion polls to tell the Cabinet

*The results of the military vote arranged by place of voting overseas and in Canada
were as follows:

	Lib.	CCF	PC
United Kingdom	20,363	24,108	17,367
North West Europe	27,904	37,257	24,067
All other theatres	2,070	1,705	1,075
Nfld	3,139	2,354	1,657
Maritimes	18,841	11,875	12,030
Quebec	8,760	1,780	2,727
Ontario	22,957	14,154	17,905
Prairies	7,500	9,535	5,478
B.C.	6,536	6,911	5,534
	118,070	109,679	87,840

(PAC, Brooke Claxton Papers, Vol. 149, Elections folder.) A Conservative opinion
survey before the election had revealed strong CCF sympathy among men overseas,
particularly in the RCAF. At one time the Conservatives feared that the CCF could
get up to 90 per cent of the service vote, but the Conservatives' heavy campaigning
among the troops and their gifts of cigarettes possibly blunted the CCF support.
PAC, John Bracken Papers, Vol. 17, Memo on Overseas Vote, 8 June 1945.

in a confidential memorandum on June 18 that 'The Liberal success is attributed chiefly to the desire for stable government, to the wide appeal of its social legislation and to the "solid accomplishments" of the administration. In the latter connection several observers mentioned the anti-inflation program as a decisive factor.'[142] That assessment probably summed it up, although other observers honed in on specific issues. Tories blamed their defeat on family allowances;[143] CCF periodicals noted that the Liberals had capitalized on the Toryism of their opponents;[144] while others, including CCF leader M.J. Coldwell, blamed both old parties for a 'quite unscrupulous' anti-socialist campaign that hurt his party severely.[145] Mackenzie King, as usual, eventually began to complain that his party's organization had collapsed and thus prevented a greater victory, a more unjustifiable gripe than usual since many Liberals believed the Prime Minister to be the greatest cross they had to bear.[146] The reasons in sum are impossible to discover for this election as for all others. What is certain is that the Liberals had remained a national party with support in all regions of the country and that no other party had achieved that status. And if elections are lost, not won, the Conservatives had misjudged the national mood, not the Liberals. The last word belongs to the Prime Minister. In a letter he wrote to Senator Wishart Robertson of the National Liberal Federation, he said that 'When account is taken of the inevitable misunderstandings and grievances which develop in the course of a long war, it is, I believe, little short of miraculous for a wartime government to survive an appeal to the people at the close of the struggle. Viewed in that light, the success of the Liberal party at the polls on June 11th was a very great triumph indeed.'[147] Miracles, yes, but miracles that the Liberal Party and Mackenzie King had worked very hard to make real.

---

1 Public Archives of Canada [PAC], W. L. Mackenzie King Papers, Diary, 16 Jan. 1945.

2 Queen's University, C. G. Power Papers, Power to King, 21 July 1943 and atts; copy in King Papers, ff. 91357ff.

3 King Diary, 22 July 1943.

4 King Papers, Power to King, 3 Jan. 1944, ff. 110591ff. Cf. *ibid.*, Claxton to King, 28 Dec. 1943, ff. C209032ff.

5 King Diary 2 Feb. 1944; Public Archives of Nova Scotia, A. L. Macdonald Papers, Diary, 2 Feb. 1944.

6 *Ibid.*, 29 Feb. 1944; King Diary, 29 Feb. 1944.

7 See J. L. Granatstein, 'Financing the Liberal Party, 1935-45', in M. S. Cross and R. Bothwell, *Policy by Other Means* (Toronto, 1972), pp. 193-4; Queen's University, Norman Lambert Papers, Diary, 8-9 Mar. 1944, 26, 28 Apr. 1944; PAC, National Liberal Federation Papers, Vol. 596, A. G. McLean to J. G. Fogo, 3 July 1944.

8 Lambert Diary, 3-7 May 1944, 17 Jan. 1945; NLF Papers, Vol. 596, Robertson to Fogo, 24 Jan. 1945; King Papers, Claxton to King, 28 June 1944, ff. C208540ff.

9 'Trends of Popular Opinion According to the Gallup Poll', in NLF Papers, Vol. 809; King Papers, Claxton to King, 28 June 1944, ff. C208540ff.

10 'Summary of Report on Public Opinion . . . 21 June 1944' in NLF Papers, Vol. 603.

11 'Special Analysis of Public Opinion . . . May-June, 1944', in *ibid.*

12 'Slogan Preference . . .' in *ibid.*

13 Macdonald Diary, 22 June 1944.

14 Power Papers, Power to P. Power, 27 June 1944.

15 E.g., King Papers, King to McLarty, 25 Aug. 1944, f. 107450.

16 King Diary, 25 Aug. 1944.

17 NLF Papers, Vol. 597, McLean to King, 2 Sept. 1944; copy in King Papers, ff. C208584ff.

18 King Diary, 5 Sept. 1943.

19 NLF Papers, Vol. 802, Kidd to McLean, 1 Sept. 1944; H. A. Kidd interview, August 1971; Power Papers, Fogo to J. W. Pickersgill, 15 Sept. 1944.

20 King Papers, Vol. 84, Mulock to King, 21 Sept. 1944.

21 Kidd interview.

22 King Papers, Bertrand to King, 31 Aug. 1944, ff. 98844-5.

23 Power Papers, Diary Memorandum, 2 Sept.-13 Oct. 1944; J. W. Pickersgill and D. F. Forster, *The Mackenzie King Record*, Vol. II: *1944-45* (Toronto, 1968), esp. p. 101.

24 Power Papers, Power to King, 1 Sept. 1944.

25 Queen's University, Grant Dexter Papers, Memo, 6 Oct. 1944; cf. King Papers, Valentine to Power, 13 Oct. 1944, ff. 110589ff.

26 Saskatchewan Provincial Archives, J. G. Gardiner Papers, W. W. Dawson to Gardiner, 30 Nov. 1944. Cf. Dawson to Gardiner, 7 Nov. 1944. For a different look at the political confusion in the West, see Public Archives of Manitoba, Stuart Garson Papers, Garson to R. M. MacIver, 29 Dec. 1944.

27 E.g., NLF Papers, Vol. 596, C. J. Bennett to McLean, 9 Jan. 1945; King Papers, Vol. 112, W. M. Southam to King, 2 Jan. 1945.

28 *Ibid.*, Vol. 99, King to W. R. Givens, 15 Jan. 1945.

29 King Diary, 1, 8 Dec. 1944. Grey North was suggested by Pickersgill.

30 King Papers, Vol. 77, King to G. Fleming, 14 Dec. 1944.

31 PAC, John Bracken Papers, Vol. 55, Bruce to Bracken, 19 Dec. 1944.

32 Owen Sound *Daily Sun-Times*, 11 Dec. 1944, cited in Paul Bennett, 'The Grey North By-Election of February 5, 1945', 8, an excellent York University undergraduate paper, 1971.

33 PAC, M. J. Coldwell Papers, Vol. 12, Coldwell to C. Fines, 3 Nov. 1944; *ibid.*, Vol. 11, Coldwell to T. C. Douglas, 9 Jan. 1945; Bennett, 12-13.

34 *Ibid.*

35 *Ibid.*, 10.

36 PAC, A. G. L. McNaughton Papers, Arthur Roebuck to McNaughton, 2 Jan. 1945; King Diary, 24-5 Jan. 1945.

37 McNaughton Papers, McNaughton to Roebuck, 24 Dec. 1944.

38 Bennett, 20; King Diary, 5 Jan. 1945; Macdonald Diary, 9 Feb. 1945. The biography, *Shields of Canada* (Grand Rapids, 1967) by L. K. Tarr, says nothing of this episode.

39 Pickersgill, II, p. 281.

40 Macdonald Papers, King to Macdonald, 29 Dec. 1944; King Diary, 3 Jan. 1945.

41 Lambert Diary, 28 Feb. 1945.

42 Toronto *Globe and Mail*, 13 Jan. 1945; King Diary, 8-9 Jan. 1945.

43 *Ibid.*, 10 Jan. 1945.

44 Progressive Conservative Party Records (Ottawa), file O-G-4a, R. Brown to H. R. Milner, 12 Jan. 1945; Toronto *Globe and Mail*, 13 Jan. 1945; McNaughton Papers, clippings from *Daily Sun-Times*, 26 Jan. 1945.

45 Bennett, 30; King Diary, 17-18 Jan. 1945; Public Record Office [PRO], Dominions Office Records, DO 35/1118, High Commissioner to Secretary of State for Dominion Affairs [SSDA], 15 Feb. 1945; *ibid.* Review of Dominions Press, 12 Apr. 1945, Series E, No. 220, the best press survey of the by-election.

46 Toronto *Globe and Mail*, 24 Jan. 1945; King Diary, 18 Jan. 1945.

47 *Ibid.*, 21, 26 Jan. 1945; Pickersgill, II, pp. 286-7; King Papers, draft dissolution announcement, 29 Jan. 1945, ff. C160965ff.

48 Bennett, 35-6.

49 Toronto *Globe and Mail*, 1 Feb. 1945. Part of this speech was prepared by George Drew and C. P. McTague. See Bracken Papers, draft on Vol. 34; *ibid.*, Vol. 17, 'Observations North Grey', 29 Jan. 1945.

50 *Ibid.*, Vol. 17, speech, 1 Feb. 1945.

51 Directorate of History, National Defence Headquarters, file 314.009(D15), Col. G. V. Gurney to Secretary, Department of National Defence, 7 Feb. 1945, quoting Sen. B. K. Wheeler; cf. Erick Estorick, preface to M. J. Coldwell, *Left Turn, Canada* (New York, 1945), pp. ix-x.

52 McNaughton Papers, Vol. 267, Note and draft letters to Bracken, 9 Feb. 1945.

53 Bracken Papers, Vol. 62, Milner to Bracken, 5 Mar. 1945; NLF Papers, Vol. 596, McLean to Fogo, 12 Mar. 1945; John Bracken interview, 1 June 1963; R. K. Finlayson interview, 1 June 1963.

54 The poll showed Case—39 per cent; McNaughton—38 per cent and Godfrey—17.8 per cent. Copy in Macdonald Diary, 9 Feb. 1945.

55 King Papers, Vol. 105, Mulock to King, 26 Jan. 1945; King Diary, 3 Feb. 1945; DO 35/1118, Macdonald to Cranborne, 31 Jan. 1945.

56 Toronto *Globe and Mail*, 5 Feb. 1945.

57 Macdonald Papers, file 11-88, W. A. Fraser to Macdonald, 19 Feb. 1945.

58 See Toronto *Globe and Mail*, 6-7 Feb. 1945; Ottawa *Journal*, 7 Feb. 1945; Bracken Papers, Vol. 35, Bruce to Bracken, 6 Feb. 1945; Vol. 7, F. J. Pickering to Bracken, 6 Feb. 1945; Vol. 35, speech by J. Diefenbaker, 27 Feb. 1945.

59 See the extraordinary conversation with McNaughton in King Diary, 7 Feb. 1945; McNaughton Papers, Grey North file, McNaughton to F. P. Brass, 12 Feb. 1945 and additional letters in *ibid*. Cf. Bracken Papers, Vol. 17, Case to Bracken, 10 Feb. 1945; DO 35/1118, High Commissioner to SSDA, 15 Feb. 1945.

60 King Diary, 5, 7 Feb. 1945; King Papers, Vol. 112, King to J. R. Stirrett, 20 Feb. 1945; *ibid*., Memo, 'North Grey By-Election', 6 Feb. 1945, ff. 160976ff.

61 *Ibid*., Vol. 113, King to Telford, 12 Feb. 1945; Pickersgill, II, p. 302.

62 Power Papers, Power to King, 17 Jan. 1945.

63 Macdonald Diary, 10 Dec. 1945.

64 Power Papers, Notes of an Interview with Rt Hon. W. L. M. King, Jan. 1945; King Diary, 29 Jan. 1945.

65 Power Papers, undated diary memo, Jan.-Feb. 1945.

66 *Ibid*., Memo re Political Situation Quebec District 21 [?] Feb. 1945.

67 *Ibid*., unheaded diary note.

68 King Diary, 20 Feb. 1945.

69 Power Papers, unheaded diary note. Cf. King Diary, 6 Mar. 1945.

70 Power Papers, diary notes, 22, 24 Feb. 1945.

71 Gardiner Papers, Fogo to Gardiner, 6 Feb. 1945; King Papers, Fogo to Turnbull, 21 Feb. 1945, ff. 123655-7.

72 NLF Papers, Vol. 596, McLean to Fogo, 1 Feb. 1945.

73 *Ibid*., Fogo to McLean, 7 Feb. 1945. See also Michael Scott, 'The 1945 Federal Election: The Liberal Party's Use of Advertisement', unpublished York University undergraduate paper, 1971, *passim*.

74 King Papers, King to Pickersgill, 26 Dec. 1944, f. C186159.

75 NLF Papers, Vol. 613, Publicity Committee minutes, 16 Feb.-12 May 1945.

76 *Ibid*., Vol. 602, 'Estimate for Advertising', 24 Apr. 1945.

77 Copies in *ibid*., Vol. 604.

78 Kidd interview; *Public Opinion Quarterly*, VIII (Fall, 1944), 445.

79 Scott, *passim*.

80 King Papers, Vol. 114, King to Wood, 24 Feb. 1945; *ibid*., Vol. 104, King to A. S. MacMillan, 12 Feb. 1945.

81 *Ibid*., Vol. 97, Memo, 27 Feb. 1945.

82 See J. L. Granatstein, *The Politics of Survival* (Toronto, 1967) chapters VII-VIII.

83 PAC, A. K. Cameron Papers, Vol. 35, T. A. Crerar to Cameron, 27 Feb. 1945; NLF Papers, Vol. 596, Fogo to McLean, 7 Mar. 1945.

84 A. R. Adamson Papers (Port Credit, Ont.), 'Study of Public Opinion . . . York West', Feb. 1945.

85 King Diary, 2 Mar. 1945.

86 Pickersgill, II, p. 337.

87 Macdonald Diary, 20 Mar. 1945.

88 Copy in PAC, L.-P. Picard Papers, Power to Picard, 14 Mar. 1945 and atts. Cf. Power Papers, Interview transcript, Reel F, side 1.

89 *Ibid.*, Diary Notes, 11 Apr. 1945; King Diary, 11 Apr. 1945.

90 Power Papers, diary notes, 9-15 Apr. 1945; *ibid.*, interview transcript; Lionel Bertrand, *Mémoires* (Montréal, 1972), p. 137.

91 King Diary, 12 Apr. 1945.

92 *Ibid.*, 16 Apr. 1945.

93 *Saturday Night*, 21 Apr. 1945, 3.

94 Neil McKenty, *Mitch Hepburn* (Toronto, 1967), p. 270.

95 King Diary, 2 Mar. 1945.

96 *Ibid.*, 14 Apr. 1945.

97 *Ibid.*, 17-18 Apr. 1945. King told Martin how glad he was to have another Harvard man in the Cabinet. Paul Martin interview, 24 July 1971.

98 King Diary, 17 Apr. 1945.

99 *Ibid.*

100 PAC, Brooke Claxton Papers, Vol. 21, Claxton to Pickersgill, 25 Apr. 1945.

101 *Ibid.*, 1 May 1945.

102 Gardiner Papers, Fogo to Gardiner, 5 May 1945.

103 Claxton Papers, Vol. 21, Claxton to Pickersgill, 25 Apr. 1945.

104 Macdonald Diary, 9 May 1945.

105 Power Papers, transcript.

106 Pickersgill interview, Aug. 1971; King Diary, 16 May 1945.

107 King Papers, Pickersgill to King, 10 May 1945, ff. D63021ff.

108 Address, 16 May 1945, in *Mackenzie King to the People of Canada* (Ottawa, 1945), pp. 5-18.

109 Bracken Papers, Vol. 92, Speech, 18 May 1945.

110 *Ibid.*, Speech, 26 May 1945.

111 *Ibid.*, 28 May 1945.

112 Claxton Papers, Vol. 27, 'To the Electors of St. Lawrence-St. George'.

113 King Papers, Address, 30 May 1945, ff. D63348-9.

114 *Mackenzie King to the People*, p. 39.

115 House of Commons *Debates*, 31 Jan. 1945. p. 6995.

116 King Papers, Vol. 98, Davidson Dunton, WIB, to Cabinet, 26 Mar., 2, 9 Apr. 1945.

117 *Public Opinion Quarterly*, IX (Summer, 1945), 237.

118 King Papers, Vol. 104, McLean to candidates, 29 Mar. 1945.

119 NLF Papers, Vol. 604, Bulletin to candidates, 25 May 1945.

120 Progressive Conservative Party Files, file F-6-G, R. A. Bell to Mrs Hargreaves, 10 Apr. 1945.

121 *Mackenzie King to the People*, p. 73.

122 *Ibid.*, pp. 104-6.

123 Kidd interview; J. W. Pickersgill claims authorship of this paragraph, too. Letter to author, 27 Mar. 1974.

124 *Mackenzie King to the People*, p. 117.

125 *Ibid.*, p. 126.

126 E.g., Regina *Leader-Post*, 5 June 1945; Halifax *Chronicle*, 6 June 1945; U.S. National Archives, State Department Records, 842.00/6-645, L. Clark to J. Parsons, 6 June 1945; PAC, Ian Mackenzie Papers, file 50-84, Mackenzie to National Liberal Committee, 6 June 1945.

127 Pickersgill, II, p. 399. Senator Lambert was offering 1 to 2 that the Liberals would get 123 seats. Lambert Diary, 8 June 1945.

128 For analyses, see H. F. Quinn, 'The Role of the Liberal Party in Recent Canadian Politics', *Political Science Quarterly*, LXVIII (Sept., 1953), 399; J. M. Beck, *Pendulum of Power* (Scarborough, 1968), pp. 241ff.; *Public Opinion Quarterly*, IX (Summer, 1945), 234-5.

129 King Diary, 11 June 1945.

130 *Ibid.*, 12 June 1945.

131 Pickersgill, II, p. 411.

132 Robert Rumilly, *Histoire de la province de Québec*, tome XLI: *Duplessis reprend les rênes* (Montréal, 1969), pp. 241-2.

133 Bertrand, p. 138; Power Papers, transcript; Norman Ward, ed., *A Party Politician: The Memoirs of Chubby Power* (Toronto, 1966), pp. 175-6.

134 Rumilly, XLI, p. 243 notes: 'Les libéraux conscriptionistes, demi-conscriptionistes, et anticonscriptionistes presenteront bien un front uni.'

135 State Department Records, 842.00/6-1245, N. Winship to J. Atherton, 12 June 1945.

136 Cf. *Saturday Night*, 23 June 1945; Power Papers, transcript; G. Rothney, 'Quebec Saves Our King', *Canadian Forum*, XXV (July, 1945), 83.

137 King Diary, 14 June 1945.

138 Toronto *Globe and Mail*, 1 June 1945; *Winnipeg Free Press*, 28 May 1945.

139 Directorate of History, National Defence Headquarters, General H. D. G. Crerar Papers, 958.C.009(D154), Crerar to J. Bickersteth, 27 Mar. 1945.

140 King Diary, 11, 12 June 1945.

141 D. C. Abbott interview, 29 Oct. 1971.

142 King Papers, Vol. 98, Confidential Memo to Cabinet, 18 June 1945.

143 E.g., PAC, R. B. Hanson Papers, Vol. 41, Hanson to G. Black, 29 June 1945.

144 Rothney, 'Quebec Saves', 83.

145 Coldwell Papers, Vol. 10, Coldwell to M. Denison, 16 July 1945; PAC, CCF Records, Vol. 103, D. Lewis to A.M. Nicholson, 13 June 1945; Gerald Caplan, *The Dilemma of Canadian Socialism: The CCF in Ontario* (Toronto, 1973), especially chapter X; Ian MacPherson, 'The 1945 Collapse of the C.C.F. in Windsor', *Ontario History*, LXI (Dec., 1969), 210-12.

146 Dexter Papers, Memo, 14 June 1945 re conversation with Ilsley.

147 King Papers, King to Robertson, 11 July 1945.

11. Conclusion: Canada's War

The election of 1945 marked the effective ending of the Second World War for Canada. Certainly the voters saw the polling on June 11 as marking the transition to peace. The fighting in the Pacific theatre continued through the summer, but this war was not one that greatly concerned Canadians, nor were many Canadian servicemen involved in the fighting. Europe had been the locale for Canada's War, and with its successful conclusion peace returned.

The country had irrevocably changed during the sixty-eight months that the war against Hitler had lasted. The population had risen from 11,267,00 in 1939 to 12,072,000 in 1945, but the birthrate had risen by 20 per cent in the same period, a reflection of the confidence Canadians had in their future. The Gross National Product, just $5.6 billion in 1939, had more than doubled to $11.8 billion in 1945, a figure that was slightly below the previous year's wartime high. To fuel this growth, federal government expenditures had soared from $680 million in 1939 to $5,136 million in 1945, an incredible jump. The wealth of the country increased, too, as did the amount paid in to the federal treasury in taxes. Income taxes increased to $809 million in 1945 from $112 million in 1939, while corporation taxes rose from $115 million to $599 million over the same period. To spend this money and administer the new functions of government, the federal bureaucracy grew vastly larger, increasing from 46,106 at the beginning of the war to 115,908 in 1945, a figure that would continue to grow with the peace.[1]

Not all the statistics were so pleasant. In November 1940 Mackenzie King could tell Parliament that the Navy's losses in action were 241, the

Army's 168, and the RCAF's 278, a death toll after more than one year of war of only 687.[2] By V-E day those totals had mounted grimly to 2,204 dead in the Navy, 17,101 in the RCAF, and 22,917 in the Army.[3] More than 40,000 dead was a terrible price to pay for the follies of European diplomacy, and it was no consolation at all to remember that the casualties were less in the Second World War than in the earlier conflict of 1914-1918.

In monetary terms the war had cost dearly as well. Colonel Stacey estimates the direct costs at $21.7 billion from 1939 to 1950, a figure that does not include the additional billions of dollars paid out after the war in pensions and care for the wounded, the crippled, and the widowed.[4]

Perhaps it was worth the cost. Hitler's Germany had been a monstrous evil, an evil beyond compare. The discoveries at the end of the war of concentration camps such as Auschwitz, Treblinka, and Belsen, and the revelation of the extent of Nazi genocide demonstrated this too well.

Still, Canadians would do well to remember that those atrocities were not the reasons they went to war in 1939 and not the reasons for which they fought and bled. Canada had gone to war in September 1939 because Britain had gone to war and for no other reason. It was not a war for Poland; it was not a war against anti-Semitism; it was not even a war against Nazism. All that came later, after the defeats in France and Flanders in May and June 1940, after Dunkirk, after the Battle of Britain. However just the war, and it was demonstrably a just war well before its end, Canada did not enter it to fight the good fight. Canadians should recollect that Canada began it with much the same status as in 1914. The achievement of the war and the war effort was that Canada entered the peace as a nation.

That national development is reflected in the statistics marking the transition of Canada from depression and despair to prosperity and power, but it is reflected even more in the areas of foreign power and public confidence. Before 1939 Canadian foreign policy had been cautious to the point of timidity, a policy reflective at once of weakness and of an overriding concern to avoid controversy. To Mackenzie King and to his Under Secretary of State for External Affairs, Dr Skelton, Canadian duality was still too fragile to be subjected to the strains that a forward policy would entail, and the two men were probably correct if unadventurous. Canada's active involvement in world affairs would have altered little or nothing, no more than a twig in a flowing current re-directs the course of the river. In such circumstances to look inward and to change what might be changed, to preserve what could be saved, was sensible. But by 1945 the world was different and Canada with it. Great powers were prostrate; new giants had stepped forward. Canada was no giant, but as the one major industrial and agricultural nation other than the United States to emerge from the war without physical destruction on its soil, Canada had a unique opportunity to advance its power and influence. During the war the struggle for increased influence had had limited success; the struggle would continue into the peace. The old policy of avoiding commitments, of 'Parliament will decide' was gone although, so long as Mackenzie King remained at the head of the government, not forgotten.

The shift in public confidence was no less profound. Before the war, the lack of policy was likely accepted uncritically by the majority of the people, isolationist, inward-looking, insular, and particularist. The long war opened eyes and widened horizons. In November 1943, 78 per cent of a national sample questioned by the Canadian Institute of Public Opinion favoured Canada's participating in the postwar maintenance of world peace 'even if that meant sending Canadian' servicemen to other parts of the world. In Quebec, 56 per cent of those questioned agreed.[5] In March 1945 fully 76 per cent of those questioned accepted the conscription of youth for a 'health-building' program, and six out of ten believed such a program ought to include military training. In Quebec, 49 per cent favoured military training and only 21 per cent disapproved.[6] Such figures would have been simply incredible before the war, and only a nation confident of its purpose and strength could produce them.

This confidence was a product of many things. The war effort, the shared sense of sacrifice and struggle in a good cause, all contributed to it. As much as anything else, however, the confidence sprang from a feeling that Canada had the resources and Canadians the ability to provide a good life for all. In addition Canadians believed that their government was a positive factor in their lives. This is reflected over and over in the public opinion polls, where large majorities indicated belief in government ownership of key industries, in government-run health insurance, in family allowances, and in other social-welfare measures.[7] In July 1944, for example, 55 per cent of a national sample expected prosperity to follow the war, and a month later 53 per cent of young Canadians questioned thought opportunities would be better after the war than before it, with only 17 per cent believing things would be worse.[8] This kind of confidence in the benevolence of government and in a positive future was a new development after years of depression and war, and much of it sprang from the government's preparations for the peace. The family-allowance scheme, the unemployment-insurance benefits, the huge sums allocated to housing, development, and job-creating reconstruction policies, however conservative their intent, changed the way Canadians perceived their world. Those wartime alterations were happily permanent, too, and a generation inured to depression and bloodshed made a new Canada.

To say that Mackenzie King led this shift in public perception to-wards a new reality is not too strong a claim. For all his caution, he had a clear idea of the direction he wanted Canada to follow, of what he wanted to prevent. So did others, but Mackenzie King was in a position to do something about his plans, and he did. His leadership in the social-welfare field, like his role elsewhere, was undramatic, his attitudes towards reform remained those he had expressed in 1918 in *Industry and Humanity* and in the 1919 Liberal Party platform, and he continued to resist the lavish expenditure of public funds. His greatest talent was for sniffing the wind, however, and he was soon attuned to the public mood. *Industry and Humanity* may have been too advanced for the 1920s, but the ideas King had put forward at the end of the Great War were right enough for the war and postwar realities of the 1940s. After the long wait, after confusion and backing and filling, King had exploded into action and created the basis of the conservative social-welfare state. He had his supporters—the influence of the higher bureau-cracy was very great, indeed crucial—but King and his government deserve credit for these reforms that altered Canadian life and reduced inequities, even if they did nothing to alter the basic distribution of power. If the government contrived to win re-election on the basis of its social-welfare policies, if it managed to hobble socialism and to check Conservatism with them, so be it. That is the way politics works. Social welfare had been one of the guiding principles of Mackenzie King's life, and unlike most politicians he managed to erect his principles into law over a generation in power.

The Prime Minister had been trained in the tradition of service and self-sacrifice, a tradition that usually means command over others but can sometimes mean something else. To King it did. He enjoyed the perquisites of power, and he had the mandarin's near-scorn for those beneath and near-obsequiousness to those above him, but he genuinely believed that he was doing 'good' things for people and for the nation. His thinking was sometimes embarrassingly simplistic, and he could refer to a Jew as 'a credit to his race', to a 'darky' servant, or to the 'masses' in his private musings in his diary. There was prejudice in him, but no more than was commonplace in men of his class, age, and up-bringing. His attitude could be patronizing, but it was also benevolent, and he deserves praise for his measures that ensured a national minimum standard of living to Canadians.

Similarly King deserves credit for his handling of conscription during the war. His resistance to compulsion was based neither on emotional nor theoretical grounds; he was not an anti-conscriptionist because he believed it the wrong way to mobilize a nation or because he believed compulsion inefficient. He was anti-conscriptionist for sheer pragmatic reasons—conscription would create more strife and division than benefits. This is the most familiar type of political cost-benefit analysis, and there is nothing wrong with decision-making of this sort, especially when the resulting judgement is so self-evidently the right one. Con-scription was an issue King correctly feared.

But if his responses to conscription were defensible, his tactics in implementing his policies were less so. Mackenzie King's goal was to keep the Liberal Party in power under his leadership as long as possible because he believed sincerely and correctly that he was the most acceptable leader to French Canada. To maintain this objective he brutally sacked Ralston because he demanded conscription, and then three weeks later reversed himself and imposed a measure of conscrip-tion. Each step was necessary, King believed, because of his fear of conspiracy. Ralston was plotting against him, possibly with the aid of his colleagues in National Defence. The generals were in revolt and the supremacy of civilian control was in danger. Both theses were probably fanciful, but significantly Mackenzie King had to create these dark shadows before he could bring himself to take drastic and difficult actions. Self-justification mattered.

King's suspicious nature was nowhere more evident than in his deal-ings with the Great Powers. His attitude to Great Britain, shaped over the years at Imperial Conferences and tempered by crises dating back to Chanak in 1922, was unfailingly one of suspicion mixed with un-abashed admiration. Nothing that happened during the war altered this. To the United States, however, King's responses seem to have changed during the war. Before 1939 the Americans were a convenient counterweight to be employed against Britain; during the war, American power waxed as Britain's waned. King's benign attitude to the United States began to disappear while his fears about American power grew, unfortunately without his taking serious action to counter it. Perhaps there was nothing that could have been done, given the war situation and the pressures on the Canadian economy. What King did do was to strike bargains with Roosevelt that ensured Canadian safety and economic stability without apparent immediate costs. These costs would become clearer as the Cold War began.

The Second World War, then, was not one in which Canada sought involvement and perhaps not one in which Canada should have been involved, at least not from the beginning. But once in the war, and once the character of the war altered to pose a direct threat to Britain and to this continent, it became Canada's war. The Great War had sped the transition of Canada from colony to semi-autonomous state; the Second World War saw this semi-autonomy alter rapidly into genuine nationhood. There would be new problems and pressures on the nation in the troubled years of the peace, but Canada's war had been won.

---

1 All data from M. C. Urquhart and K. A. H. Buckley, *Historical Statistics of Canada* (Toronto, 1965), pp. 14-19, 38, 130, 135, 621-2.

2 House of Commons *Debates*, 12 Nov. 1940, p. 51.

3 C. P. Stacey, *Arms, Men and Governments: The War Policies of Canada, 1939-1945* (Ottawa, 1970), p. 66.

4 *Ibid.*, pp. 65-6.

5 *Public Opinion Quarterly*, VIII (Spring, 1944), 161.

6 *Ibid.*, IX (Spring, 1945), 106-7.

7 E.g., *ibid.*, VIII (Summer, 1944), 291; (Winter, 1944-45), 601; IX (Summer, 1945), 236.

8 *Ibid.*, VIII (Fall, 1944), 455-6.

Index

Voyageurs de Commerce, 222

Waley, S. D., 308
Walford, General A. E., 346
Wallace, W. S., 255
War Exchange Conservation Act, 135-6, 175
War Exchange Tax, 175
war finance, 155 n.87, 186ff.; aid to U.K. (1942-5), 307ff.; billion dollar gift, 187ff., 191-4; and BCATP, 46ff.; Canadian view of (1939), 62-4; Canada-U.K. problems re, 65, 133ff.; and Hyde Park agreement, 133ff.; end of limited liability, 98; King on, 188; limits on, 312-13; in May 1940, 97; military budget (1939), 24; Moffat on, 136-7; need for U.K. orders, 51; negotiations with U.K. (1939), 59ff.; Ralston on, 70 n.88; repatriation of securities, 134-5; and Rowell-Sirois, 163ff.; settlement with U.K., 315-16; Towers on, 70 n.99; see also Hyde Park agreement, billion dollar gift
War Industries Control Board, 174-5
War Measures Act, 77
War Supply Board, 82
War Time Elections Act, 79

Wartime Information Board, 251, 358, 359, 412-13
Wartime Labour Relations Code, 280
Wartime Prices and Trade Board, 174, 177
Welland by-election, 215, 221
wheat, 63-4, 126, 324
White Paper on Employment and Income, 277-8
Whitton, Charlotte, 261-2, 285
Winch, Harold, 22-3
Winnipeg Convention, 252, 261
Winnipeg General Strike, 256
Wood, Sir Kingsley, 48, 53, 191
Woods, Walter, 262
Woodsworth, J. S., 16-17, 22, 88, 279
Woolton, Lord, 298n.
Working Committee on Post-Hostilities Planning, 317
World War I, 19, 78-9, 84, 88, 98, 99, 101, 159, 202, 204, 206, 231, 256
Wrong, Hume, 295-6, 303, 316

York South by-election, 220-1, 251, 262, 265n., 270

Zombies: see conscription; NRMA men